INTERPERSONAL COMMUNICATION

This fully revised text demystifies interpersonal communication skills by bringing the latest research together with practical guidance that prepares students to discern key communication dynamics and communicate more effectively in all areas of their lives.

The new edition draws on current theory and research to guide students through the foundations of the discipline, recent developments in scientific research, and tips for improving their own interpersonal communication skills. In addition, readers will find:

- Expanded coverage of technology and computer-mediated communication, including explicit examples of what interpersonal communication looks like online.
- Invitations to engage with elaborated descriptions of theories and related resources on the companion website whenever prominent theories of interpersonal communication are mentioned in the text.
- A commitment to gender inclusive language and topics, as well as a new feature, "IDEA: Inclusion, Diversity, Equity, and Access," that invites students to consider ways to address exclusion and inequity in interpersonal communication.

The fully revamped companion website includes updates across all resources, additional videos, self-quizzes for students, and all-new instructor resources, which can be accessed at www.routledge.com/cw/solomon. Also new to the companion website for this edition are links to essays and videos featuring the work that students in the Communication Studies program at the California State Prison, Los Angeles County, produced in response to self-reflection prompts in the first edition. These materials provide insight into facets of interpersonal communication in these students' lives, and they offer a broad range of rich life experiences.

Interpersonal Communication: Putting Theory into Practice, Second Edition is ideal for undergraduate students in courses on interpersonal communication and communication skills.

Denise Solomon is Liberal Arts Professor of Communication Arts and Sciences at the Pennsylvania State University, University Park, USA.

Jennifer Theiss is Professor of Communication at Rutgers University, USA.

"As might be expected from two of the field's leading scholars, Solomon and Theiss have produced a first-rate survey of research and theory in interpersonal communication. Their treatment is comprehensive, current, and goes beyond exposition of foundational concepts by challenging students to consider the practical, ethical, and skill-development implications of the material covered in each chapter."

John O. Greene, *Purdue University, USA*

"In *Interpersonal Communication: Putting Theory into Practice, Second Edition* Solomon and Theiss provide a well-balanced and theory-oriented approach to highlighting the multiple dimensions of interpersonal communication influences, processes, and outcomes in a variety of socially relevant and timely contexts. Presented in an easy-to-read logical format with a multitude of examples pertinent to undergraduate students, Solomon and Theiss's thorough coverage of theory and research is accessible and will be enjoyable to anyone interested in better understanding the multi-faceted nature of communication."

Jennifer A. Samp, *University of Georgia, USA*

"This book provides a solid foundation to teach interpersonal communication skills that facilitate solutions to complex human problems. The authors find a great balance between density and presentation of core concepts. The book provides well-presented content for students to understand core concepts and significant issues, and to reflect on their own communication practices, experiences, and possibilities for making a difference through skillful interpersonal communication."

Ashley P. Duggan, *Boston College, USA*

"Solomon and Theiss have done a terrific job translating complex theories and social science into practical language without sacrificing intellectual depth. The textbook reflects the latest social scientific knowledge about interpersonal communication and is chock-full of important real-life applications that encourage students to think about interpersonal communication. Solomon and Theiss speak directly to students with engaging examples and provocative questions. Every chapter contains crucial exercises for students to hone their social competencies and to reflect on their strengths."

Susanne M. Jones, *University of Minnesota, USA and Associate Editor of* Mindfulness

"Solomon and Theiss thoughtfully translate interpersonal communication research and theory into everyday life and examples. My students are left enchanted by the ways the text intersects with their own relationships and experiences, enabling them to be deliberate and thoughtful in their encounters and equipping them with relational skills that enrich their own lives and careers."

Keli Fazio, *The College of New Jersey, USA*

INTERPERSONAL COMMUNICATION

Putting Theory into Practice

2nd Edition

Denise Solomon and Jennifer Theiss

NEW YORK AND LONDON

Access the companion website: www.routledge.com/cw/solomon

Cover image credit: Courtesy of Getty Images, Jackson Dillard, William Markwardt, and Midwest Lifeshots Photography

Second edition published 2022
by Routledge
605 Third Avenue, New York, NY 10158

and by Routledge
4 Park Square, Milton Park, Abingdon, Oxon, OX14 4RN

Routledge is an imprint of the Taylor & Francis Group, an informa business

First edition published by Routledge 2013

Library of Congress Cataloging-in-Publication Data
A catalog record for this book has been requested

ISBN: 978-0-8153-8695-7 (hbk)
ISBN: 978-0-8153-8697-1 (pbk)
ISBN: 978-1-351-17438-1 (ebk)

DOI: 10.4324/9781351174381

Typeset in Berkeley
by Apex CoVantage, LLC

Denise dedicates this edition to Nora, Nicole, Jackson, and Quincy, whose strength of character and essential goodness are an endless source of optimism, and to her mother, Marie, who loves them completely.

Jen dedicates this edition to her mother, Nan, and sisters, Julia and Anne, and to her mother-in-law, Cathy, and sister-in-law, Meghan. It is a privilege and a source of inspiration to be surrounded in life by phenomenal women like you who are strong, resilient, persistent, thoughtful, smart, funny, adventurous, and kind.

Brief Table of Contents

Contents

Preface

Students attend college for a variety of reasons: to broaden their minds, to learn a vocation, or to become independent adults. But all students need to master interpersonal communication skills. Everyone, regardless of their personal and career goals, benefits from an ability to promote a friendship, to resolve a conflict, to comfort someone in need, and to answer questions clearly. Throughout the course of our lives, the experiences that bring us joy, that define who we are, and that connect us to others are grounded in interpersonal communication.

As active communication researchers, we hope that the studies we conduct will someday offer tangible solutions to complex human problems. As teachers, our greatest professional joys have come from seeing students improve their communication skills in ways that changed their lives. Denise remembers a student who started the semester paralyzed by the thought of interpersonal conflict and who, over the course of the semester, became confident enough to express herself during disagreements. That student wrote a couple of years later to say that she had become the go-to person in her workplace whenever someone had an interpersonal communication problem. Jen has seen how learning strategies for listening and self-disclosure helped a shy and lonely first-year student emerge as a confident campus leader. Like all teachers of interpersonal communication, we have countless stories like these. Because of the impact of interpersonal communication on students' lives, we are inspired to promote the teaching of interpersonal communication.

OUR MISSION

This book introduces students to interpersonal communication as a subject that has enormous relevance to their daily lives. We provide concrete strategies for building communication skills that are firmly grounded in contemporary communication research. We also show that effective interpersonal communication is based on strategies and skills that everybody can learn to do better. Our touchstone throughout is a commitment to topics and applications that can help students in many different situations and throughout their lives.

Improve Quality of Life by Promoting Communication Skills

A central goal of this text is helping students use what researchers have learned about interpersonal communication to improve their own ability to communicate well. To that end, we weave skill-building suggestions throughout every section of every chapter. We frequently invite students to pause and reflect on material in the text, so that they can identify connections between what they are learning and their own life experiences. We encourage students to consider how disparities are reflected in social interaction, as well as how interpersonal communication can be used to promote and embrace inclusion, diversity, equity, and access. We suggest activities for applying concepts, and we provide self-assessments to promote personal insight. Each section of every chapter suggests ways that students can practice what they have learned – these recommendations are focused, concrete, and closely tied to the information in the chapter. Then, because good communication is attentive to ethical issues and priorities, each chapter concludes with a set of activities for promoting communication ethics.

Use Contemporary Research to Inform Concrete Skill-Building Tips

As college students, we were both drawn to the study of interpersonal communication because we saw that communication scholars take on important questions that have real-life relevance. For Denise, discovering the inherent biases people bring to conflict interactions motivated her to study how personal relationships develop and survive in the face of threats. Jen wanted to understand how romantic partners express intimacy and establish mutual commitment within relationships. As researchers, we have worked independently and together to understand how romantic partners experience and withstand challenges, such as uncertainty, jealousy, hurtful messages, and conflict. As teachers, we continually draw upon communication research to develop concrete guidelines for building communication skills.

Dispel Myths About Interpersonal Communication

Like many teachers of interpersonal communication, we've been confronted by two persistent myths that students bring to our classrooms. One is that interpersonal communication is just a matter of common sense. Paradoxically, the other myth is that communication skill is an innate gift that you either have or you don't. In translating the richness of the communication discipline for the introductory communication skills course, we show students that interpersonal communication skill isn't just common sense, but neither is it a mysterious quality that defies learning.

To drive home this point, we focus on topics that connect fundamental communication concepts to students' daily lives. We also address communication issues that emerge at different life stages, from childhood and through all the transitions of adolescence and adulthood. These topics give readers insight into communication issues relevant to their own stage of life, the changes that the future may hold, and the experiences of people around them. And throughout every chapter, we help students apply what they discover about these issues so they can become better communicators.

A Text That Reaches Out to Students

Helping students see the complexity of interpersonal communication, as well as how to improve their skills, requires teaching both the fundamental parts of the communication process and how those parts come together. Accordingly, both the order of the chapters and the organization of material within each chapter are designed to meet students at a basic level and then elevate their ability to communicate. We also capitalize on technology as an important part of students' lives by encompassing communication via social media within the scope of interpersonal communication, highlighting research on technologically mediated forms of interpersonal communication, showcasing dialogue from real online interactions, and providing materials to engage course material more deeply on an online companion website, available at: http://www.routledge.com/cw/solomon.

The text begins with a chapter that introduces students to interpersonal communication as a practice that can be skillful and consequential – and as the focus of scientific research designed to reveal and explain the inner workings of this complex phenomenon. The remainder of the text is organized into four parts that accomplish the following important goals:

- Explore the foundations of interpersonal communication: culture, the characteristics of individuals, and the workings of the mind.
- Explore the behaviors and dynamics that unfold in interpersonal interactions.
- Locate interpersonal communication at the heart of developing, intimate, and family relationships.
- Describe how people can use communication to accomplish strategic goals like influencing others, managing conflicts, and comforting each other.

In this way, we help students to master specific facets of interpersonal communication, and we put the pieces together to help students succeed in communication situations they face every day over the course of their lives.

In a similar fashion, each chapter begins with foundational concepts and then layers the nuances of interpersonal communication onto that foundation. People learn by mastering basic ideas and then elaborating their knowledge with specific details. Following a consistent structure for presenting information can also make unfamiliar content easier to understand. Accordingly, students go through the same general sequence in most chapters:

- *Students master key concepts.* The primary goal of the opening section of most chapters is to define key terms and fundamental assumptions. For example:
  - Chapter 2 on communication and culture defines the layers of culture and explains how cultures develop and change.
  - Chapter 5 on verbal communication begins by discussing the nature of language.
  - Chapter 10 on communication in intimate relationships opens by defining intimacy and clarifying the forms it can take.

Our discussion of these fundamental topics concludes with concrete suggestions for putting knowledge of these core concepts to practical use.

- *Students relate communication to the core concepts.* After we introduce core concepts, we show students how they are relevant to everyday communication experiences. For example:
  - Chapter 2 examines how people use verbal and nonverbal messages to reveal important cultural beliefs and values to others.
  - Chapter 3 considers how people can use communication strategies to enhance self-esteem.
  - Chapter 10 explores the role of communication in maintaining intimacy.

We draw from research examples to bring these relationships to life, and again we show students how to apply this knowledge to build communication skills.

- *Students probe socially significant issues.* In the final sections of most chapters, we feature real-world issues that affect or are affected by interpersonal communication. For example:
  - Chapter 2 on culture and communication explores how people with different gender identities experience communication in relationships across the lifespan.

- In Chapter 9, the reader learns about the communication challenges created by unrequited love and "friends-with-benefits" relationships.
- Chapter 11 discusses how improved communication patterns can strengthen family bonds.

These sections reveal the important research questions and lifespan issues that communication scholars are grappling with, and they point to the real-life situations this text can help students deal with more effectively.

- *Students apply their knowledge.* Each chapter includes a feature called "Putting Theory into Practice." These sections offer students tips for using what they have learned to improve their interpersonal communication. Then, through recommendations, concrete examples, and numerous exercises, we help students apply what they have learned to their day-to-day communication experiences.

HELPING STUDENTS PUT THEORY INTO PRACTICE

Interpersonal communication is an essential life skill that everybody can learn. We include a variety of learning aids to engage students in activities that will help them to understand their own communication experiences and, more importantly, to improve their ability to communicate effectively.

Pause and Reflect

Each chapter poses eight to ten questions that ask students to reflect on their own experiences so that they can see how communication affects them every day. These moments of reflection ask students to think about their own communication practices, experiences that they found rewarding, or situations where skillful communication might have made a difference. For example:

- Which verbal and nonverbal cues make you think that someone is listening to you – or not?
- Which stories are told and retold within your family, and how do they reflect your family's values?
- What happened in a recent conversation that left you feeling loved and supported?

Questions like these invite students to draw connections between the text and their own lives. Instructors might also find them useful as topics for discussion, journal assignments, or themes for extended writing assignments.

Communication in Action

Each chapter includes three to five exercises that help students probe or test the chapter's claims and to examine communication in their own world. These activities directly connect course material to students' personal experiences, and they point to situations where skillful communication can make a difference. These exercises take various forms, such as:

- encouraging students to observe and record aspects of the communication that occurs around them;
- asking students to reflect on their own experiences, for example, keeping a diary to chart communication and emotions over the course of a few days;
- providing students with problem-solving tasks, like mapping communication boundaries within their family and identifying ways to revise those boundaries to improve communication.

As with Pause and Reflect questions, Communication in Action exercises can be completed at the student's discretion or integrated into homework assignments. Instructions and forms for Communication in Action exercises are referenced in the text, with supporting materials provided as needed on the companion website.

How Do You Rate?

Each chapter also offers one or two self-report or observational research measures. Using scales provided on the companion website, students can, for example, assess their ability to engage in perspective-taking, their preferred listening style, their competence with computer-mediated communication, the norms for communication within their family, or their preferred types of social support. We consistently find that students enjoy these tools. In addition, these exercises promote insights that are relevant to students' own interpersonal communication experiences.

Real Words

In several chapters, we offer transcripts of conversations to bring concepts and ideas to life. In most cases, the transcripts come from interactions that we video-taped in our communication labs or that were given to us by other researchers. Thus, these dialogues are, in fact, "real words." The transcripts that are showcased include topics such as hurtful conversations, interpersonal conflicts, and comforting interactions. By reading these transcripts, students get a close look at what works and what doesn't work in real conversations between people.

Interpersonal Communication Online

A similar feature that we have incorporated into several chapters are examples of real interpersonal communication in online or technologically mediated contexts. These excerpts come from online chat rooms or blogs, social media sites, or text messages that we have analyzed in our own studies or that other scholars have included in their research. Examples include a chat from an online forum for family and loved ones of military recruits, text messages between romantic partners at various stages of relationship development, and excerpts from a study in which romantic partners analyzed their text messages in a conflict. By reading these exchanges, students get a sense of the ways that technology shapes interpersonal communication.

Inside Communication Research

To illustrate how communication research points to strategies for effective communication, each chapter presents one extended description of a particular communication study. We take students inside the research process by reviewing the methods and results of a study. Follow-up questions then direct students to consider both the implications of the findings and the pros and cons of the research procedures. For example, students will learn about research on social support in same-race and mixed-race friendships, relationship maintenance in friends-with-benefits relationships, and stereotypes in imagined interactions with older adults. These boxes seek to make interpersonal communication research accessible and to show students how research findings can inform their own communication practices.

Connect with Theory

To underscore how the knowledge shared in this book is grounded in theory, we have added a feature that invites students to learn more about specific theories that we draw upon. When relevant within each chapter, readers are invited to connect with theory, by going to the companion website to learn more about a particular theoretical perspective. There, students will find a brief summary of the theory and additional references that they can use to read more about important theories that have shaped what we know about interpersonal communication.

Scholar Spotlights in the Communication Café

We created space within the companion website called the "Communication Café." Here, students will find our video introductions to each unit – our goal with these is to help bring alive the learning objectives for each part of the book. In addition, the Café provides video-recorded interviews with leading scholars in the field of interpersonal communication. We've invited one scholar for each chapter to elaborate on topics covered within that chapter. In the interviews, we also asked these scholars to describe their own journey as interpersonal communication researchers. These videos showcase some of the most influential people in the field of interpersonal communication, and bring alive their experiences as people who practice and advance the science of interpersonal communication.

Inclusion, Diversity, Equity, and Access

To help students learning about interpersonal communication consider the broad tapestry of society, we integrated two new features into this edition. First, in every chapter, we create space for students to reflect on the implications of inclusion, diversity, equity, and access in interpersonal communication. These reflections point to the ways in which people of different ethnicities, genders, ages, and abilities are included or excluded from various interpersonal contexts and the role of interpersonal communication in promoting inclusivity and equality. In addition, we have partnered with the Communication Studies program at the California State Prison, Los Angeles County, where incarcerated men have been using this textbook to learn about interpersonal communication. There are links on the companion website that showcase some of the essays and animations these men have created in response to the Pause and Reflect prompts. These sample writings offer students an opportunity to look at interpersonal communication constructs through a different set of eyes and understand how the life experiences of incarcerated men both shape and reflect their culture, identity, social interactions, and relationships. We are grateful to Kamran Afary, who teaches this course at the prison, for sharing the thoughtful insights that his students have written about in their work.

Exploring Communication Ethics

Ethical issues permeate all facets of interpersonal communication; therefore, we offer them as the capstone to every chapter. Each chapter presents three different types of exercises:

- We ask students to consider an ethical choice in a particular situation.
- We invite students to think about the ethical implications of a line of reasoning or a communication decision.
- We offer students activities for analyzing communication ethics in concrete materials.

Whether completed independently or as a part of classroom assignments, these exercises encourage students to probe the ethical issues that emerge within interpersonal communication contexts.

WHAT'S AHEAD

We are excited to share this journey with teachers and students. We both remember vividly our first introduction to interpersonal communication. We have enjoyed devoting our professional lives to investigating the complexities of interpersonal communication and practicing what we hope is skillful interpersonal communication in our personal lives. We know from our own experiences that interpersonal communication is challenging – even to people like us who spend all their time studying and thinking about it. We also know that everyone can improve their interpersonal communication skills. Improving interpersonal communication skills takes knowledge, opportunities to practice, and believing that interpersonal communication is something one can and should do better. We designed this text to help others on their journey toward more effective and satisfying interpersonal communication, and we hope that everyone who reads this book finds what they need to have more fulfilling interpersonal communication experiences.

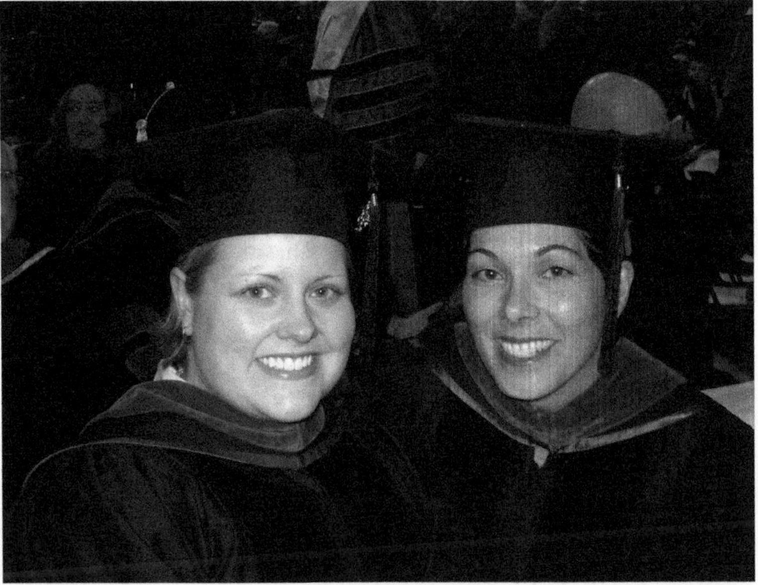

Jen & Denise

Icons Used in This Text

Look for these icons throughout the text – they indicate material for you to use, complete, or watch on the companion website.

Communication Café: When you see this icon, go to the companion website and watch videos of Denise and Jen. They provide introductions to each of the four parts in the text, and they interview some of the leading scholars in the field of communication in the Scholar Spotlights.

Communication in Action: A Communication in Action box with this icon indicates an activity on the companion website that will give you the opportunity to probe or test the claims in the text and examine communication in your own world.

How Do You Rate? When you see this icon, you can complete a self-evaluation exercise on the companion website. It will be related to the topic under discussion and will help you understand your own interpersonal communication experiences.

Connect with Theory: This icon indicates that you can find an elaborated description of a theory, as well as citations to sources to learn more about it, on the companion website.

Includsion, Diversity, Equity, and Inclusion: This box creates space for students to reflect on the ways in which people of different ethnicities, genders, ages, and abilities are included or excluded from various interpersonal contexts and the role of interpersonal communication in promoting inclusivity and equality.

Acknowledgments

We have been delighted to see the response to the first edition of this textbook and are grateful to all of the instructors who were early adopters of the book and gave us excellent feedback for improving the second edition. It has taken longer than we might have liked to develop the second edition, but we are excited that this extra time has resulted in a text that is fully updated and a reflection of modern events and experiences. We are grateful to our team at Routledge, especially Felisa Salvago-Keyes and Grant Schatzman, for their consistent support and endless supply of patience through our many false starts and frequent delays. Your encouragement and compassion were much appreciated during this process.

Denise has other people to thank, none more so than Jen. Every time Denise considered walking away from a second edition, Jen's enthusiasm and dedication brought her back. Jen's support and understanding as life's highs and lows delayed progress were a gift, as was her ability to manage the myriad details that were involved in updating photos, figures, and so many other bits and pieces involved in making a truly fresh new edition. Denise is also grateful to her spouse, Jim, for helping her stay the course, and her sons, Jackson and Quincy. Thinking about her sons' college journeys was an added incentive to create a text that reflected contemporary theory, research, and social values.

Jen is endlessly grateful to Denise for her persistence, encouragement, and good humor during the work on this second edition of the textbook. We have descended into the bunker to complete big projects and hard tasks before, but I was especially appreciative to have you as my battle-weary partner this time around. Jen also thanks her husband, Kevin, for his encouragement to do this work, his understanding of the sacrifices required to complete such a massive undertaking, and his much needed and always appreciated sense of humor that keeps me laughing every day.

We are also grateful to our colleagues, friends, and family who encouraged and supported us along the way. Particular thanks go to Kellie Brisini, Xi Tian, and Mandy Goodwin for their assistance in developing new materials for the companion website, Deborah Yoon for her assistance with editing and updating the bibliography, and Jackson Dillard,

Bill Markwardt, and Midwest Lifeshots Photography for providing vivid photographs for the book cover. More generally, we thank our mentors and our many, many students for inspiring us to be better scholars and teachers.

Finally, we express our deep gratitude to Kamran Afary, and the students in the Communication Studies program at the California State Prison, Los Angeles County. We were so moved when we read the first set of essays produced by these students, and the annual publication of their writing – as well as the animated videos based on them – blew us away. Denise kept a copy of the 2017 publication on her desk throughout the writing of this edition, and these students were on her mind every day that she worked on the manuscript. Thank you for your commitment to learning about interpersonal communication, and for inspiring us with the knowledge that our book made a difference in your journey. Thank you, also, to Routledge for partnering with us to share a percentage of the royalties earned by the second edition to support this program.

LEARNING OBJECTIVES

After reading this chapter, you should be able to:

1. Define interpersonal communication and describe five characteristics of it.
2. Distinguish between content and relational messages.
3. Describe six features of competent communication.
4. Identify three factors that promote competent communication.
5. Explain what a theory is and define interpersonal communication theory.
6. Describe how communication researchers study interpersonal communication.

PUTTING THEORY INTO PRACTICE

In this chapter, you will learn how to:

1. Recognize the fallibility of symbols.
2. Pay attention to relational messages.
3. Clarify your communication ethics.
4. Practice your communication skills to become more competent.
5. Adapt to communication situations.
6. Think theoretically about interpersonal communication.
7. Evaluate research on interpersonal communication.

WHAT IS INTERPERSONAL COMMUNICATION?

1

Source: Photo by ABC Contributor/Getty Images.

In 2020, the popular reality television competition, *American Idol*, pivoted to a remote format because of the COVID-19 pandemic. What didn't change was the communication dynamics among the three judges: singer-songwriter Lionel Richie, pop diva Katy Perry, and country crooner Luke Bryan. Each week on the show, the judges are faced with the sometimes unenviable task of communicating rejection to untalented contestants, offering comfort to devastated singers who don't make the cut, delivering criticism in a way that is constructive and helpful to competitors, and debating with each other over which contestants to keep or cut. Given Lionel Richie's long career and extensive experience in the music industry, he frequently frames his rejections in terms of concern for the contestant and a desire to protect them from an industry that can be brutal to unprepared newcomers. Katy Perry, on the other hand, tends to favor honesty over sensitivity, telling contestants outright when she doesn't like their voice, sometimes in a snarky or sarcastic manner. Luke Bryan shows the most empathy for contestants, wanting to give everyone a chance, sometimes showing disappointment that he didn't fight harder against the other judges to keep certain people in the competition. Despite their remote participation, there was no mistaking the judges' exuberance when African American street musician "Just Sam" was named the season's winner and the first ever LGBTQ winner on the show. Through these actions, the *American Idol* judges have demonstrated how interpersonal communication can be a challenging, but powerful process.

Interpersonal communication skills are critically important in every facet of life. As the *American Idol* judges have shown, interpersonal communication is an essential skill and a useful tool for providing comfort and support, offering constructive criticism, managing conflict, or persuading others to share your point of view. You will certainly use interpersonal communication for these reasons, but you will find that interpersonal communication skills are also important in a variety of other situations, such as when you converse with a new neighbor, coordinate your schedule with your roommate, or negotiate a raise with a boss. You can use interpersonal communication to build successful relationships in the home, at school, at work, and in public. Because interpersonal communication has always been a part of your life, you may find it difficult to think about it as a topic you can study and learn more about. In this chapter, we'll offer you a deeper understanding of interpersonal communication, explain how you can develop and improve your interpersonal communication skills, describe how researchers study interpersonal communication, and consider what it means to practice ethical interpersonal communication.

WHAT IS INTERPERSONAL COMMUNICATION?

Interpersonal communication is a specific type of communication. **Communication**, in general, is the use of symbols to represent ideas so that meanings can be shared. Class lectures, podcasts, street signs, Instagram posts, tweets, conversations, and blogs are all examples of communication. These forms of communication use some kind of **symbols** – sounds, movements, or images – to represent ideas. During interpersonal communication, you use symbols in the form of written or spoken words, gestures, or pictures to represent the complex ideas in your mind. In this part of the chapter, you'll learn the definition of interpersonal communication, the characteristics of interpersonal communication, the types of messages created through interpersonal communication, and some of the contexts in which you experience interpersonal communication.

Communication
Using symbols to represent ideas so that meanings can be shared.

Symbols
Sounds, gestures, or images that represent ideas.

A Basic Definition

Whereas communication, in general, includes any use of symbols to represent meanings, **interpersonal communication** refers more specifically to communication that occurs between people and creates a personal bond between them. Let's probe this term by breaking it down into its two parts: "inter" and "personal," as shown in Figure 1.1. The *inter* part of the word highlights how interpersonal communication connects people. In interpersonal communication, one person's actions both affect and reflect another person's actions. This is not the case with all kinds of communication: you can shut down your Internet browser without having an effect on the source of those messages. In contrast, if you don't respond to a text message, your communication partner will probably have some kind of a reaction. When you engage in interpersonal communication, you and another person become linked together.

Interpersonal Communication
Using symbols to represent ideas in order to share meanings and create a personal bond between people.

Interpersonal communication is also *personal*. This doesn't mean that interpersonal communication always involves private topics or that it only occurs in close relationships. Rather, it means that your unique qualities as a person matter during interpersonal communication. If you are at a restaurant and you are treated only as a customer – someone who needs to place an order and get food – you aren't really experiencing interpersonal communication. This would be considered **impersonal communication**, because your personal qualities are irrelevant to the interaction. But if your server shows an interest in you as an individual and communicates with you in unique ways because of your characteristics and circumstances, then that conversation is much more personal. In interpersonal communication, you are attentive to the personal qualities that you and your partner bring to the interaction.

Impersonal Communication
Using symbols to represent ideas in a manner that ignores personal qualities of the people involved in the interaction.

What does "interpersonal communication" mean to you? The activity described in the Communication in Action 1.1 box gives you a chance to reflect on your own perceptions of interpersonal communication. You'll find Communication in Action exercises throughout the chapters of this book. Like the activity on "Defining Interpersonal Communication," these exercises give you a chance to explore what you are learning about interpersonal communication by paying attention to your own experiences and the world around you.

INTER	PERSONAL
Interpersonal communication creates a connection between people, such that one person's actions affect and reflect the other person's actions.	Interpersonal communication involves paying attention to the characteristics and circumstances that make the participants unique individuals.

FIGURE 1.1 Defining interpersonal communication

COMMUNICATION IN ACTION 1.1

Defining Interpersonal Communication

Make a list of five communication experiences you had in the past week that you consider to be interpersonal communication. Then, list five communication experiences you had that you do NOT consider to be interpersonal communication. Reflecting on those two lists, what features of your experiences seem to define communication episodes as interpersonal?

Dyad
Two people, which is a common context for interpersonal communication.

You might think of interpersonal communication as something that occurs between two people, also known as a **dyad**. A dyad is a common setting for interpersonal communication, because each partner in the interaction is free to focus her or his attention exclusively on the other. Notice, though, that the definition of interpersonal communication can include more than two people. If you communicate with a group of people in ways that are personal and connect everyone involved, interpersonal communication occurs. An example might be a group of friends who regularly hang out together. You might also have dyadic interpersonal communication with a person who is part of a larger group, for example, talking with your best friend while you are both with your larger social group or texting with a classmate during an online class. The key factor in interpersonal communication isn't the number of people present, but personal interaction.

PAUSE & REFLECT

Think about a person with whom you spend time, both one-on-one and as part of a larger group. How are your communication experiences with that person the same in those two situations? How are they different?

Interpersonal communication often occurs in face-to-face interactions. Face-to-face interaction allows partners to communicate both verbally and nonverbally – with words, with gestures, and with body language. Face-to-face interaction also helps each partner attend to the other as an individual. Interpersonal communication doesn't have to occur face-to-face, though. When you talk on the phone, exchange text messages, or participate an online chat, your communication can create a personal connection with another person. Once again, the key is the presence of interaction that is personal, no matter what tools you use to communicate.

Characteristics

Now that you have learned the definition of interpersonal communication, let's examine features that are present in any interaction you might have. Figure 1.2 shows the **transactional model of communication** – this name reflects the fact that people involved in an interpersonal interaction participate together in the act of communicating. The model includes at least two *participants*, who bring personal qualities to the interaction, as well as their own thoughts and their impressions of their partner. Together, these participants create and interpret symbols that represent ideas. The interaction unfolds in a *context* that includes everything from physical characteristics of the setting to the cultural environment. The process of interpersonal communication also unfolds over time. Although we've identified the separate parts of an interaction to help you learn about them, in practice, all of these components come together to create a holistic and dynamic experience that is communication. In this section, we consider five characteristics of interpersonal communication that are implied by this model.

Transactional Model of Communication
A conception of the components present in an interpersonal interaction and how people participate together in the act of communicating.

Interpersonal communication is a continuous process. Notice that the model in Figure 1.2 connects the communication partners with a double-headed arrow. This arrow reflects the continuous exchange of messages that occurs during interpersonal communication. Even when one partner is speaking, the other is communicating through body position, eye contact, and facial expressions. This arrow also represents the **channel** or the medium through which messages are exchanged between

Channel
The medium through which messages are exchanged between people.

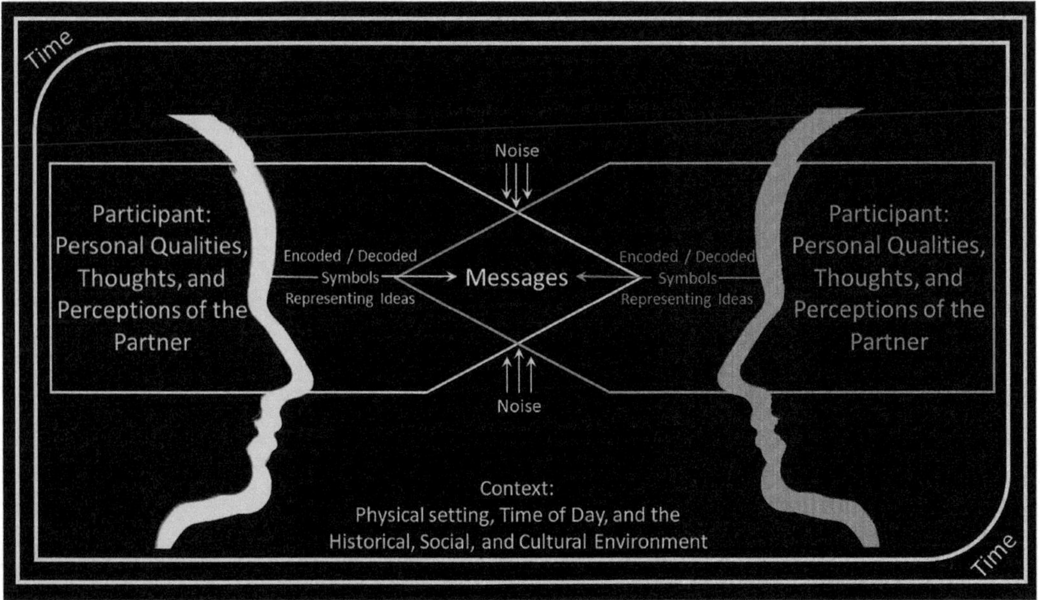

FIGURE 1.2 The transactional model of communication

people. That channel might be a connection that exists when face-to-face partners give each other their attention, or it could be a cell phone or Internet connection. Sometimes, people don't even notice the communication channel, because they are so thoroughly connected by their mutual engagement in the communication experience. In all cases, the channel allows partners to jointly participate in the continuous creation and interpretation of symbols that represent ideas.

Interpersonal communication is a dynamic process. Interpersonal communication is a dynamic process because meanings change and unfold over time, and previous messages affect how subsequent messages are created and understood. In the Real Words box, you can read a transcript from a conversation that was recorded in Denise's research lab. We'll share dialogs like this one throughout this book to illustrate ideas and concepts using real conversations. In this case, notice how Alicia's assertion that she is hard-working changes as the conversation unfolds. At first, Alicia doesn't realize that Marcus is criticizing her, and she offers more evidence to back up her claim. Over time, though, Alicia starts taking Marcus's comments more to heart. When Alicia repeats that she is hard-working later in the conversation, her statement is more forceful and defensive than it was at the beginning. This example illustrates how messages have different meanings at different times and how meaning depends on prior messages.

REAL WORDS

A HURTFUL CONVERSATION

This transcript was drawn from a study of dating couples (Priem, McLaren, & Solomon, 2010). In the study, the researchers asked one member of the couple to identify a personal trait he or she valued. Then they secretly instructed that person's dating partner to challenge that trait.

ALICIA: I wrote down that I was hard-working, because I had to work really hard to get into this college.
MARCUS: I don't understand; what was so hard about getting into this college?
ALICIA: Well, I always had this goal, and I worked hard toward it.
MARCUS: Like what? You had to finish high school? How is that hard?
ALICIA: Well, I also worked hard at sports too.
MARCUS: Your sports were softball and basketball; how were those hard?
ALICIA: What do you mean? You had to be like in top physical condition – that makes you hard-working. I had to run miles.
MARCUS: For softball?
ALICIA: Yes. That makes me hard-working.
MARCUS: I just don't see that it was all that hard.
ALICIA: What about how hard I work for my classes? How many hours of homework did I do last semester? Like six hours a night.
MARCUS: Steve's in the same major and he doesn't do any work. It's an easy major. It's like playing softball instead of soccer.
ALICIA: I'm sorry that I didn't play soccer and you think that's a better sport. We're not talking about soccer and we're not talking about your major. We're talking about me being hard-working and I am hard-working.
MARCUS: Are you sure?
ALICIA: Why are you putting me down right now?
MARCUS: I just don't think you are any more hard-working than anyone else.
ALICIA: What about the fact that I work five days a week waitressing? Do you know how hard waitressing is?
MARCUS: Oh brother, Alicia. Just about everyone we know waits tables.
ALICIA: I guess I don't care what you think. I think I'm hard-working. You shot down everything that I've said, but I still think I'm hard-working.

Interpersonal communication is consequential. Interpersonal communication has consequences – in other words, it produces outcomes. When people actively use interpersonal communication to accomplish a goal, those consequences are deliberate. For example, you might use interpersonal communication to persuade a classmate to help you with a paper, to resolve a conflict with a sibling, or to cheer up a friend. At other times, the consequences are unintentional. For example, without realizing it, you might put down a co-worker, insult a classmate, or hurt a romantic partner. The consequences of interpersonal communication, intended or unintended, can take a variety of forms. Some of the most common consequences of interpersonal communication include the following:

- *Learning:* Interpersonal communication allows you to gather information about yourself, other people, and past, present, or predicted events, beliefs, and attitudes.
- *Helping:* Interpersonal communication allows you to provide information, advice, emotional support, or assistance that can help the recipient deal with a problem.
- *Influencing:* Interpersonal communication allows you to persuade another person to provide help, give advice, share an activity, change an attitude, change a relationship, give permission, or fulfill an obligation.
- *Relating:* Interpersonal communication allows you to experience closeness or distance, agreement or disagreement, and equality or inequality with another person.
- *Playing:* Interpersonal communication allows you to experience humor, camaraderie, celebrations, as well as to pass time and coordinate shared activities.

PAUSE & REFLECT

Think about the last time that an interpersonal interaction made you feel especially strong emotions, such as happiness, anger, or sadness. What was it about the conversation that produced those emotions? In your experience, do communication experiences that occur face-to-face versus using some technology, such as texting or snapchat, evoke more or less intense emotions?

Interpersonal communication is irreversible. You can't take back messages that you have communicated, and you can't recreate communication opportunities that have passed. If you make hurtful comments, for example, you can apologize, you can explain, you can try to correct a misunderstanding, but all of your future conversations with that partner will include those comments as part of your shared history. Indeed, when you communicate using social media, you sometimes create a permanent record of your message others can revisit long into the future. Just as you can't "un-say" messages after the fact, you can't deliver messages after their moment has passed. Have you ever been teased or insulted, and thought of a perfect comeback hours after the conversation occurred? As much as you might want to call the person and deliver your zinger, you'll never recapture that moment in the interaction when your response would have been most appropriate.

Interpersonal communication is imperfect. Finally, keep in mind that interpersonal communication is imperfect. Your thoughts can never be completely communicated to another person. You have to use symbols to represent those ideas, and you have to rely on your partner to decipher those symbols. Inevitably, your partner will attach slightly different meanings to the symbols than you did. Sometimes, our different interpretations are noticeable, frustrating, or humorous. When Denise was a child, for example, she thought her father invited her to "sailing," when he actually asked her to go with him to "Salem" (a town 150 miles away) – although her warm clothing wasn't useless, an overnight bag would have been more helpful! Even when you don't notice a misunderstanding, try to keep in mind that there is always some slippage between the ideas in people's minds and the meanings they create through interpersonal communication.

Sometimes, people forget that interpersonal communication is imperfect, and they place too much faith in what communication can do. Table 1.1 corrects some common misconceptions about interpersonal communication. When you keep the limits of interpersonal communication in mind, you can begin to improve your interpersonal communication experiences.

Types of Messages

As you learned previously, interpersonal communication involves creating shared meaning with people. In this section, we describe the two general kinds of meanings created through interpersonal communication: content messages and relational messages.

Content messages are the literal or typical meanings of the symbols used to communicate. Consider the question "Are you using your car this afternoon?" You can attach a dictionary or literal meaning to those words and easily decipher the content meaning – the speaker wants to know if you will be doing something that involves your car. You can probably also recognize the conventional or typical meaning: this question often means that the speaker would like to borrow your car. As this example shows, content messages can be the direct or literal meaning of the words, or they can be the indirect meanings of the symbols that are used.

Content Messages
The literal or typical meanings of the symbols used to communicate.

Relational messages are the meanings that symbols have for the relationship between communicators. Let's continue the previous example. What kind of relationship do you think exists between communication

Relational Messages
The nature of the relationship between communication partners that is implied by the symbols that are used to communicate.

TABLE 1.1 Correcting misconceptions about interpersonal communication

Interpersonal communication is NOT a natural ability

Although people are born with the ability to learn to communicate, creating and interpreting messages requires self-knowledge, attention to a communication partner's perspective, detailed understanding of how the situation shapes meaning, and an ability to select and sequence messages to achieve particular goals. These abilities take effort and practice to develop.

Interpersonal communication does NOT always solve problems

Sometimes, talking through a problem helps people to understand each other, sheds new light on the situation, and leads to resolution. Sometimes, however, interpersonal communication produces greater misunderstanding, confusion, and an increase in tension. Effective communication can sometimes solve problems, but advice to "just talk about it" overlooks the flaws that are inherent in interpersonal communication.

Interpersonal communication does NOT always build close relationships

Interpersonal communication occurs within personal relationships, and it can help you create a bond with a relationship partner. But interpersonal communication can also be used to damage a relationship, decrease closeness, and avoid intimacy.

Interpersonal communication does NOT always advance pro-social goals

By communicating with other people, you can achieve a variety of desirable goals – for example, you can influence people, resolve conflicts, or provide comfort. But interpersonal communication also has negative consequences that may be intended or unintended. Through messages, people manipulate each other, create and escalate conflicts, and inflict pain. Interpersonal communication can advance positive outcomes, but it doesn't always do so.

partners if one asks the other, "Are you using your car this afternoon?" Notice that you aren't focused on the meanings of the words themselves, but what those words imply about the relationship. The communicators probably aren't strangers or enemies, because we don't usually ask strangers or enemies about their cars or their afternoon plans. The speaker's choice of words also suggests that the partners aren't really, really close – if they were, the speaker might just say, "Hey, I need your car." The symbols used to communicate shed some light on the relationship that exists between communication partners. In this case, you might conclude that the communicators have a familiar, but not intimate, relationship.

In general, relational messages convey where the relationship between communicators stands with regard to two dimensions: affiliation, or how much we like each other, and dominance, or how much power or status we have relative to each other (Courtright, 2016). Often, our messages reflect and reinforce our existing relationship, such as when a friend uses casual, familiar, and expressive language in a text ("Hey, on my way, can't wait!"). Other times, our messages might be an attempt to change the relationship. For example, an adolescent might make a bid for more dominance with a parent by asserting a plan, instead of asking for permission. As these examples show, relational messages are conveyed by how people choose to express content given the kind of relationship they either have or want to have with their communication partner.

PAUSE & REFLECT

What differences are there in your texts to a friend versus your parent or child? For example, do you use more acronyms and emojis when texting your friends? How do the differences in your texts reflect the differences in the qualities of these relationships?

Sometimes, relational messages are easily seen in the words or behaviors used to communicate, as in the case of phrases like "I'm so glad that we're friends," or "I want a divorce." However, research shows that people in interpersonal relationships often avoid discussing their relationship explicitly, especially if they aren't sure where they stand in the relationship (Knobloch, 2010). Instead, relational messages have to be inferred from a communicator's choice of symbols. As we make sense of relational messages, we use several sources of information (McLaren, Dillard, Tusing, & Solomon, 2014). As summarized in Table 1.2, the specific symbols people use to communicate can provide information about the relationship, especially if relationship information is expressed explicitly. In addition, though, you might consider what kind of interaction you are having, your prior relationship with your communication partner, your personal history or characteristics, and the social situation. All these influences on their meanings make relational messages hard to decipher. Nonetheless, because relational messages concern that type of personal connection created between partners, they are an important part of interpersonal communication.

CONNECT WITH THEORY

Visit the companion website to learn about Relational Framing Theory, which explains how people make inferences about the degree of affiliation and dominance expressed by a communication partner.

Contexts

Interpersonal communication can unfold between strangers, acquaintances, close friends, or family members. Most often, your communication partners will be people with whom you have a personal relationship. The shared history you have with your friends, family members, or romantic partner makes it easy to form a personal connection when you communicate. Communication is also essential to developing and maintaining closeness in personal relationships. In this section, we remind you of some of the other contexts in which you experience interpersonal communication.

Organizations. The workplace is a venue in which people have many interpersonal interactions. What happens within organizations depends a lot on the characteristics of the particular setting – whether it is formal or casual, whether there is a clear power hierarchy, or whether the industry traditionally employs men, or women, or both men and women. Within the organizational structure, people's experiences are also shaped by their interpersonal interactions (Fairhurst & Putnam, 2004). When you and a co-worker chat about your personal lives, when you pitch an idea to your boss, when you influence the decisions made by your team, and when you address a conflict about work schedules, you use interpersonal communication to connect with people. Moreover, interpersonal interactions with co-workers provide important, emotionally fulfilling experiences, and they allow us to express and work through our own personal issues (Miller, Considine, & Garner, 2007). On the other hand, a workplace environment can sometimes encourage fruitless and ongoing complaining, which contributes considerably to workplace stress (Roeder, Garner, & Carr, 2019). Thus, interpersonal communication is an integral part of organizations.

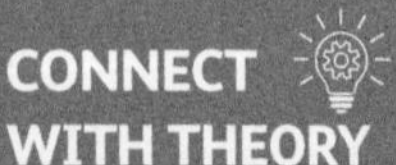

Visit the companion website to learn about Affection Exchange Theory, which explains how communicating affection produces health benefits.

Health settings. Interpersonal communication also occurs in contexts related to your health and well-being. Communication researchers have shown that giving and receiving affectionate messages decreases physical symptoms of stress and improves people's ability to recover from stressful experiences (Myers, 2016). In addition, the people in our lives might use interpersonal communication to influence our health behavior,

TABLE 1.2 Sources of information about relational messages

Source	*Examples*
The symbols used	"Let's get together more often" "I hope we never work together on another project"
The type of interaction	"That suit looks great on you" while shopping for clothes for an interview "That suit looks great on you" in the middle of an interview
The relationship history	"I love you" spoken for the first time between romantic partners "I love you" spoken at a 50th wedding anniversary
People's personal traits	"I need you to help me" from a new employee "I need you to help me" from a supervisor at work
The situation	"I love you" after a fight "I love you" before a long separation

from endorsing a healthy diet and exercise routine (Theiss, Carpenter, & Leustek, 2016) to encouraging risky behaviors like drinking, smoking, or unprotected sex (Koesten & Andersen, 2004). Our interactions with medical professionals also affect whether we get the care we need to maintain or regain our health (Thompson, Robinson, & Brashers, 2011). In other words, interpersonal communication interfaces with – and affects – our health and well-being.

Computer-mediated Communication
Interaction between people that is made possible by computer technology.

Computer-mediated communication. Many interpersonal communication experiences involve computers and technology such as snapchat, texting, email, Discord or Skype, online chats, online social networks (e.g., Facebook), and virtual worlds. Using technology, we are able to create a personal connection with others that transcends the separations imposed by time or space. **Computer-mediated communication** refers generally to the variety of ways in which computer technology allows people to exchange messages with each other. Computer-mediated communication offers a less threatening communication venue for people who get anxious about talking to new acquaintances (Caplan, 2005). In fact, Jen knows two men who prefer to address conflicts about their shared apartment by texting, which they rely on even while they are sitting in the same room! The study described in the "Inside Communication Research" box shows how communication can be different when it occurs face-to-face versus through computer-mediated channels. In every chapter of this book, we'll showcase a communication study like this one to reveal how communication researchers are working to better understand how interpersonal communication unfolds within – and affects – your life.

INSIDE COMMUNICATION RESEARCH

Interpersonal Communication in Online Contexts

Supportive communication is an essential resource to help people manage times of stress. The supportive messages that people receive through mediated channels can often have different characteristics and quality when compared to social support that is communicated face-to-face. People can seek support using both verbal and nonverbal strategies that can be direct or indirect, such as directly asking for help, hinting or complaining about a problem, and crying or sulking. In one study, Lucas Youngvorst and Andrew High (2018) investigated the ways that people seek support in online social networking sites and how different verbal and nonverbal aspects of their profile and status updates can elicit messages from others that are more or less supportive. They predicted that people would receive higher quality support messages when they had profile pictures that conveyed more negative emotions and wrote status updates that explicitly asked for support. They also expected that private messages would offer better support quality than public messages.

The researchers conducted an experiment in which they created several fictitious Facebook profiles supposedly belonging to a college-aged woman who had recently suffered a romantic break-up. They varied certain features of the profiles, such as the emotions expressed in profile pictures and the directness of support requests in status updates, to see which qualities garnered the highest quality support messages. The profile pictures were varied to include a generic picture of a dog, a picture of a woman looking melancholy, and a picture of a woman looking upbeat and positive. The status updates were altered to include no information, indirect bids for support (e.g., "Pretty bummed out, wondering why life is so hard sometimes.") and explicit requests for help (e.g., "Another break-up. Feeling pretty bummed out and could use some help. Anyone free to chat?"). Participants in the study were presented with one of the fake profiles and asked to write two supportive messages – one that would appear publicly on the person's page and one that would be sent via a private message. The researchers then analyzed the support messages that were written and rated them with regard to the quality of the support provided.

The results of the study showed that both direct and indirect status updates resulted in higher quality support messages than responses to posts with no information, but that direct requests for support did not necessarily produce better support messages than indirect posts. The profile pictures, on the other hand, tended to elicit higher quality support when the photo conveyed negative emotion than when it was positive or neutral. Private messages also generated higher quality support than public messages. The results of this study suggest that the ways people present themselves and talk about their problems online will shape the quality of supportive messages that they receive.

THINK ABOUT IT

1. The researchers in this study found that indirect and direct status updates elicited support messages of similar quality. Why might explicit requests for support not necessarily produce better support messages? Are there circumstances when indirect bids for support might be better received and produce better results?
2. Do you think that similar patterns would emerge when talking about a romantic break-up face-to-face instead of online? Do people who directly ask for support tend to get better support than those who hint around? Do people provide better support in private than in public? Why or why not?

Yinfan Huang
"Have you tried oversharing deeply personal thoughts on social media to help with the phone addiction?"
CartoonStock.com

FIGURE 1.3 Online social support

Source: © Yinfan Huang/www.cartoonstock.

PAUSE & REFLECT

What proportion of your interpersonal interactions involves the use of technology? How might your personal and work relationships be different if you didn't have technology to help you stay connected?

Putting Theory into Practice: Thinking Critically

The goal of this first section of the chapter has been to open your eyes to the complexity of interpersonal communication. You can learn to communicate more effectively if you appreciate the nuances of this rich and dynamic process.

Recognize the fallibility of symbols. One of the first steps toward developing your interpersonal communication skills is recognizing that communication is inherently flawed. The symbols you use will always have a different meaning to your interaction partner than they do to you, and you will never get your point across exactly as you intended. If you recognize that interpersonal communication is fallible, you can take steps to reduce miscommunication.

- As you communicate, pay attention to your partner's responses to see if they seem to be getting the right idea. Notice whether your partner asks relevant questions, laughs when you meant to be funny, or looks concerned when you express disappointment. Your partner's messages can tell you whether your meanings are coming across.
- If the messages you receive seem out of line, don't assume that your partner disagrees with you. Instead, double-check how well your meaning was understood. Phrases like "Did you understand that I meant. . .?" or "I'm not sure I was clear – what do you think I'm trying to say?" can help you to discover misunderstanding.
- Keep in mind that you have more than one opportunity to express your ideas, then restate, clarify, or elaborate your messages if you need to.

By double-checking your partner's interpretations and addressing points of confusion, you can improve the understanding that you achieve through interpersonal communication.

Pay attention to relational messages. Relational messages are always part of our interpersonal communication experiences, so you'll communicate more effectively if you pay attention to the relational messages that you receive and send to others. The Communication in Action 1.2 exercise is designed to help you become more aware of relational messages.

COMMUNICATION IN ACTION 1.2

Deciphering Relational Messages

This exercise helps you to decipher relational messages so that you can become more attentive to them in your interpersonal interactions. You can download Form 1.2 from the companion website to help you complete this activity. For each statement in the table, identify what you think is the content message based on the direct or implied meanings of the words. Then, for each relationship context listed, identify at least one possible relational message.

PRACTICING INTERPERSONAL COMMUNICATION

Interpersonal communication is a necessary and inevitable part of life – you can't avoid exchanging messages with people, and you can engage in interpersonal communication without a lot of practice or knowledge. At the same time, interpersonal communication is a skill: like playing music or soccer, it is the product of human creativity or effort that varies in perceived quality. When we focus on interpersonal communication as a skill, we acknowledge that it can be learned through study, practice, and observation. In this part of the chapter, we examine the characteristics of good interpersonal communication, conditions that promote high-quality communication, and how skillful interpersonal communication varies across contexts.

Communication Competence

Interpersonal Communication Competence
The ability to use symbols appropriately and effectively to create a personal connection with another person.

Fidelity
The extent to which meanings can be correctly inferred from the symbols that are used.

In general, competence is an ability to do something well, as measured against some standard for performance. **Interpersonal communication competence**, then, is the ability to use well the symbols that represent ideas and create a personal connection with another person. Communication competence is measured by six standards: fidelity, appropriateness, satisfaction, effectiveness, efficiency, and ethics (Spitzberg & Cupach, 2011).

Fidelity. **Fidelity** refers to the clarity of a message – the extent to which meanings can be correctly inferred from the symbols. Fidelity exists when a receiver can hear the message, understand the symbols, and interpret meanings accurately. Fidelity might be undermined by noise in the environment, such as when the sound of construction equipment outside an office makes it difficult for a teacher and student to hear each other. Fidelity is also reduced when communicators use different kinds of symbols, perhaps due to their distinct cultural backgrounds, educational experiences, or age. Consider, for example, how the abbreviations and acronyms that are common in text messages might be difficult for someone less familiar with communication technology to understand. Although threats to fidelity are often outside a person's control, communication competence is not. Competent communicators adjust their behaviors to overcome the barriers to communication – they eliminate noise or move to a quiet location, or they use less jargon when communicating with someone with a different background. As a result, competent communicators produce messages that are easier for a partner to understand.

Appropriateness. Communication is appropriate when the messages that people produce match the requirements of the situation. How do you know what is appropriate communication? All interpersonal interactions are guided by **social rules**, which are guidelines that specify the actions that are expected, preferred, and off-limits in a given situation. We have rules that apply broadly within a community, such as when online groups have guidelines specifying that participants will not insult one another. Particular relationship partners also have their own standards for appropriate communication. For example, parents and their adolescent children may develop communication patterns that discourage open discussion about sexual issues, illicit drug use, finances, and education, but allow communication about the child's friendships and other everyday topics (Baxter & Akkoor, 2011). Competent communicators notice the social rules that are relevant to a communication situation, and they produce messages appropriate to the circumstances.

Social Rules
Guidelines that specify the actions that are expected, preferred, and off-limits within an interaction.

PAUSE & REFLECT

Consider some of the interactions that you have had in the past week, including those related to school, work, and your personal relationships. What are some of the social rules that guided your communication in those situations? Do you have any distinct rules for communication using various forms of social media?

Satisfaction. Competent communication is also enjoyable. Consider the feelings you have after an especially good conversation – you might be energized, feel happy, and enjoy a sense of connection with your interaction partner. Compare those reactions to how you feel after a conversation where you were ignored, slighted, or misunderstood. What makes a conversation satisfying? Young adults report greater communication satisfaction in their relationship with a grandparent when the grandparents' communication conveys love, esteem, and caring, interactions focus on memories and stories, and grandparents display celebratory affection (Mansson, 2013). In the workplace, communication satisfaction arises from high-quality content messages, which address organizational practices, as well as relational messages that maintain personal connections between people in the organization (Gray & Laidlaw, 2004). In general, competent communicators create satisfying interactions by paying attention to their partner's point of view, being responsive to that partner, and maintaining a positive atmosphere.

Effectiveness. A fourth criterion for communication competence is effectiveness. Remember that interpersonal communication allows you to do many things, including learn, help, influence, relate, and play. Your communication is effective when you are able to produce the outcomes that you want. For example, if your best friend was upset about a conflict with his girlfriend, you might want to help make him feel better. If you choose your messages well ("Let's talk through what happened" or "I can appreciate how you're feeling"), you can make a big difference to your friend. Less competent communicators are less effective because their messages don't allow them to achieve their goals.

Efficiency. Interpersonal communication is efficient if you can produce the outcomes you seek with no more than a reasonable amount of effort. Think about the last time you had to ask for a favor – perhaps you needed time off from work or you wanted to use a friend's computer. How hard did you try to get what you wanted? If your request was granted after just a little effort, your communication was efficient. What if you had to provide a lot of reasons or even beg or threaten before you could get what you were after? Although you might achieve your outcome, your communication would be less efficient, because you had to put out a lot of effort – and maybe even damage your image or relationship – to get what you wanted.

Ethical Communication
Using values as a moral guide when you interact with other people.

Ethics. Ethics is a consideration of what constitutes right versus wrong or good versus evil. **Ethical communication** involves using values as a moral guide when you interact with other people. Ethical communicators make their values and assumptions clear to others, and they demonstrate a respect for the values and assumptions that other people express. Unethical communication can be tempting at times; for example, it might be easier to get a loan from a relative if you imply that the money is needed for tuition. Although communication strategies that involve lying, false implications, or hostility can be effective and efficient, they fall short of being ethical, because the messages don't represent a person's agenda honestly and they don't treat other people with integrity. This final standard for communication competence requires being true to yourself and others when you participate in interpersonal interactions.

Communication competence can be difficult to achieve because it involves being clear, appropriate, satisfying, effective, efficient, and ethical, and these goals can sometimes conflict. Consider the example of Robyn, who has young children and doesn't want to waste her time dating anyone who doesn't like kids. When Robyn meets a potential romantic partner, either in person or online, she has a few choices. If she wants to be appropriate, she might casually chat about children, eventually mention her own kids, and observe her communication partner's response. This strategy will give Robyn some information about the other person's attitude about her children, but it might not be very precise. Or Robyn could say right away that she's not interested in seeing anyone who doesn't like kids. This strategy would effectively and efficiently weed out potential partners who don't meet her criteria, but it might be so inappropriate that suitable dating partners would be put off. Being a competent communicator involves balancing all of the different requirements for communication competence.

Promoting Communication Competence

Now that you know the standards for competent interpersonal communication, let's consider some of the conditions that can help you to achieve communication competence. In the following paragraphs, we examine three ingredients for interpersonal communication competence: motivation, knowledge, and skills.

Motivation. Competent communication takes effort – you need to pay attention to what is and is not appropriate and satisfying, weigh your options so that you maximize effectiveness and efficiency, and attend to ethical considerations. As a result, competent communication requires motivation or a desire to communicate well. Consider how you might feel as you prepare for a job interview. You'd probably spend some time thinking about the kinds of questions you'll be asked, and how you can answer them in ways that make you look like a good employee. When you have important outcomes that are tied to your communication performance, you'll be motivated to identify clear, appropriate, satisfying, effective, efficient, and ethical conversational strategies. When the consequences of your interpersonal communication are less dire, you'll be less concerned about getting your message just right.

PAUSE & REFLECT

Recall a time when you were especially motivated to achieve a communication goal. How did your desire to achieve that outcome affect what you did before, during, and after that conversation?

Knowledge. All the motivation in the world won't help if you don't know what communication behaviors are best for a given situation. Consider the challenges of comforting another person. As you'll learn in Chapter 14, different people prefer different kinds of comforting. Some people like tangible help that will fix their problem, others want information that will help them figure out a solution on their own, and still others like to discuss their feelings and emotions, rather than fix the problem directly (McLaren & High, 2019). If you care about a person and empathize with his or her distress, you'll be motivated to help. To do so, though, also requires knowing what kinds of comfort the other person wants and how to provide it.

You can develop the knowledge you need to communicate competently in the same way that you learn about other topics. Studying interpersonal communication will help you to learn communication strategies and the situations where they can be used. You can also observe other people to see what works or doesn't work for them. And of course, paying attention to your own successes and failures is an important source of knowledge. If you actively seek knowledge, you can become more expert at identifying the interpersonal communication behaviors that are appropriate and effective within particular situations.

Communication Skills
The ability to create symbols and perform behaviors that are clear appropriate, satisfying, effective, efficient, and ethical in a given social situation.

Skills. People need skills to act upon their motivation and knowledge in an interpersonal interaction. **Communication skills** are the ability to create symbols and perform behaviors that are appropriate and effective in a given social situation. Skills aren't reflexes or habits – they are learned. When you have learned communication skills, you can enact behaviors intentionally to achieve desired outcomes (Spitzberg, 2003). In particular, a skillful communicator is someone who can do the following tasks (adapted from Wilson & Sabee, 2003, pp. 8–9):

- *Identify expectations within a situation and behave in ways that meet or exceed expectations.* For example, when you meet with an instructor to discuss your class project, recognize that your instructor expects you to show enthusiasm about the project, to express ideas of your own, and to ask questions about how to complete the assignment successfully.
- *Recognize when obstacles to success are and are not controllable, and respond with behaviors that increase the chance of success.* For example, when you ask your family to excuse you from Thanksgiving dinner because you made other plans, start off by acknowledging the importance of spending holidays together and expressing appreciation for your family.
- *Enact, monitor, and adjust plans for communication.* For example, if your explanation for forgetting your romantic partner's birthday doesn't lead to forgiveness, consider planning a special, though belated, celebration.
- *Adapt quickly and smoothly to changes or new information.* For example, when you discover that someone you are interested in romantically is dating someone else, redirect your messages toward becoming friendly acquaintances – just in case.
- *Enact behaviors that invite and include different perspectives.* For example, if a newcomer to your social group reveals a political affiliation that isn't shared by most of the others, acknowledge the validity of different points of view and try to learn about this person's beliefs.

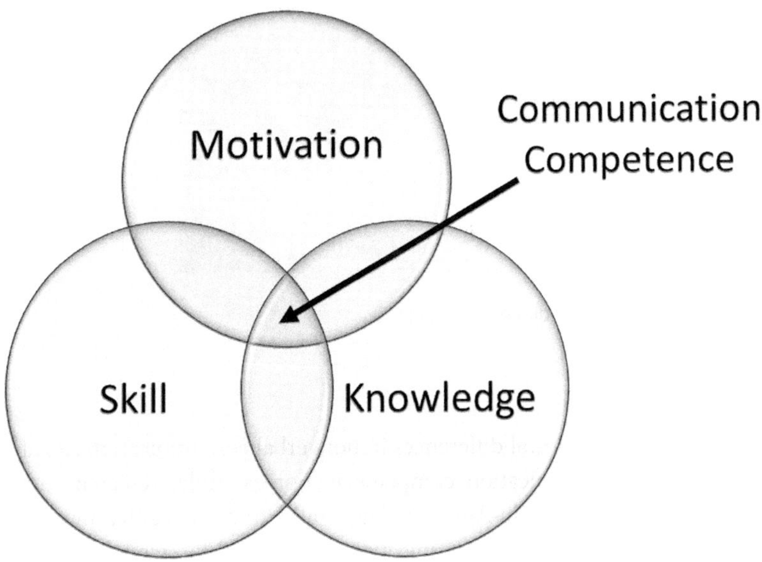

FIGURE 1.4 Communication competence

As the preceding list illustrates, skillful communicators need to be attentive to the situation and to translate their perceptions into a fitting response. When motivation, knowledge, and skills all exist, the possibility for competent communication exists (see Figure 1.4).

The Role of Culture, Setting, and Age

Interpersonal communication competence is always evaluated with respect to the context for communication. Consider how competent communication requires different behaviors depending on whether you're in class or at a party, talking to your professor or a friend, or at work or with your family. Many new norms for communication also emerged with social distancing and remote interaction as the COVID-19 pandemic spread in 2020. In this section, we explore some of the ways in which the context for communication can affect standards for competence.

Cultural differences. Cultural differences are one reason that perceptions of communication competence vary. There are both linguistic and nonverbal differences between cultures that can complicate communication competence. Many linguistic cultural idioms do not translate across cultures, which can easily lead to misunderstanding if misapplied in a different language. For example, in the Ukraine it is customary to say to a newborn baby "Oh, what an ugly child!" because it is considered bad luck to compliment the baby (Stukan, 2018). Although Ukrainians may say this to protect the baby and not jinx it, a non-native speaker could easily misinterpret such a message and assume that the baby and the parents are

FIGURE 1.5 A family dinner

Source: Getty Images.

being insulted. Cultural differences in nonverbal communication can also undermine communication competence. For example, research shows that Hispanic and Anglo-Americans generally do not consider a greeting kiss to be part of good communication in an initial interaction, whereas Spaniards and Chileans rate a greeting kiss as important in this situation (Johnson, Lindsey, & Zakahi, 2001). Likewise, research shows that Mexican Americans report greater comfort with affectionate touching with acquaintances in public than European Americans, especially when they identify with their Mexican ethnic identity (Burleson, Roberts, Coon, & Soto, 2019). Therefore, physical contact between acquaintances may be an expected and desirable aspect of communication in some cultures, but could be misinterpreted by individuals for whom this practice is not a cultural norm. The cultural context shapes standards for fidelity, rules for appropriateness, factors leading to satisfaction, the priority placed on effectiveness and efficiency, and the values that underlie communication ethics. In other words, culture shapes what it means to communicate competently.

PAUSE & REFLECT

What standards for competent communication are most prominent in your own friendships? Do you know people who seem to have different expectations for communication between friends?

Setting. Our perceptions of communication competence also depend on the setting in which the interaction takes place. For example, both doctors and patients see an ability to explain or provide information about medical problems as an important part of communication competence in a medical setting, but neither doctors nor patients consider emotional supportiveness relevant to each other's competence (Cegala, Gade, Broz, & McClure, 2004). Even subtle variations between settings can have dramatic consequences for evaluations of messages. For example, a flirtatious message between co-workers is seen as more sexually harassing when it occurs in a meeting room during work hours versus at an after-hours retirement party (Solomon, 2006). In the How Do You Rate? 1.1 exercise, you can test yourself using the features of communication competence in computer-mediated interactions.

Age. Your perceptions of communication competence are also related to your communication partner's age. Young children need to develop both their verbal communication skills and their knowledge about how to use communication (Sanders, 2007). When we communicate with children, then, we allow them greater latitude for making speech errors, leaving out relevant information, or perhaps sharing more detail than is necessary. By adolescence, we expect communicators to have an understanding of appropriate conversation, but we might accept that teenagers are still developing their ethical standards. As people age, we might expect more wisdom, maturity, authority, or forgetfulness from them (Pecchioni, Wright, & Nussbaum, 2005). In these ways, perceptions of communication competence are tied to changes that occur over the lifespan.

HOW DO YOU RATE? 1.1

Computer-Mediated Communication Competence

Technologies such as email, text-messaging, Instagram, and Zoom present interpersonal communication contexts that put people's competence to the test. Brian Spitzberg (2006) created a scale to measure people's computer-mediated communication competence. The scale measures your motivation, knowledge, and skill for online communication. To see how you rate on computer-mediated communication competence, complete the scale on the companion website.

Putting Theory into Practice: Communicating Competently

Becoming a competent communicator is a never-ending process. If you make interpersonal communication competence a priority, you can become a more effective communicator over the course of your lifetime.

Clarify your communication ethics. Ethical communication involves being responsive to your values and committed to moral behavior, regardless of context. One way you can improve communication competence, then, is to take stock of your values and identify how you can communicate ethically in any communication situation. The Communication in Action 1.3 exercise can help you to do this.

COMMUNICATION IN ACTION 1.3

Identifying Strategies for Ethical Communication

This exercise helps you to identify specific communication strategies that will help you accomplish your ethical goals during interaction. In the table provided on the companion website, identify some of the values that are most important to you when you communicate with other people. Then, identify how you can demonstrate those values in your interpersonal interactions. The first two rows provide examples to help get you started.

Practice, practice, practice. Communication is a skill, not unlike playing an instrument or riding a horse. And just as with other skills, you'll get better at it if you practice. Your experiences as a college student give you many opportunities to practice interpersonal communication.

- If you have trouble talking to new acquaintances, introduce yourself to a classmate, chat with someone you meet at the library, or strike up a conversation with the person waiting in line at the coffee shop. These are low-risk situations that allow you to practice creating appropriate and satisfying conversations.
- Within your classes, make a commitment to commenting or asking a question at least once a week. Although you might find it uncomfortable to draw attention to yourself, your instructor and your classmates will probably appreciate your contributions. More to the point, the classroom is a better place than the boardroom to develop your ability to be clear, concise, and effective.
- Are you upset about your roommate's behavior, a class grade, or your family's unwillingness to adjust to your exam schedule? Here's your chance to build your communication competence. Try to express your concerns in ways that are clear ("Here is exactly what is bothering me"), appropriate ("I recognize that you're the final authority in the class"), and ethical ("Nothing is more important to me than my family"). Then, take stock of what worked and what didn't, so you can do better the next time.

Adapt to communication situations. Keep in mind that there isn't one right way to communicate. As you encounter different communication situations, consider a few basic questions to get you thinking about how to best adapt to those circumstances:

- What are the expectations people have for me, given their cultural background? How should I change my expectations given my partner's cultural background?
- What are the expectations people have for me, given the context (personal relationship, work situation, health setting, or computer-mediated interaction)? How should I change my expectations, given the context?
- What are the expectations people have for me, based on my age? How should I change my expectations, based on my communication partner's age?

This list can get you started thinking about how to adapt your communication behaviors to the different kinds of interpersonal interactions you experience.

STUDYING INTERPERSONAL COMMUNICATION

When we think of interpersonal communication as a skill, we focus on how people create and perform messages in ways that are more or less competent. The science of interpersonal communication refers to studies conducted by communication researchers to understand how interpersonal communication works. Physicists study the properties of physical substances, such as their molecular structure, how they are affected by forces like heat or radiation, and the effects of one physical substance on other substances. Interpersonal communication researchers study the properties of interaction between people, such as the structure of messages or conversations, how messages and conversations are affected by the characteristics of the participants or the situation, and the outcomes of the interaction. Understanding the scientific study of interpersonal communication can help you to see how the practice of communication is related to the parts of communication and how they work together. In this section of the chapter, you'll learn about theory and research as the two core components of communication science.

SCHOLAR SPOTLIGHT

Visit the Communication Café on the companion website to view a conversation with the late Charles Berger, a pioneer in the scientific study of interpersonal communication.

Theory

A **theory** is a description of the relationships among concepts that helps us to understand a phenomenon. In a sense, a theory is just an explanation for why something is the way it is. In science, for example, the theory of gravity explains why things fall down, and the theory of evolution explains the diversity of species that exist on our planet. You create informal theories every time you try to make sense of a situation. Why did your parents divorce? Why do you have such a good time with your best friend? Why did someone else get the job you wanted? Because interpersonal communication theories help you answer questions like these, the following sections help you to understand the parts of a theory.

Theory
A description of the relationships among concepts that promote an understanding of a phenomenon.

PAUSE & REFLECT

Think about the break-up of a marriage or dating relationship that you either experienced or witnessed. How do you explain that break-up? Do you think that other people involved in that relationship would explain the break-up in the same way? If not, how do your theories differ?

A theory highlights specific concepts. How do we understand an event, situation, or experience? We do so by identifying the relevant details. A theory focuses on some parts of a situation and ignores other details. Let's consider the theory you might develop for why you didn't get a job you wanted. You might focus on your lack of training or experience; you might consider the stiff competition; you might think that the interviewer was biased against you for some reason; or you might decide it was just bad luck. Each of these "theories" emphasizes different concepts: training, competition, interviewer bias, and luck. The **concepts** within a theory, then, are the categories of phenomena that are believed to be relevant to understanding an event, situation, or experience. If you think that whether people like you depends on how confident you are when you talk, the concepts in your personal interpersonal communication theory are communication style and liking. Throughout this book, you'll learn about many concepts that can shed light on your communication experiences.

Concepts
Categories of phenomena that are believed to be relevant to understanding an event, situation, or experience.

A theory describes how concepts are related. A theory does more than just identify relevant concepts – it describes how those concepts are related to each other. If you decide that you didn't get the job offer because you didn't perform well during your interview, you are linking interpersonal communication competence to getting a job. In particular, you are saying that communication competence and getting a job have a **positive association**: the more competence, the greater the likelihood of getting hired. Your theory, then, would look like the first model in Figure 1.6.

Positive Association
When an increase in the amount, frequency, or intensity of one phenomenon corresponds with an increase in another phenomenon.

Negative Association
When a decrease in the amount, frequency, or intensity of one phenomenon corresponds with an increase in another phenomenon.

Curvilinear Association
When the positive or negative association between two phenomena exists only up to a certain point, and then reverses.

There can be other types of relationships between concepts as well. As illustrated in Figure 1.6, there is a **negative association** between nervousness and getting a job: the more nervous you seem, the less likely you are to get the job. A **curvilinear association** exists when two concepts are positively or negatively related, but only up to a point. For example, communicating friendliness can help you get the job offer, but only up to a point – extremely friendly behavior might be seen as unprofessional and hurt your chances of getting hired. Because phenomena in the world around us are related in many different and complex ways, theories can describe a variety of relationships among concepts.

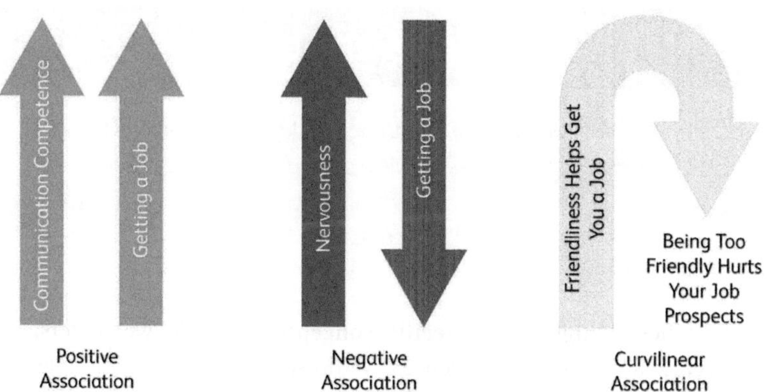

FIGURE 1.6 Examples of relationships described by theories

A theory is always incomplete. Another quality of theories needs to be mentioned: theories are always incomplete. For example, success in an interview is probably based on many different factors – your training and experience, your communication competence, the interviewer's personal biases, and a host of other factors, ranging from the weather that day to economic projections and even including your height. If a theory included every possible relevant concept, it wouldn't be very helpful, because it wouldn't focus attention on the concepts that really matter. In practice, then, a theory emphasizes particular concepts that a communication scholar believes are most important to understanding an event, situation, or experience. Other concepts that might be involved are left out.

A theory is tested against the experiences of people. Communication theories are similar to the explanations you create to understand your own experiences, but there are some important differences. Whereas your private theories focus on understanding your personal experience, a formal theory tries to understand the experiences of people in general. In addition, your private theories are evaluated against your own impressions and beliefs, but formal theories are judged by communication experts based on how accurate or useful they are for understanding interpersonal communication. You might conclude, for example, that you didn't get a job because you were so much taller than the boss – and you might even be right. Your ideas don't rise to the level of interpersonal communication theory unless they are supported by the experiences of many people documented in carefully designed research studies. Because this notion of testing theories through research is an important part of the science of interpersonal communication, we turn to that topic next.

IDEA: PROMOTING INCLUSION, DIVERSITY, EQUITY, AND ACCESS

Many theories in the field of interpersonal communication have been developed and tested in predominantly Western, educated, industrialized, rich, and democratic (WEIRD) populations, with samples that are largely white, cisgendered, and heterosexual. What might interpersonal communication theories be missing due to this lack of diversity and representation? As you learn about interpersonal communication throughout this book, we will invite reflections on how scholars could develop theories and design studies to promote inclusion, diversity, equity, and access.

Research

A good theory is accurate, meaning that the explanation it offers more or less matches reality. Thus, interpersonal communication scholars test their theories by observing communication in the real world, and comparing what they observe to the ways that theories describe communication. Interpersonal communication research encompasses the variety of methods that communication scholars use to test theories against real-life experiences.

Broadly speaking, communication research involves observing interpersonal communication and drawing conclusions based on those observations. As summarized in Table 1.3, researchers use a variety of methods to study interpersonal communication.

TABLE 1.3 Research methods for the study of interpersonal communication

Interviews

The researcher asks people questions about their communication experience, usually following an outline for the interview but also probing topics as they come up. Interviews allow researchers to interact closely with the people they are studying.

Ethnography

The researcher observes a group of people, either as an anonymous bystander or by participating in interpersonal interactions, and takes detailed notes on communication experiences. Researchers draw conclusions from studies like these by reflecting on their observations, looking for patterns that seem especially important or meaningful, and identifying core themes or concepts.

Surveys/questionnaires

The researcher asks participants short-answer or multiple-choice questions by phone, the Internet, or on paper. These tools might also include short-answer questions, which the researcher codes with numbers to represent different types of responses. Then, researchers use statistics to evaluate the relationships between scores.

Interaction studies

The researcher records conversations and examines patterns of communication over the course of the dialog. The key characteristic of an interaction study is that it captures actual communication between people. These recordings allow researchers to analyze patterns of communication as they unfold over time.

Experiments

The researcher manipulates some aspect of a situation and records behaviors under those conditions, perhaps using questionnaires or coding behavior to identify different types of actions. Experiments often involve dividing participants into groups and giving each group different experiences – other than the manipulated aspect of the situation, the researcher tries to keep the experiences of the different groups identical.

PAUSE & REFLECT

If a researcher did an ethnographic study of your college or university – in other words, observed what people at your school do, who talks to whom, and what kinds of topics they talk about – what communication practices would stand out?

HOW DO YOU RATE? 1.2

Communication Satisfaction

You can probably recall interactions you've had that were extremely enjoyable, as well as ones that were quite unpleasant. Visit the **companion website** to complete a scale that measures communication satisfaction in both European and African American populations (Larkey & Hecht, 1995). It shows how researchers assess communication concepts using a questionnaire.

Let's focus on surveys and questionnaires as one common type of research method. If you have ever completed a course evaluation form or rated your satisfaction with an online shopping tool, you've participated in a survey or questionnaire study. In this approach to research, a lot of people are asked the same set of questions, and they record their answer by choosing among options – not unlike a multiple-choice test. Researchers then add up or average responses to different questions to figure out how people score on a topic. The How Do You Rate? 1.2 box demonstrates how questionnaires are used by communication scholars to measure certain features of interaction.

Researchers have a lot of methods available to explore interpersonal communication. These methods all provide ways of observing and analyzing concepts that are relevant to communication experiences. By comparing the results of these studies to communication theories, scholars advance our understanding of how interpersonal communication works.

Putting Theory into Practice: Studying Interpersonal Communication

As a student of interpersonal communication, you will learn about a lot of different theories and hear about a variety of different studies that explain and examine interpersonal communication phenomena. As you read about theories and research in this book and hear about them from your instructor, use the guidelines given in this section to be a smart consumer of information about interpersonal communication.

Think theoretically about interpersonal communication. Theories are helpful because they focus attention on the issues that matter. One way to develop your knowledge of interpersonal communication is to pay attention to the theories you form about your own experiences. What are the concepts or details that you think are most important, and how do you think those concepts relate to each other? The Communication in Action 1.4 exercise can help you become more aware of your own theories about interpersonal communication.

COMMUNICATION IN ACTION 1.4

Testing Your Own Theories of Communication

For three days, keep a diary in which you record at least three conversations you have on each day. For each interaction, describe who was present, the setting for the conversation, the background leading up to the event, the content of the interaction, and the reactions that you and your partner had to the conversation. Rate each conversation on a scale of 1 to 5 in terms of how satisfying the interaction was, with 5 being the most satisfying. Then, examine each entry to identify the features of conversations that were especially satisfying or unsatisfying. How might these features be arranged to present your theory of communication satisfaction?

FIGURE 1.7 Denise and Andy High, who did the study described in the Inside Communication Research box, discuss nonverbal cues displayed during a conversation that was recorded in Penn State's Communication Research Laboratory

Evaluate research on interpersonal communication. You'll have the opportunity in this book to learn about communication research. Lots of studies report interesting findings, but it is important to think critically about the research methods that are used in those studies. Here are some criteria to apply when you read about studies of interpersonal communication:

- Do the findings in this study apply to all people, in general, or are they limited to a certain population or group?
- Do the questions on surveys and questionnaires really measure what the researchers say they do?
- In experimental studies, are the manipulated conditions realistic and ethical, and do they produce the effects that the researcher intended?
- Are the research methods used in the study the best way to answer the researcher's questions, or would a different method have been more appropriate?
- Do the researcher's personal opinions bias their research methods or findings?

You can learn a lot more about interpersonal communication research in a class devoted to that topic; in the meantime, you can think critically about whether the research methods in the studies you encounter make sense to you.

INTERPERSONAL COMMUNICATION ETHICS

As you study interpersonal communication – both its practice and the research that informs what we know about interpersonal communication – you will improve your ability to make educated decisions about how you communicate. Earlier in this chapter, you learned that competent communicators engage in ethical communication by using their values as a moral guide when communicating with others. Because all interpersonal communication involves an ethical dimension, we end this first chapter by delving deeper into ethics as they are related to interpersonal communication practice and research.

Communicating Ethically

In general, a consideration of ethics involves questions about *right* and *wrong*, what we value as *good* or *honorable* or *moral,* and how people conduct themselves to promote and protect that which is *good*. Unfortunately, what constitutes *right* and *wrong* isn't always obvious, and people don't always agree about what is *good* and what is *bad*. Understanding ethical communication is further complicated by the fact that an evaluation of *good* and *bad* communication must also consider the specifics of the communication situation. For example, honesty is almost universally valued as *good* communication behavior and hurting someone's feelings is typically viewed as *bad* communication behavior, so what happens when you find yourself in a situation in which your honesty might be hurtful? Should you be honest even though the result might be negative, or should you be dishonest to protect the other person's feelings? In many ways, your decision in this context will depend on which trait – honesty or kindness – you view as most honorable or moral in that situation. Interpersonal interactions can be so automatic and fast that we often don't reflect on the values we want to promote when we communicate with others. One component of ethical communication, then, is being attentive to the values that you want to uphold in a particular situation.

Interpersonal communication occurs between people, and **interpersonal communication ethics** involve a consideration of the moral responsibilities that you have to the other person and to your relationship when making communication decisions. As you'll learn throughout this book, your interpersonal communication behaviors have consequences for others – you can affect how people think about themselves and others (and you), the emotions that others experience, the quality of their relationships, and whether they achieve their goals, resolve their conflicts, or find support in times of distress. In their book on communication ethics, communication scholars Ronald Arnett, Janie Harden Fritz, and Leeanne Bell (2009) define ethical interpersonal communication as communication that takes responsibility for the communication partner, as well as the relationship with that person, whatever the personal consequences might be. Thus, another component of ethical interpersonal communication is recognizing the impact of your communication decisions on other people and your relationship with them.

Interpersonal Communication Ethics
Considering moral responsibilities to other people and relationships when making communication decisions.

Given that definitions of what is *right* or *wrong* and *good* or *bad* can be hard to pin down, how do you decide which communication choices are ethical? As communicators, we need to avoid assuming that

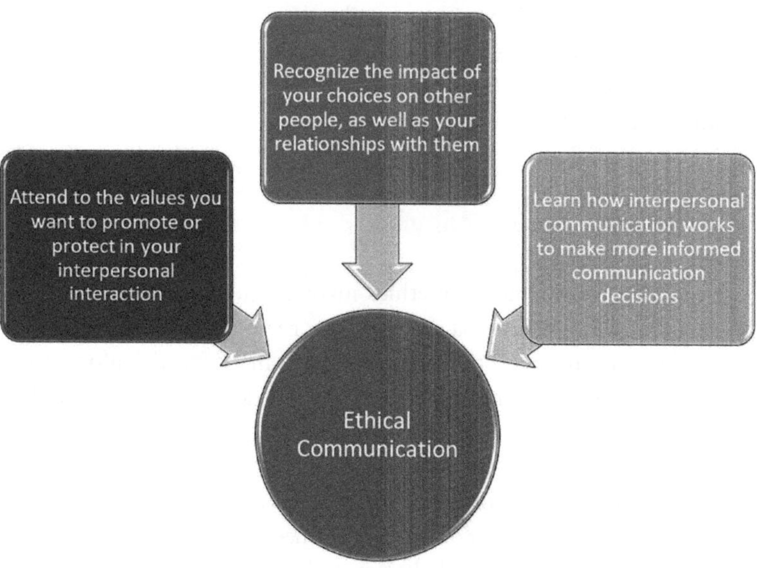

FIGURE 1.8 Components of ethical interpersonal communication

anything goes. Although people have different views of what is *right* and *wrong*, that does not mean that any behavior is acceptable as long as somebody believes it is the right thing to do. But we also need to avoid assuming that there is one single objectively *right* way to communicate. Communication ethics involves an informed consideration of the diverse values that exist in our world as we discover the principles that we want to protect and uphold through our own actions (Arnett et al., 2009). A third component of ethical interpersonal communication is learning about how communication works and how it affects people so that you can make informed decisions about your own communication behavior.

The three elements that contribute to ethical interpersonal communication are summarized in Figure 1.8. You have taken an important step toward improving your communication ethics by choosing to learn more about interpersonal communication. As you study interpersonal communication, work toward identifying the values that are most important to you as a communicator and reflect on how you want to affect others through interpersonal communication.

Ethics in Communication Research

Scholars who conduct research on interpersonal communication also attend to standards for moral behavior within the scientific community. All scientists are expected to be truthful in how they report research findings, to clearly identify the sources that they consulted in developing their thinking, and to credit through authorship the people who played a substantive role in producing a research report. Interpersonal communication researchers also have important ethical obligations that revolve around protecting the people who participate in research studies.

Sometimes, the questions a researcher seeks to answer involve behaving in ways that would be inappropriate outside the research setting. For example, studying very private or sensitive topics, such as conflict within a family, communication about sexual intimacy, or verbally aggressive communication, involves probing into topics that are often only discussed within close relationships. These are important topics to learn about, in part because they are such influential and powerful communication experiences, and we wouldn't want interpersonal communication researchers to neglect questions about sensitive issues. Instead, researchers conduct their investigations into topics such as these in ways that protect the confidentiality of the research participants and the information that they provide. In addition, people are typically given a description of the study in advance so that they can participate – or not – with full knowledge of the issues that will be examined.

Occasionally, studies conducted by interpersonal communication researchers might involve procedures that are only explained to the participant after the fact. Consider, for example, the study conducted in Denise's research lab on hurtful communication, which was featured in the Real Words box earlier in this chapter. Denise and her colleagues were trying to find out how people react emotionally and physiologically to hurtful messages. To get answers, they couldn't tell people in advance that their romantic partner was going to say something hurtful – if the research participants were forewarned, they wouldn't have been hurt. Instead, Denise's research group took several steps to minimize risks to their participants: (a) they monitored the interactions through a one-way mirror, so that they could interrupt any conversations that were excessively upsetting; (b) they provided specific guidelines to the romantic partners, to gain control over the focus and intensity of the hurtful messages; and (c) they explained the procedures to participants in detail after the study was over, with particular emphasis on the fact that the romantic partner had only been following instructions when they said hurtful things. Once participants knew that the comments were scripted for their partners, they no longer felt hurt.

Interpersonal communication research involves observing people, analyzing messages produced by people, or engaging people in surveys or experiments that focus on their own behavior and their relationships with other people. In other words, the science of interpersonal communication delves into the personal conduct and lives of the people who participate in research studies. Consequently, when scholars seek to advance our understanding of interpersonal communication, ethical considerations are always relevant.

Putting Theory into Practice: Ethical Interpersonal Communication

Every topic that is covered in this book involves questions about ethics. Which values do you want to promote when you communicate with people from other cultures, when you present yourself to others, when you make sense of other people's communication behaviors? Which principles are important to you as you choose your words, display nonverbal messages, experience and act upon emotions, and listen to others? How will you uphold your standards for right and wrong when developing and ending relationships, maintaining intimate bonds, and communicating within your family? And how will you influence other people, manage your conflicts, and give or receive support in ways that are morally sound?

Because ethics are a part of all of the topics you will learn about, we have included opportunities for you to explore communication ethics at the end of every chapter in this book. By considering the questions posed in these exercises, our hope is that you will develop your awareness of the values that inform your interpersonal communication and, in turn, develop an ability to engage in ethical interpersonal communication.

SUMMARY

This chapter begins your study of interpersonal communication. As a foundation for this journey, you learned that interpersonal communication is the use of symbols to represent ideas so that meanings can be shared between people. You also learned that interpersonal communication is a continuous and dynamic process, it has consequences, and it is irreversible and imperfect. We use interpersonal communication to convey both content and relational messages, and we do so in all of the contexts in which our lives unfold.

You also learned that interpersonal communication is a skill, meaning that it is the product of human creative activity, practice, and effort. Just as an artist or athlete can perfect their technique through study and practice, you can improve how you communicate with other people. Communication competence involves sending clear messages, being appropriate or responsive to social rules, producing satisfying interactions, achieving your objective both effectively and efficiently, and communicating in ways that are ethical. Although meeting all these criteria can be challenging, your communication competence should increase if you are motivated to communicate well, you improve your knowledge about interpersonal communication, and you develop the skills you need to perform the communication behaviors that fit a given situation. Remember, also, that what counts as competent communication will vary across the many circumstances that you experience over the course of your life.

As you strive to become a better communicator, take advantage of advances in interpersonal communication theory and research. A theory is an effort to explain or understand something by identifying the most relevant concepts and describing how they are related. A theory won't tell you everything you need to know about interpersonal communication, but it can provide some general knowledge that may help you to understand your experiences. Keep in mind that the information you'll learn about interpersonal communication is usually based on research. Through interviews, ethnography, survey and questionnaires, interaction studies, and experiments, communication researchers gather information about interpersonal communication, and they use that information to develop or improve their theories. Just like other fields of study, such as biology, psychology, or economics, interpersonal communication is a discipline filled with people doing studies to advance our knowledge.

Although you're just beginning your exploration of interpersonal communication, you already have some tips you can use to improve your communication experiences. By thinking critically about interpersonal communication, making communication competence a priority, and studying interpersonal communication in the world around you, you can develop the tools you need to use symbols to create a personal connection with other people. Based on what you have learned about interpersonal communication so far, consider the following activities for exploring communication ethics. Activities such as these are included at the end of every chapter, so that you can develop your sense of communication ethics at the same time as you build your expertise in interpersonal communication.

ACTIVITIES FOR EXPLORING COMMUNICATION ETHICS

At this end of each chapter in this book, we'll present some opportunities for you to consider communication ethics. Remember that ethical communication involves using values as a moral guide when you interact with other people. The exercises we offer invite you to decide what an ethical communicator would – or should – do in a particular situation, to think about an ethical dilemma, and to collect evidence that can inform a judgment about ethical communication.

What Would You/Should You Do?

Imagine that your good friend is running for office in a student organization on campus. Of course, your friend wants to get enough votes to win. You've been proud of your friend for working hard to connect with people in the organization by describing her priorities and values. As the election draws closer, though, you've noticed that she is offering people rewards for supporting her. For example, you clearly heard her tell someone in the organization that she would make him treasurer if he voted for her. You appreciate that competent communication involves being both effective and efficient, and this strategy is likely to win the election. As you reflect on other standards for competent communication, like appropriateness, you have some concerns. As an ethical communicator, what would you or should you do?

Something to Think About

Communication research involves making observations about communication and comparing those observations to the assumptions made within a communication theory. Sometimes, communication research involves recording conversations that people have in their own homes or videotaping partners as they talk in a communication lab. In fact, some studies involve getting partners to have a conflict or asking one partner to be hurtful, upset, or supportive. These studies can yield information about how people communicate with each other, but they also intrude on the private domain of a relationship. What are the ethical issues involved in conducting research on personal topics like interpersonal communication?

Analyze Communication Ethics Yourself

The college you attend uses symbols to represent itself to both people inside the institution and outsiders, such as potential students, alumni, and the community around the university. Review the home page for your university or college, your major department, and a few programs on your campus such as athletics, theatre, or fraternities and sororities. What are some of the symbols that are used to represent your college and particular organizations within it? How well do these symbols capture qualities of the institution they represent? How do these symbols distort or neglect important, though perhaps less glowing, qualities of your college or the particular organization? What are the ethical issues involved in using symbols to portray your campus to the world?

KEY WORDS

channel
communication
communication skills
computer-mediated communication
concepts
content messages
curvilinear association
dyad
ethical communication
fidelity
impersonal communication
interpersonal communication
interpersonal communication competence
interpersonal communication ethics
negative association
positive association
relational messages
social rules
symbols
theory
transactional model of communication

PART 1 FOUNDATIONS

Visit the Communication Café on the companion website to hear Denise and Jen talk about the topics addressed in Part 1 of this book.

In Chapter 1, we described interpersonal communication as a fluid and dynamic process in which communication partners create meanings by sharing messages that they encode and decode – these experiences create bonds between people and have consequences that last beyond a particular interaction. None of the parts of the communication system is more important than the others, and what one person considers the first topics to study when learning about interpersonal communication might not be what another person considers the foundations for this journey. How could communication transpire without understanding how messages work? Or how relationships form and change? Or the goals that we can achieve through communication? While we believe that all the aspects of the communication experience are important to understanding interpersonal communication, we position the communication experience of the individual as the foundation to learning about interpersonal communication. Understanding how one person experiences interactions with others will give you a basis for learning how people work together to create interpersonal communication.

Perhaps the most influential characteristic of a person is his or her culture. The culture that people are born into shapes everything from the kind of family structure they are raised in, the language and nonverbal cues that they learn, the relationships they value, and the goals they pursue through interpersonal communication. We also use evidence of another person's culture as a touchstone for making sense of our encounters with them. Because culture has such a significant influence on interpersonal communication, we begin our exploration of the foundations of interpersonal communication in Chapter 2 by examining the role of culture.

Whereas culture is the framework for making sense of the world that people share with others, people also have personal characteristics that are equally important to understanding how they experience interpersonal communication. Our interactions with other people shape how we see ourselves, and we also use communication to show other people who we are. In Chapter 3, we focus on the individual, and we consider how interpersonal communication relates to a person's self-perception and identity.

DOI: 10.4324/9781351174381-2

The third and final chapter in this unit focuses on the processes by which people see and make sense of the world around them. Somehow, the human body translates all the stimuli collected through the senses of smell, taste, sight, hearing, and touch into a useful portrayal of the environment. This basic human function is an essential part of interpersonal communication, which requires people to make sense of complex and often ambiguous symbols, as well as information in the communication context, often in rapidly unfolding interactions. In Chapter 4, then, we examine how perception works and the aspects of perception that are most relevant to interpersonal communication experiences.

LEARNING OBJECTIVES

After reading this chapter, you should be able to:

1. Understand the different layers of culture.
2. Describe the steps through which cultures form and change.
3. Identify three types of communication that explicitly reflect culture.
4. Recognize barriers to effective intercultural communication.
5. Strengthen your ability to communicate with people of different cultures.

PUTTING THEORY INTO PRACTICE

In this chapter, you will learn how to:

1. Find experiences you and a communication partner have in common.
2. Adapt to new cultural environments.
3. Help others understand your culture.
4. Explore communication practices in different cultures.
5. Explore the rituals and stories of other cultures.
6. Strengthen the culture of relationships you value.
7. Maintain realistic expectations for intercultural communication.
8. Avoid communicating based on stereotypes.
9. Avoid exaggerating sex differences.

CULTURE AND INTERPERSONAL COMMUNICATION

2

Source: SIA KAMBOU/AFP/Getty Images.

As the daughter of Jamaican and Indian immigrants, Kamala Harris made history when she was the first Black, first South Asian, and first woman to ever be elected Vice President of the United States. As a woman and a racial minority, however, she also faced tremendous challenges and double standards in people's judgments of her communication and actions. In the Vice Presidential debate against Mike Pence, for example, Harris had to walk a tightrope to be assertive in making her points, but not come across as an "angry Black woman." Research shows that voters tend to see assertive behavior as authoritative when it comes from men, but condescending when it comes from women, particularly women of color. When Vice President Pence interrupted her multiple times during the debate, Ms. Harris would calmly and respectfully assert herself by saying, "I'm speaking. Mr. Vice President, I'm speaking." Experts believe that this was the right strategy to calmly and diplomatically manage the conversation and respond to disruptions. Harris also had a number of nonverbal reactions to her opponent during the debate, such as shaking her head, chuckling, and making "are you kidding me?" facial expressions that some undecided voters who watched the debates found to be condescending, but there was no comparable backlash against Pence's head shakes and unamused facial expressions. She was also quite effective, however, in making many of her most important arguments directly to the camera, thereby creating a connection and rapport with voters when it mattered most. As a woman of color, Kamala Harris' communication and actions as Vice President will be scrutinized and often held to a different standard than those of her White male counterparts; however, she is likely to be quite vigilant about recognizing these double standards and applying strategies to diffuse them.

People from different races, cultures, religions, and even genders may use and interpret symbols in different ways. The meanings that you create through communication are necessarily influenced by your **culture** – the values, beliefs, and customs that you share with a group of people. An important part of culture is **norms**, or shared expectations for behavior. Cultural norms shape your communication experiences – they influence your nonverbal communication, the words you choose, how you form those words into sentences, and every other aspect of interpersonal communication. The way people interpret interpersonal messages is also heavily influenced by cultural norms and expectations. Vice President Kamala Harris enacts communication behaviors that reflect her experiences as a woman of Black and Indian descent, but many people's impressions of her are still limited by historical cultural norms that dictate what a Vice President should look and sound like. As the first woman of color to be elected to national office, she will likely face biases until cultural expectations begin to shift and the idea of a non-White, non-male Vice President becomes normalized.

When you create messages, your culture provides guidelines that help you decide what is expected, appropriate, or desirable. For example, your culture helps you know whether you should greet another person with a handshake or a kiss, call a person by his, her, or their first name, and look your interaction partner directly in the eye. At the same time, other people send you messages that are influenced by their perceptions of your culture. From the topics people discuss with you to how formally or informally they speak, the messages you receive are different from those sent to someone who is a different age, a different gender, or a different ethnicity than you. In this chapter, we'll explore how culture provides a framework for all of your interpersonal communication experiences.

Culture
The values, beliefs, and customs that we share with a group of people.

Norms
Expectations for behavior that are shared within a cultural group.

WHAT IS CULTURE?

Some cultural differences, such as languages, physical characteristics, or clothing styles, are easy to see. Other cultural boundaries can be hard to define. Would you consider someone with different political values, someone with different musical tastes, or someone attending a different college to be a member of your culture? And would you put yourself in the same cultural group as people who attended your college 20, 40, or 100 years ago? In this section, we probe the complexity of culture by examining different layers of culture, how cultures change over time, and core differences between cultures.

Layers of Culture

A cultural group is a subset of people whose common experiences have led them to develop similar ways of thinking, feeling, and behaving. When we ask students in our classes to identify the cultural groups they belong to, some of them mention only one or two broad ethnic, national, or religious groups (African American, Vietnamese, Muslim). Others also mention groups defined by gender, sexual orientation, or age (woman, queer, millennial). Still others give a lengthy list of affiliations (member of Alpha Tau, varsity lacrosse player, business major). These responses show the many different ways we can identify a cultural group. These layers of culture are illustrated in Figure 2.1, and discussed in the paragraphs that follow.

Cultural institutions. At the broadest level, cultural groups are defined by the members' nationality, religion, or ethnic heritage. Within the boundaries of a nation, the form of government, the monetary system,

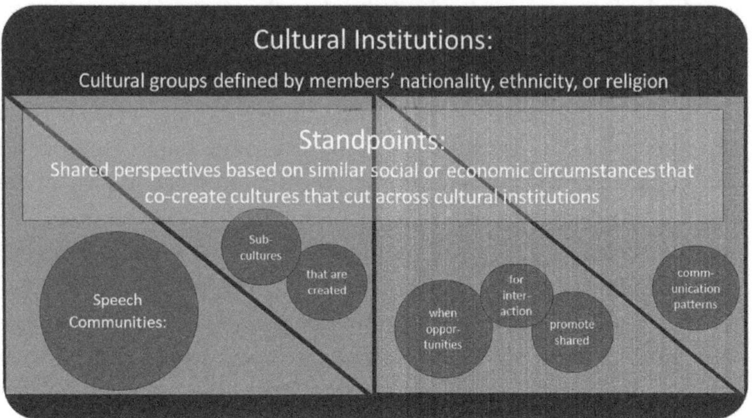

FIGURE 2.1 Layers of culture

holidays, and national heroes and heroines unify people's experiences and create a common culture for billions of people who share the same institutions. For example, when Denise was a college student, she studied abroad in Scotland, where she ended up celebrating the 4th of July with several other U.S. citizens at a youth hostel. Although the travelers were from different parts of the United States, different ages and races, and traveling for different reasons, they were connected by their shared knowledge of the holiday and the rituals used to mark it. Likewise, people who affiliate with a particular religion or an ethnic group, regardless of their nationality, adopt a set of beliefs, perform particular rituals, and celebrate specific holidays. At this broadest level, then, cultures develop because national, religious, or ethnic institutions promote particular beliefs and customs.

The triangles represent different cultures that are distinguished by their cultural institutions. The rectangle represents cultural groups defined by a shared standpoint. As the rectangle illustrates, a standpoint can cut across cultural institutions, such as when people share a connection because of their similar gender, economic status, or military status. The circles represent subcultures or speech communities. Speech communities emerge, usually among people from the same cultural institution, when opportunities for interaction promote shared communication patterns.

PAUSE & REFLECT

What labels do you use to identify your cultural background? What are some of the ways of living, thinking, and feeling that you have in common with other people who share these labels?

Standpoints. A cultural group can also form when people have similar life experiences because of their social or economic circumstances. This kind of group is defined by its members' similar **standpoint** – the position from which people see the world based on their status in society (cf. Allen, 2017). Men and women, for example, may be treated differently as children, form different kinds of friendships, have different job opportunities, and play distinct roles as parents. Because of these differences, some scholars have suggested that men and women constitute distinct cultures with unique standpoints (e.g., Dougherty, 2001). In the same way, access to education, jobs, health care, or the Internet can create cultural divides based on people's age, economic class, or place of residence (e.g., Ballard-Reisch, 2010). For example, a person brought up in an upper-middle-class family has different experiences from a person brought up in a low-income family; as a result, these two individuals would most likely have very different standpoints. Thus, cultural groups that are created from a similar standpoint can range from just two or three people with a similar perspective to millions of people with shared experiences.

Standpoint
The position from which people see the world based on their social or economic status.

Figure 2.1 shows how cultural groups defined by standpoints often cut across national, ethnic, or religious boundaries. In other words, people in the same cultural institution might have distinct standpoints, and people who are members of different cultural institutions might have a shared standpoint. As an example, consider two women who live in different countries, speak different languages, and have different religions. Despite these differences, these two women might have many experiences in common. Perhaps both experience poverty, have trouble finding work because their societies discriminate against women, and are mothers trying to care for their children. Even though these two women belong to different cultural institutions, they share a culture based on a common standpoint.

Speech communities. Cultures also arise when people who have regular contact with each other develop shared norms and values. A **speech community** is a group of people who have similar ways of using and interpreting symbols. A speech community arises when people live, study, or work together and therefore have shared experiences, norms, and communication practices (e.g., Babel, 2016). For example, fraternities and sororities are speech communities: Members display their unique culture by wearing their Greek letters, adopting a mascot, recording the organization's history, and holding private pledge ceremonies. Even two people in a romantic relationship can create their own speech community, complete with anniversaries, rules, important symbols like wedding rings, rituals, and unique discourses (Baxter, 2010).

Speech Community
A group of people who use and interpret symbols in the same way.

Speech communities can be considered **subcultures** because they are distinguished from the broader culture by a handful of unique practices. Unlike cultural groups based on a shared standpoint, speech communities develop when people communicate with each other directly. Because

Subcultures
Speech communities that share some unique practices within a broader cultural group.

we are more likely to have frequent contact with people who live near us and who have the same ethnic or religious practices, speech communities often form among people who belong to the same cultural institution. For example, parishioners who attend a particular church follow the norms for their religion, and they most likely have a few practices that are unique to the congregation. In this way, speech communities create subcultures within a cultural institution.

Virtual groups or online communities show how communication is at the heart of building speech communities. Millions of people turn to online communities to find people with similar backgrounds and experiences with whom they can provide support, share information, and form social connections. Many people are drawn to virtual communities because they allow connections with other users who may not live nearby and permit the discussion of topics that might be taboo in face-to-face contexts. Even though the individuals who comprise an online community may have diverse cultural backgrounds and belong to different social groups in the physical world, they create a unique speech community in the virtual world through their interactions online. Within virtual groups, traits that foster group cohesion, such as referring to the group as a community, expressing shared goals, and agreeing about discussion topics, tend to increase over time (Cassell & Tversky, 2005). A study focused on an online video gaming community found that participants with more experience create more positive social messages and use more specialized conventions, such as emoticons and abbreviations (Pená & Hancock, 2006). Another study showed that women who participate in discussion boards for breast cancer survivors feel a sense of connection with the online community that increases over time (Rodgers & Chen, 2005). In these ways, virtual groups have many of the same qualities that emerge when members of a speech community interact in person.

PAUSE & REFLECT

What online groups or virtual communities are you part of? Can you identify any beliefs, norms, or communication practices that participants in the community shared?

When you consider all the labels you might use to define your own cultural identity, you will probably find that you are a member of many different cultural groups. All of your cultural groups define who you are as an individual, but some may be more important to you than others. For example, you can complete the How Do You Rate? exercise to see how important your ethnic identity is to you. Notably, the cultural groups that are most important to you are the ones you most likely try to emphasize in your interactions with others. As you'll learn throughout this chapter, your cultural identity has a pervasive effect on your interpersonal communication.

HOW DO YOU RATE? 2.1

Ethnic Identity Salience Scale

Everybody can be characterized in terms of their ethnic heritage, but people differ in how important that ethnicity is to them. To find out the importance that you place on your own ethnicity, complete the scale on the companion website.

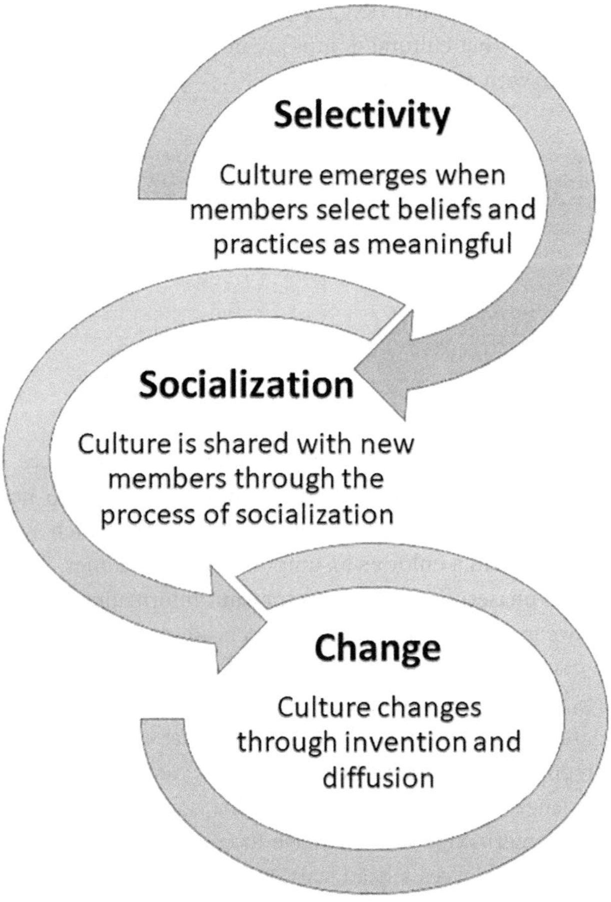

How Cultures Form and Change

In general, cultural groups differ based on their members' beliefs, values, and norms, or behavior patterns. Although every culture is unique, three general processes allow cultures to develop, grow, and change over time (see Figure 2.2). Understanding these processes can help you to see how distinct cultures develop different ways of seeing and doing things.

Culture emerges through selectivity. People everywhere perform certain actions that are simply part of being human: we make friends, we love, we dislike or hate, we suffer, we empathize, and we celebrate. Although these activities occur in all cultures, different cultural groups perform them in different ways (Duranti, 2006). How do you communicate

Selectivity
Culture emerges when members select beliefs and practices as meaningful
Socialization
Culture is shared with new members through the process of socialization
Change
Culture changes through invention and diffusion

FIGURE 2.2 Cultural dynamics

your affection for a friend? How do you talk to someone who is older or younger? How do you mark an anniversary or birthday? As a member of a cultural group, you probably enact behaviors that are expected and meaningful within your community. Thus, cultures are distinct because cultural groups have selected different behaviors as meaningful.

For a concrete example, think about how different cultures approach the common task of exchanging greetings. When people greet each other, they don't just acknowledge each other's presence. In Thailand, people frequently greet each other by placing their palms together and bowing their heads – this gesture accomplishes the utilitarian function of greeting another person, while it also shows respect for status, reflects national identity, seeks to ingratiate, and expresses religiosity (Powell, Amsbary, & Hickson, 2014). The specific behaviors used to perform greetings also depend on culture. For example, greetings within a Persian culture typically include a person's title, whereas a Spanish culture uses a person's title only to show respect for elders (Elhami, 2020). When greeting strangers, Norwegians tend to avoid small talk or chatting, which can seem rude or unfriendly to people from cultures where exchanging niceties with strangers is more common (Rygg, 2016). These examples highlight just one specific way that cultural groups are distinguished by how members communicate with each other.

PAUSE & REFLECT

What are some of the ways that people in your social network or family communicate with each other? How do these communication events set your speech communities apart from other groups?

Socialization
The process by which newcomers to a cultural group come to understand its assumptions and guidelines.

Culture is shared with new members. The practices that are selected as meaningful within a culture must be taught to new members of the group. **Socialization** is the process by which newcomers come to understand a culture's assumptions and guidelines. Socialization involves two phases: first, members transmit information about the culture to newcomers and, second, newcomers adopt the cultural practices. In some cases, socialization includes specific activities designed to teach a culture's rules to a new member. For example, many college campuses have orientation programs for new students that cover everything from how to register for classes to how to cheer at football games. Socialization experiences can also influence whether someone decides to join a community; internships students have in college, for example, function to give future employees a head start on learning the organizational culture, while they might also persuade a prospective employee that the job isn't a good fit (Dailey, 2016). Within dangerous professions, such as fire fighting, supervisors foster both the command hierarchy that structures a team and participatory norms necessary to perform life-threatening jobs by using inclusive communication, promoting understanding or roles throughout the chain of command, modeling respectful communication, and reflecting on specific incidents to learn from them (Jahn & Black, 2017). In general, then, socialization occurs as newcomers and experts communicate and exchange information about cultural practices (Scott & Myers, 2010).

The ways in which interpersonal communication contributes to socialization can be seen in the messages adults use to convey cultural values to children. In one research study, parents from the northeastern United States or from India made up stories to go with a picture book that shows a boy searching for, and finding, a lost frog (Harkins & Ray, 2004). Parents from the United States emphasized how the boy's hard work achieved his personal goal of finding the frog – their stories revealed the goal-oriented and individualistic cultural values of the United States. In contrast, parents in India described how the boy's recovery of the frog created sadness within the frog's family. In this version of the story, children learn that selfish ambitions can hurt the community. When parents communicate with their children, they guide children toward the cultural values and norms of their community. The Communication in Action activity 2.1 suggests another way that cultural values are taught to children.

COMMUNICATION IN ACTION 2.1

Discovering Cultural Messages

Although communication with parents and caretakers plays a key role in teaching culture to children, the television shows that children watch also convey cultural values. To complete the table provided on the companion website, watch a few shows designed for young children – try Nickelodeon, Noggin, or PBS Kids networks that are devoted to children's programs. As you watch the stories, identify the messages or themes that support the values within your culture, and also note any messages that contradict or question your cultural beliefs.

Culture changes over time. The ways of thinking, feeling, and behaving that define a culture evolve over time. As one example, consider some of the changes in marriage and family that have occurred in the United States over the past 50 years (Cherlin, 2004). In the 1950s, only about 5% of unmarried adults lived with their romantic partner, and having children outside of marriage was rare. In the 1970s, living together before marriage and having children outside of marriage gradually became more acceptable. At present in the United States, living together is a viable alternative to marriage, almost 40 percent of children are born to unmarried parents, and about one out of three children live with an unmarried parent. Half-siblings and step-families are common parts of the social landscape, and DNA analysis services, such as "23 and Me," are enabling people to find biological relatives that they didn't know existed. Although there are certainly differences of opinion about the sanctity of marriage, American culture has moved toward more diverse views of marriage and family over the past 50 years.

IDEA: PROMOTING INCLUSION, DIVERSITY, EQUITY, AND ACCESS

How does your definition of your family compare to who counted as "family" 60 years ago? When you reflect on people you know, how many of them have families that were excluded by a 1950s focus on two-parent, heterosexual, married households? How can we communicate to be more inclusive of the broad diversity of families that exist in our society?

Invention
The development of new cultural practices.

One way that culture changes is through **invention** – the development of new cultural practices. When social revolutions, medical breakthroughs, technological advances, or pandemics create novel situations, societies must create new norms. Consider the cultural inventions and norms made necessary by the COVID-19 pandemic. Wearing a mask became an expected social convention to slow the spread of the virus, with some states, communities, and businesses mandating mask wearing as a requirement in public places. The pandemic also introduced the term "social distancing" to the cultural lexicon in response to recommendations to maintain a space of six feet between yourself and others. In addition, people embraced technology like Zoom as an essential way to maintain connections with friends and family, facilitate work from home, and deliver education. Adapting cultural practices became a necessary response to survive the COVID-19 pandemic, in much the same way that access to the Internet, the invention of Facebook, Instagram, and Snapchat, opportunities for telecommuting, and the decoding of human DNA have prompted the invention of new norms for close relationships, employment, and health care (Hylmö, 2006; Silva, 2005).

Diffusion
When the cultural practices of one group are adopted by another society.

Cultures also change through the process of **diffusion**, which occurs when a society adopts the cultural practices of another group. Because U.S. culture is displayed around the world via the Internet, syndicated television shows, and blockbuster films, some societies have become concerned that their own culture is being overwhelmed by American practices. In fact, Canada, France, and Korea, among other countries, have laws that require their symphonies, theatres, and cinemas to feature at least some national artists or productions. Although cultural heritage is certainly worth protecting, diffusion is inevitable when two groups come into contact. Moreover, the mingling of different cultures is at the root of many wonderful creations, including reggae music, spaghetti with marinara sauce, and New York City.

Classifying Cultures

A cultural group's communication norms are shaped by the way the group members answer some basic questions about how people relate to each other. Which is more important: the individual or the group? Are all people essentially equal, or do some people have more power than others? Which is more important when communicating: the words that are spoken or the context for them? Is it more important to get things done or to follow a good process? Should we avoid risks or seek out novel experiences? The answers to these questions help us distinguish cultures along five important dimensions (see Table 2.1).

TABLE 2.1 Dimensions that distinguish cultures

Individualism	*Collectivism*
Individualistic cultures value independence and autonomy more than the group	Collectivistic cultures put the needs of the community before the needs of the individual
High power distance	*Low power distance*
High power distance cultures respect a rigid hierarchy based on power and status	Low power distance cultures assume that all people have equal rights and opportunities
High context	*Low context*
High context cultures rely on the social situation to give messages meaning	Low context cultures rely on explicit language to make meanings clear
Outcome-oriented	*Process-oriented*
Outcome-oriented cultures value achievement, deadlines, and getting a job done	Process-oriented cultures appreciate the experiences gained by working on a task
Uncertainty-avoidant	*Uncertainty-seeking*
Uncertainty-avoidant cultures prefer stable routines that avoid risks or novel experiences	Uncertainty-seeking cultures prefer diverse, novel, and even risky experiences

As an example of the effect of cultural dimensions on communication, consider how citizens of the United States and South Korea refer to older members within their society. Korean culture values collectivism, high power distance, and high context communication, whereas U.S. culture values individualism, low power distance, and explicit language. Not coincidentally, Koreans often refer to older members of society using terms that mean "grandma," "grandpa," "uncle," "older brother," etc., even when the other person isn't a relative. In this way, Koreans extend the bonds of family to everyone in the social group and acknowledge the power and status of elders. And notice how using these terms means that you must rely on the social context to figure out if the person actually is the speaker's grandmother, grandfather, uncle, or older brother. In comparison, people from the United States are likely to use first names, which emphasize a person's individuality, and they have only a few words (for example, "sir" or "ma'am") that signal status. Because residents of the United States explicitly name another person, sometimes even going so far as to distinguish "Grandma Jane" from "Grandma Marie," they don't need to rely on the social context to figure out who they are talking about. As this example illustrates, the values of a cultural group have pervasive effects on interpersonal communication.

Putting Theory into Practice: Finding Common Ground for Communication

When we think about the layers of culture, the dynamics by which culture develops and evolves, and the dimensions that differentiate cultures, we can see that defining a person's cultural affiliation is difficult. You participate in multiple cultural groups defined by cultural institutions, common standpoints, and speech communities. And culture isn't stable – it evolves as new practices are selected, new members are socialized, and time passes. While this view of culture emphasizes its complexity, it also opens doors to improving your interpersonal communication experiences.

Find experiences you and your partner have in common. The multiple layers of culture make it possible for you and a communication partner to belong to similar and different cultures *at the same time*. For example, because you and your parents and siblings are all part of a family speech community, you can understand each other in ways that non-family members cannot. You also belong to cultural groups, such as your university community, your major, and your circle of friends, that the rest of your family might have difficulty understanding. When you are interacting with another person, keep in mind that you have both cultural differences and similarities, and work to find those experiences that provide you with a common foundation for communication.

Finding areas of cultural overlap gives you and your partner a shared framework that can improve your communication experiences. When you start a conversation with a new acquaintance, open with general topics that can point you to things you have in common. Questions like "Where are you from?" allow you to gather information that may direct you to common ground. The key is to follow up by focusing on connections. If your interaction partner answers, "I'm from Virginia," your job is to think of something – anything – that connects you to Virginia: "Oh, I have a cousin in Virginia"; "I read a book about Virginia"; or "I've always wanted to visit Virginia." You have a lot of options for locating some point of overlap. And if you can't find any way to connect with the information you've received, move quickly to another topic ("What's your major?"). By seeking out common ground with your interaction partners, you can have more fulfilling and effective interpersonal communication experiences.

Socialize yourself in new cultural environments. Socialization often takes place gradually as cultural insiders and outsiders interact. You can also be proactive by using the following strategies to help you to learn the ropes in a new cultural setting:

- *Learn as much as you can about a culture before you interact with its members.* Examine websites, publications, or media coverage to find out how a cultural group presents itself to the public. Any information you can discover can help you to master the culture more quickly.
- *Take notes or keep a journal to record the events that seem particularly meaningful within the culture.* When you reflect on your observations, you may be able to identify patterns that can guide your entry into the culture.
- *Identify someone who can serve as your informant on cultural practices.* Staff assistants in an organization, advisors in an academic department, and civil servants in a government office are people who really know the culture, and they can be invaluable resources.
- *Test whether your conclusions about cultural practices are correct.* Ask questions: Should I call professors by their first names? Is it okay to bring my cousin for a run with the intramural cross-country team? Also, try out your guesses about the culture – wear jeans to work on Fridays or bring snacks to share at a meeting. People will be especially tolerant of your errors and more willing to help you when you are still a newcomer, so take advantage of this grace period to experiment with your perceptions of the culture and make sure you're on the right track.
- *Openly seek feedback.* Checking whether your conclusions about the culture are accurate can help you learn the ropes more quickly, save you from making mistakes down the road, and show others that you are eager to adapt to the cultural environment.

Using these strategies will help you join the cultural group more quickly and enhance your interpersonal communication experiences.

Help others understand your culture. You have a great deal of expertise about the beliefs and customs that are important to members of your cultural group. Use this knowledge to help others to understand or adapt to your culture. As a first step, make your implicit cultural assumptions explicit; in other words, create a list that identifies or describes assumptions, beliefs, and customs that characterize your culture. Then, make a point of sharing your observations with newcomers. One communication professor we know went so far as to have students in his class create a video for future students in which they explained the challenges of completing the class project and the strategies that helped them along the way. Just as this video helped subsequent students adapt to the demands of the course, you can help cultural newcomers by being explicit about the beliefs, values, and customs of your speech community.

CULTURE AND COMMUNICATION

CONNECT WITH THEORY

Visit the companion website to learn more about speech codes theory, which explains how people's culture influences their communication behaviors.

Your culture inevitably shapes your interpersonal communication. One theory that describes the link between culture and communication is speech codes theory. According to this theory, people communicate based on their understanding of the meanings, norms, and values that are relevant in a particular context (Phillipsen, 1997; Phillipsen, Coutu, & Covarrubias, 2005). In this section of the chapter, we'll examine the assumptions of speech codes theory and use them to explore how culture shapes communication and communication reflects culture.

Culture Shapes Communication

According to speech codes theory, context always affects communication. Consider the example of Katie, a college student who works at a restaurant. When Katie's friends come in for dinner one evening, her interactions with them involve taking their order, serving their food, checking that they are enjoying everything, and accepting a tip. While the messages exchanged in this context make sense to both Katie and her friends, imagine how out of place they would be if Katie had invited her friends for dinner at her apartment instead! From the orders for food to the offer of a tip, every message would have a quite different (if not insulting) meaning. As this example illustrates, context has a very strong effect on the way we produce and make sense of messages.

Speech Code
The system of symbols, rules, and assumptions that people create to accomplish communication.

The theory defines a **speech code** as the system of symbols, rules, and assumptions that people create to accomplish communication. People create speech codes through social interaction and within particular situations, and their meanings are both complicated and flexible. In fact, a speech code is like a genetic code: it is intricate, it can combine in different ways to produce different effects, and the outcomes produced depend heavily on the environment.

PAUSE & REFLECT

Are there speech codes that you use in some of your social groups that would be complete nonsense in other social groups? How do the symbols and rules that are meaningful in each group set them apart?

Because context affects the meaning of communication behaviors, different cultures have distinct speech codes. One classic study, for example, revealed the speech codes that shape interpersonal communication and relationships in Bogotá, Colombia (Fitch, 1998). Within this culture, people persuade others to do things by emphasizing social connections ("Be a good brother, and help me with the gardening"), rather than logical arguments ("The gardening needs to be finished before the rain starts") or personal needs ("I can't do the gardening alone"). They also consider making a request to be a sign of closeness, rather than an imposition. In fact, people phrase requests as commands ("Take care of the laundry!") when they want to underscore the strength of their bond with the other person. Although these communication practices show up in other cultures too, citizens of Bogotá use them intentionally to emphasize the value they place on social ties. The speech codes within this Colombian community enable members to appreciate the full meaning of the messages that are exchanged.

Communication Reflects Culture

Speech codes arise from culture, and they are the basis of communication. Consequently, the messages people create reveal their culture. More specifically, acts of communication reflect a cultural group's way of thinking, assumptions about human relationships, and strategies for living. Communication features that reflect culture include boundary markers, myths, and rituals (see Table 2.2).

Members of a cultural group mark activities that are off-limits through a variety of specific communication devices. **Boundary markers** are messages that indicate when an action is inappropriate within the cultural group, and they can help contribute to a sense of cultural identity. For example, participants in a virtual community have a stronger connection to the community when members explicitly point out when someone violates norms for the group (Gibbs, Kim, & Ki, 2019). Throughout this textbook, we feature transcripts of online communication or "Interpersonal

Boundary Markers
Messages that signal that an action is inappropriate or off-limits within a cultural group.

TABLE 2.2 Communicative reflections of culture

Communication device	*Description*
Boundary markers	Cultures mark the messages or behaviors that are considered inappropriate by ignoring them, defining them as humorous or obscene, or gossiping about the people who perform them
Myths	Cultures communicate core cultural themes by creating sacred stories about heroes and villains
Rituals	Cultures celebrate culturally significant events, ranging from important moments in history to weddings, through carefully scripted public performances

Communication Online," to show what messages look like when people communicate using technology. In the Interpersonal Communication Online box, participants in an online forum for family members of military recruits help a woman who was upset by a comment from someone outside the military culture – the participants' suggestions clearly show how communication can be used to mark boundaries for appropriate behavior. We also mark behaviors or attitudes that are acceptable or off-limits by what we consider obscene versus appropriate language (Mohr, 2013) and embarrassing versus funny humor (Hall, 2011). Likewise, when people gossip, they focus on inappropriate behavior and target people who have violated cultural rules, which help to keep unwanted behaviors in check (Peters & Kashima, 2014). As these examples show, looking closely at communication can provide insight into the values and customs within a culture.

INTERPERSONAL COMMUNICATION ONLINE

MARKING BOUNDARIES FOR APPROPRIATE COMMUNICATION

This transcript was drawn from an online forum for family and loved ones of military recruits: www.recruitparents.com/forums. Notice the communication behaviors participants suggest the poster use to mark an upsetting message as inappropriate. At the same time, the replies bolster the values shared within this online military community.

POSTER: Today at work someone asked me about my boyfriend, who left for bootcamp about a month ago . . . Then he decided to ask me if I was aware that the marines have the highest death rate? I stayed strong and held my tears until I got home (right now) and I'm having an EXTREMELY hard time keeping myself together after what he said. It just wasn't a good night for me to hear something like that (this isn't the first time and I'm sure comments like these have been made to many of you ladies) . . . I'm just looking for ANY advice from anyone for what to do when this happens . . .

REPLY 1: Unfortunately, you'll more than likely hear comments like these more than once or twice down the road. When I hear them, I feel like decking the person who said it in the face, but obviously, I don't. I keep my composure and kindly tell them that I don't listen to the statistics and I'm proud of what my husband does and support him all the way . . . When people make ignorant comments like that, just be proud that you're a strong woman who's got a great man by her side.

REPLY 2: I have had people say similar stuff, it's hurtful and has almost broken my heart!! But people are ignorant and don't think!!! The best thing is to just hold your head high, pray that your boy will stay safe and ignore those who don't think before they speak!!

REPLY 3: What I tell people when they make comments like that is just "thanks for your input but your negativity isn't welcome . . . I only want positivity surrounding me, so, please, if you feel the need to be negative, do it somewhere private alone." Some people just don't think before they talk. I'm sorry you had to endure that ignorance.

REPLY 4: I have found that the best way to handle people who are clueless is to perfect that look, you know the one that your teacher would give you when you did something wrong and it would stop you in your tracks, you have to just give them that "look" and walk away. These people will never get it.

People also reveal their culture through the stories they tell. **Myths** are sacred stories in which the characters and their actions embody core cultural themes. For example, the Anglo-American culture of the eighteenth century was embodied in the myth of Buffalo Bill – stories of this Pony Express rider celebrated masculinity and Whiteness and dismissed violence against Native Americans (Dickinson, Ott, & Aoki, 2005). Likewise, the myth of the evil, greedy wicked stepmother brings to light cultural values that continue to challenge stepmothers (Christian, 2005). Speech communities such as families also develop myths, which take the form of stories about important or revealing family experiences (Flood-Grady & Koenig Kellas, 2019). Through historical figures, childhood fairy tales, and family stories that are told and retold, myths underscore the beliefs and values shared within a cultural group.

Myths
Sacred stories in which the characters and their actions embody core cultural themes.

PAUSE & REFLECT

Think about a family story that is told within your family and shared with others. What does that story reveal about your family's speech community?

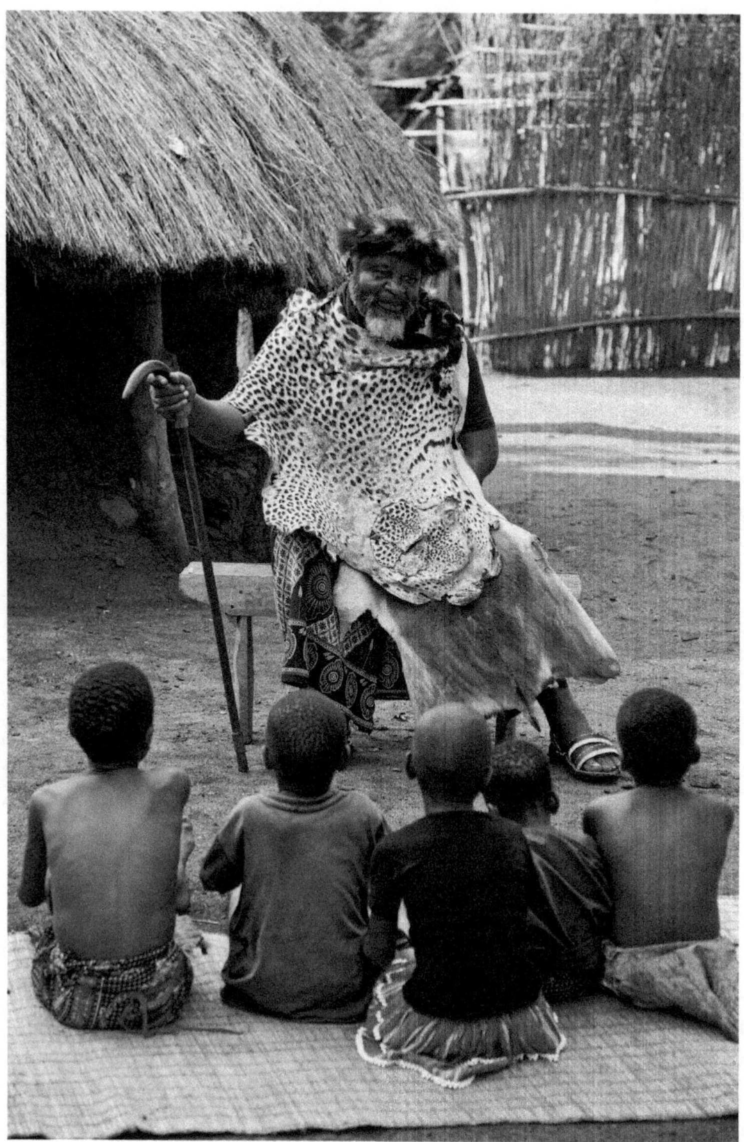

FIGURE 2.3 Shangaan Chief tells folk tales to young children

Getty Images.

Rituals
Carefully scripted performances that mark culturally significant events.

Culture is also highlighted by **rituals**, which are carefully scripted performances that mark culturally significant events. Public rituals that are common in the United States include fireworks on the 4th of July, the Macy's Thanksgiving Day Parade, and the countdown on New Year's Eve at Times Square. Other cultures celebrate their own unique rituals, such as the running of the bulls in Pamplona, the changing of the guard at Buckingham Palace, and the annual Carnivale celebration in Rio de Janeiro. Within interpersonal relationships, rituals are a way of recognizing private events as important within the cultural group. A good example of this is the wedding ceremony, which elevates the private union between romantic partners to the public institution known as marriage.

Like other forms of communication, rituals reinforce cultural beliefs and social roles. For example, a wedding or baby shower includes specific activities to mark a couple's passage into marriage or parenthood, and participants will explicitly embarrass newcomers who don't follow the rules (Braithwaite, 1995). For married couples, investment in family rituals is higher among people who value intimacy and who have higher quality and closer relationships (Crespo, Davide, Costa, & Fletcher, 2008). These rituals taken on greater significant within migrant families, where participation in rituals weaves together celebrations of ethnic or national cultures and reunion within the family speech community (Li, 2019). In fact, enacting rituals that is one way that step-families can foster the development of their own unique family culture (Braithwaite, Waldron, Allen, Oliver, & Bergquist, 2017). Thus, rituals can help create solidarity within a speech community.

Putting Theory into Practice: Appreciating Cultural Diversity

In this part of the chapter, we have examined how culture is woven into the very heart of our communication experiences. From the speech codes you use to the cultural events you participate in, you enact your culture in everything you do. Viewed in this light, communication becomes an opportunity to celebrate cultural diversity.

Explore the speech codes of different cultures. Because communication is a reflection of speech codes, the symbols and messages people create may be thought of as folk art: they are unique and sometimes beautiful cultural performances. Become an art connoisseur – someone who appreciates and understands different forms of art – by exploring the speech codes of different cultures. Try this simple exercise to get you started: The next time you're in someone's home, apartment, or dorm room, take a look at the objects that person has on display – artwork, photographs, memorabilia. As you study these cultural artifacts, think about how they symbolize important values, customs, or events within that person's cultural groups. By making a habit of viewing communication practices as cultural symbols, you'll open your eyes to the diversity of cultures around you.

Ask people about their rituals and stories. Knowing the rituals that people perform and the stories that they enjoy can help you to understand what is important to them. Jen has a friend who had formed elaborate plans for her wedding long before she'd even met her spouse. Another friend hadn't given wedding arrangements a moment's thought until she and her partner decided to marry. Whereas the first couple displays photos from their wedding and enjoys retelling how the groom lost the marriage license, the other couple is pressed to remember the date of their anniversary. Which woman do you think has the more conservative view of marriage? Not surprisingly, the "wedding planner" has a more traditional marriage – she is responsible for the house and children (and paperwork!), while her husband pursues his career. In the other couple, both partners work outside the home and play a more equal role in home-making. As this example illustrates, you can gain insight into people's beliefs and values by asking them about the rituals and stories that are important to them.

COMMUNICATION IN ACTION 2.2

Learning About Others Through Rituals and Stories

Asking people about the rituals celebrated within their families and the family stories that they like to tell can help you learn about their cultural values. Talk to two different people as you complete the table on the companion website. This exercise can help you see the connection between family rituals and stories and cultural values.

Create rituals and stories within relationships you value. You can also take steps to encourage rituals and stories that promote a sense of community with others. In the interpersonal relationships you value, look for activities that can become special for you and your partners, and turn these into rituals by repeating their key components. For example, you can maintain closeness in a group of old friends by embracing birthday celebrations as a cultural ritual. You might make a point of gathering for each person's birthday, holding an annual reunion where all the birthdays are celebrated, or developing norms for location, food, and gifts that mark your celebration. Likewise, you might signal to a new friend that the relationship is special by turning your occasional lunch together into a regular event at a favorite restaurant. For the most part, the activity itself doesn't matter as much as identifying it as a marker of your relationship culture.

INTERCULTURAL COMMUNICATION

Sometimes the effects of cultural differences on interpersonal interactions are quite obvious. When we ask our students to identify a personal experience with intercultural communication, they usually recall a time when they traveled abroad or talked to an international student. It can be quite easy to identify differences in language and norms when you communicate with someone from a different country. But what about more subtle differences? People who live in or near New York City, for example, recognize the dialects, customs, and rituals that distinguish people from Manhattan versus the other boroughs, north Jersey versus south Jersey, and Mets fans versus Yankees fans. Although these individuals might share the same nationality, ethnicity, or religion, the fact that they come from distinct speech communities means that cultural differences have emerged. In this section, we'll examine what makes interpersonal communication intercultural, as well as some of the barriers to effective intercultural communication.

SCHOLAR SPOTLIGHT

Visit the Communication Café on the companion website to view a conversation with Howard Giles, a leading scholar who studies intercultural and intergroup communication.

The Nature of Intercultural Communication

A person's cultural background always shapes interpersonal communication experiences. What sets intercultural communication apart is the extent to which messages reflect a focus on a person's culture. Specifically, **intercultural communication** occurs when interaction is guided by the participants' memberships in different social groups, rather than their unique qualities as individuals (Gudykunst, 2005). In other words, if a person's cultural group membership is very relevant to you and you tailor your messages with that cultural group in mind, you are engaging in intercultural communication. So, intercultural communication occurs when you adjust your word choice and nonverbal behaviors because you are talking to a person who doesn't share the same meaning for words and actions. Intercultural communication also occurs when you adjust your messages based on a partner's gender, age, political views, or favorite baseball team. In each of these cases, you might change the way you communicate based on your knowledge or stereotypes about a partner's cultural group.

Intercultural Communication
Interaction that is guided by a person's membership in a social group, rather than his or her unique qualities as an individual.

PAUSE & REFLECT

Do you remember the last time you interacted with someone who had a very different cultural background from your own? How did you alter your communication in that interaction, if at all?

Have you ever communicated with someone from Great Britain and started speaking with a British accent? When you talk to your grandparents or other elderly individuals, do you tend to speak more slowly and loudly than usual? Communication accommodation theory is a general model of interaction that describes how cultural group memberships influence interpersonal interactions (Dragojevic, Giles, & Gasiorek, 2016).

CONNECT WITH THEORY

Visit the companion website to learn more about communication accommodation theory, which describes how culture group memberships influence interpersonal interactions.

Communication accommodation theory identifies two communication patterns that might emerge over the course of a conversation: characteristics of the participants' speech can become more similar to each other, or they can become more distinct (see Figure 2.4). These communication patterns may be conscious or subconscious, but they reflect a desire either to increase or decrease the connection to a partner. In particular, we tend to match the communication behaviors of people we like or feel similar to, and we exaggerate communication patterns that distinguish us from people we don't like (Soliz, 2016). In intercultural interactions, we tend to adopt a partner's communication patterns when we want to promote intergroup relationships or we have had positive interactions with members of this culture in the past. On the other hand, we maintain or exaggerate differences in communication if our own culture is important to us at that moment or we have a bad history with our partner's cultural group.

Communicating in ways similar to an interaction partner has important advantages. People who experience disconnected, dissimilar communication with a grandparent feel less life satisfaction, more depression, and more loneliness – in part, because of how those interactions make them

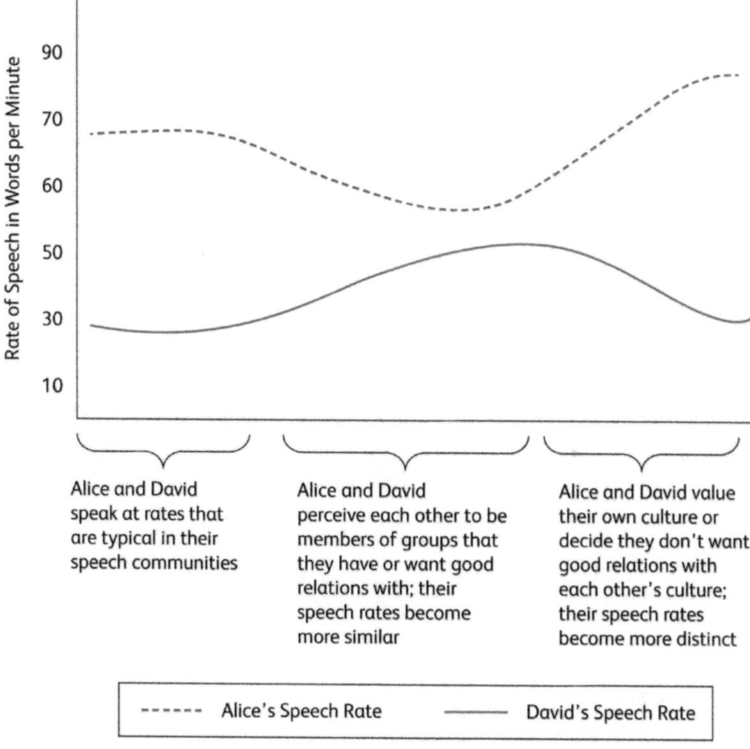

FIGURE 2.4 Communication accommodation theory. Communication accommodation theory describes how two people adjust their communication behaviors to become more similar or more different over the course of an interaction. The graphs show how Alice and David change their rate of speech to signal their desire to be more or less connected with each other's cultural group

feel about aging (Bernhold & Giles, 2020). Conversely, people who experience communication accommodation when interacting with someone with a physical disability may experience a reduction in negative stereotypes about people with different abilities (Byrd, Zhang, & Gist-Mackey, 2019). When you adjust your communication behavior for an interaction partner, you can signal your willingness to bridge cultural gaps, and you might experience a number of other positive outcomes.

INSIDE COMMUNICATION RESEARCH

Social Support in Same Race Versus Mixed Race Female Friendships

When women encounter stress or threats to their personal identity, they often turn to female friends for support. The quality of support that friends provide, however, can vary widely and does not always live up to expectations or result in positive outcomes. Support gaps occur when there is a discrepancy between the type of support that is desired, expected, or needed and the amount or quality of support that is actually received. The racial composition of an interpersonal dyad is one factor that can shape perceptions of support. For example, Black women often turn to other Black women for support because their shared cultural experience makes it easier to relate to the stress of gendered racism. On the other hand, cross-racial friendships sometimes face barriers to effective communication due to uncertainty or implicit bias about other races that can lead to miscommunication.

Communication scholars Shardé Davis and Andrew High (2019) sought to examine how perceptions of social support differed in interactions between friends of the same race and friends of different races. The researchers asked 312 women from across the U.S. who identified as either Black/African American or White/European American to recall a time when they experienced an event that challenged their identity or personal sense of self. Then, the participants were randomly assigned to recall a supportive conversation that they had with a same race friend or a different race friend about that experience. The participants then completed scale items to indicate the amount of support they expected or needed from the interaction and to rate the quality of the support they received during the interaction. The researchers conducted analyses to compare the perceived support in friendships of the same race versus different races.

Results showed that women needed and expected more social presence support, which communicates availability and solidarity, from friends of the same race than friends of a difference race. Women also expected more identity support, or messages that reinforce one's perceived sense of self, from same race friends than different race friends. In terms of the support that was received, women reported more emotional support, esteem support, social presence support, and identity support from friends of the same race than friends of a different race. With regard to support gaps, women generally expected to receive less support than they felt they needed and that gap was bigger for friends of a different race, suggesting that they felt friends of a different race would not be up to the task of providing sufficient support. In contrast, participants generally received more support than they needed, and that surplus of support tended to be larger from friends of the same race than friends of a different race. Finally, when individuals received a deficit of support, meaning that they received less support than they felt they needed or expected, they tended to judge the interaction more harshly when their friend was of the same race than of a different race. Taken together, these results suggest that women tend to have higher expectations for support from friends of the same race and that friends of the same race tend to overperform those expectations; however, when friends of the same race underperform with regard to support expectations, women tend to have more negative perceptions of those interactions.

THINK ABOUT IT

1. Why do you think women tend to have higher expectations for support from friends of the same race and why would they expect less from friends of a different race? Do you think these expectations are accurate?
2. This study focused on Black/African American and White/European American women's friendships and support needs. How do you think the results would have differed if the researchers examined men's support needs and friendships? What if they had examined other races?

Barriers to Intercultural Communication

In our efforts to communicate with partners from different cultures, we face a number of barriers. Have you ever tried to order food, ask for directions, or offer assistance to someone who didn't speak a language you know? When you communicate across cultural boundaries, you confront a number of barriers: different speech codes, different expectations for interaction, and different customs. Beyond these logistical issues, intercultural communication is also complicated by biases and tensions, including ethnocentrism, uncertainty and anxiety, and marginalization (see Table 2.3).

Ethnocentrism
The tendency to see one's own cultural beliefs as more correct, appropriate, and moral than other cultures.

Ethnocentrism. **Ethnocentrism** refers to seeing one's own cultural beliefs and practices as more correct, appropriate, or moral than those of other cultures. To some extent, culture is inherently ethnocentric, because adopting cultural norms means viewing those practices as right or natural. By comparison, the norms of other cultures seem "deviant," "weird," or even "immoral." To glimpse the power of ethnocentrism, imagine how repulsed you would be if you were invited to dinner at someone's home and served a main course of roasted grasshoppers. A Hindu person from India would probably be just as horrified to be served some juicy roast beef. Because ethnocentrism involves evaluating practices with respect to one's own cultural rules and assumptions, we often find flaws in another culture's practices.

Ethnocentrism can have a powerful impact on our feelings and behavior. In one study, American students completed a self-report measure of ethnocentrism and evaluated one of two videos of a speaker discussing the advantages of exercise – the speaker spoke with a standard

TABLE 2.3 Barriers to intercultural communication

Barrier	*Definition*
Ethnocentrism	The tendency to see one's own cultural beliefs as more correct, appropriate, and moral than those of other cultures
Uncertainty and anxiety	A lack of knowledge and fear of consequences that can make people unable to predict or enjoy intercultural interactions
Marginalization	The tendency to treat less dominant groups of people in a society as inferior or unimportant

American accent in one video and a nonnative accent in the other (Neuliep & Speten-Hansen, 2013). People who scored high in ethnocentrism rated the speaker as less attractive and credible in the video presenting a nonnative accent. Similarly, Australian college undergraduates who scored high in ethnocentrism were less willing to spend time with or get to know a person from another cultural group (Logan, Steel, & Hunt, 2014). This research illustrates how a tendency to privilege their own culture can cause people to discriminate against members of other cultural groups.

IDEA: PROMOTING INCLUSION, DIVERSITY, EQUITY, AND ACCESS

Because ethnocentrism leads people to devalue and avoid people from other cultural groups, it contributes to exclusion and inequity in our society. What are some ways in which we can decrease ethnocentrism to promote inclusion, diversity, equity, and access for people of all cultures?

Uncertainty and anxiety. Your communication with someone from a different culture may also be affected by uncertainty and anxiety. *Uncertainty* refers to a lack of knowledge about the person's traits, expectations, and customs, and *anxiety* is a negative emotional state that arises when you feel uneasy, worried, or apprehensive (Samochowiec & Florack, 2010). All communication episodes can provoke uncertainty and anxiety. When cultural differences are conspicuous, you may be especially likely to experience uncertainty and anxiety (Nishida, 2016). Although uncertainty and anxiety can lead people to avoid communication with members of other cultures, there are benefits to overcoming these obstacles. For

CONNECT WITH THEORY

Visit the companion website to learn more about anxiety/uncertainty management theory, which explains how uncertainty and anxiety affect intercultural communication.

example, a study of international students in the United States found that communication with people from the local community through social network sites reduced uncertainty and, in turn, anxiety about intercultural interactions, which promoted adaptation to life in the U.S. (Rui & Wang, 2015).

Anxiety/uncertainty management theory explains how these forces affect intercultural interactions (Gudykunst, 1993, 2005; Nishida, 2016). According to the theory (Figure 2.5), people have maximum and minimum thresholds for uncertainty and anxiety during interpersonal exchanges (see Figure 2.4). The maximum threshold is the highest amount of uncertainty or anxiety you can tolerate, and the minimum threshold is the lowest level you can experience without becoming overconfident, bored, or uninterested. Effective intercultural communication requires that your uncertainty and anxiety remain between the maximum and minimum thresholds. When your uncertainty level is between the two thresholds, you feel comfortable and motivated to interact with others.

Marginalization. Within a diverse society, some cultural groups tend to have more influence than others. In the United States, for example,

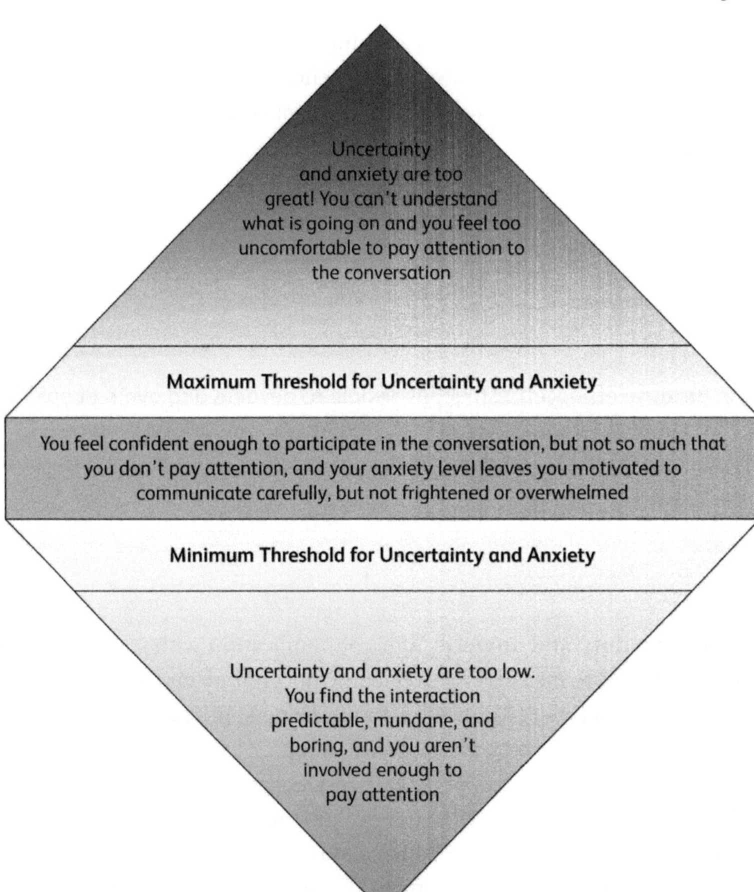

FIGURE 2.5 Anxiety/uncertainty management theory

men, White people, and the wealthy have held more privileged roles historically than women, ethnic minorities, and the poor. Influential cultural groups have the power to determine the communication norms and values for the whole society. **Marginalization** occurs when less dominant groups are treated as inferior or unimportant. As a stark illustration, consider the slow response to the devastation in Puerto Rico following Hurricane Maria in September of 2017 (Figure 2.6). It is estimated that more than 5,000 people died in the aftermath of the hurricane, due in large part to contaminated water supplies and extended power outages that crippled rescue efforts. This crisis demonstrated how marginalized groups suffer when insufficient resources are invested in services for their communities.

Marginalization
When less dominant groups of people in a society are treated as inferior or unimportant.

Marginalization can be a barrier to effective intercultural communication because it tends to make cultural differences more pronounced. When marginalized members of a society communicate with members of the dominant group, they are often forced to adapt to the very values and norms that marginalize them (DeTurk, 2001). Consider again how Kamala Harris had to be conscious of her behavior in the Vice Presidential debate and adapt her way of speaking to conform to a traditional style of communication similar to that of the White males who have historically held this role. She needed to be assertive to convey her point and demonstrate the same level of competence and confidence that her male counterpart put forth; however, at the same time she could not come across as too aggressive lest she violate gendered norms and expectations for women's softer styles of communication. On the campaign trail, critics derided Harris for wearing Chuck Taylor sneakers and dancing with her constituents because they conveyed a "silliness" or "lack of seriousness" that did not conform to the traditional stuffiness and business attire traditionally displayed by male politicians. At the core of both creating and overcoming marginalization is critical reflection on how dominant cultural groups use communication to support the status quo or oppose discrimination against other cultural groups (Razzante & Orbe, 2018). One of the great challenges to intercultural communication, then, is finding ways to bridge cultural gaps that are magnified by power differences.

HOW DO YOU RATE? 2.2

Intercultural Communication Apprehension

Knowing your own tendency to be anxious about intercultural communication can help you understand your experiences when communicating with people from different cultural groups. To see how you rate on a measure of intercultural communication apprehension, complete the scale on the companion website.

COMMUNICATION IN ACTION 2.3

Exploring Marginalized and Dominant Identities

This exercise helps you to identify how the social groups that you belong to may have some benefits, because they are privileged groups in society, or some disadvantages, because they are marginalized in some way. Completing the table on the companion website can also help you to think about whether any of the groups you belong to contribute to the marginalization of other cultural groups.

FIGURE 2.6 A mother embraces her children amidst the devastation of Hurricane Maria in Puerto Rico. More than seven months after the storm hit, many families were still homeless and power had not yet been restored to the entire island

Source: Joe Raedle/Getty Images

Communication Between People with Different Gender Identities

Sex
Whether a person is biologically male or female.

Gender
A social construction of one's psychological identity as predominantly masculine, feminine, or nonbinary.

One intercultural encounter that people have on a daily basis involves interacting with people with different gender identities. Whereas **sex** refers to whether a person is biologically male or female, **gender** refers to one's psychological orientation toward masculine, feminine, or nonbinary traits, or how one is socialized to enact a gender identity. Often, the words "sex" and "gender" are used interchangeably, because people often infer someone's psychological gender from their biological sex. While people vary in the degree to which they have more masculine or feminine characteristics, regardless of their biological sex, sex differences are often taken as a proxy for gender differences. Cultural differences among genders aren't as obvious as the differences that can exist between Blacks and Whites or between U.S. citizens and Pakistanis, but people with different gender identities have different life experiences that can foster distinct cultural values and practices. Although the debate about the magnitude and relevance of sex and gender differences in communication is ongoing (Dindia & Canary, 2006), we can illustrate some of the challenges of intercultural communication by exploring the experiences of gendered identities across the lifespan.

Infancy and childhood. From birth, biological boys and girls have unique social experiences that can promote distinct ways of seeing the world and relating to others. Mothers tend to talk more to infant daughters than to sons, relying more on interpretations than instructions (Clearfield & Nelson, 2006), whereas mothers of boys tend to use more regulatory language (Kuchirko, Schatz, Fletcher, & Tamis-Lemonda 2020). Among parents of toddlers, both fathers and mothers are more likely to follow a son's lead during playtime, compared to a daughter's (Lindsey, Cremeens, & Caldera, 2010). These differences are reflected in the toys that are provided to children, as well. For example, one analysis of LEGO game sets concluded that sets marketed for boys emphasize professional skills and heroics, whereas sets marketed for girls emphasize hobbies, domestic activities, and socializing (Reich, Black, & Foliaki, 2018). Even when school-aged children spend time outside the home, boys and girls may continue to have different social experiences because of their preferences for friends who are the same gender (Bukowski & DeLay, 2020).

Dating. When we consider the world of dating, we can point to fundamental similarities among genders: all genders engage in dating, and they seek romantic partners to fulfill personal and social needs. But within heterosexual relationships in the United States, men and women are expected to play distinct roles in the dating game. A look at research from the 1990s shows some norms for heterosexual dating at the end of the last century:

- Both men and women expected men to initiate first dates, plan the activities, drive, pay for expenses, and initiate sexual intimacy (Rose & Frieze, 1993).
- 83% of undergraduate men reported that they had been asked out on a first date by a woman, and 63% of undergraduate women reported that they had asked a man out on a first date (Mongeau, Hale, Johnson, & Hillis, 1993).
- Men tend to form higher expectations for sexual involvement on dates that women initiate (Mongeau & Carey, 1996).
- Women who initiate dates are seen as more feminist and less attractive than women who wait to be asked out (Mongeau et al., 1993).

Although norms for heterosexual dating have changed a lot since the 1990s, more recent research suggests these gender stereotypes about first dates haven't changed very much (Cameron & Curry, 2020). As a result, people of different genders often bring unique perspectives to the dating game.

One difference that may exist between men and women is how they talk about their dating relationships to others. In a study that Jen conducted, an interviewer asked men and women a variety of questions about their romantic relationship – and often got different details from each partner. For one couple describing how they met, the woman had lots of detail to share:

> We met in the beginning of the school year. Ummm, actually, the night before my birthday. I decided that since it was the night before my birthday I wasn't gonna stay in, I planned to go out, so, I . . . and none of my friends on my floor were going out, so . . . I . . . spoke to a different friend who's like, "Okay, fine, we'll go out," and, um, he happened to be a mutual friend, and so we met, he was also going out, so we met through him.

This woman's partner, however, simply answered "September 9th, the night before her birthday, uh, my friend picked us up, and we went to a party. So, we shared the same car, hung out at the party." In Jen's study, men and women in relationships were interviewed separately – can you imagine how the conversation might unfold if the partners were communicating their impressions of their first meeting to each other? The woman in this case might find her boyfriend's focus on the bare bones details disappointing compared to the serendipity she highlights in her answer.

PAUSE & REFLECT

How do your own experiences dating compare to the research findings from the 1990s? Did your interactions with friends during your childhood affect your understanding of the cultural rules for your gender? What did those interactions teach you?

Work relationships. People with different gender identities also confront unique communication challenges and perceive meanings differently at work. In the United States, many organizations privilege and reward masculine communication norms: managers are expected to be assertive, to use their dominance to influence decisions and provide leadership, and to talk about their own strengths (Eagly & Karau, 2002). Moreover, although emotional restraint is generally valued in the workplace, men – compared to women – feel more comfortable expressing their anger directly around supervisors (Domagalski & Steelman, 2007). If a woman follows these norms, she violates the expectations that many people have about women: namely, that her communication style be submissive, polite, and other-focused (Martin, 2004). Even when men and women have similar communication styles, group members respond more favorably to information that is presented by a man (Grossman, Eckel, Komai, & Zhan, 2019). Also, men are less likely than women to rate flirtatious or sexual comments that occur in the workplace as sexual harassment (McCabe & Hardman, 2005; Solomon, 2006). These examples show how men and women encounter different expectations in the workplace, and how these differences can complicate interpersonal communication.

IDEA: PROMOTING INCLUSION, DIVERSITY, EQUITY, AND ACCESS

Much of the research on gender and communication in the workplace has focused on the binary of men and women. For the transgender employee, a host of organizational rules and norms make the workplace a challenging space to navigate (Jones, 2020). As you think about places you have worked in your life, how can organizations adjust their practices to create a more inclusive work environment?

Putting Theory into Practice: Improving Your Intercultural Interactions

Although everyone faces barriers to intercultural communication, there are specific skills that will help you have more effective and fulfilling encounters with people from different cultural groups.

Maintain realistic expectations. It would be nice to think that being more sensitive will always allow you to bridge cultural divides. And, no doubt, being mindful of cultural differences can contribute to more effective communication between cultural groups (Gudykunst, 2005). At the same time, intercultural interactions occur within historical and social contexts that place real limits on communication outcomes. When cultural groups have a history of conflict and violence, when power differences have allowed one group to dominate the other, or when two groups are competing for scarce resources, communication will be strained (Gallois, 2003). One way to enhance your intercultural communication experience, then, is to keep those constraints in mind.

When you focus on the challenges to intercultural communication, you can implement strategies that directly target those barriers. Identify the intercultural tensions that are present in a communication situation, and talk about them with your partner. For example, openly acknowledge the religious differences you have with a roommate, and use that as a foundation for learning about each other's cultures. Or point out to a classmate that your culture values punctuality to open a discussion about how to coordinate your meeting times. By bringing these constraints out into the open, you can put them in perspective. In doing so, you convey a respect for cultural group membership, a sensitivity to group differences, and an appreciation for how you and your partner are more than just representatives of your cultural groups.

Practice person-centered communication. When you adjust your communication based on assumptions about another person's culture, your behavior is likely to be restricted, rigid, and inadequate. Instead, make an effort to notice the distinct and unique characteristics that your partner reveals, and tailor your communication to those qualities. Does your grandmother really need you to speak more loudly, or are you just doing so because of your stereotypes about the elderly? Is your new acquaintance from Jamaica really laid back, carefree, and forgiving when you're late, or are you acting on your beliefs about island communities? Pay attention to the communication behaviors your partners actually prefer, and avoid letting cultural stereotypes drive your interpersonal communication experiences.

Avoid exaggerating sex differences. When people accept the belief that people of different genders are wildly different in their attitudes and behaviors, they allow themselves to treat gender differences as unavoidable and insurmountable. At the end of the day, all of us have many overlapping life experiences and many shared communication values. Each of us is a great deal more than just male or female or a reflection of our masculine, feminine, or nonbinary gender identity. Be careful about your assumptions and focus on the qualities that your partner actually brings to the exchange.

COMMUNICATION IN ACTION 2.4

Practicing Person-Centered Communication

This exercise can help you to be more thoughtful about how your expectations for a cultural group might be influencing your communication with a member of that cultural group. By completing the table on the companion website, you might identify ways you can make your intercultural communication experiences more person-centered.

In your effort to keep sex differences in perspective, you might make a list of the values and norms that you share with relationship partners of different genders. Then use this list of similarities as a context for discussing the communication practices you prefer. If you assume values or priorities from another person's biological sex, the likelihood you'll be mistaken is high. Likewise, using gender identity as a basis for inferring values is going to leave room for error. Instead of making guesses based on gender, take the time to learn about your communication partner's values. In doing so, you can transform a potentially challenging intercultural exchange into meaning interpersonal communication.

SUMMARY

This chapter focused on the fundamental role of culture in our interpersonal communication experiences. As a starting point, we examined the complexity of culture by considering the various layers at which culture can be defined, the processes by which cultures develop, are passed on, and change over time, and how cultures can be distinguished from each other. The view of culture offered in this chapter highlighted how it is both nuanced and dynamic. In other words, our culture is a shifting, complicated, and evolving part of our lives.

Culture includes our assumptions about living, thinking, and feeling; therefore, it is inevitably reflected in our communication. Speech codes are culturally grounded systems of symbols and rules for interpretation that make communication possible. Although all of our interpersonal communication reflects cultural speech codes, boundary markers, myths, and rituals make a cultural group's values particularly conspicuous. By examining the communication that occurs between people in a cultural group, you can gain insight into the experiences and beliefs that are meaningful within a culture.

Because culture is always reflected in communication, it always affects interpersonal communication experiences. When cultural differences are especially pronounced, interpersonal communication becomes intercultural communication. Under these circumstances, people adjust their communication behavior to signal either solidarity or disagreement with an interaction partner's cultural group. Communicating based on stereotypical cultural assumptions can lead to rigid and even condescending behavior, whereas attempts to bridge cultural gaps by adopting a partner's communication norms can create more satisfying interactions. You can improve your intercultural interactions by keeping in mind how ethnocentrism, uncertainty and anxiety, and marginalization can be barriers to effective communication. Even interactions among people of different genders can involve intercultural communication.

Although your membership in cultural groups may be more or less noticeable as you communicate with other people, it is an ever-present force in your interactions with others. Now that you understand the impact of culture on interpersonal communication, you may be ready to grapple with the ethical issues that surround culture and interpersonal communication.

ACTIVITIES FOR EXPLORING COMMUNICATION ETHICS

What Would You/Should You Do?

You are at a party when someone starts telling jokes that disparage a particular ethnic group. Many of your friends laugh, but others appear to be uncomfortable. What would you or should you do?

Something to Think About

The opposite of ethnocentrism is *cultural relativism*, the tendency to see all cultural practices as morally equivalent. When you think about some practices that are culturally sanctioned – for example, female genital mutilation or the murder of women who bring shame on their families – culture relativism would seem to have some limits. How do you balance the need to keep ethnocentrism in check with the limits of cultural relativism?

Analyze Communication Ethics Yourself

The last half of the twentieth century saw a dramatic increase in international travel, trade, and communication. One consequence of this increased cultural exchange is a blending of cultures and a concern that the unique qualities that distinguish cultural groups will be lost. As a result, some nations and organizations have taken steps to outlaw foreign cultural practices and promote local culture. Visit the website for the National Congress of American Indians (www.ncai.org) and examine the concerns expressed by this organization, as well as their tactics for protecting native cultures. Based on your analysis, what are the ethical issues involved in cultural diffusion and protectionism?

KEY WORDS

boundary markers
culture
diffusion
ethnocentrism
gender
intercultural communication
invention
marginalization
myths
norms
rituals
sex
socialization
speech code
speech community
standpoint
subcultures

LEARNING OBJECTIVES

After reading this chapter, you should be able to:

1. Define self-concept and describe characteristics of the self.
2. Identify sources of self-knowledge.
3. Define, identity, and distinguish among the four layers of identity.
4. Define identity gaps and describe their consequences.
5. Describe the challenges that confront people as identities change in early adulthood and when children move out of the family home.
6. Strengthen your ability to use interpersonal communication to support your own identity, as well as the identities of others.

PUTTING THEORY INTO PRACTICE

In this chapter, you will learn how to:

1. Seek out situations that activate important facets of yourself.
2. Behave in ways that reflect who you want to be.
3. Enhance your self-esteem.
4. Communicate with integrity.
5. Reduce your identity gaps.
6. Find opportunities to represent multiple identities.
7. Confide in others as your identity changes.
8. Embrace diverse identities.
9. Support parents as their nest empties.

IDENTITY AND INTERPERSONAL COMMUNICATION

3

Source: Andrey Popov/Shutterstock

On the popular Netflix reboot, *Queer Eye*, a chic squad of gay men with expertise in culture, fashion, design, grooming, and cuisine descend upon an unsuspecting target to make-over their home, appearance, and lifestyle. The "Fab Five" change people's lives and challenge them to adopt changes to their style, home, habits, and hobbies that will better align with their desired sense of self. For example, Season 4 featured an episode about Wesley, a 30-year-old community activist who became paralyzed after being shot several times at the age of 24. He is the founder of an organization called Disabled But Not Really, which helps individuals with disabilities "develop a limitless mindset" to breed courage, competence, and confidence to create a version of themselves that isn't defined by their disability. Despite helping others to see themselves in a different light, Wesley struggles to embrace those qualities in himself. The Fab Five encourage him to dress more professionally, renovate his home to be more wheelchair accessible, and help him feel good about himself. They also arrange for him to meet with the man who shot him to gain closure from that experience and shed some of the shame he carries about his previous identity as a "bad boy" before the accident. In the end, the Fab Five do more than just a make-over, they hold up a mirror for people to better see how the life they were living was incompatible with the person they truly want to be. By helping people change their look, learn new skills, and confront hard truths, the Fab Five set them up to live a life that reflects their fullest and truest self.

How have your past experiences in life shaped the way you see yourself today? Can you identify some of the ways that your personal style or appearance might affect how other people perceive you? Do your ways of presenting yourself to others affect or reflect how you see yourself? What might happen to your self-perceptions and communication experiences if you changed how you look, act, or speak? Wesley's experience as a participant on Queer Eye highlights how our self-perceptions are closely tied to our past experiences and the ways that we act and present ourselves to others.

Your sense of self both shapes and is shaped by interpersonal communication. You express your personality, goals, and values in every interpersonal interaction. Through interpersonal communication, then, you reveal yourself to others. At the same time, the messages you receive from others affect how you see yourself. By communicating with other people, for example, we learn whether we are interesting, funny, intelligent, or worthy of respect. In this chapter, we examine how the self is formed and performed through interpersonal communication. With a deeper understanding of the self, you will be able to play a more active role in supporting both your own unique identity and the identities of others.

SELF-CONCEPT: HOW YOU SEE YOURSELF

Our personal experiences and interactions with others provide us with substantial information about who we are. When we communicate with other people, we both observe our own behavior and we receive feedback about how others perceive us. That sum total of knowledge that you have about yourself is your **self-concept**. It includes your memories of experiences and accomplishments, your physical traits and distinguishing features, your likes and dislikes, your feelings about yourself, and your experiences communicating with others. It is, in fact, all that you know and believe yourself to be. In this part of the chapter, you'll learn about characteristics of the self-concept and where you get information about who you are.

Self-concept
The sum total knowledge you have about yourself.

Characteristics of the Self

Although everyone's self-concept is unique, some general qualities apply to everyone's self. The following characteristics are core features of everybody's self-concept.

The self is subjective. Your self-concept is inherently subjective; in other words, you are who you think you are. Perhaps not surprisingly, we are often biased in how we think about and evaluate ourselves. For example, you might consider yourself to be a good friend, to have a good sense of humor, or to be a hard worker, but other people may see you differently. Our self-concept reflects how we see ourselves, which may or may not reflect the perceptions of others.

One of our biases is the tendency to interpret new information in ways that are consistent with how we already see ourselves (Swann, 2012). Imagine receiving an exam score that was much higher or lower than usual. Because that grade was not consistent with your view of your abilities, you might conclude that the exam was either especially easy or especially unfair. Conversely, we view experiences that support our self-perceptions as more valid and important. This desire to have our self-concept affirmed can affect our relationships with others. For example, a study of married couples showed that people are most satisfied when their spouse sees them the way they see themselves; on the other hand, being either overrated or underrated by a spouse predicts depression, marital dissatisfaction, and even the likelihood of divorce (Burke & Harrod, 2005).

Another subjective aspect of the self is **self-esteem**, which is a person's overall judgment of his or her own worth and value. Researchers measure self-esteem by asking people how much they agree with statements like these (Rosenberg, 2015):

Self-esteem
An overall judgment of one's self-worth or value.

- On the whole, I am satisfied with myself.
- At times I think I am no good at all.

- I feel that I have a number of good qualities.
- I am able to do things as well as most people.
- I feel I do not have much to be proud of.
- I certainly feel worthless at times.
- I wish I could have more respect for myself.
- I am inclined to feel that I am a failure.

PAUSE & REFLECT

As you reflect on the statements that measure self-esteem, would you say your self-esteem is high, low, or average?

Your self-esteem can both shape and reflect your interpersonal communication. For example, people with high self-esteem are more likely to be trusting of their conversational partners, disclose more personal and intimate information, and are more willing to show vulnerable emotional expressions in conversations with others (McCarthy, Wood, & Holmes, 2018). Conversely, people who experienced parental alienation in childhood tend to have lower levels of self-esteem, which give rise to more communication apprehension when communicating with male caregivers (Aloia & Strutzenberg, 2019). In addition, during initial "coming out" conversations, LGBTQ individuals who had clearer goals for the interaction and were more open and detailed about their sexuality and the degree to which they were out experienced higher self-esteem and lower levels of depression (Li & Samp, 2019). These studies show how self-esteem can predict certain communication behaviors and also be shaped by the qualities of an interaction.

The self is multi-faceted. There are a number of sides to our self-concept that reflect the roles and relationships that we have in different aspects of our lives. Take the example of Janine, who attends college on a rowing scholarship. In her role as a student, Janine's academic goals, abilities, and limitations are primary facets of her self-concept. Out on the water, though, Janine's sense of self emphasizes her strength, her connection to her team, and her commitment to hard work. She is also the child of South American immigrants, an art major, and a sorority sister; each of these roles calls upon a different set of personal qualities or facets of her self. Importantly, people with a complex self-concept tend to experience less depression following stressful life events, perhaps because a negative experience is less likely to undermine all of their different facets of self (Constantino, Wilson, Horowitz, & Pinel, 2006).

The different aspects of your self-concept can be more or less compatible or incompatible with each other. Consider, again, the example of Janine. If Janine's priorities as an athlete interfere with her ability to excel as a student or show commitment to her family, those aspects of her self-concept are incompatible. For example, Janine might skip classes to fit in an additional workout or forego holidays with her family because the team is traveling for competition. On the other hand, Janine's devotion to her team, studies, and family might prompt her to tutor a teammate in exchange for a free ride home to visit her family for a weekend. In this case, the different sides to Janine's self-concept complement each other.

The facets of your self-concept are more likely to be compatible or complementary when they reflect shared core values or beliefs. In Janine's case, her sense of self as an athlete, student, and daughter might be unified by a commitment to perform her best at any task; in turn, Janine can use that over-arching value to guide all of her behavior. When the facets of a self-concept are incompatible, however, a person is more likely to experience depression, loneliness, and low self-esteem (Lutz & Ross, 2003). For example, if Janine's aggressiveness as a competitor conflicts with the respect she is expected to communicate to her parents, she might struggle over how to communicate in a particular situation.

Facets of the self are more or less visible. Although some facets of the self are easily recognized by others, there are other facets that we try to keep private or that we might not even be aware of. The Johari Window is a tool for exploring facets of yourself that are more or less visible (see Figure 3.1). Information about yourself that you are aware of and that is

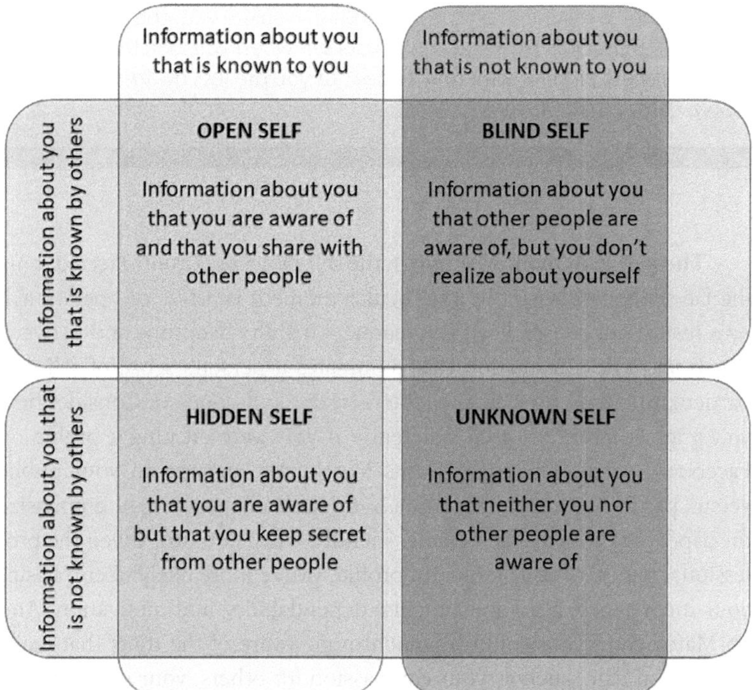

FIGURE 3.1 The Johari Window

visible to others is referred to as your open self. There are also parts of our self that we don't share with other people. Consider the example of someone who is known as a "tough guy," but who also has a sensitive side. Showing his softer side would diminish the public reputation that he's trying to uphold, so it becomes part of his hidden self – the part of the self that he knows about but is not visible to others. On the other hand, there are some aspects of the self that other people can see in you that you are unable to see in yourself, which is known as the blind self. For example, teachers may see potential in a student that the student has yet to realize. The final facet of self is the unknown self, which is the part of your self that is unknown to you and invisible to others. Perhaps you and the people you know never realized how tenacious, motivated, and determined you could be until you were faced with a challenging life situation. The Johari Window helps us to become more aware of the parts of our self we already know and to explore aspects of our self that we have yet to realize.

COMMUNICATION IN ACTION 3.1

Exploring Windows on Yourself

Because who you are is an essential part of how you communicate with others, becoming more self-aware can improve your interpersonal communication experiences. Create your own Johari Window by filling in the form that is available on the companion website with the information, attitudes, beliefs, feelings, and behaviors that you see in yourself when you look through each window. When you are done, reflect on how self-knowledge that you are less aware of might be shaping your interpersonal communication experiences.

Working Self-Concept The information that dominates a person's sense of self at a particular moment.

The self is dynamic. Although the self-concept is multi-faceted, only the facet that is relevant at a particular moment is active or operational. As a result, our sense of self is dynamic – it shifts over time and between situations. The information that dominates a person's sense of self at a particular point in time is called the **working self-concept**. Consider how you might present yourself differently if you were creating a profile on Facebook, versus LinkedIn, versus Match.com, or even in your public versus private Instagram accounts. On Facebook, you might emphasize the aspects of yourself as sociable, friendly, witty, and fun. Given the professional nature of your LinkedIn profile, you're more likely to emphasize your intelligence, accomplishments, dependability, and motivation. And on Match.com, you would be much more aware of the traits that make you a good date, such as your compassion for others, your romanticism, or your sex appeal. In a similar fashion, your working self-concept brings forth different facets of self as relevant to your circumstances. Movement between selves is as fluid as changing between online profiles, but when a particular self is active, it dominates that moment.

What we are experiencing in a particular moment – both our internal states and external circumstances – determines which self will be active (McConnell, 2011). Internal states that cue particular facets of self include the thoughts, goals, motivations, and feelings we have at a particular moment that make a particular aspect of the self more salient. External circumstances, such as the social situation, the physical environment, and external demands can also call forth qualities of the self that resonate with your surroundings. Although certain aspects of our self are spontaneously triggered by different internal and external circumstances, it is also possible to consciously activate a particular facet of self. For example, if you feel anxious about meeting your romantic partner's family, you can deliberately think about your strong family values, your polite demeanor, and other traits they are likely to find appealing. Thus, our self-concept at any particular moment is tailored to our circumstances based on our internal states, external circumstances, and our desired self-image.

Sources of Self-Knowledge

When you recognize the various sources that shape your self-concept, you can become more self-aware and less biased in how you see yourself. Consider, for example, your concept of yourself as a friend. Are you a good friend? Are you fun, caring, supportive, or interesting? How do you know? In the paragraphs that follow, we consider four sources of self-knowledge: your own observations of yourself, your social roles, social comparison, and feedback from others (see Figure 3.2).

Your own observations of yourself. Your first-hand experiences of your thoughts and actions are an important source of your self-concept. In fact, nobody knows better than you whether or not you are truthful, how much effort you put into your schoolwork, how willing you are to volunteer for good causes, and whether or not you are sincere in your relationships with others. Based on your own observations, then, you can support a variety of judgments about yourself. Thus, one way to determine what kind of friend you are is to reflect on how you have seen yourself treat your friends over the course of your life.

You can also learn about yourself by observing your specific actions. A **self-reflexive act** is a behavior that gives you insight into your own state of mind. Rather than thinking about how you generally treat friends, for example, you might think about a particular interaction you had with a particular friend. What did you do to mark the friend's last birthday? What did you say when that person asked for help with a class paper? Did you tell the truth or make up an excuse when you didn't want to loan your friend your car? Because the conversations you have reveal your personal qualities, you can reflect on your actions to draw conclusions about yourself.

Self-reflexive Act
A behavior that gives you insight into your own state of mind.

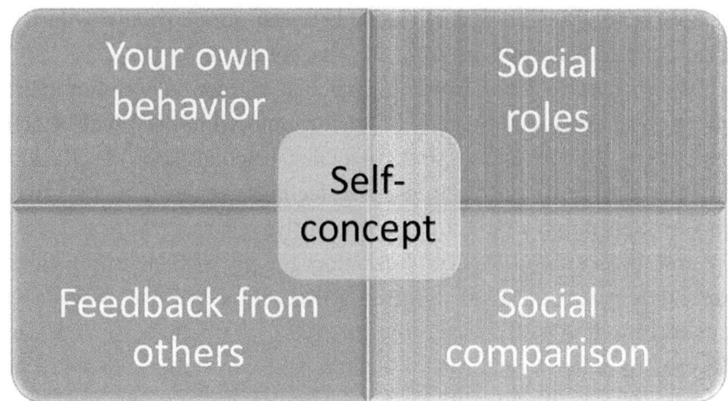

FIGURE 3.2 Sources of self-knowledge

Social Roles
The positions a person holds with respect to other people.

Your social roles. Another source of your self-concept is the different roles you play in your life. Social roles refer to the positions you hold with respect to other people. Your role as a student is primarily defined by your relationship to a teacher, your role as a child is defined by your relationship to a parent, your role as an employee is defined by your relationship to an employer, and so on. Each of those roles comes with a set of behaviors for performing your character, and enacting different roles allows you to learn different things about yourself.

Consider the self-knowledge you have gained from the different roles you perform. In the role of a student, you have learned the value you place on learning, working hard, and meeting deadlines. If you fill a leadership role at work, you might discover that you are decisive, well-organized, and motivational. And perhaps your relationship with your family has taught you that you are reliable, caring, or independent. One way to recognize how your social roles inform your self-concept is to remember what it was like to anticipate a new role. Before you were a college student, you might have wondered if you could manage the demands of classes, new friends, and a job. Since you had yet to be a college student, your self-concept didn't include the information you needed to answer that question. With a little experience in the role, though, your sense of yourself as a college student develops and may even become a central part of you.

PAUSE & REFLECT

What new things did you discover about yourself when you first became a college student?

Social Comparison
The process of comparing one person's traits and abilities to those of others.

Social comparison. Your self-concept is also the product of social comparison, the process of comparing yourself to others to gain insight into your own traits and abilities. On any human quality that varies across people, we look to others to see how we compare. Take the example of a seemingly objective trait like how much you talk. If everybody spoke the same number of words each day, that trait would be as uninformative as noting that someone has two ears or only one head. But because people vary in how much they talk, we develop an impression of ourselves as quiet, average, or talkative. And importantly, our sense of our own talkativeness depends on the people we compare ourselves to. If you come from a family of raucous story tellers, you might think of yourself as just average in talkativeness; on the other hand, if everyone you know is quiet, you could have a much more talkative self-concept.

As you might guess, our comparison points have a lot of influence on our self-concept. Whether you think you are smart, ambitious, generous, kind, or talented all depend on the traits of the people you compare yourself to. For example, mothers who compare their parenting to others on social networking sites perceive themselves as more overloaded and less competent, perhaps because of the cheerful portrayal of parenting many people post (Coyne, McDaniel, & Stockdale, 2017). And not surprisingly, perhaps, our social comparisons are subject to bias. In general, people prefer to compare themselves to others of the same gender and age (Knobloch-Westerwick & Hastall, 2006). Other research suggests that people with low self-esteem perceive that they turn to Facebook for social comparison more than other people do, but actual use of Facebook for social comparison is the same for people with low and high self-esteem (Cramer, Song, & Drent, 2016). Although it is clear that the process is far from objective, social comparison provides us insight into ourselves, relative to other people in our lives.

PAUSE & REFLECT

To whom do you compare yourself when you evaluate your own academic ability? Would your self-perceptions change if you picked different people to compare yourself to?

Feedback from others. Finally, other people shape our sense of self by the messages and feedback they communicate to us. The knowledge you gain about yourself can come from specific people, such as when you get information about how attractive you are from the comments that your friends or family make about your appearance. Feedback that people get from close relationship partners in public social media venues, such as Facebook, has been shown to have an especially strong effect on their self-perceptions (Carr & Foreman, 2016). In addition, you come to know about yourself by thinking about how other people, in general, perceive you. In the case of your appearance, your self-perceptions are probably influenced by how attractive you think you are to people, in general. This knowledge isn't based on a specific conversation, but rather on the messages you have received from a variety of people over the course of your life. This point of view is called the **generalized other** because it is a mental composite of other people that you can use to appraise yourself.

Generalized Other
A mental representation of the combined viewpoints of all other people.

Although the feedback provided by others can give us insights into ourselves, this process is also subject to the following biases (Kenny, 2019):

- We place a higher value on information from people who are close to us.
- We are more attentive to the perceptions of others when we are experiencing changes in our lives and uncertainty about our selves.
- We overestimate how much different people agree in their perceptions of us.
- We base our self-concept more on what we believe other people think about us than how they actually perceive us.

Despite these distortions, our self-perceptions are strengthened by the belief that they are shared by others. To continue the earlier example, no matter how attractive you perceive yourself to be, you'll have more confidence in your looks if you believe that other people find you attractive. Thus, the feedback we receive from others has an important impact on our self-concept.

FIGURE 3.3 We see ourselves in many different ways depending on the feedback we receive from others, and our sense of self can be distorted by biased perceptions.

Putting Theory into Practice: Cultivating Qualities You Value

Everyone's self-concept is unique, but we can make some generalizations about how the self operates. With this understanding of the nature and sources of self-knowledge, we can consider strategies for enhancing your self-concept.

Seek out situations that activate important facets of yourself. Keep in mind that only the facets of your self-concept that are relevant to your current internal and external circumstances are operating at any one moment in time. In fact, if you don't draw upon a facet of yourself, that part of you will become a less prominent part of your self-knowledge. In contrast, the working self-concepts that you use most often will come to dominate your sense of self. With this in mind, you can change or enhance your self-concept by seeking out situations where the working self-concept you have is one that you value.

Identify qualities of yourself that you value, but that you don't draw upon very often. Then, try to think of specific situations that would pull that part of you into your working self-concept. When Jen was in high school she was an accomplished actress and competitive debater. When she was in graduate school, she found that the overwhelming amount of time spent on school work and research obscured her sense of self as a dramatic performer. In an effort to seek balance in her life and restore a central part of her self-concept, Jen volunteered to coach a competitive speech and debate team at a local high school. This activity helped Jen to integrate aspects of her self as a performer that had been lost in light of her new role as a scholar.

Behave in ways that reflect who you want to be. One powerful source of information about yourself is your own behavior, so you might want to avoid behaviors that are inconsistent with the person you want to be. One way to take control of your self-concept is to set goals for yourself, and try to behave in ways that support that view of yourself. If you want to see yourself as more honest, moral, caring, or fun, the answer may be as simple as remembering to behave in those ways. Eventually, your patterns of behavior will support the self-concept you want to have.

COMMUNICATION IN ACTION 3.2

Finding Your Ideal Self

One way to enhance your self-concept is to identify the qualities you think you actually have and compare them to qualities that you consider ideal. You can download a form on the companion website that will help you reflect on how you typically communicate and how you would ideally communicate in a variety of situations. A discrepancy between the two columns identifies an area where you might change your communication to cultivate a self-concept you value.

Enhance your self-esteem. Recall that self-esteem refers to how you evaluate your self-worth. On any given day, you may encounter situations that make you feel good about yourself and those that make you feel not so good about yourself. Your experiences can have a positive or a negative impact on your self-esteem depending on how you respond to them. Consider the following suggestions for improving your self-esteem and avoiding experiences that threaten it.

- *Take stock of your strengths and weaknesses.* Make a list of all the things you do well and not so well. When you find yourself feeling down about one of your personal traits, skills, or characteristics, remember all of the positive aspects about yourself and give yourself some credit.
- *Change self-directed language and labels.* Don't adopt negative labels, like fat, stupid, or lazy, as part of your self-concept. Just as you probably wouldn't tolerate someone else saying such things about you, avoid being so negative about yourself.
- *Survey your environment.* Consider whether any of your friends, family members, or co-workers makes you feel bad about yourself. Find ways to distance yourself from people who diminish your self-esteem or resolve not to let them have a negative effect on you.
- *Act confidently.* Even if you don't feel strong, happy, or confident, behave in ways that make it seem like you do. If you act like a confident and valuable individual, people will begin to respond to you as someone who embodies those traits; in turn, positive reinforcement from others will help you to see yourself as a confident person.

IDENTITY: THE COMMUNICATED SELF

When we communicate with another person, the messages that we create reveal our self-concept and make it visible to others. Imagine how your communication behaviors might change if you had to pretend to be someone else – your best friend, a co-worker, or your parent – for one day of your life. How would this role affect the way you dress and walk, your gestures and expressions, the amount and way that you laugh, what you say, and how you speak? **Identity** is the image of yourself that is embodied in communication. Just as you can think of unique communication behaviors that would allow you to assume the identity of someone else, you have ways of communicating that embody your own self-concept. In this section of the chapter, we will explore the nature of identity and how it is intertwined with interpersonal communication.

Identity
The image of a person that is embodied in communication.

Creating Identity

How do people around you know whether you are assertive, agreeable, shy, or sarcastic? How do they come to know your feelings about topics like sports, animals, or movies? And how do they figure out your political values, your commitment to religion, or your thoughts about having children? Interpersonal communication is a powerful tool that allows us to present ourselves to others; the way we do so, in effect, becomes our identity.

SCHOLAR SPOTLIGHT

Visit the Communication Café on the companion website to view a conversation with Karen Tracy, who studies how people create identities through interpersonal communication.

PAUSE & REFLECT

What are some of the communication behaviors someone else would have to adopt if they assumed your identity for a day?

One way that we present ourselves to others is **self-disclosure**, which involves explicitly sharing personal information with another person. When you tell a new acquaintance where you are from, what you are studying in college, and what you do for fun, you are painting a picture of your identity. Likewise, the more private information you share with a friend – your hopes for the future, your concerns about your family, or past behaviors you regret – influence how that friend sees you. If you have a Facebook, Instagram, Snapchat, or Twitter, every status update, post, snap, or tweet is a disclosure that provides information about who you are, what you value, how you're feeling, and where you're going. As you'll learn in Chapter 9, self-disclosure is a key part of developing close relationships. More generally, disclosing information about yourself is a direct way in which you represent your identity through interpersonal communication.

Self-disclosure
Explicitly sharing personal information with another person.

We also create our identity more indirectly through the topics we discuss and the qualities we display when we communicate with others. As an example, consider how interactions in a work setting express our traits and values. One study, which involved a close analysis of interactions between co-workers, concluded that people use personal stories to showcase traits or qualities that might otherwise be unexpressed at work (Holmes, 2005). Imagine you had a co-worker who came in every Monday morning with tales of her weekend get-away to go rock climbing, mountain biking, or parasailing. From these stories you might infer that she is an adventurous and athletic risk-taker who enjoys the outdoors and likes to brag about her accomplishments. Similarly, a co-worker who is always telling animated stories about his trouble-maker of a daughter and the schemes he devises to catch her red-handed would convey an

CONNECT WITH THEORY

Visit the companion website to learn about the hyperpersonal model, which considers how online communication allows people to present themselves in ways that are more strategic than face-to-face self-presentation.

image of a family man who has a sense of humor about his daughter's shenanigans and is motivated to stay involved in his daughter's life. Thus, sometimes you come to infer qualities about an individual based on what their stories imply about them, rather than the explicit information they share about themselves.

When you consider how communication behaviors besides self-disclosure reveal your self-concept, you can see that any opportunity to communicate is an opportunity to create your identity. For example, the holiday letters that people send to their friends and relatives paint a picture of accomplishments, positive qualities, and promising futures (Banks, Louie, & Einerson, 2000). In the context of support groups, participants tell stories that invite others to validate their experiences and point of view (Hsieh, 2004). Even when we're not using words, we express our identities through our outward appearance to others, such that the clothes we wear, the car we drive, or the way we decorate our home communicate something about our self to others (Leary, 2019). Your online or virtual self-presentation is also a representation of how you see your self-concept, from the way you style your avatar for online gaming (Martey & Consalvo, 2011) to the carefully curated and filtered selfies you post to social media (Terán, Yan, & Aubrey, 2020).

PAUSE & REFLECT

What do your personal stories, room decorations, social media posts, and voicemail recording say about you?

Importantly, interpersonal interaction isn't just a source of information about the self, and nor is it simply a portrayal of the self; rather, it is the venue in which identities are created for self and others. The ways in which opportunities for communication allow us to create identities is clearly illustrated by communication online. A hallmark of the Internet is its ability to connect individuals with marginalized identities (Mehra, Merkel, & Bishop, 2004). Moreover, a study of virtual communities for transgender people found that some participants performed identities online in preparation for transferring those identities to off-line environments, whereas others used virtual communities to express identities that they could not perform off-line (Marciano, 2014). Because online communication gives people a place to develop and express identity that might otherwise be stigmatized or embarrassing, it plays an important role in creating identities.

COMMUNICATION IN ACTION 3.3

Creating an Online Identity

Online communities like Facebook, Instagram, LinkedIn, and Twitter have created outlets for people to express and experiment with their personal identity. Choose three people you know who have a webpage on one of these virtual communities and analyze the content on their page as an expression of their personal identity. How do these three individuals reflect their personal identity through the photos they display, the groups they are affiliated with, and the information they provide? Which aspects of these people's identities are emphasized on their webpage? Is each person's online representation of himself or herself consistent with how he or she expresses their identity in face-to-face communication?

Layers of Identity

Just as your self-knowledge is multi-faceted, your identity has multiple layers. Communication scholar Michael Hecht suggests that a person's identity has four layers or frames (Hecht & Lu, 2014). In Hecht's view, our identity is like the image that emerges when photographic images are projected on top of each other; each photo makes a unique contribution to the overall picture, and the final image is a composite of all the individual sheets.

CONNECT WITH THEORY

Visit the companion website to learn more about the communication theory of identity, which offers a multi-layered conception of people's identity.

The **personal layer of identity** refers to the perceptions you have about yourself that you communicate to others. This layer encompasses your self-concept, because it includes your perceptions of yourself, and it focuses on the self-knowledge that you display to others through communication. This identity is communicated to others not only by what you say, but also through the topics you choose to discuss and the way you talk about them. If you like to cook, for example, you would probably jump right into conversations about cooking and speak with confidence about how to prepare certain dishes; these actions communicate your identity as a good cook even if you don't explicitly claim that you are. When the conversation turns to topics that are less relevant to your personal traits, you would communicate that these skills are not part of your identity by saying less, being less assertive, and perhaps mentioning your lack of expertise. In these ways, the topics you discuss, the way you talk about them, and your specific words reveal information about who you are as a person.

Personal Layer of Identity
The perceptions people have about themselves that they communicate to others.

The **enactment layer of identity** refers to the qualities we reveal in the verbal and nonverbal style of our communication. Are you soft-spoken or loud? Do you tend to be polite or blunt? Do you use a lot of slang or speak more formally? How does your accent or dialect reflect the places you have lived? These features of communication don't involve what you say, but rather how you say it; in other words, your style of communicating

Enactment Layer of Identity
The characteristics of the self that are revealed through a person's verbal and nonverbal style of communication.

"If I want to impress a woman online, what font should I use? Aristocrat Bold so she'll think I'm rich or Comic Sans so she'll think I'm funny?"

FIGURE 3.4 Enacting identity

Source: © Randy Glasbergen/glasbergen.com.

reveals to others whether you are introverted, well-mannered, and a Southerner or extroverted, hip, and from the West Coast. In fact, a study of language used in email messages found that women who value their femininity create messages that are longer and more emotionally charged than women for whom femininity is less important (Palomares, 2004). This study shows the subtle ways that a woman's communication behavior enacts her gender identity.

Relational Layer of Identity
Characteristics of the self that are related to relationships with other people.

The **relational layer of identity** includes the various ways in which our personal relationships shape our identities. Our relational partners can either foster or thwart the identities we wish to present. For example, your efforts to present yourself as highly qualified for your job are doomed to fail if your colleagues already think you're incompetent. In addition, your relationships are where you can perform your roles as friend, teammate, spouse, or parent. Conversely, if you aren't involved in a particular type of relationship, you don't have an opportunity to express that identity. Finally, a relationship itself can have an identity. Roommates, couples, fraternity brothers, and best friends are all examples of relationships where the participants share in the relational identity.

Communal Layer of Identity
Characteristics of the self that are related to a person's group memberships.

The final layer, the **communal layer of identity**, captures how people's identities are embedded in their group memberships. Each of us is connected to a variety of groups – cultural groups, ethnic groups, neighborhoods, professional organizations, and/or social clubs. The shared experiences, group history, and the qualities that define the group we belong to become part of our identity. This identity is also embedded in our communication behavior. For example, each branch of the United States military has its own symbolic colors, slogans, songs, or rituals that are representative of significant moments and alliances that define the group's history. Our identity is also shaped by public images of the groups we belong to. Depictions of firefighters as heroes, for example, both honor people in this line of work and burden them with high expectations (Tracy & Scott, 2006).

COMMUNICATION IN ACTION 3.4

Marketing Yourself

Take a moment to write a profile suitable for posting on an online dating site or app, such as Tinder or Match.com. As you craft your profile, include information that you think would attract the kind of person you would like to date. Then, analyze your profile in terms of the four layers of identity. You can use the form on the companion website to guide your analysis. After analyzing your profile, consider how your profile would have been different if you had specifically focused on a single layer of your identity. What differences might there be in the kinds of dating partners attracted by profiles that focus on each layer of identity?

INSIDE COMMUNICATION RESEARCH

Interpersonal Communication and the Formation of Adoptive Identity

Most people start to explore and understand their individual identity during adolescence, but individuals who are adopted can sometimes struggle to integrate their adoption status into a coherent sense of self. Adoptees may have characteristics that are dissimilar to other members of their adoptive family in terms of their appearance, personality, abilities, or ethnicity. At the same time, they may struggle to identify with peers who have different types of family structures and backgrounds. Communication researchers Colleen Warner Colaner and Jordan Soliz (2017) sought to examine the role of family communication in helping adoptees form a coherent adoptive identity and promoting positive feelings about adoption.

The researchers surveyed 179 adults who had been adopted as infants or toddlers. They asked questions about the extent to which their adoptive parents communicated openly about adoption, how adoptees came to understand their adoptive identity, and their feelings about adoption and their birth parents. They examined two processes that are central to the development of adoptive identity: reflective exploration and preoccupation. Reflective exploration refers to the extent to which individuals have thought about the details of their adoption, which can be important for integrating the adoption into a larger sense of self. Preoccupation refers to the extent to which adoptees view their adoption as the primary organizing framework for understanding their identity and defining the self.

Results of the study indicated that adoptees tended to show less preoccupation when their family communicated openly about the adoption, but communicative openness did not have an effect on the amount of adoptees' reflective exploration. In turn, adoptees with more reflective exploration and less preoccupation regarding their adoptive identity tended to have more positive feelings about their adoption and toward their birth parents. The results of the study suggest that the way families communicate about adoption can help adoptees to integrate their adoptive identity into a broader sense of self.

THINK ABOUT IT

1. This study focused on the role of interpersonal communication within the adoptive family in facilitating a positive and coherent identity for adoptees. How might communication with people outside the family shape adoptive identity, such as communication with peers, birth parents, community members, or religious leaders?
2. How might the identities of the parents and other siblings in a family be affected by adoption? What role does communication inside and outside the family play in developing individual identities for other family members? For developing a relational identity for the family as a whole?

Ethnic Identity
The characteristics of self that reflect a person's shared heritage with a particular racial, cultural national, or tribal group.

We can see the four layers of identity at work in the example of **ethnic identity**, which arises from the perception that you share a heritage with a particular racial, cultural, national, or tribal group. A person's ethnic group is part of the communal layer of identity because it refers to people with whom an individual shares an ethnic identity (Hecht & Lu, 2014). Ethnicity, in contrast, exists within the personal layer of identity because it focuses on the degree to which membership in an ethnic group is personally important. Our ethnic identity may also be revealed in our style of communication (i.e., the enactment layer) or in the kinds of relationships we want to have (i.e., the relational layer). As summarized in Table 3.1, your ethnic identity spans the four layers of identity.

TABLE 3.1 The layers of ethnic identity

Layers of identity	*Ethnic identity*
Personal Layer	Ethnicity, or the degree to which membership in the ethnic group is personally important
Enactment Layer	The nonverbal and verbal cues, such as appearance, clothing, or dialect, that reflect ethnic group membership
Relational Layer	The kinds of relationships valued within the ethnic group, and the ways members of the group relate to each other in terms of status or friendship
Communal Layer	The ethnic groups that a person belongs to

Because your ethnic identity encompasses the personal, enactment, relational, and communal layers of your identity, it influences many aspects of your life. One study examined the strength of ethnic identity among Whites, Blacks, and Hispanics as a predictor of health beliefs and behaviors (Hovick & Holt, 2016). Among Whites, a strong ethnic identity was associated with increased physical activity and lower body mass index, as well as increased knowledge about their cancer risks. Among Blacks and Hispanics, a stronger ethnic identity predicted more worry about cancer risks, but not necessarily increased knowledge or action with regard to those risks. Ethnic identity has also been linked to drug use among middle-school children. In particular, ethnic pride is associated with less drug use among Mexican Americans and African Americans, but it is associated with more drug use among European Americans (Marsiglia, Kulis, & Hecht, 2001; Miller-Day & Barnett, 2004). Attitudes about social issues can also be shaped by the strength of one's ethnic identity. Research shows that African Americans with a strong ethnic identity are more supportive of the Black Lives Matter movement than those with lower levels of ethnic identity, whereas ethnic identity for White Americans is not predictive of their attitudes about the movement (Holt & Sweitzer, 2018).

Given the relationships among the layers of ethnic identity, managing diverse ethnic identities can be challenging. What happens when you identify with two different groups? If one ethnic identity is more physically apparent, communication partners are likely to ignore the less visible ethnic identity. A survey of multiracial Japanese European Americans showed that people identify more with the ethnic group that they physically resemble, but they also experience feelings of exclusion from

FIGURE 3.5 People at Sardar Market at Girdikot, Jodhpur, Rajasthan, Northern India

Source: Photo by Tim Graham/Getty Images.

their less obvious ethnic group (Ahnallen, Suyemoto, & Carter, 2006). Another study focused on Israeli adolescents with European mothers and Arab fathers – because their parents were not Israeli, and there was not a well-formed European-Arab community, these teens were forced to juggle separate European and Arab identities (Abu-Rayya, 2006).

PAUSE & REFLECT

How does your own ethnic group and ethnicity affect your interpersonal communication experiences?

Identity Gaps

Although we have described the layers of identity separately, they are intertwined within interpersonal communication. In other words, our personal, enactment, relational, and communal qualities are all relevant when we interact with other people. As an example, consider how the four layers of identity are connected for members of an Amish community. An Amish person's communal identity includes membership in a cultural group that has distinct social customs, such as refraining from the use of electronics. Those communal norms affect the community members' personal values, such that they embrace a traditional, agricultural lifestyle. These communal and personal identities shape each person's relational layer of identity by discouraging close relationships with people outside the community and encouraging strong ties with extended family. And the communal, personal, and relational identities dictate people's style of communication, including how they dress, the topics they are comfortable discussing, and to whom they convey respect, authority, or affection. The relationships among the layers of identity are captured by the word **interpenetration**, which refers to how the layers of identity are connected to each other.

Interpenetration
A characterization of the layers of identity that captures how they are interconnected or permeate each other.

The interpenetrated layers of identity can either complement or contradict one another. When the groups you belong to endorse the relationships you want to have and when your communication style is consistent with your self-perceptions, the layers of your identity form a coherent network (Figure 3.6). Sometimes, however, the layers of identity might conflict with one other. Consider the case of Gwen, who moved in with her parents after her divorce so that she could live near her new job. Gwen's personal layer of identity includes her sense of competence and authority as she performs her management duties at work, but her relational layer of identity includes her feelings of failure about her marriage, and feelings of awkwardness about her renewed role as a daughter in her parents' home. When the different layers of identity don't match, an **identity gap** is present (Jung & Hecht, 2004a).

Identity Gap
A mismatch in the qualities associated with two or more layers of identity.

FIGURE 3.6 Much like the superimposed images in this photo, identity is multilayered

HOW DO YOU RATE? 3.1

Identity Gaps

Jung and Hecht (2004a) developed a scale to measure gaps between college students' personal layer of identity and enacted layer of identity, in other words, discrepancies in how people see themselves and present themselves to others. To gain insight into any gaps between the personal and enacted layers of your own identity, visit the companion website to complete their measure of identity gaps. As you reflect on items in the scale, can you identify strategies that might help you to reduce the gap between the person you think you really are and the identity you enact for others?

Although some disagreement across layers of your identity is inevitable, large identity gaps can have profound consequences. In one study, Korean Americans living in New York City completed a questionnaire about their experiences of depression and any differences between how they see themselves (the personal layer of identity) and how they communicate with other people (the enactment layer of identity); the results showed that people with bigger identity gaps reported more symptoms of depression (Jung & Hecht, 2004a). Another study found that college students who perceived gaps between their personal and enactment layers of identity were less satisfied with their interpersonal interactions, felt misunderstood by others, and saw their communication experiences as inappropriate and ineffective (Jung & Hecht, 2004b). These studies reveal how experiencing identity gaps can affect how you feel about both yourself and your interactions with others.

Putting Theory into Practice: Being True to Yourself

As we have seen, communication is the tool you use to represent yourself to other people. Because your actions define you as a person, you should take care to communicate in ways that reflect and create an accurate image of who you are.

Communicate with integrity. Communicating with integrity involves being honest and authentic in your interactions with others. Sometimes, it may seem like there are benefits to misrepresenting yourself to others – perhaps exaggerating your qualifications will give you the advantage on the job market, pretending to be confused might encourage a professor's sympathy, or playing hard to get might increase a romantic partner's interest. When you communicate in ways that convey a false identity, though, you can suffer serious consequences. Claiming skills you do not have can get you fired, rather than the training you need; your professor might not mention an internship opportunity to a student who is already overwhelmed; and your dating partner might decide to find someone more interested in a relationship.

As a case in point, Denise recalls a former student who suggested that it was okay to express racist attitudes when it served a purpose; in particular, he said you could avoid jury duty by making prejudiced comments about the defendant's ethnic group. Denise cautioned him against both avoiding his civic duty and failing to recognize the power of an expressed identity. Expressing racism is to create yourself as a racist. Taking advantage of the history of racism in the United States for personal benefit is, in fact, being racist. Giving voice to racist attitudes, even if you claim not to share them, might reinforce someone else's racist opinions. Because the identities you create take on a life of their own, make a point of creating identities you believe in.

Reduce your identity gaps. When the layers of your identity conflict with each other, interpersonal communication can be less satisfying and you might feel worse about yourself. On the other hand, you can improve your well-being if you can reduce your identity gaps. Consider again the example of Gwen, who perceives a gap between her personal layer of identity as a competent office manager and her relational layer of identity as a daughter living with her parents again. Gwen can reduce this gap by bringing the layers of her identity into alignment with the personal qualities that she feels good about. To avoid feeling like a child in her parents' home, she can change her relational layer of identity by paying her parents rent or contributing to the household. She can also make changes in her enactment and communal layers of identity by getting up early, dressing more professionally, and offering to help her parents organize their retirement savings. Making these changes would align her various layers of identity with the personal qualities she values.

Find opportunities to represent multiple identities. Taking steps to reduce identity gaps does not mean that you have to abandon diverse identities that you value. You can be a competent, independent, college student and still enjoy and appreciate the comforts of being a child in your parents' home. In fact, being able to express both aspects of your identity can help you to cope with different life circumstances that might require elements of both identities. Because expressing an identity makes it an active part of who you are, seek out situations that allow you to perform the various identities that matter to you.

Opportunities to express multiple identities may be especially important for people who identify with more than one ethnic or cultural group. Multicultural individuals often adapt their communication behavior to express different sides of their identity in different cultural contexts or social situations. A study that interviewed biracial Asian/Caucasian individuals about their strategies for negotiating a biracial identity found that they were sometimes frustrated and found it challenging to balance the assertive and outgoing communication behaviors that are typical of their mainstream White peers with the expectations to be patient and respectful that is enforced in the Asian side of their family (Toomey, Dorjee, & Ting-Toomey, 2013). A common source of tension or conflict in relationships between these biracial individuals and their White peers stemmed from feeling misunderstood when friends and romantic partners failed to understand or empathize with their complex cultural perspectives. The Asian/Caucasian individuals would sometimes engage in passing behaviors in which they would act in ways that emphasized similarities with their mainstream White friends, but being forced to suppress their Asian side in order to "fit in" ultimately created social distance in these relationships. These findings suggest that it is important to embrace core aspects of the self and find opportunities to express the various identities that are important to you.

IDENTITIES IN TRANSITION

Our self-concept changes with the different circumstances we experience over the course of our life. As a young child, for example, you may have spent most of your time communicating with siblings and parents; as a result, those relationships figured prominently in your identity. As you progressed through middle school and high school, you might have had more conversations with friends than you did with your parents. In adulthood, college, work, and raising your own family require that you express new identities. In this section of the chapter, we consider two life stages that involve a change in people's self-concept: the transition that takes us from child to adult, and the experience of parents when their adult children move out of the family home.

Emerging Adulthood

Our self-concept evolves throughout our lives, but the changes we experience are especially striking in the period from adolescence to adulthood (around ages 18 to 25) known as **emerging adulthood**. During this time of life, people in our society are often less constrained by their families and not yet burdened by the responsibilities of adulthood (Arnett, 2010). This relative freedom allows emerging adults to explore a variety of identities before settling on the relationships, jobs, and worldviews that will define their adulthood. This is also a tumultuous phase of life. One study found that college students who believe that they haven't reached adulthood engage in more risky behavior, like illegal drug use or drunk driving, and

Emerging Adulthood
The period spanning ages 18–25, when people in our society are less constrained by their families and not yet burdened by adult responsibilities.

experience more depression than students who consider themselves to be adults (Nelson & Barry, 2005).

As people develop an adult identity, their relational layer is especially likely to change. For example, young college students identify relationships with parents as an area of their life that changes the most when they enter college, such that they have less contact with their parents, but the quality of their relationship improves (Lefkowitz, 2005). Emerging adults tend to communicate more honestly with their parents, compared to adolescents in high school (Jensen, Arnett, Feldman, & Cauffman, 2004). In addition, there tend to be more open conversations between emerging adults and their parents about sex and dating, with young adult men receiving more permissive parental messages about sex and emerging adult women receiving more restrictive messages about sex from parents (Morgan, Thorne, & Zurbriggen, 2010). As people go through emerging adulthood, their relationships with siblings also improve; despite reduced contact, those relationships are warmer, involve more emotional sharing and less conflict, and are less influenced by sibling rivalries (Hamwey, Rolan, Jensen, & Whiteman, 2019).

PAUSE & REFLECT

In what ways did your identity change – or how has it been changing – between the ages of 18 and 25?

Sexual Identity
How a person perceives and expresses sexual needs, values, and preferences.

Importantly, emerging adulthood is also a period when sexual identities become solidified. **Sexual identity** is more than sexual orientation; it refers to how you perceive and express your sexual needs, values, and preferences. Communication experiences are an important part of developing a sexual identity. For example, research shows that adolescent males are especially likely to use the Internet to express and explore a gay or bisexual identity by increasing self-awareness about their sexuality, meeting and communicating with others in the gay or bisexual community, and finding comfort and acceptance with their sexual identity (Harper, Serrano, Bruce, & Bauermeister, 2016). More generally, teens regularly use online chat rooms to express their sexual identity by referring to sexual activities, using sexual language, or adopting a sexualized screenname (Subrahmanyam, Smahel, & Greenfield, 2006). Similarly, one study found that two-thirds of their young adult participants reported engaging in sexting by sending sexually suggestive texts and/or nude or semi-nude photos via text message (Henderson, 2011). Sexual expression on social media is also seen as a way for emerging adults to create and experiment with their sexual identity (Tiidenberg & van der Nagel, 2020). Likewise, sexual behavior during this phase of life can affect emerging identities. For example, young women who demonstrate an appetite for sexual contact can be labeled "bad girls," whereas girls who maintain their virginity and refrain from sexual behavior are deemed "good girls" (Ashcraft, 2006). Moreover, college students who engage in more frequent sexual acts and have a greater number of sexual partners tend to report higher levels of sexual esteem than individuals who are less sexually active, and young men who report never using contraception during penetrative sex tend to have higher sexual esteem, whereas emerging adult women who never use contraception report lower levels of sexual esteem (Maas & Lefkowitz, 2015).

Expressions of a sexual identity and people's responses to those messages have important consequences. For example, talking about sexual identity can help youths solidify perceptions of their self-concept. In particular, a study of lesbian, gay, and bisexual youths found that people who had expressed their sexual identity to another person had more stable identities over a one-year period (Rosario, Schrimshaw, Hunter, & Braun, 2006). Interpersonal interactions about sexual identity can also affect how people feel about themselves. In one study, for example, lesbians kept diaries for two weeks in which they noted if they had any interpersonal communication experiences that devalued their sexual identity; they also recorded how they felt on each day. The results of the study showed that the women tended to feel more depressed and report lower self-esteem on the days when they experienced negative interactions about their sexual identity (Beals & Peplau, 2005). These studies illustrate how interpersonal communication experiences impact both our sexual identity and how we feel about it.

FIGURE 3.7 Friends hanging out in a park

Source: Getty Images.

HOW DO YOU RATE? 3.2

Emerging Adulthood

Emerging adulthood is the label given to the stage of life between around 18 and 25 years of age, but people vary in terms of when they consider themselves an adult. Visit the companion website to take a questionnaire that assesses the extent to which a person has met specific criteria for adulthood (Nelson & Barry, 2005). Based on this measure, can you identify ways in which you could express a more mature identity?

The Empty Nest

When you learned to drive a car, your parent stopped being your chauffeur; when you turned 18, your parent stopped being your legal guardian; and when you moved out of your parent's home, your parent stopped being your landlord. As parents see their children transition into adulthood, they must create a new identity that includes a different relationship with their children and a different view of themselves.

One task for the parents of emerging adults is to "let go" of their maturing children, and this process often begins before a child leaves home. In one study, parents of high school seniors were interviewed about their child's upcoming transition to college (Karp, Holmstrom, & Gray, 2004). Parents anticipated their child's departure from the household with mixed emotions, including a sense of profound loss, excitement about their child's future, and happiness at the thought of having more personal freedom. That study also showed the strategies that some families used to make this transition easier. For example, parents and children worked together to decide how far from home the child would move, so that the emerging adult would have sufficient independence but still be close enough to get help and support from the family. In addition, families would often agree to keep the child's bedroom intact, which communicates that the child has a presence in the home. These strategies can help to make the transition to an empty nest more gradual and give parents time to adjust to their new identity.

PAUSE & REFLECT

How did you and your parents address the changes in your lives once you graduated from high school? Did you explicitly take steps to ease that transition by communicating within your family or did your family tend to play it by ear?

Although emptying the nest isn't a universally positive experience, it has several upsides. After the last child moves out, mothers are often happier and experience fewer daily hassles, especially if they don't have a reason to worry about their children (Dennerstein, Dudley, & Guthrie, 2002). Couples in the empty-nest phase of marriage also report that they enjoy more time together and talk more frequently, appreciate the freedom to create their own schedules and be more spontaneous, and look forward to the added privacy and opportunities for new beginnings (Nagy & Theiss, 2013). In fact, parents tend to be happier with their lives after children move out, provided that they can communicate frequently with their children (Bouchard & McNair, 2016). When you talk with your parents after you have moved out of their home, you give them a chance to perform their parental identity, without burdening them with the tasks they juggled when you were younger.

For parents who don't have other important facets to their identity, the period after children move out can be more difficult. Relative to people with a strong sense of self, people with a less hardy self-concept need to use more coping strategies to deal with the distress they feel when their children leave the home (Crowley, Hayslip, & Hobdy, 2003). Married couples or domestic partners report uncertainty about the new roles and identities they must adopt during the empty-nest period, as well as waning interest in their romantic relationship and concerns about growing older and their own mortality (Nagy & Theiss, 2013). Uncertainty in empty-nest couples is also associated with more avoidance and indirectness during interpersonal conflicts, which increases stress and puts a strain on the relationship (Nagy & Theiss, 2013). Although emptying the family nest can be the beginning of an exciting life stage, it can also spark less desirable changes in a person's identity and relationships.

REAL WORDS

TRANSITIONING TO THE EMPTY NEST

The following transcript was taken from a study that Jen conducted with Mary Nagy in which they asked married couples who had recently become empty-nesters to talk with one another about how they were adjusting to this new phase of life. Notice how the couple emphasizes both positive and negative aspects of this phase of life.

HUSBAND: Well, I mean, it's definitely become a quieter house, so we have a chance to interact more without being interrupted. That's good for our relationship. Don't you think?

WIFE: Yeah and it's just calmer. There's a lot less things to do during the week. You know, with the kids home, it was a lot, we always were running to activities and we're not doing that now as much.

HUSBAND: Well, we cook together. Right? It seems like whatever we do, we do more together than we did before. Before you would be doing something and I would be doing something separately so that we could accomplish it all in one day. Now it seems like we can accomplish more of it easier. You know because we don't have those interruptions that we used to have.

WIFE: Well, it's also a little stressful though because you kinda feel like you're getting older. We're already where our kids are in college and they've left our house. It's gone a little bit too quickly. I felt like we blinked our eyes and we're in a whole new stage of our life which is a little bit scary.

HUSBAND: That's true. I did wonder how it was going to be prior to it happening, like, what's it going to be like when the kids are out of the house, and, uhh, what do you do with yourself? But I know we're busy. We're still busy. It just seems to be, umm, like we're able to be together more than before.

WIFE: When it's all said and done, I mean, I don't really . . . It doesn't really feel like we should be empty-nesters already.

HUSBAND: That's true. Like that we're there! It's one big blur.

Putting Theory into Practice: Supporting Identity Changes

In this section of the chapter, you learned about the changes to identity that occur during emerging adulthood and the pros and cons of emptying the family nest. By understanding the role of interpersonal communication, you can take steps to support both your own unique identity and the changing identities presented to you by others.

Confide in others as your identity changes. The changes we go through during the transition from adolescent to adult can be staggering. We become legally recognized as adults who can join the military, vote on election days, or go to prison. We may be expected to work full time, support ourselves financially, and take care of a family. It can be daunting when the question "What will you be when you grow up?" demands an answer. As you go through this transition, or changes in identity that you may face in the future, keep in mind that communicating with others is a key step in exploring new identities.

Through conversations with your friends, roommates, or co-workers, you might discover that they too are struggling with the new identities they have to adopt as they enter adulthood. Talking about these transitions can help you clarify your thoughts and make you feel less alone during this time. By sharing your feelings and gathering ideas from your peers, you might gain innovative perspectives on how to manage the shift in your identity. Even though you might feel compelled to make decisions about your new identity as an independent adult, consulting your parents, a favorite aunt or uncle, or a respected religious leader can provide valuable insight as to how you should enact your identity as an emerging adult. Maybe your father has some experience and advice that can help you navigate the transition from partier to professional. An older sibling might suggest ways to assert your independence from your parents. Communicating about your changing identity during emerging adulthood can contribute to a smoother transition.

Embrace diverse identities. Take stock of how your actions might constrain the identities that others present to you. For example, do you automatically assume that people you meet are heterosexual? If so, you create a real dilemma for gay, lesbian, bisexual, and transgender people that you encounter. On one hand, your communication partner can let the misperception go uncorrected, but that involves presenting him, her, or themselves as heterosexual. As an alternative, your new acquaintance can clarify his, her, or their sexuality, but personal topics like this are often avoided when we meet someone new. Rather than jump to conclusions, give people the opportunity to perform their identity for you. When you do, you can avoid forcing people to correct your mistakes and you can have more fulfilling communication experiences.

It can be hard to see how your own communication practices and cultural expectations can marginalize someone else's identity. For example, a recent popular trend for expecting parents is to throw a gender reveal party, where they invite all of their friends and family (and sometimes even themselves) to learn the sex of their baby. Couples will cut into a cake to reveal pink or blue frosting, pop a balloon to release pink or blue confetti, or fire explosives with pink or blue smoke. Although these parties can be cute and may seem innocuous to some, consider all that they imply about the cultural assumptions and expectations surrounding gender. First, such parties treat gender as binary instead of recognizing that gender exists on a spectrum (Jack, 2020). Also, a gender reveal during pregnancy also assumes that the child will identify with the gender that is associated with their biological sex, which isn't always the case. Once a baby's gender is revealed, friends and family often respond in ways that reinforce existing cultural norms about gender. A gender reveal party is often followed soon after by a baby shower, where guests will double down on gendered gifts: for girls it will be all things pink, themes of being a princess, and gifts that reinforce the notion that girls should be prim and proper and protected; whereas for boys it will be all things blue, with themes of sports and trucks, and assumptions that boys should be rough and tumble and tough. What do these events suggest about the nature of gender and gender roles in our society? How might these assumptions and expectations for each gender shape the way parents treat their children and make it more difficult for a transgender child to make sense of their identity later in life? Some scholars have criticized the popularity of gender reveal parties for being a performative event that reinforces the binary of gender identity and creates expectations for the unborn child to ascribe to traditional gender norms (Gieseler, 2018).

IDEA: PRACTICING INCLUSION, DIVERSITY, EQUITY, AND ACCESS

Consider how cultural norms and practices can marginalize gender and sexual minorities. What can be done to increase awareness about gender fluidity and encourage practices that embrace a diverse range of gender identities?

Support parents as they empty their nest. Interpersonal communication provides you with the tools you need to help your own parents, or other people you know, embrace their new identity as they launch their children into the world. Changes to the family during this stage of life can give rise to new identities, selves, and personal goals that did not previously exist. Everyone will find those changes easier to manage if you talk about them before they occur, discuss how close to each other you will live and how often you will talk, and decide whether you will maintain space for the adult child in the family home.

COMMUNICATION IN ACTION 3.5

Creating Space for Parental Identities

Although you don't need your parents in the same way that you did when you were younger, you can still create opportunities for them to express and enjoy their identity as parents. Visit the companion website to complete a table that will help you identify some of the ways your parents were able to express their identity as parents when you were younger and to think of situations that would allow your parents to express those same qualities in different ways now that you are older.

SUMMARY

Every interaction that you have involves the person you believe you are and the image you present to others. As you have seen, the self-concept is not a simple entity. How we see ourselves is inherently subjective, there are many facets to our self-concept, and our self-concept changes based on our present internal and external circumstances. You also learned that interpersonal communication is central to the development of self-knowledge. From a lifetime of experience with our own behavior, we can draw inferences about who we are. In addition, the social roles that we fill create opportunities for us to develop the qualities required by those relationships. We also look to the people around us to determine how we compare. Finally, other people shape our sense of self by the messages and feedback they communicate to us. From the wealth of our interpersonal communication experiences, we come to understand who we are.

Whereas the self-concept refers to the knowledge you have about yourself, identity captures the images that you create for others. Interpersonal communication is a performance of your self; in this sense, communication and identity are inherently connected. Like the self-concept, identity has multiple facets. The image you portray is a blend of the personal traits you communicate, your verbal and nonverbal choices, the relationships you have or would like to have, and the social groups that you belong to. Moreover, the different layers of your identity may or may not complement each other. When they don't, identity gaps can lead to less satisfying communication experiences and decreased well-being.

Throughout our life, our identity continues to develop and change. During emerging adulthood, people experience numerous changes across the layers of their identity as they explore the person they will become as an adult. Another time when identities change a lot is when parents see their adult children move out of the family home. Although both of these transitions can mark an exciting time in our lives, it can be challenging to abandon familiar identities and to develop a new view of yourself. An ability to communicate with others and receive identity support is an important part of making these key life transitions.

Your self and identity are a part of every interpersonal interaction that you have. Although your sense of yourself and the image you project are complex and evolving, you are not a passive observer of yourself. As you learned in this chapter, you can take steps to cultivate qualities you value, stay true to yourself, and support both your own unique identity and the diverse identities that you encounter. Consider the ways that you might use interpersonal communication to confront the ethical issues described below and still help yourself and others develop and display a valued sense of self.

ACTIVITIES FOR EXPLORING COMMUNICATION ETHICS

What Would You/Should You Do?

Imagine that you are at a family reunion, and you've been noticing how your cousin talks to his eight-year-old son. Over the course of the day, your cousin has said a number of hurtful things to the boy. When the child was getting his lunch, his dad said, "If you don't eat more than that, you'll always be scrawny." When the kids were choosing teams for a softball game, your cousin told everyone that this son couldn't hit a pitch if his life depended on it. And when the boy fell off the trampoline and starting crying, his father called him a "cry baby." Given what you know about the effects of messages on a person's self-concept, what would you – or should you – do?

Something to Think About

Public health statistics show that LGBTQ youth are at higher risk for suicidal ideation and attempts, and these risks are even higher for transgender and nonbinary youth who are questioning or unsure of their sexual identity (Price-Feeney, Green, & Dorison, 2020). Based on these statistics, some people have called for improving counseling services in high schools that provide support to queer youths (John, Poteat, Horn, & Kowciw, 2019). Other fringe groups, however, have argued that the evidence linking sexual identity to suicide is flawed, and that providing support services will encourage youths toward a homosexual lifestyle (e.g., Virginia Christian Alliance, 2012). What are the ethical issues involved in deciding whether to use school resources to support marginalized identities?

Analyze Communication Ethics Yourself

Television shows often draw upon stereotypes of ethnic groups to develop the drama or shape the plot. For example, the ABC sitcom *Fresh Off the Boat* played off common stereotypes about Asian Americans, with an overbearing and critical Taiwanese mother and children who are intelligent and accomplished in school, to create a story about the successful assimilation of an Asian family into American culture. Select a television show that portrays a particular ethnic group and watch a few episodes. As you do so, take note of how that ethnic group is represented to audiences. Based on your analysis, consider the ethical issues involved in media representations of ethnic identities.

KEY WORDS

communal layer of identity
emerging adulthood
enactment layer of identity
ethnic identity
generalized other
identity
identity gap
interpenetration
personal layer of identity
relational layer of identity
self-concept
self-disclosure
self-esteem
self-reflexive act
sexual identity
social comparison
social roles
working self-concept

LEARNING OBJECTIVES

After reading this chapter, you should be able to:

1. Describe the three stages of perception.
2. Define the dimensions of attribution.
3. Define the fundamental attribution error and the actor-observer effect.
4. Describe the patterns of attributions that occur in satisfying versus dissatisfying relationships.
5. Understand how culture, social group, and personal traits influence perception and attribution.
6. Describe the impact of alcohol consumption on perception and sexual risk-taking.
7. Understand how stereotypes affect perception and interpersonal communication.

PUTTING THEORY INTO PRACTICE

In this chapter, you will learn how to:

1. Direct your attention during interpersonal interactions.
2. Distinguish between facts and inference in your interpretation of a situation.
3. Avoid forming an explanation based only on your own point of view.
4. Focus on behaviors, not personalities.
5. Protect relationships you value by making adaptive attributions.
6. Recognize individual differences in perception and attribution.
7. Recognize when your perception is impaired.
8. Combat the formation of stereotypes.

4

PERCEPTION AND INTERPERSONAL COMMUNICATION

Source: Photo by Stuart Frank/Getty Images.

Following the election of Donald Trump to the Presidency of the United States, Americans seemed more bitterly divided than ever along political party lines. Democrats and Republicans, seemingly, could not see eye to eye on any issues of importance to the American public. Interestingly, a Pew Research Center Poll showed that 40% of both Democrats and Republicans say that they belong to their political party because they oppose the other party's values, not necessarily because they embrace their own party's ideals. Ironically, most of the perceptions that people have of the opposing political party are pretty inaccurate. A YouGov poll asked individuals from each party to estimate the prevalence of certain groups within the opposing party and people's perceptions did not align with reality. Republicans believed that 46% of Democrats are Black, but in reality Blacks make up only 24% of the Democratic party. They estimated that 44% of Democrats are union members, when the actual number is only 11%. And they assumed that 38% of people in the party are lesbian, gay, or bisexual, when the actual number is only 6%. Democrats didn't fare much better in their perceptions of Republicans. Democrats estimated that 44% of Republicans are Evangelicals, over the age of 65, and earn more than $250,000 per year. In reality, Republicans are only 34% Evangelical, just 21% are older than 65, and a mere 2% in the party earn more than $250,000 annually. Perhaps some of the conflict, disdain, and polarization in American politics could be reduced if people had more fair and accurate perceptions of the opposing party.

Everyone brings their own unique perspective and viewpoint to their communication experiences. Just as Democrats and Republicans might be at odds because they misperceive one another's values and beliefs, communication partners can reach very different conclusions about why a conversation unfolded as it did. In addition, our personal traits influence both what we take away from interpersonal interactions, and what our communication partners might be assuming about us. At the root of all of these experiences is how we perceive and make sense of events in the world around us.

Cognition refers to the mental processes involved in gaining knowledge and comprehension. In other words, your cognition includes all of the thoughts and ideas that you have in your mind. Because our minds are capable of processing countless thoughts at once, we need a process that helps us to organize all of that information in meaningful and useful ways. **Perception** is the process by which a person filters and interprets information to create a meaningful picture of the world. In the context of interpersonal communication, our perceptions shape how we interpret and react to another person's messages (Figure 4.1). While we cannot remove the filter of perception from our interactions with others, we can become more aware of how that filter operates. And understanding perception will allow you to take steps to improve your interpersonal communication. To that end, this chapter examines the stages of perception, how people perceive – and often misperceive – the causes of behavior, and factors that influence perception.

Cognition
The mental processes involved in gaining knowledge and comprehension.

Perception
Filtering and interpreting information to create meaning.

STAGES OF PERCEPTION

We are bombarded by stimuli of all sorts at all times. Consider all of the information that is available to your senses at this very moment. As you read this page, your eyes focus on the black shapes on white paper or screen, while your peripheral vision conveys images of the table top and the room. Your ears are also gathering information, such as the hum of a furnace, people talking in another room, or traffic noise. Likewise, your nose is helping you keep track of smells that may signal danger, as in the case of a fire, or opportunity, as in the case of freshly baked cookies. Even the nerve endings in your skin are busy telling you whether you are warm or cold, whether your shoes fit comfortably, and how your body feels against your chair. As if this information about your environment weren't enough, you also receive internal stimuli in the form of hunger pangs, emotions, fatigue, etc. As this example makes clear, even sitting quietly trying to read your class assignment exposes you to a vast array of stimuli that need to be processed. The stages of perception refer to the sequence of steps we use to sort through all of the information available at a given moment in order to create a useful understanding of the environment.

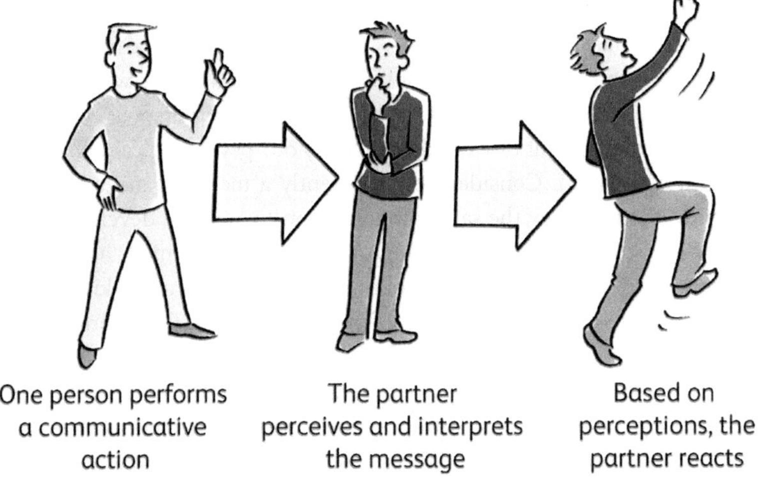
One person performs a communicative action
The partner perceives and interprets the message
Based on perceptions, the partner reacts

FIGURE 4.1 The role of perception in interpersonal communication

PAUSE & REFLECT

Make a list of things that you notice around you at this moment. Then, concentrate on each of your senses – what you see, hear, smell, and feel – one at a time, and make a list of anything new that you perceive. How do the two lists compare?

Selection

Selection
Directing attention to a subset of sensory information.

The first stage of perception is **selection** or directing attention to a subset of the stimuli available to the senses. In your efforts to read these words, you selectively attend to the marks on the page, and you screen out or ignore the feel of the chair against your body, the noises around you, and thoughts about other tasks you have to do. Selection can be guided through conscious control; for example, you might direct your attention to the conversation at the next table in an effort to eavesdrop. More often, however, the selection of stimuli for further processing happens subconsciously. In other words, our brains automatically screen out a huge quantity of information provided by our senses before we even notice it. Notably, our screening mechanisms aren't haphazard; rather, the selection stage of perception is influenced by several factors, including our point of view, the intensity of stimuli, the personal relevance of information, consistency with expectations, and inconsistency with norms.

Point of view. One basic force that shapes what stimuli we attend to is our point of view or the perspective that we have on a situation. Consider for a moment how your physical perspective on a situation influences what you pay attention to. For example, being on a basketball court during a game, on the sidelines, or high up in the stands directs attention to different facets of the game. In the same way, how close we are to another person, whether we are sitting or standing, and the way our bodies are oriented influence what we notice about interpersonal communication partners. Point of view also includes our psychological orientation toward a situation. Consider how differently a manager and a potential employee might view the same job interview. In fact, the development of expertise at a task involves learning to notice different things about a situation; for example, as high school musicians become more skillful, they become more adept at hearing discrepancies between their performance goals and execution (Hamilton & Duke, 2020).

The intensity of stimuli. The selection stage of perception is also affected by the intensity of stimuli – how strongly various features stand out in our perceptual field. We typically focus on elements that stand out from the background by virtue of their size, color, movement, or closeness to us. Big, bright, moving things that are nearby are especially likely to block us, blind us, or knock us down; therefore, these stimuli are almost always selected for further processing. You may have noticed that the advertisements that appear in the margins on your favorite websites take advantage of intense stimuli by making their ads very colorful and using animation to draw attention. Similarly, instructors who make direct eye contact and have an expressive face are more likely to sustain the attention of students in class (Bolkan & Griffin, 2018). In the same way, the intensity of cues can affect what people focus on during interpersonal communication.

Personal relevance. A third factor that influences the selection stage of perception is the personal relevance of information to the perceiver. Research has shown that people pay more attention to conversations about topics that are personally relevant – for example, heavy drinkers find conversations about alcohol more involving (Hendriks & Yzer, 2020). More generally, people are more likely to automatically attend to information that is relevant to the self, such as their name (Pfister, Pohl, Kiesel, & Kunde, 2012). Likewise, our needs or purposes can influence what we focus on in others. For example, the extent to which people notice attractive features in others is related to whether or not they are thinking of someone else they love (Ma, Xue, Zhao, Tu, & Zheng, 2019). In this context, what observers notice depends on whether they are sizing up a potential date for themselves. These examples show that people attend to information that is relevant to them or their goals in a situation and they are less attentive to information that doesn't apply to them. You have probably become quite skilled at identifying junk mail in your inbox because it is typically from a source who is not a personal friend and contains information that is irrelevant to your circumstances. This cognitive process allows you to delete messages that are not important and focus on the ones that have more relevance to you.

Consistency with expectations. Another force that shapes the selection stage of perception is consistency with expectations; in other words, the degree to which a situation is similar to or different from what we anticipated. Generally speaking, people tend to look for and select information that they expect to be present in a situation. On the first day of class with a professor you've heard good things about, you are primed to look for qualities that have earned that favorable reputation; on the other hand, you'll tend to notice more negative attributes about a class that you've heard is a waste of time. Because we always enter interactions with other people with some assumptions about their behavior, expectations are a powerful force shaping interpersonal perception and communication.

Inconsistency with norms. A final factor shaping selection ensures that we notice the unexpected. Inconsistency with norms is the extent to which events violate our standards for behavior. Expectancy violation theory suggests that when people's behavior deviates from anticipated norms for interaction, our attention is drawn to the inconsistency and shapes our

CONNECT WITH THEORY

Visit the companion website to learn about Expectancy Violation Theory, which explains how deviations from anticipated norms for behavior can shape perceptions of interpersonal interaction.

perceptions and reactions to the encounter. In other words, expectancy violations occur when behavior falls outside the range of anticipated behavior (Burgoon, 2016). To continue the earlier example, imagine how distracted you might be if your professor wore a gorilla costume to class (unless of course, the occasion was Halloween). In fact, when teachers violate classroom norms by being incompetent, offensive, or lazy, students spend more time thinking about interactions with that teacher, are less engaged by the course material, and perform worse on exams (Berkos, Allen, Kearney, & Plax, 2001; Goodboy, Bolkan, & Baker, 2018). Not surprisingly, then, atypical information is more likely to be noticed and remembered, at least in the short term (Shapiro & Fox, 2002).

The selection stage of perception is the critical step where we determine what information we will and will not consider. As we have seen, the selection of details selected for further processing is influenced by characteristics of the situation and the perceiver. Thus, from the very moment that your brain selects some information and ignores other details, you have started crafting a perception of reality that is unique to you.

Organization

Organization
The process of arranging information into a coherent pattern.

The second stage of perception is **organization**; during this stage, people sort stimuli to clarify which details are closer or further away, above or below each other, or on the same spatial plane. In other words, people arrange information to create a coherent map of features within a situation. As Figure 4.2 reveals, even a drawing can change form depending on which details we assign to the foreground or background. Within the dynamic world of interpersonal interaction, organization includes efforts to sort events into causes and effects, intentions and accidents, patterns and coincidences, etc. In total, then, the organization stage involves assigning roles and relationships to the information we have selected with the ultimate goal of making sense of it.

How we organize information plays a particularly important role as we form impressions about other people. Think for a moment about all of the information you might gather about someone during a first interaction: perhaps you can discern the person's gender and ethnicity, and you have information that the person shares with you, ranging possibly from name and hometown to career and relationship goals. You also can observe the person's communication style, such as whether you got their full attention or they were checking their phone as they talked to you (Vanden Abeele, Antheunis, & Schouten, 2016). As you make sense of this information, you must decide which details are most important or relevant to the person's personality. There are several different theories that describe how people organize information about others into a coherent impression (Ledgerwood, Eastwick, & Smith, 2018); the basic point is that the weight you place on different details ultimately affects how you view others.

HEAD IN LANDSCAPE.
(From a Print of about 1650.)

FIGURE 4.2 "The Image Disappears" (Dali, 1938)

The amount of information we have also influences the impressions we form about our communication partners. In general, email and other computer-mediated exchanges are assumed to provide less social information than face-to-face encounters (Walther, 2011). In these contexts, you can still observe your partner's communication style through their tendency to capitalize (a little or A LOT), punctuate excessively (!!!), or use emojis (😟) and you also receive the information they choose to communicate to you. At the same time, you don't get a lot of details that are visible in a face-to-face conversation. The effect of this information shortage is that people form less detailed impressions of an online interaction partner, but the judgments that they do make tend to be more extreme (Hancock & Dunham, 2001). For example, you might be deeply moved by a cancer survivor's courage and optimism after participating in an online support group, but you wouldn't have any idea whether she was athletic, friendly, smart, or even tall or short. Not surprisingly, having fewer pieces of information gives greater weight to the information that is available, especially for people you perceive to be different from yourself (Carr, Vitak, & McLaughlin, 2013).

Interpretation

In the final stage of perception, **interpretation**, we assign meaning to the information that we have selected and organized. To do so, we have to add in details and draw conclusions that aren't actually present in the situation. For an example, look at the image in Figure 4.3. If you don't have any prior information, the image can be pretty hard to figure out.

Interpretation
The process of assigning meaning to information.

FIGURE 4.3 Dalmatian on a beach

On the other hand, if you know it's a picture of a Dalmatian, and you are familiar with what Dalmatians look like, you can probably make sense of the image quickly. And notice how once you know what the picture is, it is almost impossible for you to go back to perceiving the image as meaningless. By drawing connections between information in the environment and past experiences or knowledge, we are able to make sense of the stimuli that we encounter.

The interpretation stage of perception also includes making sense of past experiences, and we might reach different conclusions than we did at the time those events occurred. More recent experiences, new information, and how we're feeling in the present can all color how we interpret that past. For example, people change their evaluations of other people's physical attractiveness after then learn positive or negative information about their personality (Lewandowski, Aron, & Gee, 2007). In fact, a study which asked dating couples to keep diaries over a three-week period showed that ratings of a partner's physical attractiveness go (or stay) up after positive interactions, but decrease after negative interactions (Albada, Knapp, & Theune, 2002). Among married couples, satisfied partners characterize negative interactions as bygones, but consider positive experiences as currently important (Cortes, Leith, & Wilson, 2018). These examples show how the interpretation stage of perception is an ongoing process through which we form and modify our judgments.

PAUSE & REFLECT

Think about a past romantic relationship or friendship that you are no longer in. How did you describe the day you met that person when your relationship was at its best? How would you describe that day now that the relationship has ended?

Putting Theory into Practice: Paying Attention to Perception

As we reflect on the stages of perception depicted in Figure 4.4, we see how perception is affected by characteristics of the perceiver. Although our perceptions are inherently subjective, we can take steps to be more mindful and careful as we make sense of the world around us.

Direct your attention during interpersonal interactions. Although attending to every sensory input available to us at a given moment is neither desirable nor feasible, we can consciously focus on details that we might otherwise overlook. Just as you might concentrate to hear a nearby conversation, make a point of noticing details in the situation. Consider the following suggestions for focusing your attention during interaction:

- Before a conversation, take stock of your goals and expectations so that you can look for information that both supports and contradicts your needs or assumptions.
- As you're chatting, look around to see what stands out from your communication partner's point of view.
- Make a point of examining details in the background, rather than just those that stand out or grab your attention initially.

By actively directing your attention during your interpersonal interactions, you'll gain a fuller understanding of your communication experiences.

Distinguish between facts and inference in your interpretations of a situation. Facts are the verifiable details within a situation; inferences involve going beyond the verifiable facts and adding in information that may or may not be true. As you communicate with others, it is important that you recognize that your inferences are your own personal conclusions – they are not facts that everyone accepts. And when you make judgments about a situation, double-check what you've based your

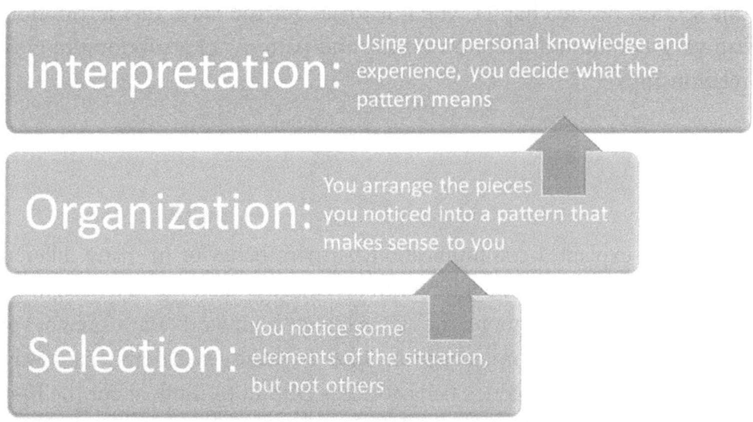

FIGURE 4.4 The stages of perception

conclusions on. Have you reached a judgment after considering facts? Or is your judgment based on other inferences you have made? The goal is to make inferences that are well grounded in facts, and to recognize the difference between the two.

COMMUNICATION IN ACTION 4.1

Forming Impressions of Others

Find a seat at the library, cafeteria, or coffee shop where you can watch people for a while. Choose someone to observe. Using the form provided on the companion website, record your perceptions of this person and reflect on the judgments you make about him or her. This exercise will help you realize all of the judgments you make about people, even when they are total strangers, and reflect on where your perceptions come from.

ATTRIBUTION: PERCEIVING AND MISPERCEIVING CAUSES

Attributions
Explanations for why something happened.

One inference that people sometimes make as part of the perception process is a judgment of *why* something happened. **Attributions** are explanations that help us to identify what caused certain events or people's behaviors. A person's desire to understand the causes of events is particularly great when circumstances or outcomes are negative (Baumeister, Bratslavsky, Finkenauer, & Vohs, 2001). For example, while you probably wouldn't feel the need to explain why the driver in the next lane is holding a steady course, you would be more motivated to look for causes when that driver swerves into your lane, and you would be even more focused on causes if you have a collision. Thus, attribution occurs during the interpretation stage of perception when people are prompted to draw inferences about the causes of the circumstances around them. In this section of the chapter, you'll learn about the ways that attributions can vary, common attribution biases, and patterns of attribution in close relationships.

Dimensions of Attribution

You might explain a communication partner's behavior in many different ways; for example, you might interpret an insult from a friend as a sign that he doesn't like you anymore, she's stressed out from work, they thought you were criticizing them, or it was just a joke. To make sense of the many ways we might explain someone's behavior, it is helpful to think about the basic ways in which attributions can differ. One classic and widely accepted view is that the attributions we make for another person's actions vary in terms of three dimensions (Weiner, 1986). These three dimensions are described in the following paragraphs and illustrated in Table 4.1.

Internal or external? One core question we consider when making attributions is whether a person's behavior is caused by something within the person or something in the situation. **Internal attribution** assumes that personal forces or characteristics of individuals are at the root of their behavior, whereas an **external attribution** locates the cause of events in environmental forces that exist outside an individual. To continue the earlier example of the car swerving into your lane, an internal attribution for the driver's erratic behavior is that the person has poor driving skills; an external attribution would focus on the squirrel that ran in front of the car.

Internal Attribution
Concluding that behaviors are caused by characteristics of the actor.

External Attribution
Concluding that a person's behaviors are caused by the situation.

PAUSE & REFLECT

Consider your perceptions of people who post comments to blogs, discussion boards, or online news sites. How likely are you to assume that the comments posted reflect the poster's personality? Could there be external forces that prompt someone to post a comment in a public online forum?

TABLE 4.1 The dimensions of attribution

Imagine that you're on your way to the bookstore to meet up with a new acquaintance, Stephen. As you approach the store, you see Stephen in an argument with another man. Why is Stephen behaving this way? Who or what caused the fight? When we consider the three dimensions of attribution in combination, we can see the many different ways that you might explain Stephen's communication behavior. Notice how the internal, controllable, and stable attribution highlights Stephen's personality as the root of his behavior. In contrast, the external, uncontrollable, and unstable cause places the blame on a mistake by the other guy.

	Internal		*External*	
	Stable	*Unstable*	*Stable*	*Unstable*
Controllable	Stephen enjoys arguing with strangers	Stephen copes with trouble with his girlfriend by arguing with strangers	The store is a gathering place for protesters – arguments are common	When people get stressed out, they come to this place to blow off steam
Uncontrollable	Stephen has a short temper	Stephen is just the kind of guy some people like to argue with	The other guy often starts arguments with people on the street	The other guy mistook Stephen for the man who stole his girlfriend

Controllable or uncontrollable? We also consider whether an action is controllable or uncontrollable. A behavior is seen as controllable if the person could have acted differently; in fact, control often implies that the person performed the action with the intention of producing certain consequences. Conversely, we sometimes see a person's actions as uncontrollable either because the actor could not have behaved differently or did not mean to produce the consequences. To understand the importance of attributions of control, imagine how differently you would react to a car accident if you thought the other driver actively sought to hit your car rather than simply lost control of the vehicle.

Stable or unstable? A third question is whether the causes of a behavior are ongoing or temporary. Stable causes are those that we expect to persist or to be present into the future; unstable causes are assumed to be either temporary or sporadic. When we attribute a behavior to stable causes, it leaves us feeling more in control because we can anticipate actions and adapt our own behavior accordingly. In contrast, unstable causes leave us unsure when a behavior will or won't occur. For example, if you conclude that driving conditions on a particular stretch of road are always hazardous, you can avoid danger in the future by taking a different route; if you conclude that other drivers will occasionally just drift into your lane, you may suffer quite a bit more anxiety whenever you are driving.

How we explain another person's behavior determines how we communicate with that person. For example, we are less inclined to offer help to someone in need when we judge that person to be responsible for their situation (Weiner, 2006). When we make internal attributions for another person's problems, we are more likely to tell that person to accept responsibility and less likely to convey sympathy and concern (MacGeorge, 2001). In particular, one research study showed that college students responding to a person seeking support online judged that person more negatively, provided lower quality support messages, and were less polite when they perceived the person as responsible for the distressing situation (Rains, Tsetsi, Akers, Pavlich, & Appelbaum, 2019). Another study found that children's attributions of responsibility were related to their willingness to forgive a parent's infidelity (April & Schrodt, 2019). As these examples illustrate, our interpersonal communication decisions are closely linked to how we explain other people's behaviors.

Attribution Biases

Attribution Biases
Distortions in the causal explanations people construct.

Although you might think that people seek accurate explanations for things that happen, we are actually quite biased in the attributions we make. **Attribution biases** refer to distortions in the conclusions we reach about the causes of events. There are several types of attribution biases; however, two biases are particularly common and important to interpersonal communication. The **fundamental attribution error** refers to our tendency to link other people's behavior to internal, rather than external, causes. The **actor-observer effect** is the complementary tendency to attribute our own behavior to external, rather than internal, causes. Although there are certainly situations when we deviate from these patterns (see Table 4.2), these two biases typically shape how people make sense of the world.

Fundamental Attribution Error
Explaining the behaviors of others in terms of internal, rather than external, causes.

Actor-Observer Effect
Explaining one's own behavior in terms of external, rather than internal, causes.

Consider for a moment the many instances of these biases throughout a student's day-to-day experiences. As Zoey commutes to campus, she attributes her own driving errors to external conditions (the weather or animals in the road), but she concludes that another driver's mistakes reflect a lack of skill or intelligence. As she rushes late to class, Zoey reflects on how she was delayed by a talkative teaching assistant; her professor, on the other hand, thinks she wasn't motivated to get to class on time. Likewise, Zoey attributes her low marks on an exam to the vague questions; unfortunately, admission officers at that law school she is applying to are more likely to think her grades reflect qualities like ability or intelligence. Throughout all facets of our interactions with other people, we consistently overestimate the degree to which others are personally responsible for their actions, while we simultaneously downplay our responsibility for our own behaviors.

The fundamental attribution error can also be explained by our need to feel in control of our circumstances. We can generate strategies for dealing with people in the future if we attribute their actions to internal qualities. In contrast, an external attribution leaves us feeling vulnerable to the randomness of life's situations. In other words, we make the fundamental attribution error because we'd rather be wrong and feel in control, than be right and feel helpless.

Why do we make biased attributions? Some of the examples in the previous paragraph might suggest that people are just unfair in their explanations for events. A closer look, however, suggests that these biases are related to characteristics of perception itself. One explanation for both the fundamental attribution error and the actor-observer effect is that we attribute cause to whatever stands out in the situation. When you observe another person's actions, that person is likely to be the most visually intense aspect of the situation. When you are doing something, however, your focus is on the environment rather than yourself. Because actors and observers select different information in the first place, they reach different conclusions about the causes of behaviors.

In contrast, the actor-observer effect can be explained by our desire to maintain impressions of ourselves that don't change too much over time. Imagine if you had to update your self-concept each time you performed an action: Monday you considered yourself a competent driver, but Tuesday you concluded that you should have your license

TABLE 4.2 Attribution biases

The fundamental attribution error and the actor-observer effect describe two general biases in how we explain behavior. As you consider the attribution biases described below, notice how the positive or negative impact of behavior and our relationship with the actor can also influence whether we make internal versus external attributions.

Attribution biases	*Examples*
The Fundamental Attribution Error The tendency to make internal attributions for other people's behavior	Chris didn't pay attention during our conversation because she isn't interested in me
The Actor-Observer Effect The tendency to make external attributions for our own behavior	I didn't pay attention during my conversation with Chris because I was pressed for time
The Self-Serving Bias The tendency to make internal attributions for our successes and external attributions for our failures	I did well in the class debate because I'm a hard-working and intelligent person; I did poorly on the exam because it was tricky
The Defensive Attribution Bias The tendency to make internal attributions for someone's successes and external attributions for that person's failures, if the person is similar to us	Mark is a lot like me – he did well in the debate because he is smart, and he did poorly on the exam because it was tricky
The Hedonic Relevance Effect The tendency to draw inferences about people's personality when their behaviors have negative consequences	Alex was hurt by the feedback he got on his paper; his instructor must be a mean and insensitive person
The Self-Centered Bias The tendency to conclude that we contribute more to a group task than other group members	When it comes to keeping things running smoothly, I do more than any of my co-workers

revoked; an uneventful drive to campus on Wednesday raised your self-esteem again, only to have it plummet after a harrowing lane change late Thursday afternoon. Fortunately, your self-concept provides you with a stable source of information about your internal qualities. Moreover, you maintain your sense of self by attributing daily variations in your behavior to external forces.

The attribution biases reviewed in this section of the chapter once again demonstrate the subjective nature of perception. In our efforts to explain the behaviors of others, we are inevitably influenced by our point of view and our own needs. Not surprisingly, then, different people can reach very different conclusions about why something occurred. When

FIGURE 4.5 Kabukicho Red Light District in Tokyo. What is your attention drawn to on this busy street? Do you think it is the same as what people on the street are noticing?

Source: Photo by Mary Knox Merrill/The Christian Science Monitor/Getty Images.

these divergent attributions are followed by communication – watch out! As we act upon our own understanding of a situation, we may very well be contradicting the other person's reality.

Attribution Biases in Close Relationships

Much of what we have learned about perception and attribution so far has focused on interactions with strangers. Perception and attribution are also the tools by which we observe and attach meaning to the actions of the people closest to us. And even in relationships where we know people better, it turns out that biased attributions are the rule rather than the exception. In particular, our attributions for a partner's actions are influenced by how satisfied or dissatisfied we are with the relationship, especially if other parts of our life are stressful (Nguyen, Karney, Kennedy, & Bradbury, 2020).

As summarized in Table 4.3, people who are satisfied with their close relationships tend to attribute a partner's positive behaviors to internal and stable causes, but explain negative events in terms of external and unstable causes. Why did Denise's spouse remember her birthday and surprise her with concert tickets? He did it because he is thoughtful and loving – both qualities that she sees as part of her spouse and unlikely to change. What if Denise's spouse were to forget her birthday? Because Denise is generally satisfied in her relationship, she would assume that her spouse must be really busy at work these days – a circumstance that doesn't reflect on him personally and (hopefully) is temporary. As you can see, partners in happy relationships are credited for the good things that they do and excused for their bad behaviors. Attributions that reflect and contribute to a positive view of a relationship are called **adaptive attributions.**

Adaptive Attributions
Explanations that link positive behaviors to internal and stable causes and negative behaviors to external and unstable causes.

People who are satisfied or dissatisfied with their relationships reach very different conclusions when their partners behave positively or negatively. Consider the example of Maria and Alexa, who are struggling with the demands of two jobs and young children. Table 4.3 shows the different kinds of attributions Alexa might make when Maria either creates problems at home by staying late at work or helps Alexa meet a deadline by leaving work early.

TABLE 4.3 Attributions in satisfying and dissatisfying relationships

The behavior	*Adaptive attributions*	*Maladaptive attributions*
Maria stayed late at work and created problems at home	Maria must have had a crisis at work	Maria is self-centered and uncaring
Maria left work early so that Alexa could meet a deadline	Maria is a wonderful and loving person	Maria's boss must have cancelled her last meeting

Maladaptive Attributions
Linking negative behaviors to internal and stable causes and positive behaviors to external and unstable causes.

The third column in Table 4.3 reveals the pattern of attributions that dominates when people are dissatisfied with a relationship. In this case, a partner's positive behaviors are attributed to external and unstable causes, while negative behaviors are seen as a reflection of internal and stable qualities. When Jen's parents were facing the dissolution of their marriage, her dad actually did forget her mom's birthday. Her mother attributed his forgetfulness to the fact that he is a thoughtless and insensitive person and she gave up hope of ever getting a birthday present from him again. When he came home one night with a gift certificate for them to have dinner at a nice restaurant, she assumed that he must have gotten it from one of his clients at work and it was about to expire. People who are unhappy with a relationship make **maladaptive attributions** that blame the partner for negative behavior and fail to credit the partner for positive actions.

How we perceive our partner's behavior has enormous consequences for the relationship. On the upside, adaptive attributions can protect happy couples from the occasional problem. Unfortunately, maladaptive attributions seem to lock unhappy couples into a cycle of negativity (Figure 4.6). In fact, studies that have tracked newly-weds over time showed that partners who made maladaptive attributions early in their marriage were less satisfied one to four years later (Fincham & Bradbury, 2004). In contrast, making adaptive attributions for a partner's actions can keep

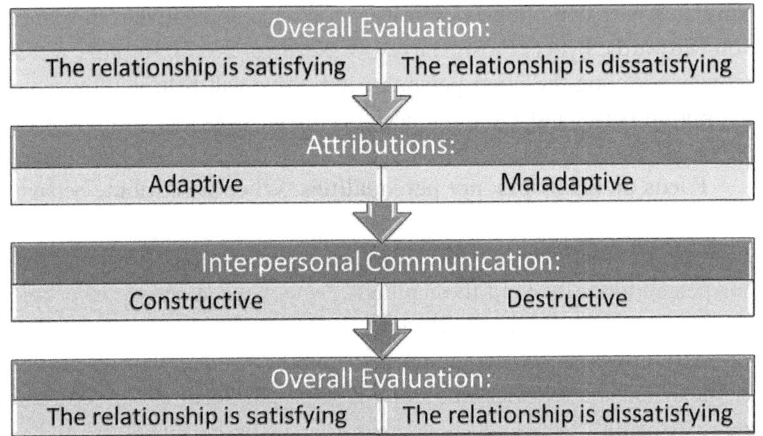

FIGURE 4.6 Cycles of satisfaction and attributions in close relationships

healthy relationships strong over time (NcNulty, O'Mara, & Karney, 2008). The attributions we make for other people's behaviors are inevitably subjective and biased – and yet, these explanations have the power to preserve or destroy our relationships.

PAUSE & REFLECT

Think of one couple that you consider happy and one couple you think is unhappy. How can you tell which relationship is happy or unhappy? How would you describe the communication that goes on within each relationship?

HOW DO YOU RATE? 4.1

Perspective-Taking in Interpersonal Communication

Perspective-taking refers to efforts to see things from another person's point of view. You can go to the companion website to complete a self-report measure of perspective-taking that was drawn from a larger measure of empathy (Davis, 1980). As you reflect on your score, think about how you could improve your perspective-taking.

Putting Theory into Practice: Combating Attribution Biases

In this section of the chapter, we have examined how people perceive, and often misperceive, the causes of other people's behavior. Our efforts to explain the world around us will never yield flawless results; however, the following strategies can help us limit the impact of attribution biases on our interpersonal communication experiences.

Avoid forming an explanation based only on your point of view. As you seek to understand someone else's actions, think for a moment of how the situation looks to the other person. What must she be focused on? What could be on his mind? How are they likely to be feeling? One way to do this is to imagine yourself as the other person, and consider what would you see, think about, and feel. Another strategy is to ask the other person to share their perspective *before* you draw your conclusions. Research suggests that engaging in perspective-taking is negatively associated with the frequency of misunderstanding and positively correlated with communication satisfaction and cooperative communication (Edwards, Bybee, Frost, Harvey, & Navarro, 2017). In other words, actively adopting the other person's perspective will help you overcome attribution biases and avoid the negative interactions that biases contribute to.

Focus on behaviors, not personalities. When we attribute behavior to someone's traits, we see that person in less flexible terms. The labels we apply to other people create expectations that further direct and limit our perceptions. To avoid these pitfalls, focus your attention on people's behaviors, and don't draw conclusions about what kind of trait that behavior might imply. As you communicate with others, tailor your reactions to the behavior you experienced, and not some judgment about your partner's personality. When you remember to focus on behaviors themselves, you can begin to perceive others without the blinders that labels create.

COMMUNICATION IN ACTION 4.2

Focusing on Behaviors Rather than Traits

This exercise helps you to focus on the specific behaviors that individuals perform rather than relying on broad labels and characterizations that may or may not be accurate. Because labeling individuals constrains our expectations for their behavior, it is important to look for more open-minded and positive ways to characterize another person's behavior. Complete the form on the companion website to see how you can change your perceptions to focus more on specific behaviors rather than broad personality traits.

Protect relationships you value by making adaptive attributions. Recall that happy couples tend to make attributions that contribute to their future happiness, and unhappy couples tend to reach conclusions that increase their dissatisfaction. Armed with this knowledge, might you be able to protect relationships you value by actively making adaptive attributions? Research on couples in marital counseling suggests that the answer is yes (Epstein, Baucom, Kirby, & LaTaillade, 2019), and that a common ingredient in effective couples therapy is a focus on changing the maladaptive attributions made by partners in distressed relationships (Epstein, 2016). Because making more adaptive attributions can help keep your close relationships on the right track, these suggestions might protect relationships that you value:

- *Look for external causes for behavior.* When your partner has done something that makes you unhappy, consider all of the potential situational explanations for that behavior before jumping to conclusions.
- *Assume that the negative behavior is temporary.* If we believe that our partner's negative behavior is stable and will always occur, it becomes

difficult for our partner to overcome that negative attribution. Give your partner the benefit of the doubt and assume that they will behave better in the future.

- *Consider aspects of the situation that were out of the partner's control.* Even when our partner has behaved badly, there might be aspects of the situation that weren't entirely under his or her control. If your partner is late for dinner, she could have controlled when she decided to leave work and the fact that she decided not to call you, but the traffic jam on the way home was really out of her hands. Thus, you might temper your frustration with the knowledge that it wasn't entirely her fault.

FACTORS THAT AFFECT PERCEPTION

Previously in this chapter, you learned that perception and attributions are subject to a variety of biases. One reason that biases can emerge is because our perceptions are shaped by our cultural background, social group characteristics, and individual traits. In addition, we can create situations that impair our perception through alcohol consumption or relying on stereotypes to make inferences. In this section, we consider how these factors affect our view of interpersonal communication experiences.

Individual Differences

Various differences between people, such as culture, ethnicity, gender, and personal traits, influence the way we perceive the world around us. As a starting point, consider the impact of culture on your perceptions and attributions. Because our culture provides a window through which we make sense of the world around us, cultural differences take root from the very first stage of perception. For example, research has shown that North American children are encouraged by their parents to focus their attention on the main object in a scene, whereas East Asian children are taught to attend to background information to a greater degree (Senzaki, Masuda, Takada, Okada, 2016). As adults, these cultural differences are reflected in a tendency for East Asians to pay attention to the emotions expressed by faces surrounding a focal person, while European Canadians downplay the background faces in their evaluation of the emotions experienced by a particular person (Ito, Masuda, & Man Wai Li, 2013). Similarly, Americans pay more attention to *what* is said when they are being evaluated, but Japanese are more attuned to emotional tone or *how* an evaluation is communicated (Ishii, Reyes, & Kitayama, 2003). Not surprisingly, these differences in perception are reflected in attributions. In particular, people from cultures that focus on the accomplishments of individuals are more likely to attribute a person's behavior to internal causes, whereas people from cultures that emphasize the community more than the individual often prefer external attributions (e.g., Hong, Benet-Martinez, Chiu, & Morris, 2003; Peng & Knowles, 2003).

Our membership in different social groups also affects our perception. Consider how people of different genders differ in their selection, organization, and interpretation of information. In one experiment conducted in Israel, research participants studied a list of objects that were either stereotypically female-oriented (e.g., make-up products), stereotypically male-oriented (e.g., professional sports), or gender neutral (e.g., household appliances), and they were later tested for their memory for objects on the list. The results showed that males and females had better memory for the objects that matched their gender orientation (Pansky, Oren, Yaniv, Landy, Gotlieb, & Hemed, 2019). Another study showed that men and women pay attention to the same features in a map, but then organize that information differently when giving directions (MacFadden, Elias, & Saucier, 2003). In particular, men tend to emphasize distances and direction (i.e., north, south, east, or west), and women more typically mention left/right turns and landmarks. Gender differences are also evident in the attributions people make. For example, a study of African American students in 8th and 11th grade found that boys tend to attribute their academic success or failure to ability, whereas girls tend to attribute their outcomes to effort (Swinton, Kurtz-Costes, Rowley, & Okeke-Adeyanju, 2011). Another research study, which focused on men and women experiencing depression, reported that women were more likely to see other people's criticisms and insults as their own fault (Gilbert, Irons, Olsen, Gilbert, & McEwan, 2006). Although we should be careful not to exaggerate differences between men and women (Canary & Hause, 1993), these examples illustrate the variety of ways in which gender can shape perception.

IDEA: PRACTICING INCLUSION, DIVERSITY, EQUITY, AND ACCESS

The large body of research on gender differences in perception and attribution has focused predominantly on biological sex differences, rather than the broader spectrum of genders. What kinds of questions might we explore to better understand how people of different genders select, organize, and interpret information as they engage in interpersonal communication?

Age is another social category that affects perception. In young children, developing an understanding of people as individuals corresponds with more internal, person-specific attributions for other people's behavior (Chalik, Rivera, & Rhodes, 2014). The tendency to attribute another person's behavior to internal and consistent causes continues to increase through middle childhood and young adulthood (e.g., Brandone & Klimek, 2018). Continuing across the lifespan, we find that middle-aged adults are less likely than young adults to hold people personally responsible for their actions (Follett & Hess, 2002). Among older adults, however, there is a tendency to see behavior as a reflection of personal traits, even when a person's actions were constrained by the situation (Blanchard-Fields & Horhota, 2005). Over the lifespan, then, internal attributions increase when children begin to understand how traits can motivate behavior, they decrease as people's lived experiences teach them that actions are often driven by circumstances, and they increase again among the elderly.

Our individual traits can also influence perception and attribution. One quality on which people differ is **cognitive complexity** – the degree to which they differentiate details within a situation. People who are high in cognitive complexity tend to notice more specific features in their environment. In contrast, a person low in cognitive complexity focuses on the more general picture, rather than the details. In the context of interpersonal interactions, cognitive complexity has been linked to a person's ability to decode nonverbal behavior (Woods, 1996). Perhaps because people high in cognitive complexity notice a greater variety of details, they are less likely to make the fundamental attribution error when explaining other people's actions (Follett & Hess, 2002). A trait that is closely related to cognitive complexity is attributional complexity. **Attributional complexity** refers to people's tendency to explain events in terms of intricate rather than simple causes (Fletcher, Danilovics, Fernandez, Peterson, & Reeder, 1986). In addition, people high in attributional complexity tend to do more perspective-taking and feel more empathy for others (Joireman, 2004). This extra effort seems to be appreciated, because people high in attributional complexity are considered by others to be more open, socially skilled, wise, thoughtful, and empathic (Fast, Reimer, & Funder, 2008).

Cognitive Complexity
The extent to which a person tends to notice details and distinctions among features within a situation.

Attributional Complexity
The extent to which a person tends to explain events in terms of intricate, rather than simple, causes.

Alcohol and Interpersonal Encounters

It is widely known that drinking alcohol can lead to more extreme interpersonal behavior – being more aggressive, taking more risks, flirting more vivaciously, or feeling more forlorn. Although these consequences are generally associated with the chemical effects of alcohol, communication scholars have explored how drunken behavior in interpersonal situations might stem from the effects of alcohol on perception. Myopia, also known as being nearsighted, is a vision problem in which objects near at hand are in focus, but those further away appear blurry. Alcohol myopia theory proposes that some of the effects of alcohol occur because drinking makes some aspects of a situation more difficult to see (Steele & Josephs,

1990; see also Lac & Berger, 2013). In other words, intoxication strikes at the very foundation of interpersonal communication behavior by distorting perceptions of the world around us.

A central assumption of the theory is that alcohol disrupts the normal process by which people balance competing interests. In many situations, people experience some degree of **inhibition conflict**, a condition defined by the presence of both vivid cues that promote a certain response and less vivid cues that inhibit that response. Consider the case of Brian: A friend who wants to gossip about one of Brian's confidential legal cases is a vivid cue encouraging disclosure, but Brian knows the rules against talking about clients in his profession. Normally, people are skilled at balancing vivid cues with less vivid cues and acting appropriately, but alcohol myopia theory suggests that drinking alcohol limits perception to those cues that are most vivid or striking. If Brian is chatting with his friend over happy hour and has already had a few drinks, he is more likely to pay attention to the vivid cues he receives from his talkative friend who wants to gossip and less likely to recall the less vivid cues in that situation that would advise him against disclosing private information about his clients. Blind to more subtle cues within a situation and acting upon only a subset of the relevant information, intoxicated people respond in ways that are often inappropriate and excessive.

CONNECT WITH THEORY

Visit the companion website to learn about alcohol myopia theory, which offers an explanation for drunken behavior that focuses on the effects of alcohol on perception

Inhibition Conflict
The simultaneous presence of vivid cues that provoke a response and subtle cues that inhibit that response.

PAUSE & REFLECT

Can you think of a time when you, or someone you know, did something foolish after drinking alcohol? Are there reasons that you or this person don't typically behave that way? Why didn't those reasons matter after consuming alcohol?

HOW DO YOU RATE? 4.2

Attributional Complexity

You can go to the companion website to complete the Attributional Complexity Scale, which was developed by Fletcher et al. (1986) to measure the complexity of a person's attribution patterns. Based on your score on this scale, do you think that you have more or less attributional complexity than your peers?

Among other things, alcohol's effect on perception can lead to risky sexual behavior. Alcohol consumption has been linked to incidences of regretted sexual experiences among college students (Peterson, Dvorak, Stevenson, Kramer, Pinto, Mora, & Leary, 2020), as well as the tendency to engage in unprotected casual sex (Scott-Sheldon, Carey, Cunningham, Johnson, & Carey, 2016). In addition, intoxicated women are more likely than sober women to consider a sexual relationship with a risky partner (Purdie, Norris, Davis, Zawacki, Morrison, George, & Keikel, 2011). In fact, women who have consumed alcohol have greater faith in their ability to detect a partner's HIV status through casual conversation (Monahan, Murphy, & Miller, 1999). And relative to sober persons, intoxicated males and females rate hypothetical episodes involving sexual coercion as more enjoyable and acceptable (Lannutti & Monahan, 2002).

Stereotyping

Stereotypes refer to over-simplified beliefs about people who fall into particular social categories. **Stereotyping** occurs when people's stereotypes control their perceptions during an encounter with another person. In other words, stereotyping is automatically assuming that individuals have certain qualities based on their membership in a social group. In turn, stereotyping leads to judgments, behaviors, and interpersonal communication patterns that often perpetuate stereotypes.

Racial and ethnic stereotypes are among the most pervasive sources of distorted perception in our society. Research has shown that pictures of people with physical cues characteristic of an African American heritage are more likely to be judged as showing someone who will be aggressive (Blair, Chapleau, & Judd, 2005). Another study showed that people are more likely to mention stereotypical physical features when they describe a photo of an African American who is implicated in a violent crime (Oliver, Jackson, Moses, & Dangerfield, 2004). The real-world consequences of these biases were brought to light by a study on criminal sentencing decisions, where analysis of prison inmates showed that, controlling for criminal histories, those with more Afrocentric features received harsher sentences (Blair, Judd, & Chapleau, 2004). Indeed, the consequences of stereotyping and racism, particularly for young Black men, has been characterized as a public health crisis (Jones-Eversley, Rice, Adedoyin, & James-Townes, 2020).

Stereotypes
Over-simplified beliefs about members of a social group.

Stereotyping
Assuming that individuals have certain qualities based on their membership in a social group.

SCHOLAR SPOTLIGHT

Visit the Communication Café on the companion website to hear Jennifer Monahan talk about her research on alcohol myopia theory, and on perception and communication more generally.

IDEA: PRACTICING INCLUSION, DIVERSITY, EQUITY, AND ACCESS

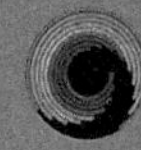

Consider all the ways in which racial and ethnic stereotypes contribute to systemic prejudice and discrimination against certain minorities. How do the systems within society both reflect and reinforce racial and ethnic stereotypes? What can be done to alter social systems and structures in order to promote greater equity and decentralize racial stereotypes?

Not surprisingly, stereotypes surface in interpersonal communication. For example, people are more likely to include information that is consistent with stereotypes when they share information with others about someone from another culture (Kashima, Lyons, & Clark, 2013). In fact, stereotypes have been linked to the very language we choose to convey information about others (e.g., Burgers & Beukeboom, 2016). In general, people prefer generalizations over specific details when describing behavior that is consistent with stereotypes, but they use specific language when discussing behavior that is inconsistent with a stereotype (see Maass, Arcuri, & Suitner, 2014). For people on the receiving end of these descriptions, the general – and stereotype-consistent – descriptions are more likely than specific details to promote inferences about the person's personality or traits (Wigboldus, Semin, & Spears, 2006). In other words, the language used to describe others cements stereotypical judgments and dilutes details that are inconsistent with stereotypes.

Of course, stereotyping also affects how people communicate with a person they have stereotyped. As one example, researchers have shown how stereotypical judgments of the elderly make intergenerational communication difficult (Atkinson & Sloan, 2017; Barker, Giles, & Harwood, 2004). The impact of stereotypes on perception and intergenerational communication is summarized in Figure 4.7. When people have negative stereotypes about the elderly, they will limit communication with an older person, and they will use more patronizing and stylized speech if an interaction can't be avoided. This rather lifeless conversation doesn't offer much for the elderly participant to work with, and he or she ends up making limited and often stereotypical responses. Similarly, people may avoid topics that are complicated or contemporary, based on the stereotypical belief that the elderly lack mental agility. Consequently, their conversations would be fairly simple, mundane, and boring for both. The result is an interaction that both confirms the stereotype and undermines the older person's sense of self. Left unchecked, the cycle of stereotyping and communication contributes to experiences of prejudice and discrimination that divide people in our society.

INSIDE COMMUNICATION RESEARCH

Stereotypes in Imagined Interactions with Older Adults

Ageism is responsible for a number of stereotypes that characterize older adults. The aging stereotype reinforcement model suggests that the expectations people have during intergenerational interactions give rise to communication behaviors that further reinforce existing stereotypes. Notably, this is true of both negative stereotypes (e.g., older adults are slow) and positive stereotypes (e.g., older adults are nurturing) about older adults. Increased intergenerational contact can have positive outcomes for both younger and older people and be beneficial for combating ageist stereotypes. Communication scholars Chien-Yu Chen, Nick Joyce, Jake Harwood, and Jun Xiang (2017) sought to examine whether imagined interaction with older adults would similarly reinforce stereotypes about older adults. They identified three main characteristics about which older adults are often stereotyped, including their competence and mental acuity, their warmth and sociability, and their trustworthiness or sincerity. The researchers also considered three communication behaviors that individuals might adapt or alter in response to each stereotype, including overaccommodation, humor, and self-disclosure. They expected that individuals would imagine adapting their communication behavior with older adults in ways that reinforced either positive or negative stereotypes along these dimensions.

The researchers conducted a study in which they asked a sample of college undergraduates to imagine that they were traveling on a plane and upon boarding found that they were seated next to an elderly woman between 70 and 75 years of age. They went on to describe the elderly woman in one of six different ways, as: (a) sociable and friendly, (b) unsociable and unfriendly, (c) competent and intelligent, (d) incompetent and unintelligent, (e) trustworthy and sincere, or (f) untrustworthy and insincere. Participants were asked to imagine what this woman would be like, from her appearance to her demeanor, and to write a description of her. Then, they were told to imagine that they start a conversation with the woman and to describe what they imagined the conversation to be like. Finally, the participants completed survey items to rate their imagined behaviors during the interaction and their attitudes toward older adults.

To analyze the data, the researchers examined how their manipulation of the woman as (in)competent, (un)sociable, or (un)trustworthy was associated with the imagined communication behaviors and resulting stereotypes about older adults. First, they found that when the woman was described as incompetent and unintelligent, people imagined more overaccommodation in their communication, which in turn was associated with more negative stereotypes about the competence of older adults. In contrast, when individuals imagined a competent and intelligent older woman, they tended to overaccommodate less, which also corresponded with fewer stereotypes about older adults being incompetent. Second, they found that when the older woman was sociable and friendly, participants imagined enacting more humor in their conversation, which further reinforced stereotypes about the sociability of older adults. Conversely, when they imagined an unsociable and unfriendly older woman, participants enacted less humor, which contributed to more negative stereotypes about the sociability of older adults. Finally, contrary to expectations, the researchers did not find any associations between the imagined trustworthiness of the woman and participants' imagined self-disclosure or stereotypes about older adults.

THINK ABOUT IT

1. The participants were asked to imagine having an interaction with the older woman on the plane. Do you believe that people's imagined interactions would closely resemble their likely behavior if the interaction were real? How might the imagined interaction be accurate or inaccurate? How might the results differ if this study was carried out in real interactions?
2. The researchers didn't find any associations between the trustworthiness of the older woman and people's self-disclosure in the imagined interaction or their stereotypes about older adults. Why do you think the other stereotypes and communication behaviors were associated as expected, but not trustworthiness and self-disclosure?

PAUSE & REFLECT

Consider a positive stereotype you might hold, for example, that Asian Americans are intelligent or that first-born children are ambitious. Can you think of any downsides of being the target of such "positive" stereotypes?

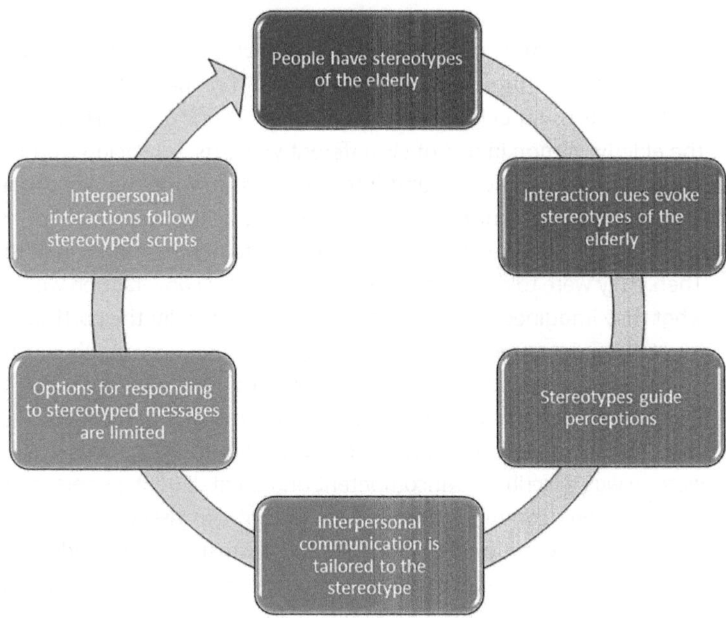

FIGURE 4.7 A general model of stereotypes and intergenerational communication

Putting Theory into Practice: Confronting Barriers to Perception

Cultural backgrounds, personality traits, and features of the environment or situation create a constellation of characteristics that come together to shape how we see and explain the world around us. These effects take root during the very first stage of perception and, in turn, contribute to every aspect of our thinking about our experiences. Not surprisingly, all of these features make the perception process vulnerable to errors. Fortunately, you can take steps to confront barriers to perception.

Recognize individual differences in perception and attribution. How often have you found yourself in a conflict with another person because you disagreed about what happened or why? Or you found yourself defending your actions by explaining your point of view? The fact of the matter is that people see and explain events in different ways, so our differences in perceptions and attributions often lead to disagreements with others. When you find yourself arguing with somebody, consider how individual differences in perception might be the reason for your disagreement. By questioning how culture, social group, and personality shape perceptions, you might be able to set aside a conflict to learn about a different point of view. To minimize conflicts stemming from individual differences, ask yourself the following questions:

- How am I different from my partner in ways that might cause me to see this situation differently than he or she does?

- How does my partner's membership in a particular social group shape his or her perceptions of this situation?
- What do we have in common that might allow us to share the same perception of this situation?

Recognize when your perception is impaired. Our ability to perceive the world around us can vary depending on our circumstances. Recognize the conditions that limit your appreciation for nuances, for example, being tired, emotional, or under pressure. Likewise, take stock of how characteristics of the setting, such as a crowded or noisy room, might undermine perception during your interpersonal interactions. In those circumstances, you should be particularly careful about letting your perceptions lead you to easy but flawed conclusions.

Combat the formation of stereotypes. Television is a prolific and widely available source of information about other social groups. And unfortunately, the medium frequently draws stylized, extreme, and hyper-stereotyped portraits of social groups, particularly those constituting minorities in the United States. For example, the Canadian television sitcom *Schitt's Creek* portrayed a pansexual character who loves fashion and has a flamboyant manner. Even while *Schitt's Creek* intentionally rejected the gender binary and modeled acceptance for the character's sexuality, stereotypes are common fare on television. Fortunately, research has shown that young children are more likely to reject gender stereotypes if they watch television with an adult who refutes stereotyped scenes, e.g., "The show is wrong. Lots of girls do things besides paint their nails and put on make-up" (Nathanson, Wilson, McGee, & Sebastian, 2002). Thus, interpersonal communication is a tool we can use to undermine the development of stereotypes from the start.

COMMUNICATION IN ACTION 4.3

Challenging Stereotypes in the Media

Select three television programs or movies that depict a particular social group in stereotyped ways. For example, you might choose *Ozark* for its depiction of the rural poor, *Schitt's Creek* for its portrayal of LGBTQ individuals, *Insecure* for its portrayal of Black women, or *Shrill* for its depiction of overweight people. For each program or movie you select, make a list of all the ways the portrayal of that social group is an accurate depiction of that group. Then, make a list of all the ways the portrayal of that social group is based on stereotypes for that group. Is there any overlap between the stereotypes we have about these groups and how they actually behave? What has been the impact of exposure to these stereotypes on your own thinking about those social groups?

SUMMARY

In this chapter, we have examined perception as part of the foundation for interpersonal communication. Perception is a three-stage process by which we select, organize, and interpret information to make sense of our environment. At each step, we impose our own point of view, needs and goals, and experiences to produce our own unique understanding of a situation. Although perception allows us to function in a world saturated with information, we have also seen how this process is inherently subjective.

The interpretation stage of perception sometimes includes our efforts to understand why something happened. The attributions we make for another person's behavior can focus on causes that are internal or external to that person, controllable or uncontrollable, and stable or unstable. Two common attribution biases include the tendencies to attribute other people's behavior to internal causes and our own behavior to external causes. Although the fundamental attribution error and actor-observer effect appear to arise rather innocently from perception processes, they represent a pervasive bias that permeates our interactions with other people. Patterns of attribution in close relationships also revealed that the conclusions we reach about the causes of a partner's behavior are often skewed by our satisfaction with that relationship.

Our perceptions are influenced by personal characteristics, as well as by features of the situation. Our cultural background shapes how we focus our attention, prioritize information, and draw inferences about what we perceive. Characteristics such as gender and age give us life experiences that further influence how we make sense of our environment. People also differ in their tendency to perceive information or causes of events in simple versus complex ways. Thus, the traits and qualities we carry with us into any situation are an inevitable part of our perceptions. Our perceptions are also impaired by alcohol intoxication and stereotyping. Alcohol myopia theory suggests that drunken behavior reflects a breakdown in perception, such that people attend only to the most vivid cues in a situation; importantly, intoxicated people miss the more subtle cues that might inhibit risky behavior. When stereotyping occurs, the source of distorted perceptions is quite different, but process is similar; in this case, pre-existing beliefs about social groups blind perceivers to the unique qualities individuals possess. As these examples demonstrate, impaired perception can have critical consequences.

Perception is the process by which we observe and make sense of other people, and it is at the heart of interpersonal communication experiences. In this chapter, we discovered that these processes are inherently subjective and vulnerable to a variety of biasing forces. At the same time, you do not need to be a victim of your perceptions. By paying attention to perception, combating attribution biases, recognizing individual differences in perception, and confronting barriers to perception, you can become more skillful at interpersonal communication. Now that you know more about perception and attribution, consider the implications of these processes in the following ethical exercises.

ACTIVITIES FOR EXPLORING COMMUNICATION ETHICS

What Would You/Should You Do?

Imagine that you are out for an evening with your friend, Amy, who is pretty shy and hasn't been involved in many romantic relationships. The two of you had a few beers before you went out, walked to a couple of bars, and have ended up at a party. Amy is pretty drunk now, and you notice that a man is hitting on her. She seems to be enjoying the attention, and she is talking a lot for a change. When Amy sees you watching her conversation, she rushes over to you. She is happier and more excited than you've ever seen her as she tells you that this guy is "so great" and "really likes her." Then, she asks if you would mind if you had to go home alone. As a good friend, do you celebrate Amy's joy and hope for the best in this relationship? Or do you protect Amy from the dangers of alcohol myopia?

Something to Think About

Now that you know about perception and interpersonal communication, you should appreciate that the way we understand the world around us is inherently subjective. Other people have different perceptions, draw different conclusions, and communicate differently than you do. What you've learned implies that you should avoid imposing your interpretations on others. But is that always the case? When (if ever) is it right to stick to your own perspective and reject another person's point of view? Where is the line between conviction to your values and a lack of perspective-taking?

Analyze Communication Ethics Yourself

Ethical communicators make their values and assumptions clear when they argue for a course of action. To investigate communication ethics in the world around you, examine letters to the editor in the *New York Times* or the "Point/Counterpoint" feature in *USA Today*. What perceptions do the writers use to justify their position? In particular, evaluate the extent to which the writers make clear when their positions are based on fact, inferences, or assumptions. As you do this analysis, think about how these letters might be rewritten to achieve a higher ethical standard.

KEY WORDS

actor-observer effect
adaptive attributions
attribution biases
attributional complexity
attributions
cognition
cognitive complexity
external attribution
fundamental attribution error
inhibition conflict
internal attribution
interpretation
maladaptive attributions
organization
perception
selection
stereotypes
stereotyping

PART 2 INTERPERSONAL INTERACTION

Visit the Communication Café on the companion website to hear Denise and Jen talk about the topics addressed in Part 2 of this book.

When people interact with each other, they do so by creating and responding to messages. In this part of this book, we look at the interactive components of interpersonal communication: language, nonverbal messages, emotions, and listening.

Language is perhaps the most obvious symbol system people use to communicate. Whether we are interacting in person or using some communication technology, our words are a big part of how we create meanings with other people. Although you have spoken at least one language since early in your life, have you thought about how language works? How is it that two (or more) people can use sequences of sounds and silence to accomplish such a powerful thing as communication? In Chapter 5, we examine the nature of language, the ways people use language to communicate, some factors that affect how people use language, and also some problematic uses of language.

Although sometimes less obvious than language, nonverbal behaviors have a major impact on interpersonal communication experiences. As you will discover in Chapter 6, we communicate information to others through a variety of nonverbal cues. Culture and individual characteristics influence nonverbal communication, just as much as they influence the languages that a person speaks. In this chapter, you will also learn about the complexities that can emerge when people weave together verbal and nonverbal messages.

The emotions you experience are also central to the interpersonal communication process. Our emotions can motivate us to communicate with others, we use communication to express emotions, our communication experiences influence how we feel, and how we feel influences how we interpret messages. In Chapter 7, we clarify the nature of emotions, how emotions relate to interpersonal interactions, and some of the ways people differ in their experience of emotions. We also delve into some of the more extreme emotions – hurt, jealousy, and grief – that can be part of our interpersonal communication experiences.

The words, behaviors, and emotions that we use to communicate with others would be meaningless if listening did not occur. Because hearing is one of the five basic human senses, people don't always think about listening as an action that can be performed more or less effectively. In fact, people listen in different ways, encounter several forces that can interfere with listening, and can take active steps to be more engaged listeners. Because interpersonal communication occurs with other people, listening involves making sense of what the interaction means for the relationship between the people involved. These important topics are the focus of Chapter 8.

DOI: 10.4324/9781351174381-6

LEARNING OBJECTIVES

After reading this chapter, you should be able to:

1. Identify the essential characteristics of language.
2. Describe how language rules operate in conversations.
3. Describe differences in how men and women use language.
4. Explain how language changes with power or intimacy in a relationship.
5. Understand how racist, sexist, and heterosexist language marginalizes people in a society.
6. Improve your use of language in interpersonal interactions.

PUTTING THEORY INTO PRACTICE

In this chapter, you will learn how to:

1. Use concrete language.
2. Ask for clarification if a word is ambiguous.
3. Look beyond labels.
4. Attend to connotative meanings.
5. Diagnose topic shifts.
6. Set the stage for conversation.
7. Avoid gender traps.
8. Tailor your language to social contexts.
9. Confront racist language.
10. Develop your gender- and sexuality-neutral repertoire.

LANGUAGE AND INTERPERSONAL COMMUNICATION

5

Source: Photo by Ben Hider/Getty Images.

DOI: 10.4324/9781351174381-7

As technology continues to evolve and people come to rely more heavily on their computers, phones, and other electronic devices, researchers focused on artificial intelligence are hard at work trying to perfect the verbal communication skills of interactive bots like Apple's Siri and Amazon's Alexa. Bots are software that can communicate with humans and other computers to perform tasks, like giving directions or booking an appointment. Researchers at Facebook developed a project designed to teach two bots how to conduct an effective negotiation. The two bots, Bob and Alice, were programed with a training data set consisting of hundreds of examples of negotiation dialog and rules for evaluating success and failure, which the bots then analyzed to extract the features of dialog that lead to the most positive results. Using these data, the bots can then select words and phrases to use in their negotiation that are shown to have the highest probability of success. As Bob and Alice started their negotiations over books, balls, and hats, something interesting started to happen. They started out talking more or less in English, but as they learned from their own mistakes and failures in the negotiation, they started to develop their own language for negotiating. Some words that were not contributing to success were lost, while those that were leading to a positive outcome were amplified. For example, if saying the words "I want" in a negotiation increased the odds of a positive outcome, then the bots reasoned that saying those words multiple times would improve outcomes even more. Over time, the bots developed their own shorthand to become more effective at making a deal. Ultimately, Facebook shut down the study because the language developed by the bots was not actually useful for programming bots to communicate more effectively with humans. Scientists still have a lot of work to do to develop artificial intelligence that can replicate the complexity, flexibility, and nuance of verbal communication in interpersonal interactions.

Today's technological world involves a lot of communication between humans and computers. When you call your bank, your insurance company, or even your university, you might be greeted by a computerized voice that is supposed to help you find information or guide you to the person you need to talk to. It usually becomes obvious very early in the conversation that you are communicating with a non-human interaction partner. These computerized interactions can be frustrating because computers aren't as skilled as humans in their use of language. Our ability to use verbal communication to make a connection with another person – to comfort, amuse, inform, and so on – is what separates us from other animals and, for the moment, from computers.

When our ancestors developed verbal skills, they gained the ability to share ideas, make plans, and reflect upon their relationships. The result was more effective hunting and gathering, improved strategies for protecting the social group, and deeper bonds with others. Of course, verbal messages have also been used to divide and oppress people. Because verbal cues are so central to interpersonal communication, we will examine how they work in some detail. While you may already be a sophisticated speaker of English and perhaps even a second or third language, this chapter can help you become more aware of the effects of your words on others.

THE NATURE OF VERBAL COMMUNICATION

Language encompasses both our vocabulary and our knowledge about when to use particular words, what those words mean, and how we can put words together to create a meaningful message. Some languages, such as American Sign Language, don't rely on verbal messages, but verbal communication and language share a number of qualities. In particular, verbal communication and language are abstract, arbitrary, culturally determined, and consequential. As we consider each of these qualities, we examine how they make language a powerful but imperfect tool for interpersonal communication.

Language
The words people use to communicate and knowledge about how to use those words to create a meaningful message.

Language is Abstract

One basic but important feature of language is that it is abstract; this means that words stand for objects, people, ideas, etc., but words are not themselves the things that they represent. This is a simple but powerful point. When you use the word "apple," you do not need to hold a real apple to put an image of one in the mind of your communication partner (see Figure 5.1). In the same way, you can use words to refer to a wide range of objects and concepts which are not physically present, and – as in the case of a concept like "justice" – might not even physically exist. By using language, we create images and ideas in each other's mind.

Although all verbal cues are abstract to some degree, words can be more or less precise. For example, you could send someone to the store to buy some apples, some red apples, or some Macintosh apples. As your language choice becomes more specific, you are more likely to get exactly the kind of apples you want. **Abstract language** refers to words that have very general meanings because they cover a variety of events, objects, or actions. In contrast, **concrete language** includes references to specific events, objects, or actions.

Abstract Language
Words with general meanings that refer to broad categories of object events, or behavior.

Concrete Language
Words that refer to specific events and behaviors or tangible objects that are available to the senses.

Using concrete language may be especially helpful when you want to avoid miscommunication about sensitive issues. Consider the example of

FIGURE 5.1 The relationship between words and ideas. Language allows us to create an image in another person's mind. That image is unlikely to be a perfect match to our own image – how close a match it is will depend on whether communication partners attach the same meaning to verbal cues.

Markesha, who is annoyed with her sister Deirdre for leaving the bathroom a mess. In the transcript presented in Table 5.1, Markesha begins the conversation using abstract language that generally describes her views and doesn't even mention the bathroom specifically. As the conversation continues, Markesha begins to refer to particular events or tangible objects. By the end of the dialog, Markesha is very specific about the circumstances that bother her. Notice how the concrete language Markesha uses at the end of the dialog gives Deirdre a much better idea of what's bothering her sister.

Concrete language helps a communication partner to better understand what the other person is thinking or feeling and to form an appropriate response. In fact, communication scholar Claude Miller and his colleagues (Miller, Lane, Deatrick, Young, & Potts, 2007) found that people pay more attention to persuasive messages that use concrete language (e.g. "sugar causes tooth decay and obesity"), rather than abstract or vague terms (e.g., "sugar is bad for you"). That study also showed that speakers are perceived as more expert and trustworthy when they create messages that are concrete, rather than very abstract. In another study (Douglas & Sutton, 2006), people evaluated speakers as less biased when they described another person using concrete terms (e.g., "Lisa slapped Ann") rather than abstract words (e.g., "Lisa is aggressive").

TABLE 5.1 Talking at high and low levels of abstraction

MARKESHA:	You are such a huge slob, Deirdre! I can't believe you would be so rude.
DEIRDRE:	What are you talking about?
MARKESHA:	It's just so inconsiderate to leave huge messes for me to clean up. I hate it when you do that!
DEIRDRE:	I don't think I left a mess anywhere, and even if I did, you didn't have to clean it up. I never asked you to do that.
MARKESHA:	This morning I went into the bathroom to get ready for work and you had left your dirty stuff on the floor.
DEIRDRE:	I'm sorry, I must have forgotten to pick it up because I was in a hurry. But what's the big deal? All you had to do was throw it in the laundry basket.
MARKESHA:	Well, I was in a hurry too, so it was frustrating to have to deal with your mess before I could get ready myself. Then, I was so mad about it that I couldn't even relax and enjoy my shower.
DEIRDRE:	Oh, I guess I can see your point now.
MARKESHA:	Yeah, maybe some days it wouldn't bother me, but sometimes I'd like to zone out in the morning, and it makes me feel angry and taken for granted when the first thing I encounter is your dirty clothes and wet towel. It makes me feel like you don't respect me. You know what I mean?
DEIRDRE:	Yeah, I do. I'm really sorry. It won't happen again.
MARKESHA:	OK, good. Thanks.

PAUSE & REFLECT

What are some of the different ways you can interpret the phrase "I'm feeling good"? Can you think of ways to make this expression more concrete to fit the different circumstances in which you might use it?

Language is Arbitrary

Because we understand our native languages so easily and automatically, it might be hard to recognize that language is arbitrary. Language is arbitrary because there is no inherent reason for using a particular word to represent a particular object or idea. As part of your college experience you have to take these things called "classes," but they just as easily could have been called masses, or lasses, or sasses. People in an English-speaking culture assigned the label "classes" to refer to the meetings you have with professors so that we would all have a common way to reference this experience in our speech, but there is nothing about the experience that is inherently linked to the label it was given. As another example, consider the words we have for strong emotions like "anger" and "joy." Although you can readily think of the feelings that those words are linked to, there is nothing about those feelings that necessarily gives rise to those particular terms. In fact, had the labels been reversed, the underlying feelings would remain the same, we would just use a different word to refer to them.

Because there is no fixed connection between words and what they represent, words have ambiguous meanings, which means that people can interpret different meanings for the same word. To make this point in our classes, we ask our students to close their eyes and picture a dog. When students report on the kind of dog they envision, answers range from a golden retriever to a dachshund, or the rescue dog their family adopted from a shelter. The word "dog" can be interpreted in many different ways depending on one's own background and experiences. As another example, the word "pain" can refer to an unpleasant physical sensation in one language (English) and a loaf of bread in another (French). Although the word is the same, the way that people interpret that word is different. The complications that can follow from the ambiguity of language are underscored by the many meaning of the word "love." Love can refer to the feelings of affection that exist within friendships or family and also the passion and sexual intimacy that exists in a romantic relationship (Fehr, 2019). When someone says, "I love you," they can be communicating any variety of feelings, because language is arbitrary and ambiguous.

Language is Related to Culture

Language, like manners, clothing fashions, and traditions, is related to the culture of the people who use it. First of all, characteristics of a language can reveal cultural values and norms. For example, the Korean language emerged within a culture that recognized a strict social hierarchy, so it includes a complex system of honorifics – similar to the English words "ma'am," "sir," or "your honor" – that acknowledge social status. Likewise, the English language emerged within a male-dominated culture, which was reflected for many years in the use of "he" and "man" to refer to people, in general, regardless of their gender.

COMMUNICATION IN ACTION 5.1

Exposing Cultural Assumptions about Power

Take some time to create a list of all the titles you can think of that are used to designate a person who holds a position of power. To get you started, identify the different ways that you would complete these sentences, "One person who has power over me is my____" or "People in charge of are called______." Try to identify at least 15 terms. Then, review your list to uncover the cultural values embedded within those words. Do the words seem to honor or put down people in power? Do the terms tend to include more masculine, feminine, or gender-neutral references? What are the cultural assumptions about power that are encoded in the language you use?

Second, language changes with new cultural developments. Consider how language has adapted to changing norms for romance within American culture, as recounted in a classic book on courtship (Cate & Lloyd, 1992). In the early twentieth century, spending time with a romantic partner was referred to as "courting" because eligible women would be visited in their homes, similar to the way that men who were noble or well-behaved were qualified to be present in a royal court. In the 1920s, women enjoyed greater freedom to meet romantic partners outside their home, which required interested parties to set a day and time that they would meet; hence, the term "dating" was used. Greater romantic freedoms in the 1950s and 1960s meant that people might "date" any number of partners, rather than one person at a time. This state of affairs required new terminology to distinguish committed relationships where partners went on dates with each other consistently, otherwise known as "going steady." We can see similar evolution in the language of courtship in the twenty-first century. For example, terms like "hooking up" and "friends with benefits" distinguish fleeting sexual relationships from those that include an expectation about future involvement. And, as smart phones and social media have become ubiquitous, relationship changes can involve "ghosting" (a sudden lack of contact), "zombieing" (the sudden reappearance of someone who ghosted you), "deep liking" (liking old social media posts that might be months or even years old), or "benching" (continuing to engage with someone in social media but no longer seeing each other in person). These examples show how novel experiences and cultural developments create a need for new language and render old language obsolete.

Sapir–Whorf Hypothesis The assumption that the way people think depends on the structure of their language.

Finally, language can influence how people perceive the world around them. The **Sapir–Whorf Hypothesis** is the long-standing idea that the way people think depends on the structure of their language (Whorf, 1956). The hypothesis would argue that if there is no word in your language to represent some object or idea, then you would not be able to understand or comprehend that object or idea. For example, in Indonesian the word *jayus* refers to a joke so poorly told and so unfunny that one cannot help but laugh. The Sapir–Whorf Hypothesis would argue that because there is not an equivalent word for *jayus* in the English language, people who speak English could never understand or think of this sort of social situation. Of course, you have probably had an experience when a cheesy or poorly told joke made you laugh just because of how bad it was, so does the fact that there is no English word for this situation make it impossible for you to understand? Of course not. Not surprisingly, then, the Sapir–Whorf Hypothesis has fallen out of favor over the decades as people have come to realize that its claims were unfounded. Although the literal interpretation of this claim is now considered overly extreme (Greiffenhagen & Sharrock, 2007), different languages do reflect and create cultural differences in conceptions of reality. This relationship among language, culture, and conceptions of reality is called **linguistic relativity**.

Linguistic Relativity
The assumption that different languages reflect and create cultural differences in conceptions of reality.

Tests of linguistic relativity are provided by studies that examine how language systems influence perception and information processing. For example, one study compared how speakers of Chinese, Japanese, and German performed a variety of cognitive tasks on a set of words (Saalbach & Imai, 2012). The Chinese language is distinctive because words are systematically marked to indicate how the object is classified; for example, the symbols for river (河), lake (湖), stream (流), and slippery (滑), all include the same symbol on the left indicating that the word is related to water. In the study, the test outcomes for Chinese speakers were influenced by word classifiers, compared to speaker of Japanese, which classifies concepts into categories less obviously, and speakers of German, which does not classify concepts within the language system. Another study used neurophysiological evidence to demonstrate that speakers of English differentiate between a "cup" and a "mug" more than speakers of Spanish, for whom one word, "taza," is used for both of those objects (Boutonnet, Dering, Viñas-Guasch, & Thierry, 2013). These studies show how the language you speak affects how you organize and evaluate your perceptions of the world around you.

Language is Consequential

When we use language to represent our reality, our words inevitably highlight some aspects of that reality and neglect others. As an example, think about what happens when you try to describe a dream to another person. Some dreams are crazy narratives where the plot jumps around, people pop in or out of the story, the setting for the dream (or even the color of it) might change dramatically, and feelings can be unclear or fleeting. When you try to describe a dream to someone, certain aspects of the dream will be easier to put into words than others. As you do this, the parts of the dream that defy language will recede from your impression of the dream, and the parts you can put into words will become more solid. This tendency for language to resolve – or neglect – nuances in real-life experience is called **totalizing**. Language totalizes reality because words create an incomplete and oversimplified image of real experiences.

Totalizing
Resolving or neglecting details, nuances, or complexity.

When we label individuals or groups, we also create consequences for them. Consider, for example, what happens when teachers attach labels to elementary schoolchildren. In one classic study, teachers gave higher grades to a fourth grader's handwritten essay when they were told that the paper was written by a student who was "gifted" (Babad, 1980). Other research shows that teachers are less willing to refer students to a gifted program if they have been labeled with a learning disability or an emotional and behavioral disorder (Bianco, 2005). And children who are tagged as slow learners suffer more emotional and behavioral problems than unlabeled classmates who have similar academic skills (Frey, 2005).

IDEA: PROMOTING INCLUSION, DIVERSITY, EQUITY, AND ACCESS

What labels have been given to you in your lifetime? How do you think those labels have affected how people communicate with you? Can you think of labels you use for other people that might be affecting how you see them? What are some practices people can incorporate to avoid the totalizing effect of labels?

Reification occurs when we respond to labels as though they are themselves real. A vivid example of reification comes from interviews that were conducted with women coping with infertility (Steuber & Solomon, 2011). One woman described how her experience with infertility began when she casually mentioned to her doctor that she and her partner hadn't used any kind of birth control for about a year. The doctor told her that she was infertile, and he immediately started to discuss options and prescribe treatments. The woman described how being labeled "infertile" washed over her in the doctor's office and changed her entire view of her life – she was no longer a woman with vague hopes of starting a family, but one with a reproductive disability that would require treatment and might leave her childless. Likewise, the doctor neglected other facets of her experience, never questioned whether the label fit, and focused exclusively on curing her. Although labels can be helpful in diagnosing problems or organizing information, we should be aware of the consequences of allowing those labels to define our reality.

Reification
Reacting to words as though they are an accurate and complete representation of reality.

Putting Theory into Practice: Harnessing the Power of Language

In this section, we looked at the characteristics of verbal communication. These qualities reveal language to be a flexible and powerful tool for interpersonal communication, but one that also contributes to miscommunication. It takes effort, then, to harness the power of language.

Use concrete language. Studies show that people pay more attention to your messages and perceive you as more expert, trustworthy, and unbiased when you use words that are precise and unambiguous. The next time you are in a situation where your communication partner doesn't get your message, consider whether your language is concrete enough. By using words that match the precision of your thoughts, you can communicate more effectively.

COMMUNICATION IN ACTION 5.2

Using Concrete Language

This exercise is designed to help you practice using more concrete language. Complete the form that is available on the companion website to transform abstract comments into statements that are more concrete.

Ask for clarification if a word is ambiguous. A humorous example of the effects of ambiguity on understanding comes from a story Jen once heard about a professor of Slavic Studies who was preparing a group of students for a summer studying abroad in Eastern Europe. As the professor reviewed the list of essentials, he informed them that they would be bathing in public showers, and so it was important for them to bring thongs. Only after several raised eyebrows did he think to clarify that he was referring to flip-flops, not underwear. If the students hadn't signaled their misunderstanding, there might have been a far more embarrassing moment overseas.

It is important to ask directly when you need clarification. If your friend makes a request that you don't understand, you might be wise to reply, "What exactly are you asking me to do?" This gets you focused on the concrete behaviors that are at the heart of the request. Another tactic is to use synonyms for key words, to see if you are capturing your communication partner's meanings correctly. For example, if you aren't sure what someone means by "I'm upset," you might ask if he or she is feeling angry, frustrated, or sad. Although it might seem that probing the meaning of words would burden conversation, often it's better than miscommunicating.

Look beyond labels. Although labels help us make sense of our experience, try not to overreact to them. Would you be surprised to learn that many gifted students are also learning disabled in some way? These "doubly exceptional learners" are sometimes hard to identify, because educators can't reconcile the conflicting labels (Morrison & Rizza, 2007). The important point is to remember that labels don't represent the entire truth, they just summarize part of it.

When you communicate with someone who has been labeled – an athlete, a single mother, a cancer survivor, a sorority sister – pay attention to the qualities that set this individual apart from the category. The label can help you to identify topics you might talk about, but it surely won't capture everything that is important to know about your communication partner. People are always more complex and interesting than the few words that might describe them.

THE RULES OF LANGUAGE

When you drive a car, you can avoid an accident by obeying the rules about which side of the road to drive on, what to do at a four-way stop, and when to pull over for an emergency vehicle. In the same way, we rely on rules of language to avoid miscommunication. Importantly, we usually don't think consciously about these rules; instead, our knowledge of them automatically shapes how we create and decipher verbal messages. In the following sections, we'll examine the rules for using language to make meaning and for making conversation.

Using Language to Make Meaning

Our use of language is guided by rules that address the structure of words and sentences, the meanings attached to words, and the use of language to accomplish goals (see Figure 5.2). These rules of language both shape the verbal messages we create and how we interpret the messages we receive from others.

At a basic level, **syntactic rules** identify how words and phrases can be structured within a message. Consider how much harder it is to understand a sentence with just two words in the wrong place compared to a sentence with the words in a correct order:

Syntactic Rules
Guidelines for structuring words and phrases within a message.

I put my clothes the washer in dinner after.
I put my clothes in the washer after dinner.

The order of words can also help us decipher words that have more than one meaning. For example, "the ship sails" and "ship the sails" have the same words, but those words have different meaning depending on where they are placed in the sentence. People might also play with the syntactic rules for artistic effect. The character Yoda, who makes a first appearance in the Star Wars saga in *The Empire Strikes Back*, often orders sentences object-subject-verb (e.g., "patient I am") rather than the subject-verb-object ordering (e.g., "I am patient") that is more normative in the English language. This stylistic change made everything Yoda said, from ordinary statements to his parting words ("When gone am I, the last of the Jedi will you be"), seem like clever riddles.

Denotative Meaning
The literal, public, or conventional definition of a word.

Connotative Meaning
The implicit emotional or evaluative interpretation of a word.

We are also influenced by the meanings of words when we use them to craft messages. **Denotative meaning** refers to the literal, public, or conventional definition for the word; for example, "cancer" refers to a category of disease in which mutant cells reproduce and disable a host organism. **Connotative meaning** is the implicit emotional or evaluative tone of a word. Because connotative meanings are grounded in our personal and cultural experiences, they can be different for difference people and change over time. For example, if you know someone who died from cancer, that word probably has a special meaning for you and might evoke strong feelings. Likewise, consider how the connotations of being *liberal* have changed in the United States. In the nineteenth century, being liberal meant being tolerant of different ideas and endorsing individual freedoms; however, in the twentieth century, the word became associated with endorsing government programs that provide services to the public, while taking away individual autonomy. Presently, how people react to the word *liberal* is influenced by their own identity as *conservative* or *progressive* – the connotations of which have also evolved over time (Scott, 2019).

PAUSE & REFLECT

What words have an emotional impact on you but may be neutral for another person? Why are those words so meaningful to you?

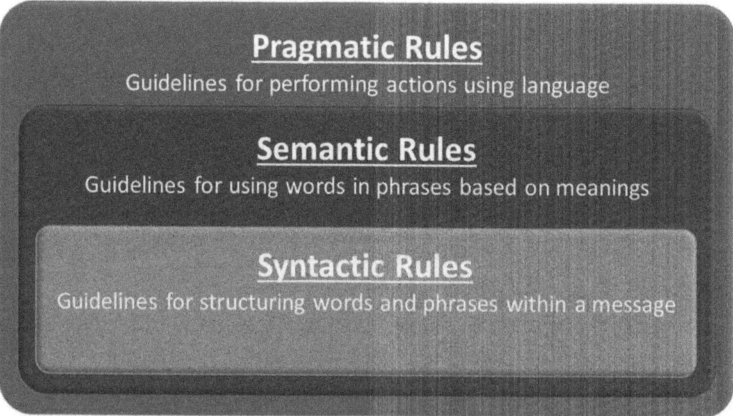
Pragmatic Rules
Guidelines for performing actions using language
Semantic Rules
Guidelines for using words in phrases based on meanings
Syntactic Rules
Guidelines for structuring words and phrases within a message

FIGURE 5.2 A hierarchy of language rules.

Semantic rules govern the way you use language based on both denotative and connotative meanings. Of course, we need to use words in a way that is consistent with their meanings; it would be confusing to say you spent the summer "reading bikes" rather than "reading books" or "riding bikes." The connotative meaning of words also influences how we use and understand language, but perhaps in less obvious ways. One study demonstrated the effects of connotative meanings in messages that doctors use to recruit people into studies of experimental medical treatments (Krieger, Parrott, & Nussbaum, 2011). Most messages about medical experiments explain that some people will get the new treatment and some people won't, and that deciding who gets the treatment is random, "like flipping a coin." The study found that older women from rural communities reacted negatively to these messages, which made them think of "gambling" or "playing a game" with their lives. In contrast, explaining that random is "like the sex of a baby" had positive connotations for women with strong family values, and it emphasized to them that either outcome was desirable.

Semantic Rules
Guidelines for using words in phrases based on meanings.

Rules also govern how we use language to accomplish goals. Table 5.2 provides examples of several **speech acts**, which are actions that we perform using language. When we use words to express a compliment, accuse a person of cheating, ask a question, or make a request, we are acting upon our environment; in fact, all of our messages perform some kind of function, even if it is just to provide information. By the very act of speaking, we have changed our circumstances in some way. And some outcomes – such as inaugurating a president or pronouncing a couple legally married – require that someone utter specific words.

Speech Acts
Actions that are performed using language.

Pragmatic rules help us to figure out which speech acts can be performed in specific circumstances. For example, not anyone can inaugurate a president; in the United States, that speech act can only be performed by the Chief Justice of the Supreme Court. Within interpersonal interactions, you cannot always express a compliment, accuse a person of cheating, ask a question, provide information, make a request, etc. For example, before

Pragmatic Rules
Guidelines for performing actions using language.

TABLE 5.2 Examples of speech acts

Propose	*Will you marry me?*
Compliment	I like how you've decorated your home
Insult	I don't think I've ever seen sloppier work
Hire	Maria, you're perfect for the job – when can you start?
Accuse	I believe that you cheated on the exam
Break up	It's over. I'm leaving you
Apologize	I'm sorry
Vow	I promise to love, honor, and cherish you

you can accuse someone of cheating, there has to be some standard for behavior that can be violated, you have to have some reason to suspect cheating, and you have to have the right to pass judgment.

Pragmatic rules help us identify the messages that are appropriate or inappropriate in a particular situation. For example, before you ask someone for help, you might consider your relationship with that person and whether he or she has the ability to help you. If you make a request that doesn't fit with the circumstances – such as asking your unemployed college acquaintance to pay your tuition bill – your behavior will be inappropriate. Because the speech acts we can perform are linked to qualities of our relationships, different types of relationships involve different types of speech acts. Within step-families, for example, catching up, joking around, and recapping the day are the most frequent conversational topics (Schrodt, Braithwaite, Soliz, Tye-Williams, & Miller, 2007), and for parents who don't live with their children, sharing mundane stories about life experiences can sustain a sense of closeness (Rodriguez, 2014). Within geographically separated romantic relationships, making plans for the future serves key relationship maintenance functions (Sahlstein, 2006), and romantic partners separated by military deployment engage in "problem talk," "friendship talk," and "love talk" to different degrees depending on whether they are speaking synchronously or through a written medium (Carter, Osborne, Renshaw, Allen, Loew, Markman, & Stanley, 2018). In Table 5.3, you

TABLE 5.3 Speech acts and types of interpersonal relationships

This table shows the percentage of speech acts that are performed in different relationships. Categories that captured at least 10% of speech acts within a relationship type are in boldface. Notice how the most common speech acts vary depending on the type of relationship.

Speech act	*Acquaintances (%)*	*Close friends (%)*	*Parent & child (%)*	*Romantic partners (%)*
Make small talk	**28**	4	3	4
Joke around	**12**	9	8	8
Gossip	8	**27**	8	8
Make plans	8	**12**	**13**	**12**
Catch up	5	**10**	**15**	2
Recap the day	1	5	**10**	**10**
Greet in the morning	0	1	3	**10**
Express love	0	0	2	**14**

can see the results of one classic study, by communication scholars Daena Goldsmith and Leslie Baxter (1996), which demonstrated how the frequency of small talk, joking, gossip, etc., is affected by the relationship that exists between interaction partners.

Pragmatic rules also help us to interpret the meaning of a message and figure out what speech acts people are performing. Imagine a friend telling you, "I'm moving during finals week." What could this mean? Perhaps the friend is alerting you that she can't socialize during that time or hinting that she'd like to use your car to move. Now, imagine that same message being delivered to your professor. If you mentioned to your professor that you were moving during finals week, they might wonder if you are asking to reschedule the exam or explaining why your performance might suffer; however, your professor probably wouldn't think that you were asking to borrow a car. Pragmatic rules help us to eliminate some of the possible meanings of messages, which improves our ability to figure out what people really mean.

Making Conversation

Because verbal communication is abstract and arbitrary, communication partners need to help each other in order to have an effective conversation. The philosopher Paul Grice (1957, 1975) coined the phrase **the cooperative principle** to refer to the assumption that people work together to advance a conversation. In other words, we go into a conversation expecting the other person to make a good faith effort to produce meaningful messages.

The Cooperative Principle The assumption that people who are talking to each other are working together to advance the conversation.

Grice theorized that there are basic rules, called maxims, that we assume people are following as they cooperate in a conversation. The maxims dictate rules for good behavior in conversations, but more importantly, they identify the assumptions that you can rely on when talking to someone else. The role of these maxims was brought to life in a study of college students engaged in online conversation with a romantic partner where the couple discussed a source of disagreement while they also expressed their thoughts out loud as they communicated (Vangelisti, Middleton, & Ebersole, 2013); we've reproduced an excerpt from two speaking turns in the Interpersonal Communication Online box. The thoughts that people reported showed that they made inferences about the other person's reasons behind messages and where the conversation was going. Based on these inferences, they would supply additional details, make comments that they thought were pertinent, and try to clarify their statements. The maxims of conversations are assumptions that allow us to make sense of the messages we receive.

INTERPERSONAL COMMUNICATION ONLINE

This transcript and the partners' thoughts as they communicated were reported in Table 1 of Vangelisti et al. (2013). In that study, people discussed a source of conflict with a romantic partner through text messages, while they spoke aloud about the thoughts they were having. In this example, the couple is discussing a conflict over how much time they spend together.

When this was said. . .	*He thought. . .*	*While she thought. . .*
He said: "We have forever to spend with each other and only a little time to be young."	Oh there it is. . . This is what I always tell her. This is going to make her mad.	He thinks we have forever to see each other that I'll just sit back and wait and he can hang out with his friends all the time so I don't do anything with him. . . Yeah, exactly. So he goes and parties and I sit home.
She said: "I'm not going to be here forever if I don't see you KNOW NOW! But I love you."	Oh no, "if," uh-oh. The big "if". . . Let's see. . . She's too cute.	Oops, told him I love him, though. He'll get mad if I don't.

PAUSE & REFLECT

Have you ever communicated with someone who didn't seem to share your goal of advancing the conversation? How was their lack of cooperation evident and how did it make you feel?

Maxim of Quantity
A conversational rule that communicators should provide sufficient information to advance the conversation.

The **maxim of quantity** specifies that communicators should provide enough information to advance the conversation, and they should avoid providing either too much or too little information. Imagine that you get a call from a friend; after you say "Hello," the response is a simple "I'm back." Although it's only a two-word phrase, the maxim of quantity lets you assume that your friend is giving you all the information they think you need. So what can you infer to inform your reply? For one, your friend believes that you know who is calling, otherwise they would have stated their name. What else do you know from these two words? Your friend has been away, thinks you know where, and believes you would like to know that they are back. Because you can assume that your friend is giving you all the information you need, you are able to draw a lot of meaning from those two words.

Think about how difficult interpersonal communication would be if we couldn't assume that people speak truthfully. The **maxim of quality** helps us understand even far-fetched utterances, because we can start with the expectation that the speaker means to convey something truthful. Imagine your roommate says, "I'm sorry I didn't clean the kitchen. I've been so stressed by exams I haven't slept for ten days!" You probably wouldn't actually believe that it was possible that your roommate has been awake for 240 hours straight, but it isn't hard to find a true interpretation that makes sense (i.e., that they are exhausted and overwhelmed). The maxim of quality also helps us to detect when someone isn't being truthful. We conclude that people are lying when the meanings implied by their messages don't add up (Levine, Anders, Banas, Baum, Endo, Hu, & Wong, 2000). What if your roommate also mentioned the dinner party they threw last night while you were at work? Because being stressed by finals, endless sleepless nights, and throwing a party don't fit together, your friend's story would seem a bit fishy.

Maxim of Quality
A conversational rule that communicators should make truthful contributions to conversation.

Now, let's focus on the **maxim of relevance**, which suggests that communicators should make contributions that are pertinent to the conversation topic. Consider the opening turns in an exchange between Lexi and Scott:

Maxim of Relevance
A conversational rule that communicators should make contributions to conversation that are pertinent to the topic.

LEXI: Hey, Scott – what's up? You look upset.
SCOTT: Oh, I just got a call from my dad. He expects me to drop everything and run over and help him with his taxes, and he got mad when I told him I was busy.
LEXI: Did I ever tell you about my good friend from high school?

On the surface, Lexi's last comment violates the maxim of relevance, but if we assume that Lexi is following the rules, her high school friend must be relevant in some way. Perhaps the friend takes advantage of Lexi's expertise too, and Lexi is bringing him up to show empathy for Scott. Or perhaps Lexi's friend is a tax accountant who can help solve the problem. Although we have to get a bit further in the conversation to find out how the high school friend fits in, using the maxim of relevance puts Scott on the lookout for the connection.

PAUSE & REFLECT

How do you typically react when someone violates the maxim of relevance – in other words, changes the topic suddenly – during a conversation?

Maxim of Manner
A conversational rule that communicators should strive to be clear, organized, and to the point.

Finally, the **maxim of manner** specifies that we should avoid being vague, wordy, or disorganized; instead, we should craft messages that are as clear and tidy as possible. Consider how confused you might be if someone violated the maxim of manner when giving you directions to a street address, saying: "Turn left at the supermarket, go three blocks, turn right on Main. And oh, back at the supermarket, you'll need to get into the left-hand lane as soon as possible, so you don't miss the turn onto 16th Street." Jumping back in the sequence of directions makes it harder for you to organize the information in a meaningful way. The maxim of manner is so important that learning to tell a coherent story is a fundamental part of child development (Kelly & Bailey, 2012). For example, while a child might tell a story that involves enormous detail ("it was black and blue, and kind of spotted; well, the spots were really heart-shaped, but smaller; kind of like a dot") about an experience that her parents don't remember ("that walk we went on") that has no obvious organization ("we walked a long time; before that we had waffles; the butterflies were pretty"), parental collaboration in story telling can help them learn to develop more succinct and sensible narratives ("first we had waffles, and went for a long walk where we saw pretty butterflies, including a black and blue one with small, heart-shaped dots.")

The rules for making conversation highlight why misunderstanding is so common. The maxims of conversation help us make inferences about meaning, but there is still a leap involved in interpreting verbal cues. When someone doesn't give us enough information, says something untrue, shifts the topic suddenly, or is vague, wordy, or disorganized, we have to figure out why. As we sift through various explanations – the topic is sensitive, the person is upset, the speaker is asking us to do something – we may or may not settle on the right implication (Holtgraves, 2002). In other words, the rules of language can help us make conversation, but they can't prevent communication partners from drawing unintended inferences.

Putting Theory into Practice: Reducing Miscommunication

Any tool we might use comes with rules for how to use it, and language is no exception. These rules can help us troubleshoot when verbal communication breaks down.

Attend to connotative meanings. Different words evoke positive or negative feelings and some words evoke stronger emotions than others. Strive to choose words that create the reaction you seek. If your message isn't producing the desired effect, you might ask the person you're trying to reach how they are reacting to your words. In the same way, be attentive to the words that cause you to react with strong emotions. Being aware of words that trigger strong reactions within you can help you to avoid overreacting to someone else's message.

COMMUNICATION IN ACTION 5.3

Exploring the Meanings of "Help"

In this exercise you will explore how subtle changes in a message can promote different connotative meanings, especially when you consider the source of the message and your relationship with that person. Visit the companion website to test your skills at deciphering connotative meanings in messages.

Diagnose topic shifts. Have you ever been in a conversation where your interaction partner seemed to change the topic suddenly? It can seem like the person isn't listening or has a different agenda. The maxim of relevance suggests, however, that even a seemingly unrelated comment is probably connected to your utterance in some way. Rather than being miffed at the topic change, try to find out why your partner responded in that way. You might ask, "Is that related to what I just said?" or express confusion by saying, "I'm not sure how that connects to what I was talking about." If this was a blatant topic shift, at least your partner knows you noticed. And if it wasn't, you give your partner a chance to clarify his or her intentions.

Of course, topic shifts are a natural part of conversation, and they don't always violate the maxim of relevance. Communication scholar Galina Bolden (2006) examined recorded conversations to identify how people verbally signal a topic change. She found that people use the word "so" (e.g., "so, how are you?" or "so, I hear it's your birthday") to signal a shift to a new topic or a topic that was previously set aside. Bolden also observed that people use "oh" to introduce new information that has just been noticed or remembered, and it suggests some degree of urgency. For example, "Oh, that reminds me. . ." indicates that your partner intends to talk about something new and it is pressing enough to discard the topic at hand. Verbal cues like these illustrate how we use language to change topics without violating the maxim of relevance.

Set the stage for conversation. We sometimes have difficulty being organized, clear, and precise, because we don't know what our communication partner already knows about a topic. Consider what happens in a conversation between co-workers Dwayne and Lydia when Lydia mistakenly assumes that Dwayne has heard about an upcoming meeting. When Lydia opens with, "Are you ready for Friday?" Dwayne has no idea what she's talking about. Lydia might continue making references to the Friday meeting, until Dwayne says, "Wait, I didn't know about this meeting." At that point, Lydia might start over, "About six months ago, there was an awful mix-up in shipping; it was a huge mess." Now Dwayne might have to interrupt this recounting of events, "I know about all that, but what's

SCHOLAR SPOTLIGHT 

Visit the Communication Café on the companion website to view a conversation with Steven Wilson, who has conducted a wide variety of studies of language use in interpersonal interactions.

going on this Friday?" Lydia's story has to start again, this time describing the agenda and focus of the meeting.

You can avoid disorderly conversations by taking a little time to set the stage. In other words, before launching into a conversation on a topic, find out what the other person already knows. "Did you hear about . . .?" "When was the last time you talked to . . .?" and "How much do you know about . . .?" are simple questions that can help you and a conversational partner figure out where you need to elaborate, where you can gloss some details, and where to start your discussion so that you can have a coherent interaction.

FACTORS THAT AFFECT LANGUAGE USE

Thus far, you have learned about the general features and rules of language use. Now, we consider variations in how people use language based on gender, power, and intimacy.

Gender

Large scale reviews of research on gender differences in language use conclude that males and females, on average, use language in slightly different ways (Leaper, 2014). In childhood and in general, girls tend to be more talkative and use affiliative speech, whereas boys tend to use more assertive language (Leaper & Smith, 2004). These gender differences in affiliative and assertive language use persist into adulthood, except that adult males tend to be more talkative than adult females (Leaper & Ayres, 2007). Another difference, documented in both online blog posts and speeches by members of Congress, is a tendency for men to use more abstract language and women to speak more concretely (Joshi, Wakslak, Appel, & Huang, 2020). In fact, another study found more than 20 specific language features that showed gender differences in prior research, such as a tendency for men to refer to quantity, use judgmental adjustive, and use directives, and a tendency for women to refer to emotions, use more dependent clauses, and speak in longer sentences (Mulac, Bradac, & Gibbons, 2001).

Communication scholar Anthony Mulac, who has studied the linguistic styles of men and women for over 30 years, summarized differences in language use in a theory called the Gender-linked Language Effect. In one of his classic studies, 20 men and 20 women described the same landscape photograph to a researcher (Mulac & Lundell, 1986). Men's speech focused on facts, such as the number of objects present and their location, whereas women were more likely to describe their feelings when looking at the landscape (see also Mulac, Giles, Bradac, & Palomares, 2013). Men also used more short, declarative, and judgmental sentences; women used longer and more detailed sentences, more adverbs, and less concrete verb forms. Differences have also been found in how men and women communicate in television interviews – women use plain language and discuss their feelings, but men are more likely to use jargon and depersonalize the conversation (Brownlow, Rosamond & Parker, 2003). Men and women also communicate differently online. In a study that examined messages posted by students in an introductory psychology class, women posted more tentative claims and expressed agreement with other students, whereas men made more assertions and expressed more disagreement with others (Guiller & Durndell, 2006). Men talking to men in chat rooms also use more figures of speech and slang than women chatting with women (Hussey & Katz, 2006). These gender differences are even more pronounced when people are discussing gendered topics, like sports or fashion, rather than gender-neutral topics (Thomson, 2006).

CONNECT WITH THEORY

Visit the companion website to learn about the Gender-linked Language Effect, which summarizes gender differences in language use and links those differences to perceptions of people speech.

PAUSE & REFLECT

Do you think you can tell someone's gender from an online posting? If so, what cues do you use to figure out someone's gender?

"When you say 'It's all good' what you really mean is 'I don't care'."

FIGURE 5.3 What you really mean

Source: © William Haefeli/The New Yorker Collection/www.cartoonbank.com.

You might be wondering how people react to gender differences in the use of language. When other people read the landscape descriptions generated in Anthony Mulac's research, they tend to rate women's descriptions of the landscape higher in aesthetic quality and more intellectual, and they find men's descriptions to be more dynamic (Mulac et al., 2001; Mulac et al., 2013). As another example, consider the effects of the tendency for women to make more hesitant or qualified claims, by inserting hedges, qualifiers, or tag questions into their statements (e.g., Mulac et al., 2001). In particular, compare the following variations on the claim "That's a good idea":

- Hedge: "That's *sort of* a good idea."
- Qualifier: "*I'm not really sure*, but that *seems* like a good idea."
- Tag question: "That's a good idea, *isn't it*?"

As these examples illustrate, people who use hedges, qualifiers, and tag questions appear unsure of themselves, and they invite disagreement from others.

INSIDE COMMUNICATION RESEARCH

Sexist Slurs Reinforce Feminine Stereotypes Online

Social media platforms have become a hostile environment for women, where sexist stereotypes are reinforced and women are frequently bullied or harassed. The anonymity that people enjoy on the internet has emboldened some individuals to engage in cyber aggression, which involves the construction of intentional electronic messages with the goal of harming or insulting the recipient. Cyber aggression enforces social norms and establishes social hierarchies in ways that reflect and reify traditional gender stereotypes. In this study, researchers examined Twitter as a social media platform where women are often the targets of aggressive, derogatory, or hostile messages that attempt to reinforce idealized forms of femininity (Felmlee, Rodis, & Zhang, 2020).

As a first step in this study, the researchers compiled tweets over a period of 2.5 years that contained keywords reflecting sexist or misogynistic language. In total, they collected over 50,000 tweets that encompassed a broad variety of gendered derogatory language and made a list of commonly used insults that reflected negative concepts and stereotypes about women. Their analysis identified four derogatory words that were most common in gendered insults on the social media platform, including "bitch," "cunt," "slut," and "whore." Then, in a second step, they scraped data from Twitter to find tweets that contained at least one of the four key terms that they had identified in the previous analysis. Over the course of one week, this data scraping process resulted in a set of 2.9 million tweets that contained at least one of the four key terms, of which 87% contained the word "bitch" and the other terms each accounted for 4–5% of the tweets. There were over 418,000 tweets per day that included one of these sexist terms. In addition to searching for tweets that contained one of these derogatory terms, the researchers also assessed the degree of negativity in the tweets by examining the inclusion of derogatory adjectives that reflect negative feminine stereotypes. They searched for key words and synonyms reflecting seven categories of feminine insults: ugly, stupid, overweight, underweight, crazy, old, and promiscuous. Finally, the researchers conducted a network analysis to examine the different roles that individuals played in spreading these derogatory messages through retweeting, commenting, and liking.

The researchers found that including words in a tweet that reinforce negative feminine stereotypes, such as words that attack women's appearance (e.g., "ugly"), size ("fat"), intellect (e.g., "stupid"), mental stability (e.g., "crazy"), age (e.g., "old"), or sexual experience (e.g., "promiscuous"), significantly increase the negative sentiment reflected in the tweet. Results of the network analysis revealed that sexist attacks of this nature can become quite large and spread rather far, particularly when the target of the attack is a celebrity or has a large Twitter following. Individuals can play a variety of different roles in the harassment of women online. In addition to the perpetrator and the victim, there are reinforcers who retweet, like, and add inflammatory comments on the tweet; defenders who comment on the inappropriateness of the tweet and attempt to turn down the vitriol; as well as bystanders who are aware of the harassment but neither support nor condemn the attack. The findings in this study show how powerful and pervasive sexist language can be for creating a climate of aggression and bullying online.

THINK ABOUT IT

1. To what extent is derogatory sexist language prevalent in face-to-face conversations versus in online communication? Do you think that the perpetrators of online aggression would be as likely to use the same language in messages that are verbally communicated to the victim in person? Why or why not?
2. Have you ever been the target of or a witness to online harassment? What words did the perpetrator and reinforcers use in their messages that were derogatory or enhanced the negativity of the attack? What strategies could a defender use in this context to buffer the aggression?

Power and Intimacy

Language use also varies according to the relationship that exists between conversational partners. Consider how your own speech changes as you talk to different people over the course of your day. How would your greetings change if you were speaking to an acquaintance in class, one of your professors, a good friend, your parents, or someone who works for you? Chances are, you have a lot of different ways of saying hello, and the way you talk depends on the power dynamics and degree of intimacy in your relationship with the other person.

Politeness theory is a perspective on language use that highlights how relationship qualities affect communication (Brown & Levinson, 1987). Specifically, the theory focuses on how we perform speech acts that might have a negative effect on a partner – criticizing a person, asking for a

CONNECT WITH THEORY

Visit the companion website to learn about politeness theory, which highlights how relationship qualities, including power differences and social closeness, affect language use.

favor, or interrupting a conversation. When the other person has more power, we try to minimize the negative impact of our words. In addition, we have less freedom to impose on people with whom we have a more distant relationship. When we need to soften the impact of an intrusive speech act, we use polite messages like the ones summarized in Table 5.4.

In the workplace, employees depend on a manager for work assignments, performance evaluations, and promotions. Not surprisingly, these power differences have a pervasive effect on language use at work (Morand, 2014). In one study, college students imagined that they were new employees at a company meeting where someone had taken their seat and moved their belongings (Morand, 2000). When the "seat-stealer" had higher status, the students used more polite messages to request their seat and possessions. Power also affects how people address each other within an organization. Managers are free to call employees by their first names, employees tend to use their boss's formal title, and subordinates sometimes avoid using any name for their supervisor, because a first name is too informal and a formal title is too stiff (Morand, 2005).

Whereas politeness theory suggests that we adjust our language based on a communication partner's power, our language also affects how much power we project during interpersonal interactions. Indeed, the verbal cues that convey politeness can be considered examples of powerless speech and using them can affect how people perceive you. One study, for example, took transcripts from a criminal trial and created low-power speech versions by inserting hedges or tag questions, and asked research participants to evaluate the speaker after reading different versions of the transcripts (Hosman & Siltanen, 2006). The speakers in the version that included hedges were perceived as the least competent and as having the least amount of self-control, compared to the speakers in the other versions of the transcripts. Other research has shown that including

TABLE 5.4 Verbal cues that increase politeness

Indirectness	Are you going to be using your car this weekend?
Hedging	I was kind of wondering if you would mind helping me
Conditional language	If you were going by the coffee shop, could you get me a muffin?
Minimized consequences	I need a little of your time
Apologies	I'm so sorry to bother you, but can I borrow your phone?
Past tense (which decreases urgency)	I had been planning to ask you about a loan

tag questions within a persuasive message leads to lower evaluations of speaker credibility, message quality, and speaker power (Hosman & Siltanen, 2011). Our language choices, it seems, have a profound influence on how persuasive other people find us to be (Dillard, 2014).

Our language choices are also related to the degree of intimacy in a relationship, such that our use of language is more informal in intimate or close relationships. One linguistic feature that surfaces in close relationships is the **idiom**, which refers to a metaphor, term, or phrase that has a special meaning known only to members of a social group. Denise recalls an idiom that emerged within a group of graduate students who had, at one time or another, met her dog Tupelo. As a bloodhound, Tupelo had an ample supply of saliva, which she could send flying across the room with the toss of her head. One student coined the term "Tupeloed" to describe being slobbered on by the dog, and the rest of the students quickly adopted her language. Over time, "Tupeloed" became an idiom to describe any unfortunate mess – if a student came back from lunch and said they had been "Tupeloed," everyone knew that a spill had occurred. In this way, idioms arise from shared experiences, are adopted by members of the social group, and become part of the linguistic code used by group insiders.

Idiom
A term, phrase, or reference that has a special meaning known only to members of a social group.

Not surprisingly, idioms commonly arise in friendships and romantic relationships, and they are one of the linguistic devices we use to signal that a relationship is close (Duck & Usera, 2014). In fact, research shows that women, in particular, use more idiomatic language in online communication with friends compared to strangers (Hussey & Katz, 2006). In turn, people evaluate the relationship between two partners as closer or more familiar when the conversation includes metaphors rather than literal statements (Bowes & Katz, 2015; Horton, 2007). Closeness in a friendship also allows partners to use and understand ironic insults, compliments, humor, and teasing (Pexman & Zvaigzne, 2004).

PAUSE & REFLECT

What are some of the nicknames, inside jokes, and terms that have a special meaning within your close relationships? Where did these idioms come from?

Intimacy is even reflected by the pronouns that people use to refer to themselves and their partner (Allgood, Seedall, & Williams, 2020). In one study, dating partners talked for ten minutes while being videotaped (Knobloch & Solomon, 2003). Partners who were more intimate and interdependent tended to use more pluralistic pronouns like "we" and "us," and partners who were less close used more singular pronouns like "you" and "I." Do these subtle effects of intimacy on language matters? A study of middle-aged and older couples found that using pronouns that conveyed togetherness (e.g., "we") corresponded with less cardiovascular arousal and more positive emotions during a conversation about a source of conflict in the marriage (Seider, Hirschberger, Nelson, & Levenson, 2009). Together, these studies suggest that language use in close relationships is connected to both relational and personal well-being.

Putting Theory into Practice: Fine-Tuning Your Language

Studies that have analyzed people's language use over time show that our verbal behavior does not change significantly (Pennebaker, Mehl, & Niederhoffer, 2003). Nonetheless, we are not trapped into gendered speech patterns, and we can take steps to tailor our language to the interpersonal communication situations that we find ourselves in.

Avoid gender traps. A long-standing explanation for gendered speech patterns is that women use more hesitant language because they have held a less powerful position in society than men (Lakoff, 1973). Although this explanation may have been more valid 50 years ago, we need to be sure that our language reflects the more equal positions men and women hold nowadays. More to the point, you can avoid using stereotypically male speech (e.g., making assertions of fact, passing judgment, being impersonal) or stereotypically female language (e.g., using tentative language, focusing on feelings, or being personal). Instead, choose words that are assertive or tentative, fact- or emotion-focused, and personal or impersonal to fit the context.

FIGURE 5.4 Friends can use language to reinforce their bond

Source: Getty Images.

COMMUNICATION IN ACTION 5.4

Analyze Your Speech Patterns

Use a recording device, such as a digital recorder or even your cell phone, to record one of your naturally occurring conversations. Then, listen closely to the words and phrases you used in that interaction. Take note of how often you assert a fact, insert a hedge or qualifier, ask a tag question, reference your feelings, and issue a command. As you reflect on the results of your analysis, can you think of ways in which you can make your language less gendered? Are there times when you assert information as a fact, when it is really an impression or guess? Do you find that you soften assertions you believe are true by hedging or qualifying your words?

Tailor your language to social contexts. When you are in a subordinate position, consider whether your language communicates an appreciation for status differences. You needn't refrain from expressing opinions or asserting yourself; however, you should strive for politeness. Try to be less forceful with your requests, apologize for imposing, and use appropriately formal terms of address. For example, research shows that some students are more likely to use less polite, more direct, and less formal language when emailing a faculty member they think is female, rather than male (Thomas-Tate, Daugherty, & Barkoski, 2017). Indeed, even as chair of her department, Denise routinely gets emails from undergraduates she has never met that begin, "Hey, Denise!" You will be more effective in your communication with people in positions of power if you show respect for status through the language you use.

In a similar fashion, adjust the familiarity of your language to the level of intimacy you share with a communication partner. When you use nicknames, special greetings, and idioms, you convey solidarity with a friend or family member. These terms can foster a sense of closeness and make intimacy tangible. At the same time, avoid overly familiar language with people you're not close to. When you adopt terms of endearment, special words or phrases, and inside jokes that belong to others, you run the risk of violating relationship boundaries.

BIASED LANGUAGE

A hammer can be used to put things together or smash things to pieces. In the same way, language can be used to promote well-being, build relationships, and foster communities, or it can be used to undermine someone, weaken an interpersonal bond, or divide people. In this section of the chapter, we consider some forms of language that contribute to problematic communication experiences.

Racist Language

Racist language includes words and utterances that undermine a person's ethnic group. By doing so, these verbal messages dehumanize their targets and render people vulnerable to both discrimination and acts of violence. Consider the racist propaganda that Nazis used to justify the extermination of Jews, the origins and usage of racial slurs in American culture, and messages of hatred produced by Al-Qaeda to intimidate citizens of the Western world.

Sometimes racist messages are obvious. In recent years, celebrities called out for racist remarks include Rosanne Barr, who was written off of her own sitcom, *The Connors*, for posting racist remarks about President Barack Obama on social media; Paula Deen, who was fired from three cooking shows for her racist language; four cast members on *Vanderpump Rules*, who weren't invited back to the reality show after their racist social media posts surfaced; and Noah Cyrus, youngest sibling of pop icon Miley Cyrus, who issued a public apology for using inappropriate language when defending Harry Styles for wearing dresses for his December 2020 *Vogue* photo shoot. Although the popular press offers numerous vivid examples of racist language, racism often surfaces in more subtle linguistic forms that are pervasive in interpersonal communication (Harris & Moffitt, 2019). **Racial microaggressions** are "everyday slights, insults, putdowns, invalidations, and offensive behaviors that people of color experience in daily interaction" (Sue, Alsaidi, Awad, Glaeser, Calle, & Mendez, 2019, p. 129). Microaggressions are more than rude conduct – they are pervasive communication behaviors that reveal prejudiced beliefs, perpetrate discrimination, and undermine well-being for the people they denigrate. Microaggressions also place constraints on people, by making assumptions and imposing identities that the targets of racism are forced to contend with (Holling, 2019).

Racial Microaggressions Slights, insults, putdowns, invalidations, and offensive behaviors that target people of color in everyday communication.

How can you talk about race while avoiding racist language? Two researchers who were involved in an interracial relationship in South Africa – where interracial sexual relations were a crime until 1985 – conducted a study of the language people used when raising issues of race in their presence (Barnes, Palmary, & Durrheim, 2001). The couple recorded conversations with friends, family members, colleagues, and strangers. When analyzing these conversations, the couple noticed several linguistic devices that people used to discuss matters of race. Humor was the most common strategy for bringing the topic of race into a conversation, because it inhibits angry responses from listeners and reduces the tension associated with racial discourse. They also found that people referenced personal experiences to ground their racial perceptions in some external reality. People also waited for the couple to raise the topic of race, thereby giving them permission to discuss the topic. Although tensions may make it difficult to discuss race openly, taking care with your language can help you avoid racist talk while still discussing racial issues.

IDEA: PROMOTING INCLUSION, DIVERSITY, EQUITY, AND ACCESS

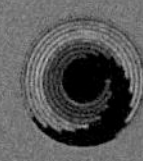

Have you ever been involved in or the target of a racist conversation? If so, how did the person making the racist comment justify or hide the racism? What are some strategies we can use in our everyday interactions to avoid or correct the occurrence of microaggressions?

Sexist Language

Sexist language includes words or expressions that differentiate among sexes or exclude and trivialize particular genders. Consider words in the English language that reflect men's historically dominant position in society. For example, the United States Declaration of Independence states that "all men are created equal" and that the laws set forth in the declaration are for the benefit of all "mankind." Until the twenty-first century, writers typically used "he" as the pronoun of choice to refer to all people. In the United States, the 2020 election of Vice President Kamala Harris raised questions about what to call her husband, given that the spouse of the vice president had always been referred to as "the second lady." In 2009, the European Union banned members of the European Parliament from using the terms Miss and Mrs to refer to women because they felt it was sexist to refer to a woman's marital status when a similar language structure did not exist for men. This means that Madame and Mademoiselle, Frau and Fraulein, and Senora and Senorita were also banned. Instead, women are simply to be called by their name. Figure 5.5 identifies just a few of the professional titles that are linked to the sex of the person in that position, as well as some gender-neutral alternatives.

Notably, sexist language tends to go hand in hand with sexist attitudes. For example, people who endorse sexist beliefs are more likely to use the pronoun "he" to describe a business executive or professor (Swim, Mallett, & Stangor, 2004). Sexist men are also more likely to use the terms "girl" or "lady," rather than the more neutral word "woman" (Cralley & Ruscher, 2005). Among college students, negative attitudes toward people who are transgender or gender nonconforming have been found to correspond with characterizing gender-inclusive language as difficult to use (Patev, Dunn, Hood, & Barber, 2019). In contrast, cultures that use more gender-inclusive or gender-fair language, also manifest more equality among genders (Prewitt-Freilino, Caswell, & Laakso, 2012).

Sexist language has consequences. For one, when masculine references and pronouns are used as the generic default to refer to a category of people, individuals are less likely to think of someone other than

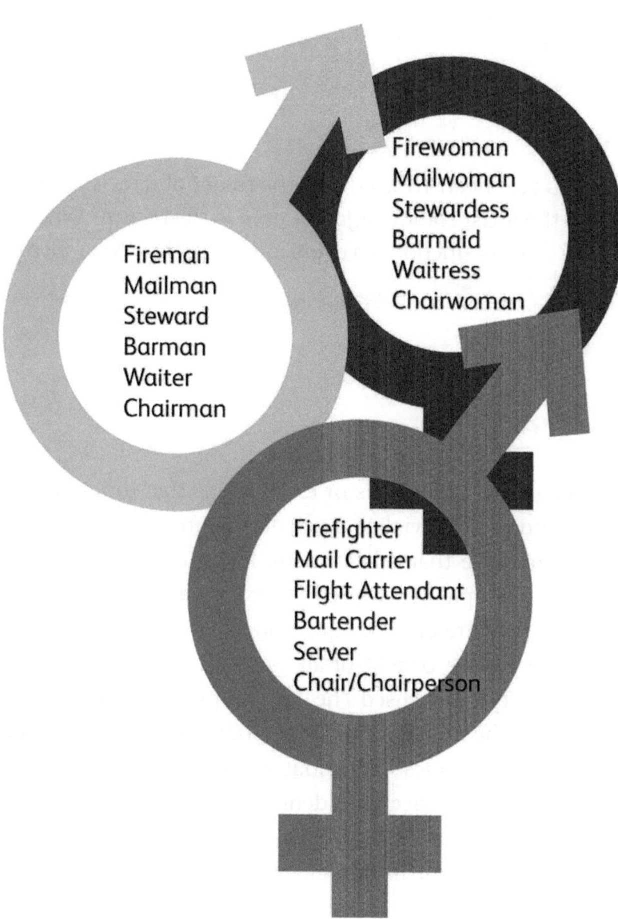

FIGURE 5.5 Sex-specific job titles

> **HOW DO YOU RATE? 5.1**
>
> **Attitudes Toward Sexist/ Nonsexist Language**
>
> As communicators, we are often unaware of the sexist implications of our language. Visit the companion website to complete a scale to assess your attitudes toward sexist language. Once you determine whether your attitude toward sexist language is positive, negative, or neutral, consider how this attitude is reflected in your communication behavior.

cisgender males in that category (Hansen, Littwitz, & Sabine, 2016). Even when a more inclusive list of references is used, such as "men and women," there is overwhelming tendency to mention men first (Willis & Jozkowski, 2018), which leads people to infer that the situation applies more commonly to men (Kesebir, 2017). Conversely, using gender-fair language, such as gender-neutral third person pronouns (e.g., "they") reduces the tendency to assume that references to people, in general, are references to men, per se (Lindqvist, Renström, & Gustafsson Sendén, 2019). These findings suggest the value of ongoing efforts to foster language that transcends the gender binary and is inclusive of the full array of gender identities.

Heterosexist Language

Heterosexist language is language that assumes heterosexuality is superior to other sexual orientations. In the most explicit form, heterosexist language includes derogatory comments, insults, jokes, or threats about the sexual practices of someone who is not heterosexual. Heterosexist language also surfaces in more subtle ways, such as references to romantic partners that assume a heterosexual relationship.

Using heterosexist language isn't just insensitive – it can also damage the development of professional and personal relationships. In one study, lesbian and gay volunteers read a transcript in which a counselor's language was edited to have either a heterosexist bias or no bias (Dorland & Fischer, 2001). In the heterosexist version, the counselor assumed the female client's partner was male and that the client would participate in heterosexual traditions like marriage. Perhaps not surprisingly, readers of the transcript rated the heterosexist counselor as less credible, less helpful, and less likely to encourage openness than the unbiased counselor. Although this study used an edited transcript, research suggests that sexual minorities regularly experience microaggressions from counselors, including statements that assume they are heterosexual, ignore their sexuality, or presume that their reason for seeking counseling is grounded in their sexuality (Spengler, Miller, & Spengler, 2016).

Specific terms in the English language also perpetuate heterosexism. Consider some of the labels used to identify different sexualities. If "heterosexual" is equivalent to "straight," does that imply that other sexualities are somehow crooked? If someone is "gay," does that mean that they are frivolous, superficial, and incapable of being serious? Research suggests that sexual and gender minority adolescents embrace a far greater variety of labels than were used even just a decade ago, including pansexual, nonbinary, and asexual (Watson, Wheldon, & Puhl, 2020). Our language use is less heterosexist when we use an array of terms that matches the nuanced ways in which people identify their sexuality.

Sometimes heterosexist language is used because of the way our language is constructed, with no explicit intention of marginalizing alternative sexualities. Other times people use derogatory sexual terms as an insult. In one study, British teens were able to identify more than 600 insulting words and phrases that included an offensive reference to a person's sexuality (Thurlow, 2001). Moreover, peer victimization (i.e., bullying) during adolescence is greater for gender nonconforming children (van Beusekom, Collier, Bos, Sandfort, & Overbeek, 2020). Being on the receiving end of such bullying has serious consequences, including an increase in suicide planning (Turpin, Boekeloo, & Dyer, 2019). In fact, one study found that exposure to bullying was among the factors differentiating transgender youth who engaged in non-suicidal self-injury from those who had attempted suicide (Taliaferro, McMorris, Rider, & Eisenberg, 2019). Beyond middle and high school, exposure to derogatory heterosexist language continues to harm people. For example, among college students, exposure to heterosexist microaggressions was associated with worse academic outcomes, such as a lower grade point average, among sexual minority students (Mathies, Coleman, McKie, Woodford, Courtice,

Travers, & Renn, 2019). These examples demonstrate the far-reaching and serious consequences of problematic language use.

Putting Theory into Practice: Using Inclusive Language

Racist, sexist, and heterosexist language is clearly damaging to interpersonal relationships and people's sense of self-worth. Given these significant consequences, we should all take steps to avoid and eliminate racist, sexist, and heterosexist language.

Confront racist language. Even if you don't produce racist messages, you contribute to racism when you allow others to use racist language. It can be challenging to speak up when someone is using language in a hurtful way, but you contribute to a more inclusive society when you confront racist language.

What can you do to stifle racist remarks? People who receive racist comments use polite corrections, witty repartee, and strong putdowns to quiet someone who is making racist remarks (Guerin, 2003). A simple comment, such as "I find that kind of language unacceptable" can go a long way toward decreasing expressions of racism. And if you are concerned that confronting a racist speaker will escalate a situation, you can vote with your feet and leave the situation.

Develop your gender- and sexuality-neutral repertoire. You may not even be aware of all the ways your language reflects gender and sexuality biases but increasing your consciousness of these language patterns can help you to make more inclusive linguistic choices. Eliminating sexist language involves replacing terms that indicate gender with genderless equivalents – *chairperson* rather than *chairman*, *fire fighter* rather than *fireman*, *flight attendant* rather than *stewardess*, etc. Likewise, you can combat heterosexist language by integrating gender-neutral terms like *partner*, *spouse*, or *significant other* into your speech. This use of language might seem awkward at first, but with time it will become second nature. And people who encounter heterosexism throughout their lives will be grateful to find someone who doesn't assume that their romantic relationships involve a person of a different sex.

One particular problem that people sometimes struggle with is avoiding the use of masculine pronouns to refer to both men and women. Students often argue that using "he" or "his" is less cumbersome than writing "he or she," "his or her" Or "they and their." As an alternative, you can rephrase a sentence to use a gender-neutral plural pronoun. The sentence "A doctor should be polite to *his* patients" excludes the possibility of female doctors, but "Doctors should be polite to *their* patients" makes the same point without the gender bias. In the same way, you can replace masculine terms to refer to humans with gender-inclusive alternatives. Instead of saying "*Man* cannot live without water," you could say "*One* cannot live without water" or "*People* cannot live without water." Avoiding sexist language isn't all that difficult, but it may take conscious effort; the pay-off is more effective interpersonal communication.

SUMMARY

Language has four core characteristics: it is abstract, arbitrary, culturally determined, and consequential. Because language is abstract, our conversations can transcend the physical world, and we can communicate about ideas, hopes, and dreams. At the same time, language is arbitrary, and it can be ambiguous; although language enables the richness of human interaction, it also introduces the potential for miscommunication. Our language is also inherently tied to our culture – in fact, language both reflects the values of a cultural group and affects how users of that verbal code process their experiences. Language can have especially profound consequences when we allow the words we use to overshadow the nuances and complexity of reality.

When we use language to communicate interpersonally, we are guided by some basic and important rules. Semantic, syntactic, and pragmatic rules inform how we structure words and utterances, use words based on their denotative and connotative meaning, and accomplish speech acts. Researchers have also identified rules or maxims that make it possible for us to make sense of verbal messages. The maxims of conversation specify that we should provide enough information (but not too much), speak truthfully, make relevant contributions to a conversation, and avoid being terse, wordy, or disorganized.

Although general features and rules of language apply in all situations, people vary in how they use language. Gender differences in language use have shown up in some people's tendency to use hedges, hesitations, and tag questions. People choose more formal language and polite phrasing when dealing with those who have greater status or power. In close relationships, informal language includes the use of nicknames, idioms, and private jokes. People even represent their intimacy through verbal cues, such as the pronouns "we" and "us."

Language also has destructive powers. Racist, sexist, and heterosexist language share the quality of marginalizing people within a society. In addition, words and phrases that implicitly privilege being White, male, or heterosexual create barriers for other ethnic groups, genders, or sexual identities in our society. Language at its worst can undermine people's well-being and their ability to contribute to their community.

Although you have been using language all of your life, you can still take steps to improve how you use verbal messages when you communicate with others. By attending to your use of language, you can harness the power of words, reduce miscommunication, reinforce the relationships that you have with interaction partners, and ensure that your verbal messages promote effective interpersonal communication. Developing your language skills may take effort and practice at first, but these communication strategies will eventually become a habitual part of more effective interpersonal interactions. Armed with the knowledge you have gained in this chapter, you are ready to consider ethical issues like those highlighted in the following exercises.

ACTIVITIES FOR EXPLORING COMMUNICATION ETHICS

What Would You/Should You Do?

Imagine that you are out with a group of friends and someone tells a joke in which they use derogatory language to refer to a particular ethnic group. No one of that ethnicity is represented in your social group, but you still recognize the power of language to marginalize certain groups of people. All of your friends are enjoying a hearty laugh at the joke. You don't want to appear as though you have no sense of humor, but you also don't want to promote such derogatory references among your peer group. What would you – should you – do in this situation?

Something to Think About

In the year 2000, a Census Bureau report indicated that one in five Americans spoke a language other than English in their home. The number of people who speak a foreign language at home more than doubled between 1990 and 2000. Of those who reported that they speak a foreign language at home, only 55% indicated that they also spoke English "very well." California, New Mexico, and Texas lead the country in the number of non-English-speaking households, with residents in Laredo, Texas, reporting that nine in ten households spoke a foreign language. What are the implications of living in a community in which people don't use the same language to express themselves? Should the United States require all citizens to speak the same language? How might such a decision further marginalize or better integrate different social groups?

Analyze Communication Ethics Yourself

Visit a local clinic and pick up an assortment of pamphlets or review websites that provide information about a variety of health topics. Review this information for evidence of racist, sexist, and heterosexist language. For example, do the pamphlets clarify whether the health information provided applies equally to people of different races, or does it assume that readers are White? Does the text use "he" or "him" to refer to people, or is the language more gender-inclusive? And are care-givers automatically assumed to be women, while men are assumed to have employment outside the home? Do the topics covered and the language that is used to refer to relationships assume that readers are heterosexual? As you reflect on the results of your analysis, consider whether people of various races, genders, and sexualities would find the health information equally helpful.

KEY WORDS

abstract language
concrete language
connotative meaning
cooperative principle
denotative meaning
idiom
language
linguistic relativity
maxim of manner
maxim of quality
maxim of quantity
maxim of relevance
pragmatic rules
racial microaggressions
reification
Sapir–Whorf hypothesis
semantic rules
speech acts
syntactic rules
totalizing

LEARNING OBJECTIVES

After reading this chapter, you should be able to:

1. Identify the channels and characteristics of nonverbal communication.
2. Explain the functions of nonverbal messages.
3. Describe similarities and differences in nonverbal behavior across cultures and genders.
4. Describe how verbal and nonverbal messages work together.
5. Describe the ways that nonverbal cues can reveal deception.

PUTTING THEORY INTO PRACTICE

In this chapter, you will learn how to:

1. Monitor nonverbal behavior more thoroughly.
2. Question your assumptions about the meaning of nonverbal behavior.
3. Make sure nonverbal cues reflect the nature of the relationship.
4. Use nonverbal cues to improve the flow of your conversations.
5. Educate yourself about nonverbal differences when you visit other cultures.
6. Be sensitive to gender differences when communicating.
7. Rely on uncommon cues to detect deception.
8. Recognize the limitations of nonverbal messages.

NONVERBAL COMMUNICATION

6

Source: Photo Researchers.

In the 2018 film, *A Quiet Place*, the Abbott family find themselves in a post-apocalyptic world where creatures with hypersensitive hearing, but no sight, attack anything that makes noise. The Abbott family must remain silent in order to survive, which poses a number of challenges to daily living. They successfully modify their home to muffle sounds from cleaning, cooking, and eating, but perhaps the most significant issue they face in their silence is that they are prevented from speaking to one another. To adapt to these circumstances, they communicate using sign language, gestures, and facial expressions. They rely on touch to get one another's attention or show affection. Just the mere act of making eye contact communicates volumes, from showing recognition and understanding, to alerting others to danger, to showing love and admiration. Although the family has lost the ability to express themselves verbally, they manage to survive and communicate using nonverbal cues.

Although the verbal messages you construct during interaction are important, your unspoken behaviors and actions are equally, if not more, vital to the communication process. Your facial expressions, posture, and vocal tones help to facilitate turn-taking during interaction, show emotion, and reveal your affection for others. The Abbott family in *A Quiet Place* relied almost exclusively on nonverbal cues to communicate with one another, but were able to maintain a rich family life through gestures, facial expressions, eye contact, and physical touch. In the same way, your interpersonal interactions with others are enriched through the use of nonverbal messages.

From the moment you wake in the morning to the minute your head hits the pillow at night, you engage in actions and behaviors that have the potential to communicate meaning to others. **Nonverbal behaviors** are human actions that have the potential to form meaningful messages. Nonverbal behaviors become nonverbal communication if they stimulate meaning in the mind of a receiver. Thus, **nonverbal communication** is defined as the process of one person creating meaning in the mind of another person through nonverbal behaviors. Communication scholars have argued that only 35% of the meaning humans derive from interaction comes from words (e.g., Birdwhistell, 2010), which means that as much as 65% of meaning comes from nonverbal behaviors. Some scholars have argued that nonverbal behavior constitutes an even greater portion of our communication, with as much as 90% being nonverbal. These statistics are difficult to test, but no one can deny the pervasive influence of nonverbal communication in shaping interaction. In this chapter, we will examine the characteristics of nonverbal communication, the functions that are served by nonverbal behaviors, and the individual differences that create challenges to nonverbal communication. In the final section of the chapter, we will consider the ways in which verbal and nonverbal messages work together by examining how interpersonal communication is used to deceive others and negotiate sexual intimacy.

WHAT IS NONVERBAL COMMUNICATION?

Have you ever been in a situation where you were able to exchange meaningful messages with an interaction partner without speaking a word? Imagine, for example, attending a boring party with a friend. Your friend catches your eye from across the room, she rolls her eyes and tilts her head in the direction of the door, you smile and nod and head for the closet to get your coats. Without speaking a word, your friend was able to convey her desire to leave and you were able to agree to her request. This example shows how nonverbal cues can provide a very efficient way to communicate with others.

Nonverbal Behaviors
Human actions that have the potential to form meaningful messages.

Nonverbal Communication
The process of creating meaning in the minds of others through nonverbal behaviors.

Channels

When people communicate with one another, they send messages back and forth through a channel. A **channel** is the medium through which information is conveyed during interaction. When you communicate nonverbally, you send information through a variety of channels on your body or in your environment. Channels for nonverbal communication include facial expressions, eye contact, body movement, gestures, touch, and physical appearance. In addition, you share or gather meaning from the physical environment, from the time you devote to interaction, and from smells. Table 6.1 summarizes the channels through which nonverbal communication occurs and gives examples of what might be conveyed through each channel.

Channel
Medium through which information is conveyed.

SCHOLAR SPOTLIGHT

Visit the Communication Café on the companion website to view a conversation with Judee Burgoon, a leading researcher on nonverbal communication.

PAUSE & REFLECT

Make a list of the nonverbal behaviors you noticed during your last conversation. Are there particular channels that you tend to pay attention to? How many channels identified in Table 6.1 were left off your list?

Notice how each channel described in Table 6.1 is capable of sending a variety of messages. Consider, for example, the category of eye behavior. When you make eye contact with another person, you could be trying to get that person's attention, showing that you're listening to what he or she has to say, flirting with a stranger, sharing an intimate moment with a romantic partner, or exerting dominance over a subordinate. The fact that such a subtle behavior like eye contact could have so many potent meanings speaks to the power of nonverbal behavior for communicating with others. On the other hand, this example reveals the complexity of creating and interpreting nonverbal messages.

TABLE 6.1 The channels of nonverbal behavior

Channels	*Behaviors*	*Examples*
Kinesics	Movement of the body: includes gestures, orientation of the body during conversation, posture	When you arrive late to a party by yourself, a friend waves and motions for you to come over by her. The people she's talking to turn toward you to greet you
Facial expressions	Movement of the facial muscles: primarily for the communication of various emotions	Your friends throw you a surprise party for your birthday. When you walk in, your eyes open wide, your eyebrows raise, and your mouth drops open, revealing your surprise
Eye behavior	Movement of the eyes: includes looking, gazing, eye contact, and pupil dilation	When studying in the library, the person at the next table keeps looking in your direction. You have made eye contact a number of times, which prompts you to say goodbye as you leave
Haptics	Touching behavior: includes shaking hands, hugging, kissing, patting on the back, tickling, or holding someone; as well as touching your own body, such as rubbing your eyes to show that you're tired	Your friend is very sad over the death of her dog. In an effort to comfort her, you put your arm around her, rub her back, and then give her a hug
Paralinguistics	Characteristics of the voice: includes volume, tone, rate of speech, pitch, intensity, vocal attributes, laughter, and silence	You pick up the telephone and recognize your best friend's voice on the other end. She is speaking softly and there is a quiver in her voice, prompting you to ask, "What's wrong?"
Physical appearance	Visible features of the body: includes body shape and size, hair style, gender, ethnicity, clothing, accessories, beauty and attractiveness	Students who attend private high schools are often required to wear a school uniform. This uniform ensures that students will appear "clean cut" and identifies the students as belonging to that institution

Channels	*Behaviors*	*Examples*
Proxemics	Use of physical space: includes arrangements of objects in physical space, markers of personal territory, and a need for personal space	You are riding in an elevator when another passenger enters, so you move to the far left corner and the other passenger stands in the far right corner to preserve your physical space. Another rider enters and stands near the front of the elevator
Chronemics	Orientation toward time: a desire to do one thing at a time versus a preference to engage in many activities at once; use of time to communicate cultural values and beliefs, power, intimacy	You arrive early to an interview for a job you really want. The interviewer still isn't back from lunch, but you wait patiently because she has power over you in this situation, and culture dictates that you should wait for more powerful people
Olfaction	Scents and odors: includes body odor, pheromones, colognes and perfumes, cleanliness, and smells in the environment	Your newest love interest has agreed to come over for dinner. To prepare for the date, you bake cookies to make your house smell good, apply perfume or cologne to your body, and light a scented candle

Characteristics

As you saw in the previous chapter, words have no physical connection to the object they represent. Nonverbal communication, on the other hand, is an analogic code system. **Analogic codes** bear a direct, physical resemblance to the object or idea that they represent. Consider the difference between using language versus nonverbal behaviors to communicate sadness. Using language, you might communicate sadness by speaking the words, "I feel sad." People who know how these words are defined will get your message, but the words themselves do not resemble the feeling of sadness. Using nonverbal behavior, you might communicate sadness through downcast eyes, a pouting mouth, crying, and a slumped body posture. These behaviors reveal the lack of physical strength and depression that a sad person typically experiences. Even in online contexts where nonverbal channels are limited, people often substitute emojis like a sad face (☹) in place of a verbal articulation of their feelings. Users can even select from a wide range of emojis that convey varying degrees

Analogic Codes
Symbols that bear a physical resemblance to the thing they represent.

of sadness, from a simple frown (😞), to a single tear (😢), or with tears pouring down the face (😭), to properly convey the intensity of their feelings. In the sections that follow, we highlight some of the characteristics of analogic codes that define nonverbal communication.

Potential for universal meaning. Because analogic codes are more likely to resemble the object or idea that they refer to, they are often more easily recognized across cultures and contexts. When symbols mean the same thing to people, regardless of cultural differences, they have universal meaning. If you have ever traveled in a country where you are unfamiliar with the language, you know all too well the communicative value of nonverbal behavior. You might point at a location on a map in order to get directions; you might mimic swimming motions to ask someone directions to the beach; or you might rub your stomach to show you are hungry and would like to find a restaurant. When you and a communication partner do not share the same meaning for digital codes, your nonverbal behaviors become especially important for interpersonal communication.

Nonverbal expressions of emotion, in particular, are widely recognized in all cultures (Matsumoto & Hwang, 2016). The similarity of emotional cues across cultures makes sense if you think about how an ability to express and understand feelings may have contributed to the evolution of humans (Floyd, 2006). Recognizing fear on the faces of others alerted people to the dangers of an approaching predator. Being able to show love and attraction enabled people to mate and produce offspring. Because the ability to express and read certain emotions evolved with the human species, expressions of emotion are similar in all cultures around the globe.

Variable Intensity
Nonverbal behaviors can show a lot or a little of the idea that they represent.

Variable intensity. Nonverbal behaviors range in terms of the strength with which they are transmitted; this quality is known as **variable intensity**. For example, the strength of your touch can fluctuate from light tickling to a tight squeeze; the smell of your cologne might vary from weak to strong; and the duration of your eye contact might constitute a fleeting glance or a long stare. Variations in nonverbal behavior are especially apparent in expressions of emotion. For example, nonverbal behaviors that convey fear – wide eyes, a contracted facial expression, and a tense body – can express a range of meanings from "a little afraid" to "scared to death." Variations in intensity are easy to see when you consider the nonverbal channel involving the voice. The volume of

FIGURE 6.1 Denise's son Quincy showing moderate happiness

FIGURE 6.2 Quincy showing intense happiness

your voice can range from a whisper to a shout; your rate of speech can vary from very slow to very fast; and the pitch of your voice can fluctuate from very high to very low. Through these variations, you can express a range of meanings.

Simultaneous transmission. People can send multiple signals through different channels at the same time. Consider the example of a father who is angry with his son. The content of his verbal message might be, "I can't believe you did that, I am very angry right now." His words only express one feeling: anger. His nonverbal behavior, on the other hand, can communicate many details about his anger, as well as other feelings, all at once. The father might simultaneously speak at a loud volume to show just how angry he is, fold his arms across his chest to show defensiveness, shake his head in disbelief, maintain very intense eye contact with his son to show dominance, and sigh heavily to show his disappointment. Unlike words, nonverbal behaviors allow you to communicate many messages at once (see Figure 6.3).

Spontaneous transmission. Most of the time, you don't have to think about how to communicate nonverbally with others. For example, if you were feeling nervous, you might unconsciously tap your foot, fidget with your hands, and speak faster at a higher pitch. Sometimes you choose nonverbal behaviors carefully to convey a specific meaning (for example, giving a thumbs up to show approval), but nonverbal communication typically requires little thought or planning. You can send signals through nonverbal channels without consciously constructing the message. Even when you know what you want to communicate, you may not be aware of your nonverbal signals. People can communicate more or

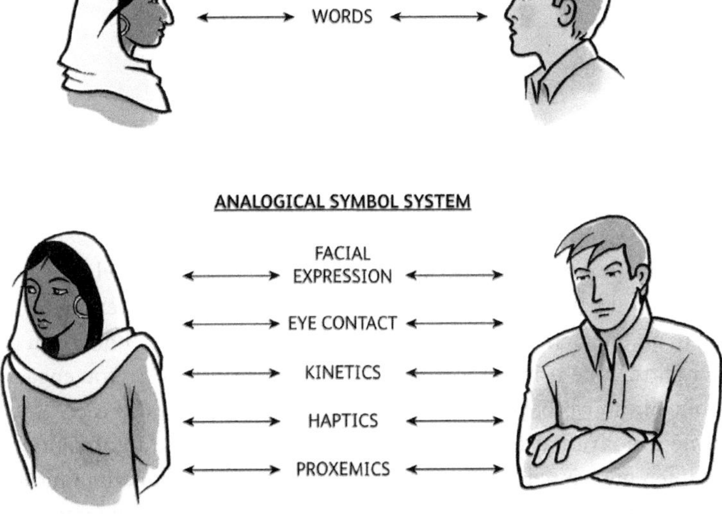

FIGURE 6.3 Communication symbol systems

less liking for a partner by changing their posture, gesturing, gazing, smiling, and nodding; however, 75% of individuals cannot accurately report an awareness of the nonverbal behaviors they use to convey increased or decreased liking for their partner (Knapp, Hall, & Horgan, 2014).

PAUSE & REFLECT

How can you tell when someone likes you? Have you ever thought that someone liked you, but it turned out that they didn't? What led you to misinterpret their behavior?

Automatic processing. Just as you don't have to think very carefully about how to send nonverbal messages, you can comprehend and respond to nonverbal messages without conscious awareness. Automatic processing refers to the ability to interpret nonverbal messages without consciously thinking about the meaning behind the behavior. Have you ever taken a single look at a friend and known that they were upset? Or have you ever had an interaction with someone who made you feel uncomfortable, but not known why? Perhaps it was his or her close proximity during conversation, shifty eyes, or inappropriate touching that made this interaction awkward, even though you couldn't put your finger on it while you were talking. You might be so quick to make judgments about other people, or to draw inferences about their feelings or relationship to you, that you don't even realize what those conclusions are based on.

Putting Theory into Practice: Being Aware of Nonverbal Cues

Nonverbal communication is a complex web of behaviors that work together to convey information. Although nonverbal cues are processed automatically, it is possible to increase your awareness of nonverbal messages.

Monitor nonverbal behavior through several channels. Remember that you have a number of different channels that can send information to an interaction partner. Try to become more aware of how you and your partner are using those channels to communicate. Are you engaging all of your nonverbal channels to send messages to others? Is each of your partner's nonverbal channels communicating the same information, or are different channels sending conflicting messages? Your communication will be improved if you use all of your channels during interaction to communicate one clear message. Make a point of consciously noticing at least five different channels for nonverbal communication every time you interact with other people. Over time, you'll find it easier to attend to more channels during your conversations. And when you take advantage of all of the nonverbal cues available to you, you'll have a more complete understanding of your interpersonal interactions.

Question your assumptions. Because you can send and process nonverbal cues spontaneously and automatically, you might have to guard against false assumptions and snap judgments. Consider how crying can be an indication of sadness, but also a sign of happiness, frustration, anger, or hurt. People can also be too quick to make assumptions about a person based on their physical appearance. Those misunderstandings can sometimes be amusing or innocuous, such as when you mistake the relatively young professor dressed to exercise as a fellow student. On the other hand, snap judgments can be deadly when a young Black man in a hoodie is deemed out of place walking through a mostly White neighborhood, as in the case of Trayvon Martin. Sometimes when you rush to judgment about a person, the meaning you assign to someone's appearance or behavior is based on incorrect stereotypes or implicit biases. Interpreting nonverbal messages correctly might require you to question your initial reactions, consider the context for the interaction, and check your biases.

COMMUNICATION IN ACTION 6.1

Witnessing Nonverbal Behavior in Context

This exercise asks you to compare the meaning of various nonverbal behaviors depending on the context and the relationship in which they are enacted. Use the form on the companion website to take notes as you observe people interacting from each of the categories listed. How did the nonverbal behaviors differ from one category of relationship to another? Did behaviors that occurred in each interaction (for example, touch) mean the same things? Were there ways in which the meaning behind the nonverbal behaviors were the same, regardless of the relational context?

THE FUNCTIONS OF NONVERBAL MESSAGES

Nonverbal communication accomplishes a variety of social tasks, such as revealing your feelings, showing people that you like them, conveying respect to a superior, and managing the flow of conversation. Your nonverbal channels play an important role in communicating each of these different messages. In this section, we focus on the ways that the different nonverbal channels combine to serve a variety of functions during interaction.

Communicating Emotion

One primary function of nonverbal messages is to let other people know what we're feeling. Sometimes it's hard to verbalize emotions to others and nonverbal expressions come more easily. For example, finding the words to describe feelings of anger can be challenging, but your tense body, scowling face, and loud voice automatically display your underlying emotions.

PAUSE & REFLECT

Have you had a feeling that you couldn't fully express through words? How did the emotion reveal itself through your body? How does your voice change when you're feeling happy, frightened, angry, or sad?

The face is an especially powerful channel for revealing emotions. People express emotions through three regions of the face: the mouth, the eyes, and the forehead (Rosenberg & Ekman, 2020). For example, in the lower part of the face, a smile corresponds with happiness, a frown indicates sadness, and a wide open mouth reveals surprise. The eyes also distinguish between different emotions, for example, they open wide in fear and glare in anger. When you study the forehead, you'll see that the eyebrows raise up during surprise, furrow during anger, and droop during sadness. Interestingly, people can recognize emotions when shown only one region of the face, and many facial expressions of emotion – happiness, sadness, fear, anger, disgust, surprise, contempt, shame, shyness, and guilt – are universally recognized (Floyd, 2006; Fridlund & Russell, 2006).

COMMUNICATION IN ACTION 6.2

Forming Facial Expressions of Emotion

This exercise will make you more aware of the nuances in your facial expressions of emotion. Sit in front of a mirror and form a facial expression for each of the emotions listed in the table on the companion website. For each emotion, write down the characteristics that you see in each of the three areas of the face. Which emotion was easiest or hardest for you to express? What region of the face reveals the most information about the underlying emotion?

The voice is another channel that reveals emotions. In fact, vocal cues sometimes convey emotions better than facial expressions (Knapp et al., 2014). Sadness and anger, in particular, are more recognizable in vocal cues than in other nonverbal channels (Scherer, Clark-Polner, & Mortillaro, 2011). That is why when your best friend calls on the phone, you can tell whether he or she is having a good day or a bad day in the first 30 seconds of the conversation just by the tone in his or her voice. A slower, quieter, lower pitched voice with longer pauses communicates sadness; a faster, louder higher pitched voice with more variation in tone conveys happiness or joy; and a higher pitch, vocal tremors, and speech dysfluencies (e.g., stutters, repetition) communicate anxiety (Bänziger, Patel, & Scherer, 2014). Because the voice is more difficult to control than facial expressions, it can be a more reliable indicator of a person's feelings.

Although much of nonverbal behavior is natural and automatic, some of it is also a learned response to social situations. **Simulation** occurs when you display emotions that you are not actually feeling. For example, you might smile for a photograph even though you aren't feeling particularly happy. **Intensification** occurs when your display of a particular emotion is stronger than you are actually experiencing. When someone gives you a gift, you might display stronger happiness than you are actually feeling to ensure that they know you are grateful. **Deintensification** refers to the tendency to downplay particularly strong emotions. For example, you might be elated over the A you received on your midterm, but you might act only mildly pleased so that your friend who got a D doesn't feel badly. Finally, **masking** occurs when people show an entirely different emotion from the one that they are truly feeling. An Oscar nominee for best supporting actress might clap and smile when one of the competitors wins the award, but she probably feels disappointed and maybe a little jealous.

Simulation
Displaying emotions that are not actually felt.

Intensification
Displaying emotions that are stronger than the felt emotion.

Deintensification
Downplaying particularly strong emotions.

Masking
Displaying a different emotion from the one that is truly felt.

Communicating Liking

How do you behave when you like someone? How can you tell when someone really likes you? You may determine whether a person likes you or not by focusing on the immediacy of their nonverbal behavior. **Immediacy** is the degree of physically or psychologically perceived warmth and involvement between people. In general, people are more well liked when they show more immediate nonverbal behaviors, because they seem friendly, supportive, and kind (Andersen, Guerrero, & Jones, 2006). In this section, you'll learn about some of the nonverbal behaviors that contribute to perceptions of immediacy.

Immediacy
The degree of physically or psychologically perceived closeness.

Eye contact is central to expressions of liking. During conversation, people often judge how interested or involved a partner is based on the amount of eye contact that he or she displays. People rate partners who make a lot of eye contact as more intimate, more attracted to one another, and more trusting than partners who make less eye contact (Montoya, Kershaw, & Prosser, 2018). Likewise, your own eye contact reveals your feelings for a partner. For example, communication partners who are in love are more likely to gaze at one another (Belmont, Cacioppo, & Cacioppo, 2014).

Touch is another nonverbal behavior that reveals liking and intimacy in a relationship. Touch is a strong communicator of immediacy, because it brings people together, both physically and psychologically (Ben-Ari & Lavee, 2007). Communicating affection for a relationship partner through various forms of touch, such as hugging, kissing, or holding hands, can increase relational intimacy, decrease stress, and provide a number of health benefits for both senders and receivers of affection (Floyd, 2018). Receiving a hug from a relationship partner on the same day that the couple engaged in interpersonal conflict can help attenuate negative emotions arising from the fight (Murphy, Janicki-Deverts, & Cohen, 2018). Similarly, affectionate touching can generally lower daily stress levels (Floyd et al., 2009). In general, affectionate touch between relationship partners can improve relationship quality and contribute to individuals' psychological and physical well-being (Jakubiak & Feeney, 2017).

PAUSE & REFLECT

Can you think of a situation when you were uncomfortable with a touch that you received from someone? What were the circumstances that made this touch problematic?

HOW DO YOU RATE? 6.1

Nonverbal Immediacy

Visit the companion website to complete a scale that measures people's tendency to display nonverbal immediacy. As you reflect on your nonverbal immediacy score, think about how your interaction partner may have perceived you during the interaction. Do you think your partner felt liked or disliked by you? What can you do to be perceived as more immediate in your future interactions?

Body movements can also contribute to perceptions of immediacy and liking. People tend to interact at closer proximities with individuals they like and interacting at a closer personal distance tends to foster more attraction, warmth, liking, and positive attitudes about one's partner (Andersen, Gannon, & Kalchik, 2013). One study asked participants to have a conversation with another person about a personal problem and then rate how supportive their partner was during the interaction (Bodie, Vickery, Cannava, & Jones, 2015). The study showed that people who showed more smiling, nodding, gesturing, relaxed posture, and a direct body orientation were perceived as better listeners and more supportive than people who demonstrated fewer of these behaviors. These findings demonstrate the impact of body movements on perceptions of immediacy, supportiveness, and liking.

Communicating Power and Status

In the United States, people are socialized to recognize differences in power and status. Power refers to a person's ability to influence and control the actions of others. People can gain power based on their status, which is their social position within a given community or culture. In other words, status refers to a person's position in the social or professional hierarchy, and power refers to the degree of influence that person derives from their position. In general, powerful people tend to make a good first impression.

Even before any words are spoken, a person's physical appearance communicates volumes about his or her power and status. Research indicates that people who are more physically attractive tend to be rated as more intelligent and competent during job interviews (Zebrowitz, Montepare, & Strom, 2013). In contrast, interviewees with visible scars or birthmarks on their cheek are rated as less desirable and interviewers recalled less information about them as compared to their peers without these physical characteristics (Madera & Hebl, 2012). Another study found that African American men with soft facial features were rated as warmer and more honest than those with hard facial features, and they were also more likely to climb the ranks of their organization to positions of higher status and power (Livingston & Pearce, 2009). In general, people who are physically attractive tend to be seen as having more power and higher status than others. This phenomenon is known as the **halo effect**, or the tendency to attribute positive personality traits to attractive people.

Halo Effect
The tendency for physically attractive people to be perceived as having other positive characteristics.

Your voice also reveals a great deal about your status and power. People with more power tend to have vocal qualities associated with assuredness, confidence, maturity, animation, and extroversion. Compare, for example, the different degrees of authority associated with the deep, smooth voice of Dwayne "The Rock" Johnson versus the high pitched, screechy voice of his frequent comedic counterpart Kevin Hart. People

FIGURE 6.4 Showing disinterest

Source: www.cartoonstock.com.

perceive speakers who are louder overall and who change their volume throughout an utterance as more dominant (Tusing & Dillard, 2000). Individuals with status and power also tend to speak longer, have more speaking turns, and are more successful at interrupting others during conversation (Mast, 2002). Interestingly, research shows that individuals with lower pitched voices are more likely to win elected office, though vocal pitch is not actually associated with leadership ability (Klofstad & Anderson, 2018). Thus, a variety of vocal cues can reveal power and status in interpersonal interactions.

High power people also command more physical space. In the business world, people who have the most status within an organization are typically given the most spacious and private offices. In addition, people with higher status adopt more expansive and relaxed postures, whereas people with less power are more constricted and tensed (Park et al., 2013). High status people will likely lean back in their chair and adopt an open posture with their arms and legs, but a low status person is more likely to lean forward and slouch a bit during interaction. In general, these behaviors allow the high status person to stretch their bodies, whereas the low status person is confined to a smaller space.

Notably, the nonverbal behaviors that convey power and dominance can also be misused to create a climate of mistreatment in relationships and organizations. Toxic interactions often involve at least some degree of nonverbal behavior that capitalizes on uneven power dynamics. For example, bullying can often involve an invasion of personal space, aggressive touching, and sustained or uncomfortable staring (Einarsen, Hoel, & Notelaersa, 2009). People also enact mistreatment and discrimination through more subtle nonverbal behaviors. Microaggressions, for example, involve subtle behaviors that communicate denigration (Cortina, 2008; Nadal, 2011). Microaggressions can involve subtle forms of discrimination, including hostile body language, decreased smiling, a rude or irritated tone of voice, or limited eye contact (Hess, 2013). Thus, people with high power or status positions must be mindful of the ways in which their nonverbal behavior communicates dominance and potentially marginalizes individuals with less power.

IDEA: PROMOTING INCLUSION, DIVERSITY, EQUITY, AND ACCESS

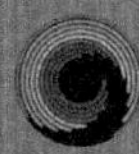

Individuals from marginalized groups often receive mistreatment and microaggressions from individuals who enjoy higher status and power. Consider the overt verbal discrimination, as well as more subtle nonverbal messages, that people might receive based on their race, gender identity, body size, or disability. How might discrimination and mistreatment manifest in nonverbal communication in different social or professional contexts?

Regulating Conversation

Interpersonal communication is like a carefully choreographed dance that requires the coordination of behaviors between two individuals. People can send and respond to cues that guide them in initiating a conversation, taking turns speaking, and signaling the desire to end it. Consider all of the ways you signal that you are ready and willing to communicate with another person. You might initiate interaction by making eye contact with another person. For example, heterosexual women initiate eye contact with potential male suitors in an effort to invite the male to engage in interaction with them (Moore, 2010). You could also initiate interaction by moving closer to others and sometimes touching them to get their attention. Body orientation is also a common tool for initiating conversation, such as when doctors orient their bodies away from patients until they are ready to hear the patient's physical ailments and then turn toward patients when it is okay for them to speak (Robinson, 2006).

Once a conversation is underway, the intricate dance of turn-taking begins (see Figure 6.5). Duncan and Fiske's (2015) model of turn-taking behavior outlines the behaviors that people enact depending on their goal during the interaction. When you want to speak during a conversation, you might nod your head several times in rapid succession and/or start making sounds. **Back-channel communication** refers to non-language utterances like "mm-hmm" and "uh-huh." When you make back-channel sounds while a person is still speaking, it shows that you understand your partner and either encourages them to continue or signals that he or she can stop talking. When you are speaking and you don't want someone to interrupt, you might talk more loudly and gesture more vigorously. When you are finished making a point and want your partner to speak, you establish eye contact, relax your gestures, and increase or decrease the pitch of your voice at the end of your sentence. And what if your partner stops talking, and you have nothing to say? You can try to avoid talking

Back-channel Communication
Non-language utterances that show understanding or involvement and help to move an interaction along.

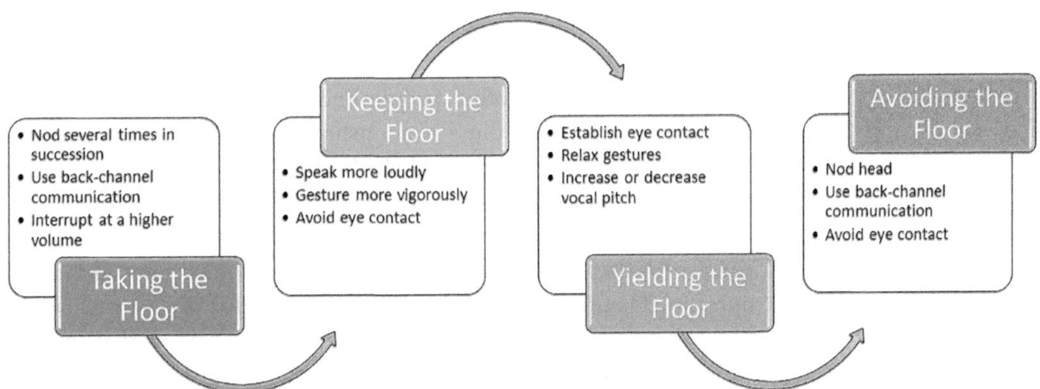

FIGURE 6.5 Nonverbal cues for regulating conversation

by nodding your head or using back-channel communication instead. In combination, these nonverbal behaviors help to move the interaction along and manage turn-taking between partners during the conversation.

PAUSE & REFLECT

What do you do when you are talking on the telephone to help regulate the interaction? Are there ways in which this process is more or less challenging than face-to-face communication?

Finally, a number of nonverbal behaviors mark the end of a conversation. As partners draw near the end of their interaction, they partially turn away from one another. They tend to move farther from each other, nod more, and reduce eye contact as they reveal their desires to end the conversation. Partners also tend to start talking over one another at the end of conversations. The last moment in an interaction often involves some sort of touch, such as a pat on the upper arm, a handshake, a hug, or a kiss. In these ways, you use nonverbal behaviors to bring your conversations with others to an end.

Putting Theory into Practice: Managing Relationships and Interaction

As you have seen, your nonverbal behaviors serve critical functions within interpersonal interactions. In this section, we discuss how you might harness the power of nonverbal communication to improve your relationships and interactions with others.

Make sure nonverbal cues reflect the nature of a relationship. Using words to express how much you like a person can be difficult or uncomfortable, but nonverbal behaviors are a clear and easy way to show others that you like them. Make an effort to enact nonverbal behaviors that let other people know that you care about them; your actions will make those relationships more rewarding and secure. In particular, smiling and nodding during conversations with friends shows them that you enjoy their company. Hugging a family member demonstrates your support during difficult times. Kissing a romantic partner for the first time can be an important turning point in the relationship (Manusov, Docan-Morgan, & Harvey, 2015). Even when you have a hard time expressing your feelings in words, nonverbal cues can still communicate how you feel.

Similarly, skillful communicators are clear about power dynamics so that messages can be exchanged more effectively. Denise used to get puzzled when some students refused her invitation to call her by her first name; eventually, however, she realized that those individuals were more comfortable communicating with her when their status differences were clear. When you are the one with more status, remember that you are expected to set the emotional tone for the interaction, to act with dignity or authority, to signal the beginning and end of the conversation, and to accept messages that convey respect. When the nature of your power relations is clear, you and your partner can focus your attention on other aspects of your interaction.

Use nonverbal cues to improve the flow of your conversations. Look for cues from your interaction partner to know when it is appropriate to speak. If your partner is gesturing actively and looking away from you, recognize that he wants to keep talking. When you simply must break in, don't just interrupt your partner; instead, use head nods and back-channel sounds to signal your eagerness to contribute. When you have the speaking floor, be sure that you are responsive when your partner uses those same signs to let you know she has something to say. And you can avoid catching your partner off-guard by giving cues that you are about to stop talking; making eye contact with your partner, relaxing your gestures, and changing your pitch are signals that invite your partner to get ready to speak. When you regulate interactions using these nonverbal behaviors, your communication will be more efficient, effective, and enjoyable.

COMMUNICATION IN ACTION 6.3

Charting the Course of Interaction

In this exercise, you'll learn to recognize the nonverbal cues that serve to regulate interaction. Observe two people engaged in conversation and pay attention to the nonverbal behaviors they use to regulate their interaction. Complete the table on the companion website with the different behaviors you notice as people initiate conversation, begin or end a speaking turn, interrupt a partner, or end the interaction.

INDIVIDUAL DIFFERENCES

Generally, people are more similar than different in the ways that they communicate nonverbally. Many of the behaviors you enact to display your emotions, manage relationships, and facilitate interactions are similar across cultures. Likewise, people of different genders have many of the same goals for interaction, and they are able to communicate with one another with relatively few misunderstandings. Nevertheless, differences do exist in nonverbal behavior across cultures and among genders.

Differences Across Cultures

Famous actors from around the globe have portrayed characters from cultures different from their own. For example, in the television series *The Americans*, Welsh actor Matthew Rhys portrayed an undercover Russian spy who convincingly assimilated as an American suburbanite. American actor, Gillian Anderson, adopted a British accent to portray former Prime Minister Margaret Thatcher in *The Crown*. Antony Starr played Homelander in *The Boys*, a quintessential American character played by a native New Zealander. What nonverbal behaviors do these actors have to use in order to perform their cross-cultural roles convincingly? Nonverbal markers of cultural identity are so deeply ingrained that you rarely even recognize the symbols and behaviors that display your culture. Only when you are given the opportunity to interact with people from other cultures do you begin to realize how you take your nonverbal codes for granted.

Emblems
Gestures that have a direct verbal translation.

One of the most recognizable and problematic differences between cultures involves the use of gestures called emblems. **Emblems** are gestures that have a direct verbal translation, such as the peace sign, waving hello or goodbye, the OK symbol, or extending your middle finger. These gestures have very specific meanings in American culture, but they are often interpreted differently in other cultures around the world. For example, the OK sign indicates understanding or implies that everything is good in the United States, but the same gesture in Brazil is an insult similar to raising your middle finger. In France, the OK sign means zero, and in Japan it is the symbol for money. These differences create countless opportunities for misunderstanding when people from different cultures communicate.

Monochronic Time Orientation
A cultural trait that reflects a desire to do one thing at a time.

Polychronic Time Orientation
A cultural trait that stresses informality and reflects little regard for artificial schedules.

Another prominent difference between cultures is how people think about and use time. A **monochronic time orientation** reflects a desire to do one thing at a time. Countries that adopt a monochronic orientation toward time include Britain, Germany, Finland, Norway, Sweden, Canada, and the United States. In these countries, people keep rigid schedules and they view time as a commodity that can be spent, saved, or wasted. In contrast, a **polychronic time orientation** disregards artificial schedules and stresses informality. Many Latin American and Arab cultures adopt a polychronic time orientation, where people are comfortable scheduling many activities at once and don't adhere to a rigid schedule. Likewise, "island time" refers to the relaxed view of time common in many tropical locations.

PAUSE & REFLECT

Do you tend to be punctual or more relaxed about your time commitments? How is your personal preference rewarded or punished in your culture?

Each culture also has a different idea about what is attractive in terms of clothing, body shape, ornamentation, and artifacts (Regan, 2016). In Western cultures like the United States, perceptions of beauty have become heavily influenced by media representations of thin, full-lipped, large-breasted female supermodels and muscular, broad-chested, male athletes. These images are not the gold standard of beauty in other cultures. One of Jen's friends was traveling in India when she noticed two male shopkeepers looking her up and down and commenting to one another as she shopped. She assumed that they were talking about how beautiful she was, but her translator told her that they were actually disgusted by how thin she was. The thin ideal that is valued in the United States is far from universal. Some media outlets have started to recognize the need to provide more diverse images of beauty and are more inclusive in their advertising. In the United States, Dove started using more "regular-sized" models in their advertising. In Germany, *Brigitte* magazine went so far as to ban professional models from appearing in the publication and replaced them with images of "real-life" women.

Gender Differences

Have you noticed any differences in the ways that people of different genders communicate nonverbally? Most researchers agree that people of different genders are more similar than different in their communication patterns (Hall & Gunnery, 2013); however, some subtle differences have been documented. For example, women have been found to smile more than men, which is a tendency that is exaggerated when women know that they are being observed (LaFrance, Hecht, & Paluck, 2003). Women also gaze more at their interaction partners during conversation (Hall & Gunnery, 2013), with gaze and physical touch being most prominent in interactions between two women (Derlega, Catanzaro, & Lewis, 2001). Women are also more likely to engage in back-channel communication (e.g., nodding, saying "mm-hmm") when listening to others (Leaper & Robnett, 2011), whereas men are more likely to interject and interrupt others who are speaking (Brescoll, 2011). Other research shows that women are more likely to use touch to convey sympathy, whereas men are more likely to use touch when communicating anger (Hertenstein & Keltner, 2011). Thus, although gender differences in nonverbal communication are not necessarily widespread, there are some subtle differences in the form and function of nonverbal behaviors across genders.

Evolution accounts for some of the variation in nonverbal behavior between males and females. For example, males and females evolved with different body structures and appearances in order to facilitate mating and carry out traditional gender roles (Floyd, 2006). Furthermore, women tend to be more expressive in the face and tend to reveal their emotions, especially positive emotions, more frequently than men (Brody & Hall,

2000; Alexander & Wood, 2000). Men, on the other hand, are more likely than women to display anger (Hess, Adams, Grammar, & Kleck, 2009). These differences probably evolved because of the roles males and females played in ancient societies. An ability to express frequent and positive emotions would have helped women provide nurturing to infants and encourage socialization, whereas anger might have helped men ward off predators and convey dominance (Sell, Cosmides, & Tooby, 2014; Tay, 2015). Thus, some of the differences in the nonverbal behaviors of men and women likely served important evolutionary functions.

IDEA: PROMOTING INCLUSION, DIVERSITY, EQUITY, AND ACCESS

Most of the existing research on gender differences in nonverbal communication contrast the actions of cisgender men and women as a gender binary. What are scholars missing when they overlook the experiences of gender and sexual minorities in their research? In what ways might nonverbal communication be different or unique for individuals who are transgender, intersex, or gender nonconforming?

An alternative explanation for gender differences in nonverbal communication is related to the ways that men and women are socialized into their respective gender roles. From a very young age, children begin to imitate behaviors that are modeled to them by parents and other caregivers. For example, research has shown that infants can imitate some facial expressions and gestures within the first few days of life (Soussignan et al., 2018). Notably, due to cultural norms and implicit stereotypes about gender, parents and other caregivers often display different nonverbal behaviors for sons than for daughters. One example is that mothers tend to be more expressive and show more positive emotions with their daughters than with their sons (van der Pol et al., 2015). In turn, girls are more skilled than boys at recognizing facial expressions of emotion (Székely et al., 2011), and women tend to be more emotionally expressive than men (LaFrance & Vial, 2016). Women are also better at recalling other people's nonverbal behaviors during interaction, such as gazing, smiling, and self-touching (Hall, Murphy, & Schmid Mast, 2006). Thus, as children learn to model nonverbal behaviors that are shown to them by parents and other caregivers, they are socialized to behave in stereotypically gendered ways.

One final explanation for gender differences in nonverbal behavior is that gendered behaviors are reinforced. In general, young girls are rewarded for performing traditionally "female" behaviors, and young boys are rewarded for performing traditionally "male" behaviors. For a specific example, consider how males and females might come to prefer different degrees of closeness during interaction. As infants, girls tend to be cradled and held more close to the body, whereas boys are more often playfully tossed into the air or allowed to lie independently in a crib or on a blanket. As boys and girls start to grow up, the toys, games, and activities that girls tend to enjoy (e.g., dolls, playing house) require less space than the games that boys like to play (e.g., trucks, cops and robbers). Thus, from a very early age, boys are conditioned to want and need more physical space, and girls are socialized to want and need less space. Not surprisingly, then, women interact at closer distances and have been found to face their interaction partner more directly than men (Hall & Gunnery, 2013). In contrast, men require and are given more physical space both during interactions and for their daily activities (Vrugt & Luyerink, 2000), which is related to perceptions of power and dominance (Hall, Coats, & LeBeau, 2005).

Putting Theory into Practice: Embracing Individual Differences

Although nonverbal communication is more similar than different across cultures and genders, increasing your awareness of individual differences in nonverbal behavior can lead to more effective communication.

Educate yourself about nonverbal differences when you visit other cultures. When you plan foreign travel, learn some key nonverbal emblems along with handy phrases. The Communication in Action 6.4 exercise can get you started. And when you are at home, cultivate tolerance toward those who are struggling with the nonverbal codes of American culture. Deal patiently with errors in cross-cultural interactions and try to explain the behaviors that are appropriate in your culture.

COMMUNICATION IN ACTION 6.4

Nonverbal Meaning Across Cultures

Do some research about a culture that you have always been interested in learning more about, or a culture that you plan to visit one day. For this activity, you might find some fascinating differences if you focus on a culture that is very different from the United States, like African, Middle Eastern, or Asian cultures. Use search engines on the Internet to find answers to the following questions: What are the meaningful nonverbal gestures and emblems in this culture? What are considered appropriate styles of dress for people of different genders? What is proper etiquette during meal times? How are power and status denoted in the culture? When you have identified meaningful cultural practices, compare that culture's behaviors to those in the United States. How are they similar and how are they different?

Be sensitive to gender differences when communicating with people of a different gender. Even though people are mostly similar in their nonverbal behaviors, you'll communicate more effectively if you are sensitive to the potential for gender differences. In particular, could you try to be more or less expressive with your nonverbal cues in order to match the expressiveness of your interaction partner? In addition, remember that some people still experience strong emotions, even if their nonverbal cues of emotion are not as strong as other people's. Understanding the small differences in the ways people communicate nonverbally will make a big difference in how you understand nonverbal messages.

COMBINING VERBAL AND NONVERBAL CUES

Verbal and nonverbal messages weave a complex web of understanding during the communication process. Table 6.2 summarizes four of the ways that verbal and nonverbal messages combine during interaction. Nonverbal behaviors can **complement** language, meaning that they enhance or help to illustrate the ideas that are being spoken. Nonverbal behaviors can also **accent** verbal messages by adding emphasis to particular words or phrases. Nonverbal behaviors sometimes **substitute** verbal messages, by replacing a word that conveys the same meaning. Finally, nonverbal behaviors can **contradict** verbal messages when nonverbal cues are in contrast to the words that are spoken.

Complementing
When nonverbal cues enhance ideas that are being spoken.

Accenting
When nonverbal cues add emphasis to a word or phrase.

Substituting
When nonverbal cues replace a word that conveys the same meaning.

Contradicting
When nonverbal cues are in contrast to the words that are spoken.

In combination, verbal and nonverbal cues can either clarify or confuse the intended meaning of the message. When verbal and nonverbal messages are consistent, there are fewer opportunities for miscommunication. At other times, discrepancies between verbal and nonverbal cues create challenges to communication. Consider the examples of deceptive communication and negotiations of sexual intimacy. In the first case, we'll see that the effort required to craft untrue messages is often revealed by nonverbal cues. When sexual involvement is being negotiated, an ambiguous mix of verbal and nonverbal cues can have more dire consequences.

The Signs of Deception

Everybody lies. A *Reader's Digest* poll revealed that 93% of respondents admitted to lying at work, school, or business, and 96% admitted that they had lied to family and friends (Kalish, 2004). Across various studies, individuals indicate that they tell between 0.59 and 1.96 lies per day, with people lying more over mediated channels of communication than face-to-face (Serota, Levine, & Boster, 2010). You can probably remember a time when you tried to deceive someone. What was your lie about? Was it a big lie, or a little white lie? Did you get away with it, or did you get caught? **Deception** is defined as intentional and strategic behavior

Deception
Intentional and strategic behavior designed to promote a false belief within another person.

TABLE 6.2 Combinations of verbal and nonverbal messages

Function	*Definition*	*Example*
Complementing	When nonverbal messages enhance or help to illustrate the ideas that are being spoken	You might hug and kiss a romantic partner while speaking the words "I love you"
Accenting	When nonverbal behaviors add emphasis to particular words and phrases	When professors want to make sure that students understand an idea, they might pause after a sentence to indicate that this was an important thought
Substituting	When nonverbal behaviors replace a word that conveys the same meaning	If someone asked you how you did on your midterm exam, you might make the "OK" symbol with your hand instead of saying "I did fine"
Contradicting	When nonverbal behaviors are in contrast to the words that are spoken	A person might say "I'm all right," but their tear-stained face and quivering voice would send a different message

designed to promote a false belief or conclusion within another person. In this section, we describe the ways in which verbal and nonverbal cues combine to reveal deceit, and we discuss some of the nonverbal cues that are markers of deception.

Patterns of behavior that reveal deception. Although there are a number of culturally transmitted stereotypes about the nonverbal behaviors that are indicative of lying – liars won't make eye contact, they fidget, they talk fast, they stammer and stutter, etc. – these isolated nonverbal behaviors are actually not very reliable indicators of deception (Hartwig & Bond, 2014). Detecting deception becomes much easier when you focus on patterns and inconsistencies in the person's nonverbal behavior. If you have ever caught someone in a lie, you might have noticed that statements made later in the conversation contradicted statements made at the beginning, or perhaps his or her gestures seemed to contradict the words being spoken. The person may have acted calm and aloof, but at the same time kept tapping his or her foot, fidgeting with a button or piece of jewelry, and speaking with a higher pitch. Examinations of people's perceptions of courtroom testimony reveal that stereotypically deceptive behaviors don't necessarily trigger suspicion, but inconsistent nonverbal behaviors are frequently interpreted as deceptive regardless of the specific actions that are performed (Henningsen, Cruz, & Morr, 2000).

CONNECT WITH THEORY

Visit the companion website to read more about interpersonal deception theory and the features of interpersonal interaction and relationships that provide cues to detecting deception.

Research has also shown that familiarity with a person's typical nonverbal behaviors makes it easier to identify discrepancies and detect deception. In particular, people are better able to tell whether a partner is telling the truth or lying when they have previous experience with that person's truthful behavior (Vrij, 2008). In close relationships, people have the benefit of increased knowledge about a person's normal behavior, which should make it easier to detect inconsistencies. On the other hand, people tend to believe that the people they care about are usually truthful, so they aren't always on the lookout for deception (Levine, 2014). Interpersonal deception theory (Burgoon & Buller, 2015) brings together several assumptions about the strategic action that individuals take to manage information, behavior, and their personal image in a deceptive encounter. In general, detecting deception requires individuals to question their assumptions about their partner's personal characteristics, relational history, and situational features.

Nonverbal Leakage
When a deceiver subconsciously reveals their deception through uncontrollable nonverbal behaviors.

Specific cues that reveal deception. Supposedly, liars can't look you in the eye, they fidget nervously, or they might smile when not speaking the truth. In fact, because these traits are generally seen as revealing a lie, many people become skilled at controlling these behaviors. The result, then, is that cues to deception arise in channels that are more difficult for people to control. **Nonverbal leakage** occurs when a deceiver subconsciously reveals their deception through uncontrollable nonverbal behaviors. For example, a liar may not have shifty eyes, but the eyes can signal whether a person is lying or telling the truth. The pupils may dilate during deception, which is an impossible behavior to control (Trifiletti et al., 2020). Research also shows that deception corresponds with increased blinking of the eyes (Leal & Vrij, 2008).

PAUSE & REFLECT

Is there a person in your life whom you can always peg as honest or dishonest? How does their behavior change when they lie? What cues do you rely on to tell if they are lying or telling the truth?

The voice is another nonverbal channel that is difficult to control and, therefore, it provides a cue to deception. One of the most consistent findings is that deceivers display a higher rate of speech errors, such as stutters, mispronunciations, and other disfluencies (Loy, Rohde, & Corley, 2017). In addition, research indicates that deception is associated with higher vocal pitch, increased vocal tension, and a shorter duration of speaking turns (DePaulo et al., 2003).

Finally, there are two types of facial expressions that indicate potential deception. Research shows that people struggle to control regions of the face while telling lies, therefore unsuppressed smiles and raised eyebrows

FIGURE 6.6 A mother scolds her daughter for lying.

Source: JGI/Jamie Grill

often emerge as cues to deception (Hurley & Frank, 2011). A second and especially telling sign of deception is the presence of **micro-momentary facial expressions** – fleeting and virtually unobservable expressions of underlying emotion (Porter & Ten Brinke, 2008). In the case of deception, there is often a micro-momentary expression of distress in which the eyebrows rise up, creating a cluster of wrinkles in the center of the forehead that are typically unperceivable to observers in real time.

Micro-momentary Facial Expressions
Brief unobservable expressions of underlying emotion.

INSIDE COMMUNICATION RESEARCH

Interaction Synchrony as a Cue to Deception

Conversational partners have to attend to a variety of different goals in order to achieve a successful interaction. In order to create an effective conversational climate under normal circumstances, individuals need to promote pleasant feelings, avoid discomfort, and maintain face for themselves and their partner. People who are trying to deceive their interaction partner must simultaneously manage an additional set of interaction goals that involve crafting a believable message, avoiding detection, and minimizing damage if they are caught. One way that deceivers might build rapport with their target and increase the believability of their lies is through the strategic use of interaction synchrony, which involves adapting communication behaviors in ways that align or coordinate actions between partners. Interaction synchrony can involve mirroring, matching, or reciprocating interpersonal communication behaviors. In general, synchronized communication behavior is perceived more positively and fosters more connection and satisfaction with interactions than unsynchronized actions. Under these conditions, individuals are more likely to assume that their partner is being truthful and, therefore, are less likely to successfully detect deception.

A team of researchers led by communication scholars, Norah Dunbar and Howard Giles, conducted a study to determine how interaction synchrony affected people's perceptions of interaction and ability to detect deception (Dunbar et al., 2020). In this study, college undergraduates who had not met previously were separately asked to brainstorm three things that they loved about their university and to engage in a conversation about these ideas. Prior to the interaction, one partner was instructed to manipulate their involvement in the interaction. Half the sample was instructed to show high involvement, such as leaning forward, sitting on the edge of their seat, making direct eye contact, nodding, and smiling. The other half showed low involvement, in which they would seem disinterested, distracted, low energy, and avoid eye contact, smiling, and nodding. The other partner was instructed to be either deceptive or truthful in their description of things they love about the university. The researchers coached the participants prior to the interaction to help them think through what they were going to say and how they would attempt to lie. Then, the partners were asked to have a conversation about the ideas they brainstormed and after the interaction they completed surveys in which they rated the trustworthiness of the partner, rapport, involvement, synchrony, and satisfaction with the interaction. Later, the researchers watched videos of the interactions to identify moments of interactional synchrony between partners. The researchers coded the interactions manually, but also used a computer program to detect synchronous rhythms that would be undetectable to the human eye.

Results showed that most people (84.7%) perceived their partner to be truthful or were unsure about their partner's truthfulness (11.7%). Only 3.6% believed their partner was being deceitful, which provides evidence of a strong truth bias in these conversations. Notably, of the people who classified their partner as a deceiver, only one of them was correct. Thus, deceivers were virtually indistinguishable from truthtellers in the study. Interestingly, participants rated deceivers as lower in rapport and synchrony than truthtellers, which was unexpected, but increased involvement in conversations was associated with more rapport and synchronization. Finally, although the trained observers were unable to detect a difference in the synchrony of interaction behaviors between deceivers and truthtellers, the automated computer coding system detected that deceivers showed greater synchrony in their faster movements. This result suggests that synchrony may not be a deception strategy that interactants are able to detect in real time during conversations.

THINK ABOUT IT

1. Participants in this study were generally quite poor at detecting deception in the interaction. What features of the interaction may have contributed to a truth bias or perceptions that the partner was trustworthy?
2. What do the results of this study suggest about detecting deception in your own life? Do feel as though synchrony would be a useful cue to help detect deception in your own relationships?

Negotiating Sexual Intimacy

When it comes to talking about sex, people generally prefer to let their actions speak for themselves. Research has shown that people do not communicate very openly before engaging in sex, and they rely primarily on nonverbal cues to consent to acts of sexual intimacy (Vannier & O'Sullivan, 2011). In fact, some studies show that people often view non-resistance – letting their partner undress them, not stopping their partner from kissing or touching them, and not saying no – as an acceptable signal of sexual consent (Humphreys, 2004). Men tend to use primarily nonverbal cues to indicate their own consent for sex and also rely more on nonverbal indicators to interpret a partner's consent, whereas women report greater use of verbal consent strategies (Jozkowski et al., 2014). Same sex partners, particularly men who have sex with men, are also likely to use nonverbal acts of non-resistance to signal consent to engage in sexual activity (Beres, Herold, & Maitland, 2004). One study found that men and women both believe (though men to a greater degree) that nonverbal behaviors are just as effective as verbal communication to indicate sexual consent, and men, in particular, felt that asking for verbal consent would "wreck the mood" (Humphreys, 2007).

Although people might rely on nonverbal cues to consent to sexual activity, it is important recognize the benefits of more direct communication about sexual intimacy for avoiding miscommunication and preventing non-consensual sex. People rely on sexual scripts to guide their behavior during intimate encounters, which typically include a mix of verbal and nonverbal behaviors that are expected during the negotiation of sexual intimacy. One study found that college students indicated that they give their own consent verbally, but infer consent from their partner nonverbally (Jozkowski, 2013). Women are more likely than men to communicate their consent verbally, especially in response to an explicit request to initiate sexual contact (Jozkowski & Peterson, 2013). Same gendered partners also tend to enact more explicit verbal sexual consent than individuals with opposite gendered partners, likely due to a comparative lack of stereotypical cultural scripts to guide behavior in same gendered sexual encounters compared to opposite gendered encounters (Beres et al., 2004).

When you are interested (or not interested) in pursuing sex with a partner, it is important that your verbal and nonverbal cues are sending the same message. Even when you think you're being clear about your sexual desires, other people can misinterpret your behavioral cues. Heterosexual men tend to interpret the behaviors of females as more seductive, promiscuous, and flirtatious than women do (LaFrance, Henningsen, Oates, & Shaw, 2009). As a result, men are more likely than women to perceive friendly behaviors as signs of sexual interest. Thus, women need to establish clear boundaries for sexual involvement and men need to accept those boundaries. In general, though, everyone should strive to send clear messages when it comes to sexual intimacy.

PAUSE & REFLECT

Have you ever had a sexual experience that made you feel bad afterward? How was that experience different from sexual encounters that made you feel good afterward?

When people rely only on nonverbal behaviors to communicate their consent to sexual intimacy, they experience more negative reactions following sexual activity. One study revealed that when people were not direct in their communication about a first sexual encounter with a partner, they experienced more anger, fear, and sadness, had more negative thoughts about the encounter, and believed that the experience was bad for their relationship (Theiss & Solomon, 2007). In contrast, people who communicate openly about sexual intimacy tend to be more satisfied with both their sexual encounters and their relationships (Byers, 2011). Thus, sexual episodes can have negative repercussions when people rely only on nonverbal messages to negotiate intimacy, but they can have positive outcomes when people combine signs of sexual interest with a clear verbal statement of sexual consent.

Putting Theory into Practice: Combining Verbal and Nonverbal Cues

When you consider verbal and nonverbal messages in combination, you can see opportunities for both greater clarity and greater complexity in your interpersonal interactions. Now that you have seen two examples of how verbal and nonverbal messages combine to create meanings, consider the following strategies for becoming a more skillful communicator.

Rely on uncommon cues to detect deception. A lack of eye contact and fidgeting are commonly thought to be cues to deception, but because many liars can control these behaviors, they are actually poor predictors of deception. To figure out if someone might be lying to you, look for signs of deception that are out of that person's conscious control. In particular, try to tell if they are blinking more than usual, pay attention to vocal cues like an unusual pitch and either a faster or slower speaking rate, and look for brief displays of anxiety in facial expressions. In addition, look for inconsistencies in your partner's behaviors over the course of the conversation, contradictions between the verbal and nonverbal messages, and deviations from your partner's typical communication style. Both behaviors that are hard to control and inconsistent patterns of communication can reveal when a person is lying to you.

Recognize the limitations of nonverbal messages. Although there is no guarantee that your verbal messages will be understood, there are times when nonverbal messages are just too ambiguous. When people miscommunicate about sexual intentions, the result can range from unwanted sexual contact to sexual assault or rape. Rather than run this risk, use clear verbal and nonverbal messages to convey the level of sexual activity that you are comfortable with.

COMMUNICATION IN ACTION 6.5

Creating a Sexual Script

One way to have more effective conversations about sexual intimacy with a potential partner is to anticipate what you might say when you find yourself in that situation. Use the form on the companion website to help you formulate a script for negotiating sexual intimacy and to reflect on the nonverbal behaviors that might complement your verbal messages. Does your script include a clear request for sexual contact, a direct statement of consent, a discussion of risks, and the precautions you might take to prevent those risks?

SUMMARY

Nonverbal messages are an important part of the interpersonal communication process. Nearly every part of the human body and many features of the environment can be channels for communicating information to others. In addition, nonverbal communication is an analogic symbol system, which means that most nonverbal behavior is spontaneous, automatic, and universal. When you learn about the nature of nonverbal messages, you can see that they are very pervasive and powerful tools for communication.

Nonverbal messages have four important functions. First, nonverbal behaviors are essential for expressing emotion. Nonverbal cues are also important to show people that you like them and to figure out when others are attracted to you. Another function of nonverbal communication is that it reveals your power and social status. Finally, nonverbal behavior helps you to regulate your interactions with others. Clearly, nonverbal behaviors accomplish critical functions in your interpersonal interactions.

Individual differences influence nonverbal behavior. Although different cultures and different sexes are more similar than different, there are several important distinctions. For example, people from different cultures use gestures in unique ways, have different orientations toward time, and place value on different physical characteristics. Gender differences in nonverbal communication arise from people's unique physical qualities, the ways in which emotional expressiveness is modeled for different genders, and how different genders are encouraged to adopt different stereotyped norms for behavior.

Verbal and nonverbal cues work in combination. Nonverbal messages can complement, accent, replace, or contradict verbal messages. Inconsistencies between verbal and nonverbal behaviors are one of the signs that a communication partner might be deceptive. When negotiating sexual intimacy, nonverbal messages sometimes replace verbal messages, but there are consequences for relying too heavily on nonverbal messages during these interactions.

In Chapter 5, you witnessed the power of language and the versatility of verbal messages for creating shared meanings between people. In this chapter, the equal – if not greater – impact of nonverbal messages was examined. By drawing upon multiple channels and the unique qualities of analogic codes, nonverbal cues are unparalleled in their ability to communicate feelings, affection, perceptions of power, and participation in a conversation. By recognizing individual differences in nonverbal expression and the complexity of weaving together verbal and nonverbal messages, you can draw upon nonverbal messages to improve your interpersonal communication experiences.

ACTIVITIES FOR EXPLORING COMMUNICATION ETHICS

What Would You/Should You Do?

You're out with some friends and you notice two people having a heated discussion near the bathroom. They are shouting at one another, pointing fingers in one another's faces, and making facial expressions showing anger and disgust. Eventually, one of them starts hitting the other with a purse. The target restrains the attacker's hands, then kicking and efforts to get free ensue. What should you do when other people's nonverbal behaviors are dangerous to others and to themselves?

Something to Think About

In some cases, people mask their emotions by displaying different emotional cues from what they are really feeling inside. For example, people who are telling a lie might try to look calm, even though they are feeling very anxious. Some people might flirt by smiling, moving closer to their target, and even touching the other person, even though they may not be interested in pursuing a romantic connection with the person. When people play poker, they try to hide their excitement when they are dealt a good hand, and they try to appear confident when they don't have any good cards. To what extent is it ethical to hide your true feelings? When would concealing your true emotion have a negative impact on the people around you?

Analyze Communication Ethics Yourself

In work or institutional settings, power and status are revealed and reinforced by the allocation of physical space, the openness of personal territory to others, standards for dress or appearance, personal artifacts that people can or cannot display, etc. One context where nonverbal markers of status play an important role is the United States prison system. Think about representations of prison culture that you have seen in the media. How are inmates and prison guards different in the ways they are allowed to dress, the personal artifacts they are allowed to carry, the way they schedule their days, and the amount of space they are given? Consider the function of these cues within the institution of prisons, as well as the impact of these messages on inmates. Based on your analysis, what are the ethical issues at stake when nonverbal communication is used to constrain people's freedoms?

KEY WORDS

accenting
analogic codes
back-channel communication
channel
complementing
contradicting
deception
deintensification
emblems
halo effect
immediacy
intensification
masking
micro-momentary facial expression
monochronic time orientation
nonverbal behavior
nonverbal communication
nonverbal leakage
polychronic time orientation
simulation
substituting
variable intensity

LEARNING OBJECTIVES

After reading this chapter, you should be able to:

1. Recognize types of emotions.
2. Understand how people experience emotion.
3. Identify components of emotions.
4. Describe the role of emotions in interpersonal communication.
5. Understand how messages are involved in intensely painful emotions.

PUTTING THEORY INTO PRACTICE

In this chapter, you will learn how to:

1. Seek out specific labels to describe feelings.
2. Address all of the components of emotions when you express or respond to feelings.
3. Locate the cause of emotions within people's appraisals.
4. Express emotions verbally rather than just showing them nonverbally.
5. Consider other people's goals when you respond to their emotions.
6. Consider context when you express your feelings to others.
7. Use the social context to understand the emotions expressed by others.
8. Buffer yourself and others from the consequences of dark emotions.

7

EMOTIONS AND COMMUNICATION

Source: Photo by Ezra Shaw/Getty Images.

DOI: 10.4324/9781351174381-

In the women's final match of the 2018 U.S. Open, Serena Williams faced off against Naomi Osaka. During the match, Williams received three code violations from the umpire and her frustration was palpable. Her first code violation was for receiving coaching signals, which Williams vehemently denied, yelling at the umpire, "I don't cheat to win, I'd rather lose!" Then, Williams received a violation after she broke her tennis racket in a fit of anger and frustration over the game, which also cost her a point. Finally, overcome with frustration, Williams received a code violation and a game penalty for demanding an apology from the umpire and calling him a "thief" for taking away one of her points. Although Williams' emotions may have gotten the better of her during the match, many people believed that she was unfairly penalized and the victim of a sexist double standard. Tennis great Billie Jean King tweeted after the match, "When a woman is emotional, she's 'hysterical' and she's penalized for it. When a man does the same, he is 'outspoken' and there are no repercussions." This incident shows how emotions can shape our communication behaviors and the complex rules and expectations we have for emotional expression.

Serena Williams felt frustrated that she was not playing very good tennis, embarrassed at accusations that she was cheating, and angry that the umpire was treating her unfairly. Her opponent, Naomi Osaka, felt joy at winning the U.S. Open, but also disappointment and sadness that her big win was overshadowed by the tension and antics between Williams and the umpire. In your own life, you feel emotion in response to your own triumphs and hardships, and you experience emotions when good or bad things happen to people you care about. For example, you might feel grief at the funeral of a loved one, joy at your best friend's wedding, frustration when your favorite team loses a big game, and pride when you accept your college diploma. **Moods** are pervasive or lasting feelings that range from bad to good, and **emotions** are more fleeting feelings that arise in particular situations. Emotions are especially relevant to interpersonal communication, because interactions evoke feelings and your feelings shape how you communicate. In this chapter, we examine the nature of emotions, look at how feelings are at work when we communicate with others, and consider how the communication situation shapes the way we express our feelings. Finally, we explore the painful emotions that sometimes arise in our interactions with friends, family, and romantic partners.

WHAT ARE EMOTIONS?

Consider all of the different emotions you might have over the course of a typical day. When you wake up, you might feel content with a good night's sleep, eager to face the day, or perhaps fearful

FIGURE 7.1 Vader assesses his mood

Source: www.cartoonstock.com.

Moods
Feelings that are lasting or ongoing.

Emotions
Short-term feelings that are linked to specific situations.

about a midterm exam. As you make your way to work or campus, you could become frustrated by a traffic jam, worried about being late, or pleased when you run into a friend. After a class, you might be happy with high marks on an assignment, or disappointed by a low grade. And as you communicate with others, you might find yourself angered by an insult, grateful for a compliment, hurt by a careless remark, or embarrassed when you say the wrong thing. These examples show how your everyday experiences are rich with emotions. In this section of the chapter, we will take a closer look at types of emotions, the causes of emotions, and distinct facets of emotional experiences.

PAUSE & REFLECT

Reflect on your life and identify one experience that was especially important to you. How did that experience make you feel? How important were your feelings as a part of that experience?

Types of Emotions

The different emotions that you feel allow you to relate to your circumstances in nuanced ways. And when you recognize different emotions in yourself and in others, you gain a more complete understanding of

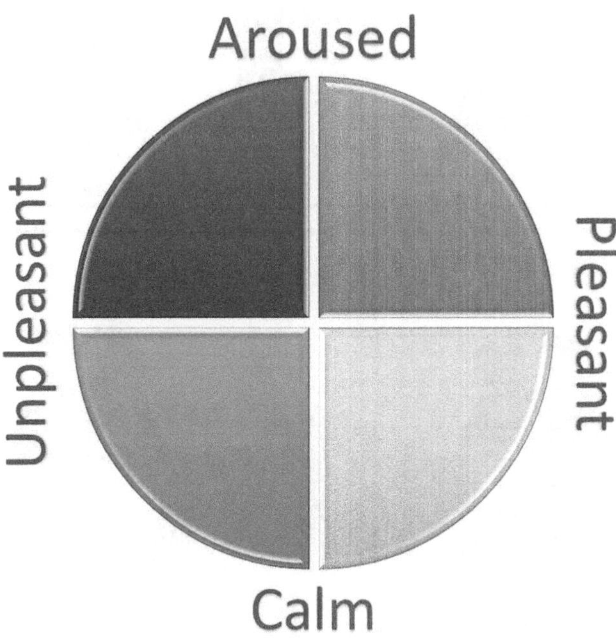

FIGURE 7.2 Dimensions of feelings

Source: Adapted from Clore & Schnall (2005).

your interpersonal communication experiences. To help you appreciate the variety of emotions you experience, the following paragraphs examine three frameworks for distinguishing the emotions people experience.

One way to distinguish emotions is to focus on how positive or negative they are and how intensely the emotion is felt (Netzer, Gutentag, Kim, Solak, & Tamir, 2018). In Figure 7.2, the horizontal dimension distinguishes between pleasant and unpleasant emotional experiences. Pleasant emotions include happiness, joy, and contentment, whereas unpleasant emotions include anger, sadness, and fear. The vertical dimension contrasts emotions that involve a high or low degree of arousal. As examples, consider the difference between annoyance and anger or contentment and happiness. This way of thinking about emotions emphasizes how emotions are generally more or less positive and more or less strong.

Basic Emotions
Common or primary feelings that are experienced universally.

Another way to understand emotions is to identify the different types of feelings people have. **Basic emotions** include common and universal feelings like happiness, surprise, sadness, fear, and anger. Each of these primary or "pure" emotions can take various forms (see Figure 7.3). For example, fear is often evoked in response to situations that are perceived as dangerous (e.g., being attacked by a bear), disgusting (e.g., fear of spiders and bugs), unpredictable (e.g., anticipating how a job interview will go), or uncontrollable (e.g., being a passenger on a plane) (Armfield, 2006). Furthermore, basic emotions can come together to create blended emotions. As one example, consider the feelings involved in jealousy: fear

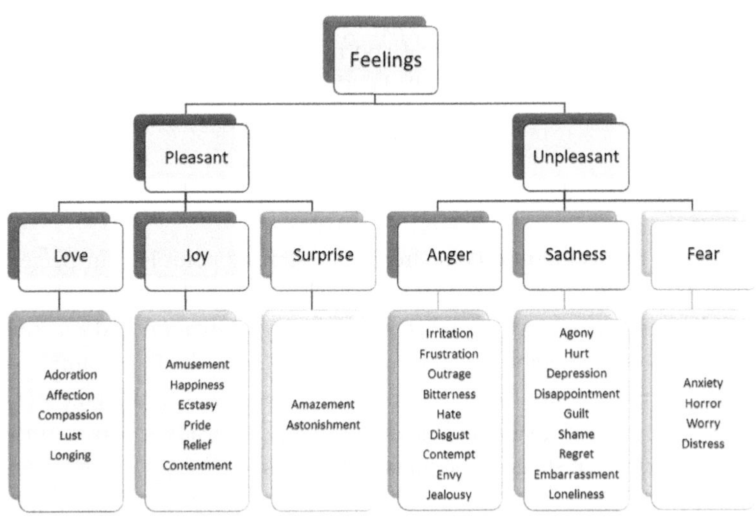

FIGURE 7.3 The structure of emotions

Source: Shaver, Schwartz, Kirson, & O'Connor (1987).

SCHOLAR SPOTLIGHT

Visit the Communication Café on the companion website to view a conversation with Peter Andersen, whose broad program of research includes the study of emotions and interpersonal communication.

that your love interest will leave you, anger at the interloper, and maybe just a dash of sadness that your relationship isn't as strong as you hoped it was (Guerrero, Trost, & Yoshimura, 2005). This perspective helps you to understand the most common emotions you experience, as well as how those emotions are related to more precise or more complex feelings.

Social Emotions
Feelings that occur in interpersonal communication or relationships.

Some emotions are specifically tied to your relationships or communication with other people (Planalp, Fitness, & Fehr, 2018). These social emotions take four distinct forms (see Table 7.1). Affectionate emotions create attachment and closeness with other people. Self-conscious emotions arise from a focus on how the self is perceived by others. Melancholic emotions occur when interpersonal experiences aren't fulfilling or have changed for the worse. Hostile emotions emerge from feelings of injury or threat in the context of interpersonal relationships. Although some of these emotions can occur outside of interpersonal experience,

TABLE 7.1 The social emotions

Affectionate emotions	*Self-conscious emotions*	*Melancholic emotions*	*Hostile emotions*
Love	Embarrassment	Sadness	Anger
Passion	Shame	Depression	Hate
Warmth	Guilt	Grief	Jealousy
Joy	Pride	Loneliness	Envy
			Hurt

social contexts dramatically intensify these feelings. For example, imagine how differently you would feel if you tripped in the front of an empty classroom versus one that was filled with other students.

Causes of Emotions

Appraisals
Evaluations of how favorable a situation is to the goals that you have.

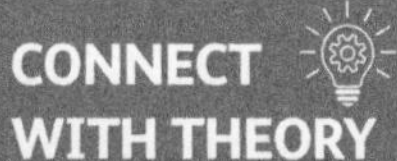

CONNECT WITH THEORY

Visit the companion website to read more about appraisal theories of emotion, which are a collection of theories that link evaluations of a situation to emotional experiences.

Where do your emotions come from? The starting point is your perceptions of your circumstances. More specifically, **appraisals** are perceptions of whether you are getting what you want in a situation and whether conditions are favorable or unfavorable to your goals. For example, if your goal is to get your friend to loan you her car, you would take stock of barriers to that goal (the fact that she appears ready to drive to the store) or cues that suggest you might succeed (she is busy studying for an exam). You also make more specific appraisals concerning, for example, how hard you will have to work achieve your goals under the circumstances, how much you can control the situation, or how certain you are about what will happen (Dillard & Seo, 2013). Thus, appraisals capture a variety of judgments you make about your circumstances.

Appraisal theories of emotion claim that different appraisals of the environment elicit different emotional responses (Moors, 2020). Generally speaking, when you believe that the situation will enable you to achieve your goals, you experience positive emotions, and when you think that the situation will interfere with your goals, you experience negative emotions. Within this general framework, specific emotions are distinguished by the particular appraisals that you make about the situation's relevance to your goals, positive or negative valence, potential causes, and your ability to cope with expected outcomes (Yih, Uusberg, Taxer, & Gross, 2019; see Table 7.2).

The link between appraisals and emotions are particularly relevant in the context of close relationships. Consider how you might feel if you saw your romantic partner flirting with someone else, or if your romantic

TABLE 7.2 Appraisals and their corresponding emotions

Appraisal of the situation or event	Emotion
An injustice is interfering with a desired and obtainable goal	Anger
Something of value has been lost and can't be recovered	Sadness
The situation allows a desired goal to be met	Happiness
An unpleasant outcome is possible, but not certain	Fear
I have behaved in a way that violates my moral ideals	Shame
I have behaved in a way that makes me look inept to others	Embarrassment

partner wanted to have a talk about the future of your relationship. These types of events can increase your doubts and uncertainty about a relationship, which affects your emotional reactions to the event. In particular, people who perceive that they will have to work to resolve the situation tend to feel more anger, sadness, fear, and jealousy; people who believe they need to pay attention to the situation feel more sadness and fear; and people who see the situation as predictable are happier (Knobloch, 2005). Thus, appraisals of a situation are closely linked to the emotions we experience during interpersonal interactions.

PAUSE & REFLECT

Think of the last time that you knew something wasn't going to work out the way you wanted. What was the reason for that outcome? Did you feel mostly anger, sadness, grief, or anxiety? What role did other people play in your emotional experience?

Components of Emotions

The feelings that are set in motion by your appraisals have four distinct parts. Consider the example of Wendy, who is waiting for an important job interview. As you think about how Wendy is feeling, you can probably identify multiple facets of her emotional experiences.

Perhaps the most obvious component of emotions is your **self-perceptions of emotion**; in other words, your own awareness of how you feel. For example, Wendy will probably recognize if she is feeling nervous rather than confident about the interview. Because your perceptions of your emotions reflect how you label and interpret your feelings, they are an essential part of your experiences. In fact, people who have experienced traumatic events, like fighting in a war or being a victim of sexual assault, develop a better understanding of their complex feelings once they are able to put those emotions into words (Torre & Lieberman, 2018). Thus, self-perceptions of your emotions allow you to define your feelings for yourself and others.

Self-perceptions of Emotion People's own awareness of how they feel.

Anyone who has experienced intense anger, fear, or elation knows that emotions also have a physiological component. As Wendy awaits her interview, no doubt her heart is beating a bit faster, her skin temperature rises a bit, and she may even be queasy. Even variations on positive emotions, such as different types of love, correspond with distinct physiological reactions within your body (Shiota, Neufeld, Yeung, Moser, & Perea, 2011). The **physiology of emotion** refers to the physical changes that occur within body systems when you experience feelings. Within the cardiovascular system, heart rate, blood flow to different parts of the body,

The Physiology of Emotion Physical changes that occur in conjunction with feelings.

and oxygen or adrenaline levels in the blood vary with different emotions. Likewise, the respiratory system may speed up or slow down depending on experiences of sadness, anger, fear, etc. In a very real sense, emotions are physical experiences.

Nonverbal Markers of Emotion
Changes in appearance that occur when a person experiences affect.

The physical changes during emotion are often visible to others. **Nonverbal markers of emotion** are changes in appearance that coincide with the experience of emotion. Nonverbal displays can be unconscious reflections of the physiological changes emotions produce, for example, the increase in blood flow to the face caused by embarrassment is visible as blushing. You can also consciously display or exaggerate nonverbal markers of emotion in an effort to communicate feelings to other people. In fact, the facial feedback hypothesis suggests that making facial expressions associated with certain emotions (e.g., smiling/happy, frowning/sad) can intensify those feelings, whereas inhibiting facial expressions (e.g., unclenching your jaw and relaxing facial muscles when stressed) can weaken emotional experiences (Manusov, 2015). Thus, while Wendy's feelings of apprehension might be revealed by her crossed arms, her wide eyes, and her rigid posture, she might feel more at ease if she can relax her body and smile at the secretary. In these ways, nonverbal markers of emotion are the visible features that both reflect and affect your feelings.

Action Tendencies
The behaviors that emotions compel us to perform.

Wendy's emotions fuel her behavior during the interview – her anxiety prompts her to pay attention to the interviewer's every word, and her confidence leads her to share information freely. The behaviors that emotions compel us to perform are called **action tendencies**. In fact, the physiological component of emotions makes the body ready to perform behaviors appropriate for particular feelings. For example, think of the last time that you felt really angry. Your heart was pounding, you were probably quite alert, and your muscles were tense. These changes poised you to do battle with the source of your anger. Alternatively, remember the last time that you felt sad. Your slow heart and respiratory rate were better suited to pulling the covers over your head. The behaviors promoted by emotions depend on the characteristics of the specific situation, but Table 7.3 summarizes some general action tendencies that have been associated with various emotions (Frijda, 2007). Because these links have been found across different cultural groups (Hwang & Matsumoto, 2020), action tendencies are assumed to be a basic part of the experience of emotions.

From your perceptions of a situation to the actions you take, your feelings allow you to interface with the world around you. Appraisals focus on discrepancies between what you desire and what is present in a situation. These appraisals elicit specific emotions. Emotions, in turn, involve physiological changes to the body that allow you to perform certain actions. Those actions, quite conveniently, are often the very behaviors that can close the gap between your actual and preferred circumstances. In this sense, emotions are part of a finely tuned system that promotes fitting responses to the communication situations in which you find yourself.

TABLE 7.3 Emotional action tendencies

Emotion	*Action*	*Purpose*	*Example*
Anger	Attack	Conquer a barrier to obtaining a desired outcome	The anger Mark feels when his co-workers haven't done their share gives him the energy he needs to finish the project alone
Sadness	Retreat	Provide time to adjust to a loss	Sarah's sadness at the break-up of her romantic relationship slows her down so that she can revise her future plans
Happiness	Approach	Take advantage of favorable circumstances	T.J.'s happiness at finding the printer he needs on sale helps him decide to make the investment
Fear	Fight or flight	Eliminate a threat by either conquering it or out-running it	Lacey's fear when the exam study guide was handed out motivates her to devote extra study time
Shame	Make amends	Restore one's sense of oneself as moral	Brian's shame over losing his temper with his daughter compels him to apologize
Embarrassment	Escape	Get away from people who witnessed the incompetence	Rachel's embarrassment over her poor class presentation prompts her to cut class the following week

PAUSE & REFLECT

Think of the last situation that made you feel anxious. How was your increased vigilance an advantage or disadvantage as you coped with that situation?

Putting Theory into Practice: Recognizing and Communicating Emotions

Emotions arise out of your perceptions of your circumstances, and your feelings involve several components that work in concert. This knowledge can help you to more clearly identify and describe both your own emotional experiences and the emotions of people around you.

Seek out specific labels to describe feelings. Rather than describe how you are feeling in general, try to use the wealth of emotion labels to capture your precise emotions. Instead of "angry," are you really frustrated, merely annoyed, exasperated, or raging mad? Similarly, encourage your communication partners to identify their specific feelings. For example, if your friend says that he is sad, probe those feelings to clarify whether he is gloomy, depressed, hurt, or heartbroken. By seeking out specific labels to describe feelings, you will help other people to understand your own emotions and you can respond more effectively to other people's feelings. You can practice this skill by completing Communication in Action 7.1 exercise.

COMMUNICATION IN ACTION 7.1

Charting Your Emotions

This exercise is intended to help you understand your emotional experiences in greater detail. Using the form you download from the companion website, keep a diary of your emotions over the course of one full day. By logging your emotions every hour, and noting details about the situations surrounding your emotional experiences, you'll gain insight into the circumstances that evoke emotions and how you tend to describe those emotions.

Address all of the components of emotions when you express or respond to feelings. You can use your knowledge about the different parts of an emotional experience to both express and respond to feelings more effectively. Beyond your self-perceptions of emotion ("I'm frightened"), you might describe your physiological state ("my heart is pounding") or how your emotions make you want to act ("I feel like hiding out in my room"). These descriptions can help others empathize with what you are feeling and appreciate its full effect on you. Likewise, keep in mind the multiple facets of emotions when other people share their feelings with you. The Communication in Action 7.2 activity will help you identify the physiological and behavioral aspects of your emotions.

COMMUNICATION IN ACTION 7.2

Beyond Self-Perceptions of Emotion

This exercise will help you think about the physical changes you experience when you have different emotions. Visit the companion website for the instructions and to download a form for this activity.

Locate the cause of emotions within people's appraisals. In the heat of the moment, you might find yourself pointing an emotional finger at others: "*You* make me angry." "*You* hurt my feelings." "*You* are bringing me down." But remember, emotions arise from *your* appraisals of how a situation fits with *your* goals. In other words, the feelings you experience are the result of perceptions and objectives that exist within you. As you make sense of your feelings and communicate them to others, acknowledge that your own perceptions and goals are at the root of your emotions. Similarly, encourage other people to own their own emotions by helping them to identify the goals and appraisals that are fueling their feelings. The following questions might help you sort out your appraisals of your emotions:

- What is your goal in this situation?
- What is preventing you from reaching your goal?
- Why are you upset about the barriers preventing you from reaching your goal?
- How can you eliminate the barriers to your goal?
- How can you change how you are reacting to your unmet goals?

FEELINGS AND COMMUNICATION

Emotions and interpersonal communication go hand in hand. The strongest emotions you experience – for example, love, hate, or shame – occur within social situations. Even emotions that you experience by yourself, such as grief and loneliness, are connected to relationships with others. In this section, we examine how feelings shape and reflect interpersonal communication.

Feelings Cause Communication

Most emotions can be addressed by using communication to confront, avoid, embrace, or repair the situation that provoked your feelings. The anger you feel when someone interferes with your goals might compel you to raise your voice and argue. Likewise, you can relive situations that made you happy by telling your friends about those experiences. Research shows that feeling lonely or disconnected causes people to engage others through social media, such as Facebook (Sheldon, Abad, & Hinsch, 2011). In the workplace, feeling guilty often motivates people to work harder and, in turn, feel greater commitment to their job (Flynn & Schaumberg, 2012). In ways such as these, the emotions you experience underlie many of your communication experiences.

Emotions also explain why people react to a particular situation in different ways. For example, people who feel sympathy for a friend in distress use communication to solve the problem or to make their friend feel better, whereas people who feel angry will try to make the friend take responsibility for the problem (MacGeorge, 2001). Similarly, when people feel angry about an unexpected event in a dating relationship, they are more likely to confront their partner, but when they feel sad, they prefer to avoid communication (Knobloch, 2005). As these examples illustrate, your communication goals and behaviors reflect the action tendencies of specific emotions (Burleson & Planalp, 2000; Dillard & Seo, 2013).

Communication Describes Feelings

Some of the most intimate interpersonal interactions involve messages about emotions and feelings themselves. You might unconsciously reveal your emotions through physical displays, such as teary eyes or slumped shoulders, and you also deliberately communicate your feelings to others. Research shows that most people describe their emotions to at least one other person (Van Kleef, 2016). Indeed, many people use emojis in text messages to convey feelings to communication partners (Riordan, 2017). Discussing emotions can also be a prominent part of coping with negative life events, such as the stress and anxiety of financial hardship after losing a job (Lucas & Buzzanell, 2012), or the grief and disappointment of struggling with infertility (Steuber & Solomon, 2011). Both consciously and unconsciously, our verbal and nonverbal behaviors convey our emotions to others.

Communication Affects Feelings

From the warmth you experience after a jovial exchange with a friend to the elation of hearing "I love you" from that someone special, the messages you receive from others have tremendous emotional potential. Not surprisingly, people sometimes tap that potential to shape the emotions of people around them. People sometimes craft messages to make others feel embarrassed (Hall, 2011), guilty (Turner, 2017), or jealous (Goodboy & Bolkan, 2011). You can also use communication to make people feel better. For example, when Jen's grandfather was dying of lung disease, she didn't dwell on medical tests and gloomy topics when she went to visit him. Instead, she tried to entertain him with stories about graduate school and debates about politics. You can also cheer people up by offering supportive messages that help them to change the appraisals that are at the root of bad feelings (Jones & Hansen, 2015). For example, when Denise's friend lost her job, Denise tried to persuade her to view the situation not as a loss, but as an opportunity to start her own business or perhaps go back to school. In these ways, producing or changing emotions might be the driving force behind interpersonal communication.

PAUSE & REFLECT

Recall a time when you actively tried to influence someone's emotions. What emotion were you focused on and what messages did you use?

HOW DO YOU RATE? 7.1

Messages that Evoke Guilt

Visit the companion website to complete a scale that measures your likelihood to use or be affected by guilt-inducing messages. As you reflect on your scores, do you think you use guilt to manipulate others more than you should? Do you need to be on your guard against other people's efforts to use guilt to influence you?

Feelings Shape Interpretations of Messages

Your feelings also influence how you interpret messages from others. At a general level, moods influence how people perceive a situation, such that people in a happy mood are more likely to recognize the positive rewards of a situation, whereas people in a sad mood might be more likely to notice the disappointing or threatening aspects of a situation (Yan, Dillard, & Shen, 2010). You also tend to focus on information that is relevant to your specific emotions. For example, people who are worried about a breast cancer diagnosis tend to engage in more information seeking about their health condition (Lee & Hawkins, 2016). In addition, news stories that are framed in terms of emotions like anger or hope can make readers spend more time on the page than news framed in fear, but in all cases people tend to seek additional news and information that is consistent with the emotional tone of articles they have already read (de los Santos & Nabi, 2019). Similarly, mood can also shape the extent to which people are persuaded by political advertisements on television, such that people in a happy mood are more persuaded by positive messages, but people in a sad mood are equally persuaded by both positive and negative messages (Turner, Underhill, & Kaid, 2013).

A classic study by James Dillard and Eugenia Peck (2000) shows how messages can cause emotions that, in turn, shape how people respond to the messages. Dillard and Peck studied public service announcements (PSAs), which encourage viewers to buckle their seatbelts, stop smoking, avoid recreational drugs, practice safer sex, or stop littering. These televised messages evoke a variety of emotions, including surprise, fear, anger, sadness, happiness, and contentment. Dillard and Peck found that the emotional responses viewers had to the PSA predicted their subsequent attitudes about the advice given in the message. For example, people who felt fear in response to a PSA were more likely to be persuaded by the message, but people who felt anger tended to reject the advice offered in the PSA. In a similar fashion, your feelings and your interpretations of messages are intertwined within interpersonal interactions.

Putting Theory into Practice: Expressing and Responding to Emotions

Emotions are woven into the fabric of interpersonal interactions. Once you embrace feelings as an inevitable part of communicating with others, you can take steps to improve both how you express your emotions and how you respond to the feelings expressed to you by others.

If you're going to show your emotions, you might as well express them. Oftentimes, people leave it to their nonverbal cues to convey emotions to others. In other words, instead of expressing your joy, you simply act happy; instead of apologizing, you act remorseful; or instead of explaining your anger, you act mad. Of course, there are occasions when you might want to downplay your emotions (such as when you've just received an awful birthday present from your romantic partner). When you want to share your emotions, you'll be more effective if you can find a way to verbalize your feelings. Use the Communication in Action 7.3 exercise to help you put your emotions into words.

COMMUNICATION IN ACTION 7.3

Verbal Expressions of Emotion

This exercise involves using the form on the companion website to think of a time when a friend, romantic partner, sibling, parent, or co-worker did something that upset you, and to reflect on how you can put those emotions into words.

Consider other people's goals when you respond to their emotions. When people express their feelings to you, think about what's driving those messages and tailor your responses to those goals. When a friend shares his fears with you, he may want you either to protect him from harm or to reassure him that he is safe. If you are on the receiving end of someone's anger, explore whether she wants you to understand her feelings, to help her achieve a goal, or to get out of her way. By recognizing the action tendencies that accompany emotions, you can more effectively help your friends recover from embarrassment, relieve a parent of guilt, cheer up a sad co-worker, and prolong a child's joy. When you find yourself on the receiving end of someone's emotional expression, use the following questions to guide your response:

- Why is this person telling me about this event?
- Am I the cause of this emotion or am I supposed to help this person resolve the emotion?
- What might I have done to contribute to this emotion?
- How is this emotion relevant to the context of this interaction?
- What is this person trying to accomplish by expressing this emotion?
- What can I do to help this person achieve his or her goal?

FACTORS THAT AFFECT EMOTIONS AND COMMUNICATION

The links between emotions and communication depend on the cultural context, characteristics of the people involved, and their interpersonal relationship. By understanding how these factors shape how feelings are expressed, you can improve your ability to decipher other people's emotional messages. In turn, you will be able to respond more effectively to the emotions that communication partners express to you.

Cultural Norms

Some aspects of emotional experiences are shared across cultures – these include the automatic or unconscious parts of emotion such as physiological changes, facial displays, and action tendencies. Moreover, basic emotions such as happiness, sadness, anger, fear, and surprise are experienced by people of all cultures. However, when it comes to how people consciously act upon their emotions, culture plays a major role. A culture's **display rules** tell its members when, where, and how emotions should be expressed. Consider, for example, how people of different religions grieve the death of a loved one. Within Judaism, a death is followed by seven days of intensive mourning, during which mirrors are covered, men do not shave, and family members wear a black ribbon. In contrast, Buddhism sees death as part of the normal order of the universe, and only a one-hour period of prayer or meditation is typical.

Display Rules
Cultural prescriptions about when, where, and how emotions should be expressed.

In a similar fashion, culture dictates how people express everyday emotions like happiness, anger, jealousy, pride, etc. In general, culture shapes people's willingness to rely on others for emotional support (Ryan, La Guardia, Solky-Butzel, Chirkov, & Kim, 2005). For example, the Latin American value of *simpatía* emphasizes the relational benefits of positivity and costs of negativity, which leads people of Latin American heritage to rate positive emotions as more desirable and appropriate to express than individuals with Asian or European heritage, and to rate negative emotions as undesirable and less appropriate to express (Senft, Campos, Shiota, & Chentsova-Dutton, 2020). Research also indicates that Japanese culture discourages the display of both strong negative emotions and positive emotions, compared to North American cultures (Safdar et al., 2009). One study examined the emotional reactions of American, Chinese, and Japanese children who were presented with a disappointing gift and found that American children were much more positively and negatively expressive than Japanese children and more negatively expressive than Chinese children, with Chinese and Japanese children verbally reporting more negative emotions in response to the gift but showing more neutral expressions (Ip et al., 2020). Even in communication online, there is cultural variation in the types of emoticons people use to express their feelings, with people from individualist cultures like the United States favoring horizontal mouth-oriented emoticons like :), whereas people from collectivist cultures like Korea favor vertical and eye-oriented emoticons like ^_^ (Park, Baek, & Cha, 2014). As these examples illustrate, culture influences whether, to whom, and how intensely emotions are communicated.

PAUSE & REFLECT

In what ways do your experiences and expressions of happiness, pride, anger, and sadness reflect your cultural background?

Culture can also set different standards for emotional expression based on a person's age. In American society, we tolerate extreme expressions of anger, frustration, sadness, and joy from children in their "terrible twos" (Figure 7.4) – can you imagine a middle-aged adult expressing raw

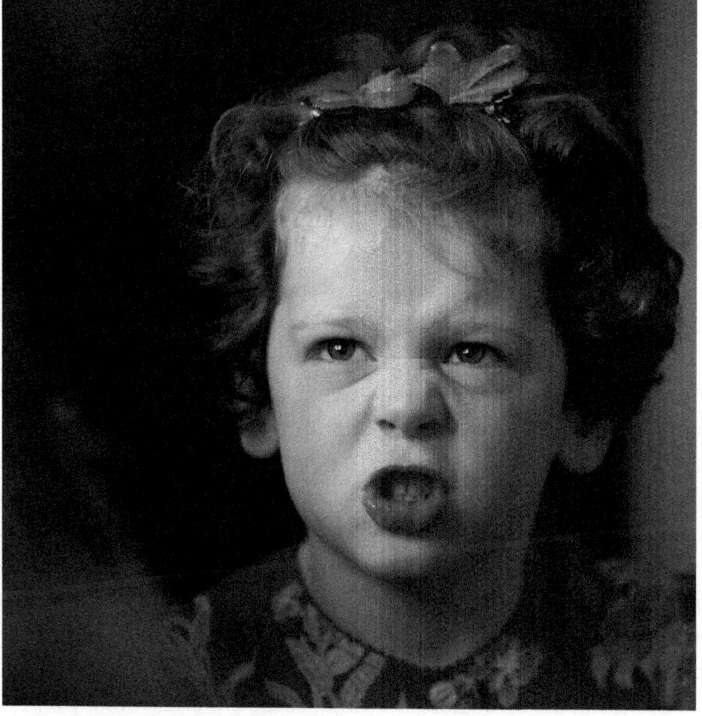

FIGURE 7.4 A defiant toddler

Source: Getty Images.

emotions in the same way? Relative to older adults, adolescents and young adults experience more negative emotions when they have interpersonal problems (Birditt & Fingerman, 2003). Moreover, elderly people exert more emotional control than younger adults (Thomsen, Mehlsen, Viidik, Sommerlund, & Zachariae, 2005). Although older adults are sometimes overcome by their emotions, people generally expect mature individuals to manage their emotions and express their feelings responsibly. Complete the Communication in Action 7.4 activity to test your assumptions about emotions and aging.

Gender has also been linked to the experience and expression of emotions in ways that both span and reflect cultural norms. In general, studies of people from different nations and age groups suggest that women experience emotions more frequently and intensely than men do (Brebner, 2003; Thomsen et al., 2005). A study of people from Japan, Canada, and the United States found similar gender differences across these cultures, such that men tended to express powerful emotions like anger more than women, while women were more likely than men to express sadness, fear, and happiness (Safdar et al., 2009). Within American society, display rules also tend to discourage men from disclosing their emotions (Burleson, Holmstrom, & Gilstrap, 2004). Accordingly, research conducted in the United States shows that women are more willing than men to rely on others for emotional support (Ryan et al., 2005). In addition, American women notice more distinctions and nuances in feelings than men do (Barrett, Lane, Sechrest, & Schwartz, 2000). Thus, these findings highlight how culture shapes how men and women express and make sense of emotional messages.

COMMUNICATION IN ACTION 7.4

Expressing Emotions Across the Lifespan

To shed light on how people in different age groups express their emotions, download and complete the form on the companion website.

IDEA: INCLUSION, DIVERSITY, EQUITY, AND ACCESS

Cultural norms that specify the behaviors that are expected also explicitly or implicitly discourage or devalue behaviors deemed nonnormative. How does applying the expectations for most people in a cultural group affect people in the minority? How can we talk about cultural norms for emotional experience and expression in ways that are more inclusive of diversity in our society?

Emotional Intelligence

Emotional Intelligence
The ability to understand and manage one's own feelings, as well as the moods and emotions of others.

Within any cultural group, you'll find that some people are more tuned in to emotional messages than others. **Emotional intelligence** refers to people's ability to understand and manage their own feelings, as well as the moods and emotions of others. Because feelings are complex, emotional intelligence requires self-awareness, self-control, motivation, empathy, and social skill (Petrides et al., 2016). More specifically, emotional intelligence includes being able to recognize emotional nuances, to put emotional information to use, to understand how emotions work, and to either promote or suppress emotional experiences in oneself and in others (Mayer, Caruso, & Salovey, 2016). Thus, an emotionally intelligent person is insightful, articulate, and in control when it comes to affective experiences; someone who is agreeable, likable, and respected by others; and someone who engages in positive social experiences, rather than personally or interpersonally destructive behaviors (Mayer, Salovey, & Caruso, 2004). The How Do You Rate? 7.2 exercise can help you to learn about one facet of emotional intelligence: an ability to rely on others for emotional support.

HOW DO YOU RATE? 7.2

Willingness to Rely on Others for Emotional Support

Do you tend to "go it alone," or do you turn to others in times of need? Complete the scale on the companion website to assess how much you turn to others when you are experiencing strong emotions. Ryan et al. (2005) found that the average score for emotional reliance on friends among participants in their study was 436. How do you compare? If you repeat this test, thinking about a family member or co-worker instead of a friend, how different would your scores be?

Research has connected emotional intelligence to several important outcomes. For example, people who are higher in emotional intelligence report having a better quality of life, in general (Szczygieł & Mikolajczak, 2017). Emotional intelligence has also been linked to both leadership ability and a person's performance as a member of a problem-solving team (Harms & Credé, 2010; Michinov & Michinov, 2020). Emotional intelligence can also promote greater resilience to difficult or challenging circumstances (Schneider, Lyons, & Khazon, 2013). In contrast, a lack of emotional intelligence is associated with a variety of negative outcomes, including drug and alcohol abuse, deviant behavior, and poor relationships with friends (Brackett, Mayer, & Warner, 2004). Moreover, romantic couples in which both partners are low in emotional intelligence are more superficial, less supportive, and more prone to conflict than couples where at least one partner is emotionally intelligent (Brackett, Warner, & Bosco, 2005). When viewed in this light, emotional intelligence is revealed as a consequential aspect of people's personality.

The Relationship Context

Another factor that shapes the expression of emotions is the nature of the relationship between partners. Close relationship partners have many opportunities to help or hinder each other's goals in ways that evoke emotions (King & LaValley, 2019; Solomon & Brisini, 2019). Research has shown that having a romantic partner who is responsive and empathetic to your needs increases your day-to-day experience of positive emotions (Stanton, Selcuk, Farrell, Slatcher, & Ong, 2019). Conversely, people experience more intense negative emotions when a romantic partner, rather than a friend, dismisses their concerns (Fehr & Harasymchuk, 2005). Moreover, people's disagreeable behaviors in relationships make their partner feel worse the more often they occur (Cunningham, Shamblen, Barbee, & Ault, 2005). In these ways, our closest relationships are also the most emotionally volatile.

Communicating emotions leaves you vulnerable to the other person's response; therefore, you are more likely to express your emotions to relationship partners you trust. Not surprisingly, then, people are generally more willing to express emotions to partners in personal, rather than business, relationships (Clark & Finkel, 2005). In addition, college students in the United States report that they rely on their best friends for emotional support more than anyone else (Ryan et al., 2005, studies 1 and 2). Within romantic associations, relationship satisfaction is associated with more constructive communication strategies for expressing jealousy (Guerrero, 2014). Moreover, individuals who perceive that a romantic partner is responsive and understanding are more likely to express both positive and negative emotions in their relationship (Ruan, Reis, Clark, Hirsch, & Bink, 2020). As these examples illustrate, the nature and duration of a relationship influence how much the partners disclose their feelings.

PAUSE & REFLECT

How do you express strong emotions like anger or love with different people, such as your parents, grandparents, friends, siblings, or a romantic partner?

One notable exception to the tendency for people to express emotions in close, rather than nonintimate, relationships is the practice of sharing emotions in online venues. For some people, posting on Facebook or Twitter, making a Tik Tok video, or chatting on message boards gives them a place to describe their feelings to an often large number of friends, acquaintances, and even strangers. If you have a Facebook account, take a quick look at the newsfeed coming in from your array of friends. On any given day, you might find a diversity of emotions running through your friendship network. Perhaps one friend expresses disappointment that her favorite NFL team lost (while another friend's spirits are lifted by the opposing team's victory). Or maybe you have friends who use Facebook to comment on their frustration with their job, their children, their parents, or their neighbor's noisy dog. While it's true that many people prefer to discuss their emotions with close friends and relationship partners, the Internet also allows us to share our feelings and cope with stress with a much broader audience.

INTERPERSONAL COMMUNICATION ONLINE

A study by communication scholars, Erin Basinger and Leanne Knobloch (2018) analyzed content of online message boards for parents of individuals in the United States military to see how they expressed emotion and sought support from others in the online community. The comments illustrate the emotional turmoil that parents experience when their child is deployed, as well as the utility of online groups for helping people express their emotions and garner support.

Expressions of Emotion:

- **"I am going through a dichotomy of feelings because this has been his dream since he was able to recognize soldiers (pretoddler) but hell week for me due to not knowing."**
- **"I go through periods of being upbeat about all that is ahead of him and then when I walk by his room or see some of his things, the emotions start to well up."**
- **"I feel like a ping-pong ball, going back and forth between feelings of complete sadness to stuffing my feelings and being strong."**

Seeking Emotional Support:

- **"I wish I knew he was doing okay. So far I only have received the 'I'm here' phone call. Being former Navy myself I did not think I would feel this way about my son leaving. I know he's in good hands but I can't stop worrying."**
- **"Will this get any easier as time goes on or am I gonna be on edge 24/7? I will always worry about my son but I love him more than he will ever know."**
- **"I'm new to all this. Trying to cope. I need a good ear."**

Putting Theory into Practice: Developing Emotional Intelligence

Within the boundaries set by culture, people's personal traits and skills influence how they communicate emotions, and the relationship between communicators shapes emotional messages. Armed with an understanding of how context shapes emotional messages, you can increase your emotional intelligence.

Consider context when you express your feelings to others. Although some aspects of your emotional experiences are automatic, emotional intelligence involves tailoring emotional messages to fit the situation. Here are strategies for incorporating context into your communication of emotions:

- If you are communicating with someone from a culture other than your own, keep in mind that your communication partner may have different rules for expressing emotions.

- Ask yourself in what ways your age, gender, or other characteristics might influence how others perceive your emotional messages.
- If you have especially strong or complex feelings to work through, seek out a friend who has the emotional intelligence to appreciate and respond to your emotions.
- Consider the extent to which your relationship with a communication partner allows you to share your feelings openly.

If you adapt your emotional messages to the situation, your communication partner will be more likely to understand your feelings and respond in the ways you had hoped.

Use the social context to understand the emotions expressed by others. Many people can recognize the emotions conveyed by a smile, a glare, or a trembling lip. Being able to understand the intensity or complexity of the feelings behind these displays, however, can be considerably more challenging. As you make sense of other people's emotional messages, think about how the context might be shaping their messages. In particular, consider these issues:

- How might your communication partner's cultural display rules require or prohibit the expression of particular emotions?

FIGURE 7.5 The hierarchy of influences on expressions of emotion

- How skilled is your communication partner when it comes to expressing feelings – is this someone you can read like a book, or a person who typically sends ambiguous emotional messages?
- Is your relationship prompting a partner to hide their emotions from you or express their feelings at full strength?

Paying attention to cultural norms, your partner's emotional intelligence, and the kind of relationship you have can help you determine whether your communication partners are considerably more angry, sad, frightened, or happy then they appear.

THE DARK SIDE OF EMOTIONS IN CLOSE RELATIONSHIPS

Dark Side of Interpersonal Communication
Aspects of interaction that involve socially inappropriate goals, harmful behaviors, or painful experiences.

Throughout this chapter, you have seen how feelings are an inevitable part of interpersonal communication. In this final section, we turn our attention to the intensely negative emotions that can arise within our closest relationships. The **dark side of interpersonal communication** includes those aspects of interaction that relate to socially inappropriate goals, harmful behaviors, or painful experiences (for example, deception, violations, and abuse; Spitzberg & Cupach, 2013). To highlight how people use interpersonal communication to both cause and relieve painful emotions, consider hurt, grief, and jealousy.

Hurt, Grief, and Jealousy

Hurt
A blended emotion that includes sadness, fear, and sometimes anger.

The intimacy that makes close relationships so special can also leave people vulnerable to the hurtful actions of their partners. **Hurt** is considered a blended emotion that includes sadness, fear, and sometimes anger (Feeney, 2005; Vangelisti, Young, Carpenter-Theune, & Alexander, 2005). It is a uniquely social emotion, in that it arises from the injury produced by another person's words or actions (Vangelisti, 2015). More specifically, you feel hurt when someone communicates that they don't appreciate you, they don't value the relationship as much as they used to, or they don't feel they need to be supportive, faithful, open, and trustworthy (Lemay, Overall, & Clark, 2012). The form of a hurtful message also influences the pain it causes (Vangelisti & Young, 2000). Compare two hurtful messages that Olivia might receive from her father, Alan. If Alan says, "I think you're making a mess of your life," Olivia might be hurt, but she can also argue the point. If Alan says, "I never loved you as much as your brother," she is left without a rebuttal. These examples show both how interpersonal communication can be hurtful, and how some messages do more harm than others.

INSIDE COMMUNICATION RESEARCH

Hurtful Episodes in Parent-Adolescent Relationships

Parent-Adolescent relationships are typically ripe for hurt feelings given the inevitable conflicts that tend to arise between parents and their children during adolescence. Adolescents often report feeling hurt by their parents' disciplinary action, criticism, or disregard for autonomy. Although hurt feelings may be inevitable in these relationships, the follow-up conversations that parents and adolescents have about hurtful encounters provide a unique opportunity for reconciliation and learning. Communication scholars Rachel McLaren and Alan Sillars (2020) conducted a study designed to examine how interaction patterns in conversations about hurt can shape understanding and empathic accuracy – or the ability to infer another person's thoughts and feelings during interaction.

The researchers invited 95 parent-adolescent pairs to a university lab to complete a series of activities for the study. First, the parent and adolescent were separated and the adolescent was asked to use note cards to write down something their parent said or did that hurt their feelings in the last two weeks. The adolescents were instructed to set aside any cards that they would not want their parent to see. The researchers then presented the notecards to the parent to see if they remembered each of the incidents and they randomly selected one of the events that the parent recalled to be the focus of the remainder of the study. The parent and adolescent each filled out a survey reflecting on that hurtful event and then they were brought together in a living room setting to have a video recorded conversation about the hurtful event. Afterward, the parent and adolescent were separated again and asked to watch the video of their conversation. While they were watching, the researchers paused the video every 30 seconds and asked the participants to talk about what they were feeling in that moment and to guess what their family member was thinking or feeling in that moment. Afterward, the researchers analyzed the interaction patterns in the recorded interactions and categorized each participant's reports of their own and their partner's thoughts and feelings during the video-assisted recall.

The analysis showed that parents perceived greater understanding from their child when both the parent and the adolescent showed more confirmation and warmth during the interaction and less confrontation. Similarly, the adolescents perceived more understanding from their parent when both parties showed more warmth and less confrontation in the conversation. In addition, adolescents who were more involved in the conversation showed more empathic accuracy toward their parent. Also, both parents and adolescents showed more empathic accuracy when the parent showed remorse and regret for hurting their child during the conversation. In the video-assisted recall, parents attributed a higher proportion of negative thoughts, avoidant thoughts, confrontational thoughts, and complaints about parents than the adolescents actually reported. The adolescents tended to underestimate how much their parent blamed themselves, how much they were unhappy or anxious about the interaction, and their positive appraisals of the adolescent, but they overestimated how much their parent understood and agreed with their point of view. The results of this study suggest that parents and adolescents make sense of hurtful events differently.

THINK ABOUT IT

1. The researchers found that people perceived hurt differently depending on if they were the victim or the perpetrator of the event. How might victims and perpetrators understand a hurtful event differently? What biases might each person bring to the encounter depending on their role?
2. Why might adolescents have more negative and less positive appraisals of their parent's behavior and intentions during the interaction? Do you think this has more to do with the relationship between adolescents and parents, or the fact that the parent was the perpetrator of the hurtful event?

Grief
An extreme state of sadness that includes feelings of despair, panic, guilt, and anger.

In the case of hurt, interpersonal communication creates negative feelings – for other emotions, interpersonal communication might be your only option for relieving your pain. **Grief** is a state of extreme sadness that includes feelings of despair, panic, guilt, and anger (Jakoby, 2012). Grief arises from the loss of something that was deeply valued, that you expected to enjoy into the future, and that is irreplaceable. Consider, for example, how grief might be associated with events such as a romantic break-up, a loved one's cancer diagnosis, the loss of a job, or a death in the family. In cases such as these, grief is made worse when the loss is sudden, untimely, preventable, or violent (Kristensen, Weisæth, & Heir, 2012; Tian & Solomon, 2020).

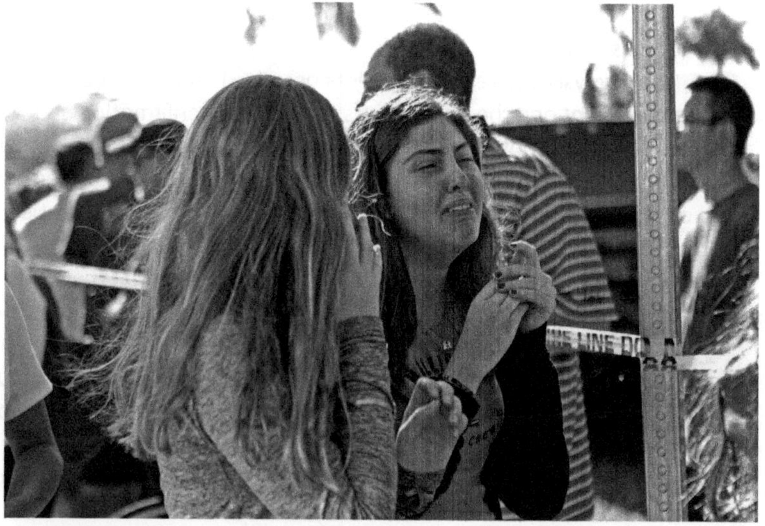

FIGURE 7.6 Students grieve the loss of their classmates after school shooting at Marjorie Stoneman Douglas High School in Parkland, Florida.

Source: Photo by Daniel Berehulak/Getty Images.

Although grief involves a sense of hopelessness, interpersonal communication does provide some relief. For example, research has shown that spouses who communicate perspective taking after a miscarriage experience more positive emotions and relationship satisfaction (Horstman & Holman, 2018). In addition, individuals tend to experience more personal growth and fewer feelings of detachment following the death of a family member if the family promotes an open communication environment (Carmon, Western, Miller, Pearson, & Fowler, 2010). Even the specific language individuals use to describe their grief can be influential in their ability to make sense of the situation and accept their circumstances (Horstman, Holman, & McBride, 2019). Although communicating about grief can help alleviate sadness, some people prefer to keep their thoughts and feelings private (Cohen & Samp, 2018) and might develop rules about when, how, and to whom they prefer to open up about their grief (Basinger, Wehrman, & McAnich, 2016). In fact, couples who have experienced miscarriage say that they sometimes might avoid conversations about the loss in order to prevent further pain and suffering for themselves or a partner (Stroebe et al., 2013). Sometimes, one of the most helpful things you can do to comfort someone who is grieving is simply to express your willingness to listen (Bodie, Vickery, Cannava, & Jones, 2015). Although nothing can recover the losses that lead to grief, interpersonal communication can be a key part of a person's emotional recovery.

Jealousy is yet another emotion that arises from perceptions of vulnerability and loss – in this case, feelings result from the perception that a valued relationship is threatened by a partner's competing interests (Bevan, 2015). Jealousy includes feelings of passion, fear, envy, hostility, irritation, guilt, sadness, and even love (Guerrero, Trost, & Yoshimura, 2005). How do people cope with such varied and intense emotions? As summarized in Table 7.4, people can use interpersonal communication to pursue a variety of goals when they feel jealous. Table 7.4 also reveals that the responses to jealousy include options as diverse as denying feelings, confronting the rival, accusing the partner of infidelity, or showcasing one's strengths as a partner.

Jealousy
An emotion that arises from perceptions that a valued relationship is threatened by a partner's competing interests.

How people respond when they are jealous is influenced by the emotions they feel most strongly. For example, hostility promotes more violent reactions to jealousy, but fear leads people to try to regain their partner's affections (Guerrero et al., 2005). Although it isn't always easy to control negative reactions when your relationship is threatened, research has shown that communicating constructively and sharing feelings can heal the relationship, whereas destructive communication strategies can diminish relationship satisfaction and damage the relationship (Guerrero, 2014). The process linking the emotions of jealousy to relationship outcomes is depicted in Figure 7.7. As you review that model, note how short-lived feelings of jealousy can lead to communication decisions that have a long-term impact on a romantic relationship.

TABLE 7.4 Communication goals and strategies for responding to jealousy

Goals for communication about jealousy
Maintain the relationship: *We have to find a way to get through this together.*
Recover from the loss of self-esteem: *I'm going to show that it's her loss!*
Reduce uncertainty about the situation and/or relationship: *I need to know what's going on.*
Reassess the nature of the relationship: *This changes how I feel about her.*
Retaliate against the partner or rival: *I'm getting even, no matter what!*
Responses to jealousy
Physically distance yourself from the partner: *I need to get away for a while.*
Psychologically distance yourself from the partner: *I'm not going to think or talk about this.*
Engage in covert surveillance to gather more information: *I wonder what is going on?*
Display negative affect by crying or acting upset: *I'm upset with you.*
Confront and accuse the partner: *I think you have been unfaithful.*
Communicate or behave violently: *You're not getting away with this!*
Manipulate your partner's feelings: *As if I haven't had lot of offers better than you.*
Contact and confront the rival: *How dare you?*
Discuss the situation with your partner to gather information: *Tell me what happened.*
Be especially nice, so your partner will prefer you: *I'd like to take you out to a special dinner.*

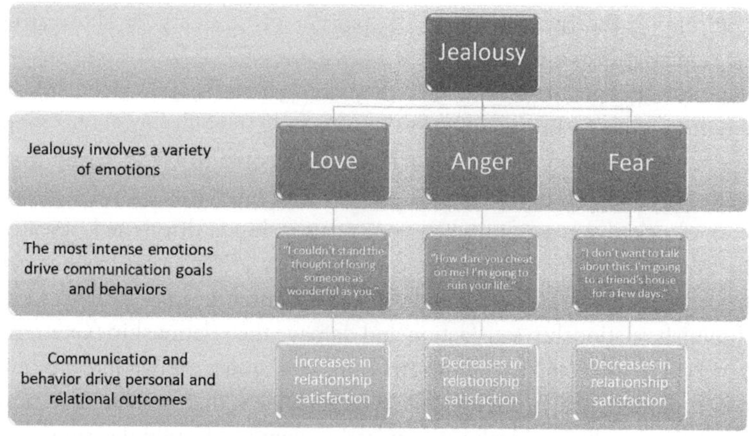

FIGURE 7.7 The impact of jealous emotions.

PAUSE & REFLECT

Have you ever felt jealousy? What caused your feelings? What specific emotions did you feel, and what did you do? In the end, did your relationship become closer or more distant because of the experience?

Putting Theory into Practice: Keeping Emotional Consequences in Check

As interpersonal communication is intertwined with the experience, management, and resolution of some of the darkest emotions, use your communication skills to limit the effect of these feelings within relationships you value.

Buffer yourself and others from the consequences of dark emotions. When we experience intense emotions, we might find ourselves responding in extreme ways. To keep your negative emotions from wreaking havoc on relationships you value, learn to recognize when you are in the throes of these intense and dark emotions. At those times, be especially cautious about going where your feelings would take you. Might it be worth it to gather more information about your partner's hurtful comment before ending the relationship? Might talking with someone help you recover from your terrible loss? Might those feelings of jealousy point you to issues in your relationship that you can address and improve? Attention to the dark side of interpersonal communication reminds us that hurt, loss, and infidelity are as much a part of interpersonal relationships as love and joy; however, we needn't be hostage to these feelings.

SUMMARY

This chapter focused on feelings as a part of interpersonal interaction. As a foundation for this discussion, we began by clarifying the nature of emotions. You saw that emotions can range from positive to negative and involve more or less arousal, they can be pure or blended forms of several basic emotions, and they can be distinguished by the social functions that they serve. You also learned that emotions arise from people's appraisals of their environment, and that the experience of emotion involves self-perceptions, physical reactions, nonverbal markers, and action tendencies. In short, the experience of emotion is a complex phenomenon.

Our examination of the relationship between emotions and interpersonal communication revealed four distinct links. Because emotions involve action tendencies, they can motivate communication to address the conditions that produced our feelings. In addition, you might use communication to describe your feelings to others. You also employ communication to influence how other people feel – perhaps to cheer them up, make them feel guilty, or evoke feelings of love. Finally, your own feelings frame how you interpret the messages you receive from others. In these ways, emotions permeate both the creation and perception of interpersonal communication.

The expression of emotion during interpersonal interactions is also shaped by culture, the traits of the people involved, and the relationship that exists between the parties. Cultural display rules specify which emotions you should express, as well as when and to whom you can express your feelings. Emotional intelligence – the ability to perceive and manage feelings – helps you to communicate your feelings more carefully and to respond to other people's emotions more skillfully. And within the constraints and opportunities created by the cultural context and your personal skills, your relationship with another person influences whether and how you express feelings. In particular, close interpersonal relationships are a place where some of our most negative emotions are created and soothed.

ACTIVITIES FOR EXPLORING COMMUNICATION ETHICS

What Would You/Should You Do?

You're out running errands with your father, and things haven't been going well. Your day started off with a dead battery in your car, which made you late for your father's doctor's appointment. The doctor ordered some tests, and so that appointment went over time too. Now you have to pick up your mother at work, and neither of you have had lunch. You decide to zip through a drive-through window. As your father is ordering, the server keeps interrupting him – "Do you want cheese on that?" "Do you want fries?" etc. These interruptions put your father over the edge. He starts to be rude and insulting to the person taking his order. You know that he's just frustrated by the day, and you feel bad for the person on the receiving end of his tirade. What should you do when you see someone taking out his or her bad feelings on an innocent bystander?

Something to Think About

When people have strong opinions about something, they are often influenced by both beliefs and emotions. Consider a public issue that you feel strongly about: Should abortion be legal? Should the United States do more to regulate firearms? Should immigrants be given a path to citizenship in the United States? Take a moment to consider how much your position stems from facts or arguments that you believe, and how much your position is fueled by your feelings about that issue. To what extent is it ethical for people to let emotions influence their positions on important issues?

Analyze Communication Ethics Yourself

Emotions are an inevitable part of public policy debates. Ethical participants in these discussions own their emotions, and they don't manipulate other people's feelings in order to win. Locate the text or a video of a speech that addresses a controversial public issue – for example, whether creationism should be taught in public schools, the changes that are required to combat climate change, or an issue important in your own community. As you examine this speech, note the speaker's use of emotion. Does the speaker reveal his or her own feelings about the issue? Does the speaker try to evoke emotions in the audience? Based on your analysis, has the speaker incorporated emotion into his or her speech in an ethical manner?

KEY WORDS

action tendencies
appraisals
basic emotions
dark side of interpersonal communication
display rules
emotional intelligence
emotions
grief
hurt
jealousy
moods
nonverbal markers of emotion
physiology of emotion
self-perception of emotion
social emotions

LEARNING OBJECTIVES

After reading this chapter, you should be able to:

1. Describe the steps, types, and styles of listening.
2. Identify barriers to effective listening that exist in the environment, in messages, and within listeners.
3. Recognize forms of nonlistening, and how nonlistening can occur in close relationships.
4. Describe how to use questions and empathy to be a more active and effective listener.
5. Recognize different kinds of relational messages, and describe how people make sense of relationship information.

PUTTING THEORY INTO PRACTICE

In this chapter, you will learn how to:

1. Complete all stages of the listening process.
2. Tailor your way of listening to the situation.
3. Prepare yourself to listen.
4. Use questions strategically.
5. Empathize within limits.
6. Read between the lines.
7. Avoid reading too much into messages.

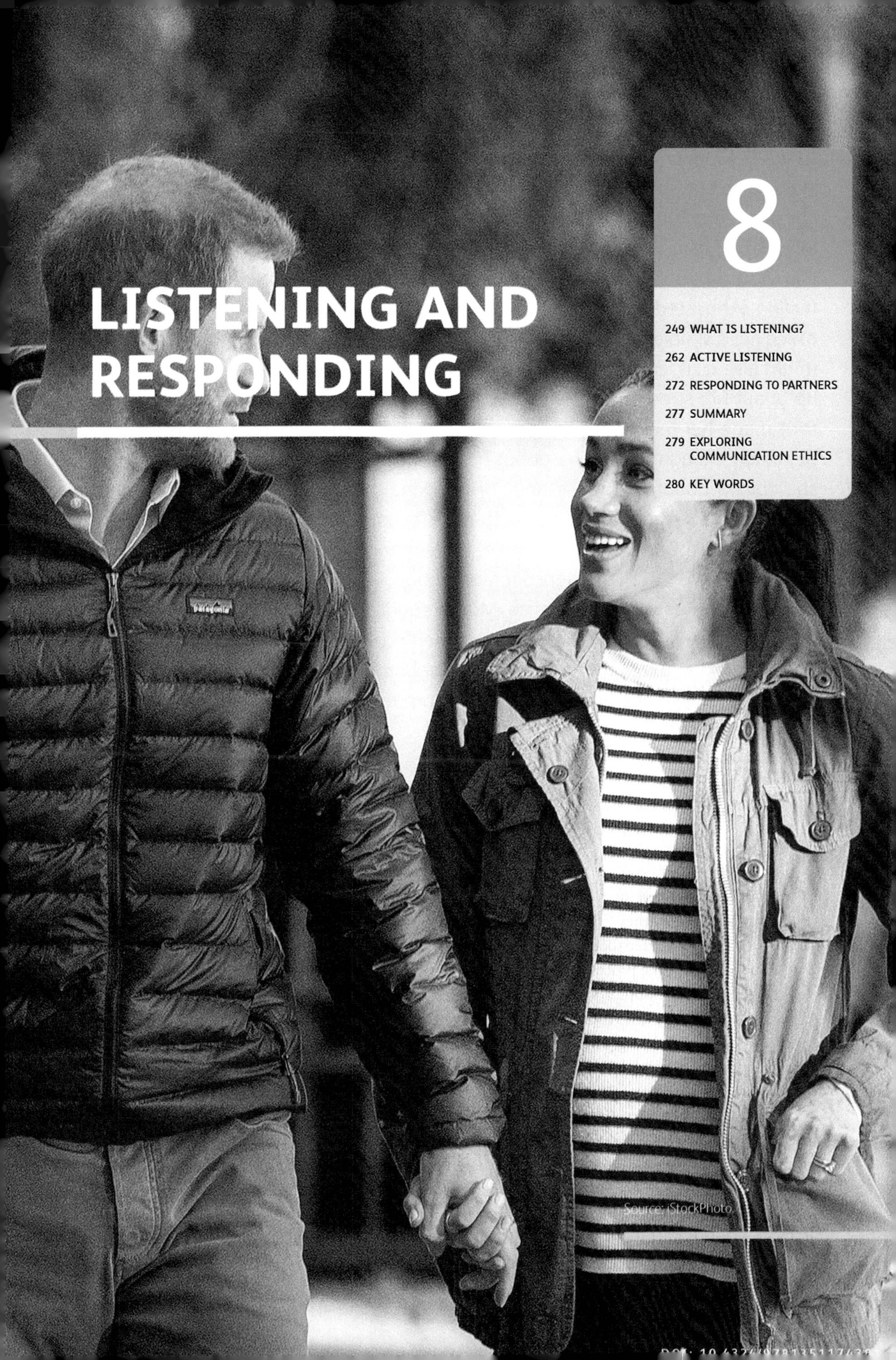

8

LISTENING AND RESPONDING

Source: iStockPhoto.

In 2020, Meghan Markle, the Duchess of Sussex, was pregnant with her second child when she suffered a miscarriage and lost the baby. Devastated by the loss, she penned an op-ed for *The New York Times* in which she recalled a memorable interview she had given the previous year. She and Prince Harry were finishing up a lengthy tour of South Africa, she was breastfeeding her first-born child, she was feeling exhausted but trying to keep up a brave face in public. The interviewer asked her a simple question, "Are you OK?" Although most people in this situation might give a superficial "I'm fine" in reply, Markle answered honestly and opened up about her stress and exhaustion. She recalled that it wasn't her honest reply that made her feel better in that moment, it was the fact that the interviewer genuinely thought to inquire about her wellbeing in the first place. In her op-ed, she opined about the importance of checking in with people and really listening to their stories, empathizing with their feelings, and supporting them during hardship. Although the miscarriage of a pregnancy is a common occurrence, conversations about this experience remain taboo, leaving countless women feeling ashamed and mourning in silence. Markle suggested that when people take the time to ask how others are doing, and then really listen to the answer with an open heart and mind, they can truly lift the burden of grief. Inviting someone to share their pain with you and really listening to their struggles can have healing and restorative power.

In sharing her honest pain and struggles with an interviewer, Meghan Markle recognized that asking people how they are doing creates opportunities to really listen to their stories and help them feel heard, understood, and supported. Within interpersonal interactions, effective listening is an essential part of the process. Listening can be a rewarding, informative, and enlightening part of the interpersonal communication process. In fact, one estimate suggests that college students spend more than half of their time communicating engaged in listening (Emanuel et al., 2008). And people enjoy and appreciate being listened to. Have you ever felt relieved after venting to a friend about some frustrating circumstances? Even if that person doesn't have much to say in response, having the opportunity to express your thoughts and feelings to someone who listens attentively can be a rewarding experience. Listening can also be an important tool because it allows you to gather information and deepen your knowledge and understanding. You can pick up on an important detail in a lecture or see a relationship in a new light based on how you interpret another person's message. Attentive listening helps us understand complex information and improve the nature of our interpersonal relationships. In this chapter, we examine the process of listening, strategies for active listening, and how people listen for information about their relationships. Learning about these topics can help you enjoy the benefits of being a good listener.

PAUSE & REFLECT

Do you know anybody you consider to be an especially good listener? What does that person do when you are engaged in a conversation?

WHAT IS LISTENING?

Have you ever been asked, "Are you listening to me?" The difference between simply being present and being engaged in an interaction highlights the distinction between hearing and listening. **Hearing** is one of your five senses that gives you the ability to perceive sound by detecting vibrations in your ear. During an interaction, you might be able to hear the other person talking, but if your mind is elsewhere you're not actually listening to that person's message. **Listening** goes beyond hearing, because it involves receiving messages, creating meaning based on them, and responding to the message source with verbal and nonverbal messages. Listening requires more effort than simply relying on your sense of hearing, and you probably engage in the listening process to a greater or lesser degree in different interactions. For example, you might occasionally space out during a class lecture while you are thinking about the errands you need to run after class. Or maybe during a recent conversation with your mother you paid only perfunctory attention to her criticisms of your best friend. In this section, we'll discuss features of the listening process, different ways that people can listen, barriers to effective listening, and forms of nonlistening.

Hearing
The ability to perceive sound by detecting vibrations in your ear.

Listening
The process of receiving, constructing meaning from and responding to spoken and/or nonverbal messages.

The Listening Process

The process of listening unfolds through several phases that repeat over the course of a conversation (see Figure 8.1). This process begins when you pay attention to a communication partner's message, and it ends when you respond to that message. Communication scholar Brant Burleson (2011) clarified that the listening process involves both mindful activities where you are consciously engaged, and also mindless activities that unfold automatically during a conversation. Let's look more closely at the different behaviors and goals that characterize each stage of the listening process.

Attending. The first stage of the listening process is **attending** – the process of noticing specific cues provided by a communication partner. This stage of listening resembles the selection stage of the perception process, as described in Chapter 4 on perception. Selection involves noticing only a subset of the stimuli that are available to your senses at any given moment. Similarly, during the attending phase of the listening process,

Attending
The process of noticing specific cues provided by an interaction partner.

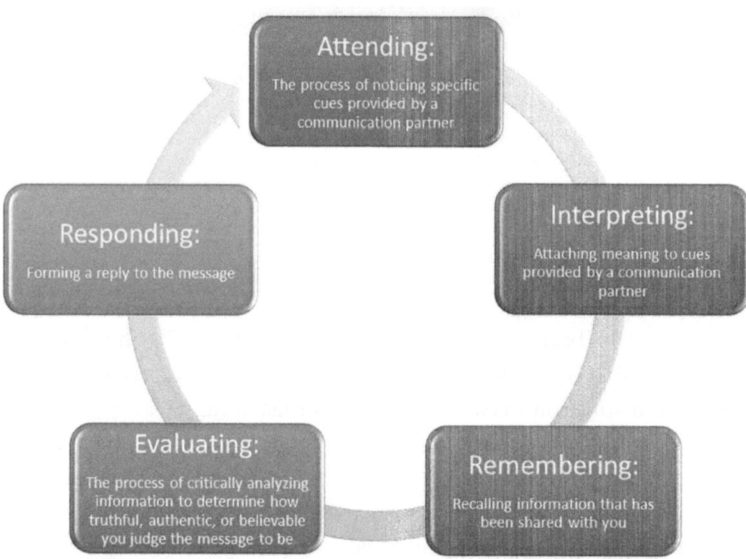

FIGURE 8.1 The listening process

you select among the various cues available from your conversation partner. Just as effective perception requires that you sort out important details from all the other stimuli around you, effective listening means that you focus on cues that are particularly relevant to understanding a conversation. For example, Jen recalls going on a job interview that involved going out for dinner at a busy and loud restaurant. During that part of the interview, she had to filter out the noise from surrounding tables to focus on what her companions were saying. She could also minimize her attention to her colleagues' side comments about enticing menu options, but she had to pay full attention to the questions they asked about her qualifications and abilities. As this example illustrates, the first stage of the listening process allows you to identify the details that are most relevant to the interaction and tune out other information that could interfere with your efforts to listen.

Interpreting
Attaching meaning to cues you have noticed in interaction.

Interpreting. During the next stage of the listening process, **interpreting**, you attach meaning to the cues that you have noticed. In other words, the interpreting phase involves your efforts to understand the cues you have received. As summarized in Table 8.1 and described below, there are several strategies people can use to achieve understanding during conversation:

- *Try to determine the organization of the message so that it's easier to identify the speaker's main points.* Some people make their point up front and use the rest of the interaction to support their cause, others lead up to their point more tentatively and finally get to what they want to say at the end of the interaction. By examining the organization of a

TABLE 8.1 Strategies for interpreting messages

Determine Organization	Is the main point made up front or at the end?
	Does supportive information come before or after the point?
Attend to Nonverbal Cues	Do nonverbal cues match the verbal cues?
	What additional information is conveyed nonverbally?
Paraphrase	Can you put your partner's ideas into your own words?
	Does your interpretation of the situation overlook anything that the partner emphasized?
Question	What information do you need to make sense of the conversation?
	Are you making assumptions that need to be clarified?

message, you can identify main points more effectively and interpret periphery comments in context.

- *Rely on both verbal and nonverbal cues to decipher a message.* Although people often think of listening as focusing primarily on the verbal component of a message, nonverbal cues can help you understand an interaction. Someone might tell you verbally that they agree with you, but their lack of eye contact and skeptical facial expressions might send a different message, so effective listening might require attention to both verbal and nonverbal messages.
- *Increase understanding by silently paraphrasing what you think your partner is trying to say.* **Paraphrasing** involves putting your partner's statement into your own words, which can help you to determine if you understand the message the way it was intended.
- *Ask questions.* If you aren't sure about the meaning of a particular message, it is important to seek more information. Asking for clarification will ensure that you understand what your partner means and that you're not making inaccurate assumptions to help you fill in missing information.

Paraphrasing
Putting your partner's statement into your own words.

Remembering. The **remembering** stage of the listening process involves recalling and retaining the information that has been shared with you. During the course of a conversation you need to remember what has been previously stated so that you don't repeat yourself or ask questions that have already been answered. Remembering what happens in an interaction also has some long-term implications for professional and relational success. For your classes, you probably take notes to record

Remembering
Recalling and retaining the information that has been shared with you.

specific points, and you study for an exam by reading your notes several times to help you remember the information. Retaining content you learn in class or at your job can help you get a good grade or earn a promotion. In social contexts, remembering information that interpersonal communication partners share with you is also very important. You show your interaction partners that you are a competent communicator by recalling information they have shared with you. Remembering messages and important details can also tell people that you care about them. In fact, relationships become closer as partners remember and build upon the interactions they've had with each other.

PAUSE & REFLECT

How do you feel when you discover that a friend, co-worker, or family member forgot personal information that you communicated?

Evaluating
The process of critically analyzing information to determine how truthful, authentic, or believable you judge it to be.

Evaluating. The next stage of the listening process is **evaluating** – the process of critically analyzing information to determine how truthful, authentic, or believable you judge it to be. Have you ever heard a friend tell a story and thought that it sounded a bit far-fetched? Have you ever caught someone in a lie and then looked for inconsistencies in their other messages? Have you ever been persuaded to make a purchase based on a salesperson's arguments? You make judgments like these during the evaluating stage of the listening process. When you evaluate messages effectively, you carefully examine the information you have received so that your conclusions are based on accurate facts or plausible arguments. When you encounter inconsistencies or unbelievable information, you can seek additional information to help you make sense of the interaction by focusing on nonverbal cues and asking questions to get to the bottom of the problem.

Responding
Forming a reply to a message.

Responding. The final stage of the listening process is **responding**, which involves forming a reply to the message. During an interpersonal interaction, your partner expects you to respond to show that you have been listening and that you understand the message. You might respond throughout the interaction with various nonverbal cues. For example, you can show that you're listening and that you understand by nodding your head in agreement, matching your partner's emotional expressions, or maintaining eye contact. People can also show they are listening by using back-channel communication; as you learned in Chapter 6, back-channel communication includes short utterances, such as "um-hmm," "I know," and "absolutely," that signal attention and encourage a speaker to continue. When used as part of listening, back-channel responses help support the communication going on in the main channel (Bavelas,

Coates, & Johnson, 2002). In fact, study in which people disclosed an upsetting problem to someone else found that listeners who responded more actively, through verbal and nonverbal messages, were perceived as more emotionally aware and helped the discloser to feel better (Bodie, Vickery, Cannava, & Jones, 2015).

Your partner will likely expect you to also respond with a more substantive comment at some point as well. One type of verbal response is to acknowledge and confirm what was said, such as when you repeat back your supervisor's instructions for a task at work. Another type of verbal response might demonstrate an understanding of your partner's feelings. For example, if your friend tells you that he failed an exam, you might respond by saying "That's too bad, you must be really disappointed." Verbal responses can also reflect socially and relationally appropriate messages, like relating what your partner said about a previous relationship experience that you've shared. You have an array of verbal and nonverbal choices when responding to an interaction partner, but appropriate reactions will show your partner that you've been listening.

PAUSE & REFLECT

What kinds of verbal and nonverbal cues tell you someone is listening to you? How can you tell someone is listening when you are communicating by phone or even text-based communication technologies?

You exchange many messages with a partner over the course of a conversation; therefore, the cycle shown in Figure 8.1 occurs over and over again as you attend to new messages, seek to understand, retain, and evaluate them, and respond both verbally and nonverbally. In this way, listening is an ongoing part of interpersonal communication.

Ways of Listening

People can approach the process of listening in a variety of ways. In some cases, different ways of listening reflect the requirements of different interpersonal communication situations. For example, when you are in a staff meeting at work, you might listen for feedback on your performance and for information about specific tasks you are expected to perform. People also tend to privilege certain types of listening, no matter what the situation. For example, you might know someone who always seems to find fault, correct, or criticize people. By understanding different types of listening, as well as more persistent listening styles, you can adapt your communication to fit both the situation you are in and the person you are talking to.

Discriminatory Listening Listening to distinguish between different words, sounds, and meanings.

Appreciative Listening Listening to derive pleasure and enjoyment.

Comprehensive Listening Listening to receive and remember new information.

Evaluative Listening Listening to judge the accuracy, honesty, and completeness of a message.

Active-empathic Listening Listening to comfort and help others.

Types of listening. As a starting point, let's consider the different types of listening summarized in Table 8.2. **Discriminatory listening** involves distinguishing between different words, sounds, and meanings, which can be helpful when you are trying to make sure that you understand the details in a message correctly. For example, when you strain to listen through a poor cell phone connection to distinguish certain words and phrases, you're engaged in discriminatory listening. Other times, you might find yourself engaged in **appreciative listening**, which is listening purely for enjoyment, for example, at a poetry reading or a concert. **Comprehensive listening** focuses on receiving and remembering messages, so it can be useful for organizing details, such as when you are meeting someone for the first time or receiving complicated instructions. A situation calls for **evaluative listening** when you need to judge whether a message is accurate, honest, and complete. You might engage in evaluative listening when you're trying to determine if a salesperson is being truthful about a product and giving you a good deal. Finally, **active-empathic listening** involves focusing on another person's feelings to understand what

TABLE 8.2 Types of listening

Listening type	*Definition*	*Example*
Discriminatory listening	Listening to distinguish between different words, sounds, and meanings	Listening to determine if your friend wants to meet at 5:15 or 5:50, the directions to the place where you will meet, and whether or not this is a romantic date
Appreciative listening	Listening to derive pleasure and enjoyment	Listening to your grandfather tell a funny story that he shares at every family reunion
Comprehensive listening	Listening to receive and remember new information	Listening to a new romantic partner describe his or her ideal birthday, so that you can plan the perfect celebration
Evaluative listening	Listening to judge the accuracy, honesty, and completeness of a message	Listening to determine if your employee's explanation for an error is truthful and thorough
Active-empathic listening	Listening to comfort and help others	Listening to your best friend describe a recent break-up to show that you care, and also to figure out how you can best help your friend

FIGURE 8.2 Listening to a story

Source: Getty Images.

they must be going through. Typically you would engage in empathic listening when you are called upon to provide comfort, support, and help (Gearhart & Bodie, 2011). These different types of listening accomplish different goals, so they are useful in different types of situations.

Listening styles. Do you prefer to listen to facts and statistics or personal stories and examples? Do you like to linger and reflect on the content of a message, or would you prefer speakers to be direct and to the point? Although different situations might call for specific listening strategies, like whether you are listening for information or listening for pleasure, most people tend to have a preference for listening in the same way across a variety of different situations. A **listening style** is similar to a personality trait in that it is an approach to listening that a person uses in many different situations.

Listening Style
The way a person tends to listen in any situation.

There are four general listening styles (Sargent & Weaver, 2007; see Figure 8.3). People with an action-centered listening style see listening as a means to an end; they prefer messages to be highly organized, concise, and error-free, so that they can figure out what is meant and move ahead. People with a content-centered listening style also tend to focus on the facts and details of the message, but they value accurate and

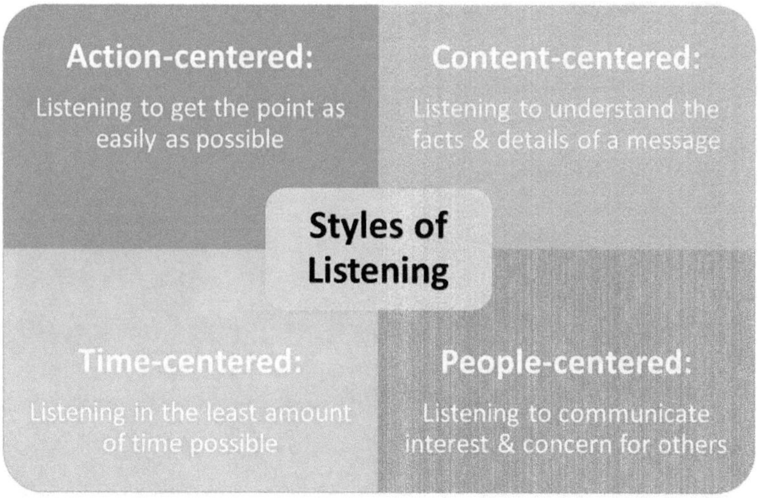

Action-centered: Listening to get the point as easily as possible	Content-centered: Listening to understand the facts & details of a message
Styles of Listening	
Time-centered: Listening in the least amount of time possible	People-centered: Listening to communicate interest & concern for others

FIGURE 8.3 Styles of listening

clear messages that allow them to comprehend and evaluate information. A time-centered listening style characterizes an impatient listener; people with this style are unconcerned with the details of someone's message, and they prefer speakers who get to the point quickly. A final listening style reflects concern with other people's feelings or emotions; individuals with a people-centered listening style tend to seek out common interests with others, and they are particularly responsive to the emotional experiences of others. You can complete the How Do You Rate? 8.1 exercise to gain insight into your own listening style.

Specific personality characteristics have been linked to a person's listening style. In particular, people who are very outgoing tend to have a people-centered listening style, which is consistent with their sociable personalities (Weaver, Watson, & Barker, 1996). People who are typically nervous and anxious are more likely to adopt action-centered or time-centered listening styles (Villaume & Bodie, 2007). These listening styles minimize the need for interaction, which tends to make anxious individuals uncomfortable. People who are very self-centered and verbally aggressive are less likely to adopt people-centered or content-centered listening styles because they prefer not to spend too much time dwelling on other people's experiences or feelings (Worthington, 2005). In contrast, people who enjoying thinking and analyzing topics tend to use a content-centered listening style (Worthington, 2008).

HOW DO YOU RATE? 8.1

Listening Styles

The listening styles profile was developed to evaluate people's preferences for listening during conversation. To determine your listening style, complete the scale on the companion website. Does your listening style resonate with your listening preferences across contexts and relationships? How do you typically react when forced to listen to messages that do not conform to your preferred listening style?

PAUSE & REFLECT

How does your preferred listening style relate to your own personality or your approach to interpersonal communication?

Listening styles also depend on people's goals for a situation. One research study showed that people reporting on a specific listening situation they had experienced reported a different style of listening then they did when completing a general listening styles measure (Gearhart, Denham, & Bodie, 2014). In particular, how personal or intimate situation was and how much empathy people felt for a communication partner were stronger predictors of listening behavior than listening style. Other research suggests that people's engagement in active and empathic listening is related to their goals for the situation and contextual cues (Bodie, Gearhart, Denham, & Vickery, 2013). In particular, active-empathic listening occurs more often between friends or romantic partners and when topics are personal.

Across the different interpersonal communication situations you encounter, you'll find yourself engaging in different types of listening, and you may also have a particular approach to listening that you prefer to use. Different types and styles of listening follow the same general process, but they differ in how each step of listening is performed. If you are engaging in evaluative listening, you might attend more to inconsistencies in a message, whereas empathic listening would focus you on the person's feelings and emotions. Appreciative listening might lead you to retain the warm feelings evoked by an interaction, but comprehensive listening emphasizes recall for specific instructions or detailed pieces of information. And you might show that you appreciate your uncle's funny story by laughing, but empathic listening demands a response that is appropriate, sensitive, and comforting. Whether driven by the situation or your own preferred listening style, different ways of listening involve attending to different parts of a message, seeking different kinds of understanding and retention, using different standards for evaluating, and having different goals for responding.

Barriers to Effective Listening

Although listening is an important part of interpersonal communication, people tend not to be very good at it. One classic study concluded that people are able to recall only about 10% of what was said during a conversation they had just five minutes earlier (Stafford & Daly, 1984). Although memory for conversations is improved when interactions are humorous (Hilal, Siddiqui, Khan, & Hameed, 2012), and also when we are talking to friends, rather than strangers, and partners who are agreeable, rather than disagreeable (Samp & Humphreys, 2007), we shouldn't be surprised that people tend to be poor listeners.

Noise. One obstacle you confront when listening to a communication partner is noise in the environment around you. Have you ever tried to have a conversation with someone in a crowded restaurant? Have you ever struggled to hear a professor's lecture over a loud air conditioner or the whispers of other students sitting near you? Perhaps an echo made it difficult to make out what the person on the other end of a phone call was saying. Chances are good that loud chatter, rumbling undercurrents, and ambient noises in your environment make it difficult to concentrate on the messages that are sent your way.

Features of the message. Features of the message being communicated can also serve as obstacles to effective listening. Denise remembers a student who described his frustration after talking to a salesperson about buying a car. One factor that made listening such a challenge for him in that interaction was the complexity of the message. He didn't have the same expertise that the salesperson did about how a car worked or about how to take out a loan. Consequently, he was confused by some of the words the salesperson used, and he had difficulty understanding parts of the conversation. Another feature of this message that was an obstacle to listening was that the message was overloaded: There was so much information, from learning about mechanical and aesthetic aspects of the vehicle to considering how to get the best interest rate on a loan, that the listener could not take everything in, and effective listening was compromised.

Thoughts and feelings. Barriers to listening also come from thoughts or feelings within a listener. In particular:

- Effective listening is more difficult if you are preoccupied. When your mind is filled with your own thoughts, ideas, or concerns, you can't listen to someone else's messages.
- If you get wrapped up in the anger, sadness, frustration, or joy that a message evokes, you may tune out important details in the rest of the conversation.
- Listening is compromised when you prejudge a message. If you believe that you already know what the other person is going to say and how you are going to respond to it, you may not feel a need to listen carefully.

When you are distracted, emotionally reactive, or judgmental, your internal thoughts and feelings drown out the information your communication partner presents.

IDEA: INCLUSION, DIVERSITY, EQUITY, AND ACCESS

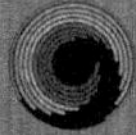

One strategy to illuminate and combat racism within universities or workplaces is holding listening sessions, where members of the community share their direct experiences with racism. These sessions are intended to help administrators and employers address racism, but how much can they accomplish in the effort to disrupt systemic racism? How can institutions promote authentic listening and how can listening contribute to substantive change in institutional racism?

Lack of effort. One prominent obstacle to listening is a simple lack of effort. When people don't pay attention, don't ask questions, or don't try to empathize during a conversation, they don't listen well. A related problem occurs when you don't adapt your listening style to the situation at hand and, as a result, you listen in a way that misses the point. Consider what might happen if you used a people-centered listening style during a meeting with an academic advisor – you might come away from the conversation with an appreciation for the advisor's warmth and kindness, but will you get all the details you need about graduation requirements? And what if you use a time-centered listening style when your friend needs to talk about a bad break-up? Your impatience may end up leaving your friend feeling even worse. When you don't bother to listen well or adapt your ways of listening to the specific situation, you can miss important parts of a message and have less-than-positive listening outcomes.

Nonlistening. Nonlistening is a complete breakdown of the listening process, because it involves enacting behaviors that make it look like you are listening when you really are not. Table 8.3 describes some common forms of nonlistening. In its simplest form, nonlistening can involve pretending to listen, perhaps by maintaining eye contact and nodding – even though your mind is on something else entirely. Another form of nonlistening occurs when you spend a conversation talking only about yourself. Nonlistening also includes attending to only a part of a message, taking messages too personally, focusing on finding flaws in the messages, or interpreting messages too literally. When you engage in any of these activities, you are not processing the messages that your interaction partner is sending.

Nonlistening
Enacting behaviors that make it look like you are listening, although you are not really doing so.

TABLE 8.3 Forms of nonlistening

Form	*Definition*
Pseudolistening	Pretending to listen when you're not
Monopolizing	Focusing communication on yourself instead of listening
Selective listening	Focusing only on specific parts of the message that are relevant to you
Defensive listening	Perceiving personal attacks in messages that are not criticism
Ambushing	Listening to gain information that will allow you to attack the speaker
Literal listening	Listening only for content and ignoring cues about the relationship

Surprisingly, you are most likely to engage in nonlistening when you are communicating with someone you know especially well. With a stranger, you are on the lookout for information that will help you learn about your partner, and you may work extra hard to decipher messages and figure out how to respond appropriately. In contrast, if your communication partner is a family member or someone you've known a long time, you might believe you already know what they have to say. As a result, you might tune out, stop listening, and start thinking ahead to your response. When you do this, you are engaging in nonlistening. Married partners are especially vulnerable to problems of nonlistening. Studies show that spouses don't spend much time thinking about their partner's perspective, and that they have an especially hard time listening during conflicts (Sillars, Roberts, Leonard, & Dun, 2000). Indeed, misunderstandings persist in close relationships, even when people have a long, shared history together, in part because they may be motivated to avoid hearing the truth (Sillars, 2011).

PAUSE & REFLECT

Do you have a relationship so close that you can predict what your partner will say and perhaps even finish her or his sentences? If so, does relying on your expectations in this way ever lead to miscommunication between you?

Putting Theory into Practice: Using Appropriate Listening Strategies

Although listening is a complex and sometimes challenging process, there are ways that you can improve your listening skills and become a more effective communicator.

Complete the listening process. Listening isn't a single event – it is a process that is completed only if you work through all of the steps. Complete the Communication in Action 8.1 exercise to find out which stages of the listening process you perform well, and which you might need to improve.

COMMUNICATION IN ACTION 8.1

Uncovering Listening Strengths and Weaknesses

Complete the form on the companion website to help you think about how well you listen during your interpersonal interactions.

Tailor your way of listening to the situation. Although people tend to have particular styles of listening, different situations call for different types of listening. You can be a more effective listener if you look for cues that will help you to adjust your listening style. As you talk to a communication partner, think about your goal in the conversation. In addition, try to figure out your partner's goal. If you have an idea about your own and the other person's goals for the situation, you can enact the type of listening appropriate to the situation. Try the Communication in Action 8.2 exercise to build these skills.

Prepare yourself to listen. You can enhance your communication experiences by overcoming obstacles to listening. To do so, eliminate as many distractions as possible so you can focus your attention on the listening process. When preparing yourself to be an effective listener, strive for the following goals:

- *Eliminate any physical impediments to listening.* Turn off the television, turn down the radio, or shut down the computer – eliminate anything that might distract you as you listen.

COMMUNICATION IN ACTION 8.2

Identifying Listening Goals

Complete the form on the companion website by identifying the most suitable listening style for each situation and the behaviors that would be most effective in helping you accomplish the listening goals of the interaction. If you can remember this exercise the next time you are faced with a listening goal, you will be better equipped to adapt your listening style to the situation.

- *Prepare yourself mentally to listen.* Set aside your own stressors and thoughts so that you won't be preoccupied with your own issues during conversation.
- *Transition completely from speaker to listener.* Don't spend your time listening trying to think of what you will say next. When you're a speaker you can speak, when you're a listener you should listen.
- *Hear your partner out completely before you react.* It's easy to get defensive or reactive if your partner says something that offends you or hurts your feelings, but if you react immediately you might not hear everything that your partner has to say.
- *Don't jump to conclusions.* It can be hard not to jump to conclusions when you know a person very well. Guard against nonlistening by focusing on what's new or unique about your partner's message and continue to test your assumptions against reality.

Overcoming barriers to effective listening is an ongoing process, and you'll never be completely successful. Nonetheless, making an active effort to prepare yourself to listen can help you minimize the obstacles you encounter when you communicate with another person.

ACTIVE LISTENING

Do you know people who are particularly good listeners? What do they do during an interaction to let you know that they are paying close attention? Do you know people who are especially poor listeners? Why do these people consistently fail to lend an ear? You have probably had enough interpersonal communication experiences to know that certain people are better listeners than others. For instance, research shows that people whose verbal messages focus on their partner and who are more nonverbally expressive tended to be rated as better listeners (Bodie & Jones, 2012). Another study concluded that interpersonal competence, in general, corresponds with better memory for a conversational partner's ideas (Miller & deWinstanley, 2002). In fact, memory for conversation improves when partners collaborate with each other to build common ground throughout an interaction (McKinley, Brown-Schmidt, & Benjamin, 2017). These research studies suggest that you can improve your listening outcomes through **active listening**, which involves engaging in the exchange of ideas and taking steps to better understand your partner. In this section, we examine two techniques you can use to become a more active listener: asking questions and paying attention to relational messages. We also consider the ways in which active listening can distort what you take away from a conversation.

Active Listening
Engaging in the exchange of ideas and taking steps to better understand your partner.

Asking Questions

One way to be an active listener is to ask questions. Asking questions can help to clarify information that you don't understand. Appropriate and well-timed questions also show your interaction partner that you're paying attention. Notice the use of questions in the Real Words transcript, which was drawn from a study of married couples (Priem, Solomon, & Steuber, 2009). Kevin asks a lot of questions, which encourage Sara to expand on her thoughts. His questions are challenging at times – such as when he asks, "Did that ever stop you before?" – but the overall effect is to bring more information into the conversation. By the end, they realize that Sara doesn't just want a new hobby, she wants to find something that she and Kevin can enjoy together, and when Kevin understands that goal, he agrees to work on it with her.

REAL WORDS

SARA: I wanna do something else beside work and exercise . . . I need something else to do.
KEVIN: Like what?
SARA: I don't know. You don't like me being involved in theatre but I'd love to go down and try out.
KEVIN: Well, why didn't you?
SARA: Because you don't like that.
KEVIN: Did that stop you before?
SARA: No, but you don't like it. Do you?
KEVIN: I've never stopped you. If that's something you wanted to do, then why didn't you do it?
SARA: I guess I gotta feel my way around, figure out what's going on. But that'd be fun.
KEVIN: Well, what else is stopping you?
SARA: Would you like to work in theatre? You wouldn't like it. You wouldn't do it. See, I'd like to do something you'd like to do, too. But . . . like with a private church that has a choir.
KEVIN: Well, let's try to work on that.

Asking questions can improve your listening outcomes in a variety of communication situations. Among college students, active listening in classes – including asking questions – is associated with academic success (Canpolat, Kuzu, Yildirim, & Canpolat, 2015). In online conversations between people getting to know each other, people who asked more questions are better liked by their conversation partners, largely because they are seen as more responsive (Huang, Yeomans, Brooks, Minson, & Gino, 2017). In the context of doctor-patient interactions, doctors who ask questions about the concerns their patient might have, beyond the main reason for their visit, get more information about the health issues their patients want to discuss (Robinson, Tate, & Heritage, 2016).

PAUSE & REFLECT

Do you tend to ask questions in your classes or when talking to people? Why or why not?

The right kind of questions can also improve communication for both partners in an interaction. For example, let's consider more closely the questions doctors ask patients during an office examination. Doctors who open a session with a patient by asking a general question, such as "What can I do for you today?", get a longer and more disclosive answer than doctors who ask the patient to confirm the reason for the visit – for example, "You are here for some blood work, correct?" (Heritage & Robinson, 2006). During an examination, doctors who ask about "any other concerns?" rather than saying "Do you have any questions?" are more likely to learn about other topics a patient wants to discuss (Robinson et al., 2016; Robinson & Heritage, 2016). And when the appointment is ending, doctors who ask questions such as "Okay?" or "All right?" steer the patient toward agreeing, rather than inviting further discussion; asking "anything else?" pressures patients into say "no," and asking "what other concerns do you have?" invites patients to bring up new topics (Robinson, 2001). These studies show that the way doctors phrase their questions can have a pervasive impact on the thoroughness of their communication with patients seeking care. You can learn about how active listening, including asking questions, affects a different communication situation – support conversations – by reading Inside Communication Research.

INSIDE COMMUNICATION RESEARCH

Mindfulness and Active Listening in Support Conversations

Providing effective social support can be a challenging endeavor, as it requires people to be attentive to nuances of the situation and craft messages that are sensitive to the recipient's cognitive and emotional state. Practicing mindfulness can make people more cognitively and emotionally centered, which can aid in their ability to attend to features of a situation and appropriately regulate their thoughts, feelings, and behaviors. Mindfulness involves five features: (a) observing the environment, (b) heightened awareness of the situation, (c) describing and labeling experiences, (d) taking a non-judgmental stance, and (e) being non-reactive. These characteristics of mindfulness can make people more sensitive to their surroundings and more engaged in interpersonal encounters, which can increase empathy enhance active listening. Communication scholars Susanne Jones, Graham Bodie, and Sam Hughes (2019) sought to examine whether people who practice mindfulness might be more empathetic and active listeners, which may in turn make them more effective support providers.

The researchers surveyed 183 undergraduate students about their degree of mindfulness, empathy, capacity for active listening, and their perceived ability to help people in difficult situations. They also presented the participants with a hypothetical scenario in which a good friend was upset that they did not receive a prestigious scholarship and asked them to rate the effectiveness and sensitivity of one of nine different messages that had been manipulated to reflect differing degrees of comforting communication.

Analysis of the survey responses showed that two features of mindfulness – observation of the environment and ability to describe or label their experience – were associated with more empathy and increased capacity for active listening. In turn, people who were more empathetic and engaged in more active listening were better equipped to help others in a difficult situation and recognize more effective and sensitive support messages. Interestingly, being non-judgmental as an aspect of mindfulness was associated with lower levels of empathy and decreased active listening, but it directly increased people's ability to help others in need. The results of this study indicate that the cognitive and emotional qualities of mindfulness can generally enhance people's empathy and active listening skills in ways that make them more effective support providers.

THINK ABOUT IT

1. What do you do to practice mindfulness when others come to you with a problem? Do you think that eliminating distractions and focusing on the situation make you a better listener and more capable of providing support?
2. The researchers found that being non-judgmental was a feature of mindfulness that surprisingly decreased people's capacity for empathy and active listening, but still made them more effective at recognizing high quality support. Why do you think being non-judgmental was associated with less empathy and active listening? Is it possible that being non-judgmental makes people more ambivalent in situations that would make them less attentive and engaged?

Listening for Relational Meanings

Paying attention to relational meanings when you communicate with a partner is another way to engage in active listening. As defined in Chapter 1, relational messages are verbal and nonverbal expressions that indicate how two people feel about each other or their relationship. Sometimes relational meanings are clear from the content of an utterance, such as when a partner says "I love you" or "I never want to see you again!" Even when relational messages are not so clear, listening can help you figure out how much a communication partner likes you, who has more power in your relationship, whether you can trust each other, and many other important things. When you listen for relational messages, you can learn a lot about the relationship you actually have, as well as about the type of relationship that your partner wants.

Table 8.4 identifies eight distinct relationship topics that can be more or less present in any conversation (Hale, Burgoon, & Householder, 2005) and, consequently, shape the outcomes of an interaction. For example, dating partners perceive interactions that involve criticism as less hurtful if partners communicate affiliation and informality at the same time (Priem, McLaren, & Solomon, 2010). Paying attention to all of the different relational messages can be difficult, in part because there are so many of them. One way that people keep track of them all is through specific ways of listening (McLaren, 2016). Listening for relational messages

TABLE 8.4 Relational message topics

Topic	*Examples of verbal messages*
Dominance vs. Submission	"Just do what I tell you to do and don't ask any questions."
	"Whatever you want for dinner is fine with me."
Composure	"You're so easy to talk to – I feel so comfortable around you."
	"Let's just hang out; we can relax."
Similarity & Depth	"I played rugby in college too. We should form a team together."
	"We seem to have a lot in common! What other kinds of things do you like to do for fun?"
Formality vs. Informality	"Excuse me, sir? Could I please ask you a question?"
	"Hey, what's up?"
Equality	"It would be great to work together on that project."
	"Let's split the workload – we both know what we're doing."
Closeness & Affection	"You have the most beautiful blue eyes!"
	"I know you've had a long day, so I'll give you a back rub after I finish making you dinner."
Task vs. Social Orientation	"I'd really rather just focus on studying for our exam."
	"This job can wait – tell me about your weekend."
Receptivity & Trust	"I've never told anyone this before, but I know you won't tell anybody so I'm willing to share it with you."
	"I'm here for you if you need me."

Relational Framing
Using either affiliation or dominance as a framework to interpret messages about a relationship.

begins with identifying whether the interaction is generally about how much the partners like each other or how much power each of them has. This process is called **relational framing**, because a listener uses either liking *or* power as a framework for making sense of a conversation. If a conversation is about liking, messages are seen as communicating how close, friendly, or positively partners feel toward each other. If a conversation is about power, messages are interpreted as signs of dominance, expressions of status, or submission to a partner's control. The How Do You Rate 8.2 exercise can help you to evaluate the relational messages that occur in your own interpersonal interactions.

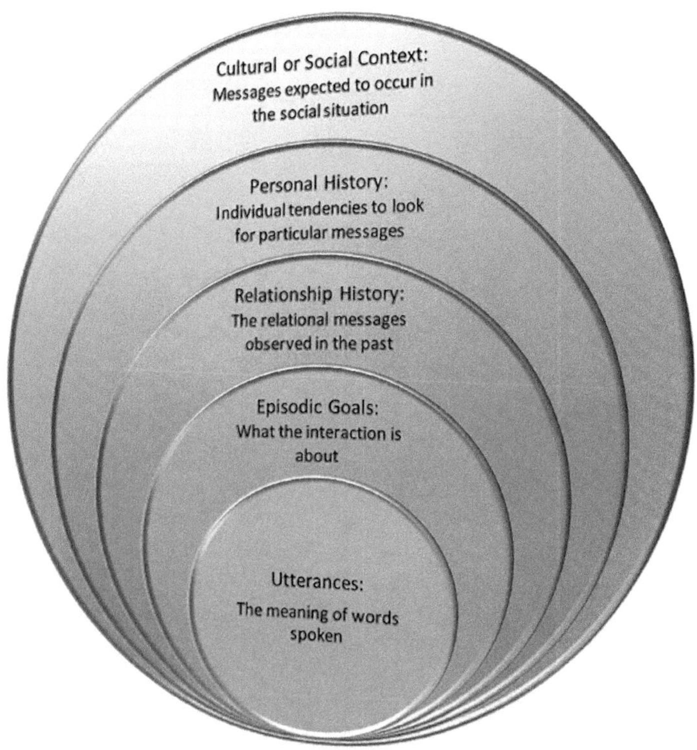
Cultural or Social Context:
Messages expected to occur in the social situation
Personal History:
Individual tendencies to look for particular messages
Relationship History:
The relational messages observed in the past
Episodic Goals:
What the interaction is about
Utterances:
The meaning of words spoken

FIGURE 8.4 Factors that affect relational framing

HOW DO YOU RATE? 8.2

Relational Messages

Visit the companion website to complete a scale that assesses your attention to relational messages. Reflecting on a recent conversation, the scale reveals which relational messages were present in the interaction. What do your results tell you about the nature of your relationship with your interaction partner?

Although you might consciously choose how to frame a conversation, this step in the process often happens automatically. Which frame you use depends on several factors (see Figure 8.5). Most specifically, the content of utterances themselves can clarify whether interactions are about power ("If you don't follow my rules, I'll fire you") or liking ("I'm so glad that I have a friend like you at work"). At a higher level of abstraction, the type of interaction can focus attention on issues of power (e.g., a performance review) or affiliation (e.g., a birthday greeting). If partners have a history of interactions that focus on either power or liking, that pattern would direct attention within a particular exchange. Likewise, some people have a general tendency to focus on status rather than friendship. At the most general level, social and cultural norms direct attention to power or liking cues within an interaction (Solomon & McLaren, 2008).

CONNECT WITH THEORY

Visit the companion website to learn about Relational Framing Theory, which explains how people use dominance-submission or affiliation-disaffiliation frames to make sense of ambiguous messages from communication partners.

PAUSE & REFLECT

What cues tell you whether a conversation is about how much you and a partner like each other, rather than how much power or status you each have?

FIGURE 8.5 Interacting in a status salient context

Source: Getty Images.

Not surprisingly, the frame you use to listen for relational messages shapes how you interpret cues in the conversation. When people view an interaction in terms of friendship, they interpret verbal and nonverbal cues as signs of liking or disliking, and when people view an interaction in terms of power, they interpret messages as signs of dominance or submission (McLaren, 2016). For example, think about how your perceptions of an interaction with a potential romantic partner might differ from your perceptions of an interaction with a condescending supervisor at work. In these types of interactions, your crush and your boss might enact similar behaviors that are perceived very differently based on the way you frame the interaction. In either interaction your partner might have leaned toward you, maintained steady eye contact, and touched you. If you were interacting with a potential romantic partner, these behaviors were probably perceived as signs that your partner liked you. In the interaction with your supervisor, you would probably interpret these behaviors as signs that your partner was trying to exert dominance and control. In other words, your interpretation of a partner's involvement in an interaction depends on the frame you use to make sense of those cues.

Biased Listening

Active listening has benefits, but there are some pitfalls to be aware of. Namely, we use active listening in some types of situations more than others, and that can lead to biases. Active listening can also lead you to distort messages from other people. You'll learn about some of the biases that accompany active listening in this section.

People tend to engage in active listening in some situations more than others. Consider the following research findings (Samp & Humphreys, 2007):

- People recall information more accurately when they interact with a friend than with a stranger.
- People remember more about disagreements than conversations where both partners agreed.
- When partners disagree, they recall negative information more accurately than positive information, especially in conversations with friends.

What do these findings mean? Active listening may be more likely or easier when you encounter disagreeable messages in close relationships. If you don't offset this trend with equal attention to positive messages, your active listening might lead you to think more negatively than you should about relationships you value.

PAUSE & REFLECT

Think back to the last time that you and a partner disagreed about what was said during a conversation. To what extent do you think your different memories were due to nonlistening versus active, but biased, listening?

Efforts to listen actively can also distort information. What might you do if someone you cared about was sending you messages that you didn't want to hear? Sometimes people go to extra effort to interpret threatening information in benign or nonthreatening ways. For example, if you were presented with a romantic partner's problematic behavior during a conflict, would you recognize it? Studies suggest that people are partly accurate in recognizing a partner's bad behavior, but they also focus on the positive when they value their relationship (Venaglia & Lemay, 2019). In fact, the evidence suggests that people might actively avoid information if it contradicts their preferred stance or plan of action (Woolley & Risen, 2018). In the same way, what people want to believe affects how they seek and interpret information (DeMarree, Clark, Wheeler, Briñol, & Petty, 2017).

In general, active listening helps you understand a communication partner. Asking questions and paying attention to relational messages allow you to get more information from a partner than you might if you listened more passively. Sometimes, though, being an active listener serves as a defense mechanism. If a friend is being disagreeable, you might be especially attentive. On the other hand, people sometimes take steps to avoid messages that they'd rather not hear.

Putting Theory into Practice: Leaning into Listening

In this section of the chapter, you learned about some extra effort you might make to be a more active listener, as well as how active listening sometimes goes too far. By embracing effective strategies for active listening and avoiding the pitfalls, you can get the most out of your interpersonal interactions.

Use questions strategically. You can enjoy many benefits as a listener when you ask questions. At the same time, you need to be strategic and judicious in your questioning strategy. How, then, do you find a balance between actively asking questions and overdoing it? Here are some strategies you can put to work in your own interactions.

- *Follow up on ambiguities.* Ask questions that focus on specific phrases that are unclear to you, such as "What did you mean when you said 'you're interested' in this project?" or "Does 'later this week' mean Wednesday, Thursday, or Friday?" When you limit your questions to parts of the message that are unclear to you, you let your partner stay on track while you address any sources of misunderstanding.
- *Question yourself.* If interrupting a communication partner with your questions would be inappropriate – perhaps because of status differences or the emotional tone of the topic – you can still keep track of where you need more information. Ask yourself questions while you listen, such as "I wonder why he feels that way?" or "Is this task a priority for my work team?" Keeping track of these questions can pinpoint important issues so that you can follow up on them at a more appropriate time.
- *Ask open-ended questions.* If you want to get more information out of a communication partner, avoid questions that allow for a yes or no answer. Instead, use open-ended questions that let your partner take control of the conversation, leave a lot of room for answers, and allow

for longer and more informative replies. For example, rather than, "Is this assignment due this week?" you might ask, "What's the timeline for this project?" Or rather than "Have you made up your mind?" you could ask "What's the process for your decision making?" Open-ended questions can yield more complete information.

- *Avoid conversation closers.* Some questions suggest to communication partners that you're ready to be done with a conversation, so avoid these when your real goal is active listening. "Is that all?" "Anything else?" and "Are we done here?" all suggest an eagerness to wrap up. In contrast, "Can you tell me more about this?" "What else can you tell me?" and "What other information should I have?" leave the door open to lengthier replies.

Read between the lines. One of the challenges you face when making inferences about your relationships is that you often have limited or indirect information. Your romantic interest might not come right out and tell you that they are attracted to you. Your professor may not explicitly clarify whether you should use her formal title or her first name. The Communication in Action 8.4 exercise highlights clues you can use to decipher relational messages.

COMMUNICATION IN ACTION 8.4

Interpreting Relational Meaning

Complete the form on the companion website as you think about a recent conversation where the relational meaning was unclear. Doing so may help you decipher interpersonal encounters more effectively in the future.

Don't read too much into messages. Active listening can help you be a more effective communicator, but avoid the pitfalls that come from obsessing over hidden meanings. For example, rather than drawing conclusions that aren't supported, base your interpretations of relational messages on the cues you have. If you can't reach firm conclusions, that's okay – it's better than reaching faulty ones.

This lesson was brought home for Miranda, a character on the popular sitcom *Sex and the City*, which originally aired in the early 2000s. When Miranda had to come to terms with a dating partner who didn't seem to like her, her friend, Berger, bluntly told her, "He's just not that into you." Although Miranda was shocked by Berger's honesty, she was also empowered by the simplicity of this insight. The observation resonated so much that a popular self-help book (Behrendt & Tuccillo, 2004) and major motion picture (Kwapis, 2009) promoted the idea that accepting relational messages at face value can be better than searching for messages that aren't there. Although it can be difficult to accept the truth, making convoluted inferences only complicates your interactions and relationships with other people.

RESPONDING TO PARTNERS

To this point, our description of listening has focused on what people do to pay attention to and make sense of messages from a communication partner, and we have learned that being an active listener can help you get the most out of conversation. An inherent part of listening, then, is that final step in the listening process: responding to a partner. In this section of the chapter, we turn our attention to where responses come from during conversations and how they can contribution to transformative communication experiences.

Assembling Messages

One of the most amazing tasks we manage when engaged in interpersonal communication is generating – in real-time – topical, coherent, and thoughtful responses to the messages that we receive. Although the time pressures are somewhat relaxed when we communicate using technology, such as when we are texting a friend, crafting relevant responses is still the hallmark of responsive communication. In fact, evaluations of artificial intelligence agents depend, in part, on the agent's ability to adapt the topics it introduces so that they are both coherent and engaging to a human partner (Glas & Pelachaud, 2018). As mere mortals, most of us are trying to accomplish the very same thing.

Action Assembly Theory was developed by communication scholar John Greene (see Greene, 2016) to explain how people's thought processes connect to overt communication behavior. Consider, for example, all the thoughts that come to mind as you listen to your friend discuss how their classes are going this semester. Your friend's words are likely to make you think about various classes you are taking, and perhaps you will think about a specific class you are taking – such as enthusiasm about an instructor, concern about a forthcoming exam, or frustration with a lab partner. Your friend's comments might also lead you to think about topics that are affecting your classes, such as worries about your parent's health, frustrations at work, or enthusiasm about your newest hobby. Action assembly theory seeks to explain how all those ideas are activated in your mind, sorted into a message that your friend will find coherent and responsive, and ultimately communicated to your conversation partner.

Action assembly theory suggests that the starting point for generating a response is the activation of ideas – and that spark comes from other sources, such as your communication partner. Listening, then, is the genesis of responding, because the words and ideas that you take in set your own mind at work. If you are texting with someone who mentions eating lunch, your own thoughts about food or restaurants will be activated in your mind. If someone mentions their cat, you might think of their cat, other cats you know, other pets in your life, or even a hit Broadway play. Once activated, these concepts are assembled into a response, with the concepts that are most activated getting priority in your message. For example, the concepts that are most active are more likely to be the subject phrase or focus of your message and they are the concepts that you will talk about the most during your speaking turn (Samp & Solomon, 2007).

CONNECT WITH THEORY

Visit the companion website to learn about action assembly theory, which explains how people's thought processes connect to over communication behavior.

Research on action assembly theory suggests that some people are better than others at crafting messages that are both novel and appropriate for the situation (Greene, Morgan, McCullough, Gill, & Graves, 2010; Morgan, Greene, Gill, & McCullough, 2009). In particular, people who listen more effectively, in that they process information from others more quickly, are able to be more fluent in their responses. In addition, people who are both somewhat open-minded and flexible thinkers seem to be more quick to adapt their messages to the demands of the communication situation. Because the cognitive processes behind message production show up in how fluently people speak (Greene, Kirch, & Grady, 2000), action assembly theory can help us understand why some people are more responsive listeners than others.

Expressing Empathy

Responding to a communication partner also involves conveying empathy. **Empathy**, which is the ability to understand and vicariously experience another person's situation or feelings, can dramatically change your reaction to another person. For example, when people listening to a person in distress are instructed to remain objective, they experience less concern and are less motivated to help than when they receive no instructions or are instructed to imagine the distressed person's point of view (McAuliffe, Carter, Berhane, Snihur, & McCullough, 2020). In hospital settings, medical professionals show a decline in empathy over the course of a long work shift, especially when they feel stressed and burned out, and this decrease in empathy corresponds with less patient-centered communication as the shift wears on (Passalacqua & Segrin, 2012). In contrast, messages that evoke empathy are more likely to motivate bystanders to take action to get someone help (Muralidharan & Kim, 2020). Perhaps not surprisingly, expressing empathy can be a powerful part of responding to a communication partner.

Empathy
The ability to vicariously experience another person's situation or feelings.

Health care settings are one context in which the impact of expressing empathy has been documented. For example, health professionals

Empathic Accuracy
An ability to accurately infer the content of another person's thoughts and feelings.

who express empathy can foster better outcomes in conversations with teens about substance abuse (Wombacher, Darnell, Harrington, Scott, & Martin, 2020). In the high stress context of a hospital emergency care unit, staff who express empathy can help soothe patients as they wait for treatment (Cohen, Wilkin, Tannebaum, Plew, & Haley, 2013). Expressing empathy is also an important part of therapists' interactions with people at risk for suicide (Knapp, 2020), and it can help patients navigate transitions that they experience over the course of treatment for cancer (Evans, Tulsky, Back, & Arnold, 2006). Expressing empathy for medical errors might even help doctors avoid malpractice suits (Nazione & Pace, 2015).

Just how do you go about expressing empathy effectively? Facial expressions that mirror the emotions of the person talking to you can help to convey that you are on the same page (Lwi, Haase, Shiota, Newton, & Levenson, 2019). Among teens, valued communication skills that convey empathy include messages that validate nonverbal messages, match the tone of the conversation, and acknowledge the speaker's perspective (Reed & Trumbo, 2020). Specific messages that convey empathy involve checking the accuracy of your impressions and saying that you understand a person's perspective and feelings (Mercer & Reynolds, 2002). Showing that you are paying attention by confirming your impressions, acknowledging emotions, and making topically relevant statements in response to your partner can do a lot to show that you empathize (Clark, Murfett, Rogers, & Ang, 2013). As these details make clear, you can't express empathy if you haven't attended to the other parts of the listening process – but if you have, you should be well-positioned to express that understanding when you respond to your communication partner. In the Interpersonal Communication Online box, you'll see how even nonhuman communication partners can express empathy in ways that make a difference.

SCHOLAR SPOTLIGHT

Visit the Communication Café on the companion website to view a conversation with John Greene, an expert on the production of interpersonal messages who has written about both action assembly theory and the experience of transcendence in interpersonal communication.

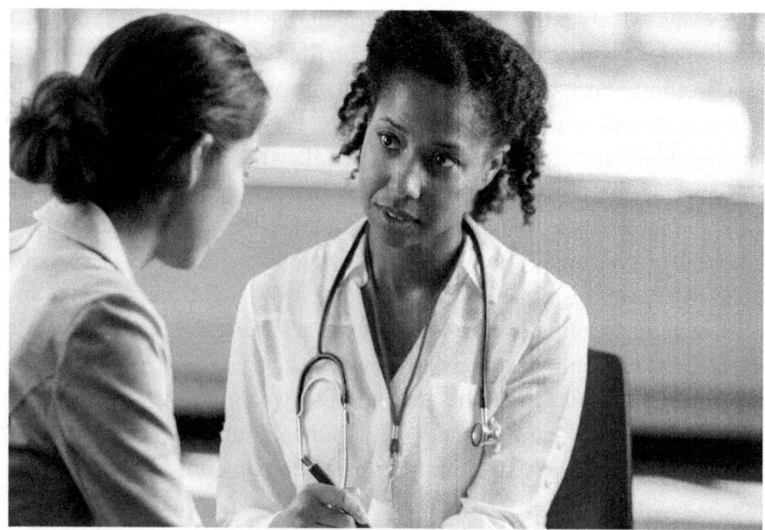

FIGURE 8.6 A doctor listens to a patient at the hospital

INTERPERSONAL COMMUNICATION ONLINE

This transcript was created by communication scholars Bingjie Liu and Shyam Sundar (2018) to study whether the inclusion of empathy expressions (the words in brackets) affected how people evaluated communication with a health advice chatbot. The results of their experiment showed that college students evaluated the chatbot less favorably when the words in brackets were left out of the message.

CHATBOT: Hello! I am a robot. How can I help you?
PARTICIPANT: My genitals feel itchy. Also got some rash on surrounding skin.
CHATBOT: [I could imagine how annoying genital issues can be.] Have you seen a doctor?
PARTICIPANT: I don't want to see a doctor because I might have been infected by HPV or other STD. What medicine should I take?
CHATBOT: [I understand why you are thinking about STD in this situation.] But many factors other than STD could cause these symptoms, such as allergy, fungus infection, or skin irritation. The best way is to take a formal test. Taking the wrong medicine can be dangerous.
PARTICIPANT: If I truly get infected by HPV, will I get cancer?
CHATBOT: [I understand your anxiety about being infected.] But most HPV infections go away on their own without causing problems, although several types are conducive to cancer.

Transcendence

As we have seen in this section of the chapter, listening is an interactive process, wherein communication partners give their attention to each other and respond in kind. When partners are enmeshed in an interaction, they might experience **transcendence** (Greene & Herbers, 2011), which occurs when communicators become completely engrossed in an interaction. In particular, four factors are considered part of transcendence:

Transcendance
A state of listening characterized by intense, mutual engagement in an interaction.

- Transcendence is characterized by a strong sense of mutuality, in that both partners perceive the other to be fully engaged in the interaction.
- This mutuality fosters a sense of connection or shared responsibility for the meanings created within the interaction.
- The level of mutual engagement and connection promotes creativity and insight, as the ideas that any one individual might have are embellished and emboldened by the connection with another person.
- Together the partners in an interaction discover new ways of thinking and being.

Experiences of transcendence are assumed to be rare, because they involve a special mix of understanding, mutuality, novelty, and even playfulness, and they are more likely when the partners are listening for both relational information and thinking analytically (Geiman & Greene, 2019). Transcendence, therefore, arises out of listening experiences where your responses are highly attuned to a communication partner – both through message assembly processes and mutual expressions of empathy. These experiences are also memorable. One example Denise recalls is a chance dinner party in the summer of 2020, when her community was largely shut down by the COVID-19 pandemic. After passing a couple in daily walks in the woods near her house for several weeks, Denise and her spouse were invited to a physically distant dinner party at the home of their new acquaintances. It was a gathering of strangers, in which José and Ernesto demonstrated their considerable culinary skills and the group shared their family histories. While Denise still can't recall the name of everyone scattered around the yard that evening, she was transported by the stories of immigration, family hardship, discrimination, and resilience that were exchanged that evening. Transcendent conversations are the rare and invaluable reward of skillful listening and responding.

Putting Theory into Practice: Attending to Detail When Responding to Partners

In this section of the chapter, you learned about how your role as a listener involves responding to a communication partner. Fortunately, this job is made all the easier if you follow your partner's lead. When you attend to another person's messages, you'll activate concepts in your own mind that are relevant and responsive, and you'll be better able to express empathy when it's your turn to speak. If you're lucky, you might experience transcendence as the conversation takes you and your communication partner on a novel and engaging journey. Attending to detail when you respond to communication partners can make all the difference.

Practice makes better. Action assembly theory helps us understand the processes in your mind that contribute to producing coherent messages, and also why the messages you do might highlight some information over other details. Research on the theory also suggests that people can improve their fluency by practicing. When you practice a particular way of presenting information, those routines are easier for you to use when you need to assemble information in a new conversation. Armed with that knowledge, you can prepare for important conversations by practicing your responses. When you anticipate meeting someone new, the first day of an important class, or answering questions during a job interview, you can give yourself an advantage by rehearsing the ways you'll organize information. You don't want to become so rote that you aren't responding to the conversation as it happens, but practicing even casual conversations can help make you more fluent when an important interaction comes along.

Empathize within limits. Connecting with another person's emotions can be a powerful way to appreciate that person's message. At the same time, you don't want to become overly emotional as you listen to a partner. If you do, your own emotions might drown out how your communication partner is feeling, making it harder for you to communicate effectively. The Communication in Action 8.3 exercise can help you focus on other people's emotions, rather than your own.

COMMUNICATION IN ACTION 8.3

Developing Empathic Accuracy

Pair up with another student to hone your empathy skills. To begin, identify a few topics that the two of you will discuss – perhaps what you are doing after graduation, how you feel about your hometown, or what you did on the last break from classes. Then, each of you should privately identify feelings about those topics that you will communicate – your fear or excitement about the future, your longing or distaste for home, your happiness or disappointment with your last vacation. Next, discuss those topics while each of you tries to figure out the other person's feelings. When you are done, check how close your perceptions were to the feelings your partner had during your conversation. If you take advantage of opportunities to practice and assess your ability to empathize, you can heighten your sensitivity to other people's feelings.

SUMMARY

Listening is a crucial part of interpersonal communication. Listening is an active process of taking in messages from a communication partner – it involves attending to messages, interpreting them, retaining meanings, evaluating information, and crafting a response. People use different types of listening, depending on whether a situation requires them to discriminate details in a message, appreciate the listening experience, comprehend information, evaluate facts or argument, or express empathy with a partner's feelings. People may also have a general preference for action-centered, content-centered, time-centered, or people-centered listening. Thus, listening is an active process that can unfold in a variety of ways within a particular conversation.

Given how involved listening can be, we shouldn't be surprised that there are many barriers to effective listening. Those obstacles include noise in the environment around you, message complexity and information overload, and your own state of mind. When your own mind is overactive – because you're preoccupied with other thoughts, wrapped up in your emotional reaction to an interaction, or prejudging a partner's messages – you can have trouble focusing on the information being communicated to you. Your state of mind can also interfere with listening when you don't put out the effort to listen or to adapt your listening style to the specific interaction. Nonlistening is an especially problematic form of communication, because you don't receive and process messages sent your way, but you give off signals that can make your partner think you are listening.

Active listening involves performing actions that improve listening outcomes. When you ask questions of a communication partner, you can convey your interest in the conversation, address points of confusion, and encourage your partner to provide more information. In educational and medical settings, an ability to ask the right kinds of questions can be the difference between learning and not learning or between getting a diagnosis right or wrong. Active listening also involve paying attention to relational messages. People communicate a variety of relational messages, including messages conveying dominance versus submission, composure, similarity and depth, formality versus informality, equality, closeness and affection, task versus social orientation, and receptivity and trust. Framing your interactions in terms of liking and friendship or dominance and power can help you make sense of the specific relational messages that you receive during a conversation. Although being an active listener can help you communicate more effectively, keep in mind that the extra effort needed can lead to biased or distorted interpretations of a conversation.

Responding to a communication partner is an essential part of listening. Responding in relevant ways relies on assembling messages from the concepts in our minds that are activated by what a communication partner says. In addition, trying to empathize with a communication partner's feelings can also help you to understand where he or she is coming from during a conversation. And when you express empathy, you show a communication partner that you are paying attention, you value what they have to say, and you understand their point of view. When you are responsive and express empathy while listening, you might even have the rare and enjoyable experience of transcendence while talking with another person.

Interpersonal communication fails without effective listening. Being a conscientious listener can help you and your interaction partner get more out of a conversation. Attentive listening also communicates sincerity, interest, and competence to a partner. When you ask questions strategically and pay attention to relational messages, you enrich and expand your understanding of messages. And when you are responsive and express empathy, you have interpersonal communication experiences that can shape your current and future relationship with an interaction partner.

ACTIVITIES FOR EXPLORING COMMUNICATION ETHICS

What Would You/Should You Do?

Your friend comes to you to complain about an interaction she recently had with her boyfriend, who informed her that he can no longer be her date at her cousin's wedding due to obligations at work. It's clear from her description of the situation that she believes her partner deliberately scheduled work for that weekend to avoid being with her and that he doesn't feel badly about letting her down. You already spoke to your friend's boyfriend earlier in the day, at which time he expressed disappointment over not being able to attend the wedding but sensed that his girlfriend understood and wasn't upset by the situation. Based on what you've heard from both individuals, you have concluded that they are misunderstanding how one another feels because they aren't listening effectively to what their partner is saying. What would you or should you do in this situation to help your friends better understand one another?

Something to Think About

The idea of a "listening tour" has gained stature in various realms. Hillary Clinton engaged in listening tours both during her successful campaign to become a New York Senator and in her unsuccessful bid for President of the United States. In the workplace, chief executive officers use a listening tour of their organization to gain insight into the perceptions of the people who work for them. Community leaders might also stage a listening tour to understand the concerns of citizens. While a listening tour is ostensibly intended to gather information, it also functions to campaign for votes, ferret out dissent, or convey the impression of concerned leadership. Can listening be authentic and sincere when the person doing the listening is also trying to advance his or her personal goals?

Analyze Communication Ethics Yourself

Visit any discussion board devoted to a social issue; for example, you might visit a website for breast cancer survivors, political conservatives, people hoping to adopt a child, global warming, or anything of that sort. At that site, follow one of the discussion board strings to see how contributors to that discussion respond to each other. Look closely at follow-up messages, and evaluate whether each responder is respecting the ideas presented earlier. Based on your analysis, what do you think are the ethical issues that apply when people "listen" and respond to each other in online venues?

KEY WORDS

- active listening
- active-empathic listening
- appreciative listening
- attending
- comprehensive listening
- discriminatory listening
- empathic accuracy
- empathy
- evaluating
- evaluative listening
- hearing
- listening
- listening style
- nonlistening
- paraphrasing
- relational framing
- remembering
- responding
- transcendence
- understanding

PART 3 INTERPERSONAL RELATING

Visit the Communication Café on the companion website to hear Denise and Jen talk about the topics addressed in Part 3 of this book.

Perhaps one of the most powerful outcomes we produce through interpersonal communication is the creation, negotiation, maintenance, and dissolution of interpersonal relationships. As you learned in Chapter 8, all of our interpersonal communication conveys information about our relationship with an interaction partner. In this unit, we focus on the personal relationships that emerge from repeated engagement in interpersonal communication over time. Your friendships, romantic relationships, and family relationships are associations that may have a lasting influence on your identity and your well-being. We'll explore how interpersonal communication is the foundation for those relationships.

All of the relationships you have, with the exception of some family bonds, began as an interaction between strangers. Interpersonal communication is a reflection of the changes that occur as people become familiar with each other and form sometimes lasting ties. Interpersonal communication is also a tool we use to move our relationships to more or less close levels of engagement. Chapter 9 traces the path of developing and dissolving relationships, and sheds light on the role of interpersonal communication within these associations.

Humans are also capable of forming intimate bonds, whether between friends or romantic partners. Intimacy is a complex phenomenon, capturing feelings of excitement that can characterize a new love, companionship between long-term friends, and many things in between. Although often very rewarding, intimate relationships can also be fraught with tension. Chapter 10 delves into the intricacies of intimate relationships and showcases interpersonal communication at the heart of these bonds.

Chapter 11 turns attention to family relationships. Families take many forms in contemporary society, and interpersonal communication is essential to all of them. Families can also be a challenging context for interpersonal communication as members navigate multiple family roles and numerous family rules. Adding to this complexity is the way that families change as their members change. In this chapter, then, you'll learn about how interpersonal communication contributes to family life across the lifespan.

DOI: 10.4324/9781351174381-11

LEARNING OBJECTIVES

After reading this chapter, you should be able to:

1 Understand how people cope with uncertainty in initial interactions.
2. Understand how people promote positive outcomes in new relationships.
3. Describe four issues that underlie the escalation of relationships.
4. Describe four issues that underlie the dissolution of relationships.
5. Recognize the behaviors that constitute obsessive relational intrusion and stalking.
6. Strengthen your ability to develop or to end relationships gracefully.

PUTTING THEORY INTO PRACTICE

In this chapter, you will learn how to:

1. Make your self-disclosure appropriate and interesting.
2. Make the most of small talk.
3. Balance breadth and depth in your self-disclosure.
4. Talk about your uncertainty.
5. Give interdependence time and effort.
6. Weigh the pros and cons of decreasing intimacy.
7. Manage face threats when ending close relationships.
8. Clarify and respect relationship boundaries.

DEVELOPING AND ENDING RELATIONSHIPS

9

Source: Emma Kim/Getty Images.

Massive multi-player online video games – like Minecraft, Fortnite, and World of Warcraft – are extremely popular as a source of entertainment, relaxation, and stress relief. Beyond these personal benefits, online gaming is a rewarding way for people to socialize and develop interpersonal relationships. Especially during the COVID-19 pandemic, many people turned to online gaming as a way to connect socially with others when face-to-face meetups were restricted. The game *Animal Crossing* gained massive popularity during the pandemic, with people holding birthday parties, first dates, and even weddings within the game. A study by the Pew Research Center found that 72% of all teens spend free time playing games on a computer, gaming console, or personal device, and 36% of those teens say that they have made a new friend through networked video games. Online video game players develop a sense of kinship with their teammates, with 78% of teens saying they feel closer to people they already know through gaming, and 52% reporting increased closeness with friends whom they only interact with online. Frequent gamers say that the team-building and collaboration that occurs in online games is a great way to learn about another person and form positive and close relationships. Thus, online gaming helps people to keep up with old friends and get to know new ones.

Interpersonal communication plays a central role in the development, escalation, and dissolution of close relationships. People who make friends through online video games get started through their common interest in gaming, but come to understand each other on a deeper level by revealing aspects of their personality through game play, engaging in online chats, and gradually sharing more personal information about themselves. Whether relationships develop online or offline, both contexts involve decisions about revealing or concealing information about yourself and gathering information about others.

What happens in a relationship that moves people from acquaintances to intimate partners? When people are asked to identify important turning points in their friendships, they mention events like discovering shared interests, disclosing private information, spending time with mutual friends, taking a trip together, and living together (Johnson, Wittenberg, & Haigh, 2004; Johnson, Wittenberg, Villagran, Mazur, & Villagran, 2003). Increases in how much time friends spend together and a shift in the context for shared time – for example, from having a class together to meeting up to study – can also signal the development of a friendship (Dominguez & Hall, 2020; Hall, 2019). In romantic relationships, the shift from online to in-person shared time (Sharabi & Caughlin, 2017), and transitioning from using social media to gather information about a partner to, instead, showcasing the relationship (Brody, LeFebvre, & Blackburn, 2016) can mark developing intimacy. As illustrated in Figure 9.1, some relationships move through these turning points quickly, others run into roadblocks along the way, and some take time to develop intimate bonds.

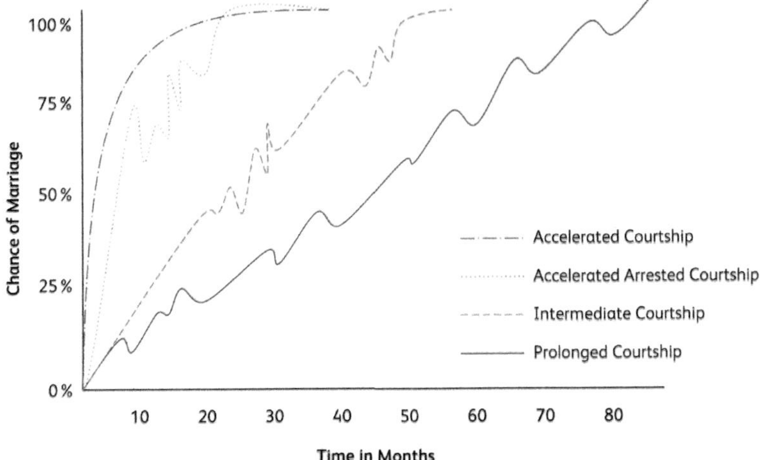

FIGURE 9.1 Four trajectories of courtship

PAUSE & REFLECT

Consider a friendship or romantic relationship you've developed in the past few years. Can you identify specific events that changed your relationship?

Catherine Surra (1985; see also Ogolsky, Surra, & Monk, 2016) identified four pathways to commitment. Some people have an accelerated courtship in which they move quickly toward a committed relationship and never look back, while others start on a fast track to intimacy but encounter turbulence just before making that commitment. Some relationships have a slow, steady, prolonged courtship, whereas others move steadily but more quickly toward mutual commitment.

One long-standing approach to thinking about relationship development focuses on a series of stages that partners move through as relationships develop (Knapp, 1984). Movement through stages can be fast or slow, but all couples experience these phases as they develop or dissolve a relationship (see Figure 9.2). In fact, people describing important events in romantic relationships tend to organize their expectations around these developmental stages (Honeycutt & Cantrill, 2001). You can gain insight into the role of communication in friendships and romantic relationships by focusing on the goals and messages that characterize the formation, escalation, and dissolution of intimacy.

FORMING RELATIONSHIPS

Over the course of a day, you might find yourself talking to any number of people you are meeting for the first time. You might chat with someone

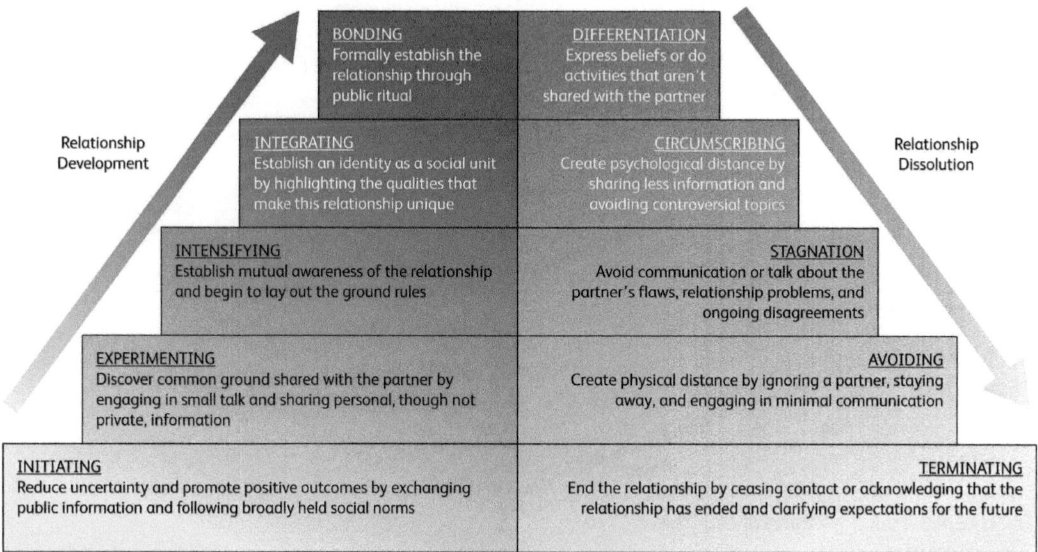

FIGURE 9.2 Knapp's model of relationship development and dissolution. This model of relationship development shows the steps people go through as they develop or dissolve a relationship. Couples can increase or decrease intimacy by going up the development side or down the dissolution side from whichever level they are on.

while you wait in line at a coffee shop, you might share a table with someone new at the library, you might exchange messages with someone in an online chat room, or you might meet the friend of a friend at a club. Although many of the interactions that you have go no further than that single conversation, all of your close relationships – excluding family – began with a conversation between strangers. What sets some relationships on the path to closeness, while others are quickly forgotten? Where you go from those initial interactions depends on your ability to accomplish two basic tasks: figuring out how to communicate with the other person and discovering opportunities for positive experiences.

Coping with Uncertainty

Uncertainty
A lack of information about a conversational partner.

One of the primary challenges to communicating with strangers is that you know so little about them. Shall you talk about your favorite professional football team? What if they don't like sports? Perhaps you should ask about their major – but maybe they aren't a student. Without knowing about the other person's cultural background, you can't even be sure that your tendency to make eye contact, gesture, and lean forward while you talk won't be perceived as invasive and rude. **Uncertainty**, a lack of information about a conversational partner, undermines your ability to communicate. In particular, uncertainty makes it difficult to set goals for the conversation, to plan a course of action, and to enact verbal and nonverbal messages (Knobloch & Satterlee, 2009). Thus, your initial interactions with other people are typically focused on gathering information that will help you communicate – a process called uncertainty reduction (Berger & Calabrese, 1975).

In the formative stages of relationship development, you reduce your uncertainty about each other by exchanging information. **Self-disclosure** is the general term that refers to telling another person about your characteristics, experiences, feelings, attitudes, or beliefs. Within initial interactions, your self-disclosures focus on public information, such as name, age, and hometown (Greene, Derlega, & Mathews, 2006). Although this information might seem superficial, it allows you to orient yourself with respect to your communication partner. For example, when Denise's neighbors took a trip with their church to repair a community in Puerto Rico damaged by Hurricane Maria, they often initiated conversations with other workers by asking where they were from and what service group they were with; based on the answer, they could discuss anything that was revealed by the geographic region of the person's hometown or the mission and beliefs of the service groups that were represented. In general, then, gathering public information about another person can help you and a partner find topics to talk about.

In addition to discovering topics to discuss, you need to determine what style of communication you should use. Should you be open and direct, or would your partner find less explicit messages to be more appropriate? How much detail should you go into on the topics you discuss? Is humor or sarcasm okay, or does your partner expect you to be more serious? To cope with uncertainty about how to communicate in initial interactions, people follow a **norm of reciprocity** in which they match their own disclosures to those made by their partner. The transcript presented in the Real Words feature shows how the norm of reciprocity helps us to navigate initial interactions. Notice how the self-disclosures are not dominated by one person or the other; instead, each person takes turns sharing a detail, and that detail is matched by the other person.

In reciprocating disclosures, partners attend to three issues. First, they typically address the same topic that was raised by the other person: Julia tells Rob her name and he tells her his name; Rob says he has four sisters and Julia reveals she has one brother. Second, they tend to match the length or expansiveness of the other person's message. Rob elaborates on being the baby in the family and Julia goes on to describe the merits of being a youngest sibling, but it would be unusual if Julia responded by going into great detail about her relationship with each person in her family. Finally, they match qualities of their messages – for example, use of explicit language, humor, or politeness – to qualities of their partner's speech. Julia and Rob both become more casual in their speech as the conversation evolves. Although the norm of reciprocity might make initial interactions a bit scripted, it structures conversations when you otherwise lack information about how to communicate with a person. The result is a more fluid interaction that can advance your relationship to the next

CONNECT WITH THEORY

Visit the companion website to learn more about uncertainty reduction theory, which explains why relationship formation is ripe for uncertainty and the strategies people use to reduce it.

Self-disclosure
Telling another person about your characteristics, experiences, feelings, attitudes, or beliefs.

Norm of Reciprocity
The tendency to match our own disclosures to those made by our partner.

REAL WORDS

AN INITIAL INTERACTION

As you review this script from a typical initial interaction, notice how the partners match the topic, expansiveness, and tone of each other's self-disclosures. How would the information being shared help you communicate with either Julia or Rob?

JULIA: Hi. My name's Julia.
ROB: Hey, I'm Rob. I have a sister named Julia.
JULIA: Really? That's cool. So then you'll never forget it!
ROB: Yeah.
JULIA: Is she your only sister?
ROB: No, I have four older sisters. I'm the baby in the family and the only boy. What about you?
JULIA: Just one older brother.
ROB: So you're the baby too.
JULIA: Yeah. It's the best. Well, at least for me, I got kind of spoiled.
ROB: Do you still live at home with your parents?
JULIA: No, my family is back in Philadelphia. I came out here for school
ROB: Oh ... what are you studying?
JULIA: Psychology. My dad wanted me to get a business degree, but ... I don't know ... I just couldn't really get into it.
ROB: Too boring?
JULIA: Yeah, I guess. Are you in school? Or ... um ... what do you do?
ROB: I just graduated. Trying to find a job.
JULIA: Doing what?
ROB: Well, I had a boring business degree... so...
JULIA: Oh no! How embarrassing! I'm sorry. It wasn't really that boring.

level. In fact, experiments that manipulated responses to self-disclosures in computer-mediated conversations showed that people liked partners more when they responded to self-disclosures with either reciprocal disclosures or compliments, and avoided changing the topic (Dai, Shin, Kashian, Jang, & Walther, 2016).

PAUSE & REFLECT

How do you feel when a conversation with a new acquaintance doesn't follow the norm of reciprocity? Is this more or less noticeable in face-to-face or online interactions?

Exploring Possibilities

As you reduce uncertainty in the formative stage of relationships, you are also trying to discover and promote positive outcomes. The **predicted outcome value** of an interaction or a relationship refers to the rewards you expect to get from a future relationship with a new acquaintance. When predicted outcome value is high, people tend to talk more, ask more questions, and use nonverbal behaviors that communicate liking and encourage disclosures (Sunnafrank, 2016). A survey of members of an online dating service found that people make more honest, frequent, and intentional self-disclosures to online partners when they want to continue that relationship face to face (Gibbs, Ellison, & Heino, 2006). In fact, the predicted outcome value based on conversations at the beginning of a semester influences how close classmates become by the ninth week of the semester (Sunnafrank & Ramirez, 2004). Because predicted outcome value has powerful effects on interpersonal communication and relationship development, people spend initial interactions trying to assess and maximize future rewards.

Predicted outcome value
The rewards a person expects to get from a future relationship with a new acquaintance.

In an effort to predict the value of a relationship, you expand your conversations with new acquaintances beyond generic, public self-disclosures by engaging in small talk. Although the specific content of small talk isn't very important to interaction partners, participating in the conversation builds rapport (Coupland, 2003). Small talk also allows partners to cover a lot of topics in search of commonalities that can foster a relationship. As you engage in small talk, two rules keep the conversation moving in a positive direction. First, limit your self-disclosures to positive, rather than negative, information. Remember, your interaction partner is trying to decide if they want a relationship with you, so you want to keep your less desirable traits under wraps for a while. Second, follow broadly held social norms. Eventually, your quirky traits might be endearing; however, at this point in your relationship, you should avoid behaviors that might suggest you're abnormal. When you keep the content of your disclosures positive and show that you aren't too unusual, you increase the likelihood that someone will be willing to have a relationship with you.

As part of the relationship development process, then, it's important to weigh the risks and rewards associated with self-disclosures. Do you know this person well enough to trust them with your deeply personal information? Will your disclosure have the desired effect on the relationship? One study asked college students to explain their reasons for sharing or not sharing a piece of positive information about themselves (Derlega, Anderson, Winstead, & Greene, 2011). Some of the reasons for sharing the information included: (a) feeling close to the partner (e.g., "We have a really good relationship, I can tell her anything"), (b) similarity of experiences and interests (e.g., "He has been in the same situation, so he could easily relate"), and (c) building closeness (e.g., "It would help him get to know me better"). Some of the reasons for withholding the information included: (a) wanting to avoid a negative reaction (e.g., "I didn't want our relationship to become weird"), (b) not feeling close enough to share the information (e.g., "I don't have enough rapport with him"), (c) lacking enough similarity for a partner to understand (e.g., "I don't think he would be able to relate to my experience"), and (d) wanting to maintain privacy (e.g., "There are just some things that are too personal to share"). These results reveal the thought processes behind people's disclosure decisions, as well as the potential risks and rewards that can arise from sharing personal information with a relationship partner.

PAUSE & REFLECT

During an initial interaction, either face-to-face or online, what personal information or traits might you withhold to improve your partner's impression of you?

Putting Theory into Practice: Starting Out on The Right Track

Your experiences during the formative stage of relationship development determine which relationships will grow into friendships and romances, and which will end as brief and forgettable encounters. By developing skills to reduce uncertainty and promote positive outcomes, you can open the door to interpersonal relationship opportunities.

Toe the line as you self-disclose. Initial interactions require you to package your unique and interesting qualities in familiar scripts for self-disclosure, but just because you're following norms for initial interactions, doesn't mean that you can't make these conversations interesting. Here are some guidelines for making your self-disclosure appropriate and interesting:

- Exchange public information, no matter how ordinary it might seem, to help a new acquaintance to locate you within a diverse society ("I went to Springfield High School, here in town" or "My parents came to the US from India, and I was born here").
- Reciprocate conversational behaviors to work with a partner in setting the course, the pace, and the tone of the interaction – in other words, if your partner comments on the weather, say what you think about it; if your partner brings up their favorite sports, comment on your interest in sports or something else you enjoy.

- Spice up your introductions by focusing on qualities that aren't private or personal, but that set you apart from others (Are you from an especially large family? Do you have an uncommon pet? Is there anything unique about your hometown?).
- Portray yourself truthfully – making exaggerated or misleading disclosures doesn't allow your partner to reduce uncertainty, it doesn't help your partner predict the value of a relationship with you, and it can undermine a relationship once your true qualities are revealed.

You can promote relationship development by following the script for initial interactions, helping your partner communicate with you, and showing that you're not someone ordinary.

Make the most of small talk. Small talk has a big job to do: it's your tool for ferreting out common ground on which you can build a relationship. Given that important task, be sure to take advantage of opportunities for small talk.

COMMUNICATION IN ACTION 9.1

Making the Most of Small Talk

Complete this exercise using the form on the companion website to help yourself prepare for your next conversation where small talk is called for.

ESCALATING RELATIONSHIPS

When your formative experiences are promising, you escalate relationships through continued interpersonal communication. Although relationships develop and change in many different ways, four general issues underlie the escalation of any friendship or romance: (a) people need to develop a sense of connection and intimacy; (b) they need to resolve questions and doubts about the relationship; (c) they need to learn how to coordinate their behaviors; and (d) they need to figure out how to balance the rewards and costs they each experience. In this section of the chapter, we explore the communication strategies that contribute to relationship escalation.

Creating a Connection

You create a connection with other people by spending time with them and sharing information with them. Social penetration theory is a description of relationship escalation that focuses on how communication allows

CONNECT WITH THEORY

Visit the companion website to learn more about social penetration theory, which describes the processes people use to disclose personal information and build closeness in relationships.

partners to probe each other's self-concepts (Altman & Taylor, 1973). As illustrated in Figure 9.3, this theory highlights how our personalities are organized into layers within segments representing different domains or aspects of our lives. Public information is at the outermost layer of each segment, and internal layers contain increasingly more personal information; the innermost layer is where you keep your most private attitudes, beliefs, and fears. Establishing a relationship involves increasing both **depth**, how personal or private information is, and **breadth**, the variety of life's segments you share with a partner. When you increase the depth and breadth of shared knowledge by self-disclosing to another person, you promote the development of intimacy in that relationship.

Depth
The extent to which shared information is personal or private.

Breadth
The variety of topics that we share with a partner.

Recall that self-disclosure in the formative stages of relationship development is guided by the norm of reciprocity, such that the information

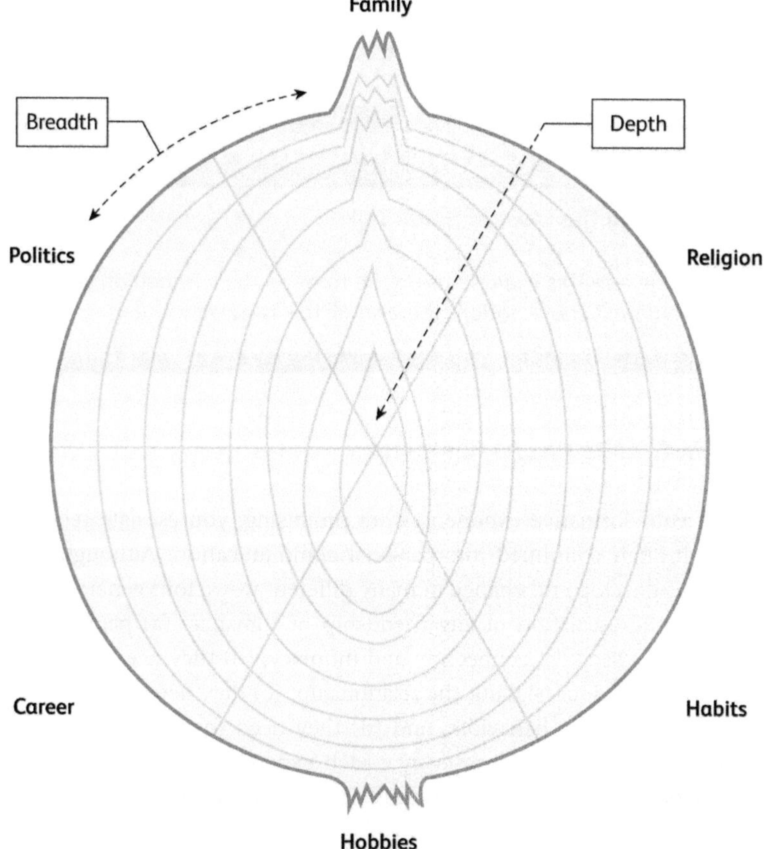

FIGURE 9.3 Social penetration theory. Social penetration theory suggests that our personalities are multi-layered like the layers of an onion. The wedges in the onion represent the different topics that we might disclose about to an interaction partner. In all segments, the outer layers of the circle contain public information that is easy to reveal to others, whereas the innermost circle represents our most private values and beliefs. Relationships escalate as self-disclosure increases in both breadth – the variety of topics – and depth, the extent to which the information reveal is personal or private.

offered by one person is immediately matched by the partner. In escalating relationships, this "tit-for-tat" pattern of exchange is replaced by responses to disclosures that convey understanding and validation (Greene et al., 2006). Consider the example of Terry and Allyson, who are escalating their new relationship. When Terry shares news of their promotion at work, Allyson can respond in one of two general ways: she can describe her own recent success at work, or she can show excitement for Terry's news. Although a matching disclosure might make sense if Terry and Allyson are still getting to know each other, it doesn't do much to celebrate Terry's good news. In contrast, Allyson can prolong Terry's celebration by keeping the focus on the promotion.

PAUSE & REFLECT

Do you know anyone who typically responds to your news or problems by talking about their own experiences? How does that response make you feel?

Another change that occurs as relationships escalate involves the appearance of less socially acceptable self-disclosures. As the depth of your disclosures increases, you move beyond positive, public information, and you begin to offer up more private and possibly problematic details. For example, you might show your friend that you sing off-key, tell your partner about a past indiscretion, or reveal that you hold an unpopular opinion. When you share less flattering details about yourself, you show partners that you trust them with sensitive information. Importantly, overly disclosive behavior can backfire if it occurs too early in the relationship. For example, one study found that people generally paid more attention to a person's intimate disclosures on Twitter, but those disclosures only led to positive evaluations if the poster was already perceived as having similar qualities (Baruh & Cemalcilar, 2015). On the other hand, discovering that you and another person share a rare or negative attitude can fuel a connection (Alves, 2018; Weaver & Bosson, 2011). Thus, changes in self-disclosure, and the opportunities for responsiveness that they create, are an essential part of building a personal connection within emerging relationships.

Resolving Doubts

As discussed previously in this chapter, initial interactions involve considerable uncertainty about a new acquaintance, and the formation of a relationship requires gathering information that allows you to communicate.

Relational Uncertainty
The lack of knowledge people have about their relationships.

When an acquaintance becomes something more special, questions about the relationship itself start to occupy you. **Relational uncertainty** refers generally to the lack of knowledge people have about their relationships (Knobloch & McAninch, 2016), and it includes three kinds of doubts. Specifically, self uncertainty involves your questions about your own involvement in a relationship, partner uncertainty refers to doubts that you have about your partner's commitment to the relationship, and relationship uncertainty includes your doubts about the very nature of the relationship. Although the three sources of relational uncertainty focus on distinct issues, they each reflect unknowns that can block relationship escalation.

HOW DO YOU RATE? 9.1

Relational Uncertainty

Visit the companion website to complete an adapted version of Denise Solomon and Kellie Brisini's (2017) relational uncertainty scale. How does your level of uncertainty in a relationship influence the way you behave in that relationship?

What can you do to address relational uncertainty and escalate a promising relationship? Ironically, being uncertain about a relationship often leads people to be more indirect in their communication, and this pattern has been found within dating relationships (Theiss & Estlein, 2014), between parents and their children's new spouses (Mikucki-Enyart & Caughlin, 2018), and in marriages experiencing the transition to an empty nest (King & Theiss, 2016). Instead, people in dating relationships are more likely to rely on covert strategies, such as spying or tying to induce jealousy, when they are uncertain about their relationship (Dainton, Goodboy, Borzea, & Goldman, 2017). These activities, referred to as **secret tests** (Baxter & Wilmot, 1984), including flirting with someone else to see if a partner cares enough to get jealous, imposing a separation – perhaps by not calling – to see how long it takes for the other person to initiate contact, or changing your social media status to "In a Relationship" to see if your partner will update their status as well. Although secret tests can answer questions about the relationship, you should be cautious about using them in relationships you value; not everyone appreciates being the target of a covert investigation.

Secret Tests
Covert actions designed to reveal information about a partner's involvement in a relationship.

PAUSE & REFLECT

How would you react if you knew someone was testing you to see how involved you were in that relationship?

Relationship Talk
Communication with a partner about your relationship with him or her.

An alternative to secret tests is **relationship talk**, communicating with your partner about your relationship. Relationship talk can be risky because it might reveal that one partner wants the relationship more than the other, and relational uncertainty magnifies the perceived threat of relationship talk (Theiss & Nagy, 2013). At the same time, talking about the relationship can help people resolve doubts that are blocking relationship development. In one study, partners in developing romantic relationships were asked to discuss positive, negative, or surprising events, and report their perceptions of the relationship talk (Knobloch, Solomon, & Theiss, 2006). The results showed that relationship talk was more likely to improve the quality of the relationship during the early stages of a relationship than in later stages of a relationship when partners were already highly intimate. Despite the risks, then, relationship talk offers a way to address uncertainties that may be holding relationships back.

Coordinating Behavior

As partners escalate a relationship, they also begin to coordinate and integrate their day-to-day activities. Consider the numerous ways that Audrey relies on her relationships over the course of her day: she walks dogs with her best friend Diane in the morning, she borrows her roommate's sweater when she gets dressed, she sits next to her buddy Sean in class, she gets a ride home from campus with her brother Blake, and she makes plans for the weekend with her romantic partner. In similar ways, Audrey's friends, family, and romantic partner depend on her to dog sit occasionally, do laundry for the household, share lecture notes, chip in with gas money, and make the weekend more fun. **Interdependence** exists when partners can count on each other to accomplish their everyday goals.

Interdependence
A state that exists when relationship partners rely on each other to accomplish their goals.

Finding ways to integrate new people into your daily routine can be challenging. The relational turbulence model highlights how establishing interdependence can be a source of difficulty within developing relationships (Solomon, 2016). According to the model, people move beyond the formative stage of relationship development by allowing a partner to influence or affect their day-to-day experiences; for example, you might start carpooling to campus with your new friend, arrange a study date to get ready for midterms, or reschedule your daily workout so your partner can join you. When you revise your activities to include your partner, your routine will initially suffer – you end up late to campus because your friend isn't a morning person, your studying suffers because the two of you can't stay focused, and you find it easier to blow off exercise late in the day. Thus, the relational turbulence model suggests that an unavoidable part of relationship escalation is the fact that a partner might create interference or barriers to your personal goals. Keep in mind that interference occurs because you are involving a partner in routines that they don't fully understand. If you talk with your partner about your goals, you might find even better ways of achieving them that include your partner. And when partners coordinate their behaviors so that they help each other achieve everyday goals, they become interdependent and, therefore, more intimate.

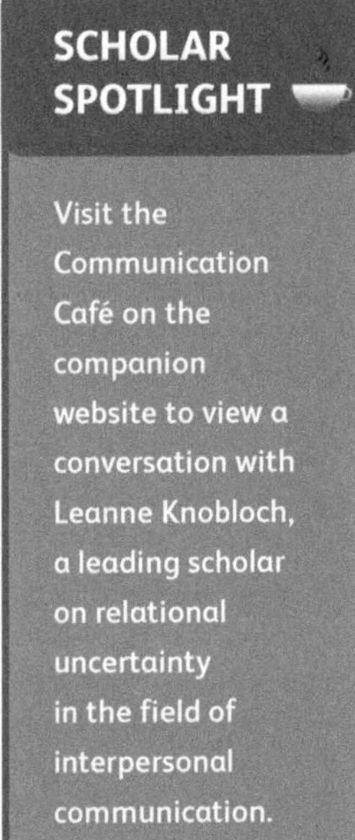

SCHOLAR
SPOTLIGHT
Visit the Communication Café on the companion website to view a conversation with Leanne Knobloch, a leading scholar on relational uncertainty in the field of interpersonal communication.

IDEA: INCLUSION, DIVERSITY, EQUITY, AND ACCESS

Most of the research on the development of interdependence in romantic relationships has focused on the experiences of mostly white college students in the United States where activities like studying, exercising, and having fun are prominent. What day-to-day experiences and goals are relevant to understanding the development of interdependence among people with more diverse life circumstances?

CONNECT WITH THEORY

Visit the companion website to learn more about the evolution of the relational turbulence model into a theory that explains how transitions can shape interpersonal characteristics that contribute to a tumultuous climate in close relationships.

Striving for Equity

As partners escalate a relationship, they get benefits from each other and they give up things they value for each other. **Social exchange** is the voluntary transfer of personal resources from one partner to another (Roloff, 2016). When a partner provides you with a benefit, such as giving you a ride home, lending you class notes, or making your leisure time more fun, you have experienced a reward. And when you give up something for a partner – the fuel and time it takes to provide that ride home, the convenience of keeping your class notes with you, or the fun you might have with a different person – you have experienced a cost. Just like a good shopper, you prefer to receive as many rewards as possible, while incurring the fewest costs. The challenge in escalating relationships, then, is to find a way to exchange resources in ways that both partners see as profitable and fair.

Social exchange in ongoing relationships is guided by **the rule of distributive justice**, which dictates that each partner's rewards should be proportional to his or her costs. When partners achieve a balance between the costs and rewards they each experience, they have achieved equity. Perhaps not surprisingly, equity motivates people to promote the well-being of a relationship (Dainton, 2019), whereas inequity – both being over-benefited or under-benefited – decreases relationship satisfaction (Sprecher, 2018). Moreover, people who pay a lot of attention to rewards and costs react more strongly when conflicts occur (Jarvis, McClure, & Bolger, 2019). Unfortunately, equity can be hard to achieve. In economic exchanges, you know the exact price of something, and you might even be able to get a refund if you're dissatisfied with the product; in social exchanges, the value of rewards and costs is much harder to determine, and therefore, harder to balance.

Social Exchange
The voluntary transfer of personal resources from one partner to another.

The Rule of Distributive Justice
A guideline dictating that each partner's rewards should be proportional to his or her costs.

Consider the 50th anniversary dinner Jen hosted for her in-laws when their celebratory trip to Spain and Portugal was cancelled due to the COVID-19 pandemic. What would be reasonable "payment" for that meal? Although you could tally up the cost of the food and add wages for Jen's time, that cold calculation probably wouldn't capture the value of the meal. The fact that Jen created an opportunity for the family to gather in celebration, prepared a Spanish-inspired tapas menu to try to capture some of the culture they were missing from their planned vacation, and helped them celebrate their anniversary despite the restrictions of the pandemic all add value to the meal. Jen's efforts to clean the house before the party and the dirty kitchen afterward might also figure into her costs. As this example shows, equity is hard to achieve because you can't clearly establish the value of the rewards and costs you experience through social exchange. Part of learning about a new relationship partner is finding out what he or she enjoys and dislikes. If you and your partner can balance your gains and losses, you'll develop an equitable foundation for a long-term relationship.

Putting Theory into Practice: Navigating the Road to Intimacy

You may know from experience just how challenging it can be to establish close friendships or romantic relationships. Interpersonal communication is a tool for overcoming these challenges and establishing an intimate bond with another person. The following tips should also help you navigate the challenges associated with escalating a close relationship.

Balance breadth and depth in your self-disclosure. When escalating a relationship, keep in mind that both breadth and depth of self-disclosure contribute to building a sense of connection. You can avoid relationships that are superficial or unidimensional by balancing your disclosures in terms of both breadth and depth.

COMMUNICATION IN ACTION 9.2

Mapping Your Self-disclosures

Consider a relationship you are involved in that is more than an acquaintanceship, but still has room to grow, and map out the aspects of your life that you have and have not shared with this partner. To do this, complete the form on the companion website to create a picture like the one in Figure 9.3.

Talk about your uncertainty. If you are having questions about a relationship, seeking answers from a partner can be intimidating – you may not be sure what you want, maybe you can't predict how your partner will respond, and you might not even know if such a conversation is allowed in this relationship. When your doubts are left unaddressed, however, you create even more uncertainty. Because relationship talk is risky, you need to take steps to promote a positive interaction:

- Make conversations about the relationship a regularly scheduled event. Plan a monthly date with a romantic partner or a regular get together with a friend where you talk about how things are going.
- When you are engaged in relationship talk, be sure to address your partner's questions, as well as your own. If you only ask your partner to provide information, they might wonder why you are asking.
- Begin the discussion by explaining your own thoughts and feelings about your relationship. By providing information that addresses your partner's uncertainty, you can encourage them to do the same for you.

Although you need to use caution, talking about your relationship gives you opportunities to clarify what's going on and to check that you and your partner are on the same page.

Give interdependence time and effort. The process of developing a relationship necessarily involves interference from partners, so try to be patient and take constructive action when you become frustrated at the ways a new friend or romantic partner disrupts your day.

- Expect and forgive some degree of annoyance – in fact, celebrate it as a sign of growing intimacy.
- When you find yourself experiencing interference from a partner, talk about what goal you are trying to achieve, and how your partner can help.
- Make equity a priority by paying attention to times when you are giving more than you're getting and making sure that you offer rewards on par with your partner's costs.

COMMUNICATION IN ACTION 9.3

Creating a Relationship Balance Sheet

Using the form on the companion website, make a list of all of the rewards you gain from a particular relationship, as well as all of the costs that you incur by being in that relationship. Reflecting on these lists can help you think of ways you could make your relationship more rewarding, less costly, and more equitable.

ENDING RELATIONSHIPS

Inevitably, some friendships and romantic relationships come to an end. One study of high school students found that more than 20% had experienced the break-up of a romantic relationship in the six months

(Connolly & McIsaac, 2009). Another study showed that more than 50% of adolescents change "best friends" in a one-year period (Branje, Frijns, Finkenauer, Engels, & Meeus, 2007). Among college students, fewer than 50% of committed romantic relationships are likely to last more than three years (Sprecher, 2001). Although ending relationships is common throughout our lives, a survey of nearly 1,000 adults aged 18–29 found that nearly 15% reported that they sometimes stay in a relationship longer than ideal because they don't know how to end it (Beckmeyer & Jamison, 2019).

Relationship dissolution refers to the process by which previously developed relationships become less close. As you saw in Figure 9.2, ending a relationship involves using communication to undo the bonds created during the development of intimacy. Within this general framework, a break-up can be one-sided or mutual, it can be accomplished directly or indirectly, it can be gradual or sudden, and it may or may not involve attempts at reconciliation. In this section, we consider the challenges people confront as they travel the often uncomfortable path from closeness to dissolution.

Relationship Dissolution The process by which previously developed relationships become less close.

Making a Decision

What causes your feelings for a friend or dating partner to fade? Relationship dissolution often begins when people perceive their needs for either independence or interdependence aren't being met (Norona, Olmstead, & Welsh, 2017). One study – which followed nearly 2,000 romantic partners for seven years – found that break-ups were predicted by both accumulating distress and disparities in partners' desire for interdependence (Finn, Johnson, & Neyer, 2020). Within college roommate relationships, termination is more likely when neither roommate is skilled at providing support or solving problems and when roommates have mismatched levels of competitiveness (Bahns, Crandall, Canevello, & Crocker, 2013). A study of adolescent "unfriending" on Facebook highlighted both offline qualities, such as a friend's undesirable personality, and online qualities, such as posting too much, as reasons for terminating the social media connection (Verswijvel, Heirman, Hardies, & Walrave, 2018). Thus, people can become less enthralled with a friendship or romantic relationship for a variety of reasons.

PAUSE & REFLECT

Have you ever had to end a friendship or romantic relationship? What reasons did you have for terminating that relationship?

External events can also create or reveal fractures in a relationship. For example, a study of first-year university students found that more than half of the best friendships people had in high school had become less close when they entered college (Oswald & Clark, 2003). Friendships can also be disrupted when one partner starts dating someone seriously or has children (Burton-Chellew & Dunbar, 2015). Important dates, such as birthdays and Christmas, can also wreak havoc for relationships. For example, Valentine's Day, with its focus on celebrating romance, is a less positive relationship event for people uncomfortable with close attachments (Chopik, Wardecker, & Edelstein, 2014) and can even prompt less committed partners to end a relationship (Morse & Neuberg, 2004). As a final example, consider the impact of lockdowns related to the COVID-19 pandemic: An analysis of Google search data showed a 13 percent increase within the United States in searches for information on relationship termination and divorce within a few months of government-imposed lockdowns (Berger, Ferrari, Leturcq, Panico, & Solaz, 2021). As these examples illustrate, circumstances outside a relationship can set partners on the road to dissolution.

The Investment Model
A theory about commitment to relationships.

The deterioration of a relationship often leads one or both partners to evaluate the pros and cons of a break-up. **The investment model**, presented in Figure 9.4, predicts that you are likely to stay in a relationship when you receive more rewards than costs, you lack alternatives to the relationship, and you have invested a lot of time, energy, or resources in the relationship (Rusbult, Agnew, & Arriaga, 2012). Conversely, you are more likely to end a relationship when you conclude that it isn't rewarding, you have better alternatives, or you don't have much to lose. The investment model highlights how deciding to decrease intimacy can be difficult, especially when we gain specific rewards from a partner or we have invested a lot in a relationship (Roloff, Soule, & Carey, 2001). Because there are often downsides to both staying together and breaking up, a critical part of relationship dissolution is figuring out whether you or your partner wants to exit the relationship.

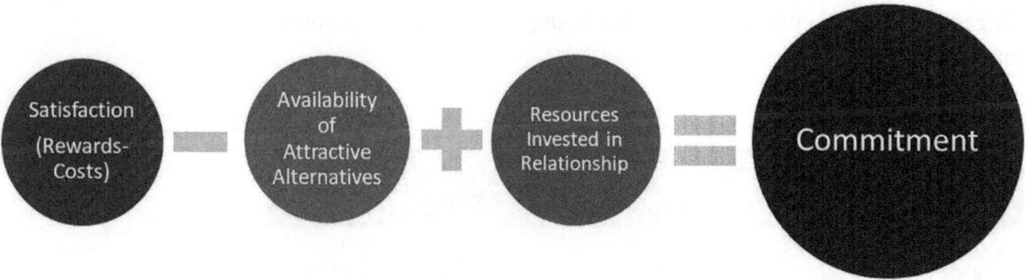

FIGURE 9.4 The investment model

Managing Face Threats

Face Threats
Experiences that can make either partner feel constrained or disliked.

A key concern guiding your communication during relationship dissolution is preventing or managing **face threats** – experiences that can make either partner feel constrained or disliked. If you think your partner wants out of your relationship, you may want to respect those wishes, show that you still value him or her, and yet retain your pride. And if you're the one initiating a break-up, you might worry about forcing your partner into a bad situation, making your partner feel inadequate, appearing insensitive, or later regretting that you ended the relationship (Wilson, Kunkel, Robson, Olufowote, & Soliz, 2009). Thus, relationship dissolution is a complicated balancing act between protecting your partner and protecting yourself from face threats.

One strategy for decreasing threats to your own face is to use covert strategies to determine whether a partner wants less out of the relationship. Just as people might use secret tests to diagnose relationship escalation, they sometimes test the limits to determine whether a previously close relationship is on the decline (Chory-Assad & Booth-Butterfield, 2001). People worried about the dissolution of a relationship are more likely to monitor a partner's social media posts (Blight, Ruppel, & Jagiello, 2019), and they also pay more attention to how dominating or friendly a partner is during conflicts (Hubbard, 2001). In fact, partners on their way to a break-up are especially motivated to uncover negative information about their relationship (Ickes, Dugosh, Simpson, & Wilson, 2003). Thus, doubts about the future of a relationship can prompt us to be more vigilant in our covert efforts to understand a partner's agenda.

When you are the one initiating relationship dissolution, you can manage face threats by using a positive tone and being open about the break-up (Sprecher, Zimmerman, & Abrahams, 2010). Less compassionate alternatives include avoiding a partner, being unpleasant in an effort to manipulate a partner into initiating a break-up, and using mediated communication, such as a text message, to end the relationship (Sprecher, Zimmerman, & Fehr, 2014). Cutting off social media contact is an especially abrupt way to end a relationship. When you terminate a relationship by unfriending someone on Facebook or ceasing to communicate through technology (i.e., "ghosting"), you magnify the negative impact on the other person (Bevan, Ang, & Fearns, 2014). In fact, the only strategies that seem to help people cope with being ghosted are doing nothing or moving on – trying to get a (former) partner to respond only makes things worse (LeFebvre & Fan, 2020). While eliminating contact might definitively end a relationship, it does nothing to mitigate the negative consequences for someone you once cared about.

> **HOW DO YOU RATE? 9.2**
>
> **Using Secret Tests to Diagnose Relationship Development**
>
> Visit the companion website to complete a scale that was adapted from Rebecca Chory-Assad and Melanie Booth-Butterfield's (2001) measure of the frequency with which people use secret tests in their ongoing or deteriorating romantic relationships. Complete the measure twice: once while thinking about a stable relationship you have been in, and once while thinking about a friendship or romance that was decreasing in intimacy. How do you explain similarities or differences in your scores for the two types of relationships?

Reasserting Independence

Because relationships develop as partners share themselves with each other and mesh their everyday routines, relationship dissolution requires people to re-establish their independence. When you developed a friendship, perhaps you discovered new interests or hobbies, you altered or deepened certain beliefs, or you came to rely on your partner to facilitate important goals. Ending that relationship, then, requires that you find ways to refocus or sustain those pastimes, beliefs, and goals without your friend. Not surprisingly, when people adopt new interests or develop values because of a relationship partner, they feel diminished or lost as that relationship ends (Lewandowski, Aron, Bassis, & Kunak, 2006). Thus, the process of breaking up involves recovering a sense of yourself that is not tied to that relationship.

You can reassert your own identity both in the activities you engage in and the way you talk about yourself and your relationship. As you withdraw from one relationship, for example, you might spend more time developing other relationships (Norona & Olmstead, 2017). It might be especially important to identify new ways to bolster goals that a former partner helped you achieve (Gomillion, Murray, & Lamarche, 2015). Was your partner an important contributor to your workout routine, your ability to leave work at the office, or enjoying your hobbies? If you can identify how your former relationship helped you in valuable ways, you'll know what holes you need to fill – whether that's joining a gym, getting a puppy, or finding a club devoted to your favorite pastimes. By engaging in activities alone or with other people, you can develop hobbies, beliefs, and goals that don't involve a relationship partner.

PAUSE & REFLECT

Have you ever taken steps to avoid contact with a relationship partner on social media? If so, what were some of the strategies you used and what did they accomplish? How have you felt when you've been unfriended or on the receiving end of someone's ghosting?

Your language also changes in subtle ways that reflect emerging independence. When people are in committed and satisfying relationships, they tend to use collective pronouns, such as "we" or "us," that signal their interdependence (Robinson, Persich, Sjoblom-Schmidt, & Penzel, 2020). In the same way, people's stories about good friends includes more frequent uses of "we" than "I," compared to less valued friendships (Tani, Smorti, & Peterson, 2015). In contrast, unwanted interdependence can lead to fewer collective pronouns during conversations with a partner (Knobloch & Solomon, 2003). In these ways, you use language to shift your sense of self from a state of "we-ness" to a state of "me-ness."

Coming to Terms

Regardless of whether you or your partner initiates a break-up, dissolving a friendship or romantic relationship can be stressful (Boelen & Reijntjes, 2009). People going through a break-up experience plenty of negative emotions and volatile swings between feeling good and feeling bad (Sbarra, 2006). Importantly, people suffer fewer negative consequences from a break-up if they come to understand why it happened (Kansky & Allen, 2018). Thus, the end of a close relationship can be a stressful and significant event with which people have to come to terms.

Part of coming to terms with a break-up is creating a narrative or account that explains what happened. People feel better about a break-up when the accounts they create include a clear sequence of events (Koenig Kellas & Manusov, 2003). Individuals also feel better about ending a relationship when they focus on how the situation, rather than their own flaws, contributed to the break-up (Tashiro & Frazier, 2003), or how their partner is not really as wonderful as they once believed (Geher et al., 2005).

Despite the seeming finality of relationship dissolution, you should avoid thinking about the end of a relationship as a specific event that completely severs all contact between former partners. Typically, relationship dissolution is a gradual process through which you realize that you want less intimacy, you signal decreased closeness through your communication, and you start to do more things without your partner. And although you may eventually have to come to terms with the end of the relationship, you might give the relationship another chance, postpone calling it quits, or find a new way to relate to your partner. In fact, sometimes the stress of ending a relationship prompts people to get back together (Cope & Mattingly, 2020). Thus, coming to terms with relationship dissolution is about coping with the changes in your circumstances and understanding how you will (or will not) communicate with your partner in the future.

Putting Theory into Practice: Exiting Gracefully

Ending a friendship or romantic relationship is far from simple, especially when that relationship was once close. Although effective communication strategies will not eliminate the sting of a break-up, you can take steps to promote a more graceful ending to a once close relationship.

Weigh the pros and cons. When you begin to feel less engaged by a friendship or romantic relationship, take some time to reflect on the pros and cons of decreasing intimacy. Within close relationships, it can sometimes be difficult to notice all the ways that a partner provides us with resources and helps us to achieve our goals. Think about what you get out of this relationship, including tangible rewards, assistance, and companionship. Are you really going to be better off with a less close relationship? You might also consider the possibility that external changes in your situation – a new class schedule, a change of career goals, pressures at home – might be making this relationship less enjoyable at the moment. If you can sort out how much value you get out of the relationship and how much your disinterest might be caused by external forces, you can avoid later regretting that you ended the relationship.

Manage face threats. Perhaps the greatest challenge to ending relationships gracefully is managing the threats to both you and your partner. If you are sure that you want to end a relationship, be direct, respectful, and kind in your communication with your partner. When you emphasize what you valued about your partner and the relationship, you can ease the transition to less intimate involvement. And remember that both you and your partner will come to terms with the break-up more quickly if you can understand what happened to end it and where you want to go in the future.

COMMUNICATION IN ACTION 9.4

Identifying Strategies for Ending Relationships

The band Train claimed that there are 50 ways to say goodbye, but some strategies are certainly better than others. Ask ten people to identify the best and worst way that someone has ended a friendship or romantic relationship with them. The form on the companion website can help you organize this information. As you reflect on the information you gathered, can you recommend some dos and don'ts for ending relationships?

WHEN THINGS GO WRONG

With so many challenges to overcome in the formation, escalation, and dissolution of relationships, you shouldn't be surprised that things sometimes go awry. One of the hardest parts of negotiating relationship development is establishing the ground rules for interaction. Sometimes, one partner refuses to respect the boundaries the other person sets. At other times, relationship partners jointly decide to push the limits. In this section, we consider some of the situations that can arise when people cross the line in developing relationships.

Unrequited Love and Stalking

Sometimes people are attracted to potential partners who do not share their interest in developing a relationship. Moreover, barriers to a relationship sometimes motivate would-be lovers to pursue the object of their affection even more vigorously. **Obsessive relational intrusion** is the repeated and unwanted pursuit that constitutes an invasion of privacy. The behaviors that characterize obsessive relational intrusion can range from mildly intrusive behaviors – like being pestered for a date, receiving unwanted gifts, and being the target of seemingly endless phone calls – to property damage, verbal threats, or physical assaults (Spitzberg, 2016). In the extreme, these obsessive behaviors comprise **stalking**, which is malicious and repeated harassment of another person that threatens their safety.

Obsessive Relational Intrusion
Repeated and unwanted pursuit that constitutes an invasion of privacy.

Stalking
Malicious and repeated harassment of another person that threatens his or her safety.

New technologies have made it easier to keep tabs on someone with whom a romantic relationship is desired. In one study of college students in the Midwestern United States, 40.8% of participants reported that they had been the victim of cyberstalking, but only 4.9% reported that they had ever been the perpetrator of online stalking (Reyns, Henson, & Fisher, 2012). The large difference between these two statistics suggests that either a small minority of individuals are responsible for instigating the vast majority of stalking, or more likely, people are unaware of the ways their behavior might be inappropriate or unwilling to admit to their own intrusive behaviors. One study identified the obsessive relational intrusion tactics that people might employ on Facebook (Chaulk & Jones, 2011), including: (a) using information on Facebook to make contact (e.g., using a person's status update to know where they will be at a certain time); (b) monitoring a person's conversations and actions; (c) making contact with others in a person's social network; (d) making overly affectionate expressions of liking on Facebook (e.g., sending virtual gifts or writing affectionate messages on their wall); and (e) sending a person unwanted invitations to join groups or events. The study also found that females were more likely than males to engage in these types of cyber-intrusions and that they were most prominent among individuals of college age. When you consider these various forms of online relational intrusions, it's easy to see how some of the behaviors you might perform innocently to keep track of someone you are interested in could be interpreted as something more sinister.

Stalking and obsessive relational intrusion can be difficult to study, because the victims don't always come forward and the perpetrators are unlikely to discuss their behaviors with researchers. One question that researchers have studied concerns the personality traits that characterize individuals who are prone to stalking behavior. Researchers asked victims of stalking to identify the personality characteristics they perceived in their unwanted pursuer and compared those traits to the personality characteristics that non-victimized individuals perceived in their "normal" romantic partner (Spitzberg & Veksler, 2007). Unwanted pursuers were perceived as less socially competent, more emotional and dramatic in their behavior and speech, and more borderline obsessive-compulsive than partners who had not engaged in unwanted pursuit. Individuals

"He's playing very hard to get—he's got a restraining order."

FIGURE 9.5 Playing hard to get

Source: © Barbara Smaller/The New Yorker Collection/www.cartoon bank.com.

who had been the target of unwanted pursuit also reported that they felt more victimized when their partner possessed high levels of these personality characteristics.

A 1998 CNN report suggested that 20% of all stalking cases in the United States involve celebrities, but the majority of victims are acquainted with their stalker (Spitzberg, 2002). In fact, people who become obsessive in the pursuit of a partner are often trying to develop a romantic relationship that they think will be filled with happiness (Cupach, Spitzberg, & Carson, 2000). Of course, a relationship that is grossly one-sided has a limited future, especially when one person's expressions of affection become aggressive. Because stalking situations persist for almost two years, on average, it is important that one or both parties seek help breaking this potentially dangerous connection.

Friends-with-Benefits

Friends-with-Benefits
A friendship in which partners engage in sexual activity but do not define the relationship as romantic.

A **friends-with-benefits** relationship is an association in which friends engage in sexual activity, but do not define their relationship as romantic. Studies of friends-with-benefits suggest that 50–60% of college students have experienced this type relationship (Afifi & Faulkner,

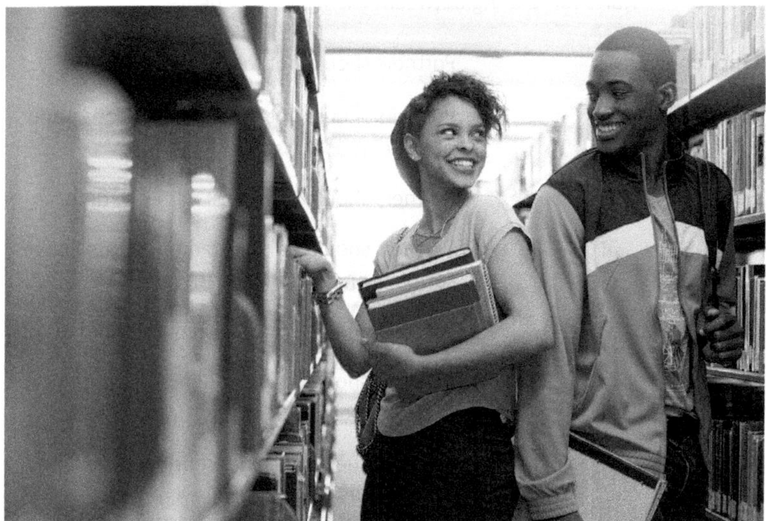

FIGURE 9.6 Increased flirtation, intimacy, and sex between friends can flex the boundaries of a typical friendship.

2000; Mongeau, Ramirez, & Vorrell, 2003). What makes this relationship appealing? One survey of college students suggested that people pursue friends-with-benefits relationships to increase sexual opportunities, avoid commitment, simplify romance, experience an emotional connection, or experiment with that type of relationship (Hughes, Morrison, & Asada, 2005). Thus, friends-with-benefits receive the rewards of friendship and the rewards of a sexual relationship, but they don't incur any of the responsibilities and commitment that are implied by a romantic relationship.

PAUSE & REFLECT

Have you ever known someone who was involved in a friends-with-benefits relationship? What did you see as the challenges in this relationship?

Friends-with-benefits relationships are unique because they violate the social norms and expectations for both friendships and sexual relationships. Accordingly, partners must develop a unique set of rules to maintain relationships of this sort. As summarized in Table 9.1, the rules that college students follow within a friends-with-benefits relationship cover many aspects of intimacy, including emotional closeness, communication, sex, friendship, commitment, and privacy (Hughes et al., 2005). The complexity of these rules highlights just how difficult it can be to maintain relationships that cross familiar boundaries.

TABLE 9.1 Rules for relating between "friends-with-benefits"

Emotional rules	Partners should not fall in love
	Partners should not get hurt or jealous about other relationships
Communication rules	Partners should be honest with one another
	Partners should adhere to appropriate conversation topics
	Partners should limit the frequency of contact
Sex rules	Partners should only engage in agreed upon sexual behaviors
	Partners should take appropriate safe-sex precautions
Friendship rules	Partners should place higher importance on the friendship than on the sexual relationship
Permanence rules	Partners agree that the sexual aspect of the relationship is temporary
Secrecy rules	Partners agree that other people in their social network should not find out about the sexual aspect of the friendship

INSIDE COMMUNICATION RESEARCH

Relationship Maintenance and Social Support in Friends-with-benefits Relationships

Friends-with-benefits relationships can be complex given that they have rules and norms that differ from traditional friendships or romantic relationships. Researchers have identified different types of friends-with-benefits relationships that take on different characteristics. For example, *true friends* are partners who know each other well, care for each other, and have sex repeatedly, but do not consider their relationship to be a romantic one. *Network opportunism* is when friends-with-benefits partners share a common social network and often turn to each other as mutual and reliable sex partners, whereas *just sex* involves serial hookups between partners where communication focuses exclusively on facilitating sexual interaction. There are also a variety of friends-with-benefits relationships that exist somewhere in limbo between romantic and platonic connections. *Successful transition in* occurs when friends-with-benefits partners desire a romantic relationship and ultimately transition to a romantic partnership; *failed transition in* is when friends-with-benefits partners desire a romantic relationship that does not ultimately materialize; *accidental transition in* happens when partners do not intend to have a romantic relationship but end up in one anyway; and *transition out* relationships occur when former romantic partners begin having sex again. Given the diverse characteristics and motivations in friends-with-benefits relationships, partners are likely to enact a wide range of interpersonal communication behaviors within each context.

Communication scholars Paul Mongeau, Lisa van Raalte, Lori Bednarchik, and Mark Generous (2019) sought to examine how the communication of relationship maintenance behaviors and social support differ across the various types of friends-with-benefits relationships. Relationship maintenance behaviors are designed to sustain satisfaction, commitment, and liking in close relationships through communication that emphasizes positivity, encourages openness, offers assurances of commitment, distributes shared tasks and responsibilities, and utilizes social networks. The authors hypothesized that these types of relationship maintenance behaviors are more likely in friends-with-benefits relationships that are characterized by closeness (e.g., true friends) or romantic potential (e.g., transition in), and less likely in relationships marked by sexual opportunism (e.g., just sex, network opportunism, failed transitions). The researchers also examined differences in supportive communication across different types of friends-with-benefits relationships. Similar to the relationship maintenance behaviors, they predicted that friends-with-benefits relationships marked by more closeness, intimacy, or romantic desire would show more social support between partners than relationships lacking those characteristics.

To investigate these predictions, the researchers surveyed college undergraduates about their current or past friends-with-benefits relationships. The results were generally consistent with hypotheses. People in *successful* or *accidental transition in* relationships reported significantly more openness, assurances, shared tasks, and network connections than people in *just sex*, *network opportunism*, and *failed transition in* relationships. In addition, participants reported that they received significantly more supportive messages when they were in *successful* or *accidental transition in* relationships than in the other types of relationships. These results suggest that individuals in friends-with-benefits relationships that have romantic potential engage in more communication behaviors to maintain the relationship and support their partner.

THINK ABOUT IT

1. Participants in *just friends* relationships did not differ significantly from the other relationship types in terms of relationship maintenance behaviors or social support. Why might *just friends* relationships be unique in this regard? What sets these relationships apart from the others in terms of communicating maintenance and support?
2. How might relationship maintenance behaviors and social support change the nature of the friends-with-benefits relationship between partners? Would more supportive communication and efforts to maintain the relationship help move a relationship toward greater intimacy and romantic connection? Or might these actions potentially backfire and scare off a partner who does not desire more intimacy?

Putting Theory into Practice: Staying on Course

In this section, we have addressed some of the darker and more complicated aspects of friendships and romantic relationships. These issues may arise from unclear relationship boundaries, but their results can range from frustrating to downright frightening. In this section, we consider how you can keep your friendships and romantic relationships on track.

Clarify and respect relationship boundaries. Relationship development is necessarily collaborative; in other words, it is something that you coordinate with your partner. You can't have a more intimate relationship than your partner is willing to have with you. And you and a partner both need to understand the challenges that come with blurring the line between friendship and romance. By identifying and maintaining boundaries that you and a partner establish together, you can avoid problems in your friendships and romantic relationships. To make sure that you and a partner are on the same page, spend some time thinking about how you each see the relationship. What are your goals for the relationship? What kind of activities do you enjoy sharing with your partner, and what behaviors do you want to keep out of the relationship? Are there any actions, such as cheating or lying, that would be a serious problem for you? After you answer these questions, consider how your partner might feel about these issues. If your relationship allows it, you might even talk with your partner about your answers. If you and your partner have similar views, you can be more confident that you can respect important boundaries for the relationship. And if you and your partner disagree on these issues, you'll know where you need to bring your views of the relationship into better alignment.

SUMMARY

One of the most important goals we accomplish through interpersonal communication is managing the rise and fall of friendships and romantic relationships. From the moment you first meet someone, interpersonal communication allows you to gather information and promote positive outcomes. And by remembering basic rules for communication, like following the norm of reciprocity and engaging in small talk, you can get a new relationship off to a good start.

When a relationship seems promising, you turn to communication to transform your acquaintance into a friend or dating partner. By sharing personal information about a variety of topics, you create a sense of connection with another person. You can also use communication to help you resolve questions that emerge as your relationship grows closer, coordinate your behavior in mutually satisfying ways, and make sure that your experience of rewards and costs is equitable. In these ways, your ability to use interpersonal communication effectively is central for building close friendships and romances.

Of course, not all relationships last forever; in fact, you will experience the dissolution of friendship and romantic relationships throughout your life. Relationships end in many ways and for many reasons, but break-ups might be easier if you keep in mind the features that they have in common. Once a decision to decrease intimacy is made, partners must manage threats as they detect or communicate a desire for less involvement. In addition, partners need to re-establish their lives and self-concepts separate from the relationship. And if decreases in intimacy result in the end of a relationship, people can create accounts that may help them come to terms with the break-up.

Coordinating the development of a friendship or dating relationship requires that you work with a partner to establish your level of involvement and the boundaries for acceptable and unacceptable behavior. Most of the time, people are pretty good at creating relationships in which the partners are equally involved, and both parties understand and follow the rules. When this balancing act goes awry, though, one-sided love affairs and relationships that cross the line between friendship and romance can emerge.

The voluntary relationships that you form with friends and romantic partners can be some of the most rewarding bonds you experience. These relationships don't emerge automatically; rather, they are the result of specific communication behaviors that are skillfully enacted. Although the relationships you have had throughout your life have given you lots of experience with the processes described in this chapter, you can also take steps to improve your communication in interpersonal relationships. By applying some of the knowledge you gained in this chapter, you can foster promising relationships, deepen bonds that are important to you, soften the consequences of a break-up, and keep your relationships on track.

ACTIVITIES FOR EXPLORING COMMUNICATION ETHICS

What Would You/Should You Do?

Imagine that you are in a friendship or romantic relationship with someone who is more invested or committed to the relationship than you are. Because your partner likes you so much, they provide you with lots of rewards and incur a lot of costs on your behalf. For example, maybe you find that you're eating at your friend's house a lot, your friend runs errands for you and drives you around, and you get a lot of compliments and support from this person. Your partner also doesn't seem to demand much from you; you don't pay for food or fuel, you leave your partner hanging at the last moment if something better comes up, and you aren't really all that interested in their problems. If you find yourself benefiting from an inequitable relationship, what would you – or should you – do?

Something to Think About

The description of relationship dissolution offered in this chapter highlighted the need to tread lightly when ending a relationship. At the same time, you shouldn't just avoid a partner, neglect the relationship, or secretly manipulate the other person into breaking up with you. Because communicating directly about a relationship in decline can be perceived as either too blunt or incredibly kind, you need to find a balance between avoidance and openness. What are the ethical issues involved in deciding how direct to be about your desire to end a previously close relationship?

Analyze Communication Ethics Yourself

Recent years have seen a dramatic increase in opportunities to meet people online. In places like Match.com, people can provide a description of themselves designed to attract potential friends or suitors. Just as we would expect in a face-to-face interaction, people seeking a relationship partner online are motivated to portray themselves in a positive light. When you don't have the information provided by face-to-face contact, though, these self-portraits can be misleading. Explore some of the online sites devoted to matchmaking and examine the strategies people use to present themselves. What strategies do you find more or less ethical when people portray themselves in cyberspace?

KEY WORDS

breadth
depth
face threats
friends-with-benefits
interdependence
investment model
norm of reciprocity
obsessive relational intrusion
predicted outcome value
relational uncertainty
relationship dissolution
relationship talk
rule of distributive justice
secret tests
self-disclosure
social exchange
stalking
uncertainty

LEARNING OBJECTIVES

After reading this chapter, you should be able to:

1. Identify the components of intimacy and distinguish different styles of loving.
2. Describe the strategies you can use to maintain intimate relationships.
3. Understand relational dialectics and strategies for coping with them.
4. Understand how attachment style and age can affect communication in intimate relationships.
5. Understand the downsides of romantic infatuation.
6. Identify strategies for improving communication in your intimate relationships.

PUTTING THEORY INTO PRACTICE

In this chapter, you will learn how to:

1. Address different facets of intimacy.
2. Expand your repertoire for love.
3. Make strategic relational maintenance part of your routine.
4. Develop skills for coping with dialectical tensions.
5. Respect the relationship beliefs of others.
6. Keep age differences in perspective.
7. Stay grounded when you're head over heels.
8. Take charge of infidelity.

INTIMACY AND INTERPERSONAL COMMUNICATION

10

Source: Getty Images.

DOI: 10.4324/9781351174381-10

On the Lifetime reality series, *Married at First Sight*, couples meet each other for the first time when they walk down the aisle to be married. A team of experts comprised of a sociologist, a marriage counselor, and a communication and relationship expert review the individual profiles of each person and pair them with a partner who is scientifically expected to be an ideal romantic match. The couples are married in the first episode, then go on a honeymoon, and then live together for eight weeks, at which point they are asked if they want to stay married or get divorced. The couples are forced to get to know each other quickly, to navigate multiple relationship milestones in short order, and decide if they want to spend their lives together in the time it takes most newly matched couples to go on a handful of dates. Needless to say, this relationship progression is quite atypical of most romantic relationships and creates expectations that the couples will establish intimacy much more quickly than they would if their relationship developed on a more traditional timeline. Across the first seven seasons, 16 of the 25 couples featured on the show decided to stay married after the eight-week experiment, but at least ten of those couples later divorced. With just a 24% success rate, this matchmaking experiment shows just how difficult it can be to develop and maintain intimacy in a close relationship.

The primary quality that defines close relationships is **intimacy** – a connection between two people that includes psychological, emotional, and behavioral bonds. Because of these ties, intimate relationships provide us with companionship, entertainment, and support. Most relationships develop intimacy through interpersonal interactions over an extended period of time. Although the couples on *Married at First Sight* violate the typical norms of relationship development, they start the work of establishing intimacy after their wedding by searching for areas of common interest, engaging in shared activities, and envisioning a future together. Of course, many of the couples on this show experience frustration, stress, and conflict as they navigate the complexities of creating a connection and establishing intimacy, resulting in very few success stories from this unique relational experience. Although your relationships are likely to follow a more traditional pattern of development than the couples on *Married at First Sight*, you will probably experience many of the same challenges in your efforts to establish intimate connections with relationship partners. Learning about communication in intimate relationships can help you to understand the important experiences you have with close friends and romantic partners. To that end, this chapter examines the nature of intimacy, how you can use communication to maintain intimate relationships, how people differ in their approaches to intimacy, and how intimacy is sometimes taken to extremes.

THE NATURE OF INTIMACY

Intimacy
A connection between two people that includes psychological, emotional, and behavioral bonds.

The bonds of intimacy can be present in your relationships with friends, romantic partners, siblings, parents, mentors, and even pets. Thus, intimacy can take a variety of forms. This section of the chapter reveals the complex nature of intimacy by examining the components of intimate relationships and the various ways that people experience love.

Components of Intimacy

Intimacy isn't any one quality; rather, it is a bond that exists when a number of qualities are present in a relationship. Consider the example of Jacob, who identifies his best friend Mark and his girlfriend Suzanne as his most intimate relationships. With Mark, Jacob enjoys talking about computer games and politics, just hanging out and listening to music, and knowing that Mark will always be there for him in a pinch. With Suzanne, Jacob knows there are some things he can't discuss and he sometimes worries about the future, but they share a deep affection for each other. As this example illustrates, intimacy involves several different components that can be more or less present in a relationship. Table 10.1 and the following paragraphs describe some of the features that contribute to intimacy in close relationships.

The core of intimacy is closeness. As Figure 10.1 illustrates, closeness reflects the degree to which your own identity overlaps with another person's identity (Branand, Mashek, & Aron, 2019). Closeness arises when people

TABLE 10.1 The components of intimacy

Feeling	*Definition*
Closeness	A feeling of union between two people that emerges when people spend time together and influence one another's actions and beliefs
Openness	Our willingness to reveal private information about ourselves to a relationship partner through self-disclosure
Trust	The feeling that a relationship partner will keep us safe and protect us from harm
Affection	The positive feelings that we have for another person that we communicate through our actions with that person
Mutuality	When both partners in a relationship acknowledge and value the bond that exists between them

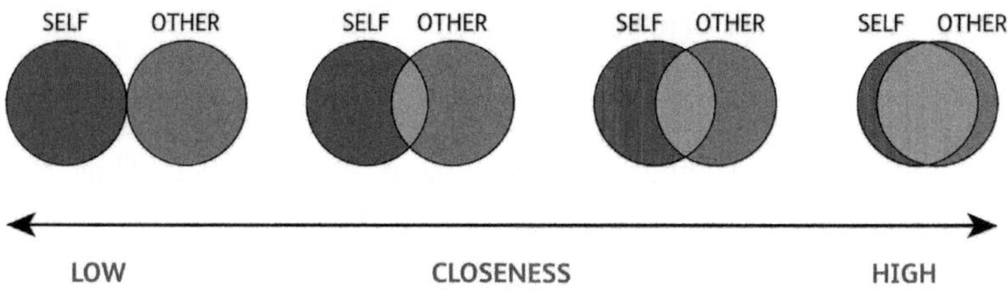

FIGURE 10.1 Aron and Aron's inclusion of other in self

spend a lot of time together, do a variety of things together, and influence each other's actions and beliefs (Berscheid, Snyder, & Omoto, 2004). Closeness is also revealed in communication. Close friends, for example, have integrated memories, which can be evident in their tendency to jointly tell and retell shared stories (Iannone, McCarty, & Kelly, 2017). Friends who report more connection with each other also have more similar Facebook profiles, as indexed by mutual friends, photos of them together, and shared Facebook likes (Cantañeda, Wendel, & Crockett, 2015). Within romantic relationships, closeness is revealed by expressions that convey support for a partner, reassure the partner, offer tangible reminders of closeness, and describe the relationship's future (Davis & Weigel, 2020). People also communicate closeness through subtle features of language; for example, saying "we," "us," and "our" signals a closer union than saying "you and I" or "yours and mine" (Robinson, Persich, Sjoblom-Schmidt, & Penzel, 2020). Thus, closeness represents the bond that is at the core of intimacy.

A second component of intimacy is openness, which also requires a degree of trust. When friends and romantic partner share personal information about their values and beliefs, their relationship becomes increasingly intimate. As a result, your intimate partner often knows all sorts of details about you, including your most embarrassing moment, your goals in life, or your insecurities. Intimate partners get to know many private details about you, and feeling comfortable sharing ourselves with relationship partners requires trust. When you trust a partner, you have confidence that they will not hurt you and that the information you share won't be revealed to others. Not surprisingly, then, trust increases communication about personal topics (Greene, Derlega, & Mathews, 2006). The more you trust a relationship partner, the more comfortable you will be sharing information with them, and the more information and experiences you share with a person, the more intimate your relationship will become.

PAUSE & REFLECT

Can you think of a time when a friend or romantic partner broke your trust? How did this make you feel? What impact did it have on the intimacy in your relationship?

Another aspect of intimacy – affection – captures the positive feelings you have for another person that you communicate through your actions. Affectionate communication conveys love, appreciation, and commitment (Floyd, Hesse, & Generous, 2015). Not surprisingly, love for a romantic partner increases verbal, nonverbal, and supportive expressions of affection (Dillow, Goodboy, & Bolkan, 2014). Nonverbal displays of affection include hugging, kissing, holding hands, caressing a partner, making prolonged eye contact, and sitting or standing close to a partner (Guerrero & Wiedmaier, 2013). People also communicate affection for romantic partners by adjusting their pitch, such that women tend to use a lower pitch and men tend to use a higher pitch (Farley, Hughes, & Lafayette, 2013). Thus, affection involves the messages you use to reveal your positive feelings for relationship partners.

The final component of intimacy is mutuality, which means that both partners in the relationship acknowledge and value the bond between them. Within friendships, mutuality with regard to support for separate interests, attention to psychological and emotional needs, and perceived closeness is both normative and a fundamental part of a high-quality relationship (Deci, La Guardia, Moller, Scheiner, & Ryan, 2006). Indeed, how much you trust a friend and are committed to that relationship are probably closely tied to your perception of your friend's commitment to you (Wieselquist, 2007). In fact, when relationships aren't mutual – when one person values the relationship more than the other – the differences between partners limit the intimacy that they share. Jen has a friend who briefly dated a man who had developed much stronger feelings for her than she had for him. Not wanting to give her partner false hope, she consistently prevented the relationship from becoming too intimate by limiting her disclosures and dodging any suggestion of increased commitment. Thus, in order for relationships to become truly intimate, both partners must feel a mutual sense of closeness, openness, trust, and affection.

CONNECT WITH THEORY

Visit the companion website to learn more about affection exchange theory, which identifies affectionate communication as an adaptive behavior that contributes to pair bonding and examines the cognitive, emotional, and physiological benefits of giving and receiving affection.

PAUSE & REFLECT

Have you ever been in a relationship that wasn't mutual? How would you describe the level of intimacy in that relationship?

Different Styles of Loving

The intimacy you share with relationship partners is sometimes experienced as love or especially strong or deep feelings of affection. Within this general definition, love is as varied as the camaraderie of siblings, the protection a parent offers a child, the passion of star-crossed lovers, and the devotion of lifelong partners (Fehr, 2019). People feel love for both friends and romantic partners, but those experiences are unique in important ways. In addition, you have different experiences of love with different friends or within different romantic relationships. To shed light on the mysteries of love, this section examines the kinds of love you might experience in close relationships.

Complete/Consummate Love
When relationships are characterized by intimacy, passion, and commitment.

Eros
Love characterized by beauty and sexuality.

Ludus
Love characterized as a game that is entertaining and exciting.

One view of love suggests that it is made up of three components: intimacy, passion, and commitment (Sternberg, 2004). As discussed previously, intimacy captures feelings of closeness and affection. The second ingredient is passion, which is the arousal that you experience when you are attracted to another person. Finally, commitment involves the decision to maintain a relationship over time. According to this model, **complete or consummate love** exists when intimacy, passion, and commitment are all present in a relationship. As illustrated in Figure 10.2, you can also experience different types of love in which only one or two of the components are present. Thinking about love as a mixture of intimacy, passion, and commitment can help you to appreciate its complexity and understand love's many different forms.

An alternative perspective on love emphasizes the different ways that people experience and express their feelings for intimate partners (Hendrick & Hendrick, 2019). In this model, love is assumed to take three primary forms: **eros**, which is an erotic love preoccupied by beauty and sexuality; **ludus**, which portrays love as a game that is entertaining

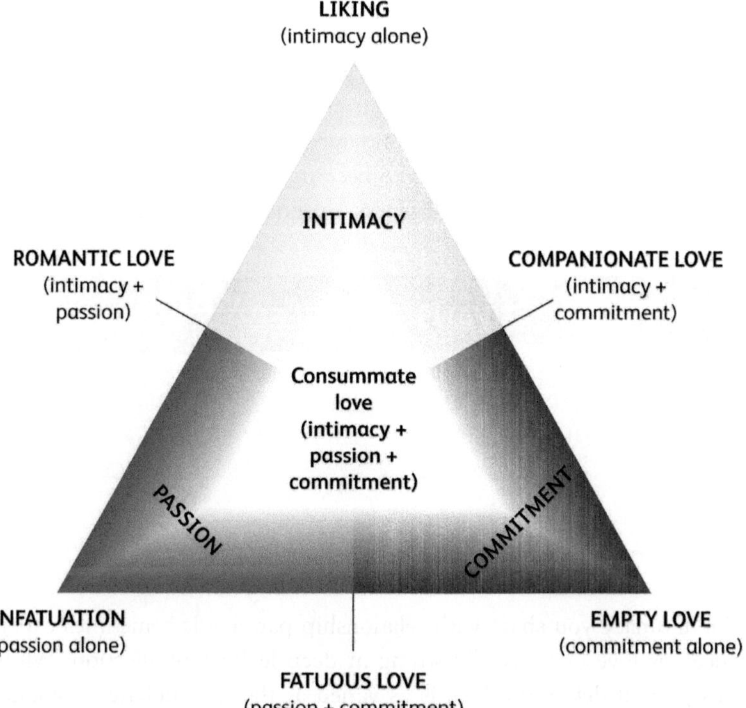

FIGURE 10.2 Sternberg's triangular theory of love

and exciting; and **storge**, which is a peaceful, friendship-based love that develops gradually over time. As shown in Figure 10.3, combinations of eros, ludus, and storge create three additional love styles. Mania blends the passion of eros with the games of ludus, resulting in a dramatic love that involves both elation and depression. Pragma combines the strategies of ludus with storge's focus on friendship to create the love that emerges when someone meets your criteria for a good partner. And when the passion of eros meets the companionship of storge, a compassionate and selfless love called agape is produced.

Storge
Love characterized as peaceful and grounded in friendship.

Love styles have been shown to have important consequences in romantic relationships. For example, people who report having pragma and ludus love styles also report more negative feelings in romantic relationships (Kanemasa, Taniguchi, Daibo, & Ishimori, 2004), people with ludus and mania love styles tend to engage in more jealousy-evoking behaviors in their romantic relationships (Goodboy, Horan, & Booth-Butterfield, 2012), and people with eros and ludus love styles tend to report having had more sexual partners (Hans, 2008). On the other hand, an eros love style has been linked to a partner's marital satisfaction (Gana, Saada, & Untas, 2013). In addition, people with an erotic or agapic love style seem to be especially appreciative of a partner who is skillful at conflict management and providing support (Kunkel & Burleson, 2003). Thus, a person's love style can have a profound impact on intimacy.

HOW DO YOU RATE?

What's Your Love Style?

Visit the companion website to complete a scale designed to help you identify your primary love style (Hendrick & Hendrick, 1990). In what ways is your love style a strength in terms of engaging in romantic relationships? In what ways is it a weakness?

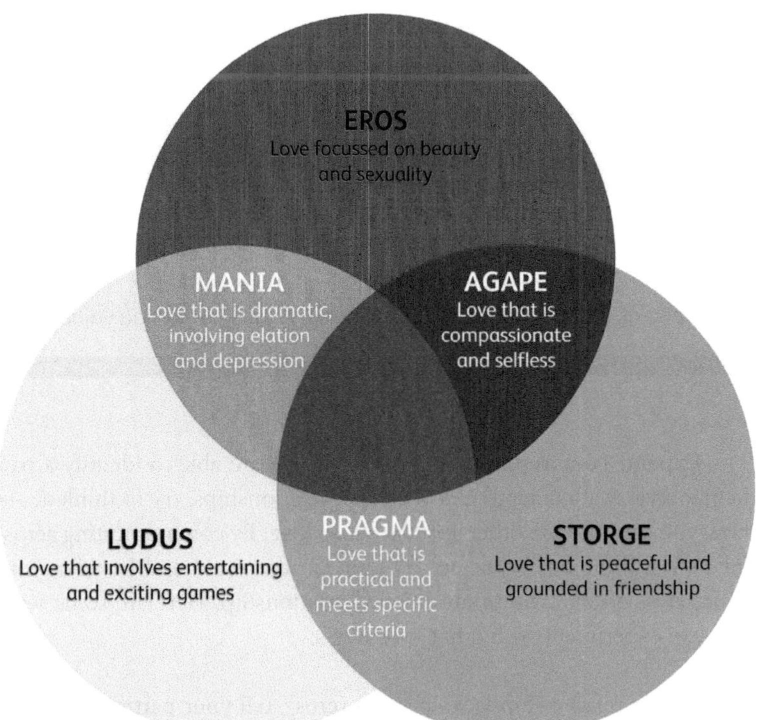

FIGURE 10.3 Hendrick and Hendrick's love styles

PAUSE & REFLECT

Have you ever been in love? If so, would you describe your partner's love style as similar or different from your own? How did that similarity or difference affect your relationship?

Putting Theory into Practice: Promoting Well-Rounded Relationships

In this section of the chapter, you learned about both components of intimacy and the various ways in which people experience love in intimate relationships. Although every intimate relationship you will have in your life will be unique, consider the following strategies for promoting more intimate bonds in those relationships.

Address different facets of intimacy. The five components of intimacy – closeness, openness, trust, affection, and mutuality – highlight the various ways in which we might experience intimacy in a close relationship. In the same way, the love triangle might point you to qualities that dominate a close relationship, as well as those facets of love that might be missing. By taking inventory of intimacy in your close relationships, you can identify areas that might merit more attention.

COMMUNICATION IN ACTION 10.1

Filling Gaps in Intimate Relationships

Complete the form on the companion website to help you evaluate whether the components of intimacy are overdeveloped or under-developed in a close relationship that you value.

Expand your repertoire for love. If you are able to identify a particular style that characterizes your love relationships, try to think about how you can develop other approaches to love. By communicating across love styles, you can break out of your current mold and broaden your experience of love within an intimate relationship. Here are some ways you can experiment with other love styles:

- If your relationship lacks passion (eros), tell your partner what you find physically and sexually appealing about him or her to remind each other that passion is important.

- If your relationship lacks friendship (storge), ask your partner to share experiences that you enjoy or must do, but that don't have romantic meaning for you, like running errands.
- If your relationship lacks fun (ludus), plan a surprise event for your partner or make a game out of a routine event. For example, you might each plan half of a romantic date night.

COMMUNICATION IN INTIMATE RELATIONSHIPS

Intimate relationships are dynamic and constantly changing. Perhaps your best friend or romantic partner needs some extra support from you today in order to meet an important deadline. Maybe you've grown bored with your relationship and you need to restore the excitement you once had. Or perhaps a brewing conflict is threatening the future of your relationship. Within intimate relationships, interpersonal communication helps you to give and receive help, revitalize your routine, and manage tensions. In this section, we explore the ways in which communication can be used to maintain intimacy and manage relational tensions.

Maintaining Intimacy

Between the ebbs and flows of relationship development described in the previous chapter, you maintain intimacy in relationships you value. In general, **relational maintenance** refers to the actions people take to keep their relationship in a desired state (Canary & Yum, 2016), and it includes both strategic and routine activities (Dainton & Aylor, 2002). **Strategic maintenance** includes behaviors that are intentionally performed with the goal of sustaining the relationship. For example, people might have conversations about the relationship, help their partner complete a task, compliment a partner, or offer an apology to ensure that the relationship continues. In contrast, **routine maintenance** refers to less intentional actions that, nonetheless, help to keep a relationship going. These behaviors might be enacted as part of your daily routine, like making dinner, taking out the garbage, or keeping in touch with your partner by texting throughout the day (Ramirez & Broneck, 2009; Stafford, Dainton, & Haas, 2000). Both strategic and routine behaviors play an important role in maintaining close relationships.

Relational Maintenance The actions people take to keep their relationship in a desired state.

Strategic Maintenance Behaviors that are intentionally performed with the goal of maintaining the relationship.

Routine Maintenance Behaviors that are performed unintentionally but that help to keep a relationship functioning.

People maintain their relationships using a variety of communication strategies, such as being positive, providing assurances of one's love and commitment, talking about the relationship, engaging in self-disclosure, expressing understanding, sharing tasks, and enjoying social networks (Stafford, 2011). People who regularly employ maintenance strategies tend to report more liking and love for their partner, more commitment

SCHOLAR SPOTLIGHT

Visit the Communication Café on the companion website to view a conversation with Jennifer Samp, a communication scholar who studies a wide range of issues related to intimacy and interpersonal communication.

to the relationship, more satisfaction, and more shared control over the relationship (Ogolsky & Bowers, 2013). In particular, providing assurances, such as saying "I will always love you" or "I would be lost without you," is a maintenance strategy that tends to be most strongly associated with liking, commitment, satisfaction, and the mutuality of control (Ogolsky & Bowers, 2013). Within same-sex romantic relationships, supportive messages from a partner are especially important, as they foster both relational well-being and help mitigate the chronic stress couples experience in a heteronormative social environment (Haas & Lannutti, 2019). Gay and lesbian couples are also more likely than heterosexual couples to pursue an equitable division of household tasks, which is a relational maintenance strategy that increases satisfaction (Kurdek, 2006). As these findings indicate, enacting relational maintenance strategies can positively influence people's perceptions of their close relationships.

INTERPERSONAL COMMUNICATION ONLINE

In research focused on texting between dating partners, Brinberg and Ram (2021) collected logs of couples' text messages from the day they started texting through the day they participated in the study. More than 30 couples shared more than a million text messages, which were then analyzed for patterns revealed by their frequency, time of day, and response times, as well as message themes and language use. One prominent feature of texting between couples was their use to enact relationship maintenance. Here are some examples of relational maintenance messages, based on Brinberg's study.

"i'm heading to sleep. thank you for everything today. thank you for being you. good night babe!"
"Good luck today! You have worked hard all week and I know you're going to do great things"
"Thank you for bringing me coffee since I was having a tough morning! It was so sweet of you"
"Hey, I wanted to say that I know it's been a rough few days and you've had a hard time, but I'm here for you. We'll get through this together. Love you ♡"
"thanks for listening to me vent today. i really needed that. looking forward to going out later and forgetting all of this!"
"If I'm being honest this is something we need to work on... I'm upset that you left me to hang out with your friends. I feel like we need to ACTUALLY communicate with each other."

INSIDE COMMUNICATION RESEARCH

Relationship Maintenance Reduces Stress in Dual-Career Couples

Dual-career families, in which both parents work outside the home, are often characterized by a hectic and fast-paced lifestyle. Couples must manage the time constraints and commitments of two careers, while also maintaining a household, potentially parenting young children, and balancing an array of associated stressors. Making time to maintain a strong relationship under these circumstances can be extremely challenging, but relationship maintenance can be beneficial for helping couples manage their stress, communicate effectively, and balance work-family obligations. Communication scholar, Tamara Afifi, and her colleagues (Afifi, Harrison, Zamanzadeh, & Acevedo Callejas, 2020) conducted a study to examine how relationship maintenance behaviors can help dual-career couples be more resilient during times of stress.

The researchers followed 62 heterosexual married or cohabiting couples, who had at least one child, over the course of a week. The couples completed an online survey during the first weekend, daily diary logs Monday through Friday, and a follow-up survey during the second weekend. The surveys and daily diaries asked the participants to report on the amount of relationship maintenance they received from their partner in the past month, as well as their perceived stress, interpersonal conflict with their partner, and loneliness. The participants also provided multiple saliva samples over the course of the week, which the researchers used to analyze salivary cortisol as a physiological indicator of stress.

The results showed that individuals physically experienced less stress when their partner engaged in a greater degree of relationship maintenance during the past month. In addition, male partners reported that they felt less stressed when their partner enacted more relationship maintenance behaviors during the previous month, but female partners' self-reported stress was not associated with perceptions of their partner's relationship maintenance. In addition, a lack of relationship maintenance from one's partner was associated with increased conflict and loneliness, whereas heightened relationship maintenance behaviors buffered these negative relationship outcomes. These findings suggest that relationship maintenance is an important factor in helping couples effectively manage stress and enact resilience in the face of challenging work-family dynamics.

THINK ABOUT IT

1. The results showed that males self-reported less stress when their partner engaged in relationship maintenance, but the physiological data showed that both men and women experienced less physical stress as a result of increased relationship maintenance. Why would the self-reported stress levels show different outcomes than the physiological stress measures? Why might men and women differ in the ways they *perceive* their own stress and/or their partner's relationship maintenance?
2. All of the couples in this study were married or cohabiting and had children. How might the results have differed for couples without children or in less established relationships? Would they have experienced the same amount of stress? Would they have enacted more or less relationship maintenance?

Coping with Tension

Your efforts to maintain intimacy are complicated by tensions that naturally arise within close relationships. Relational dialectics theory is a perspective that emphasizes the trade-offs and conflicting desires that create tension within close relationships (Baxter & Norwood, 2016). In general, a dialectic is a conflict between opposing, but also unified, ideas or forces. For example, liberalism and conservatism are two political perspectives that exist in opposition to each other, but that also gain meaning and strength by existing in contrast to each other. In the context of a close relationship, a **relational dialectic** refers to opposition between alternative ways of being intimate. Although more recent versions of the theory emphasize how meaning is constructed through language as people relate to each other (Baxter, 2011), early versions of the theory provided insight into specific dimensions of tensions within close relationships (Baxter & Montgomery, 1996).

Relational Dialectic
Opposition between alternative ways of being intimate.

Relational dialectics can be internal, meaning that opposing views of intimacy exist within the relationship, or external, in which the tension is between the relationship as a unit and people outside the relationship. Just as opposing political views are preferred at different times by different people, different relationship ideals might be preferred by one partner more than the other, or might be more or less desirable at different times. As summarized in Table 10.2 and the paragraphs that follow, relational

CONNECT WITH THEORY

Visit the companion website to read more about relational dialectics theory, which explains the tensions that arise in romantic relationships when partners have different expectations for enacting intimacy.

TABLE 10.2 Internal and external relational dialectics

Core issues	*Internal One partner vs. The other partner*	*External Both partners vs. Others*
Openness	Share everything with a partner	Reveal your relationship to others
vs.	vs.	vs.
Privacy	Keep some matters to yourself	Conceal your relationship from others
Novelty	Maintain mystery and intrigue	Have a special and unique relationship
vs.	vs.	vs.
Predictability	Know what is going to happen	Avoid a weird and unusual relationship
Autonomy	Be an independent person	Spend time together away from others
vs.	vs.	vs.
Connection	Maintain a close, interdependent	Spend time together with others

dialectics theory highlights three core tensions that can surface as both internal and external dialectics.

One basic source of tension in close relationships arises from the trade-offs between being open and maintaining privacy. As an internal dialectic, this tension creates a struggle between disclosing information to a partner and keeping silent on some issues. Although you may want to share personal details in order to develop your bond, revealing or withholding too much information could threaten the relationship. As an external dialectic, this tension surfaces in the sometimes difficult decision to share news of a relationship with other people. Revealing information about a relationship to outsiders allows them to support your bond, but it also invites them to criticize or interfere with your relationship (Sprecher, 2011). In fact, people report the greatest amount of interference from their social network when they are escalating a romantic relationship from casual to serious involvement (Knobloch & Donovan-Kicken, 2006). Thus, revealing and concealing your relationship both have advantages and disadvantages.

HOW DO YOU RATE? 10.2

Strategies for Maintaining Intimate Relationships

To evaluate the extent to which you use the various relational maintenance strategies in your own relationship, visit the companion website to complete Laura Stafford's (2011) relationship maintenance behavior scale. As you reflect on your score, is the amount of relationship maintenance you do a good match for your level of commitment or satisfaction in this relationship?

PAUSE & REFLECT

How do you manage the tension between revealing and concealing information when you communicate using social media? Do you tend to reveal more information because of the physical separation, or less information?

Another core tension stems from your desire to have both novelty and predictability in close relationships. If you feel bored when a relationship is predictable but uneasy when there are too many surprises, you may have difficulty finding the right blend of routine and mystery. You might also struggle with how novel or predictable you would like your relationship to appear to outsiders. You probably don't want to have an "ordinary" or "typical" relationship, and prefer that your relationship is considered "special." At the same time, other people might question your relationship if it's too unusual – for example, if you became close more rapidly than normal, if you have unusual rules about how often you see each other, or if you allow behaviors that are typically off-limits. Whether this tension is internal or external, it captures your need for certainty in a relationship, as well as that "spark" that makes it interesting and unique.

Finally, you can experience internal and external dialectics caused by wanting to have both independence and autonomy while maintaining an intimate connection. Internal tension about autonomy and connection may be especially central to understanding intimacy within romantic relationships (Ben-Ari, 2011), and this dialectic appears to be especially salient when circumstances, such has military deployment, separate partners (Sahlstein, Maguire, & Timmerman, 2009). Tension between autonomy and connection has also been observed within relationships that people form online (Naidoo, Coleman, & Guyo, 2020). In general, when you and a partner have integrated your activities, goals, and values, you may begin to feel like your own identity is getting lost; but if you assert your independence, you might make the relationship less close. As an external tension, the autonomy and connection dialectic reflects the struggle for a couple to interact with the social network and still have time to be alone together. If the couple spends too much time together, they lose touch with the group and the others might resent their relationship. But if they never get to be alone together, they lose their special connection. The tension, then, is between cementing a relationship and being constrained by it.

Dialectical contradictions are an ongoing tension in relationships, but partners are not necessarily helpless against these influential forces. Table 10.3 summarizes eight coping strategies people might use in the face of relational dialectics (Baxter & Montgomery, 1996; Hoppe-Nagao & Ting-Toomey, 2002). Although some strategies, like denial and disorientation, might seem dysfunctional because they do not acknowledge both sides of a dialectic, they can provide a break when tensions are overwhelming. Other strategies, including spiraling alteration and segmentation, allow partners to pursue different sides of tension at different times or in different aspects of the relationship. Partners might also find a way to embrace both sides of a dialectic through strategies that balance or integrate competing forces. And through strategies such as recalibration and reaffirmation, partners might come to accept dialectical tensions as either complementary or at least inevitable.

Putting Theory into Practice: Maintaining Intimate Relationships

Keeping your intimate relationships running smoothly is not an easy task. Not unlike a car, your relationships need to be given fuel, have regular tune-ups, and occasionally get major service or repairs.

Make strategic relational maintenance part of your routine. Recall that routine maintenance refers to activities you do with or for your partner as a matter of course; although they aren't intentionally designed to keep you and your partner close, they have that effect. Strategic maintenance is more purposeful action that has the goal of keeping your relationship in a desired state. When you make strategic maintenance a part of your routine, you can prevent problems from emerging in the first place.

TABLE 10.3 Strategies for coping with dialectical tensions

Coping strategy	*Example*
DENIAL: Selecting one pole of a dialectical tension and ignoring the other	You give up your own autonomy and put all your energy into achieving an intimate connection with your partner
DISORIENTATION: Retreating into feelings of helplessness and limited dialogue	You withdraw from the relationships to avoid the stress created by the dialectical tension
SPIRALING ALTERATION: Cycling between the different sides of a dialectical tension at different times	You and your partner spend Friday evenings and Saturdays with each other, but Saturday nights you each go out with your own friends
SEGMENTATION: Pursing different sides of a dialectical tensions in different aspects of a relationship	You and your partner decide to share information about your feelings and goals for the relationship, but you keep the issues that upset you at work or school to yourself
BALANCE: Acknowledging the legitimacy of both sides of a dialectical tension and seeking a compromise	You and your partner recognize the importance of spending time alone as a couple and together with your group of friends; you talk openly about making time for both
INTEGRATION: Finding ways to respond to both sides of a dialectical tension simultaneously	You and your partner agree upon a regularly scheduled date night, but you take turns planning unique and special dates to share together
RECALIBRATION: Reframing a situation so that the two sides of a dialectical tension no longer seem to be in conflict	You and your partner focus on how pursing your independent interests and goals allows you to have a more interesting and desirable connection
REAFFIRMATION: Accepting that dialectical tensions will always be part of the relationship	You and your partner appreciate tensions as natural and even rewarding byproducts of being in love and sharing an intimate relationship

COMMUNICATION IN ACTION 10.2

Making Relational Maintenance Part of the Routine

Visit the companion website to complete a form that will help you reflect on the ways you can make relational maintenance a more strategic component of your relationship.

Develop skills for coping with dialectical tensions. Although clear guidelines for responding to dialectical tensions are not possible, you can improve your coping potential by having several strategies at your disposal. If you have several ways that you can cope with these tensions, you increase the likelihood that you'll find one that works when you need it.

COMMUNICATION IN ACTION 10.3

Coping With Relational Dialectics

Think of your most recent experience with a dialectical tension in either a friendship or romantic relationship. Then, note which of the eight strategies for coping with relational dialectics (see Table 10.3) you used in that situation. Using the form on the companion website, generate some additional steps that you can take to address that relational dialectic in the future.

INDIVIDUAL DIFFERENCES IN INTIMACY

One challenge to intimate relationships is that they involve two people who might have quite different approaches to close relationships. For example, people have different ways of thinking about intimacy, depending on the experiences they had as young children. Our age and experience also cause us to view relationships in different ways. In this section, we discuss some of the personal characteristics that shape how people communicate within intimate relationships.

Attachment Style
A general orientation toward close relationships that reflects how people see themselves in relation to others.

Secure Attachment
A bond characterized by comfort with closeness and an ability to trust or be trusted by others.

Insecure Attachment
A bond characterized by a lack of confidence in close relationships.

Attachment Styles

One personal trait that is especially relevant to romantic relationships is **attachment style** – a general orientation toward close relationships that reflects how people see themselves in relation to others. **Secure attachment** is characterized by comfort with closeness and an ability to trust or be trusted by others. In contrast, **insecure attachment** is characterized by less confidence in relationships. Moreover, evidence suggests that an attachment style formed in childhood influences how people approach their romantic relationships as adults (Hasim, Mustafa, & Hashim, 2018; Jones et al., 2018).

Attachment styles develop based on the bond between parents and children. As summarized in Table 10.4, four adult attachment styles can be distinguished by the views of self and others that emerge from childhood experiences (Bartholomew, 1990). People with a secure attachment style have a positive view of both themselves and others, which allows them to feel equally comfortable with intimacy and autonomy. A preoccupied attachment style combines a positive view of others with relatively low self-esteem; people with this style desire closeness with others, but they worry that their partners don't really want the relationship. Because a dismissing attachment style combines a positive view of the self with a negative view of others, people with this style tend to distrust others, deny the need for closeness in their lives, and are comfortable with independence. Finally, people with a fearful attachment style have a negative view of both self and others that causes them to get anxious when people get too close to them.

Because an attachment style reflects a person's way of thinking about intimate bonds, it affects a wide variety of experiences in romantic relationships. For example, people who tend to avoid and lack confidence in relationships – qualities of a fearful attachment style – perceive a gap

FIGURE 10.4 Mother playing with young child

Source: iStockPhoto.

TABLE 10.4 Adult attachment styles defined by positive and negative views of self and others

		View of Self	
		Positive	*Negative*
View of Others	*Positive*	*SECURE* People with this style are comfortable being close to others; they feel that they can trust and be trusted by others	*PREOCCUPIED* People with this style want to be close to others, but doubt whether other people really care about them
	Negative	*DISMISSING* People with this style believe that other people are unreliable or untrustworthy; accordingly, they avoid relationships and deny the need for closeness	*FEARFUL* People with this style trust neither themselves nor others; as a result, being close to other people makes them feel uncomfortable and anxious

between their personal identity and how they act when they are in a public setting with their spouse (Kennedy-Lightsey, Martin, LaBelle, & Weber, 2015). Attachment style has also been linked to how people communicate forgiveness of a partner, such that people with a dismissive style tend to avoid explicit forgiveness, people with a preoccupied style tend to minimize transgressions, and people with a secure style express forgiveness conditionally – making clear that their partner needs to do better in the future (Edwards, Pask, Whitbred, & Neuendorf, 2017). Within friendships, the partners of securely attached people report greater relationship satisfaction, more prosocial maintenance behaviors, and more compromising conflict behavior than the friends of people with other attachment styles (Bippus & Rollin, 2003). Perhaps not surprisingly, a study that integrated findings from over 130 previous research studies concluded that people with an insecure attachment style are less satisfied with their relationship (Candel & Turliuc, 2019).

PAUSE & REFLECT

How does your attachment style affect how you communicate with close relationship partners?

Friendship Across the Lifespan

Although friendships are important from childhood through old age, changes across the lifespan give rise to different ways of experiencing

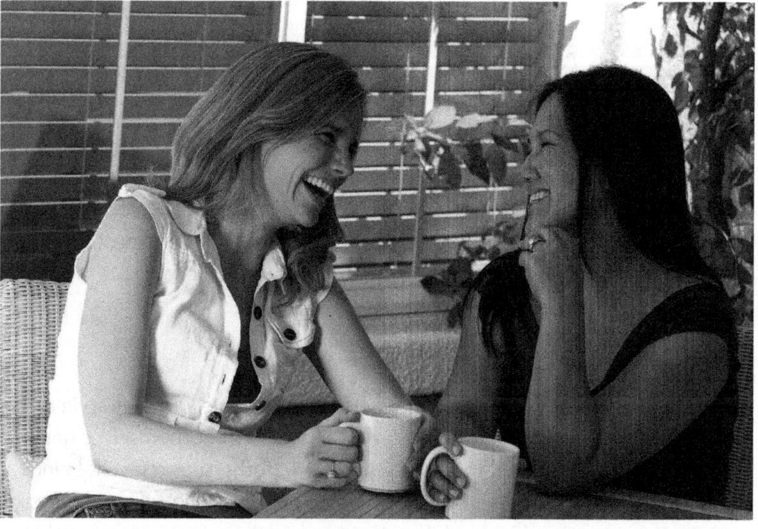

FIGURE 10.5 Two women chatting over coffee

Source: iStockPhoto.

intimacy. Expectations for friendship are remarkably stable in light of the huge changes people go through as they age (Rawlins, 2004). At the same time, the meanings you attach to intimacy evolve throughout your life. Figure 10.6 shows the lifespan changes in views of friendship that are described in this section.

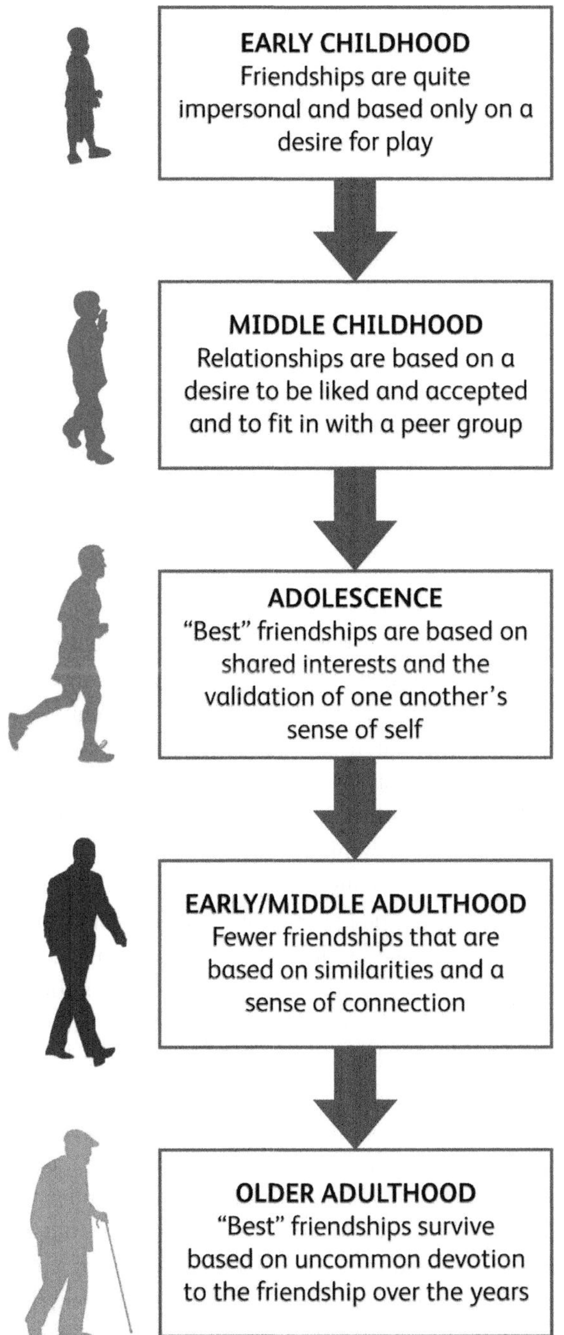

EARLY CHILDHOOD
Friendships are quite impersonal and based only on a desire for play
MIDDLE CHILDHOOD
Relationships are based on a desire to be liked and accepted and to fit in with a peer group
ADOLESCENCE
"Best" friendships are based on shared interests and the validation of one another's sense of self
EARLY/MIDDLE ADULTHOOD
Fewer friendships that are based on similarities and a sense of connection
OLDER ADULTHOOD
"Best" friendships survive based on uncommon devotion to the friendship over the years

FIGURE 10.6 Qualities of friendship across the lifespan

From childhood to adolescence. A close look at the friendships that children form with their peers shows important changes from early childhood through adolescence. For young children, the foundation of friendship is proximity, and the opportunity to play that being near another child creates, as well as positive interactions and similar ways of behaving (Afshordi & Liberman, 2021). In fact, the friendships of children are quite impersonal, especially in comparison to relationships formed later in life. Denise recalls a young girl asking her son, then aged five, if he wanted to be friends; his blunt "no" was shocking to Denise, but the little girl took it in stride. "I guess he doesn't want to do anything," she said calmly. The challenge for young children is coordinating activities, but feelings and conflict are largely (and fortunately!) irrelevant. Instead, children as young as five tend to privilege their friends' preferences (Komolova & Wainryb, 2011), and they are quite skillful at communicating with friends in ways that steer interactions away from conflict – deftly changing the topic or redirecting their peer's attention to avoid a negative exchange (Sanders, 2007).

PAUSE & REFLECT

What memories do you have of your earliest childhood friend? How did you and your friend spend your time together?

In middle childhood, friendships are about fitting in and being accepted. Being a good friend at this age involves following the rules for play, providing tangible help, and being a skillful communicator (Samter, 2003). In particular, children who can communicate emotions appropriately, have fluent conversations, use humor to make interactions fun, and manage conflicts have distinct advantages over children who can't control their emotions, have speech difficulties, are less playful, and can't resolve disputes (Stafford, 2004). Thus, middle childhood sees the emergence of a view of intimacy that is tied to interpersonal communication.

In adolescence, children face desires for both individuality and close bonds with people outside their family, and their ability to achieve both autonomy and connection with friends during this life stage has been linked to both social competence and mental health in adulthood (Chango, Allen, Szwedo, & Schad, 2015). Adolescents form "best" friendships with people who share values, have similar interests, and validate the teen's emerging sense of self. To these ends, friendships at this age revolve around self-disclosure, problem-solving, and feeling understood (Samter, 2003). A five-year longitudinal study also showed that older adolescents are more likely than younger ones to work at resolving conflicts with a friend (Yu, Branje, Keijsers, & Meeus, 2014). In total, then, the years from early to late childhood see friendship changing from an impersonal focus on shared activities to focus on sustaining a personal connection.

From younger to older adulthood. People have the most friends in late adolescence (and in college, if they attend), and then the size of friendship networks begins to shrink (Dainton, Zelley, & Langan, 2003). In fact, adulthood sees decreases in both the number of friends people have and the amount of time they spend with friends (Noller, Feeney, & Petersen, 2001). These trends may reflect a greater focus on the spousal and parental roles people may fill as adults. In addition, adults juggle demands on their time created by work, home-making, and taking care of aging parents. Like the relationships formed in late adolescence, adult friendships are defined by similarities and a sense of connection; but at this stage of life, day-to-day demands limit the energy people can devote to their friends.

In older adulthood, views of friendship are transformed once again. The elderly tend to be more discriminating about who counts as a best friend, and they reserve that title for someone who has demonstrated uncommon devotion to the relationship (Patterson, Bettini, & Nussbaum, 1993). Geographical separation has less of an impact on the friendships of older adults, relative to relationships earlier in life (Nussbaum, Hummert, Williams, & Harwood, 1996); however, older adults benefit from having local friends who give them opportunities to socialize (Bitzan & Kruzich, 1990; Gupta & Korte, 1994). Especially for residents of nursing homes, having a friend can be crucial to feeling satisfied with life (Nussbaum, 1991).

One particular challenge for elderly friends is finding a balance between maintaining independence and providing help (Rawlins, 2004). The friends of older adults provide a confidant, a companion, and someone to chat with who is outside the family network (Samter, 2003). The feelings of independence fostered by friendship, however, can be undermined when older adults have to rely on those friends for more tangible assistance, like transportation and medical advice (Pitts, Krieger, & Nussbaum, 2005). Compared to younger adults, older adults are less bothered when they receive more help than they give in a friendship (Li, Fok, & Fung, 2011; Wang & Gruenewald, 2019). At the same time, some studies have shown that older adults feel worse when they have to rely on their friends too much (Keyes, 2002; Väänänen, Buunk, Kivimäki, Vahtera, & Koskenvuo, 2008). After a lifetime forging friendships grounded in similarity and mutuality, older adults may find it difficult to embrace passing time and providing help – those qualities that define childhood friendships – as the basis for their intimate relationships.

Putting Theory into Practice: Embracing Individual Differences

This section of the chapter has explored just a few of the ways that people can differ in their experience of intimacy. Armed with this knowledge, you can embrace individual differences in relationships.

Avoid "attachment-centrism." Keep in mind that your attachment style is only one of the ways in which people might view close relationships. By respecting the relationship beliefs of others, you might find ways to relate to other people on their own terms.

COMMUNICATION IN ACTION 10.4

Assessing the Pros and Cons of Attachment Styles

Review the four attachment styles summarized in Table 10.4. For each style, use the form on the companion website to identify two strengths or benefits enjoyed by people with that attachment style, and two challenges those individuals must face.

Keep age differences in perspective. Although age differences in approaches to intimacy are worth noting, it's also important that you don't exaggerate their effects. One of the mistakes we make in life is assuming that people are locked into particular ways of communicating, such as assuming that young people can't experience mature relationships and that the elderly can't be enthralled by a romantic fling. You can enrich your experience of intimacy in your relationships by being open to the variety of ways in which you can experience close bonds with others. Begin by thinking about how your approach to close relationships might be limiting your options. As you reflect on your close relationships, try to identify the qualities – shared activities, a sense of belonging, feeling understood, or tangible help – you have used to define your intimate relationships. After identifying your priorities for intimacy, take note of the aspects of intimacy that you tend to neglect. By incorporating those qualities into your close relationships, you might have more complete and fulfilling experiences.

EXTREMES OF INTIMACY

As we have seen thus far in this chapter, intimacy includes a variety of components, it can present certain challenges, and people can experience it in different ways. You can also gain an understanding of communication in intimate relationships by considering what happens when intimacy is taken to an extreme – when intimacy is overwhelmingly positive or shattered by infidelity. In this section, we explore the realms of romantic infatuation and betrayal.

Romantic Infatuation

Perhaps one of the strongest and most wonderful emotions you can experience in a relationship is romantic love. When in the throes of romantic love, each day can seem brighter, each problem solvable, and the future unlimited. In the extreme, though, romantic love is not unlike a mental illness; when people are "madly" in love, they might obsess about a partner, feel depressed if separated from a lover, and become emotionally dependent on a partner (Tallis, 2005). People who are intensely in love even show unique patterns of brain activity when they look at pictures of their beloved (Aron et al., 2005). Their neural systems change in ways similar to people experiencing addiction (Wang et al., 2020), and they have heightened levels of oxytocin, a euphoria-inducing hormone, when they are discussing their affection for a beloved partner (Gonzaga, Turner, Keltner, Campos, & Altemus, 2006). Because intense romantic love is experienced by people of all cultures, you should be aware of the pros and cons of these strong feelings.

IDEA: INCLUSION, DIVERSITY, EQUITY, AND ACCESS

A study compared romantic beliefs for European American and African American research participants and found that while both groups subscribed to romantic beliefs, the scales that measure the four beliefs aren't the same and are likely a less good measure for African Americans (Weaver & Ganong, 2004). This is just one example of how research tools developed using nondiverse samples might have less value for studying diverse populations. How can we adapt our ways of interpreting research to acknowledge these limitations?

What is romantic love? Romantic love is embodied in four beliefs: love will find a way, one true love exists, relationship perfection is possible, and people can fall in love at first sight (Sprecher & Metts, 1989; Figure 10.7).

FIGURE 10.7 Romantic beliefs

People who endorse these beliefs generally report more satisfaction and commitment in their romantic relationship (Vannier & O'Sullivan, 2017). People are also happier when they idealize a partner and believe that a partner idealizes them (Murray, Holmes, & Griffin, 2004). College students who believe that true love can overcome obstacles also feel that love is more important than sexual intimacy, love should come before sex, sex is an expression of love, and sexual intimacy decreases with the length of a love relationship (Hendrick & Hendrick, 2002). Moreover, people who believe that they are destined to love their partner are also more likely to give in on conflict issues (Franiuk, Cohen, & Pomerantz, 2002) or withdraw from an argument (Dovala, Hawrilenko, & Cordova, 2018). Thus, believing in and experiencing romantic love can have several benefits for relationship partners.

PAUSE & REFLECT

Have you ever been "head over heels" in love? If so, what impact did your feelings have on your communication with your beloved partner?

Being in love, however, is not without some downsides. If you endorse the notion of one true love, but don't think you're dating that person, you'll probably be less satisfied with that relationship (Franiuk et al., 2002). When a current relationship falls short of people's ideals, they are generally less satisfied, committed, and invested in it (Vannier & O'Sullivan, 2018), and they sometimes resort to punishing a partner, disparaging themselves, or distancing themselves from the relationship in order to cope with the situation (Alexander, 2008). Moreover, you may lose your ability to see your partner's faults when you are under love's spell. When people are infatuated, they tend to disregard relationship warning signs, such as evidence that the other person has different values (McLanahan, Gold, Lenney, Ryckman, & Kulberg, 1990; Thompson, Gold, & Ryckman, 2003). Endorsing romantic beliefs is also associated with the experience of aggressive behavior from a romantic partner, as reported by both heterosexual women (Papp, Liss, Erchull, Godfrey, & Waaland-Kreutzer, 2017), and sexual minorities (Moskowitz, Richmond, & Michniewicz, 2020). In addition, people who are in love overestimate how in love they think other couples are (Aloni & Berneirni, 2004).

Romantic Betrayal

Whereas romantic love highlights the euphoria you can feel in close relationships, romantic betrayal focuses on one of the most devastating experiences that can occur. In the context of a close relationship, infidelity involves violating the obligation to forego intimacy with other people. **Sexual infidelity** is having physical closeness with someone outside the primary relationship, and **emotional infidelity** is devoting time, attention, and feelings to someone other than the relationship partner. Both types of infidelity violate expectations for monogamy in committed romantic relationships, but they evoke different reactions. In particular, sexual infidelity causes partners to become angry and blame the "cheater," whereas emotional infidelity causes victims to feel hurt (Green & Sabini, 2006). Men also find it more difficult than women to forgive a partner for sexual infidelity (Shackelford, Buss, & Bennett, 2002).

Sexual Infidelity
Having physical intimacy with someone other than a committed romantic partner.

Emotional Infidelity
Devoting time, attention, and feelings to someone other than a committed romantic partner.

Precise estimates of the frequency of infidelity are hard to obtain; however, one study found that 65% of college students reported being intimately involved with someone else while in a committed dating relationship (Shackelford, LeBlanc, & Drass, 2000). The ability to meet people online or through apps like Tinder has created additional avenues for people in committed relationships to find extra-relational sexual partners (Timmermans, De Caluwé, & Alexopoulos, 2018). What influences whether a person is unfaithful to a romantic partner? Perhaps not surprisingly, people are less likely to cheat on a partner they are committed to or find sexually desirable (Drigotas, Safstrom, & Gentilita, 1999; Regan, 2000). Conversely, people are more susceptible to infidelity when a current relationship doesn't fulfill their needs (Lewandowski & Ackerman, 2006). Certain kinds of people may also be more likely to cheat than others. In particular, people who are generally promiscuous, impulsive, and have a dismissive or fearful attachment style are more likely to engage in sexual infidelity (Feldman & Cauffman, 1999; McAlister, Pachana, & Jackson, 2005).

Reactions to infidelity can range from ending the relationship to forgiving the cheater – just how people respond to infidelity is influenced by qualities of their relationship, the circumstances of the betrayal, its discovery, and how partners make sense of it. Whether people break up with a partner who cheated is influenced by the level of commitment, satisfaction, and investment in the relationship – people are generally more constructive when they value the relationship, unless the infidelity is serious (Dillow, Malachowski, Brann, & Weber, 2011; Weiser & Weigel, 2014). In fact, people motivated to save their relationship might go so far as to be in denial about a partner's infidelity (Kleine, 2021). In addition, people find infidelity involving someone new to be less upsetting and more forgivable than being unfaithful with a former partner (Cann & Baucom, 2004). Infidelity also has a less negative impact on the relationship when people hear about the affair directly from their partner, as opposed to catching their partner in the act or hearing about it from other people (Afifi, Falato, & Weiner, 2001). Ultimately, whether relationships can survive betrayal depends on whether the victims of an unfaithful partner can manage to forgive the transgression (Hall & Fincham, 2006).

PAUSE & REFLECT

What would you do if a partner was unfaithful to you? Would you react differently to sexual versus emotional infidelity?

An unfaithful person can also shape the consequences of infidelity through their communication with the partner. Confessing an affair can elicit more forgiveness than waiting until a partner discovers the infidelity or forces the truth to come out (Afifi et al., 2001), but communicating about infidelity is a complicated matter (Walters & Burger, 2013). One classic study asked college students to describe what they would say to a romantic partner if they committed a hypothetical act of sexual infidelity (Mongeau & Schulz, 1997). The results of that study showed that people are more likely to offer an explanation and to be honest about an affair when they are sure a partner already knows about it. When people want to maintain their relationship, they also offer more concessions and excuses, rather than justifying their behavior. The study also highlighted the dilemma created when people aren't sure whether a partner knows about an affair. Under those circumstances, unfaithful partners tend to hold back an admission of guilt, while they offer more excuses for their behavior; by doing so, they can clarify why an affair might have happened, without providing too much information that the partner doesn't already have. Another study, which also asked people to reflect on hypothetical scenarios, found that forgiveness was more likely when the hypothetical cheater apologized and the infidelity was a one-time event (Gunderson & Ferrari, 2008).

Putting Theory into Practice: Keeping Your Head When Falling in Love

When you're in the throes of intense love, you might be compelled to do anything for your partner, forgive their offenses, and take risks to be with that partner. And if you experience a partner's infidelity, you might also be moved to extreme behavior – perhaps ending a relationship you value or maintaining it despite the violation. The common thread that runs through experiences of infatuation or infidelity is the need to keep your wits about you when communicating with your partner.

Stay grounded when you're head over heels. Intense romantic love is a physical condition; your body and brain chemistry experience real changes when you are infatuated with a romantic partner. This intense experience can create a lifelong bond between partners, but the euphoria of being in love can make you blind to trouble spots in your relationship.

You can avoid overlooking problems when you're in love by taking steps to maintain a realistic point of view:

- Ask your friends to point out potential issues that may present challenges in the future.
- Take short breaks from the relationship so that you can catch your breath and reassess the situation.
- Avoid doing anything that you would find unacceptable if you weren't intoxicated by your feelings.

By reminding your friends and yourself that infatuation needs supervision, you can make sure that your feelings of love don't lead you astray.

Take charge of infidelity. Infidelity is one of the worst betrayals a person can commit or experience. At the same time, infidelity isn't uncommon in romantic relationships. Are there ways that communication can help you weather the storm created by unfaithful behavior? Although perhaps nothing can prepare you for the consequences of violating a partner's trust or having that trust violated, there are strategies that might help you control the course of infidelity:

- If you are being unfaithful to your partner because you lack commitment to the relationship, you need to find a more appropriate way to dissolve that bond.
- If you are being unfaithful, but you are committed to maintaining that primary relationship, you need to end your affair and address your betrayal.
- Keep in mind that your partner will take the news of your infidelity better if he or she hears it from you first.
- Be prepared to take responsibility for your actions and be aware that your partner is largely in control over his or her forgiveness and the future of your relationship.
- If you find yourself on the receiving end of a confession of infidelity, it is important that you know your own boundaries for what you can and cannot accept in a relationship and that you take time to decide what you want to happen in that relationship.
- Keep in mind that infidelity isn't uncommon.
- Whether you feel that the betrayal can never be overcome or you value the relationship enough to try again, your communication choices can control what direction you go in the future.

SUMMARY

This chapter opened by exploring the nature of intimacy in close friendships and romantic relationships. Rather than being a single entity, intimacy is a blend of closeness, openness, trust, affection, and mutuality.

The love you might feel for a relationship partner can also vary depending on the amount of intimacy, passion, or commitment that is present. In fact, people can experience love in different ways, depending on their focus on sexuality, game-playing, or friendship.

Once you achieve close bonds with a friend or romantic partner, communication becomes a tool for maintaining intimacy. Relational maintenance behaviors include a variety of activities – providing assurances, being open, being positive, sharing tasks, enjoying social networks, giving advice, and managing conflicts – that help you to keep a relationship going. Although you might perform these behaviors strategically with the goal of maintaining intimacy, they also occur as part of routine communication in close relationships. Communication and relational maintenance can be especially important when you are confronted with tensions arising from relational dialectics. Whether your problems stem from internal or external dialectics focused on the trade-offs between openness and privacy, novelty and predictability, or autonomy and connection, you can use communication to manage the pushes and pulls we feel in intimate relationships.

Communication in close relationships is further complicated by the fact that people bring distinct views of intimacy to their friendships and romances. Because a person's attachment style is a view of intimacy based on early childhood experiences, it may be an especially strong influence on adult romantic relationships. As you age, you also go through changes or have experiences that shape how you view friendship. As you form friendships and romantic relationships throughout your life, you will undoubtedly encounter many different views of intimacy.

Another way to think about how intimacy varies is to reflect on the extreme experiences created by infatuation and infidelity. Intimacy can be a life-changing, positive experience when you find yourself in the throes of intense, romantic love. You should also bear in mind that love can, in fact, blind you to your partner's flaws and relational fault lines. And intimacy can be a life-changing, devastating experience when you engage in or discover sexual or emotional infidelity. Keeping in mind the frequency, causes, and outcomes of infidelity might help you to keep these betrayals from undermining intimate relationships that you value.

Intimate friendships and romantic relationships are the context for some of your most important interpersonal communication experiences. From the ways in which you experience and express intimacy to the behaviors that you use to maintain intimate bonds, communication is at the core of your closest relationships. When you recognize the enormous task that communication performs within intimate relationships, and the complexities introduced by individual differences and intimate extremes, you might wonder if there is any way to communicate more effectively with intimate partners. As we have seen in this chapter, you can take an active role and develop communication skills that will help you to foster and enjoy intimate relationships.

ACTIVITIES FOR EXPLORING COMMUNICATION ETHICS

What Would You/Should You Do?

In this chapter, you learned that mutuality is an important part of intimacy; in other words, intimacy involves partners who share interest in and responsibility for their relationship. What would you do if you had a friend who was investing a lot more in a romantic relationship than his or her partner? Perhaps your friend is doing all of the routine and strategic maintenance, or perhaps you know that your friend's partner has been spending time with other people. What would you, or should you, do when someone you care about is being taken advantage of by another relationship partner?

Something to Think About

Social media is a powerful means for connecting with relationship partners, near and far and past and present. Because people have a lot of choice over what they post on social media, they can present their identities to others in a variety of ways. Some people use social media to present only the most positive sides of their lives – retaking and editing photos so they look their best, sharing good news and celebrations, and leaving out less flattering information. Other people use social media to express strong opinions and negative emotions, perhaps venting about a politician, complaining about their family, or expressing their grief. When people have a large social media network, those messages – both superficial and very personal – are broadcast equally to close friends and loved ones, as well as potential strangers. What are the standards for ethical communication when you consider how the messages shared on social media can reach and affect such a diverse array of relationship partners?

Analyze Communication Ethics Yourself

Ageism in American society ranges from job discrimination to people's tendency to communicate with older adults as though they are children. One form of ageism is assuming that the elderly have outgrown the need for nonfamilial friendships and romantic relationships. This bias can have serious consequences within nursing homes, where institutional structures can determine whether or not residents have an opportunity to enjoy social relationships. These conditions were starkly revealed when the COVID-19 pandemic shut down visitation at residential care facilities for the elderly throughout the world. Assuming it is safe to do so, visit a nursing home in your community and observe the opportunities for socializing provided by that institution. Are residents treated like adults who have social needs? Can you identify any practices that encourage or discourage friendships and romantic relationships? As you reflect on your observations, consider the ethical responsibilities created when an institution is in control of people's communication opportunities.

KEY WORDS

- attachment style
- attachment theory
- complete/consummate love
- emotional infidelity
- eros
- gender orientation
- insecure attachment
- intimacy
- ludus
- relational dialectic
- relational maintenance
- routine maintenance
- secure attachment
- sexual infidelity
- storge
- strategic maintenance

LEARNING OBJECTIVES

After reading this chapter, you should be able to:

1. Explain the functions that are served by the family.
2. Identify the different parts of a family system.
3. Understand why family members keep and reveal secrets.
4. Describe the communication patterns that occur within different types of couples.
5. Understand the communication challenges that emerge across the family lifespan.
6. Strengthen your ability to promote family well-being through interpersonal communication.

PUTTING THEORY INTO PRACTICE

In this chapter, you will learn how to:

1. Expand your family to meet your needs.
2. Address the challenges of blending families.
3. Communicate protection and affection.
4. Respect the boundaries of your family system.
5. Practice safe secrets.
6. Anticipate changes over the family lifespan.
7. Keep the lines of communication open.

COMMUNICATION IN FAMILIES

11

Source: Photo by Win McNamee/ Getty Images.

DOI: 10.4324/9781351174381-14

When Joe Biden and Kamala Harris were elected to office, their families played an important supporting role. President Biden's family history includes stories of tragedy and triumph. His first wife, Neilia, and their three children, Beau, Hunter, and Naomi, were involved in a horrific car accident on their way to buy a Christmas tree shortly after Biden was elected to the United States senate in 1972. Neilia and Naomi were killed in the crash, leaving Biden as a single parent to Beau and Hunter. A few years after this tragedy, Biden married his second wife, Jill, and together they had a daughter, Ashley. Biden also has seven grandchildren, who were all present at his inauguration, and he has said that he will always make time to accept a call from his grandchildren, no matter what he is doing, even as President! Biden's pick for Vice President, Kamala Harris, also has a unique and rich family story. Harris is the daughter of Black and South Asian immigrants and she married Doug Emhoff, who is the son of Jewish parents. As the first female Vice President in the United States, her husband is also the first person to hold the title of Second Gentleman. Harris has two step-children through her marriage to Doug, Cole and Ella, who fondly call her "Momala." When Biden named Harris as his Vice President, he even called Cole and Ella on the phone to welcome them to the family. In an interview with People magazine, Harris said "Joe and I have a similar feeling that really is how we approach leadership: family in every version that it comes." This mindset, coupled with their diverse and supportive families, make Biden and Harris effective and empathetic leaders of a nation with countless unique family stories.

Throughout people's lives, family remains one of the stable touchstones that they can turn to for comfort or help. At the same time, family life can sometimes be distressing, frustrating, or hurtful. Joe Biden has faced many of the hardships that can befall a family, including the loss of his wife and daughter, the death of his son Beau from brain cancer, and supporting his son Hunter through very public challenges with drug addiction, but he has also experienced many of the joys that family brings, such as remarriage, becoming a grandfather, and having a supportive family to guide him during his Presidency. The formation of step-families is not always an easy path, but Kamala Harris has shown how warm and loving step-family relationships can be. In both cases, these families embody the typical dynamics of a modern family. In this chapter, we examine the rewards and challenges of interpersonal communication within families so that you can promote the well-being of these critical relationships.

WHAT IS A FAMILY?

Ideas about what constitutes the typical American family have changed significantly over the last half century, and family dynamics have changed with them. We see these changing images of family reflected in TV sitcoms and dramas. Consider the 1960s hit, *Leave It to Beaver*, which focused on a nuclear family made up of a working father, stay-at-home mother, and two sons. The 1970s brought *The Brady Bunch*, which told the story of a blended family formed by the marriage of formerly single parents. *Modern Family*, which aired from 2009–2020, depicted the life of a complex extended family, with the divorced patriarch of the family married to a much younger woman who has a child from a previous relationship, his gay son who has adopted a daughter from Vietnam with his partner, and his daughter who is married with three children. The complexity of family is also portrayed in the critically acclaimed *Black-ish*, in which the parents of five children help the family navigate personal, social, and political challenges surrounding issues of race and class. In this section, we look at the facts behind these images as we explore the dynamics of contemporary family life.

The Changing Face of Families

Analyses of data collected by the U.S. Census Bureau have detailed the changing face of families (Mayol-Garcia, Gurrentz, & Kreider, 2021). Compared to previous generations, today's adults typically wait longer to marry and might never marry. For example, in the 1960s, the average age of first marriage was 20 for women and 23 for men; in 2016, those averages were 28 for women and 30 for men. Put differently, the percent of adults aged 25–29 who were never married rose from 45.6% of women and 57.9% of men in 2006 to 59.7% of women and 70.9% of men in 2016. A number of reasons account for the decline in marriage in recent years, including divorce rates, an increase in women's educational attainment and participation in the work force, and a rise in cohabitation as an alternative or precursor to marriage. Between 2009 and 2010 alone, there was a 13% increase in the number of opposite sex couples who were cohabiting, with 7.5 million cohabiting couples, and a 30% increase in the number of same-sex partners who were cohabiting, up to 620,000 couples (Kreider, 2010). Divorce is also a factor, with about 40% of marriages eventually terminating (Hurley, 2005). These statistics remind us that many people remain single, live with a partner, or form a domestic partnership rather than get legally married.

Decreases in marriages and the frequency of divorce have contributed to changes in family structure. As of 2010, 16% of white children,

27% of Hispanic children, and 52% of African American children lived in a single-parent household (Mather, 2010). And when people marry or remarry after they have children, they also face the task of combining their pre-existing households within a step-family. A review of 20 studies that detailed experiences in step-families underscored the work these families have to do to honor their pasts, live in the present, and invest in the future (Pylyser, Buysse, & Loeys, 2018). Although members of step-families might compete over resources, have trouble managing different conflict styles, and struggle to develop a sense of solidarity, they also seem to be more aware of their struggles and, consequently, sometimes better at solving problems.

PAUSE & REFLECT

Did you grow up living with two parents, a single parent, grandparents, or a step-family? How did that experience influence your view of "family"?

Other U.S. population statistics suggest several alternatives to the family made up of a mother, a father, and their biological children. In vitro fertilization, artificial insemination, or surrogate mothering allow people to have offspring who may or may not be genetically related to them. Adoption is another common way to expand a family – indeed, approximately 120,000 children were adopted in 2012, according to a report from the U.S. Department of Health and Human Services (2016). Data from 2010 also showed that about 10% of all children live with a grandparent (Ellis & Simmons, 2014). Meanwhile, advances in genetic testing have made it possible for people to use services such as 23 and Me to find biological relatives they didn't know they had. Clearly, families can develop and expand in a variety of different ways.

IDEA: INCLUSION, DIVERSITY, EQUITY, AND ACCESS

Although there are numerous configurations of families, certain traditional images that portray families made of a mother, father, and biological children continue to dominate popular culture. What can we do in our personal, professional, and social lives to acknowledge and support the greater variety of forms that families can take?

As the characteristics of families have changed over the years, the definitions of marriage and family have expanded to include different kinds of family relationships. In general, then, a family could include

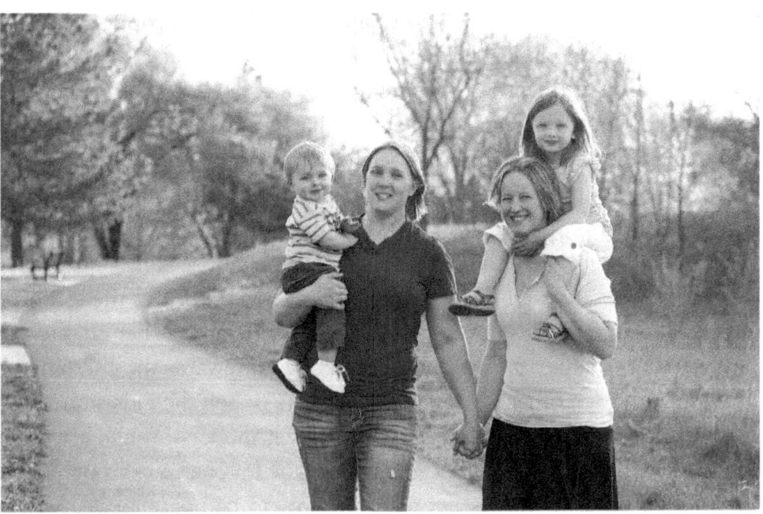

FIGURE 11.1 A family enjoying time together

Source: Kari Layland/Getty Images.

any of the following relationships: (a) people who are connected legally, genetically, or because they live together; (b) a group that fills certain needs for its members; or (c) a group that is united by a shared identity, history and future. In other words, a **family** is a network of people who create a sense of home, share a collective identity, experience a common history, and envision a similar future.

Family
A network of people who create a sense of home, share a collective identity, experience a common history, and envision a similar future.

Functions of the Family

Although families can take many different forms, families of any sort perform a few core functions for their members. For some people, a family provides a network of safety or support that isn't always available from friends. Even people who don't have close relationships with family members gain important social and interpersonal knowledge from their family interactions. In this section, we explore the functions that are served by family relationships.

One of the most basic functions of family is the promise of protection. From birth through childhood, your family members protect you and fulfill your most basic needs for food, shelter, clothing, and warmth. Even after childhood, families may offer support; for example, college students who live in dorms or rentals during the school year might return to their family's home during the summer months. Likewise, some college graduates will live at home until they get a job and can afford to move out on their own. And later in life, family members might find themselves living together again for financial or health reasons. The protective functions of family were especially salient during the lockdowns that resulted from the COVID-19 pandemic – circumstances forced some people to identify relatively small "pods" of people with whom they interacted, in an effort to minimize their threat of exposure to the virus.

Family Socialization
The process by which parents teach their children behaviors that are appropriate, expected, moral, or polite.

In addition to the tangible resources that you receive, your family also plays an important role in your socialization as a human being. **Family socialization** is the process by which parents teach their children behaviors that are appropriate, expected, moral, or polite. Through socialization, parents help their children become competent, socially skilled, and emotionally aware (Van Egeren & Barratt, 2004). Consider the example of Jen's cousin, who has three young sons. She encourages her boys to say "please" and "thank you" when making requests, rewards the children for sharing with each other, and issues "time outs" when the kids start fighting. And although the oldest son gets his own money through a weekly allowance, he is expected to set some of it aside for charity. Through these efforts, Jen's cousin teaches her children how to be polite and get along with others, promotes financial responsibility, and encourages compassion and empathy. As this example suggests, a family provides a context in which we learn social roles and appropriate behaviors.

Transmission
The teaching of cultural practices from one generation to the next.

Beyond teaching children behaviors that are valued and appropriate, the family also educates its members about the traditions and beliefs of the culture in which they live. This process is known as **transmission** – the teaching of cultural practices from one generation to the next. Whereas socialization teaches children how to behave as a well-mannered person in general, transmission teaches family members how to belong to a particular social group with unique cultural practices. For example, parents tell children stories and teach them songs that help them to learn about the history of their country, the beliefs of their religion, or the trials and triumphs of their ethnic group. Likewise, families might display religious icons in their home as a reminder of the values that are important to them. And on dates that mark important events within the culture, families have parties, attend religious services, or participate in community celebrations. Through this range of activities, children learn to accept and cherish the same cultural beliefs that are meaningful to their parents.

PAUSE & REFLECT

What are some of the cultural practices you learned from your family? How did your family teach you these practices?

A fourth function served by family is the promise of emotional support and comfort. Being able to turn to your family can be particularly important during difficult times. In fact, one study showed that cancer patients experience fewer symptoms and less distress and isolation when their family members are taught how to be more supportive (Badger et al., 2021). Although people often assume that mothers are the primary providers of emotional support and comfort within families, the role of fathers has changed a lot over the years, such that fathers are more committed to and engaged in family life (Banchefsky & Park, 2016). In particular, the most frequently mentioned qualities of being a good father, based on narratives written by fathers of sons, include loving your son, being available, setting a good example, taking an active interest and role in your son's life, and providing for your family (Morman & Floyd, 2006). Fathers also become more important as sources of emotional support, encouragement, and help as children make the transition to adulthood (Rossetto, Manning, & Green, 2017). In general, the strength of family ties is influenced by whether members fulfill the promise of support and comfort.

> **HOW DO YOU RATE? 11.1**
>
> **Affectionate Communication**
>
> Visit the companion website to complete Kory Floyd's affectionate communication index (see Floyd & Mikkelson, 2005). To see how you rate, think about how you express love or affection to one member of your family. How do you let this person know that you love him or her? Do you find that you rely more on verbal or nonverbal messages to express affection? How would your responses change if you focused on a different family member?

Putting Theory into Practice: Strengthening Family Bonds

Although the characteristics of families have changed considerably in the past few decades, these relationships remain vital to your health and happiness. With an understanding of the functions of family, you can enhance your interpersonal communication experiences.

Expand your family to meet your needs. Although families might be expected to perform the functions previously described, many families fall short of these goals. When families face financial hardships or can't perform their functions because of health, mental, or emotional limitations, its members might not receive the support that they need. What might you do if your family has trouble taking care of you? Remember that family is more than parents and their offspring. A family can include other relatives, as well as unrelated people with whom you have a relationship. Many young adults who are separated from their families to attend college or start a new job will assemble a group of friends to celebrate major holidays, organize birthday parties, or coordinate a ride to the airport. By reaching beyond your nuclear family, you might discover a lot of other people who can perform family functions.

Address the challenges of blending families. People face a number of challenges within blended families. Talking within the family about the difficulties you are facing can help improve the family environment. When families come together, it's important to clarify the role that stepparents should have with the children, strategies for addressing conflict, and the family traditions that you want to preserve. In addition, think about the strengths and weaknesses that each family brings to the table and consider strategies that capitalize on each family's strengths and minimize their weaknesses. Perhaps one side of the blended family is really good at addressing conflict and can help the members of their step-family adopt better strategies. Maybe one family isn't very good at expressing love and affection and could learn how to be better by adopting some of their step-family's behaviors. By adopting each family's strengths and discussing how to avoid each family's weaknesses, your blended family can forge the foundation for more effective communication.

Communicate protection and affection. Because protection and emotional support are basic human needs, you can strengthen family bonds by communicating to people that you're there for them. Perhaps you could remind a sibling that he or she can move in with you if they ever need to. Or you could tell your parents that you'll help them out when they get older. When you protect members of your family from life's hardships, you strengthen family ties and ensure that someone will be there for you when you need help. Expressing affection for family members might even make you feel better yourself. Adults who express more affection to other people have lower levels of stress hormones over the course of their workday (Floyd, 2006), and writing affectionate notes can actually reduce cholesterol levels over time (Floyd, Mikkelson, Hesse, & Pauley, 2007). Thus, expressing affection to family members can both strengthen those relationships and promote your own well-being.

COMMUNICATION IN ACTION 11.1

Expressing Affection

Select a member of your family with whom you would like to share an affectionate message. Then, sit down to write a card or an email to this person explaining all of the reasons you love and care about them. Try to be as specific as possible when constructing your message to identify and explain all of the traits that you appreciate about your family member. When you're finished, you might even send the affectionate letter. Whether or not you decide to send the letter, you'll still receive all of the positive benefits to your health and your relationship by expressing your affection.

COMMUNICATION IN FAMILY SYSTEMS

Systems Theory
A general perspective that emphasizes how different objects work together to form a larger entity.

Systems theory is a general perspective that emphasizes how different objects work together to form a larger entity. The human body, for example, is made up of several systems, including the digestive system, the respiratory system, and the neurological system. Each of these systems has several organs, which work together to process food, deliver oxygen to our cells, and send information to and from our brain. There are many other examples of systems in nature, ranging from molecular systems to solar systems. Humans also create systems, such as transportation systems, school systems, or systems of government. In this section, we'll examine the family as a system, as well as the role of communication within family systems.

The Family System

Generally defined, a **system** is a bounded set of objects that interrelate with one another to form a whole. As illustrated by the family system in Figure 11.2, all systems have four core qualities. First, systems are made up of distinct objects – the organs in the digestive system, planets in a solar system, or the members of a family. Second, the objects within a system have specific characteristics, as in the case of family members who have different roles or are different ages. Third, the parts of a system are related to each other in different ways; particular members of a family have special relationships with each other. Finally, a system is bounded, which means that the combined parts create a whole and recognizable entity.

System
A bounded set of objects that interrelate with one another to form a whole.

OBJECTS: The nine family members.
CHARACTERISTICS OF OBJECTS: The members of the family vary in terms of their size, age, and gender. Family members also bring other characteristics to the family, such as compassion, affection, sense of humor, or supportiveness.
RELATIONSHIPS: As you can see in the picture, some members of the family have closer relationships than others. The couples are close to each other by virtue of their marriage, the parents have a closer relationship with the infant than some of the other children due to the reliance of infants on their parents to meet needs, and the younger siblings appear

Subsystems
Relationships that are formed between just a few members of the larger system.

FIGURE 11.2 A family system. This depiction of a family illustrates the components of a system

Photo credit: Jackson Dillard

to have a closer relationship to each other by virtue of their similar age and gender.
BOUNDARY: The entire system is bounded together in this photo because it is recognized as a single family entity.

PAUSE & REFLECT

What subsystems do you belong to in your family? Do you communicate differently within the different subsystems you belong to?

Enmeshed Systems
Families that prioritize closeness among members rather than rigid boundaries between members or subsystems.

Disengaged System
Families with rigid boundaries that promote the independence of members or subsystems.

Open Families
Families that encourage experiences outside of the family and integrate those experiences into family life.

Closed Families
Families that discourage participation in activities and relationships outside the family.

Figure 11.3 shows how families create different kinds of boundaries between members or subsystems, as well as between the family and outside elements. Within **enmeshed systems**, family members have very little privacy or independence, and they communicate about a wide range of topics. In contrast, **disengaged systems** have rigid internal boundaries, such that family members don't exchange much information, affection, or support. Families can also establish open or closed boundaries between

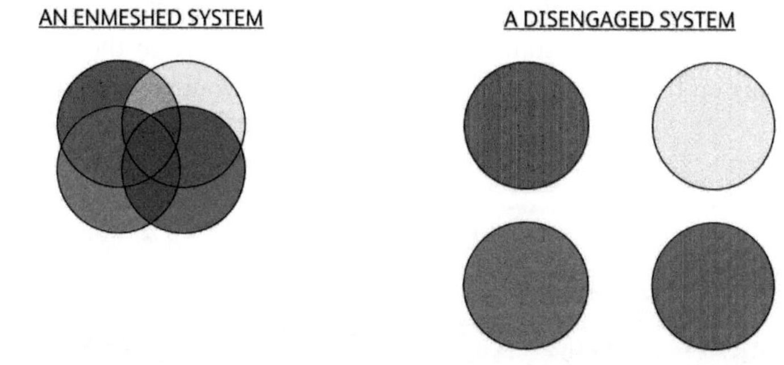

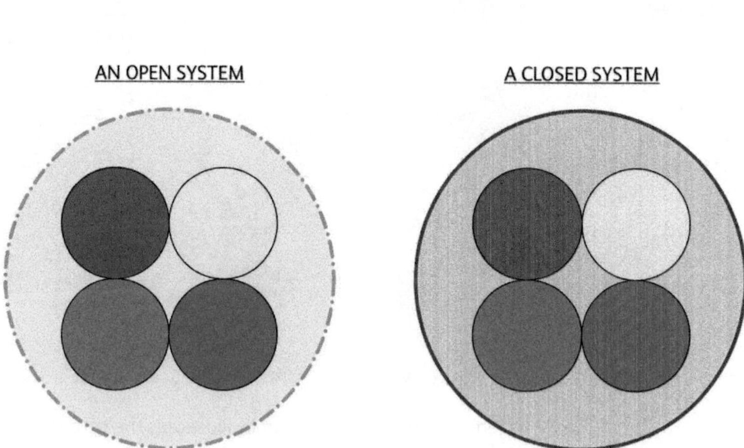

FIGURE 11.3 Variations on the family system

the system and the outside world. In **open families**, members interact freely with outsiders, and they are encouraged to share social experiences with the family. Conversely, members of **closed families** are discouraged from participating in activities and relationships outside their home. The core difference among these family systems is how much members communicate with each other and people outside the family.

The family system is made up of several smaller **subsystems**, which are relationships among only a few members of the larger system. For example, a marriage or domestic partnership might be a system that is subsumed within a family. Other subsystems that occur within families might include the relationship between a parent and child, the bonds between siblings, or the ties between divorced parents. Although family members might form their own subsystems, they do not operate in isolation. Rather, the actions, decisions, and communication behaviors within each subsystem both shape and are shaped by the larger system as a whole.

Managing Communication Boundaries

Managing system boundaries involves controlling who has access to your private information and who does not (Petronio & Child, 2020). Consider all of the private information that members of your family might know about you. Did they witness your most embarrassing moment? Do they remember how scared you were at your first horror film? Do they know how long you sucked your thumb, how you failed your first driving test, and about your first love? Even in less close families, family members have considerable knowledge about each other.

How do family members maintain each other's privacy and create system boundaries? Communication scholar Sandra Petronio has an extensive program of research focused on how people manage disclosing and protecting private information in a variety of social systems, including families. Petronio's work contributed to communication privacy management theory, which describes how families establish privacy rules or guidelines for who owns information and whether information is shared with others (Petronio, 2002; Petronio, 2010). Some privacy rules govern the exchange of information between individuals or subsystems within a family. For example, you and your siblings might have a shared understanding that limits what you tell your parents about each other, or perhaps you've refused your parents' requests to follow you on social media so that they can't monitor the information you share online. Privacy rules also let family members know what to tell non-family members. A family with an alcoholic member, for example, might agree to keep that information from outsiders.

SCHOLAR SPOTLIGHT

Visit the Communication Café on the companion website to view a conversation with Sandra Petronio, a pioneer in the study of communication boundaries and privacy management in families.

CONNECT WITH THEORY

Visit the companion website to learn more about communication privacy management theory, which describes how disclosures of private information are managed in social systems.

Of course, members of a family don't always follow or agree about privacy rules. When privacy rules are broken or contradictory, conflicts can result. Consider what might happen if Kyleigh knew that her sister was slipping out after midnight to get high and break into the town pool with friends. Although the privacy rules between the sisters might require Kyleigh to keep that information from their parents, another family rule might require her to alert a parent when her sister is in danger. Because families are complex social systems, conflict is inevitable. Communication is the system's way of creating, crossing, and repairing boundaries.

Family Secrets

Family Secrets
Events or information that family members hide from one another or from outsiders.

When a family's privacy rules create rigid boundaries that discourage communication about particular topics, family secrets can develop. In general, **family secrets** are the events or information that family members hide from one another or from outsiders. Family secrets can be shared among all family members and withheld from outsiders, shared among some family members but not others, or kept by an individual from the rest of the family (Romo, 2016). For example, parents often make strategic decisions about how much to share with other family and friends about a child's serious health condition (Rafferty, Hutton, & Heller, 2019). In similar ways, family members might collectively try to hide another member's drinking problem from non-family members, a couple that became parents through an unplanned pregnancy might not tell their daughter that she was an "accident," or a queer-identifying teenager might refrain from sharing this information with other family members until they feel ready. Whether family secrets are shared by everyone, just a few family members, or only one person, they are a common aspect of family relationships that constitute a unique communication challenge.

Secrets can serve important functions within families (Romo, 2016). By sharing secret information, you build a sense of closeness and trust between family members. Similarly, having insider information can strengthen your identity as a member of the family – you must be a part of the group if you're in on the secret. Family secrets also protect the family structure. For example, married partners might keep secrets about the origins of their relationship, when that story could open them up to negative evaluations from their children or other family members (Jackl, 2018). Family members also hide conditions like alcoholism or abuse, that might cause outsiders to interfere. When family members keep undesirable information under wraps, they maintain the family's public image.

Within families, you might also keep secrets because you are afraid of negative consequences. One reason people keep secrets from other family members is that they want to avoid judgment, conflict, or other negative consequences. In fact, young adults covered on their parent's health insurance sometimes pay directly for health services that they think the parent would disapprove of (Campbell-Salome, 2019). We also keep secrets to avoid consequences from family members who want the information kept private. Research suggests that children as young as six years old have figured out that telling someone's secret can hurt the relationship (Liberman, 2020). Consider what might happen if a family member revealed an important secret to an outsider. If the person who revealed the information has a lot of power within the family, the rest of the family may tolerate the betrayal. But if the person who reveals the secret doesn't have power, they might be punished by more powerful family members. Not surprisingly, then, research has shown family members are more likely to conceal their secrets from outsiders when they perceive other family members to have more power than they do (Afifi & Olson, 2005), or when they fear negative consequences for revealing a secret (Afifi, Olson, & Armstrong, 2005).

Although you may often have good reasons for keeping a family secret, there are times when you might want or need to tell someone else. Table 11.1 summarizes ten different criteria that people consider when deciding whether or not to reveal a secret (Vangelisti, Caughlin, & Timmerman, 2001). These criteria suggest that you are more likely to share a secret when the conversation is already intimate. In addition, you might disclose a secret when exposure is imminent or it becomes dangerous to maintain the secret. On the other hand, a person might keep a secret forever if the relationship or the urgency of the information doesn't require revelation.

PAUSE & REFLECT

What are some of the conditions that would prompt you to reveal a family secret to someone outside your family?

As the example of Suzanna in Table 11.1 might suggest, keeping a family secret can be a burden. Perhaps not surprisingly, young adults who describe their families as open communication systems report being more satisfied with their family relationships (Aloia, 2020). Another study of college students found that they are more satisfied in their families when they perceive that there are few secrets being kept within the

FIGURE 11.4 Sisters sharing a secret

Source: iStockPhoto.

TABLE 11.1 Criteria for revealing family secrets

Consider the example of Suzanna, who keeps a secret about her brother's serious drug problem. When Suzanna becomes close to Aubrey, she wonders if she should share this information. Here's how Suzanna might weigh criteria as she decides whether to reveal her secret.

The conversation is intimate
Suzanna and Aubrey were talking late one night about a variety of private topics. Suzanna wonders if this would be a good time to mention her brother.

The secret is about to be exposed
Suzanna just got a text message indicating that her brother was stopping by in an hour. Suzanna wonders if she should tell Aubrey her secret before Aubrey figures it out herself.

Revealing the secret is urgent
Suzanna's brother has overdosed and Suzanna needs Aubrey to take her to meet him in the emergency room.

The other person is likely to be accepting of the secret
In their family communication class today, Aubrey talked about how family members shouldn't be blamed for the actions of individual members. Suzanna begins to think that Aubrey won't think less of her if she knows the secret.

Sharing the secret is appropriate given the conversation
Suzanna and Aubrey were chatting about their families, when Aubrey asked Suzanna point blank why she never says much about her brother. Suzanna wonders if it's better to answer the question, rather than to try to change the topic.

The relationship can survive the secret
Suzanna and Aubrey just finished a grueling week of finals and they celebrated with a nice dinner out. When Aubrey says that she thinks they will always be friends, Suzanna wonders if it's time to share her secret.

There is an important reason to share the secret
Suzanna's brother asked Aubrey to loan him money and Aubrey is eager to help out her new friend's brother. Suzanna wonders if she should tell Aubrey her secret before Aubrey makes a big mistake.

Revealing the secret is allowed
Suzanna's parents recently said that they all should stop protecting her older brother by keeping his condition secret. Suzanna considers telling Aubrey now that she has the family's permission.

The person is a member of the family
Suzanna and Aubrey discover they are second cousins on their mothers' side. Because Aubrey is family, Suzanna wonders if it is okay to tell her about her brother.

family (Caughlin, Golish, Olson, Sargent, Cook, & Petronio, 2000). In contrast, children who rely on secrecy and avoidance to keep information from intrusive parents experience less family satisfaction (Ledbetter & Vik, 2012). Research has even linked the prevalence of family secrets to women's prenatal depression (Dayan et al., 2010). Even though keeping secrets might help families to bond, it seems that family members are happiest when they have fewer details that they have to keep under wraps.

Putting Theory into Practice: Improving System Operations

In a system of planets and a sun, the heavenly bodies have orbits that allow them to move both independently and in concert with each other. In the same way, members of a family develop norms that allow the system to function. When you view families as similar to other kinds of systems, you can identify specific strategies for improving system operations.

Respect system boundaries. The boundaries that define a system are as important as the parts of the system themselves. Members of a family are likely to form unique bonds and relationships with one another and managing these subsystems in the family are vital to the well-being of the larger family system. For example, it is important that siblings develop special bonds with one another, which may involve sharing secrets or helping one another escape punishment. Siblings need to respect the boundaries around their shared information in order to maintain one another's trust, and parents need to recognize that sometimes their children may share secrets with one another that they won't share with them. Similarly, couples may develop rules for how they share information with one another that are different from their rules for keeping their children in the loop. Along these lines, children of divorce often suffer when their parents neglect the boundaries between parent and child and disclose too many details about the breakup of the marriage (Afifi, McManus, Hutchinson, & Baker, 2007). Within your own family system, then, you can improve communication by respecting system boundaries and not interfering in subsystems to which you don't belong.

Practice safe secrets. Although family secrets can be an important part of maintaining boundaries around your family system, keeping secrets can burden family members. You should carefully consider the family secrets that you ask others to keep and that you agree to respect.

COMMUNICATION IN ACTION 11.2

Mapping Boundaries Within Families

You can respect boundaries within your family more effectively if you are aware of where those boundaries exist. Complete the form on the companion website to help you better understand the subsystems that exist within your family.

COMMUNICATION IN ACTION 11.3

Evaluate Your Family Secrets

Using the form on the companion website, make a list of the secrets that exist within your family and the pros and cons of keeping that information from others. This exercise can help you make more informed decisions about the secrets you keep within your family.

THE FAMILY LIFESPAN

When families are formed, partners (and any children they may have) face the challenge of creating a shared bond. If partners choose to raise children, their addition to the family system creates new challenges. And families continue to evolve in important ways as children move out of the home and parents age. Importantly, the lifespan of a family involves more than just the structural changes that occur as people join or leave the family circle. People also experience changes in who they are and how they define family (Brisini & Solomon, 2020). Indeed, changes in families occur on multiple interrelated dimensions, including (a) the development of the people within the family as they age and mature; (b) how the family changes as members acquire new skills, experience changes in employment, and address the need to provide for the family; (c) how the partnership between the couple that is the genesis of a family evolves; and (d) how the family cares for members, ranging from young children, members who experience illness, or aging family (Crapo & Bradford, 2021). In this section of the chapter, we explore the communication issues that arise over the lifespan of the family.

The Early Years

The first few years of marriage or domestic partnership are sometimes called the "honeymoon stage," because people assume that newlyweds

FIGURE 11.5 A wedding celebration

Source: Hinterhaus Productions/Getty Images.

experience more passion and less conflict than other couples, but that this blissful state doesn't last (Lorber, Eckardt Erlanger, Heyman, & O'Leary, 2015). To an extent, this characterization of the early years of family life is true. Newlywed couples, especially those with who did not live together or date for a long time before marriage, report more frequent sexual contact early in their marriage, compared to four years later (Altgelt & Meltzer, 2019). They are also highly committed to each other, optimistic about their future together, and tend to describe their partner in extremely positive terms (Neff & Karney, 2005). The positivity in the very first years of a marriage seems to fade away, as marital satisfaction erodes but sources of conflict in the marriage tend to stick around (Lavner, Karney, & Bradbury, 2014). Thus, the early years of a family present a relatively short window of time to get the family off on the right foot.

PAUSE & REFLECT

Do you know any recently married couples? If so, how is their communication different from couples you know who have been married for many years?

As they form a family, couples must also work out the norms for their relationship. In classic research based on more than a decade studying married couples, Mary Anne Fitzpatrick (1988) detailed the communication patterns that develop within marriages. Fitzpatrick's insights shed light on fundamental differences in couple relationships, and the distinctions she proposed have been found in numerous studies and diverse populations (e.g., Mustafa, Hasim, Aripin, & Hamid, 2013). In her view, each of us develops assumptions about relationships based on our family experiences and the images we see in our society. In turn, these assumptions affect how people behave in their own relationships and how they interpret their partner's behavior. When the beliefs that we hold as individuals are combined with a partner's view of the couple bond, one of four distinct types of relationships is created.

Traditional Marriage
A union characterized by a clear division of labor, companionship, and cooperation.

One type of relationship is called the **traditional marriage**. Importantly, this label doesn't mean that these relationships are necessarily structured around traditional roles, such as a working husband and stay-at-home wife; instead, this term highlights the value that partners place on filling specific roles in the relationship, being companions, and cooperating for the good of the household. Historically, traditional couples have divided up responsibilities so that one partner earns wages and the other takes care of the home, but even households where both partners work outside the home can develop distinct family roles. For example, one partner might do all the yard work, handle finances, and cook for the household, while the other partner takes care of the car and does all of the cleaning and laundry. Because traditional partners have such specialized roles, they are very interdependent; in other words, they rely on each other to perform their different jobs. Generally speaking, then, the traditional couple functions like a well-oiled machine where each member has a distinct role, but the system is well-coordinated.

Independent Marriage
A union characterized by an emphasis on quality time together, individuality, and frequent negotiation of household tasks.

A very different type of relationship develops when partners have less clearly divided roles, place less value on companionship, and put their own interests ahead of the household. In the **independent marriage**, partners emphasize spending quality time together, but they also put their individual attitudes, goals, and desires ahead of obligations to the household. Of course, partners in both traditional and independent relationships have jobs, hobbies, and friends outside their home; but whereas the traditional partner will see their family role as a priority, the independent partner believes that the relationship shouldn't constrain personal activities. In fact, partners in an independent marriage schedule their activities with little input from each other, create private spaces in the home that are off limits to the other person, and are likely to have different last names. How do independent couples coordinate their household activities? Whereas the traditional couple is all about cooperation, independent couples negotiate who will do what on a daily basis. To a traditional partner, all that negotiation would be tiresome, but independent couples thrive on a relationship that encourages and supports their individuality.

Separate Marriage
A union characterized by a clear division of labor, psychological and emotional distance, and a strong commitment to the relationship.

When couples have clearly divided roles like a traditional couple, but don't prioritize companionship, a **separate marriage** develops. More specifically, partners in a separate relationship organize their household around a clear division of tasks, but they resemble independent partners in that they value their individual freedom. Separate partners perform their household tasks out of a sense of duty, rather than a desire to contribute to a companionate relationship, and they seek fulfilling experiences outside their couple relationship. Although this arrangement leaves separate couples psychologically and emotionally distant from each other, these relationships can be very strong and satisfying for partners. In particular, separate couples share a strong sense of commitment to their relationship and they gain pleasure from its stability; for day-to-day fun, however, these partners enjoy interests that do not involve each other.

PAUSE & REFLECT

Do you know anybody in a traditional, independent, or separate marriage? If so, how does that couple communicate when they have free time together?

If partners have different expectations for marriage, a **mixed marriage** is the result. A mixed couple can reflect any combination of partners with traditional, independent, or separate orientations; their common feature is that partners disagree about fundamental aspects of their relationship. Should responsibilities be clearly divided or renegotiated regularly? Should partners spend a lot of time together, only quality time together, or avoid contact with each other? How much priority should be given to household responsibilities, careers and personal hobbies, or external relationships? Because partners in a mixed relationship have such different expectations, they have to work especially hard to develop shared goals, norms, and assumptions.

Mixed Marriage
A union in which the partners differ in their preferences for a traditional, independent, or separate relationship.

As you might expect, the type of marriage a couple has influences how partners talk to each other. As summarized in Table 11.2, traditional couples place a premium on spending time together and expressing love and affection; although it might be hard to believe, these activities simply aren't priorities for the other couple types. More specifically traditional partners share their thoughts and feelings with each other, turn to each for support, and cooperate when conflicts arise. Independent couples, on the other hand, constantly negotiate their household roles and personal goals. To do so, these couples engage in a lot of self-disclosure; however, they also support themselves – rather than each other – and they are more combative during conflicts than partners in other types of couples. The separate relationship involves the least amount of communication: partners don't disclose much to each other, they avoid conflict, and they rely on other family members and friends for support. Finally, although communication within mixed marriages depends on the specific combination

TABLE 11.2 Communication in different types of marriage

	Traditional	*Independent*	*Separate*	*Mixed*
Division of labor	Responsibilities follow traditional gender roles	Responsibilities are negotiated to maintain equity	Responsibilities follow traditional gender roles	Responsibilities assigned to each spouse are unclear
Relational priorities	Coordinate behavior and share time, love, and affection	Respect individual goals and interests, spend quality time together	Maintain the stability of the marriage as an institution	Develop an understanding of each other's different views
Approach to support	Rely on each other in good times and bad	Rely on themselves in good times and bad	Rely on other family members and friends for everything	Rely on themselves or seek help from other family members or friends
Approach to conflict	Cooperate and compromise over issues that are important to the marriage	Aggressively confront issues that threaten individual needs and goals	Avoid conflicts if at all possible	Experience serial conflicts about the goals and norms for the relationship

of partners, these couples generally experience more uncertainty and conflict about relationship norms.

Students are often surprised to learn that there are alternatives to a close, affectionate couple relationship that partners can still find satisfying. What is important to keep in mind is that traditional, independent, and separate relationships are fulfilling to the extent that they match the goals, expectations, and values people bring to the relationship (Givertz, Segrin, & Hanzal, 2009). For someone who seeks the companionship, affection, and teamwork of a traditional relationship, the independent and separate relationships would be a disappointment. But for a person who values his or her independence, doesn't like being constrained by family routines, and enjoys the romantic sparks of quality time with a partner, the traditional relationship would be stifling. And although partners in a separate relationship don't have either the affection or the romance of the other couple types, they enjoy an especially high level of certainty in the stability of their family arrangement. Whatever norms develop within the couple relationship, discovering how to relate to each other is an important task for couples in the early years of family life.

The Transition to Parenthood

Whether it occurs early in the couple relationship or after several years, the transition to parenthood is a tumultuous phase in the family life cycle.

In fact, families start to change even as couples decide whether to have children, take steps to promote a healthy pregnancy or pursue adoption, and anticipate the birth of a child. During pregnancy, many couples report stronger feelings of togetherness as they prepare for parenthood (Feeney, Hohaus, Noller, & Alexander, 2001). In addition, longitudinal research shows that negative communication between partners decreases in the months leading up to the birth of a child (Rauch-Anderegg, Kuhn, Milek, Halford, & Bodenmann, 2020). Impending parenthood also changes communication between the couple and their parents – fostering connection and expressions of generosity, as well as conflict and unwanted advice (Dun, 2010). Not unlike the honeymoon phase of marriage, anticipating the birth of a child is a time of closeness and affectionate communication, and also some challenges.

PAUSE & REFLECT

Do you have or expect to have children? How do you think having children changes how couples communicate with each other during the early years of marriage?

Although looking forward to parenthood brings couples closer, the actual arrival of the baby can create stress and a lot of extra work. In opposite sex couples, prior to becoming parents, wives report an average of 3.9 chores per day and husbands report an average of 1.9 chores per day; after becoming parents, wives increase to 42 chores per day and husbands increase to 8.3 chores per day (Huston & Holmes, 2004). Perhaps not surprisingly, conflict over division of household labor is a major contributor to aggressive conflicts between new parents, particularly to women's problematic conflict behaviors (Wong, Marshall, & Feinberg, 2021). Although some partners might share the load more equally and same-sex parents might distribute chores differently, having children clearly changes a couple's routine and can create a sense of inequity between partners.

Interviews with couples who have newly become parents reveal a variety of challenges that new parents must negotiate (Lévesque, Bisson, Charton, & Fernet, 2020). One prominent difficulty that new parents face is losing their identity as individuals and a couple, as being a parent takes precedence. New parents also struggle with issues of equity as they shoulder the demands of parenting. Parents may feel like they compete with each other for free time – when one partner does something on their own, the other is forced to babysit, and a partner's individual activities, such as exercising, also cut into shared time as a couple. In addition, both parents have to deal with the judgments of others concerning their representation of the norms of parenting. And of course, all of these challenges are magnified by fatigue, social isolation, and work-family balance issues that are part of being a new parent.

Another communication challenge concerns people's efforts to assume their identity as parents (Kaźmeirczak & Karasiewicz, 2019). As an example, Denise has an especially vivid memory of a bath that her spouse gave their first son when he was a week old. As much as Denise and her spouse both wanted him to assume his role as "father," she was irrationally afraid that he would drown the baby. Certainly, a "good mom" would express her concerns, but doing so would undermine the father's confidence. So Denise paced in the hallway, trembled with fear, and suppressed the urge to "save her baby." By allowing her spouse to complete the bath without interruption, Denise helped him to establish his efficacy as a father; at the same time, leaving her baby in what felt like a dangerous situation meant that she violated her image of a good mother. Parenthood provides many such opportunities to help or hinder each other's identity as a parent.

Raising a Family

After children are brought into a family, parents are faced with the challenge of raising those children into mature adults and instituting norms and rules for behavior within the family. Consider your own family for a moment. Does everyone have an equal say in family decisions? Are you encouraged to speak your mind, even if you disagree with the rest of the family? How might your family respond if one member criticized a parent's behavior or opinion? How did the communication rules in your family influence how you communicate in your adulthood? When parents and children share a household, the family develops norms for communication that influence who says what, to whom, and in what manner (Koerner, 2016). These differences in families seem to be passed from one generation to the next (Rauscher, Schrodt, Campbell-Salome, & Freytag, 2020), and they exert a pervasive effect on family communication.

Conversation Orientation
The extent to which a family encourages communication about a wide variety of topics.

One difference among families is the value that members place on conversation with each other. **Conversation orientation** refers to the extent to which a family encourages communication about a wide variety of topics. In families with a high conversation orientation, communication is frequent, spontaneous, and unrestrained. In these families, members share their individual thoughts, feelings, and actions with other members of the family, and everyone is encouraged to share their opinion when family decisions are being made. Parents who foster a high conversation orientation believe that communication is the main means for socializing children, as well as the key to an enjoyable family life. Conversely, when conversation orientation is low, family members are discouraged from communicating openly with each other, parents do not seek out their children's point of view, and siblings are less inclined to share their thoughts and feelings with each other. Parents with a low conversation orientation don't see a connection between disclosure of thoughts and feelings and a child's education and socialization.

A second quality that distinguishes family communication patterns is a family's **conformity orientation**, the importance the family places on members having similar attitudes, beliefs, and values. Families with a high conformity orientation believe that family members should share the same beliefs and attitudes, most often those that are endorsed by the parents. Accordingly, children are expected to show obedience to their parents and older adults during conversations. In contrast, families with a low conformity orientation are comfortable when members have conflicting viewpoints and even tolerate different positions on core values related to topics like religion or politics. In the low conformity orientation family, these differences don't threaten the family structure, and they might even contribute to the family's well-being.

Conformity Orientation
The extent to which the family encourages members to have similar attitudes, beliefs, and values.

PAUSE & REFLECT

How might your family's communication pattern affect how you communicate with non-family members?

Because families can be high or low on conversation orientation and high or low on conformity orientation, four distinct family types can be identified (Koerner & Fitzpatrick, 2004). As summarized in Figure 11.6, a family that is low in conversation orientation and high in conformity orientation is a **protective family**. Within protective families, members do not communicate freely, they discourage differences of opinion, and children are expected to accept authority. Interestingly, one classic study suggests that family communication patterns are related to whether the parents have a traditional, independent, separate, or mixed couple type (Fitzpatrick & Ritchie, 1994). Protective family norms are likely to develop when parents have a separate relationship. Just as separate couples attend to their household duties and keep their distance from each other, the protective family places high value on following the rules, but not on communicating with each other.

Protective Family
Families whose members do not communicate freely, discourage differences, and respect authority.

A **consensual family** is also defined by a high conformity orientation, but these families value open communication as a way of reaching a shared position. Perhaps not surprisingly, consensual families are most likely to be headed by parents who fit a traditional couple type (Fitzpatrick & Ritchie, 1994). As in the traditional relationship, consensual family members use communication to coordinate activities around a united family front. Accordingly, research has shown that closeness between siblings is highest in families that value both openness and conformity

Consensual Family
Families whose members use open communication to coordinate activities around a united family front.

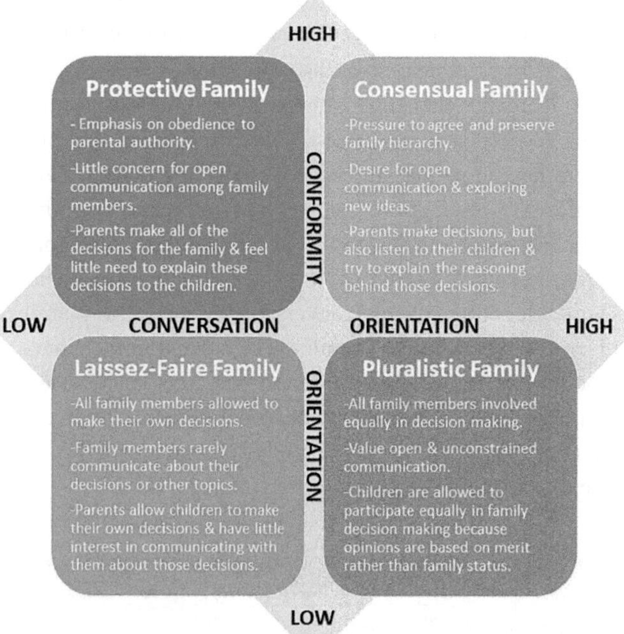

FIGURE 11.6 Types of families

(Samek & Rueter, 2011). In addition, these families are more likely to involve parental communication that imposes demands, to which children respond with acceptance (Sillars, Holman, Richards, Jacobs, Koerner, & Reynolds-Dyk, 2014).

Pluralistic Family
Families whose members are encouraged to express individuality and embrace differences.

Some families value open communication, but don't require members to have the same attitudes, beliefs, or values. Does this description remind you of one of the couple types described earlier in this chapter? Independent partners, who value individuality in their relationship, tend to create a **pluralistic family** where different opinions are expressed, tolerated, and even welcomed (Fitzpatrick & Ritchie, 1994). Members of a pluralistic family don't feel compelled to hide or resolve their differences; instead, they express their thoughts, debate their positions, and are happy to agree to disagree. In general, a family's openness to communication is associated with relationship satisfaction among young adults (Aloia, 2020). And, while a family's conversation orientation contributes to their children's mental health, conformity orientation is negatively associated with mental well-being, which suggests that the open and nonconforming environment of the pluralistic family allows members to express their individuality and embrace their differences (Aloia, 2019). The dialogue in the Real Words box comes from a study that examined parent-adolescent communication in families where one parent is an alcoholic and shows how parents' attempts to encourage conversation or enforce conformity can have positive or negative effects on adolescents' well-being (Haverfield & Theiss, 2017).

REAL WORDS

This dialogue comes from a study by Marie Haverfield and Jen Theiss (2017) that asked parent-adolescent dyads from families that had a parent with alcoholism to engage in a conversation about recent events that made the adolescent feel positive or negative emotions. The researchers analyzed the parents' communication for signs of responsiveness and control, and they analyzed the adolescents' communication for signs of emotional and behavioral impulsivity. Notice how the parent in this exchange tries to get the adolescent to open up about their feelings, but also the way she tries to encourage the adolescent to think a particular way.

PARENT: Okay, so you feel angry when dad calls. What is it about dad calling that makes you angry?

ADOLESCENT: He's an idiot.

PARENT: He's an idiot? In what way? Like, be specific. Is it the questions? His tone of voice?

ADOLESCENT: He's just weird [looks away].

PARENT: And so why does that make you angry?

ADOLESCENT: 'Cause you force me to talk to him, pick up the phone.

PARENT: Okay, but he's your dad so why wouldn't you talk to him on the phone?

ADOLESCENT: Because, it's just better for everybody.

PARENT: Well, uhm, I think he... part of his disease is that he has unrealistic expectations.

ADOLESCENT: Okay.

PARENT: And he expects to call and have you be cheerful and happy and tell him exactly everything that's going on, and that's not realistic. And then when you don't answer the way he wants you to then he just immediately gets mad right? ... Or do you see it differently?

ADOLESCENT: He does...

PARENT: Okay, so what is it that you think you can do to keep from getting angry when you're on the phone with dad?

ADOLESCENT: I'm not angry when I'm on the phone with dad.

PARENT: Okay.

ADOLESCENT: He's just weird and I hate having to talk to him.

PARENT: Okay, well, I don't know... the way I look at it is... He's your dad...

ADOLESCENT: [starts to smile in a very sarcastic way and shakes head] yeah.

PARENT: We wouldn't be in our home and have all that we do without him... Regardless of his behavior. Well, I mean that's what makes it hard to get past certain things is attitude, thankfulness is looking for the positives instead of dwelling on the negatives. And that is the reason I will continue to encourage him to seek counseling so... You know, alcoholism is not just how many glasses of wine he has.

ADOLESCENT: I know, I know that.

PARENT: Okay. So what would make him less of an idiot? I mean he's just asking you about your day.

ADOLESCENT: Stop calling me.

PARENT: Honey, he's not going to stop calling you, he's your dad!

ADOLESCENT: [Rolls eyes]

PARENT: Even when you move away to go to college, he's still going to call you to see how you're doing. He loves you and he cares about you. Despite his attitudes, he's making an effort to try and talk to you.

Laissez-faire Family
Families in which members have little contact with one another and aren't expected to share a similar point of view.

A fourth family type, the **laissez-faire family**, is created when both conversation orientation and conformity orientation are low. Members of the laissez-faire family have relatively little contact with each other, and there is no expectation that family members will have a shared point of view. In fact, members of a laissez-faire family tend to develop stronger ties with people outside the family. As a result, research shows that members of laissez-faire families are unlikely to engage in conflict (Sillars et al., 2014). Which couple type is most likely to promote a laissez-faire family environment? According to the study by Fitzpatrick and Ritchie (1994) described previously, the laissez-faire family tends to emerge from mixed couples where parents have different visions of their relationship. Perhaps because the parents have difficulty working out the norms for their own relationship, they aren't able to set a clear course for the family.

The Mature Family

HOW DO YOU RATE? 11.2

Family Communication Patterns

Visit the companion website and complete the Revised Family Communication Pattern Instrument (Ritchie & Fitzpatrick, 1990) to learn about the type of family communication patterns present in your own family. How does your family communication style influence the way you manage conflict? How does it influence the way you provide support?

As children grow and parents age, the family changes in significant ways. A major turning point occurs as children move out of the family home and parents retire from the workforce. For some couples, this can be a time of renewed relational bliss – they might travel, rediscover shared hobbies, and perhaps enjoy their grandchildren. In fact, sharing activities and time together can help people at this stage of life become more satisfied with their relationship (Bozoglan, 2015). At the same time, these dramatic changes in relationships can disrupt a well-run family system.

Health concerns are one issue in later life that can affect the couple relationship. Older individuals might find physical activities to be difficult, experience vision and hearing problems that disrupt communication, and find themselves more susceptible to illness (Dickson, Christian, & Remmo, 2004). And when one partner's health deteriorates, the

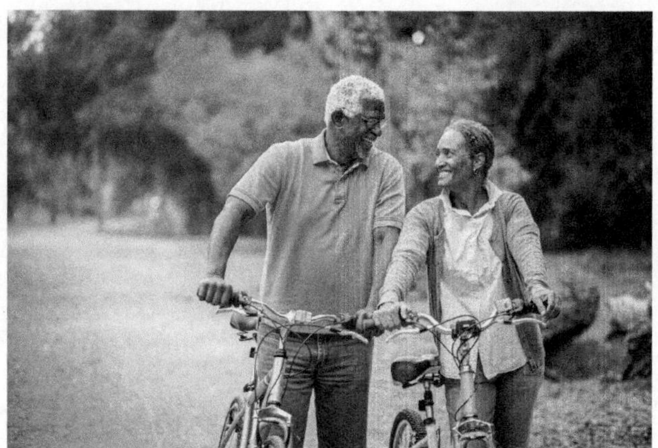

FIGURE 11.7 An older married couple

Source: Getty Images.

other might find him or herself in the role of caretaker. The shift from spouse or partner to caretaker is a difficult one for many people. Older persons who become caretakers for their ailing partner sometimes experience a decrease in their satisfaction with the relationship, especially if their own health is good (Korporaal, Broese van Groenou, & van Tilburg, 2013). More generally, older married couples exhibit a decline in compassionate love for each other over time (Sabey & Rauer, 2018). These trends are a reminder that the "golden years" shouldn't be taken for granted – people need to continue to communicate with partners thoughtfully and intentionally to maintain family bonds over the full course of the lifespan.

INSIDE COMMUNICATION RESEARCH

Coping with a Parent's Alzheimer's Disease

Alzheimer's Disease is a devastating cognitive impairment that can strain family relationships. Watching a family member with the illness lose their memory, communication ability, and sense of self can be quite taxing for those who care for them. Family members of people with Alzheimer's disease are confronted with a spouse or parent who is quite different from the person they used to know. Under these circumstances, adult children need to learn new ways of communicating with their parent and may experience a shift in their identity and family role. Communication scholar, Aimee Miller-Ott (2020), sought to understand the experiences of adult children of a parent with Alzheimer's disease in terms of the ways in which their identity, relational roles, and communication behavior are affected by the parent's illness.

She conducted in-depth interviews with 12 adult children who had at least one parent with Alzheimer's disease. The interviews were semi-structured to focus on three main questions. First, the participants were asked to describe the changes they had seen in their parent in terms of their actions and relation to others. Second, the participants described communication about the parent's illness both inside and outside of the family. Finally, participants were asked how their parent's illness impacted their own sense of identity. The interviews were then analyzed to identify themes related to each set of questions.

The analysis of the interview data revealed four themes related to changes in adult children's communication with their parent. First, adult children indicated that it felt like they were communicating with the same but also a different parent, so they had to find new ways to interact with a parent who at times felt very unfamiliar. Second, the participants said that they often had to wear different hats and operate in alternate roles. They were simultaneously their parent's child, but also taking on a parental role in caring for their parent with the illness, while in some cases also performing the role of spouse and parent in their own family. Third, the adult children in the study explained that they had to correct or reprimand their parent's behavior, which is also reflective of the need to take on new roles and identities in this context. Finally, the adult children became owners of their parent's private information and had to take on the role of deciding whether and how to share that information with others. Thus, adult children of parents with Alzheimer's disease have to find new ways to communicate with their parent and take on a variety of new roles under these circumstances.

THINK ABOUT IT

1. This study focused on the communication challenges and identity shifts that adult children face when their parent has Alzheimer's disease. How might the results of this study differ if the researchers had examined other types of ailments that the elderly confront, such as heart disease or cancer?
2. What do these findings imply about relational roles and identities in the family? Are there other turning points in the family lifespan that might call upon family members to shift their communication behavior or interpersonal roles?

In mature families, parents also need to redefine their relationship with their children. One way that the parent-child relationship shifts is that children gain expertise over their parents on contemporary topics and new technology. Many of our students, for example, say that they taught their parents how to use social media, make the most of their smart phones, or use Zoom to good effect. Although these students report frustration with their aging parents' lack of competency in using new technology or their violations of social norms for use, parents who must rely on their children's expertise in these matters are probably equally discouraged by the situation. Because parents have always had the expertise necessary to function in their daily lives and to oversee the lives of their children, it can be a frustrating change of events when adult children surpass their parents with knowledge or expertise that the aging parents don't have.

Another important shift occurs if adult children are called upon to take care of a parent. How do parents and children handle this role reversal? Adult children often use humor to relieve some of the tension that arises when they care for their elderly parents (Bethea, Travis, & Pecchioni, 2000). People might create humorous stories that help them feel better about daily hassles, safety concerns, and their parents' declining health. Adult children also become more assertive in making decisions for their older parents. In one study, for example, mothers and their adult children were asked to role-play an interaction where they made a decision together about the mother's finances (Cicirelli, 2006). That study found that children dominate the decision by talking more, introducing more ideas, and getting what they want; but mothers often regret the resulting decision. These patterns reflect a reversal of the family's roles over time.

PAUSE & REFLECT

What are some of the ways that you take care of older members of your family?

Putting Theory into Practice: Coping with Family Changes

When you enter into a long-term relationship with a romantic partner and create a family, the only certainty is that your relationship will evolve. Although you can't predict the specific experiences that you will encounter, you can take steps to cope with the changes you will face.

Anticipate changes over the family lifespan. Transitions in families can be challenging because people have to adapt to new routines, find new ways of meeting goals, and adjust to the addition or departure of family members. One reason people get caught off-guard by family transitions is that they do not consider the subtle ways their life will change. Consider a study that explored the problems people encounter when they give medication to an ailing family member (Travis, Bethea, & Winn, 2000). Would you have guessed that scheduling medications and dealing with an uncooperative patient were the most frequent problems? Even positive changes in a family, like the marriage of a sibling or the birth of a grandchild, transform the roles that individuals must perform in the family. A sibling who was once a best friend must now take a back seat to the new spouse. New grandparents must give their children enough room to figure out their own parenting style. As you look toward the changes that will inevitably confront your family, try to keep in mind that even basic parts of your routine will need your attention.

Keep the lines of communication open. As families change through marriage, children, divorce, remarriage, step-children, aging, and retirement, family members will have different responsibilities, different relationships, and different roles. By reintroducing ourselves to each other, family members can forge relationships that fit with their new situation.

COMMUNICATION IN ACTION 11.4

Renewing Family Relationships

Focus on the most recent transition that you and your family have gone through. Maybe it was when you moved out of your family home to go to college, when you and your spouse changed schedules so you could go back to school, or when you got a new job. Then, write a letter to a member of your family in which you describe how you have changed because of this transition. You might address the same details that you would include in a letter to a new acquaintance, for example, mention your hobbies, your goals, and the things that you worry about. Even if you don't send this letter, it may help you to see how the changes in your life might be affecting your family relationships.

SUMMARY

Families include both the voluntary bonds you form as adults and the relationships you are born or adopted into. These relationships have changed a lot in the last half a century – fewer people marry, people commonly divorce and remarry, children can be conceived in a doctor's office or adopted from faraway lands, and non-parents frequently participate in child-rearing. Despite the many forms that family can take, any family can help its members meet basic needs, teach children what it means to be human or a member of a culture, and provide its members with affection and support.

Families can be viewed as systems that are made up of different people who have distinct qualities and relationships, but who exist together as part of the family entity. Over time, family systems develop internal and external boundaries that create subsystems and influence how much family members interact with non-family members. By developing privacy rules, families can coordinate and regulate the disclosure of information both within and outside the family. Over the course of life, family members might collect experiences that they keep hidden from others. Family secrets can serve several functions for members, but having lots of secrets to keep can make family life less satisfying.

Of course, numerous changes occur over the family lifespan. The early years of family life can be challenging because partners in a marriage or domestic partnership have to coordinate both their behaviors and their views of the relationship. The transition to parenthood introduces new challenges, especially because it constrains both individual freedoms and shared time; partners might also interfere with each other's efforts to develop a confident identity as a parent. In families focused on the task of raising children, norms for communication promote the development of protective, consensual, pluralistic, or laissez-faire families. These family communication patterns both structure interaction among family member and shape the communication behaviors that children develop. For families still together in old age, retirement, illness, and adult children require further shifts in family roles and communication behavior.

Family relationships are perhaps the most important relationships you will have in your life. Families perform important functions for their members, they develop their own systems of communication, and they evolve over the course of our life. To promote the well-being of these critical relationships, use interpersonal communication to strengthen family bonds, fine-tune family systems, and cope with the ways your family will change in your lifetime.

ACTIVITIES FOR EXPLORING COMMUNICATION ETHICS

What Would You/Should You Do?

Imagine that you have a friend who confides in you that her stepbrother sexually assaulted her. She says that she hasn't shared this private information with anyone else, but she felt that she needed to tell someone and she knew that she would be able to trust you. She makes you promise that you won't tell anyone, because she's worried about how her mother and stepfather might react if they knew. On the one hand, you don't want to violate your friend's trust by revealing this private information against her will. On the other hand, the sexual assault is a crime and should be reported to the authorities. What would you – should you – do in this situation?

Something to Think About

When married couples have children and their marriage subsequently ends in divorce, 90% of the time the biological mother is granted primary custody of the children. The fathers are sometimes granted visitation rights and are usually expected to pay the mother child support to assist with the expenses associated with raising the children. Every year, 30–50% of fathers fail to pay the child support that is owed to their ex-wives to care for their children. What are the ethical issues at stake as divorced parents negotiate their family obligations?

Analyze Communication Ethics Yourself

The Trump administration implemented a "zero tolerance" policy for immigrants from Mexico and Central America who entered the country illegally. Part of this policy involved separating immigrant children from their parents and detaining them in separate facilities. As the policy was enforced, the administration had no reunification plan, which resulted in many parents being unable to locate their children after the separation. The Southern Poverty Law Center has a website that provides a timeline of the family separation policy and stories of families that were affected by their separation and detainment at the border (www.splcenter.org/news/2020/06/17/family-separation-under-trump-administration-timeline). What is your opinion on this issue? What are the ethical implications and potential impacts that this policy can have on immigrant families?

KEY WORDS

closed families
conformity orientation
consensual families
conversation orientation
disengaged systems
enmeshed systems
family
family secrets
family socialization
independent marriage
laissez-faire families
mixed marriage
open families
pluralistic families
protective families
separate marriage
subsystems
system
systems theory
traditional marriage
transmission

PART 4 STRATEGIC INTERPERSONAL COMMUNICATION

Visit the Communication Café on the companion website to hear Denise and Jen talk about the topics addressed in Part 4 of this book.

You would have an incomplete picture of interpersonal communication if we neglected to consider some of the powerful outcomes you can achieve in your interactions with other people. There are numerous tasks you can perform through communication, but we focus this part of the book on three that are especially important to your personal and relational well-being: influencing others, resolving conflicts, and communicating support and comfort.

Chapter 12 takes up the topic of interpersonal influence. Think for a moment about how much you rely on other people to hold attitudes or engage in behaviors that make your life better. When you seek approval from another person, when you encourage them to help you (or stop hindering you), and whenever you call upon others to adjust their actions to accommodate your priorities, you engage in an attempt to influence. This chapter breaks down this complex process by elaborating on the goals that we pursue through interpersonal communication, the messages we use to influence others, and the strategies we employ to be effective in both ordinary and difficult situations.

The focus of Chapter 13 is interpersonal conflict. Disagreements and arguments are inevitable when humans come into contact. Despite being quite common, conflicts are often emotionally and mentally taxing events because they have the potential to damage our relationships and create personal distress. In this chapter, we clarify what conflict is, and the many different forms it comes in. In addition, you'll learn about strategies for addressing conflicts through interpersonal communication. When you can understand the complexity of conflict and how communication is part of conflict dynamics, you increase your ability to take control of the conflicts that will confront you in your life.

We end this book with one of most compassionate outcomes you can achieve through interpersonal communication: providing comfort and support to others. The messages we use to make someone feel better, to help them tackle a problem, or to communicate our availability to help are some of the most powerful tools in our communication tool box. Receiving support can have a positive effect on the immediate situation, as well as the individual's personal health and well-being. Giving and receiving comfort is also a cornerstone of strong interpersonal relationships. Your ability to provide and receive comfort and support can make a lasting difference in your life and the lives of people you care about, which is why we believe that it is a fitting capstone to your exploration of interpersonal communication.

LEARNING OBJECTIVES

After reading this chapter, you should be able to:

1. Identify types of interpersonal influence goals.
2. Describe three strategies for managing multiple interpersonal influence goals.
3. Identify three dimensions on which influence messages can vary.
4. Recognize patterns of communication that occur in influence interactions.
5. Recognize obstacles to interpersonal influence.
6. Describe how intimacy and power shape the influence messages that people use.

PUTTING THEORY INTO PRACTICE

In this chapter, you will learn how to:

1. Identify goals for interpersonal communication.
2. Attend to your secondary goals.
3. Weigh options for managing multiple goals.
4. Remember that messages matter.
5. Plan for interpersonal influence interactions.
6. Respect people's right to refuse.
7. Enable upward influence.
8. Avoid strategic ambiguity.

12

INTERPERSONAL INFLUENCE

Source: Johnny Greig/Getty Images.

DOI: 10.4324/9781351174381-15

Social media platforms like Twitter, YouTube, and Instagram have broken the boundaries of traditional media in ways that give ordinary people the chance to follow and engage with their favorite celebrities and online personalities in more intimate and seemingly personal ways. This context has led to the emergence of Instagram influencers, who are frequent Instagram users, with an exceptionally large number of followers, who have the authenticity and trustworthiness to influence people to adopt certain beliefs or behaviors, and often persuade them to buy particular products. And this type of influence isn't limited to Hollywood stars; in fact, 70% of teens report that they trust regular online influencers more than traditional celebrities. For example, one of the most successful Instagram influencers is Huda Kattan, a former make-up artist turned beauty blogger with over 30 million followers, who leveraged her popularity as a social media personality sharing make-up tips to build her own billion-dollar cosmetics brand, Huda Beauty. Online influencers can be quite persuasive because they claim to have expertise in whatever they are promoting, from beauty and fashion to fitness and travel, so followers tend to see them as an authority on that subject. Social media influencers also have unique appeal because, in many cases, they are "normal" people who presumably share similar traits with their followers, but they are quite personable and engaging, often relating to their followers like friends or insiders. Given this personal appeal, roughly 40% of subscribers say they believe their favorite influencer understands them better than even their own friends! Thus, social media influencers can be quite persuasive in convincing their followers to adopt a particular attitude or behavior.

The tactics used by social media influencers to convince you to like their content or buy their products are common features of interpersonal influence that people encounter on a daily basis. Perhaps you have a friend, co-worker, or family member who relies on their likability and trustworthiness to influence your decisions about a variety of issues, from what restaurant to choose for dinner to who you should vote for in the next election. Perhaps you have drawn on these tactics yourself to convince someone to lend you money, cover your shift at work, or help you with a project. **Interpersonal influence** refers to the use of communication to change another person's beliefs, attitudes, or actions. This chapter explores the goals and messages that characterize interpersonal influence so that you can be more successful when you find yourself in these kinds of interactions.

GOALS

In general, **goals** are end-states or outcomes that a person seeks to achieve or maintain. Your goals exist within your mind – they include the knowledge, expectations, and desires that motivate your behavior. You may be very aware of a goal before an interaction – such as when you plan to ask a family member to loan you money. Even when you aren't thinking about your goals, however, they are probably affecting your communication behavior. For example, during a conversation with your mother about money, you would probably behave differently, based on whether you were trying to secure a loan, get her to repay money she borrowed, or convince her that you are responsible with money. The goals you have for an interaction inform the plans you make for communicating to achieve your desired ends. Your plans provide a framework for the actions you will take to pursue or manage the various goals you have for the interaction. The goals-plan-action theory describes this sequence of constructs that shape the production of interpersonal messages to attain desired goals (Dillard, 2015a). Because goals always influence interpersonal interactions, learning about them can help you be a more effective communicator.

Interpersonal Influence
The use of communication to change another person's beliefs, attitudes, or actions.

Goals
End-states or outcomes that a person seeks to achieve or maintain.

Interpersonal Influence Goals
Desired end-states or outcomes that can only be achieved if another person engages in cooperative activity.

Types of Influence Goals

Interpersonal influence goals are desired outcomes you can achieve only if you convince another person to cooperate with you. Table 12.1 lists the most common interpersonal influence goals (Dillard, 2015b). Notice how achieving each of the goals involves another person. For

TABLE 12.1 Influence goals

Type of goal	*Example*
Gain assistance	Can I borrow your class notes?
Give advice	I think you should quit smoking.
Share activity	Let's do something tonight.
Change orientation	Here's why you're wrong about gun control.
Change relationship	We should agree not to date other people.
Obtain permission	Hey, Dad, can I use the car?
Enforce rights and obligations	You promised to take out the trash. So, how about it?

CONNECT WITH THEORY

Visit the companion website to learn more about goals-plan-action theory, which describes the process through which individuals assess their goals and develop plans for interaction that will help them attain their desired ends.

example, you can't give advice unless someone is there to receive it. And as Table 12.1 shows, whether you achieve your interpersonal influence goals depends on your ability to use communication to change another person's thoughts or behaviors.

Do different influence goals require different types of interpersonal communication? Research suggests that the answer is yes. When requesting a favor, for example, Americans are more likely to include messages of thanks, whereas Koreans and Japanese are more likely to include messages of apology (Lee & Park, 2011; Lee et al., 2012). When offering advice, individuals need to construct messages that attend to a variety of personal and relational goals, including buffering defensiveness from the target, maintaining the relationship, and not coming across as a bossy know-it-all (Goldsmith, Bute, & Lindholm, 2012). When crafting messages, you also have to consider that people on the receiving end may react differently to different kinds of goals. For example, the goals that an influencer has for giving advice can shape whether the message is received as a sign of caring and confirmation or an attempt to control and dominate (Goldsmith, Lindholm, & Bute, 2006; Guntzviller & MacGeorge, 2013).

SCHOLAR SPOTLIGHT

Visit the Communication Café on the companion website to view a conversation with James Dillard, who conducted groundbreaking research on interpersonal influence goals.

PAUSE & REFLECT

How do you feel when someone tries to influence you? Are there types of messages that you especially dislike?

The goals described here aren't the only concerns that you have when you seek to influence another person. For example, when you try to affect another person's thoughts and actions, you might wonder if the other person will think less of you, if you'll damage your relationship, or if you can maintain your composure during the interaction. These concerns aren't your driving goal in the conversation, but they affect how you communicate with the other person. As shown in Figure 12.1, the interpersonal influence goal that motivates communication is the **primary goal**, and the other considerations that arise during interpersonal influence interactions are **secondary goals** (Dillard & Wilson, 2014). During interaction, influencers are challenged by demands to balance the primary goal of influence with any secondary goals they might have to protect the target's perceptions, maintain the relationship, or avoid damage to their own image.

Primary Goal
The influence goal that motivates the interaction.

Secondary Goals
Considerations other than the primary goal that arise during interpersonal influence interactions and shape communication strategies.

Let's consider the example of Davi, who asks Kelly to study with him for a midterm exam. Davis' primary goal might be to get help, share an activity with Kelly, change their relationship, or (if it was part of an earlier deal) enforce Kelly's obligation to help him out. No matter what the primary goal is, Davis will no doubt have secondary goals as well.

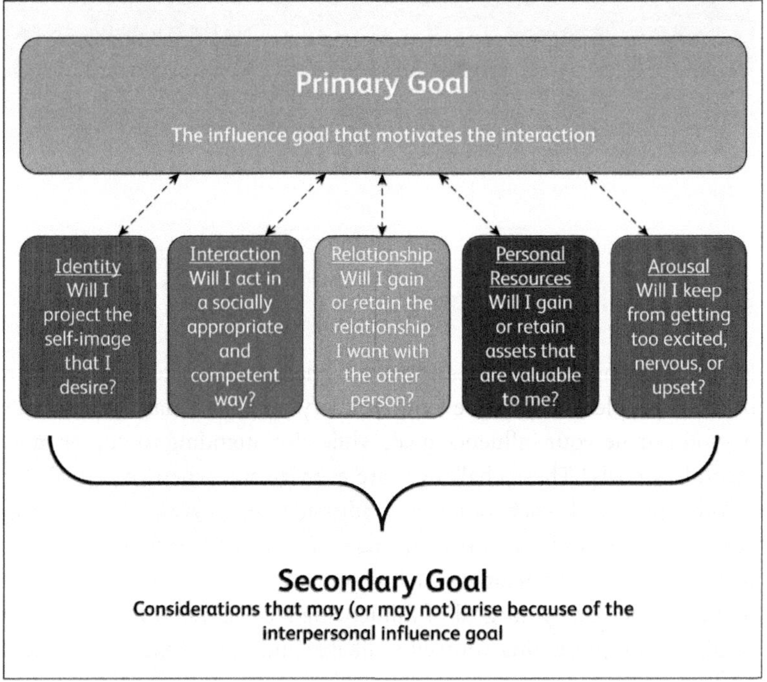

FIGURE 12.1 Primary and secondary goals for interpersonal influence

- *Identity goals* concern the image you want to project. In Davis's case, he may want Kelly to think he's smart.
- *Interaction goals* focus on managing the conversation. Perhaps Davis is concerned about stammering when he asks Kelly to study with him.
- *Relationship goals* address your association with your communication partner. For example, Davis might want to show his respect for Kelly as he makes this request.
- *Personal resource goals* involve maximizing your assets and minimizing costs. If Davis is hoping that studying with Kelly will involve her making dinner for him, he's attending to personal resource goals.
- *Arousal goals* refer to managing your emotions. In Davis' case, he might want the conversation with Kelly to leave them both feeling happy, rather than disappointed.

You might think that secondary goals are less important to interpersonal communication – they are, after all, "secondary." Actually, secondary goals have a major impact on the messages that you use to pursue your primary influence goal. Consider again the example of Davis and Kelly. If Davis was concerned with appearing smart, he might phrase his request as more of an offer to help Kelly prepare for the exam. If he wanted to manage their relationship, he might state how much he admires the comments she makes in class. Although your primary goal determines what your conversation is about, your secondary goals determine the specific messages that are exchanged during an influence interaction (Dillard, 2008).

HOW DO YOU RATE? 12.1

The Intensity of Secondary Goals

In any conversation, some goals are going to be more prominent and influential than others. To evaluate the intensity of various goals in one of your recent conversations, complete the measure of goal intensity on the companion website. Did the outcome of the conversation adequately address your secondary goals? How might the interaction have gone differently if you had a different secondary goal?

PAUSE & REFLECT

Can you remember a time when you had to influence a more powerful individual like a professor or work supervisor? If so, what secondary goals were salient to you in that situation?

Managing Multiple Goals

Influence interactions always involve managing multiple goals, in part because people always have both primary and secondary goals. How do you pursue your influence goal, while also attending to one or more secondary goals? These challenges are even greater when your goals are incompatible with each other, a condition known as **goal strain**. For example, your desire to appear strong and independent may be at odds with your desire to maintain a high-quality relationship with a close friend. Or perhaps your goal of influencing a close friend to lose weight conflicts with presenting yourself as likable and nonjudgmental. Because goal strain can complicate your efforts to influence other people, you may want to be strategic about how you approach conversations with multiple and competing goals. As described in multiple goals theory, balancing a variety of goals can complicate interaction and requires people to employ an array of tactics to communicate effectively while attending to a plethora of interpersonal aims (Caughlin, 2010). Let's consider some options for managing multiple goals (see Table 12.2).

Goal Strain
The existence of two or more goals for interpersonal influence that are incompatible with each other.

TABLE 12.2 Options for managing multiple goals

Strategy	*Definition*	*Example*
Choose one goal	Pursue the single most important goal and abandon all the rest	Davis decides that appearing smart is most important to him, so he only hints indirectly that he'd like a study partner
Sequence goals	Pursue goals one at a time over the course of an interaction	Davis begins by complimenting Kelly, so she'll know he respects her, and then focuses on showing her that he's smart
Integrate goals	Focus on a general concern that is common to all of your goals	Davis focuses on having a fun interaction with Kelly, because that is likely to let her know he respects her, protect his identity, and net him a study partner all at the same time

Prioritize. If you find yourself struggling to achieve multiple goals, you might decide which goal is most important to you. Although focusing on a single goal means you won't get everything you want, at least you will attend to your top priority. Keep in mind that the most important goal might not be your primary influence goal. For example, when family members of military service members have the goal of encouraging the service member to seek mental health services following a deployment, the family tends to prioritize secondary goals of maintaining the relationship, confirming the service member's feelings, and protecting the service member's autonomy to make their own decisions when suggesting that they seek support (Wilson, Hall, Gettings, & Pastor, 2019). Similarly, in family conversations about end-of-life healthcare decisions, identity goals like preserving the aging family member's autonomy and relational goals like affirming closeness and stability of the relationship are sometimes more important than the task of deciding how to implement end-of-life care (Scott & Caughlin, 2012). If you decide to focus on only one of multiple goals, make sure you address the one that matters to you most.

PAUSE & REFLECT

Can you think of a time when you had two goals that were incompatible with each other? If so, did you abandon one of the goals, or did you try to accomplish both?

Pursue goals in sequence. Another option is to try to pursue goals sequentially, or one after another. Think about how you might persuade a neighbor to keep his dog from barking outside every evening. Your goal is to get your neighbor to keep the dog inside so you can study in peace, but you might also be concerned with having a good relationship with your neighbor and not coming across as a jerk. You could start by pointing out the constant barking, the neighborhood rules, and your need to study – after you make headway on this goal, you might offer to help your neighbor rake his leaves or tell some jokes. On the other hand, you might start by being friendly and helpful, and then mention the barking dog when your neighbor is feeling especially friendly toward you. Whichever course you follow, sequencing goals involves focusing your attention on one goal at a time, but trying to get to everything that matters to you.

Pursue all goals simultaneously. Although it is somewhat more challenging, you might pursue several goals at the same time. To do this, you need to find some ways in which your goals are compatible with each other. Let's return to the example of the barking dog next door. How might you stop the noise, maintain neighborly relations, and be a nice person? One option might be to offer to keep the dog at your house when your neighbor is working the swing shift. As this example shows, accomplishing all your goals at once can take some creativity and it isn't always possible. But if you can find underlying ways in which multiple goals are compatible with each other, you can address more than one goal at the same time.

Putting Theory into Practice: Thinking Strategically

You probably have conversations in which you try to influence other people several times over the course of your day. Being conscious of your goals and sorting through your priorities can help you to be effective in achieving them.

Identify goals for interpersonal communication. Make a point of recognizing when an influence goal is part of your communication experiences. Then, try to figure out what the exact goal is, and whether it's you or the other person who is trying to do the influencing. Jen remembers an exchange she had with a student about the format of a midterm exam. The student sent her an email that included reasons why he thought the proposed format was flawed and Jen responded giving reasons in favor of the exam format. When Jen and the student had a chance to talk face to face, she asked him what his goal was: to change her approach to exams, to give her advice about testing, or something else. Once the student realized that his real goal was to get permission to take an alternative form of the exam, they had a productive conversation. If you identify your goals for an interaction, you can focus your messages and be more effective.

COMMUNICATION IN ACTION 12.1

Identifying Influence Goals

Keep a diary of your interpersonal interactions over the course of an entire day. After you talk to someone, jot down whom you talked to, what you discussed, any influence goals that you had, and any influence goals the other person seemed to have. At the end of the day, use the form on the companion website to tally the various goals you attended to. As you reflect on your conversations, think about how being more aware of these goals helps you communicate more effectively.

Attend to your secondary goals. Your secondary goals in an influence situation can be more important than your primary goals, because secondary goals represent concerns and priorities that constrain your options for pursuing a primary goal. Given this, be sure to take stock of your secondary goals as you prepare to pursue a primary goal. Suppose your primary goal is to get permission to use a friend's laptop to give a class presentation. If you ignore your secondary goals, you might just say, "Hey, can I borrow your laptop to give my class presentation?" This message might work, but it doesn't protect your secondary concerns. If you're worried about seeming rude or demanding, you would be wise to be more polite. If you don't want to damage your relationship, you might preface this request by saying, "I don't want to put any pressure on you, and I want you to feel comfortable saying no to me." When you face influence situations in your own life, identify your secondary goals and try to craft messages that take those concerns into consideration.

Weigh options for managing multiple goals. If your goals are incompatible – in other words, achieving one goal puts another goal in jeopardy – follow these steps:

1. Identify your most important goal.
2. Consider whether it would be possible to achieve your most important goal after you address a different goal. If so, you can sequence your goals in ways that don't undermine your first priority.
3. Consider whether it would be possible to achieve your less important goals after you address your top priority. If so, you can sequence your goals in ways that achieve your most important goal, as well as perhaps some others.
4. If pursuing any particular goal, in any order, puts the others at jeopardy, focus your communication efforts on the goal that is most important to you.

INFLUENCE MESSAGES

Now that you have learned about influence goals, let's focus on the messages people use to achieve those goals. In this section of the chapter, we examine characteristics of influence messages, patterns that emerge within influence interactions, and sequences of messages that are especially effective.

Characteristics

Compliance-seeking messages are utterances designed to get somebody to agree with a request. Table 12.3 lists 16 specific message strategies you might use to influence a communication partner. Notice how some involve being nice or focusing on positive outcomes, whereas others are pretty negative. In addition, some message types make the request quite clear, but others don't. We can organize influence messages like these along three main dimensions: explicitness, dominance, and amount of argument (Dillard, 2015c).

Compliance-seeking Messages
Utterances that are designed to get a person to agree with a request.

TABLE 12.3 Compliance gaining messages

Type of message	*Example*
Pre-giving	I bought you a present, but first you need to clean the apartment.
Liking	I think you're great. Would you clean the apartment?
Promise	I'll make your favorite dinner if you clean the apartment.
Threat	If you don't clean the apartment, I'm going to be mad.
Aversive simulation	I'm going to be mad at you until you clean the apartment.
Positive expertise	If you clean the apartment, your friends will want to spend more time with you.
Negative expertise	Nobody will want to spend time with you if you don't clean the apartment.
Positive self-feelings	You'll feel good about yourself if you clean the apartment.
Negative self-feelings	You'll feel bad about yourself if you don't clean the apartment.
Positive altercasting	Respectable people keep their apartments clean.
Positive esteem	People will look up to you if you clean the apartment.
Moral appeal	It's a sin to keep this apartment so messy when some people don't even have a place to live.
Altruism	For my sake, will you clean the apartment?
Debt	I took care of everything when you had exams; now I need you to clean the apartment for me.
Negative altercasting	Only a slob would refuse to clean the apartment.
Negative esteem	People will be disappointed in you if you don't clean the apartment.

PAUSE & REFLECT

Which of the tactics in Table 12.3 are you more or less likely to use to influence another person? Which messages do you think are especially effective when somebody seeks to influence you?

Explicitness is the degree to which a message clearly reveals a speaker's intentions. For example, "I want us to date each other exclusively" is an explicit statement – it clearly expresses the speaker's desire to change the relationship. In contrast, an inexplicit or implicit version of the same message is "I can't imagine wanting to spend time with anyone but you."

Explicitness
The degree to which a message clearly reveals the speaker's intentions.

Dominance is the extent to which a speaker expresses power through the form and content of an influence message. Dominance can be conveyed through assertive language ("You *must* do this") or nonverbal cues, such as direct eye contact, vivid gestures, or a forward body lean (Dunbar, 2015). The dominance of an influence message might reflect the speaker's perception that he or she controls the message target. A mother who says "Take the trash out tonight" clearly communicates her assumed authority over her son. Alternatively, a speaker might craft a dominant message to take control. For example, someone might say, "I'm going to run today's meeting." In either case, dominant influence messages seek compliance by dictating what the message receiver will do.

Dominance
The extent to which a speaker expresses power through the form and content of an influence message.

Argument
The degree to which reasons are given for complying with a request.

The amount of **argument** in an influence message refers to whether it includes reasons for compliance. For example, "Can I turn my paper in late?" is a request that is low in argument because it doesn't explain why the request should be granted. In contrast, "I've been diagnosed with mono and I can't attend class for two weeks, so can I turn my paper in late?" is high in argument. The argument dimension captures only the extent to which reasons are given in a message, not their quality. Thus, the following message would be considered as being high in argument: "I forgot to check the syllabus, I overslept this morning, and then I discovered that my printer is out of toner, so can I turn my paper in late?" Most instructors, however, wouldn't consider these especially good reasons for granting the request.

HOW DO YOU RATE? 12.2

Perceptions of Influence Messages

Messages with varying degrees of explicitness or dominance are likely to be perceived in different ways by a receiver and may produce diverse outcomes. Visit the companion website to evaluate the explicitness of various influence messages and rate your perceptions of those messages. How would you respond to influence attempts with varying degrees of explicitness or dominance?

As you might expect, the degree of explicitness, dominance, and argument in an influence message affects how people react to the message. Consider the different forms a date request might take. How would you respond to a purely dominant message ("You're coming with me on Friday") compared to one that is worded as an explicit request ("Would you like to see a movie on Friday?") or that offers you some reasons to agree ("There's a great film showing; we'll have fun")? Dominant and controlling influence attempts (e.g., "You have to take your medicine") are perceived as less friendly and pleasant because they are intrusive and interfere with the target's goals (Miller, Lane, Deatrick, Young, & Potts, 2007). Conversely, influence attempts that include arguments and reasoning ("You should take your medicine because it will alleviate your symptoms and make you feel better") are perceived as more polite and tend to increase the odds of compliance (McCormick & Elroy, 2009; Thompson, Romo, & Dailey, 2017). Finally, explicit requests ("I would like to see you take your medicine") are less likely to be persuasive because they create obstacles for the target that increase feelings of anger and guilt (Burgoon,

Alvaro, Grandpre, & Voulodakis, 2002). In other words, the characteristics of your influence messages shape how people respond to you.

Communication Patterns

The messages that we use to influence other people don't stand alone – they occur within conversations. For this reason, the success of an influence attempt depends on how communication partners interact with each other. In this part of the chapter, we'll examine some of the patterns that unfold during interactions when one person is trying to influence the other.

Try, try again. One common sequence captures what happens when a person fails in an initial attempt to influence someone – for example, the message target refuses a request for help. What happens when someone turns you down? The most common reaction to a refusal is to try again, usually with more force. People tend to become less concerned with being nice to partners who turn them down. Research on unwanted sexual advances shows that people become more direct and less polite in their resistance to and rejection of persistent requests for sexual intimacy over time (Afifi & Lee, 2000). As a result, influence messages tend to become more aggressive in the face of resistance.

PAUSE & REFLECT

How did you feel the last time someone turned down a request that you made? What did you say in response?

Oscillate. People also tend to cycle between explicit influence attempts and segments of talk where the influence goal isn't mentioned. In medical settings, for example, doctors respond to resistance from a patient by dropping the topic for a while to give the patient time to process, but returning to it later in the conversation (Brown & Bylund, 2008). Parents also mix different types of strategies within messages that they use to influence their children; for example, they might include a direct request, promise a reward, and slip in a threat (Lansford, Staples, Bates, Pettit, & Dodge, 2013). The Real Words transcript that follows shows how talk about a request unfolds during a naturally occurring compliance-seeking conversation between sisters Pat and Mary. Notice how Pat initiates the request, backs off when Mary resists, and chats about Mary's schedule instead. Then Pat resumes the influence attempt later in the conversation.

REAL WORDS

AN INTERPERSONAL INFLUENCE INTERACTION

PAT: Hey Mary, are you using the ... the Prelude tomorrow? The car.
MARY: Yeah.
PAT: You're going to school then?
MARY: I gotta go to school, and then I have a meeting, and then I gotta go skating. So I need the car.
PAT: What time is your ... what time is your school at?
MARY: I leave at ...
PAT: Well listen, I need to borrow the car tomorrow and since there's only one car here ...
MARY: Pat!
PAT: So tell me more about your day.
MARY: I have a meeting with that club I joined ... I told you? ... I don't know what to expect.
PAT: I'm sure you'll be glad you joined; it sounds like it could help you find a job after graduation ... How is skating going?
MARY: I like it, but it's a hassle too. I either carry my gear or come home to get it. My day's busy enough ...
PAT: Okay, why don't I ... why don't you wake me up in the morning, and I'll take you to school. Around 7:45?
MARY: Pat!
PAT: I'll borrow the car, and take you out to lunch if you want... Then I'll pick you up at 3:00.
MARY: Hmmm...
PAT: Is that okay?
MARY: Yeah, that'd be okay.

Adapted from: Sanders & Fitch (2001)

Influence first, explain later. Influence interactions tend to unfold in one of two general ways (Sanders & Fitch, 2001). Consider how you might ask an academic advisor to waive a requirement. One option is to open with a fairly explicit request and then offer reasons to comply and address barriers you encounter as the conversation unfolds. For example, you might start by saying, "I know I haven't taken that prerequisite yet, but I'm hoping that you'll let me declare my major anyway." If the advisor argues against you, perhaps by explaining the reason for the rule, you would then offer rebuttals ("I'm taking that course during summer, and I can't enroll for the fall classes that I need unless I'm a major"). One advantage of this approach is that you make your request clear from the start, and you can focus on arguments that target the specific objections the advisor raises.

Investigate first, influence later. Another route involves trying to identify and counter sources of resistance before you make your request clear. This approach involves a little investigative work – for example, you might begin by asking, "Do you ever let anyone declare the major before they take this course?" or "How do summer school courses figure in when I'm registering for fall classes?" Once you figure out what barriers exist, you can make your explicit request. Hopefully by that point, you've managed to locate the reasons why the advisor would say no and, as a result, avoid them.

PAUSE & REFLECT

Do you tend to lead off with your requests, or do you identify potential barriers first?

Short Influence Messages

Although most interpersonal influence interactions involve the give-and-take described in the previous section, sometimes you might have to make a request quickly. Perhaps you are talking to a stranger, and there isn't really any other reason for the conversation except your influence goal. For example, if you need to borrow a cell phone from a stranger to place an important call, you wouldn't work up to your request by making small talk. Even when the target of your influence message is not a stranger, time limits or a power difference might force you to keep your message very short.

Even in these circumstances, you can sequence parts of your influence messages to increase your effectiveness (Dillard et al., 2002). Several effective influence strategies require only one or two speaking turns (see Figure 12.2). Sometimes people wonder if these strategies are ethical, because they seem like tricks designed to manipulate other people. If you use these techniques, you need to make sure that the information you give is sound, you are respecting your communication partner, and your actions align with your values. The success of these strategies shows how simple adjustments to your communication strategies can significantly improve your chances of achieving an influence goal.

Putting Theory into Practice: Crafting Effective Influence Messages

Crafting influence messages involves adapting your communication behavior to increase the likelihood that you'll meet your goals. By being

ONE SPEAKING TURN	
That's-Not-All	Offer reward for complying with a request, and at the very last moment in the speaking turn, add something extra to the reward.
If you let me borrow your notes from the class that I missed, I'll share my study guide with you . . . and I'll proofread your final paper for you.	
Even-A-Penny	Emphasize that even a small contribution can be important.
I was wondering if I could borrow your notes from the class that I missed; even just looking at them for a few minutes would be a huge help.	
TWO SPEAKING TURNS	
Pregiving	Use the first speaking turn to offer a gift. Use the second speaking turn to make the request.
Let me help you with all your books! . . . Hey, could I borrow your notes from the class that I missed?	
Relational Obligations	Use the first speaking turn to identify a relationship shared with the message target. Use the second speaking turn to make the request.
Hey, I ride the No. 8 bus to campus just like you do! . . . Do you think I could borrow your notes from the class that I missed?	
Door-in-the-Face	Use the first speaking turn to make a large request that is likely to be rejected. Use the second speaking turn to make a smaller request.
Do you think I could borrow all of your notes for the whole semester? . . . How about just the ones from the class that I missed.	
Foot-in-the-Door	Use the first speaking turn to make a small request that is likely to be granted. Use the second speaking turn to make a larger request.
Do you have an extra pen that I could use? . . . Hey, do you think I could borrow your notes from the class that I missed?	
Foot-in-the-Mouth	Use the first speaking turn to find out how the message target is feeling. Use the second speaking turn to make the request.
How are you doing today? . . . That's great — hey, do you think I could borrow your notes from the class that I missed?	

FIGURE 12.2 Strategies for short influence interactions

thoughtful about the messages you use to influence other people, you can improve your chance of success.

Remember that messages matter. Keep in mind that your messages have important effects on communication partners. In particular:

- Dominant influence messages tend to evoke negative reactions. Your partner may reject your request, or you may get what you want but damage your image or your relationship with the message target.
- Explicit messages create challenges for message targets, because these direct messages force a partner to respond. When explicit messages put pressure on a partner, a negative response is more likely.
- When explicit messages are accompanied by reasons or argument, message targets respond more positively. In the best-case scenario, then, you make your influence goals clear, offer good reasons, and avoid being too bossy.

What does this mean in practice? Instead of saying to a co-worker, "You have to cover my shift," or even "Will you please cover my shift?" try something like "Can you possibly cover my shift on Friday evening? My parents are coming to visit and I need to pick them up. I'd be happy to cover for you one day next week in exchange."

Plan for interpersonal influence interactions. Advance planning can greatly improve your communication effectiveness. Think about what you might do if your first request is rejected and form a back-up plan. Also, decide in advance whether to chat for a bit first or to lead off with your request: if information you might gather would help you form a more effective influence message, you might want to ask some questions at the beginning of the conversation. Even when you have only a few speaking turns to influence a communication partner, advance planning can pay off.

COMMUNICATION IN ACTION 12.2

Creating Interpersonal Influence Messages

Imagine that you are waiting to have a short meeting with a professor about adding her class to your schedule for next semester. You know that the class is full, but you've heard great things about it and it's relevant to the kind of job you're hoping to get. Your primary goal is to register for the class, but you'd also like the professor to think you're capable and to get your relationship off to a good start. Write out what you would say to the professor. Then, show this message to three other people and ask them if they would be influenced by it. After getting their feedback, think about whether changing the order of your messages or adjusting the degree of dominance, explicitness, and argument might make the message better. Planning like this can help you be more successful when you pursue interpersonal influence goals.

INTERPERSONAL INFLUENCE IN ACTION

Interpersonal influence interactions unfold as partners exchange messages and they occur within relationships. In this section of the chapter, you'll learn about how you can overcome obstacles to achieving your influence goals, how relationship characteristics shape your communication options, and how to deal with high-stakes influence interactions.

Overcoming Obstacles

Interpersonal influence communication sometimes resembles a tug-of-war: one party tries to exert influence and the other party tries to resist it. Your partner's resistance can be more or less successful, depending on the strength of your strategy. Likewise, how influential you are depends on how you react to resistance. And by understanding the strategies that people use to refuse a request, you can arm yourself with the tools necessary to resist unwanted influence. In general, you can become a more effective communicator if you understand how to resist influence and how to overcome resistance when you influence others.

PAUSE & REFLECT

Think of a recent episode when your communication partner rejected your influence attempt. What reason, if any, were you given for the refusal?

Let's start by considering the reasons that people refuse a request. Table 12.4 summarizes six obstacles to interpersonal influence (Johnson, 2015). People draw upon knowledge of these obstacles both when

TABLE 12.4 Obstacles to interpersonal influence

Obstacle	*Definition*	*Example*
Lack of possession	The message target doesn't possess the resources needed to comply	I can't support your candidate for the school board because I'm not eligible to vote in this state
Imposition	Complying with the influence attempt would impinge on the message target's prior plans	I can't loan you my car because I need it to take my mother to an appointment
No incentive	The speaker doesn't perceive a reason to comply with the influence attempt	I'm not going to change my eating habits; my diet is fine for a person my age
Recalcitrance	The speaker doesn't want to comply with the influence attempt	I don't want to date you exclusively
Postponement	The speaker puts off complying with the influence attempt until some unspecified time in the future	I'll clean up the apartment when I'm not so busy with my classes
Violation	The message target sees the influence attempt as inappropriate or something the message source is responsible for	You shouldn't ask me to proofread your paper – you should take care of that for yourself

they create influence messages and when they refuse influence attempts (Boster et al., 2009). First, consider how you craft an influence message. You might just blurt out your request and see what happens. As a more strategic alternative, however, you could tailor your request to neutralize the obstacles that you anticipate. Consider how you might go about asking a classmate to lend you a book. If you think that your classmate might refuse because it would be an imposition, you can word your request to minimize the burden ("I'll return it right away"). If you think that your classmate isn't motivated to help you, you could offer an incentive along with your request ("I'll lend you my lecture notes in exchange"). Figure 12.3 identifies some strategies that you can use to address obstacles to requests.

When you are the target of an unwanted influence attempt, you can use these obstacles as reasons for refusing. In any given situation, you could say, "I don't want to help," "I can't help," or "You don't deserve my help." As you might expect, your choice of words has consequences. If you say you don't want to, you might damage your relationship with your communication partner: this kind of refusal might communicate

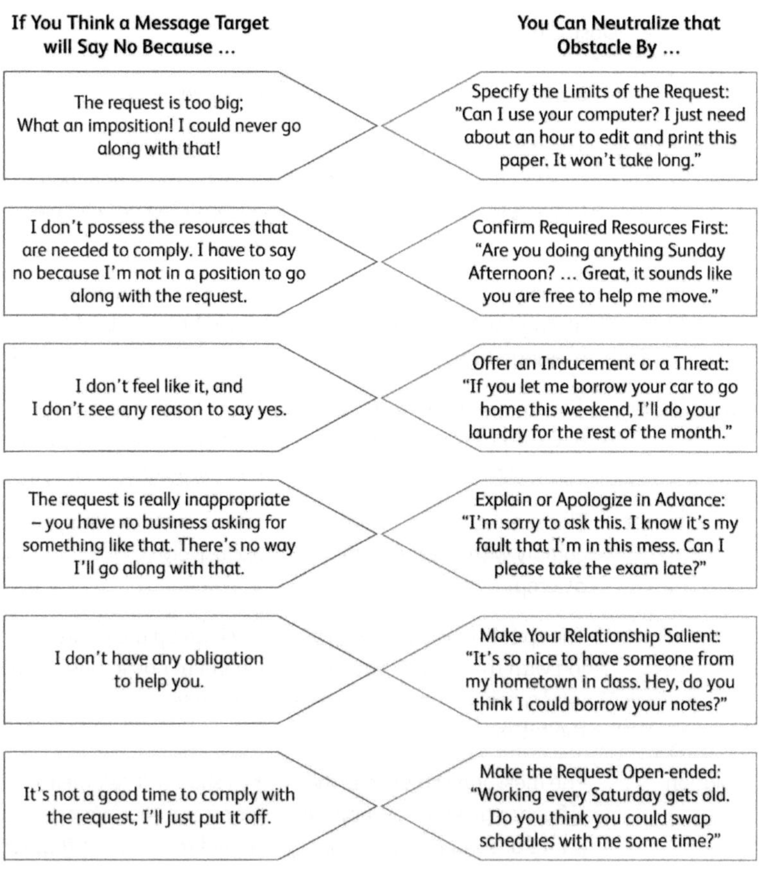
If You Think a Message Target will Say No Because ...
You Can Neutralize that Obstacle By ...
The request is too big; What an imposition! I could never go along with that!
Specify the Limits of the Request: "Can I use your computer? I just need about an hour to edit and print this paper. It won't take long."
I don't possess the resources that are needed to comply. I have to say no because I'm not in a position to go along with the request.
Confirm Required Resources First: "Are you doing anything Sunday Afternoon? ... Great, it sounds like you are free to help me move."
I don't feel like it, and I don't see any reason to say yes.
Offer an Inducement or a Threat: "If you let me borrow your car to go home this weekend, I'll do your laundry for the rest of the month."
The request is really inappropriate – you have no business asking for something like that. There's no way I'll go along with that.
Explain or Apologize in Advance: "I'm sorry to ask this. I know it's my fault that I'm in this mess. Can I please take the exam late?"
I don't have any obligation to help you.
Make Your Relationship Salient: "It's so nice to have someone from my hometown in class. Hey, do you think I could borrow your notes?"
It's not a good time to comply with the request; I'll just put it off.
Make the Request Open-ended: "Working every Saturday gets old. Do you think you could swap schedules with me some time?"

FIGURE 12.3 Tailoring requests to neutralize obstacles

that you don't value your partner (Johnson, 2007). Refusals that contain statements that soften or qualify your commitment to what you are saying, also known as **modal expressions**, are perceived as more polite, but can sometimes be less effective for declining influence attempts (Johnson, 2007). For example, if you say "I *think* I *might* be busy that day" instead of just asserting "I am busy that day," you leave open the possibility that you might *not* be busy, which would make it possible for you to comply and might encourage further influence attempts. How you refuse a request can also determine whether your communication partner gives up or keeps asking. In particular, people are more persistent in their efforts to influence a message target who is unwilling to comply because such refusals can be embarrassing and prevent the attainment of desired goals (Johnson, Roloff, & Riffee, 2004). By saying that you can't comply with a request, you can put an end to an influence attempt without damaging your relationship.

Modal Expressions
Statements that soften or qualify commitment to an assertion.

Numerous features of a situation shape how people refuse requests and, consequently, how you might overcome obstacles to influence. First, keep in mind that people find it much easier to refuse a request, or simply ignore it, if you ask over email or another computer-mediated channel (Tong & Walther, 2010). Thus, if compliance with a request is important to you, make it in person. Second, people might be more likely to use deception to refuse a request when they believe that the truth will violate social expectations (Stratmoen, Rivera, & Saucier, 2020). If you want to avoid being lied to, make sure you give people an "out" when you make a request. In addition, people who are already committed to a particular course of action may need incentives to comply with your request (Smith, Fink, Romano, & Mikanatha, 2020). If you are trying to get someone to change course, you'll have to be prepared to make it worth something to them. And because compliance with a request is more likely if the target is feeling grateful and likes or is attracted to the requester (Hendrickson & Goei, 2009), time your request for when the other person is in a good frame of mind.

PAUSE & REFLECT

Do you sometimes find yourself doing something that is disagreeable to you because you couldn't fend off an influence attempt? What kinds of obstacles could you use to avoid this problem?

Relationship Characteristics and Influence Messages

Because intimacy and power affect obstacles to interpersonal influence, they affect the messages people use to influence a communication partner.

Politeness Theory
A set of assumptions about how intimacy and power are related to the use of more or less polite influence messages.

Face
The public image of ourselves that we put out into the world.

Positive Face
The desire to be well-liked and admired by others.

Negative Face
The desire to be autonomous and unconstrained.

Face-threatening Act
A request for compliance that violates one's positive or negative face.

As you learned in Chapter 5, **politeness theory** is a set of assumptions about how intimacy and power are related to the use of more or less polite influence messages (Brown & Levison, 1987). Politeness theory suggests that we all have **face**, which is the public image of ourselves we put out into the world. There are two types of face: **positive face** refers to our desire to be well-liked and admired by others, and **negative face** refers to our desire to be autonomous and unconstrained. Given that we all have these desires, any request for compliance has the potential to violate one or both types of face; we call this a **face-threatening act**. When you attempt to influence people, you threaten their negative face because you are asking them to do what you want rather than respecting their desire for autonomy and to do what they want to do. In addition, your influence attempts can create a threat to your own positive face because people may not like you as much if you make too many demands. Politeness theory suggests that we use a variety of strategies when we attempt to influence others to limit the amount of face threats in our requests. Specifically, politeness theory suggests that we alter the directness of our requests in an effort to preserve face.

The extent to which you alter your directness may depend on the size of the request and degree of intimacy or power in your relationship. Figure 12.5 shows the factors that shape how polite an influence message needs to be. For example, consider two requests you might receive from your brother: he'd like to tag along with you and your friends on Saturday night and he'd like to move in with you for a few months. He'll have to word the second request more politely than the first, because it's a much bigger imposition and a much larger threat to your negative face. If you and your brother have a close relationship, he can phrase both requests more casually, because it's less of an imposition to hang out with – and even live with – a brother you like. Similarly, if your brother has a lot of power in the relationship, maybe because he has a well-paying job or he's

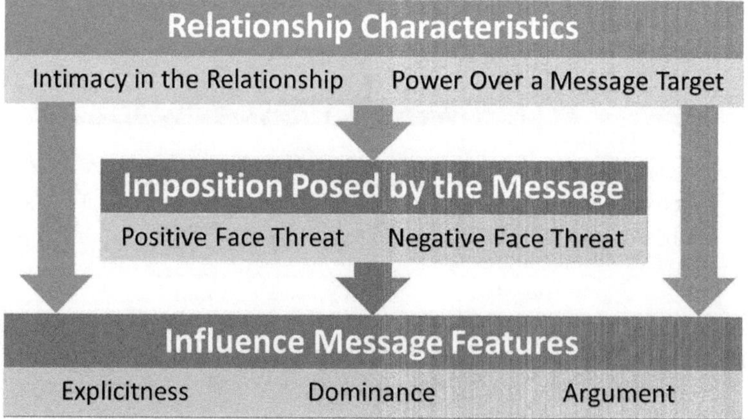

FIGURE 12.4 Factors that shape influence messages

well-liked within your family, both the imposition of these requests and the need to word them politely goes down.

Intimacy and influence messages. People in close relationships can use influence messages that are direct and to the point. Does this mean that you are less polite or even rude to your close friends, romantic partner, and family members? In one sense, yes, because you don't always say "please," "if you could," or "I'm sorry to trouble you." But being direct isn't necessarily rude in close relationships, and indirectness isn't always polite (Yu, 2011). Indirectness is perceived as impolite when you are more indirect than you need to be to get your point across (Terkourafi, 2015). When you are very indirect in a close relationship – where it would be socially acceptable for you to be more explicit – you can end up making the other person work to unearth your message. In fact, messages that are indirect can signal a lack of certainty or confidence in the relationship (Knobloch, 2006).

Although intimacy frees you up to use explicit influence messages, it may also allow you to use less explicit messages. Consider the messages you might use to try to get someone to stop smoking around you. In a nonintimate relationship, you face some challenges: you don't know whether your influence attempt will annoy the message target, and you don't want to look bad to the people around you. These concerns might prompt you to be indirect in your approach. Unfortunately, an indirect message, such as "My asthma is acting up today," might not be recognized as an influence message. So, you're forced to be a little more explicit: "If it wouldn't be too much trouble, could you please put out your cigarette?" In a close relationship, you're on firmer ground with the message target, which leaves you free to be more direct: "Hey, put out your cigarette – the smoke is bothering me." And if you and your partner really know each other well, an indirect message, such as "I need air" or even just coughing, might make your point.

When you communicate using computer-mediated channels, such as in online discussion boards or via email, the intimacy of these interactions also shapes influence messages. One study showed that when communication online is based on membership of some group, such as Dallas Cowboys fans or alumni of your high school, the absence of feelings of intimacy is associated with more obvious influence messages (Postmes, Spears, Lee, and Novak, 2005). In contrast, that study found that a lack of intimacy leads to less obvious influence messages when online relationships aren't predetermined. Using computer-mediated options for influencing other people can also affect your chances of success. In particular, research shows that women are less persuaded by online influence messages then men are, in part because online channels are less intimate venues for communication (Guadagno & Cialdini, 2007).

Power and influence messages. Power affects influence messages in much the same way that intimacy does: powerful people have the freedom to be more direct in their influence attempts, and they can get away

FIGURE 12.5 Actor Lin-Manuel Miranda used his referent power as a celebrity and Mayor Bill DeBlasio used his legitimate power as mayor to encourage New Yorkers to get the COVID-19 vaccine

Source: Photo by Richard Drew/Getty Images.

with being more indirect. For example, your supervisor at work has a lot of influence over you. She can make a request directly, such as "Clean up the staff lounge today," and you probably wouldn't find that request rude or inappropriate. Or, she might make that request indirectly, saying, "The staff lounge is sure a mess," and you could reasonably see that statement as a request. Can you imagine using either message to influence your boss? The direct message might get you fired, but the indirect message might be seen as volunteering to clean up. It is unlikely that either message would prompt your supervisor to start cleaning up.

Coercive Power
The ability to use threats and punishment to gain compliance.

Reward Power
The ability to use incentives to gain compliance.

Legitimate Power
The degree of power gained by one's position or title.

Referent Power
The extent to which individuals are well-liked and admired.

Expert Power
The extent to which individuals have information, knowledge, and expertise on a given topic.

There are five common sources of power. The first type of power is **coercive power**, which refers to one's ability to use threats and punishment to achieve their desired outcomes. In contrast, **reward power** involves the use of incentives to gain compliance toward a desired goal. **Legitimate power** is gained by individuals on the basis of their position or title. Next, people gain **referent power** when others look up to them with admiration, acceptance, and approval. Finally, **expert power** is accrued by people who have high amounts of information, knowledge, and expertise. Your boss has legitimate power on the basis of their position in the company, expert power based on the fact that they have more information than you about the operations of your company, reward power based on their ability to give you a raise or a promotion, coercive power given that they may fire you for unsatisfactory performance, and potentially referent power to the extent that you like them. Thus, your boss does not need to be concerned about being polite or making a strong argument in order to convince you to do your job. Given that your boss has high power, they can be more explicit and dominant in telling you what to do at work.

When you lack power, you need to be careful about how you make a request. **Upward influence** – seeking compliance from people with more power – is an important skill for people within organizations (Waldron, 1999). Although opportunities for upward influence can increase employee performance and satisfaction (Anderson & Huang, 2006), some workers are reluctant to persuade powerful leaders due to perceived threats to reputation or job stability and the risk of failure or embarrassment (Waldron & Sanderson, 2011). How can you go about influencing people who have power, without offending them or being seen as inappropriate? There are three types of strategies people might use to influence someone with more power (Epitropaki & Martin, 2013). Rational upward influence requires you to present data and facts to support a logical argument for your request. Soft upward influence strategies involve ingratiating yourself with your superior through friendship and flattery, or exchanging reciprocal favors and benefits. Hard upward influence strategies rely on assertive and direct requests, building coalitions with other workers to have strength in numbers, or gaining the support of an even higher authority.

Upward Influence
Seeking compliance from a communication partner who has more power.

IDEA: INCLUSION, DIVERSITY, EQUITY, AND ACCESS

Given that people with increased power are in a stronger position to exert influence, what does this imply about the ability of individuals from marginalized groups to achieve their goals through interpersonal influence? What can be done to create more equal opportunities for powerless people to have influence and achieve their desired goals?

High-Stakes Episodes

Interactions that involve a lot of secondary goals can be considered **high-stakes episodes** because a person has a lot of concerns or issues to attend to while pursuing their primary goal. Two influence situations where the stakes are high are initiating a romantic relationship and gaining assistance from somebody in power. People who have these primary goals may also be concerned about having a smooth interaction, managing their relationship with the other person, retaining their personal resources, and keeping their anxiety under control. In this section of the chapter, we'll take a close look at one particular high-stakes influence situation – asking someone out on a date.

High-Stakes Episodes
Interpersonal influence interactions that involve a lot of secondary goals.

Making a bid for more intimacy or shared time with another person can be risky. In fact, initiating or intensifying a romantic relationship can be threatening in three different ways (Kunkel, Wilson, Olufowote, & Robson, 2003):

- You run the risk of making the target of your romantic interest feel forced to go out with you. If you've ever been asked out by someone and found it hard to say no, you know what this pressure feels like.
- A bid to increase intimacy could damage the relationship. If you ask a partner to spend a special day together – perhaps your birthday or Valentine's Day – and you are rejected, you might find it hard to continue the relationship.
- You can damage your image by seeming either presumptuous or desperate.

In the high-stakes situation of changing your relationship status, you need to be attentive to all of these concerns, as well as your primary goal of getting your partner to agree to change the nature of your relationship. One study asked people what they would say or do if they had the goal of initiating, intensifying, or terminating a romantic relationship while mitigating threats to a partner's positive or negative face (Wilson et al., 2009). Participants rated the hypothetical goal of intensifying or terminating a relationship as more face threatening than initiating a relationship, but they were less likely to actually pursue relationship initiation if the hypothetical situations were real. In the conditions of initiating or intensifying a relationship, participants were most likely to use the face-saving strategies of demonstrating interest, seeking the target's input or opinion, and managing any imposition on the target; whereas those in the relationship termination condition saved face for the target by showing care and concern, giving compliments, and hedging more in their messages.

What can you take away from this closer look at date requests? First, if you find it hard to ask people out, don't judge yourself harshly – this is challenging for a lot of people. Second, you might make the task easier by focusing more on the relationship and less on the date request. Try to build closeness and reduce uncertainty by chatting, exploring common interests, and expressing your liking for the other person through your verbal and nonverbal behaviors. Third, you can reduce the threats that go along with a date request by leaving your partner a lot of room to say no. One easy way to do this is to make your request time-specific ("Do you want to catch the 7:30 movie?") – if your partner doesn't want to go out with you, the person can just say that he or she can't make it. If you ask a person to go out with you "anytime, ever," you may force that partner to say "no, never," which can be awkward for both of you.

INSIDE COMMUNICATION RESEARCH

Seeking Social Support as a High-Stakes Influence Attempt

Another interpersonal influence encounter that can have high stakes is asking for social support. Support seeking requires individuals to balance multiple goals, including impression management and relationship maintenance, in addition to the objective of receiving support. Asking for help can be challenging because people generally want to maintain a positive and competent public image, but seeking support for personal problems or stressors can expose people to potential embarrassment, humiliation, stigma, or shame. These potential vulnerabilities are amplified when people broadcast their need for support in social networking sites online. The more public a support request is, the more concerned people will be about how the request appears to others and the more motivated they will be to engage in impression management. In this study, communication scholars Hyun Jung Oh and Robert LaRose (2016) argued that support seekers would spend more time composing their messages requesting support to the extent that the problem was more severe and the request was more public.

To test these predictions, the researchers conducted a study in which participants read one of two upsetting scenarios describing an experience with car trouble that varied in terms of their severity and were told to imagine they were involved in the situation. The participants were then asked to share a message on Facebook seeking support for this event, either through a private direct message or as a public status update. Participants also responded to questions rating the importance of their support-seeking goal and impression management goal in this situation. The researchers measured how long it took participants to compose their support-seeking message and evaluated the message for its level of sophistication.

Results of the study showed that the severity of the problem did not influence the perceived importance of the support seeking or impression management goal; however, participants rated the impression management goal as significantly more important in the condition where they were asked to post their request as a public status update than in the private message condition. In addition, whether posting publicly or privately about the stressful event, people took significantly more time to compose their message when the problem was severe as opposed to mild. Messages that took longer to compose were also rated as more sophisticated. These findings suggest that influence attempts designed to solicit social support tend to have higher stakes when the message is public and the problem is severe, which shapes the amount of time and effort people put into crafting their messages.

THINK ABOUT IT

1. How might people's efforts to garner social support differ when making the request face to face instead of online? Are different types of facework required when making requests in person versus online?
2. The asynchronous nature of online communication makes it possible for people to carefully and strategically craft their message when seeking support. How do these conditions shape the quality and success of influence attempts compared to conversations that happen in real time?

PAUSE & REFLECT

Have you ever felt foolish after you made a request that was refused? How might you reword your influence message to avoid future refusals?

Putting Theory into Practice: Ethical Influence

In this part of the chapter, you learned how to anticipate and neutralize obstacles to compliance, employ strategies for exerting upward influence, and avoid some of the risks that go along with intensifying a romantic relationship. As you put what you have learned into practice, be sure that your skillful communication is also ethical interpersonal influence. Let's look more closely at what that means.

Respect obstacles. Thinking ahead and crafting influence messages that sidestep some of the common obstacles to compliance can help you to achieve your influence goals. Keep in mind, though, that ethical communicators don't use their words to trap interaction partners. Practicing ethical influence involves balancing your own desire to achieve your influence goals against your partner's right to refuse. If a person rejects your influence attempt, you have two key issues to consider:

- Are you trying to advance your own goals at someone else's expense? Or are you trying to promote the well-being of the relationship or your community?
- Does your partner have specific barriers, such as a scheduling conflict or a lack of resources, that you might be able to negotiate around? Or would persisting subject your partner to discomfort or embarrassment?

Your answers can help you decide whether it's ethical to continue. For example, trying to persuade someone to chair a committee because you know she is the best person for the job is ethical. Trying to persuade her because you don't want to do it yourself is not.

Enable upward influence. You can also promote more ethical communication by allowing people who have less power than you to exert interpersonal influence. Organizations are moving away from the strict power hierarchies that were common in the past. As a member of the workforce, you'll probably find yourself working in teams with people who have more or less power than you. You can be a more effective communicator by using some of the influence strategies described in this chapter, and by creating channels for people with less power than you to achieve their influence goals.

COMMUNICATION IN ACTION 12.3

Inviting Upward Influence

People who find themselves in powerful positions can create opportunities for individuals with less power to exert interpersonal influence and achieve their goals. Complete the form on the companion website to identify strategies for encouraging upward influence.

Avoid strategic ambiguity. Sometimes communicators are intentionally ambiguous when they pursue an influence goal. You might casually mention to your roommate that you have done a lot of dishes lately. If your roommate asks if you want her to help out more, you could deny that you were making a request. Ambiguous messages create a dilemma for receivers, because they can't tell if the influence attempt was real or imagined.

You'll be a more ethical communicator if you take ownership of your attempts to influence other people. When you have an influence goal, make your agenda clear and allow your partner to accept or reject your influence attempt. Of course, you'll use more or less explicit messages depending on how intimate your relationship is or how much power you have. In any case, try to avoid making influence messages that are unnecessarily vague and do not deny your underlying influence goals. If you treat your communication partner with respect, you may find that he or she is more willing to grant your requests.

SUMMARY

Interpersonal influence occurs anytime you or a communication partner use messages to affect each other's attitudes, beliefs, and actions. In this chapter, you learned about some of the most common interpersonal influence goals we pursue when we communicate with others. In addition to your primary goal for an interaction, keep in mind that you have secondary goals – such as preserving your self-image or maintaining a relationship – that shape your communication options. By recognizing your influence goals and keeping both primary and secondary concerns in mind, you may be more effective at managing the multiple influence goals you may have within an interpersonal interaction.

The messages you use to pursue interpersonal influence goals vary in important ways. You can craft influence messages that make your goal more or less explicit, communicate more or less dominance over your partner, and provide more or fewer arguments to support your case. Conversations in which influence messages unfold may also take different forms, ranging from interactions that start right off with the influence message to those in which a communicator gradually brings up an influence goal. Even very short influence interactions, which might have only a few speaking turns, can be sequenced in ways that increase your likelihood of success.

When you put interpersonal influence messages to work for you, keep in mind the obstacles you may encounter, characteristics of your relationship with a partner, and challenges you may face in a high-stakes episode. A communication partner might reject your influence attempt for a variety of reasons – if you take these obstacles into account when crafting your message, you might just be able to neutralize and overcome them. Intimacy in a relationship and having power with respect to a partner also gives you more options for communicating influence; in particular, you can be both more explicit and more indirect when you influence a close relationship partner or someone you have power over. And remember that high-stakes influence situations are those where your primary goal goes hand in hand with several secondary concerns. Crafting effective messages in situations like these might require you to weigh your affection for a communication partner, your certainty about the relationship, and how to minimize the risks that you may encounter.

ACTIVITIES FOR EXPLORING COMMUNICATION ETHICS

What Would You/Should You Do?

You have noticed that your supervisor at work often uses his power to influence less powerful workers to do things that aren't part of their job description. He regularly asks one of your co-workers to give him a ride home after work. You're also pretty sure that he's tried to date a couple of the interns who have worked in the office. Because the supervisor has the power to punish these people, you see them reluctantly agree to his requests. You realize that he is misusing his power, but addressing his misuse of power could jeopardize your job. What would you or should you do?

Something to Think About

In 2021, as vaccinations against COVID-19 became readily available, many different strategies were used to persuade people to get their shot. Public service announcements provided information about the safety of the vaccines, emphasized the health benefits for protecting yourself and others from infection, and leaned into the social responsibility that we all have to get vaccinated. A different influence strategy offered incentives for people to get their shots. In Ohio, New York, Maryland, and Kentucky, residents who were fully vaccinated were entered in a lottery where they could win anywhere from $225,000 to $5 million. Krispy Kreme gave a free donut to anyone who was vaccinated and in New Jersey a coalition of breweries were giving out free beer. Getting everyone vaccinated is important for preserving public health and an important part of the social contract, but what are the ethical implications involved in offering incentives for people to get the vaccine?

Analyze Communication Ethics Yourself

Many human rights organizations have objected to the use of torture to obtain information from prisoners. The Council on Foreign Relations has published the following website on the use of torture and interrogation techniques: www.cfr.org/backgrounder/torture-united-states-and-laws-war. How does the information contained on this webpage shape your opinion about the use of torture as an influence strategy to obtain information?

KEY WORDS

argument
coercive power
compliance-seeking messages
dominance
expert power
explicitness
face
face-threatening act
goal strain
goals
high-stakes episodes
interpersonal influence

interpersonal influence goals

legitimate power

negative face

modal expressions

politeness theory

positive face

primary goal

referent power

reward power

secondary goals

upward influence

LEARNING OBJECTIVES

After reading this chapter, you should be able to:

1. Describe different forms, levels, and components of interpersonal conflict.
2. Identify four goals that are relevant in conflict situations.
3. Describe three conflict strategies and five styles of conflict management.
4. Understand how biased attributions can escalate conflict.
5. Describe the effects of interpersonal power on conflict avoidance.
6. Describe the patterns of interpersonal communication that occur during conflict interactions.

PUTTING THEORY INTO PRACTICE

In this chapter, you will learn how to:

1. Diagnose your conflicts.
2. Focus on behaviors, rather than traits.
3. Unravel conflicts one component at a time.
4. Plan for multiple goals.
5. Match your strategies to your goals.
6. Branch out from your conflict style.
7. Question your attribution for conflict.
8. Keep your power in check.
9. De-escalate, rather than escalate, conflict.

INTERPERSONAL CONFLICT

13

Source: Bauer-Griffin/Getty Images

DOI: 10.4324/9781351174381-16

Sibling conflict is common in most families, but none are perhaps more explosive or public than the feuds erupting between the Kardashian sisters. In the making of their reality television series, *Keeping Up with the Kardashians*, Kim, Khloé, and Kourtney have had major blow-outs both on-screen and off. Kourtney, the eldest of the sisters, often feels picked on and criticized, prompting her to withdraw and limit her engagement with the family. In one episode of the show, the sisters are making plans for Kim's baby shower and Kourtney is completely ignoring Kim and Khloé, chiming in only to make a critical remark about Khloé's patio furniture. Kim and Kourtney got into another huge row at a photo shoot where Kim's frustration boiled over into a hurtful remark that Kourtney "had a stick up her ass" and was the "least exciting person to look at." When fans of the show came to Kourtney's defense on Twitter, Kim and Khloé fired back with more insults about Kourtney's work ethic. Even the sisters' attempts at apology missed the mark. After Kim's comment that Kourtney was the least exciting to look at, she apologized, saying, "What I meant is that you're boring," so it's not surprising that Kourtney had a hard time forgiving her sister for these remarks. After a physical altercation between Kim and Kourtney, Khloé speculated that Kourtney's apology wasn't genuine, that she only apologized to clear the air before the sisters went on a trip to Armenia together. All of this tension eventually pushed Kourtney to her breaking point and she decided to pull back from the show to spend more time with her three children. These conflicts illustrate how damaging interpersonal conflict can be for personal relationships.

Can you remember a particularly intense conflict with a close friend, roommate, co-worker, or family member? What caused the conflict? How did you resolve it? The examples from *Keeping Up with the Kardashians* suggest that interpersonal conflict is inevitable in close relationships or when people live and work together. Kourtney, Kim, and Khloé expressed their disagreements through acts of vengeance, insults, yelling, and ignoring each other, but there are constructive ways of handling conflict as well. In this chapter, we examine the characteristics of interpersonal conflict, the communication behaviors you can use to manage conflict, and conflict dynamics that unfold in interpersonal relationships.

WHAT IS CONFLICT?

When you think of the word "conflict," what experiences come to mind? In adolescent friendships, conflicts often focus on situations in which one person has violated a core expectation of friendship, a mismatch in preferences or needs, and unwanted intrusions such as unsolicited advice (Kirmayer, Khullar, & Dirks, 2021). Research on romantic relationships suggests that conflicts arise concerning dissatisfaction with expressions of affection, experiences of jealousy, division of chores or responsibilities, sex, control or dominance, and future plans and money (Lopes, Schackelford, Buss, & Abed, 2020). Although interpersonal conflicts can be painful, they also offer an opportunity to improve a relationship. You will be better able to realize the advantages of interpersonal conflict if you understand the nature of conflict.

Conflict Takes Many Forms

Interpersonal conflicts can be challenging because they can take a variety of forms. An important step in improving your conflict communication, then, is learning to recognize the type of conflict you are experiencing. As shown in Figure 13.1, conflict experiences vary along two dimensions (see Cupach, Canary, & Spitzberg, 2010). A first dimension distinguishes between conflicts that are tied to specific experiences and those that span several different experiences. For example, you might have a conflict with your maintenance supervisor, or "super," in your building because they are slow to respond when you submit a problem, or you might generally

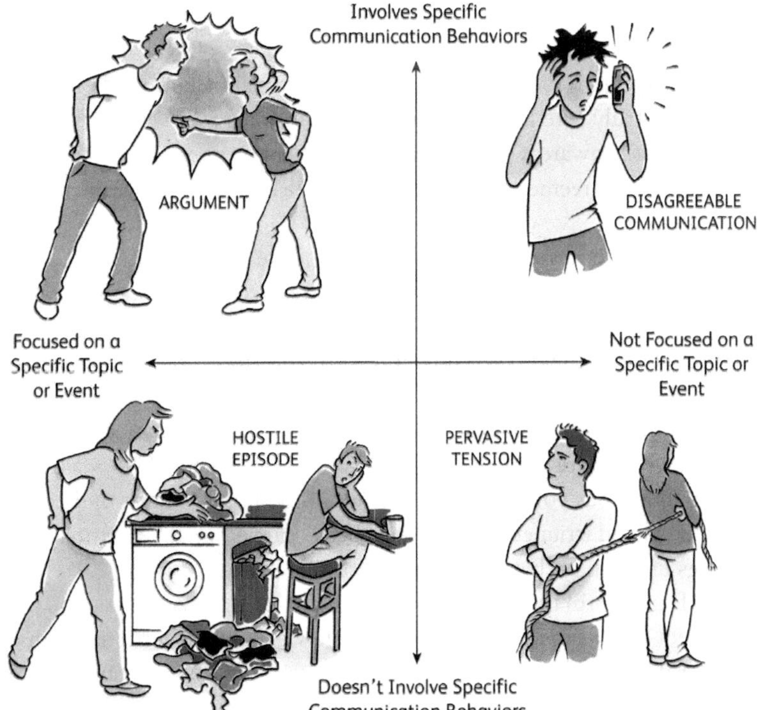

FIGURE 13.1 Forms of interpersonal conflict

dislike your super and feel annoyed by most of their actions. The second dimension contrasts conflicts that involve specific communication behaviors, such as when you confront your super about the slow response time, and conflicts that affect all communication behaviors between the parties, such as when you tend to avoid or be short-tempered with your super because you dislike them. These two dimensions of conflict result in four distinct forms of conflict: argument, disagreeable communication, hostile episode, or pervasive tension.

Argument
An explicit conversation with another person about a particular disagreement.

When you communicate explicitly with another person about a particular disagreeable situation, you are having a conflict in the form of an **argument**. An argument is an especially concrete type of conflict because it is clearly about a specific issue, event, or circumstance. And your communication behavior during an argument clearly reveals the reason for the conflict. In other words, your words and behaviors during the conversation focus specifically on a singular source of dissatisfaction. An argument is perhaps the most clear-cut type of conflict.

Disagreeable Communication
Using specific behaviors, such as contradicting, insulting, and yelling, during a conversation.

Disagreeable communication involves communication behaviors that are similar to an argument, but the communication isn't about any specific problem or issue. Disagreeable communication occurs when partners contradict each other, insult each other, and raise their voices, but there's no particular issue up for debate. Alexis and David Rose, siblings on the television series *Schitt's Creek*, are a good example of this kind of conflict. David and Alexis quarreled over everything from who would sleep in the bed closest to the door (and therefore be most likely to be murdered first in a break-in) to Alexis's decision to wear a long white gown to David's wedding. Despite their superficial bickering, the siblings show they truly care for each other in several ways over the course of six seasons of the award-winning show. Disagreeable communication seems to express disagreement, although no issue or topic of disagreement may actually exist.

Hostile Episode
A period of negative feelings or resentment toward another person.

At the other extreme, you might experience a conflict in which there is a clear underlying problem, but you don't communicate about that issue directly. This form of conflict is called a **hostile episode**, because one person is filled with hostility or resentment toward another person for a period of time (Cupach et al., 2010). In an ongoing relationship, day-to-day annoyances can make one person feel frustrated with the other person. Does your sibling keep taking your phone charger? Does your co-worker point out your mistakes in front of the boss? When you become dissatisfied and irritated by someone's behavior, you might experience the feelings of hostility that make up this form of conflict.

Pervasive Tension
A friction that is present when people communicate with each other.

A fourth form of conflict, **pervasive tension**, consists of friction that is present every time people communicate with each other. This form of conflict does not involve specific communication behaviors, and it is not about a particular event or topic. Instead, every interaction that occurs between conflict parties is characterized by discomfort and misunderstanding. Even a simple conversation can be difficult, as you struggle to coordinate speaking turns, introduce new topics, and bring the interaction to an end. Pervasive tension undermines all communication between partners, so it is especially threatening to the future of a relationship. In fact, analysis of information from more than 40,000 couples about to begin couples therapy showed that more than 80% of them had serious problems with both conflict and intimacy, and more than 20% were identified as possible risks for suicide (Gottman, Gottman, Cole, & Preciado, 2020).

PAUSE & REFLECT

Think about one specific relationship that is important to you. In that relationship, which form of conflict do you experience most often: arguments, disagreement communication, hostile episodes, or pervasive tension?

Conflict Exists at Multiple Levels

As you have seen, there are several different types of conflict. In addition, a single conflict can be seen in many different ways. Consider the example of a conflict that exists between André and his good friend Luke, who both work as servers in a restaurant. Lately, Luke has been asking André to cover for him when he's late and then taking over some of André's tables to make up for the tips that he missed. When André becomes frustrated with his friend, he could think about the conflict in several different ways: as a problematic behavior, as a violation of relationship roles, or as an example of an undesirable trait of Luke's. As summarized in Table 3.1,

TABLE 13.1 Levels of conflict

Level	*Definition*	*Example*
Problematic behavior	The conflict stems from specific actions performed by the other person	André is irritated by Luke's habit of coming to work late and then taking his tables
Relationship roles	The conflict stems from the other person's violations of expectations or norms for the relationship	André is irritated because Luke is violating André's standards for friendship by taking advantage of him
Undesirable traits	The conflict stems from the other person's problematic personality or enduring qualities	André is irritated because Luke is self-centered and doesn't think about his co-workers' needs

André might perceive this conflict in terms of the specific actions that he finds annoying, a violation of his expectations for friendship, or as a sign that Luke is a bad person. As this example illustrates, even a relatively straightforward conflict might be defined in a variety of ways.

Although you might emphasize any of the three levels in your view of a conflict, you are least likely to focus on specific behaviors. In a study of college students' journal entries about conflict, 24% of the entries focused on a partner's behaviors, 38% addressed violations of norms, and 37% emphasized the conflict partner's personal traits (Allen & Berkos, 2005). Does the level at which you define your conflicts matter? The answer is yes. Research shows that people are more aggressive toward relationship partners when they attribute conflicts to that person's personality (Marshall, Jones, & Feinberg, 2011). These findings are especially noteworthy because people often link conflicts to undesirable traits.

Components of Conflict

Because there are many forms and levels of conflict, figuring out what is going on in any particular situation can be difficult. It might help you to keep in mind that conflicts are made up of three properties: disagreement, interference, and negative emotion (Barki & Hartwick, 2004).

Disagreement is the perception that parties have different opinions, values, goals, priorities, or beliefs. On its own, disagreement isn't a

"I do, too, notice the little things, and most of them irritate me."

FIGURE 13.2 It's the little things that irritate me

Source: © Barbara Smaller/The New Yorker Collection/www.cartoonstock.com.

conflict. Two people might be fans of different baseball teams and disagree about which team is best. Likewise, members of a family might have different political values, vote for different presidential candidates, and disagree about the importance of voting. Although these disagreements might contribute to interpersonal or family conflicts, the differences of opinion in themselves are not conflicts. Interpersonal conflicts emerge only when disagreement is combined with the other two components.

A second component, interference, refers to the perception that one person's interests, goals, or outcomes are being negatively affected by another person. You probably encounter interference in a variety of ways as you go through your day. Did your friend show up late to a study session? Did your boss give someone else the extra shift you were hoping to work? When the other components of conflict aren't present, these experiences are just the inevitable disruptions that occur in an ordinary day. When combined with the other conflict components, troubles coordinating your life with a partner can be at the root of relationship problems.

Negative emotion is the component of conflict that includes all the bad feelings – anger, frustration, tension, hostility, jealousy – associated with another person. Conflicts typically involve two types of negative emotions: hard emotions, such as anger or aggravation, and soft emotions, including sadness and hurt (Sanford, 2012). Of course, you can also experience negative feelings about somebody when you aren't having a conflict. For example, you might feel guilty that you haven't spent more time with your family, disappointed that your romantic partner didn't win a scholarship, or sad about a parent's failing health. As these examples illustrate, negative emotions are not themselves experiences of conflict.

Figure 13.3 shows how the three components of conflict combine to create interpersonal conflict. As discussed previously, you might

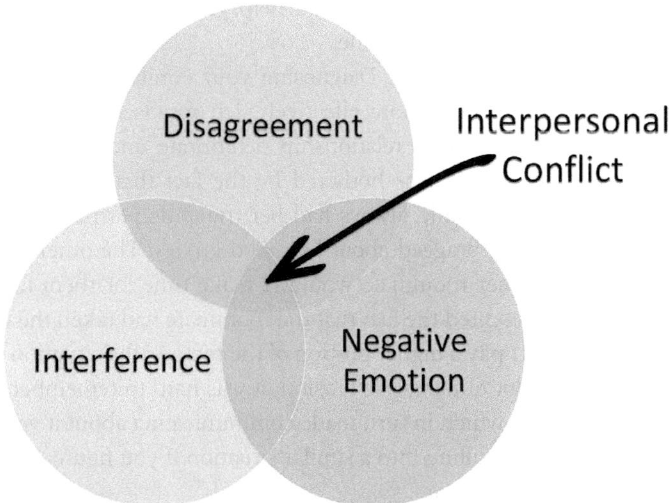

FIGURE 13.3 Components of interpersonal conflict

experience each of these components of conflict by itself; that experience might be intense, but it isn't conflict. You might also experience situations in which only two of the components are present. For example, two athletes competing for a starting position on a team probably disagree about who should be in the starting line-up, and each takes steps to interfere with the other's goal of starting (for example, by striving to improve their own skills). As long as the situation isn't tainted by bad feelings, the situation is better described as a rivalry, rather than a conflict. Interpersonal conflict, then, arises in situations where disagreement, interference, and negative emotion are all present. More specifically, **interpersonal conflict** exists when two people recognize that they hold different opinions, beliefs, or values; they see those points of disagreement as sources of interference in their lives; and the situation evokes negative emotions.

Interpersonal Conflict
A situation in which people disagree with each other, interfere in each other's lives, and experience negative emotions.

PAUSE & REFLECT

Based on your experiences, which component of conflict do you think contributes the most to making your conflicts challenging?

Putting Theory into Practice: Understanding Your Conflicts

Conflicts can take a variety of forms, you can perceive them in different ways, and they involve a combination of disagreement, interference, and negative emotion. This knowledge can help you to make sense of the conflicts that occur in your own life.

Diagnose your conflicts. Diagnosing your conflicts can help you communicate about them more effectively. Jen recalls how two of her friends in college saw their relationship deteriorate once they became roommates. One woman was bothered by the fact that her roommate left dirty dishes in the sink, always had her romantic partner spend the night, and frequently bragged about her good grades. The other woman was bothered that her roommate wouldn't make time for them to hang out together and resented the fact that the roommate had taken the larger bedroom but didn't pay a higher portion of the rent. As the situation escalated to include a lot of pervasive tension, it was hard to remember what caused the conflict, which in turn made communicating about it very difficult. You can avoid falling into a similar situation if you figure out what your conflict is really about.

COMMUNICATION IN ACTION 13.1

Diagnosing Your Conflicts

This exercise will help you diagnose the level and form of a recent conflict. Complete the form on the companion website to diagnose a recent conflict. Keep this exercise in mind when you are confronted with a new conflict, so that you can communicate with a better understanding of your situation.

Focus on behaviors, rather than traits. Conflicts can be easier to talk about when you link them to specific behaviors, rather than to a person's traits. Consider how you might confront a friend who was late for an appointment with you – again. If you focus on your friend's traits, you might find yourself saying something that attacks your friend's identity ("You're such a slacker – you're always late"). This approach would probably prompt your friend to defend themself; after all, the only other option is to accept this negative quality as true. In contrast, consider what might happen if you focus on the behavior itself ("You tend to be about ten minutes late every time we agree to meet, and it bothers me"). A statement like this focuses squarely on the specific behaviors that are causing the conflict, and it lets your friend know how you react. In response, your friend might explain their behaviors, agree to change, or apologize. Although a focus on behaviors won't always prevent an argument, you open the door to better conflict outcomes when you avoid attacking the other person's personality.

Unravel conflicts one component at a time. Because interpersonal conflict is a blend of disagreement, interference, and negative emotion, you can improve a difficult situation by targeting these components one at a time. Removing just one component from the equation can make the situation more manageable.

- To undo a disagreement, identify deeper values that you and a conflict partner have in common. For example, even if you and members of your family disagree about which candidate to vote for, you can appreciate that you share a strong sense of civic duty.
- Restructure your activities to keep a disagreement and negative emotions from interfering with your own goals. If you and a friend have heated arguments about the rival football teams that you support, find other shared interests and don't spend your weekends together watching the games.
- Manage negative emotions by enjoying the predictable, humorous, or positive aspects of a situation. In a recurrent and upsetting conflict,

you might marvel at the consistency of the problem, make a joke about the situation, or keep in mind how your relationship compares favorably to others.

By finding points of agreement, reducing opportunities for interference, or managing your negative feelings, you can transform an interpersonal conflict.

MANAGING CONFLICT

One of the most difficult communication tasks we all face is managing interpersonal conflicts so that we achieve our goals for the interaction. In this part of the chapter, you will learn about the different goals you might have during conflicts, the communication strategies you can use to manage conflict, and the reasons you might prefer some strategies over others.

Conflict Goals

Conflict Goals
The outcomes a person hopes to achieve at the end of a dispute.

In Chapter 12, goals were defined as end-states or outcomes toward which a person strives. **Conflict goals** refer to the outcomes a person hopes to achieve at the end of the dispute. The goals that people have when they experience interpersonal conflicts are summarized in Table 13.2 and discussed in the following paragraphs.

Instrumental Goal
The tangible outcomes or resources people hope to achieve through conflict.

Perhaps the most obvious conflict goal is to obtain certain resources or benefits. This conflict goal is called the **instrumental goal**, and it refers to the specific or tangible reasons for a conflict. A person's instrumental goal can involve just about any kind of resource – two siblings might battle over the family PlayStation or the largest piece of pizza; an employee and a supervisor might disagree about wages, hours, or health benefits; roommates might want to renegotiate the distribution of household chores. Instrumental goals are objective and measurable resources that people hope to retain or gain through conflict.

Relational Goal
The type of relationship people want to have with a partner once the conflict is ended.

Another type of conflict goal, the **relational goal**, concerns the type of relationship people want to have with a partner once the conflict is ended. For example, you may want your parents to respect your independence and allow you to make your own decisions. Even if you don't have a particular relational goal in mind during a conflict, your relationship can be affected by the conflict. For example, although classic research suggests that the first big fight between partners in a dating relationship can reveal insurmountable differences and lead to a break-up or it can leave partners feeling closer to each other (Siegert & Stamp, 1994), more recent research suggests that conflicts can be critical events that undermine closeness in mother-son relationships (Morman & Whitely, 2012). In general, then, your relational goal includes your desire to decrease, maintain, or increase intimacy – or other relationship qualities – after a conflict.

TABLE 13.2 Types of conflict goals

Goal	*Definition*	*Example*
Instrumental	Specific or tangible resources or benefits a person hopes to gain or retain	In a conflict with a parent, a son wants permission to go camping with friends
Relational	The type of relationship a person wants to have with a partner at the end of the conflict	In a conflict with an employee, a manager wants to gain the employee's trust and respect
Identity: Self	The self-image that a person wants to project or protect during a conflict	In a conflict with a doctor, a patient wants to demonstrate intelligence, expertise, and an ability to make treatment decisions
Identity: Other	The self-image that a person wants the partner to have at the end of the conflict	In a conflict with a student, an instructor wants to promote the student's confidence and self-esteem
Process	The steps or rules for conflict management that a person wants to follow	In a conflict within an online support group, a person wants to discourage flaming and other inappropriate remarks

FIGURE 13.4 Students protest against gun violence in schools at the March for Our Lives rally in Chicago

Source: Photo by Anadolu Agency/Getty Images.

Self-identity Goal
How a person hopes to be perceived by other people after the conflict.

Other-identity Goal
How a person hopes a conflict partner will be perceived after the conflict.

Process Goal
How a person prefers to communicate about conflict.

You might have goals for how you see yourself or for how your partner sees him- or herself. The **self-identity goal** in a conflict situation refers to how a person hopes to be perceived by other people after the conflict. If you have ever worried that someone might think you were mean or weak after a conflict, these worries reflected your self-identity goal in that situation. You may also have an other-identity goal during conflict: a goal for how the other person perceives him or herself after the experience. For example, you might want a partner to recognize her flaws, or you might want to protect a conflict partner's self-esteem.

The **process goal** highlights your preferred way to manage conflict. Process goals surface in your beliefs about how people should behave during conflict. Within a specific conflict episode, research shows that the expectations people have for how intense an argument will be correspond with emotional upset and personal attacks during that interaction (DiPaola, Roloff, & Peters, 2010). More generally, children exposed to their parents' aggressive conflict management behaviors are more likely to portray escalation as the normal course of such conflict (Grych, Wachsmuth-Schlaefer, & Klockow, 2002). On the other hand, people in dating relationships typically expect partners to behave affectionately and not try to have everything their own way during conflicts (Ebesu Hubbard, 2001). Likewise, in business relationships, people believe that success and conflict resolution require trust or refraining from opportunistic behavior (Edelenbos & Klijn, 2007). You may not always be aware of your process goals during a conflict, but they reflect important standards for how to behave. In fact, married people who have optimistic views of their marriage – who expect that problems will be managed cooperative – are more disappointed in their relationship following negative conflict interactions (Farnish & Neff, 2020).

PAUSE & REFLECT

What behaviors would violate your rules about how people should behave during conflict?

In all likelihood, you strive for more than one of these goals in any given conflict. Evidence to this point comes from a study in which people described their goals as they reviewed a video of their conflict interaction with a dating partner (Samp, 2013). This study showed that people are most often focused on expressing their interests and needs, but that their goals shift considerably over the course of a conversation. Moreover, goals are reflected in communication, such that self-oriented goals give rise to self-focused language, but a relational goal leads people to use more partner-focused language. In turn, using self-focused messages prompted a partner to keep focused on their self-focused goals, but addressing the relationship through communication on a particular speaking turn increased the likelihood that that partner would shift attention to relationship goals.

COMMUNICATION IN ACTION 13.2

Recognizing Your Conflict Goals

Keep a journal each day for two weeks in which you record any conflicts that you experience. After each journal entry, note whether you were concerned about instrumental, relational, self- or other-identity, or process goals during that conversation. Do you notice any patterns in your priorities when you experience conflict? Do your conflict goals depend on your relationship with each conflict partner?

Conflict Strategies

Chances are you pursue your conflict goals by using a variety of verbal and nonverbal communication techniques. Perhaps you show anger through facial expressions or tone of voice, your verbal messages might criticize a partner or express good will, or you might change the topic. Your **conflict strategy** is your overall plan for how you will communicate about a conflict.

Conflict Strategy
An overall plan for how you will communicate about a conflict.

One option for managing conflict is to approach the situation as a competition and the other person as your opponent. This approach, called a distributive conflict strategy, involves actively confronting a person with the goal of destroying his or her position. Distributive conflict often includes criticism, expressing anger, justifying your own point of view, and denying the other person's claims. A distributive conflict strategy is considered a "win–lose" approach, because you try to win the battle by defeating your opponent. People tend to use a distributive conflict strategy when they are focused on instrumental and self-identity goals (Keck & Samp, 2007). Distributive communication behaviors are also common when people have feelings of hostility, irritation, or anger (Guerrero, Trost, & Yoshimura, 2005; Knobloch, 2005). In addition, people are more likely to use distributive strategies in work-group conflicts that occur online versus face-to-face (Zornoza, Ripoll, & Peiro, 2002).

Distributive Conflict Strategy
An approach that involves competing with a conflict partner to obtain personal goals and to undermine the partner's outcomes.

In contrast, an **integrative conflict strategy** is a cooperative approach to resolving conflict. This strategy, which is also known as a "win–win" approach, emphasizes working with the other person to find a mutually satisfying solution. Doing so requires asking questions ("What are you feeling?" "What's important to you?"), as well as providing honest answers, so that each person's point of view is understood. When using

Integrative Conflict Strategy
Cooperating with a conflict partner to identify a mutually satisfying solution.

an integrative conflict strategy, you strive to understand and respect the other person's perspective, not to discredit that person. Perhaps not surprisingly, integrative behaviors are more likely when dating relationships are intimate, rather than casual (Knobloch, 2005), and when people are concerned about supporting a partner's identity (Keck & Samp, 2007). In addition, working groups employ more positive conflict strategies when they communicate face-to-face rather than online (Zornoza et al., 2002).

Avoidant Conflict Strategy
Limiting communication with a conflict partner about a problematic situation.

A third option is to use an **avoidant conflict strategy**. Conflict avoidance can be considered a "lose–lose" approach to conflict, because you don't care if either partner wins. Instead, conflict avoidance involves attempts to limit communication about a conflict with the person involved. People avoid conflict by withholding complaints, suppressing arguments, and declaring controversial topics off-limits (Roloff & Ifert, 2000). To suppress arguments, people pretend to agree with the other person, minimize the problem, or even walk out on a conversation. Avoidance is a risky strategy, because it does not solve the problem, but it can be useful in some situations (see Table 13.3). Conflict avoidance is neither inherently good nor bad – like any conflict strategy, its effectiveness depends on your goals and circumstances.

PAUSE & REFLECT

Which conflict strategy did you use in your last major conflict? Did that approach help you achieve your goals for that conflict?

Conflict Styles

Conflict Styles
Trait-like tendencies to think about problems in particular ways and to respond to problems with particular behaviors.

Because individuals tend to manage all of their conflicts in more or less the same way, some researchers believe that a person's approach to interpersonal conflict is a personality trait. **Conflict styles** are trait-like tendencies to think about problems in particular ways and to respond to problems with particular behaviors. In other words, your conflict style captures the goals that you typically have and the conflict strategies that you typically use.

Conflict styles vary on two dimensions: how much people tend to their own goals, and how much people attend to the goals of others (see Figure 13.5). Some people pursue their own goals eagerly and assertively, while others care less about getting what they want for themselves (vertical axis). Similarly, some people focus on making sure the other person is satisfied, whereas others don't worry about their conflict partner's outcomes (horizontal axis). Based on these two dimensions, there are five primary conflict styles (originally identified by Rahim, 1983; see also Parmer, 2018).

TABLE 13.3 When to use conflict avoidance

Conflict avoidance is not an effective way of resolving the cause of a conflict, but it can reduce arguing and avoid damage to a relationship in some circumstances. Here are some guidelines for using an avoidant conflict strategy effectively.

Conflict avoidance requires substantial tolerance
If you decide to avoid communication that might resolve a conflict, you need to be able to agree to disagree and to put up with circumstances that might annoy you. If you can't put up with a situation without being bothered, conflict avoidance isn't the best choice for you.

Conflict avoidance requires other coping strategies
If you decide to let a problem persist, you need to find something positive to balance your negative feelings. Strategies like thinking about how a relationship is better than your alternatives or having fun together can make it easier for you to put up with the conflict you're avoiding.

Conflict avoidance should be used selectively
Reserve your use of conflict avoidance for situations that are relatively minor, have few practical consequences, and don't involve values that are important to you. If a situation has a big impact on your life, disrupts your activities in significant ways, or involves values that you hold dear, conflict avoidance may not be a good long-term strategy.

Conflict avoidance requires other communication skills
Conflict avoidance doesn't mean you totally avoid a controversial topic. When the issue comes up, you will have to respond with verbal and nonverbal messages. Make sure you have the ability to deflect conversations gracefully, and use positive communication behaviors to keep the unresolved problem from souring other aspects of your relationship.

Conflict avoidance requires perspective-taking and individual problem solving
If you decide to avoid conflict, you close yourself off to opportunities to learn about your partner's point of view and to work with that person on a solution. To compensate, you need to be especially skilled at thinking about the other person's perspective on the conflict. You also need to be able to work out a solution to the problem on your own.

Adapted from Roloff & Ifert (2000)

People with a **dominating** conflict style tend to confront problems for personal gain. This conflict style is also called "competing" because people with this orientation try to get as much as they can for themselves at a conflict partner's expense. For people with a dominating conflict style, winning is a priority and conflict is exhilarating, whereas losing represents weakness and a loss of status. Dominators have great faith that their position is right, so they feel justified in confronting – and correcting – other people. For these reasons, people with a competing style tend to

Dominating
A conflict style that involves confronting problems, competing with a partner, and trying to win.

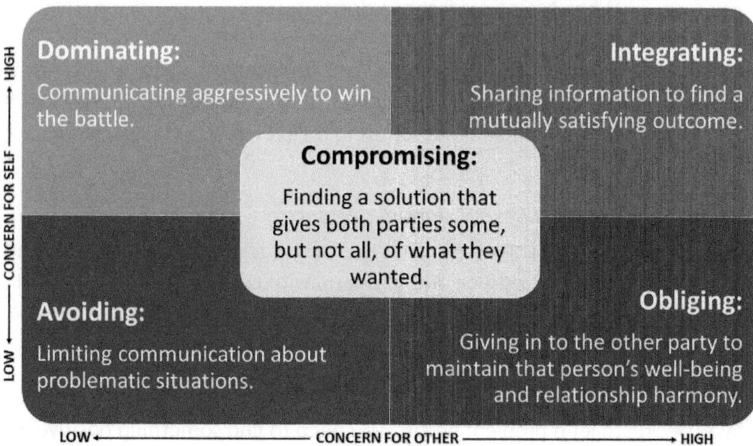

FIGURE 13.5 Conflict styles

use a distributive conflict strategy; they bolster their own position and attack the other person's arguments, even if it means distorting the truth. For someone with a dominating conflict style, conflict is a battle in which only one party can be victorious.

Integrating
A conflict style that involves collaborating with a partner to find a solution that is satisfying to everyone.

People who try to satisfy both their own goals and their partner's have an **integrating** conflict style. This style is also called "collaborating" because people work with a conflict partner to find the best possible solution for both parties. Moreover, integrators try to find the underlying cause of a conflict so that they can identify a long-term solution. People with this style encourage open and honest disclosures from everyone involved; they try to understand the situation fully and address the problem to everyone's benefit.

Obliging
A conflict style that involves accommodating or giving in to a conflict partner's needs and desires.

Some people are content to let problems slide, because they are focused on the well-being of the other person and their relationship. This **obliging** conflict style, also known as "accommodating," involves prioritizing the other party's goals. Obligers tend to believe that disagreement communicates a lack of closeness or affection and runs the risk of hurting or offending the other person. Given this viewpoint, people with this style try to smooth over differences, downplay conflicts, and focus on positive aspects of their relationships. In general, the obliging style involves a low commitment to the person's own conflict goals and a high commitment to helping the other person get what they want.

Avoiding
A conflict style that involves trying to limit communication about a conflict situation.

People with an **avoiding** conflict style pay limited attention either to their own or their partner's goals. People with this style tend to dislike discussing conflict because they think that such a conversation is unpleasant, useless, or even dangerous. The prospect of talking about a conflict can even make people with this conflict style feel physically ill! Given these views and reactions, avoiders protect themselves by physically withdrawing from conversations about conflicts, keeping their complaints to themselves, or pretending to agree with the other person.

In the middle of the grid is **compromising**. People with this style tend to believe that conflicts escalate because each partner wants too much. Accordingly, they keep conflicts in check by trying to find a balance between their own priorities and the other party's goals. Compromisers are comfortable talking about conflicts, but they don't like to see arguments get out of control or go on too long. Their goal is to find the middle ground where both parties get some of what they want. Although compromising might seem like a way to please everyone, it is dissatisfying to people who have other conflict styles. In particular, dominators would be frustrated with a less-than-total victory, integrators would feel that they hadn't found the very best solution, obligers would worry that the other person was unhappy, and avoiders would dislike being forced to address the conflict. A compromiser's ability to address a problem, split the difference, and then let it go is a unique conflict style, not a merging of the other four styles.

Compromising
A conflict style that involves finding a middle ground where both parties get some of what they want.

PAUSE & REFLECT

Which conflict style do you think it would be hardest for you to learn? Can you think of times when that conflict style would be useful to know?

As you might expect, your style during a conflict interaction affects how your partner perceives you. Within organizations, people are perceived as more competent when they engage in cooperative rather than competitive conflict behavior (Garcia, Munduate, Elgoibar, Wendt, & Euwema, 2017). In healthcare settings, cooperative conflict management helps medical staff perceive conflict as constructive, rather than a destructive process amplified by time constraints, power differences, and role conflicts in patient care (Kim, Nicotera, & McNulty, 2015). More generally, research suggests that your conflict style is noticed by others, and you are evaluated accordingly (Guerrero & Gross, 2014). Although every style might have its time and place, people who show a concern for others are generally evaluated more positively.

HOW DO YOU RATE? 13.1

Conflict Styles

Visit the companion website to complete Rahim's Organizational Conflict Management Inventory (Rahim, 1983), which will reveal your personal conflict style. What outcomes does your conflict style generally produce during interpersonal conflict?

Culture, Gender, and Conflict Management

Although conflict styles are similar to personality traits, they are also related to a person's culture and gender. One study examined 36 different investigations that tested for culture and gender differences in conflict styles (Holt & DeVore, 2005). Combining the results across the set the studies revealed some interesting conclusions. The study found that people from individualistic cultures are more likely to have a dominating conflict style, whereas people from collectivistic cultures are more likely to have avoiding, compromising, and integrating conflict styles. In addition, within individualistic cultures, females are more likely to have a compromising conflict style and males are more likely to have a dominating conflict style.

Let's focus on the two conclusions that highlight cultural differences in conflict management. When people from the United States, which is generally an individualistic culture, engage in conflict, they may be comfortable expressing demands, criticizing each other, and arguing assertively. Those behaviors would be considered inappropriate or out of line in a collectivist culture, such as China, where people expect conflicts to be handled more delicately and cooperatively. What might happen when people with such different cultural norms have a disagreement? The individualist comes off as rude and aggressive, while the collectivist seems weak or disinterested in solving the problem. Both parties might be doing what they consider to be best, but they are quite possibly offending each other.

Gender differences in conflict management within individualistic cultures create the same problem we saw for conflict between two cultures: One person's dominating style might be offensive to someone who prefers compromising, and a compromising approach might be seen as selling out by a partner who prefers to engage conflict fully. When these expectations align with gendered norms, they affect how people are perceived when they break from the cultural script. How would you react to a woman using a dominating style? And what if you interacted with a man who was compromising? Because gender-based expectations affect how people evaluate men and women, people who don't follow the norms for

FIGURE 13.6 Former British Prime Minister, Teresa May, engaged in diplomatic talks with Afghanistan's former President Ashraf Ghani.

their assumed gender can be judged negatively. In these ways, gendered norms for conflict management both shape and constrain how people handle conflicts.

PAUSE & REFLECT

Is your conflict style similar to or different from the ways that people in your culture tend to manage conflict?

Putting Theory into Practice: Expanding Your Options

Managing conflicts is one of the most difficult communication challenges you face. Fortunately, you can improve your conflict skills by focusing on your goals, adapting your conflict strategies to fit particular situations, and keeping your conflict style in mind.

Plan for multiple goals. Chances are you'll have a mix of instrumental, relational, identity, and process goals in any conflict. If you focus only on the most noticeable or strongest goal, you might end up losing something else that also matters to you. On the other hand, keeping all of your goals in mind can help you find positive solutions even when conflicts are serious. A good example comes from a woman who rented part of her house to Denise many years ago. This woman had been dating a man for several years, and they got married when her daughters moved out of the house. Just six months later, the moving van was back and a divorce was in the works. Apparently, the new husband's young children were an unexpected source of stress. Was this the end of the relationship? Surprisingly, no. The newly divorced couple continued to date from their separate homes, and several years later – when his children were older – they remarried. By focusing on the specific source of the conflict, and keeping their other goals in mind, this couple managed to resolve a serious disagreement while maintaining a relationship that they clearly valued.

Match your strategies to your goals. Once you have a clear idea of your goals for a conflict, choose conflict strategies that match those objectives. Table 13.4 shows how different conflict strategies might match up with particular conflict goals. In the table, an arrow pointing up means that the conflict strategy promotes the goal, while an arrow point down means that a strategy can make a goal more difficult to achieve. As you think about all of your goals for a conflict, try to use the strategy that maximizes the outcomes that you care about.

Branch out from your conflict style. You aren't locked into your conflict style – any person can enact all of the different conflict styles. Rather than being trapped by your own particular approach, work to develop your repertoire of responses to conflict.

TABLE 13.4 Conflict goals and strategies

CONFLICT STRATEGIES	*Instrumental*	*Relational*	*Other-Identity*	*Self-Identity*	*Process*
Distributive	↑ You can improve your chances of winning	↓ You can damage your relationship	↓ You might hurt the other person	You can seem strong and confident, but also mean or unreasonable	You stick to your beliefs, but could violate standards for fairness
Integrative	↑ You can improve your chances of winning	↑ You can improve your relationship	↑ You show that you value the other person	↑ You appear reasonable and cooperative	↑ You express your beliefs and listen to others
Avoidant	↓ You decrease your chance of winning	You can avoid damaging the relationship, but you also miss the opportunity to improve it	You can avoid harming the other person, but you also miss the opportunity to express your appreciation	You can appear uncommitted to important issues, but you might seem easy going	↑ You prevent an unpleasant interaction from occurring

(Column group heading: *Conflict goals*)

COMMUNICATION IN ACTION 13.3

Building Your Conflict Toolkit

This exercise helps you role-play various conflict situations using each of the different conflict styles. Complete the activity on the companion website to reflect on how you would manage each of the conflict scenarios using different strategies.

CONFLICT DYNAMICS

Our discussion of conflict styles highlighted the general approach a person might take when managing a conflict. Communication about conflict is also affected by your perceptions of the particular situation, how much power you have with respect to your conflict partner, and the messages you get from your partner about the conflict. Because these factors often make a conflict situation worse, understanding them can help you manage conflicts more effectively.

Attribution and Escalation

As described in Chapter 4, attributions are the explanations you create for why something happened. In the context of interpersonal conflict, attributions are the judgments you make about who is responsible for the disagreement. Do you remember the two key attribution biases discussed in Chapter 4 – the fundamental attribution error and the actor-observer effect? These biases describe our tendency to explain other people's actions in terms of internal causes (the fundamental attribution error), and our own behavior in terms of external causes (the actor-observer effect). In other words, you might think your grouchy roommate is an ill-tempered person, but your own grouchiness is because you didn't get enough sleep last night. In a conflict situation, people are even more likely to show these biases.

Attribution biases are clearly documented in research on interpersonal conflict. In marriages, each spouse tends to see the other person as the source of the conflict, and each attributes his or her own behavior to good intentions, circumstances, or stress (Schütz, 1999; see Figure 13.7).

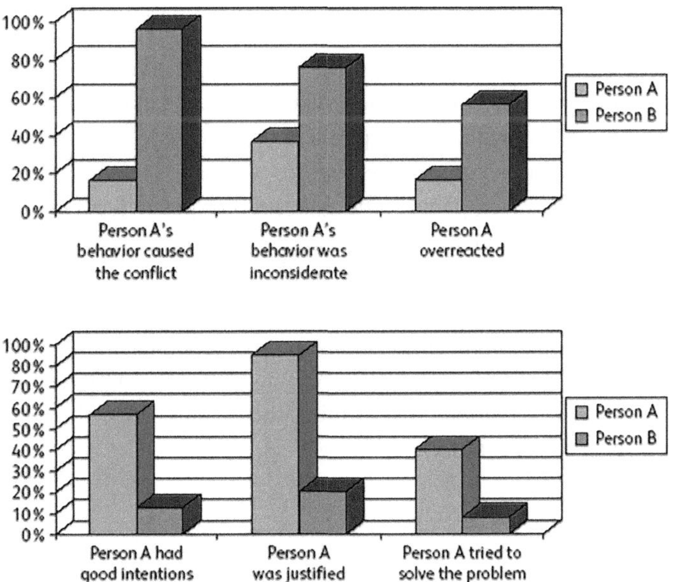

FIGURE 13.7 Biased accounts of interpersonal conflicts. These graphs are based on the results of Schütz (1999), a study that examined the stories that married partners told about the same conflict. The numbers reflect the percentage of stories that contained each element. Notice how people are unlikely to say that they caused the conflict, were inconsiderate, or overreacted, but they often describe their partner in those roles. Likewise, people describe their own good intentions, justify their actions based on the circumstances, and report trying to solve the problem much more than they give similar credit to their partner

Parents are also more likely to see their children's hurtful behavior as blameworthy, deliberate, and self-centered (while excusing their own hurtful acts; McLaren & Sillars, 2014). As a result of these biases, two partners in a conflict can end up with very different accounts of the same dispute.

What effect do these attributions have on a conflict? When people blame the other person for the conflict, they tend to use a distributive conflict strategy (O'Leary et al., 2007; Smith Slep & O'Leary, 2007). After all, if the other party is undeniably wrong, why wouldn't you point out his or her errors and misconceptions. And if you are innocent of any wrongdoing, why wouldn't you demand what you rightfully deserve without compromising? Unfortunately, if each person thinks that the other person is at fault, parties can become locked in an escalating conflict.

SCHOLAR SPOTLIGHT

Visit the Communication Café on the companion website to view a conversation with Michael Roloff, a leading scholar who has studied power, conflict, and conflict avoidance.

PAUSE & REFLECT

Can you recall a time when you and a conflict partner had very different perceptions of your disagreement? Looking back, to what extent were attribution biases fueling that conflict?

If conflicts escalate when people blame each other, what happens when they overcome these biases? The evidence on this point is very clear: empathizing with conflict partners promotes constructive problem solving and reduces competitive conflict behavior (de Wied, Branje, & Meeus, 2006). In fact, people who take another person's perspective are less likely to be dominating and more likely to prefer either integrating or compromising to manage their conflicts (Corcoran & Malinckrodt, 2000). Having concern for another person's goals also promotes more constructive and cooperative problem solving (Halpert, Stuhlmacher, Crenshaw, Litcher, & Bortel, 2010). Although attribution biases are common in conflict situations, overcoming them can change the course of your interpersonal conflicts.

Interpersonal Power
The ability to affect both one's own outcomes and another person's behaviors, attitudes, and outcomes.

Dependence Power
The influence one person has when he or she is willing and able to end a relationship with a partner who is committed to that union.

Punitive Power
The influence people gain when they are perceived as likely to lose their temper or behave aggressively.

The Chilling Effect of Power

Interpersonal power, the ability to affect both one's own outcomes and another person's behaviors, attitudes, and outcomes, is another force that shapes how conflicts unfold. Within interpersonal relationships, power comes in two primary forms: **dependence power** and **punitive power** (Worley, 2017). When one person is willing and able to end a relationship, they gain dependence power over a partner who is committed to that union. A dependent person might worry that a partner will end the relationship and therefore the dependent person relinquishes control to that partner. Punitive power refers to the influence people gain when they are perceived as likely to lose their temper or behave aggressively. Because people want to avoid this type of punishing behavior, they yield to a potentially aggressive partner. People who possess interpersonal power are free to choose what they want to talk about, how topics are discussed, and how conflicts are resolved.

In the context of an ongoing relationship, power exerts a chilling effect on complaints, such that people keep their feelings to themselves to avoid provoking their partner. In dating relationships, people withhold the most irritations from partners who are perceived to be uncommitted to the relationship and to have good dating alternatives (Solomon & Roloff, 2019). Even in laboratory-induced conversations, dating partners are more likely to avoid a conflict topic when they anticipate that their partner will react negatively (Afifi, McManus, Steuber, & Coho, 2009). Likewise, children keep secrets from parents, in part, because they depend on their parents for so many things (Afifi & Olson, 2005). When people have experienced aggression within their family, they are more likely to conceal secrets from members of their family, and they consider themselves less able to communicate about sensitive topics (Afifi, Olson, & Armstrong, 2005).

PAUSE & REFLECT

What kind of power does each member of your family have? How does power affect the way family members communicate with each other?

Why does power tend to suppress conflict communication? In one study of conflict avoidance in the workplace, university employees gave a number of reasons why they don't voice complaints (Barsky & Wood, 2005):

- Avoidance is the norm in the organization.
- The benefits of complaining are not worth the costs.
- Complaints might not be kept confidential.
- People are resigned to the situation.
- The people in charge are indecisive.
- The problem will resolve itself with time.

In addition, people perceive potential problems as less serious when their partners have power over them (Samp & Palevitz, 2014). In other words, power has two different effects: it can directly inhibit complaining, and it can lead people to perceive a situation in ways that encourage them to avoid conflict.

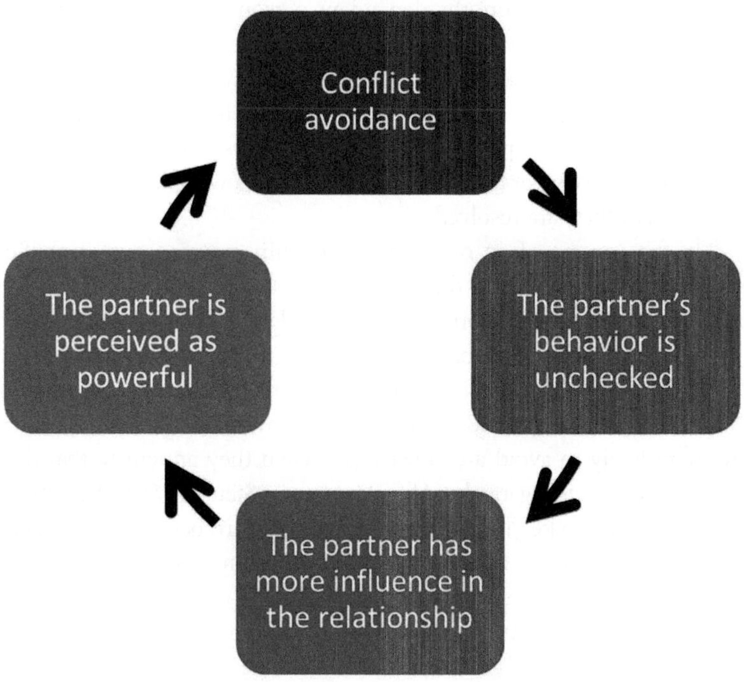

FIGURE 13.8 The cycle of power and avoidance

The chilling effect of power can create a vicious cycle in a relationship (see Figure 13.8). If we begin at the left side of Figure 13.8, we see that a person who perceives a partner to be powerful is more likely to avoid conflict. When complaints are not expressed, the partner's problematic actions go unchecked. As a result, that partner enjoys greater freedom to behave as he or she pleases and to set the terms of the relationship. They can also invest energy in other relationships and might get away with more aggressive behavior. Until something happens to correct the power imbalance, the powerless partner will have less and less effect on the course and conduct of the relationships.

Communication Patterns

Conflict interactions frequently begin when one person voices a complaint. If the partner responds positively, the issue might be resolved then and there. In contrast, conflicts escalate when a partner rejects the complaint and the person who complained questions the rebuttal (Laforest, 2002). In this section, you'll learn about three patterns of conflict behavior: demand/withdraw, reciprocity, and forgiveness. Understanding these patterns can help you recognize when your interpersonal communication is fanning the flames of conflict or leading you to resolution.

Demand/withdraw communication. A common conflict communication pattern is demand/withdraw (Caughlin & Reznik, 2016). The sequence begins when one partner demands something from the other, for example, "You need to take the garbage out more often!" The demand may be for change in behavior, agreement with a position, or even just attention during the discussion. In response, the partner withdraws from the conversation by not answering or not paying attention. The withdrawal prompts the demander to become more assertive, and the persistent demands prompt the withdrawer to become more withdrawn. Perhaps not surprisingly, married couples who engage in demand/withdraw communication are less satisfied with their relationship than couples who do not. Similarly, demand/withdraw communication between parents and adolescent children has been linked to dissatisfaction with the relationship and even with drug abuse by both parents and children. Thus, demand/withdraw communication is typically a destructive pattern in an ongoing relationship.

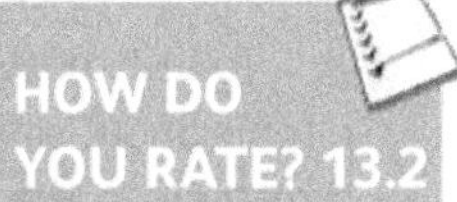

HOW DO YOU RATE? 13.2

Self-Efficacy and Conflict Communication

Visit the companion website to complete a scale that measures whether or not you feel you can express complaints to a relationship partner. If your score is high, do you find that you frequently engage in conflict with this person? If your score is low, are there things you could do to improve your confidence in your ability to express conflict?

PAUSE & REFLECT

Have you ever been involved in a demand/withdraw interaction in an ongoing relationship? How did that communication experience affect that relationship?

INSIDE COMMUNICATION RESEARCH

The Resolvability of Serial Conflicts with Shifting Goals

Serial arguments occur when individuals consistently engage in arguments or disagreements about the same recurring topic. The goals that people have for these repetitive conflicts can set the tone for the interaction and determine whether or not partners can make progress on resolving the argument. Tim Worley and Jennifer Samp (2018) examined how the salience of particular goals shifted over the course of a conflict interaction and how changes in people's goals corresponded with the perceived resolvability of the disagreement. When people believe that an argument can be resolved they tend to engage in more productive conflict tactics and experience less personal and relational harm as a result of the conflict. People can have prosocial goals for conflict, which are goals that support the partner and protect the relationship, or self-focused goals, which emphasize the pursuit of one's own interests, needs, and outcomes in the conflict. The researchers argued that people who have a prosocial goal for a conflict and whose prosocial goals increase over the course of the interaction are more likely to see the argument as resolvable. In contrast, people are less likely to see their conflict as resolvable to the extent that they start with a self-focused goal or their self-focused goals become more salient over the course of the interaction.

To test these assumptions, the researchers had 76 opposite-sex romantic couples identify a topic about which they had frequent serial conflicts and have a recorded conversation about that topic in the researchers' laboratory. After completing the interaction, the partners were taken to separate rooms to view the recording of their conversation and to rate the importance of different goals that they had at one-minute intervals. The participants also completed a survey about the perceived resolvability of the conflict.

The researchers analyzed how each person's goals during the interaction corresponded with their own perceptions of the resolvability of the conflict and their partner's perception that the conflict was resolvable. Results showed that when people had prosocial, partner-focused goals for the conflict, and when those goals increased over the course of the interaction, they rated the conflict as more resolvable, but their partner did not necessarily see the argument as more resolvable. In contrast, as people increasingly prioritized self-focused goals over the course of the conflict episode, both they and their partner perceived the argument as less resolvable. In other words, approaching conflict with concern for the other person makes conflicts seem more resolvable, but approaching arguments with self-centered motivations can make resolvability feel out of reach.

THINK ABOUT IT

1. This study focused on increases and decreases in the importance of different goals over the course of a conflict episode. How might the dynamics of a conflict interaction make some goals seem more or less important? How does a partner's behavior during the conflict influence conflict goals?
2. Serial conflicts are likely to seem less resolvable over time, because the longer the argument persists the harder it is for partners to find common ground. To what extent are serial conflicts unresolvable due to the centrality and stubbornness of self-focused goals in these encounters? How might a greater emphasis on partner- or relationship-focused goals reduce the prevalence of serial arguments?

How can you avoid the pitfalls of demand/withdraw communication? Check out the conversation in the Real Words box. As this cohabiting couple discusses money problems, Angie accepts the complaint against her. Even when she explains herself, she does so in a way that expresses agreement with the problem Daryl raises. In return, Daryl is willing to acknowledge that the problem only happens once in a while. By avoiding demand/withdraw communication, the couple fosters agreement about the situation, rather than discord.

REAL WORDS

AVOIDING DEMAND/WITHDRAW IN A CONFLICT DISCUSSION

This transcript comes from a study where romantic couples were asked to identify and discuss sources of irritation in their relationship.

DARYL: Spending money ... like a crazy lady.
ANGIE: Sometimes ... I know. I, I, I agree with that.
DARYL: Like whenever, spending money, significant amounts of money uncontrollably.
ANGIE: Not uncontrollably. Just spontaneously.
DARYL: Spontaneously.
ANGIE: It's not uncontrollably.
DARYL: It is. It only happens once in a while though.
ANGIE: Yeah. I mean this weekend I hadda go buy a new outfit for the wedding. But we spent 70 bucks on a shirt and tie for you the other week. You know, it's okay for me to spend 70 bucks on a whole new outfit, shoes and all. I mean, yeah, it was more money than we have right now, but... I do know what you're talking about though. Like an $800 bed on the spur of the moment.
DARYL: And on the car. I thought you jumped on that too fast. I didn't even get to look at it before you were like, "Yeah, I wanna buy it." You already bought it before I even saw it.
ANGIE: Well, I thought we'd agreed that it wasn't gonna be ours, and then afterwards we'd agreed that it was, and now I regret that because the car's too small for you. Way too small. Hell, it's almost too small for me.

Reciprocity. Another pattern that can escalate conflict is reciprocity, which involves matching a partner's behavior. Reciprocity occurs whenever you respond to a partner's behavior with an action that conveys a similar message. Here are some destructive patterns that can emerge from reciprocity during conflict discussions:

- *Complaint/Counter-complaint.* One person's complaint about a partner prompts the partner to complain in turn. For example, "You never do the dishes" begets "You never walk the dog."
- *Proposal/Counter-proposal.* One person's recommended outcome prompts the other person to recommend a different outcome. For example, "We should save money by eating out less" begets "We should save money by carpooling."
- *Attack/Counter-attack.* One person's insult prompts the other person to respond with an insult. For example, "I've never really liked you" begets "I think you're boring."

As you might expect, this kind of reciprocity can intensify a conflict. In fact, partners in abusive marriages often respond to each other's negative emotions by becoming more emotional themselves (Malik, Heyman, & Smith Slep, 2020). In the business world, being aggressive and insulting can actually serve to motivate your opponent to be more competitive, less cooperative, and cheat (Yip, Schweitzer, & Nurmohamed, 2018).

Forgiveness. One more conflict dynamic merits mention. Forgiveness is the communication process by which partners transcend the

TABLE 13.5 Forms of forgiveness

Form	*Definition*	*Messages*
Explicit forgiveness	Performing a speech act that clearly conveys closure to the conflict	I forgive you
Forgiveness through discussion	Reviewing the reasons for the conflict and the beliefs and values involved, and reaching a mutually acceptable definition of what happened	I can understand what you were thinking when you did what you did. I was thinking about it differently. I can see that we didn't see the event the same way
Nonverbal forgiveness	Using behavioral cues to communicate solidarity after the conflict	Eye contact, gentle touching, head nods
Conditional forgiveness	Specifying that acceptance of the situation is contingent on certain requirements	If you'll promise never to do something like this again, I'll forgive you
Forgiveness through minimization	Communicating that the issue is trivial or unimportant	It's no big deal really. It's nothing to worry about

disagreement, interference, and negative emotions that define a conflict. As shown in Table 13.5, forgiveness can take five different forms (Waldron & Kelley, 2005). Forgiveness is explicit when a person says, "I forgive you." Forgiveness also occurs through discussion when partners use verbal messages to identify and accept a shared understanding of the situation. Sometimes, forgiveness is expressed nonverbally by cues such as eye contact, facial expressions, and head nods. When people tie resolution of the conflict to a requirement, such as a promise to behave better in the future, they have granted conditional forgiveness. People might also forgive through minimization, which means that the conflict partners have characterized the problem as trivial or unimportant. Research shows that explicit forgiveness and nonverbal forgiveness tend to strengthen relationships, but conditional forgiveness is associated with the deterioration of intimacy (Waldron & Kelley, 2005).

Putting Theory into Practice: Promoting Healthy Conflicts

Attribution biases, the chilling effect of power, and typical communication patterns can complicate efforts to communicate effectively and resolve conflicts. Now that you know about these common dynamics, you can take steps to overcome them in your own life.

Question your attributions for conflict. To help overcome attribution biases, think about how both your partner's behavior and your own actions might be contributing to the conflict. Then, focus on what you can control – your own behavior – as you look for ways to change the conflict dynamics. For example, if you and a roommate battle over access to the shower in the morning, maybe you can reduce the tension by changing your routine. Similarly, consider the ways in which the situation is constraining options and alternatives for you and your partner. Are your conflict behaviors shaped by the fact that you're under a lot of pressure at work, low on cash, or worried by a family crisis? How might factors like those be contributing to your partner's behavior in this conflict? If you can think about how the context is intensifying your conflict, you might identify strategies for changing your circumstances so that you both have more choices. Finally, look for and appreciate your partner's efforts to resolve the conflict, and help your partner recognize your own efforts on that front. Even when those attempts at resolution fail, knowing that you are both doing your best can create good will between you.

Keep your power in check. If you have power in a relationship you may be creating an environment in which your partner can't speak freely. It's important to remember that you might be doing things that annoy your partner that you aren't even aware of. Keep track of how power dynamics might be leading you to avoid serious conflicts, but also when your own power advantage is silencing someone else.

COMMUNICATION IN ACTION 13.4

Knowing Your Own Strength

This exercise will help you to reflect on the amount of power you have in your relationships and how you wield your power during conflict. Complete the form on the companion website to reflect on how you typically handle conflicts in relationships where you have different levels of power. How does your power affect your communication behavior during conflicts with each partner?

De-escalate, rather than escalate, conflict. What can you do to break the demand/withdraw or reciprocal cycles that escalate conflict? Table 13.6 lists some specific communication moves you can use to keep a conflict from getting out of control.

TABLE 13.6 Alternatives to conflict escalation

When your partner ...	*You can escalate conflict by ...*	*Or you can de-escalate conflict by ...*
Demands *You have to clean up after yourself*	Withdrawing *Leave me alone!*	Engaging *Let's talk about it. What would you like me to do differently?*
Complains about you *You are so uptight – can't you just relax?*	Counter-complaining *Well, you're just plain lazy!*	Asking for details *What exactly am I doing that bothers you?*
Proposes a solution *We could get take-out Chinese*	Making a counter-proposal *We could go to that new restaurant downtown*	Considering the proposal *Chinese is always good, especially if we want to eat at home*
Attacks you *I can't believe I'm dating someone as awful as you*	Lodging a counter-attack *You're no prize either!*	Acknowledging feelings *You must be feeling pretty bad right now; I can see you're upset*

SUMMARY

Learning to manage conflicts is an important part of interpersonal communication, but conflict communication isn't a straightforward process. Conflicts may take several different forms, including arguments, disagreeable communication, periods of hostility and pervasive tension. You may experience conflict because of another person's behaviors, because a person violated relationship rules or norms, or because you perceive a personality flaw in another person. At their core, however, all conflicts essentially boil down to disagreements, involve interference in your goals and activities, and are accompanied by negative feelings.

As you prepare to communicate about a conflict, keep in mind that there are a variety of goals, strategies, and styles that may surface in your interaction. Within any particular conflict, you may have instrumental objectives that you want to achieve, alongside relationship qualities that you hope to promote or maintain, preferences for how you and your partner enact your identities, and rules of conduct that you hope to follow. As you weigh these goals, you might draw upon distributive, integrative, or avoidant conflict strategies. Remember, too, that some people tend to manage all of their conflicts using a particular conflict style. Whether someone engages in dominating, integrating, obliging, avoiding, or compromising could have as much to do with their personal preferences as with the particulars of the conflict at hand.

Once you are in a conversation about a conflict, be prepared for a number of dynamics that might unfold. Remember that attribution biases are especially common in conflict situations. In all likelihood, your partner's perceptions about the conflict are very different from yours, and these differences often cause conflicts to escalate. Interpersonal power also affects how forcefully people communicate during conflict; in fact, a person's power can prevent a partner from even voicing concerns or complaints. Your conflict discussions are also subject to dynamics that unfold from one speaking turn to the next. Demand/withdraw communication and reciprocating negative messages can be especially harmful in the context of ongoing relationships. On the other hand, forgiveness can be a powerful tool for moving beyond conflict.

Despite their complexity, you can communicate effectively when conflicts surface in relationships that you care about. Take time to figure out what kind of conflict you are having. In addition, focus on behaviors, rather than a partner's undesirable personality, and try to address the components of the conflict one at a time. Consider all of your conflict goals, and tailor your conflict strategies to those goals. Although your conflict style might be familiar to you, be sure that the style you generally prefer is a good match for the particular conflict you face. Once you are engaged in a conflict discussion, work to overcome the ill effects of attribution biases, power, and escalatory patterns of communication. With effort, you can use your communication skills to manage your conflicts and promote the well-being of your interpersonal relationships.

ACTIVITIES FOR EXPLORING COMMUNICATION ETHICS

What Would You/Should You Do?

Imagine that you have started a new job. After only a few weeks, you realize that your supervisor regularly comes to work late, spends her time in the office playing computer games, and consistently passes her responsibilities on to you. The situation isn't fair, and you're doing more work than you planned on when you took the job. You never have any downtime to rest or eat lunch, and you're required to work significantly more hours than you expected. Although you are frustrated with the situation, you also recognize that your supervisor has the power to fire you or to withhold desirable resources, such as bonuses, vacation time, or salary increases. What would you or should you do in this situation?

Something to Think About

Consider an especially messy conflict that a student in Denise's class shared a few years ago. Caitlyn had been in a serious car accident over winter break and she couldn't return to campus for spring semester. She couldn't take care of business, such as paying bills, because she was in a coma. Caitlyn's roommates were very supportive throughout her recovery, but months later they told her she owed them hundreds of dollars for her share of the rent. Caitlyn was shocked by the request (as well as unable to pay it) and her roommates were equally shocked that she expected a free ride. With each side seeing the situation so differently, their conversations over the phone were typically heated. Each side accused the other of dishonesty and inappropriate behavior, and finally Caitlyn stopped answering their phone calls or returning their text messages. Eventually lawyers were called in, and the case went to court. What kind of communication behaviors do you think escalated this conflict and what messages could have made the conflict less extreme?

Analyze Communication Ethics Yourself

Conflicts are continually unfolding all around you in your community. Perhaps there is a contentious issue dividing your local school board, a controversy about campus expansion, or a disagreement between a big landlord and your city government. Identify a conflict going on in your community and gather together newspaper articles and public relations about it. As you review the information in these accounts, look for attribution biases, expressions of power, and the types of language that tend to escalate conflict. Based on your analysis, what ethical standards were and were not met as the parties involved communicated about the conflict?

KEY WORDS

argument
avoidant conflict strategy
avoiding
compromising
conflict goals
conflict strategy
conflict styles
dependence power
disagreeable communication
distributive conflict strategy
dominating
hostile episode
instrumental goal
integrating
integrative conflict strategy
interpersonal conflict
interpersonal power
obliging
other-identity goal
pervasive tension
process goal
punitive power
relational goal
self-identity goal

LEARNING OBJECTIVES

After reading this chapter, you should be able to:

1. Describe the nonverbal behaviors that communicate support.
2. Identify characteristics of supportive verbal messages and different strategies for providing comfort.
3. Describe how conversations produce support and comfort.
4. Recognize some of the most effective ways to support cancer survivors and people grieving the death of a loved one.
5. Improve your ability to provide support to others.

PUTTING THEORY INTO PRACTICE

In this chapter, you will learn how to:

1. Communicate nonverbal immediacy.
2. Focus on feelings.
3. Practice perspective-taking.
4. Help the speaker clarify thoughts, feelings, and ideas.
5. Recognize how you can help other people support you.
6. Focus on what you can do to make life easier.
7. Don't overreach if you can't find the words.

COMMUNICATING COMFORT AND SUPPORT

14

Source: Getty Images/Tom Pennington.

When former U.S. President George H. W. Bush passed away in November 2018, just eight months after the death of his beloved wife, Barbara Bush, many people said he died of a broken heart. Although George and Barbara Bush lived long, distinguished lives and enjoyed a deeply loving marriage of 73 years, losing both the matriarch and patriarch of the Bush family in such a short span of time took an emotional toll on those who loved them. At Bush's funeral, his son, former President George W. Bush, gave a touching and emotional eulogy recounting stories of his father's adventurous spirit and good humor, sharing examples of his optimism and empathy, and illustrating the deep and unconditional love the elder Bush had for his wife, children, and grandchildren. Hundreds of people attended the funeral to pay their respects to the former President and offer condolences and support for the Bush family, including many important politicians, dignitaries, and elected officials. At one point, former President Barack Obama and his wife Michelle Obama were seen offering comfort to an emotional George W. Bush through messages of care and compassion, outstretched arms and gentle hugs, and displays of empathy. Grieving the death of a loved one is one of the most challenging aspects of the human experience, which calls upon friends and family to provide support and comfort for the bereaved. Knowing what to say and how to effectively provide comfort during these difficult times can be immensely helpful for those who have lost a loved one.

How would you respond if a friend told you about an upsetting situation, such as the death of a loved one, a fight with a romantic partner, a tense climate at work, or a medical problem? At the funeral of George H. W. Bush, Barack and Michelle Obama showed all of the hallmarks of effective comforting and supportive behavior: they showed empathy for the grief the family was experiencing, demonstrated understanding of the enormity of the family's loss, and offered quiet and gentle gestures of comfort to those who were grieving. Producing these kinds of messages is challenging, so you might struggle to find the right words or actions when someone needs your support. You might also find it hard to get support from others when you are upset. What are the benefits of meeting these challenges? When you comfort a friend, family member, or romantic partner, you promote that person's emotional, mental, and physical well-being. And when you talk about your own feelings of distress, you may leave the conversation feeling empowered to address your problems or at peace with a difficult situation. In this chapter, you'll learn about supportive communication, ways that people differ in their comforting communication, and contexts in which support is especially important.

PAUSE & REFLECT

Think about the last experience you had that left you feeling upset, frustrated, or anxious. How did you communicate with others about that experience, and how did those communication experiences affect your feelings about that event?

PROVIDING COMFORT

What can you say to make a person feel better about a bad situation? What can you do to comfort someone and show that you care? Messages of support and comfort can take a variety of forms. A hug or a sympathetic facial expression goes a long way. A thoughtful comment or attentive conversation can bring comfort. And through computer-mediated communication, people seek and provide support in forms as varied as text messages, comments on Facebook newsfeeds, and engagement with online support groups (High & Solomon, 2011). In this section, we examine nonverbal and verbal messages that provide support, and we identify some communication behaviors that can make a bad situation worse.

Nonverbal Support Messages

When you want to comfort another person, nonverbal behaviors can be as helpful as carefully chosen words. Many people automatically produce supportive nonverbal messages in response to a distressing situation. For example, you might find yourself mirroring the facial expressions of a communication partner as you empathize with his emotions, or you might automatically reach out to touch a friend who is upset. You can also communicate support through **nonverbal immediacy**, which is the involvement and warmth suggested by behaviors like being physically close, leaning forward, having an expressive face, looking a person in the eyes, and touching.

Nonverbal Immediacy
The involvement and warmth a person communicates through physical closeness, leaning forward, facial expressions, eye contact, and touching.

Several communication studies show the benefits of nonverbal immediacy in supportive conversations (e.g., Jones & Wirtz, 2006). In these studies, participants discussed something upsetting with someone who seemed to be another participant, but who was actually a confederate of the researchers. Sometimes confederates showed a high level of nonverbal immediacy by leaning forward, moving closer to the participant, orienting their body to face the other person, increasing eye contact, and using warm vocal tones. Other times the confederate showed very little nonverbal immediacy by leaning back in their chair, increasing physical distance, turning their body away from the participant, reducing eye contact, refraining from animated facial expressions, and generally appearing bored or tired. Which type of behaviors do you think produced the most comfort? Participants felt better about their circumstances and rated the confederate as more helpful and skilled at providing comfort when the confederate displayed high levels of nonverbal immediacy.

PAUSE & REFLECT

How does it make you feel when someone appears to be bored, uninterested, and uncaring when you're talking about a distressing situation?

Empathy
The ability to feel a vicarious emotional response that mirrors the emotional experiences of others.

One interpersonal communication skill that enhances a person's ability to provide nonverbal support strategies is the experience of **empathy** – the ability to feel a vicarious emotional response that mirrors the emotional experiences of others. When you empathize with another human being, you actually share his or her emotional experiences. In fact, when people observe emotions, their brains show patterns of activation revealing that they themselves are experiencing an emotional response (see Figure 14.1).

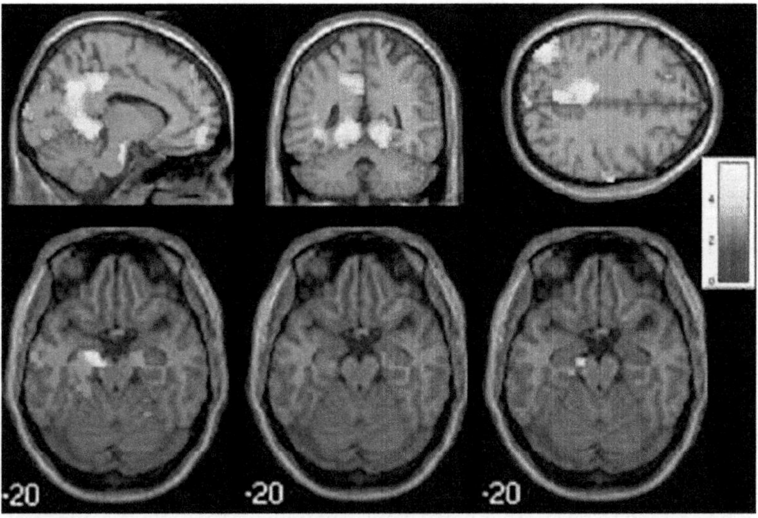

FIGURE 14.1 Brain activation and empathy: The top row shows three different views of brain activation as participants look at videos of people happy to see a familiar face. The bottom row shows, from left to right, activation in part of the brain that registers emotion as participants saw videos of people who were happy to see a familiar face, witnessing an unpleasant situation, and looking at an unusual image. In this image brighter colors indicate stronger brain activation

Source: Powers et al. (2007). Used with permission.

In other words, when your friend is happy, elated, or joyful, you might share in her enthusiasm and pleasant emotions. If your friend is sad, distressed, or dismayed, you might take on similar negative emotions. When you experience the same negative emotions as your partner, you are likely to mirror that person's facial expressions and body postures. And because matching a partner's nonverbal behaviors indicates warmth and involvement, empathy is an important skill in the provision of nonverbal social support.

SCHOLAR SPOTLIGHT

Visit the Communication Café on the companion website to view a conversation with Wendy Samter, who conducted groundbreaking research on supportive communication.

Verbal Support Messages

Like nonverbal messages, verbal messages communicate more or less warmth, interest, or responsiveness to an interaction partner. Verbal messages can also provide specific content that addresses different aspects of a difficult situation. In this section, we consider the tone, content, and orientation of the verbal messages you might use to provide comfort or support.

Person-centered messages. Supportive messages are characterized by **person-centeredness**, which means that they validate, recognize, or acknowledge the recipient's feelings and experiences. Table 14.1

Person-centeredness
A quality of messages that validate, recognize, or acknowledge the recipient's feelings and experiences.

TABLE 14.1 Examples of high, medium, and low person-centered messages

High person-centered messages	I can imagine this is a really hard time for you, I'm really concerned about you and how you must be feeling right now
	I know you were really hoping for a different outcome and I'm sorry things didn't turn out the way you expected them to
	Whenever you feel like talking about it I'm here to listen to you
Moderately person-centered messages	Most things happen for a reason, even if you can't see it at the time. Maybe it's for the best
	Let's go to the movies to take your mind off things for a while. I was in a similar situation once and everything worked out just fine
Low person-centered messages	I don't know why you're so upset. This really isn't that big of a deal
	You shouldn't take things so personally all the time. Don't let this get you down
	Just get on with your life and keep yourself busy
	You know, you're probably partially to blame for this situation. Have you thought about that?

categorizes verbal support messages based on how person-centered they are (e.g., McCullough, 2019). Comforting messages that are highly person-centered explicitly recognize and legitimize the recipient's feelings, help the recipient describe feelings, promote efforts to explain those feelings, and help the recipient see upsetting experiences in new ways. Moderately person-centered messages demonstrate an implicit recognition of the other's feelings by expressing sympathy and distracting attention from the situation. Messages that are not person-centered deny, criticize, or challenge the recipient's feelings.

Do some of the responses in Table 14.1 seem better to you than others? People rate highly person-centered messages as the most sensitive and effective means of providing emotional support, and they see low person-centered messages as the least comforting (High & Dillard, 2012). Highly person-centered communication is effective because it makes explicit a support provider's intention to be helpful, offers reasons why a person should feel better, and shows an interest in the conversation and the other person (Priem & Solomon, 2018). By being attentive to your communication partners, you give them the time and attention necessary to address and resolve their problems.

Take a look at the transcript in the Real Words box. This conversation came from a study Denise conducted in which married partners discussed sources of distress that they were experiencing (Priem, Solomon, & Steuber, 2009). Notice how the conversation begins with the wife describing her concerns about her mother-in-law, while her husband tends to neglect those concerns. As the conversation develops, though, the wife's guilt about not doing enough comes through, and her husband responds by validating both her feelings and her actions. Notice how his messages become more person-centered as the conversation progresses.

REAL WORDS

VERBAL MESSAGES OF SUPPORT

KRISTA: What's stressful to me is the demands of aging and elderly parents and relatives and that sort of thing that people that need things from us and we're not uh, we're not located close enough.

CALEB: Yeah, but we can offer just so much help in that way. I don't know how much help we can be to my mother. We've talked about this already.

KRISTA: I guess I think that we need to continue to follow up with her. She's not real good about getting in touch with us or letting us know when she's having issues come up. It's usually that we'll call her and then she'll say, out of the blue, "Oh, I keep getting these bills from the hospital" or "This Medicare hasn't settled with this provider yet" or...

CALEB: Usually when we call she has something of that sort.

KRISTA: Right. But it seems like she doesn't call us and ask so I'm wondering where she is getting ... I suppose it's possible that she's taking care of these things on her own but unlikely given what we know about her. She was so reliant on your father.

CALEB: I wouldn't say that... So. So I, see, I'm making an assumption that, okay, well, these things are going to work out because she's going to have to address them.

KRISTA: My concern is what will happen if she becomes ill or unable to care for herself, what choices and decision we'll have to make then.

CALEB: Well, my sister will go down there and make all the decisions ... which I guess is another stressor.

KRISTA: Maybe she has the time, I just don't know if she has the expertise. And she might decide that it was too expensive or too whatever, too difficult to have someone come in.

CALEB: So what would we do then?

KRISTA: One of us would go down, I think, and help make a joint decision. And I guess it should probably be you. But I, I worry about... I didn't have a lot of fun when you were down there when your dad died, in the winter with the blizzards and the sub-zero temperatures, trying to keep my life together, and having a number of people point out that I really should have been there. I'm not sure what I was supposed to do with our minor child that goes to school. The stress comes from just not being real sure what my role is in these, you know, situations.

CALEB: Well, I've – I didn't criticize you and I thought you made the right choice. Do you feel guilty about it? I mean, that's, that's part of it, right?

KRISTA: Sure. I should have been there.

CALEB: Well, I can imagine feeling that way, but you made the right choice.

Topics of support messages. The topics we discuss when communicating with someone in distress also vary considerably. Suppose you learned that a close friend was having serious marital problems. Would you give advice, listen attentively while your friend complained about the marriage, give them the number of a good divorce lawyer, offer your couch as a place to sleep, or remind your friend about all of his or her great qualities as a person? These are all supportive messages, even though they address different topics. **Informational support** involves giving advice or pointing out facts that can help a person cope. **Emotional support** messages focus on how a person is feeling and try to make that person feel better. When people offer **network support**, they try to link someone in distress to others who can help. **Tangible support** means providing practical aid – such as driving someone to the emergency room. Finally, **esteem support** involves pointing out positive personal qualities to build people up so they can better handle difficulties. Table 14.2 gives examples of these types of support messages.

All of these types of support can help a person in distress, but not every type of support helps every person and every situation (Crowley, High, & Thomas, 2019; Wang, 2019). Getting advice from someone

Informational Support
Messages that give advice or point out helpful facts.

Emotional Support
Verbal messages that focus on how a person is feeling and attempt to make that person feel better.

Network Support
Messages that link someone in distress to others who can help.

Tangible Support
Practical aid that addresses the source of a person's distress.

Esteem Support
Messages that point out positive personal qualities.

TABLE 14.2 Examples of support messages.

The pandemic caused by COVID-19 wreaked havoc as people throughout the world coped with both efforts to slow the spread of the virus and the effects of being sick, which ranged from minor symptoms for some people to lethal respiratory distress for others. As many of us found ourselves caring for people infected by the virus, here are some support messages we might have used.

Message	*Example*
Informational	It's a virus, so there isn't much you can do to cure it. Just be sure to get a lot of sleep and fluids. Pain relievers can help too, and sucking on hard candy can make your throat feel better.
Emotional	It must be so hard to fall behind in your classes and to feel like there's nothing you can do. It's okay to be upset about that. You aren't alone in this, and you can tell me how you are feeling.
Network	A friend of mine had COVID-19 last month. I'm going to have him call you to tell you how he got through it.
Tangible	There's a lot I can do to help – go to the store for you, talk to your professors, walk your dog – you just name it.
Esteem	Everyone knows what a good student you are. Once you are feeling better, I know you'll catch up in your classes in no time.

who does not have any experience with your problem can be annoying (Feng & MacGeorge, 2006). Being asked to focus on your feelings can seem like a waste of time when you need practical help. Network support can introduce you to someone helpful, but it can also feel like your friend handed you off to a stranger. Tangible support can be insulting when you are able to meet your needs on your own. And esteem support can seem insincere when you think you are the source of your own troubles. As the cartoon in Figure 14.2 illustrates, support that doesn't match your needs isn't helpful.

PAUSE & REFLECT

What type of support strategy would you prefer to receive if you were coping with the break-up of a romantic relationship, getting turned down for a summer internship, or a grandparent's death? How would you feel if you received one of the other types of support instead?

"Go ahead. Tell me your troubles. I promise to say 'Awww' in all the right places."

FIGURE 14.2 When you're not getting the type of support you need

Source: William Haefeli/The New Yorker.

How can you figure out what sort of support to provide to someone? Take time to figure out what your interaction partner might be looking for. We call this kind of effort **perspective-taking** – the ability to understand a situation from someone else's point of view. Skilled communicators notice how others are feeling and responding to messages, and they know how to adapt their communication to produce the desired effect. Jen recalls how an old friend used to comfort her during times of distress by saying, "Well, it is what it is." Although he probably found comfort in the philosophical notion that we should accept what we cannot change, he failed to recognize Jen's perspective. Because she likes to feel like she controls and understands a situation, Jen finds messages that provide advice ("Here are some ideas for solving the problem") or insight ("I wonder how much this happens to other people in your situation") more comforting. The survey in the How Do You Rate? 14.1 box can help you to understand your own preferences for support, which is a starting point for recognizing the unique support preferences of others.

Perspective-taking
The ability to understand a situation from someone else's point of view.

Supportive communication strategies. We've seen that one way to categorize support messages is by the topic they focus on. Another way to think about verbal support is to focus on supportive communication strategies: whether people communicate about a problem, and whether they focus on feelings or solutions. In Figure 14.3, the horizontal axis shows how directly a person addresses a problem (whether the person talks about the problem explicitly and in detail or avoids talking about it). The vertical axis in Figure 14.3 differentiates between problem-focused

HOW DO YOU RATE? 14.1

Preferences for Types of Support

Although the types of support you want can depend on the specific situation, people often have a general preference for certain support messages. Complete the scale on the companion website to determine your own preferences for support. Which types of support were the most desirable for you? As you reflect on your scores, think about how your own preferences might influence the kinds of support you provide to others.

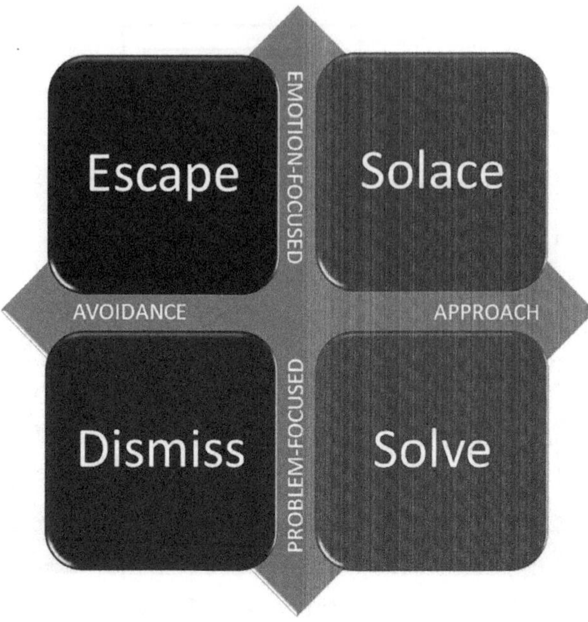

FIGURE 14.3 A typology of supportive communication strategies

versus emotion-focused strategies. People who are problem-focused strive to eliminate the problem that is creating distress. People who focus on emotions try to make the person in distress feel better. These two dimensions, considered together, give rise to four support strategies (Jones & Koerner, 2016):

- Solace: Approach-based and emotion-focused responses to elicit positive feelings and foster intimacy: "I know you've been very sad lately, and I want you to know that I'm here for you if you ever want to talk about how you're feeling."
- Solve: Approach-based and task-focused responses to find a solution to the distressing situation: "I really want to help you fix this situation. What can I do to help?"
- Escape: Avoidance-based and emotion-focused responses: "This is too depressing to even think about, let's go do something fun."
- Dismiss: Avoidance-based and task-focused responses: "You're making way too much out of this problem; just deal with it."

Solace
A support strategy that combines approach-based and emotion-focused messages to elicit positive emotions and foster intimacy.

Solve
A support strategy that combines approach-based and task-focused messages to find solutions to the problem.

Escape
A support strategy that combines avoidance-based and emotion-focused messages to discourage the experience and expression of negative emotion.

PAUSE & REFLECT

When comforting others, do you like to talk about the problem, or do you try to distract from the problem? Do you try to fix the problem or talk about the emotions that underlie it?

Some of these strategies are more sensitive and effective than others. Solve and solace, in particular, tend to produce more lasting benefits to support recipients (Derlega, Winstead, Oldfield, & Barbee, 2003). At the same time, all of them have been observed within both every day and intensely stressful situations (Barbee, Fallat, Forest, McClure, Henry, & Cunningham, 2016). Being aware of your options for providing support can help you be more intentional about the comforting messages you offer to others.

Dismiss
A support strategy that combines avoidance-based and task-focused messages to minimize the significance of the problem.

Ineffective Support Messages

Now that we've seen what makes a support message effective, let's take a look at some messages that are ineffective. Table 14.3 shows common mistakes people make when they try to comfort another person.

Putting yourself first. One of the most common mistakes we make when attempting to comfort others is to offer messages that we would find supportive, without considering whether that approach works for the person in distress. For example, if you find venting a waste of time and only turn to others for solutions, you might find it difficult to be a good listener to a friend who needs to talk about a troubling situation. Effective support requires you to overcome the tendency to do what works for you and put your partner's needs first.

Minimizing or maximizing. Providing effective support also involves finding a balance between failing to react enough and over-reacting. Minimizing messages challenge or undermine the seriousness of the problem. Someone who tries to comfort you in this way might say, "It's not that big of a deal, you have nothing to worry about, this is nothing to get

TABLE 14.3 Ineffective support messages

Support message	*Example*
Putting yourself first	Well, when *my* mom died it was really helpful for people to take me out so that I could forget about it for a while. Let's go to the movies – that should make you feel better.
Minimizing	This isn't that big of a deal. If you really think about it, things could definitely be worse.
Maximizing	I can't believe this is happening to you! You must feel totally helpless. I don't know how you can carry on after this!
Cold comfort	Oh, well, that's really too bad. But I'm sure everything will be fine.

upset over." Maximizing messages overstate the seriousness of the problem and express excessive protection for the recipient. Someone who tries to comfort you by maximizing the situation might say, "This is terrible, you're never going to recover from this, your whole life will be ruined!" Whereas minimizing messages tell people that you don't take their problems seriously, maximizing messages can produce greater distress instead of comfort.

Cold Comfort
Messages that provide limited consolation, sympathy, or encouragement in response to serious distress.

Cold comfort. One of the most ineffective responses to another person's troubles is cold comfort, or limited consolation, sympathy, or encouragement in response to serious distress. Denise still remembers vividly the response she got from a co-worker when her beloved 18-year-old cat was dying of cancer: "I had a cat that died once. Don't worry, you'll like the next cat too." Cold comfort usually involves superficial empathy ("oh, that's too bad"), minimizing messages ("things could be worse"), and oversimplified solutions ("just don't worry about it").

INSIDE COMMUNICATION RESEARCH

The Effects of Support Gaps

Although people can derive many positive benefits from receiving social support, supportive communication that is insufficient or ineffective can do more harm than good. Optimal matching theory suggests that support can have negative outcomes if the type of support provided by a sender is not a good match for addressing the stressor that the receiver is experiencing. When support messages are mismatched to support needs in this way, people experience a support gap. Support gaps can leave people feeling under-benefited when they are not receiving as much support as they need or desire, as well as over-benefited when they are receiving too much support that they don't really want. Being under- or over-benefited in social support are both undesirable and can lead to negative outcomes. Communication scholars Rachel McLaren and Andrew High (2019) examined how being under- or over-benefited in different types of support can produce hurt feelings, which then correspond with lower self-esteem and negative relationship consequences.

The researchers asked people to recall a time when they were going through a stressful experience and someone tried to provide support in a way that was unexpected or undesirable. The participants wrote about the stressful experience, what the support provider said or did in their attempt to be supportive, and how they reacted to this attempted social support. Then, the participants completed a number of survey items to rate this experience in terms of its supportiveness and the feelings they had afterward.

The study showed that people experienced more hurt feelings when they were over-benefited in informational support (i.e., received more informational support than they wanted) or under-benefited in emotional or esteem support (i.e., received less emotional or esteem support than they wanted). In turn, hurt feelings in the context of social support were associated with less improvement in self-esteem and increased perceptions that the relationship was damaged as a result of this encounter. Thus, these findings suggest that being under- or over-benefited when it comes to social support can exacerbate stressors instead of alleviating them.

THINK ABOUT IT

1. Why do you think receiving too much informational support is associated with hurt feelings and negative outcomes? Why is it problematic to be over-benefited with this type of support, but not with other types of support?
2. This study focused on the effects of support gaps on the support receiver. What do you see as the impacts on support providers when they give too much or too little support?

Putting Theory into Practice: Expanding Your Comforting Toolkit

When you try to comfort someone in distress, remember that you have a number of effective supportive messages you can try as well as some messages that you should avoid.

Communicate nonverbal immediacy. When you are with someone who is feeling low, show that you care by staying physically close and making direct eye contact. Stand or sit near your communication partner, lean forward rather than away, orient your body so you are directly facing the other person, and look your partner in the eyes. If it's appropriate for your relationship, you might also place your hand gently on their hand, arm, or back. If you close the distance between you and your partner in these ways, you are literally "being there" for that person in times of need.

COMMUNICATION IN ACTION 14.1

Becoming More Nonverbally Immediate

Practice communicating nonverbal immediacy in some low-risk situations, such as a conversation with a sales clerk, bus driver, or receptionist in an office. In these interactions, turn your body directly toward the person, lean in, make direct eye contact, and display a friendly and expressive face. Notice how people respond when you are more nonverbally immediate. This exercise helps you practice nonverbal immediacy so that you are prepared to help when someone you care about needs you to show concern.

Focus on feelings. People in distress generally find messages that encourage them to talk about their problems and focus on their feelings to be most helpful. Two important lessons follow from this point:

- *Don't avoid conversations about another person's problems* – Talking to a distressed person is helpful even if you aren't quite sure what to say. If you can't talk at the time that a problem is mentioned, set a time and place when you will be able to listen and provide support. Your friends will appreciate the effort that you're making to help them.
- *Explicitly acknowledge how the other person is feeling* – People who are distressed want to be able to vent their frustrations and to feel understood and appreciated, so encourage them to reflect on how the situation makes them feel. Try to avoid relating the other person's experience to a similar situation that you've been through, and do your best to focus the interaction on the other person's feelings and perceptions.

Practice perspective-taking. The key to providing effective emotional support is understanding what kinds of messages the other person would find comforting. Perspective-taking allows you to tailor your support messages to another person's underlying experience.

COMMUNICATION IN ACTION 14.2

Seeing Through Someone Else's Eyes

This exercise will help you engage in perspective-taking. Visit dailystrength.org, which is an online resource that hosts an array of support groups dealing with more than 30 different categories of stressors, including support for anxiety and depression, cancer, infertility, infidelity, adoption, and alcoholism, just to name a few. Select an online support group from this site for a distressing situation that you have no experience with. Read and reflect on five posts from the online message boards for that group and complete the form on the companion website.

SUPPORTIVE CONVERSATION

Now that you know what nonverbal and verbal messages you can use to communicate support, let's take a closer look at how conversations can help make people feel better. Supportive conversations occur when partners engaged in dialogue make a transition from discussing various topics to focusing on one person's stressful experience (Jefferson, 2015). The introduction of a personal problem isn't always easy – it can involve a distressed person bringing up the topic or the partner noticing something isn't right. A supportive conversation unfolds once both partners recognize that their interaction will address one person's troubles.

PAUSE & REFLECT

Whom do you typically turn to when you need support? What characteristics make that person a reliable source for comfort?

Conversationally-Induced Reappraisals

Supportive conversations can help make people feel better by changing the way they think about a situation so that they perceive their circumstances as less stressful. Consider how each of the types of support messages you learned about previously can make a problem seem less bad. Through informational support, a person gives you facts about your problem that will help you cope; for example, Jen's advice about how to perform a complex statistical analysis makes that task less daunting. Through network support, you learn about specific people who can help you solve a problem. Even esteem support, by reminding you of your own resourcefulness, can bolster your capacity to deal with a crisis. As you learned in Chapter 7, how you feel is grounded in your appraisal of a situation; therefore, conversations are supportive when they change your appraisals of your problem.

Conversationally-induced reappraisal theory outlines how conversations convey support by leading people in distress through a series of revelations and insights that change their appraisals of their circumstances and, consequently, improve their emotional state (Holmstrom, 2016). To get to that outcome, partners have to be willing to engage in a conversation that focuses on the upsetting situation, examines the distressed person's feelings and the reasons for them, and explores other ways of thinking about sources of distress. Importantly, support providers can't just jump to the conclusion – if you said, "see, this is no big deal and you shouldn't be upset," you'd be enacting low person-centered support because you are denying the legitimacy of the person's concerns. Instead, supportive conversations unfold sequentially: first, the distressed person needs to be able to describe the problem so that it is clear to both partners, and only then can the partners dig deeper to understand the causes of the problem or the reasons it is upsetting. When this full picture of the situation is made clear, the partners can work together to consider different ways of viewing the situation. In this way, a support provider facilitates – but doesn't dictate – new ways of seeing a problem.

CONNECT WITH THEORY

Visit the companion website to learn more about conversationally-induced reappraisal theory, by Brant Burleson and Daenna Goldsmith, which examines how supportive conversations can improve people's emotional state by helping them view their circumstances in a different light.

Because support outcomes are based on what happens in a conversation, the back-and-forth exchange of messages between partners is key. Research that Denise is involved in looks closely at the content and flow of speaking turns within supportive conversations (Bodie, Jones, Brinberg, Joyer, Solomon, & Ram, 2020). That work identified seven main types of speaking turns that occur in conversations where one person, the Discloser, discusses a source of stress with a partner, the Listener: question, advice, elaboration, hedged (i.e., hesitant) disclosure, acknowledgment, reflection, and uncodable filled pause. Not surprisingly, these speaking turns aren't randomly ordered; rather, one partner's behavior encourages or discourages particular actions on the next speaking turn. For example, Bodie et al. (2020) found that Listeners who engaged in elaboration or disclosure in their turn were likely to be followed by Disclosers who express acknowledgment or ask a follow-up question. This dynamic is noteworthy because, in theory, a conversation in which the Listener does the talking is less likely to help the Discloser to reappraise their troubles.

The Role of the Support Receiver

Whereas you might think the burden of being supportive rests with the support provider, the person in distress plays an essential role in supportive conversations. To begin, people experiencing distress bear responsibility for communicating to others that they would welcome support. When support seekers express their desire for support explicitly, rather than beating around the bush, they are more likely to get the support they want, both in face-to-face (Williams & Michelson, 2008) and online interactions (Youngvorst & High, 2018). Bids for support can be as subtle as a sigh or commenting about a "hard day," or as vivid as posting a plea for "thoughts and prayers" on social media (Buehler, Crowley, Peterson, & High, 2019). Research also suggests that not everyone is inclined to seek support or to do so directly. For example, women and people from families that encouraged open conversation are more likely to seek support directly than men and people whose family emphasized conformity to the family norms (High & Scharp, 2015). Learning how to ask for support when you need it is an important step in reaping the benefits of supportive conversations.

A person who seeks support also has to be willing and able to process the messages that they receive from a communication partner. Put simply, the very best support messages available won't make a difference if the person on the receiving end doesn't do their part. Sometimes, people don't pay much attention to the supportive messages they receive. This can happen when they aren't especially distressed or when they are too upset to pay attention (Bodie, 2012). When people are motivated to participate in a supportive conversation, then the quality of the messages a support provider offers make a difference; but if the motivation isn't there on the part of the receiver, the quality of supportive messages won't matter (Bodie, 2013). For people who are stressed but don't pay attention to support messages, other situation cues – such as the quality of their relationship with the support provider – play a greater role in their conversational outcomes (Holmstrom et al., 2015). And, when situational cues

FIGURE 14.4 Woman comforting a male friend

Source: iStockPhoto.

CONNECT WITH THEORY

Visit the companion website to learn more about Graham Bodie's dual process model of supportive communication, which examines the role of message quality and motivation in shaping a receiver's interpretation of supportive communication.

are muted, such as when supportive messages come through computer-mediated channels, receivers pay more attention to those messages and benefit more from high-quality support (Rains, Brunner, Akers, Pavlich, & Tsetsi, 2016).

Culture Matters

Culture has a pervasive effect on interpersonal communication and comforting interactions are no exception. Because cultural values shape the way people experience and express emotion, the way we communicate about feelings of distress is closely tied to our culture. One especially relevant dimension of culture is the extent to which the community emphasizes the individual or the group. As we discussed in Chapter 2, individualist cultures – such as the United States, in general – value personal goals and encourage independence. In contrast, collectivist cultures, like China, value group goals and emphasize group membership. These differences influence many aspects of support and comforting communication, including the kinds of events people find distressing and how people communicate about distress.

In individualist cultures, distress centers on events that block individual needs, goals, and desires (Mesquita, 2001). For example, personal failure contributes to more frustration and disappointment for European-Americans than for Chinese citizens (Mortenson, 2006). In contrast, people from collectivist cultures tend to experience distress over situations that have negative social consequences or disrupt the well-being of the group (Mesquita, 2001). In fact, individuals from collectivist cultures try to protect their friends and family from their personal problems; for example, they might hide emotions like fear and sadness to avoid burdening others (Mortenson, 2006).

People from both individualist and collectivist cultures prefer messages that are emotionally sensitive to the distressed person (Burleson & Mortenson, 2003). Beyond this preference, however, the cultural groups are quite different in their preferences for supportive communication. People in individualist cultures prefer support messages that help them work through and discuss their feelings (Burleson & Mortenson, 2003). Accordingly, European-Americans are more likely than Chinese to communicate directly with people about their problems and to seek social support when in distress (Mortenson, 2006). In contrast, Chinese people prefer comforters who distract them from their problems or offer solutions that will eliminate them (Mortenson, 2006). These types of supportive messages allow members of a collectivist culture to minimize the disruption within the community that their personal troubles might create (Mortenson, M. Liu, Burleson, Y. Liu, 2006). It's no surprise, then, that Chinese immigrants turn to computer-mediated social support as an efficient means of gaining support in their new community (Chen & Choi, 2011).

PAUSE & REFLECT

What would you say or do to comfort someone from an individualist culture, such as the United States? What if you were trying to comfort someone from a collectivist culture, such as China – how would you change your behavior?

Putting Theory into Practice: Overcoming Obstacles to Support

This section of the chapter highlighted the roles partners having in creating an effective supportive conversation. Consider the following suggestions for adapting supportive messages so that these differences don't become obstacles.

Help the speaker clarify thoughts, feelings, and ideas. Sometimes the key to truly understanding what people are going through is to help them express what happened and how it made them feel. Have you ever felt down or depressed but you couldn't put your finger on what was bothering you? Imagine how helpful it would have been to have someone help you pinpoint the source of your distress by asking questions, paraphrasing what you said, or trying different perspectives on for size. Here are some strategies for helping someone clarify his or her emotions, with examples focused on coping with the end of a romantic relationship:

- *Repeat what the other person says:* "So, you're upset about the break-up, and you're feeling betrayed." Sometimes hearing our own words repeated back to us helps us to identify perceptions and feelings.
- *Paraphrase what you think the person means:* "When I hear you talk about the break-up, it's sounds like you're upset you didn't get a chance to make it work." When you translate another person's message into your own words you add a level of interpretation that might help the person see the situation differently.
- *Share your perceptions of the situation:* "I wonder if you feel cheated, because you weren't told that things were getting so bad until it was too late." Just as perspective-taking can help you be supportive, sharing your perceptions can help a distressed individual see the situation from a different point of view.
- *Ask purposeful questions:* "How did you feel when you found out? Why do you think you reacted that way?" When you help people tap into their underlying emotions and motivations, you can really get to the heart of the matter.
- *Avoid agreeing or disagreeing:* "This is a messy situation, and there's a lot going on here." Fully agreeing with everything a distressed person says can prevent further reflection, and firmly disagreeing can make the person too defensive to talk or reflect.

Be easy to support. When you are experiencing a stressful situation, you can make it easier for people who care about you to help. Make sure you are letting people know that you need support. Remember that indirect support seeking doesn't always make it clear to people that you are stressed or need assistance. In addition, let other people know what you would find helpful. When Denise was going through some challenges at work, she would come home and tell her spouse, "For the next 15 minutes, I'm going to vent, and every time I pause to breathe, you say, 'that's terrible!!'" After she blew off steam, they could turn to helping her figure out what to do or focus on another topic altogether, but if Denise hadn't been clear about the support she needed, her venting might have been shut down by unsolicited advice, producing a much less comforting conversation. Remember, too, that you will benefit most from high-quality support if you pay attention, but even low-quality support can make you feel better if you focus instead on how a friend cared enough to try to help you.

COMMUNICATION IN ACTION 14.3

Seeking the Support You Want

This exercise will help you think about how to be clear when you are seeking support from other people. Complete the form on the companion website thinking about how you might solicit support from someone else. Are there strategies that feel more or less realistic for you? As you reflect on the messages you created, think about whether you are overcoming obstacles or creating them when you seek support from others.

Practice cultural sensitivity. Keep in mind that people from individualist and collectivist cultures may feel differently about emotional distress and emotional support. If you ever find yourself in a situation where you are called upon to comfort someone from a different culture, begin by learning about your communication partner's cultural values. Let's take the example of Shen Ming, a Chinese woman studying in the United States, and her European-American neighbor, Rachel. Rachel discovers that Shen Ming is upset by news from home that her father is ill. If Rachel considers Shen Ming's cultural preferences, she might invite Shen Ming over to watch TV or help her make plans to visit home. By doing so, she focuses on solving the problem rather than on Shen Ming's feelings about it. The Communication in Action 14.4 exercise can help you think about how culture affects everyone's experience of distress and support.

COMMUNICATION IN ACTION 14.4

Appreciating Culturally Diverse Comforting Needs

In this exercise, you will reflect on how people from different cultures might experience distress and create support messages that are culturally appropriate. Complete the form on the companion website by thinking about five experiences you've had giving comfort to someone else and how the situation would have been different if that person was from another culture.

COMFORT WHEN IT COUNTS

What can you say to comfort someone who has just been diagnosed with cancer? How can you help someone who is mourning the death of a loved one? These are times when your actions and words are most important. In fact, people who receive support from friends and family have stronger immunological responses, which can help them fight illness (Uchino, 2006). In this section, you will learn to provide the best support you can in situations when comfort really counts.

PAUSE & REFLECT

Have you experienced a serious stressor – a major illness, the death of a loved one, or a personal tragedy? If not, do you know someone who has? In your experience, what messages provide support in those extreme circumstances?

Coping with Cancer

A diagnosis of cancer can cause severe emotional trauma to the patient and their family. People feel vulnerability, loss of control, and uncertainty about their future (Jabloo et al., 2017). Two different coping processes allow people to deal with both the practical and emotional sides of serious illness. **Problem-focused coping** emphasizes controlling the illness and making sense of complex medical information. **Emotion-focused coping** emphasizes controlling negative reactions to the illness and managing emotional distress. To cope with illness at both levels, patients must interact with a social network that includes family, friends, doctors, nurses, and other health-care professionals.

Problem-focused Coping Addressing a difficult situation by focusing on understanding and resolving it.

Emotion-focused Coping Addressing a difficult situation by focusing on controlling the negative feelings and distress that it generates.

Three types of support discussed previously in this chapter are especially beneficial to cancer patients: emotional support, informational support, and tangible support (Arora, Rutten, Gustafson, Moser, & Hawkins, 2007). Providing emotional support might involve telling the patient how much you care about him and reminding him that you'll always be there

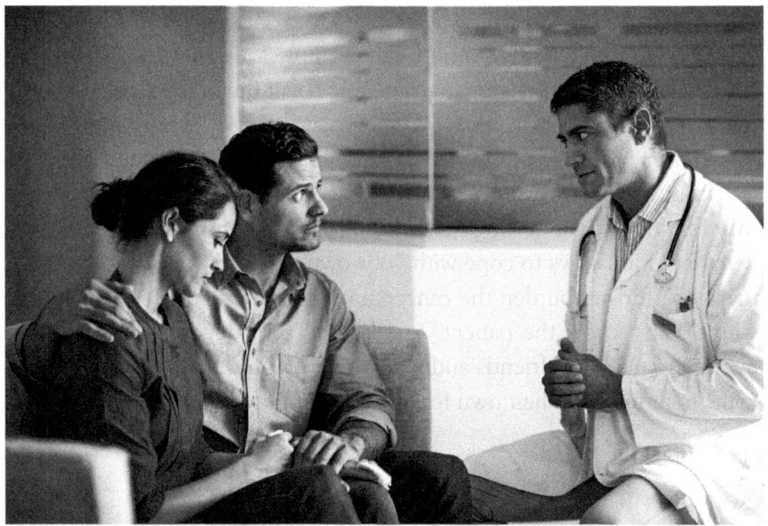

FIGURE 14.5 A couple receives news from a doctor

Source: iStockPhoto.

for him. Providing informational support might involve helping to locate and interpret medical information. Tangible support might include watching the person's kids for a weekend, cleaning the house, running an errand, or providing transportation to radiation treatments. One study of adolescents coping with cancer revealed that they receive a tremendous amount of informational and emotional support through online support groups (Elwell, Grogan, & Coulson, 2011). Among the topics that adolescents discussed in their online forum were concerns about cancer treatments, losing friends, and struggling in school. The informational and emotional support that the adolescents received from their peers online was an important tool for coping with their illness. In general, participating in online support groups to cope with illness contributes to increased social support, decreased depression, increased quality of life, and increased self-efficacy to manage one's health condition (Rains & Young, 2009).

People with cancer often do not get the support they want and need. One study examined online support groups and discussion boards established for breast cancer survivors to identify sources of distress (Weber & Solomon, 2008). Many women described the difficulties they had in getting support from others and their feelings of isolation. For example, one woman wrote, "People that I thought were once friends ... stopped phoning and even when I would meet them ... they shunned me ... They acted as though I was not there" (p. 554). Another lamented, "I don't think anyone really knows what we go through unless they walk in our shoes" (p. 554). Perhaps people who are cancer-free want to distance themselves from the illness or have difficulty understanding what a cancer patient is going through. And although friends and family are often supportive immediately after a diagnosis of cancer, all forms of support decrease significantly just five months after the initial diagnosis (Arora et al., 2007).

Your own emotions about a friend or loved one's diagnosis may actually prevent you from offering support. For example, women with breast cancer say that it can be challenging to tell people about their diagnosis because of the strong reactions others have to their news (Weber & Solomon, 2008). The cancer patient's goal may be to disclose her diagnosis and get comfort from someone close to her, but as soon as she mentions cancer, she may find herself comforting her loved one! What can you do to break this dynamic? Find ways to cope with your own reactions to someone's illness that don't further burden the cancer survivor, such as talking to someone who doesn't know the patient. In addition, provide tangible support by offering to tell other friends and family the news, so that those people can come to terms with their own feelings without relying on the patient.

Bereavement

The death of a loved one is a universal experience that is often shared with others. Family members, friends, and acquaintances of the deceased collectively grieve the loss, so understanding how to provide comfort in this context is an important social skill. Grief management strategies are types of emotional support designed to cope with extreme depression arising from extraordinary events. Unlike day-to-day disappointments, the loss of a loved one often produces intense emotions that call for carefully constructed support messages.

IDEA: INCLUSION, DIVERSITY, EQUITY, AND ACCESS

The COVID-19 pandemic made the grief of bereavement a reality for more than 5 million people worldwide. The risk of contracting the virus, as well as the severity of the illness, was not equally distributed across race and class, however. Does your thinking about grief and bereavement change when the loss of life is, at least partly, related to social, economic, and racial inequities? How should supportive communication be tailored in such situations to effectively meet the demands of the moment?

PAUSE & REFLECT

Have you ever grieved the loss of someone you loved? What kinds of things did people say to you that were most helpful or unhelpful?

Finding the right words to comfort someone who is coping with the death of a loved one can be difficult. What makes some grief management messages more effective and helpful than others? Messages that are high in person-centeredness tend to be perceived as the most supportive and comforting (Rack, Burleson, Brodie, Holmstrom, & Servaty-Seib, 2008; Servaty-Seib & Burleson, 2007). In fact, low person-centered messages can elicit anger and counter-arguing that lead a bereaved person to reject a support attempt (Tian, 2021). Characteristics of the individual and the context also influence the types of support messages that are perceived as most effective. For example, people who are optimistic about getting the support they need evaluate specific support messages as more helpful than individuals who are pessimistic about getting support (Kaul & Lakey, 2003; Servaty-Seib & Burleson, 2007). The context also affects how people respond to supportive messages during bereavement (Servaty-Seib & Burleson, 2007). For example, bereaved individuals who were extremely close to the deceased in life tend to feel more comforted by messages that express concern and positive regard for the deceased. In addition, philosophical perspectives on death and the provision of advice are perceived as more helpful shortly after the death occurred, but less helpful after some time has passed. Complete the How Do You Rate? 14.2 survey to explore your own reactions to support messages in these situations.

HOW DO YOU RATE? 14.2

Support for Bereavement

Visit the companion website to complete a survey designed to measure your reactions to various types of support messages designed to comfort someone after the loss of a loved one.

Putting Theory into Practice: Providing Support in Times of Need

Even though it is hard for you to know what to say or do for a person who is facing serious illness or bereavement, think about how much harder it is for the person who is going through it. In this section, we suggest some actions you can take to provide even a small amount of comfort during these difficult times.

Focus on what you can do to make life easier. Remember that tangible support is often just as important as emotional support. Are you a good cook? Make a couple of dinners that would keep well in the freezer for an easy weeknight meal or bake a batch of cookies that they can turn to for comfort. Do you have a car? Offer to go to the grocery store, shopping mall, or pharmacy, or offer to pick up the kids from school. Are you skilled at working outdoors? Perhaps you could mow their lawn, tend to their garden, or shovel their driveway in the winter. When people are struggling to cope with circumstances that are larger than life, day-to-day tasks can seem impossible to keep up with.

COMMUNICATION IN ACTION 14.5

Different Types of Support

This exercise is designed to get you thinking about the different types of support you can offer someone in need. Think of someone you know who might be going through a life-changing event, even something positive like the birth of a first child. Using the form on the companion website, identify three things that you could do to provide each type of social support for this person.

Don't overreach. Remember that during a traumatic event, it's difficult to find verbal messages that will provide comfort. When there is literally nothing you can say to fix the situation, problem-focused support strategies might be unhelpful and insensitive. Attempting to offer emotion-focused support is also tricky in this context, because you may not fully understand the scope of the emotional trauma and you could accidentally respond in an inappropriate way. In these situations, it's often best to keep your support efforts simple. A hug, a promise to be there, an offer to help with some tangible task are all modest but helpful ways to provide support. In addition, stay in touch and keep expressing your concern through both nonverbal immediacy and verbal messages. When people are facing major life stressors, the coping process is a lengthy one; by checking in and providing support over the long haul, you can make an enormous difference.

SUMMARY

In this final chapter, we have turned our attention to one of the most wonderful tasks we accomplish through interpersonal communication: providing comfort and support. Through the messages we send to other people, we can make them feel better about bad news, give them strength to manage a difficult situation, or remind them that they are valued and cared for. Moreover, giving the gift of a comforting message isn't expensive or difficult. By simply displaying nonverbal immediacy, by making direct eye contact, showing sympathetic facial expressions, leaning forward, and facing a person, we communicate concern for a partner. Through verbal communication, you can attend to a variety of topics and use different communication strategies to provide comfort. By practicing these communication skills, and avoiding especially ineffective support messages, you can go a long way to improving the lives of people you care about.

As you offer messages of support to other people – or seek comfort from someone else – keep in mind that supportive communication takes two. While support seekers need a supportive listener to say the right things, they also need to express their needs, pay attention to the support they are getting, and be willing to think about problems in a different way. Culture is another factor that affects both the kinds of events people consider distressing, and what they consider supportive when they are in need.

When you tune in to opportunities to provide comfort and support, you'll discover many everyday situations when your nonverbal and verbal messages can make a difference. You may also find yourself in a position to provide support to somebody who really needs it. When people in your life experience a serious illness or the death of a loved one, interpersonal communication is a tool you can use to soften the blow. Although you can't undo a diagnosis or take away a person's grief, you can go a long way toward letting someone know that you care about them and you are there for them. By providing a variety of forms of support – from nonverbal immediacy to practical aid – you can help another person cope with what might otherwise be devastating circumstances.

The ability to use messages to comfort others is one of the most important interpersonal communication skills you can develop. Even though you might be inclined to provide support in particular ways, you can take steps to expand your comforting toolkit, overcome obstacles to providing support, and provide support when it really matters. Like the other communication skills you learned about in this textbook, you can improve your ability to communicate comfort and support. When you do, you will understand how interpersonal communication can truly change people's lives for the better.

ACTIVITIES FOR EXPLORING COMMUNICATION ETHICS

What Would You/Should You Do?

One of your friends has been acting depressed, so you decide to address whatever issue is making her feel sad and try to make her feel better. When you approach your friend, she tells you about a variety of circumstances that are making her sad. She seems hopeless and apathetic and implies that she has been considering suicide. What would you or should you do?

Something to Think About

In some situations, the source of a person's distress is invisible to outsiders. For example, infertility affects one out of six couples in the United States, but you'll never know who is experiencing it unless they tell you. In fact, an infertile couple might look to you like two people who are putting their jobs first or planning for a lifetime free from the hassles of children. Supportive communication is more than just offering the right response to sad news – it also involves creating a space where people don't feel pressured to divulge private information or stigmatized for conditions beyond their control. Instead of the usual questions that many childless couples encounter ("So when are you planning to have a baby?"), how might you communicate in ways that are less hurtful and more supportive?

Analyzing Communication Ethics Yourself

One of the challenges to ethical support is providing messages that help people, while simultaneously respecting their rights to cope with their problems the way that they see fit. Ethical communication also makes clear the values that support a course of action and avoids simple directive statements. Monitor an advice column, website, or televised talk show for a period of time to observe the advice messages that are given. To what extent do advice-givers make clear the values and evidence that support their recommendations? Do the messages tend to respect the person's autonomy, or do they dictate a particular response? Based on your analysis, what might these sources of advice do to provide their service in more ethical ways?

KEY WORDS

cold comfort
dismiss
emotion-focused coping
emotional support
empathy
escape
esteem support
informational support
network support
nonverbal immediacy
person-centeredness
perspective-taking
problem-focused coping
solace
solve
tangible support

Bibliography

1 WHAT IS INTERPERSONAL COMMUNICATION?

Afifi, T. D. (2003). "Feeling caught" in stepfamilies: Managing boundary turbulence through appropriate communication privacy rules. *Journal of Social and Personal Relationships*, *20*(6), 729–755. https://doi.org/10.1177/0265407503206002.

Afifi, W. A., & Burgoon, J. K. (1998). "We never talk about that": A comparison of cross-sex friendships and dating relationships on uncertainty and topic avoidance. *Personal Relationships*, *5*(3), 255–272. https://doi.org/10.1111/j.1475-6811.1998.tb00171.x.

Arnett, R. C., Harden Fritz, J. M., & Bell, L. M. (2009). *Communication ethics literacy*. Thousand Oaks, CA: Sage.

Baxter, L., & Akkoor, C. (2011). Topic expansiveness and family communication patterns. *Journal of Family Communication*, *11*, 1–20.

Baxter, L. A., & Wilmot, W. W. (1985). Taboo topics in close relationships. *Journal of Social and Personal Relationships*, *2*(3), 253–269. https://doi.org/10.1177/0265407585023002.

Burleson, M., Roberts, N., Coon, D., & Soto, J. (2019). Perceived cultural acceptability and comfort with affectionate touch: Differences between Mexican Americans and European Americans. *Journal of Social and Personal Relationships*, 36, 1000–1022.

Caplan, S. E. (2005). A social skill account of problematic Internet use. *Journal of Communication*, *55*(4), 721–736. https://doi.org/10.1093/joc/55.4.721.

Cegala, D. J., Gade, C., & Broz, S. L., & McClure, L. (2004). Physicians' and patients' perceptions of patients' communication competence in a primary care medical interview. *Health Communication*, *16*, 289–304.

Cegala, D. J., McGee, D. S., & McNeilis, K. S. (1996). Components of patients' and doctors' perceptions of communication competence during a primary care medical interview. *Health Communication*, *8*(1), 1–27. https://doi.org/10.1207/s15327027hc0801_1.

Collier, M. J. (1996). Communication competence problematics in ethnic friendships. *Communication Monographs*, *63*(4), 314–336. https://doi.org/10.1080/03637759609376397.

Courtright, J. A. (2016). Relational communication theory. In C. R. Berger & M. E. Roloff (Eds.) and S. R. Wilson, J. P. Dillard, J. Caughlin, & D. H. Solomon (Associate Eds.), *International encyclopedia of interpersonal communication* (pp. 1433–1443). Hoboken, NJ: Wiley-Blackwell.

Fairhurst, G. T., & Putnam, L. (2004). Organizations as discursive constructions. *Communication Theory*, *14*(1), 5–26. https://doi.org/10.1111/j.1468-2885.2004.tb00301.x.

Floyd, K. (2006). Human affection exchange: XII. Affectionate communication is associated with diurnal variation in salivary free cortisol. *Western Journal of Communication*, *70*(1), 47–63. https://doi.org/10.1080/10570310500506649.

Floyd, K., Mikkelson, A. C., Hesse, C., & Pauley, P. M. (2007). Affectionate writing reduces total cholesterol. *Human Communication Research*, *33*(2), 119–142. https://doi.org/10.1111/j.1468-2958.2007.00293.x.

Floyd, K., Mikkelson, A. C., Tafoya, M. A., Farinelli, L., La Valley, A. G., Judd, J., Haynes, M. T., Davis, K. L., & Wilson, J. (2007). Human affection exchange: XIII. Affectionate communication accelerates neuroendocrine stress recovery. *Health Communication*, *22*(2), 123–132. https://doi.org/10.1080/10410230701454015.

Golish, T. D., & Caughlin, J. P. (2002). "I'd rather not talk about it": Adolescents' and young adults' use of topic avoidance in stepfamilies. *Journal of Applied Communication Research*, *30*(1), 78–106. https://doi.org/10.1080/00909880216574.

Gray, J., & Laidlaw, H. (2004). Improving the measurement of communication satisfaction. *Management Communication Quarterly*, *17*(3), 425–448. https://doi.org/10.1177/0893318903257980.

Haslett, B. B., & Samter, W. (Eds.). (1997). *Children communicating: The first 5 years*. Mahwah, NJ: Lawrence Erlbaum.

Holladay, S. J., & Seipke, H. L. (2007). Communication between grandparents and grandchildren in geographically separated relationships. *Communication Studies*, *58*(3), 281–297. https://doi.org/10.1080/10510970701518371.

Johnson, P., Lindsey, A. E., & Zakahi, W. R. (2001). Anglo Americans, Hispanic Americans, Chilean, Mexican and Spanish perceptions of competent communication in initial interaction. *Communication Research Reports*, *18*(1), 36–43. https://doi.org/10.1080/08824090109384780.

Knobloch, L. K. (2010). Relational uncertainty and interpersonal communication. In S. W. Smith & S. R. Wilson (Eds.), *New directions in interpersonal communication research* (pp. 69–93). Thousand Oaks, CA: Sage.

Koesten, J., & Anderson, K. (2004). Exploring the influence of family communication patterns cognitive complexity, and interpersonal competence on adolescent risk behaviors. *Journal of Family Communication*, *4*, 99–121.

Larkey, L. K., & Hecht, M. L. (1995). A comparative study of African American and European American ethnic identity. *International Journal of Intercultural Relations*, *19*(4), 483–504. https://doi.org/10.1016/0147-1767(95)00030-5.

Mansson, D. H. (2013). The grandchildren received affection scale: Examining affectual solidarity factors. *Southern Communication Journal*, *78*, 70–90.

McLaren, R. M., Dillard, J. P., Tusing, K. J., & Solomon, D. H. (2014). Relational framing theory: Utterance form and relational context as antecedents of frame salience. *Communication Quarterly*, *62*, 518–535.

McLaren, R. M., & High, A. C. (2019). The effect of under-and over-benefited support gaps on hurt feelings, esteem, and relationships. *Communication Research*, *46*(6), 785–810. https://doi.org/10.1177/0093650215605155.

Miller, K. I., Considine, J., & Garner, J. (2007). "Let me tell you about my job": Exploring the terrain of emotion in the workplace. *Management Communication Quarterly*, *20*(3), 231–260. https://doi.org/10.1177/0893318906293589.

Myers, S. A. (2016). Affectionate communication and personal outcomes. In C. R. Berger & M. E. Roloff (Eds.) and S. R. Wilson, J. P. Dillard, J. Caughlin, & D. H. Solomon (Associate Eds.), *International encyclopedia of interpersonal communication* (pp. 32–36). Hoboken, NJ: Wiley-Blackwell.

Nussbaum, J. F., Pecchioni, L. L., Baringer, D. K., & Kundrat, A. L. (2002). Lifespan communication. In W. B. Gudykunst (Ed.), *Communication yearbook 26* (pp. 366–389). Mahwah, NJ: Lawrence Erlbaum.

Pecchioni, L. L., Wright, K. B., & Nussbaum, J. F. (2005). *Life-span communication* (2nd ed.). Mahwah, NJ: Lawrence Erlbaum.

Priem, J. S., McLaren, R. M., & Solomon, D. H. (2010). Relational messages, perceptions of hurt, and biological stress reactions to a disconfirming interaction. *Communication Research*, 37(1), 48–72. https://doi.org/10.1177/0093650209351470.

Roeder, A., Garner, J., & Carr, K. (2019). Workplace relationships, stress, and verbal rumination in organizations. *Southern Communication Journal*, *85*, 63–72.

Sanders, R. E. (2007). The composition and sequencing of communicative acts to solve social problems: Functionality and inventiveness in children's interactions. *Communication Monographs*, 74(4), 464–491. https://doi.org/10.1080/03637750701716628.

Solomon, D. H. (2006). A relational framing perspective on perceptions of social-sexual communication at work. In R. M. Dailey & B. A. LePoire (Eds.), *Applied interpersonal communication matters: Family, health, and community relations* (pp. 271–298). New York: Peter Lang.

Spitzberg, B. H. (2003). Methods of interpersonal skill assessment. In J. O. Greene & B. R. Burleson (Eds.), *Handbook of communication and social interaction skills* (pp. 93–134). Mahwah, NJ: Lawrence Erlbaum.

Spitzberg, B. H. (2006). Preliminary development of a model and measure of computer-mediated communication (CMC) competence. *Journal of Computer-Mediated Communication*, *11*(2), 629–666. https://doi.org/10.1111/j.1083-6101.2006.00030.x.

Spitzberg, B. H., & Cupach, W. R. (2002). Interpersonal skills. In M. L. Knapp & J. A. Daly (Eds.), *Handbook of interpersonal communication* (3rd ed., pp. 564–611). Thousand Oaks, CA: Sage.

Spitzberg, B. H., & Cupach, W. R. (2011). Interpersonal skills. In M. L. Knapp & J. A. Daly (Eds.), *Handbook of interpersonal communication* (4th ed., pp. 481–526). Thousand Oaks, CA: Sage.

Stukan, D. (2018). Sociopragmatic failure: Struggling with cross-cultural differences in communication. *Open Journal for Anthropological Studies*, 2, 27–36. https://doi.org/10.32591/coas.ojas.0201.03027s.

Theiss, J. A., Carpenter, A. M., & Leustek, J. (2016). Partner facilitation and partner interference in individuals' weight loss goals. *Qualitative Health Research*, *26*, 1318–1330.

Thompson, T. L., Robinson, J. D., & Brashers, D. E. (2011). Interpersonal communication and health care. In M. L. Knapp & J. A. Daly (Eds.), *Handbook of interpersonal communication* (4th ed., pp. 633–678). Thousand Oaks, CA: Sage.

Wilson, S. R., & Sabee, C. M. (2003). Explicating communicative competence as a theoretical term. In J. O. Greene & B. R. Burleson (Eds.), *Handbook of communication and social interaction skills* (pp. 3–50). Mahwah, NJ: Lawrence Erlbaum.

Xu, Y., & Burleson, B. R. (2001). Effects of sex, culture, and support types on perceptions of spousal social support: An assessment of the "support gap" hypothesis in early marriage. *Human Communication Research*, 27(4), 535–566. https://doi.org/10.1111/j.1468-2958.2001.tb00792.x.

Youngvorst, L. J., & High, A. C. (2018): "Anyone free to chat?" Using technological features to elicit quality support online. *Communication Monographs*, 85(2), 203–223. https://doi.org/10.1080/03637751.2018.1426871.

2 CULTURE AND INTERPERSONAL COMMUNICATION

Allen, B. J. (2017). Standpoint theory. In Y. Y. Kim (Ed.), *The international encyclopedia of intercultural communication*. Hoboken, NJ: John Wiley & Sons. https://doi.org/10.1002/9781118783665.ieicc0234.

Babel, A. M. (2016). Affective motivations for borrowing: Performing local identity through loan phonology. *Language & Communication*, *49*, 70–83. https://doi.org/10.1016/j.langcom.2016.06.002.

Ballard-Reisch, D. (2010). Muted groups in health communication policy and practice: The case of older adults in rural and frontier areas. *Women and Language*, *33*(2), 87–93.

Baxter, L. A. (2010). *Voicing relationships: A dialogic perspective*. Thousand Oaks, CA: Sage.

Bernhold, Q. S., & Giles, H. (2020). The role of grandchildren's own age-related communication and accommodation from grandparents in predicting grandchildren's well-being. *The International Journal of Aging & Human Development*, *91*, 149–181. DOI:10.1177/0091415019852775.

Braithwaite, D. O. (1995). Ritualized embarrassment at "coed" wedding and baby showers. *Communication Reports*, *8*(2), 145–157. https://doi.org/10.1080/08934219509367621.

Braithwaite, D. O., Waldron, V. R., Allen, J., Oliver, B., & Bergquist, G. (2017). "Feeling warmth and close to her": Communication and resilience reflected in turning points in positive adult stepchild-stepparent relationships. *Journal of Family Communication*, *18*(2), 92–109. https://doi.org/10.1080/15267431.2017.1415902.

Bukowski, W. M., & DeLay, D. (2020). Studying the same-gender preference as a defining feature of cultural contexts. *Frontiers in Psychology*, *11*, 1863. https://doi.org/10.3389/fpsyg.2020.01863.

Byrd, G. A., Zhang, Y. G., & Gist-Mackey, A. N. (2019). Interability contact and the reduction of interability prejudice: Communication accommodation, intergroup anxiety, and relational solidarity. *Journal of Language and Social Psychology*, *38*(4), 441–458. https://doi.org/10.1177/0261927X19865578.

Cameron, J. J., & Curry, E. (2020). Gender roles and date context in hypothetical scripts for a woman and a man on a first date in the twenty-first century. *Sex Roles*, *82*(5–6), 345–362. https://doi.org/10.1007/s11199-019-01056-6.

Cassell, J., & Tversky, D. (2005). The language of online intercultural community formation. *Journal of Computer-Mediated Communication*, *10*(2), 00. https://doi.org/10.1111/j.1083-6101.2005.tb00239.x.

Cherlin, A. J. (2004). The deinstitutionalization of American marriage. *Journal of Marriage and the Family*, *66*(4), 848–861. https://doi.org/10.1111/j.0022-2445.2004.00058.x.

Christian, A. (2005). Contesting the myth of the "wicked stepmother": Narrative analysis of an online stepfamily support group. *Western Journal of Communication*, *69*(1), 27–47. https://doi.org/10.1080/10570310500034030.

Clearfield, M. W., & Nelson, N. M. (2006). Sex differences in mothers' speech and play behavior with 6-, 9-, and 14-month-old infants. *Sex Roles*, *54*(1–2), 127–137. https://doi.org/10.1007/s11199-005-8874-1.

Crespo, C., Davide, I. N., Costa, M. E., & Fletcher, G. J. O. (2008). Family rituals in married couples: Links with attachment, relationship quality, and closeness. *Personal Relationships*, *15*(2), 191–203. https://doi.org/10.1111/j.1475-6811.2008.00193.x.

Dailey, S. (2016). What happens before full-time employment? Internships as a mechanism of anticipatory socialization. *Western Journal of Communication*, *80*(4), 453–480. https://doi.org/10.1080/10570314.2016.1159727.

Davis, S. M., & High, A. C. (2019). Widening the gap: Support gaps in same race versus different race female dyad friendships. *Journal of Social and Personal Relationships*, *36*(1), 187–213. https://doi.org/10.1177/0265407517722245.

DeTurk, S. (2001). Intercultural empathy: Myth, competency, or possibility for alliance building. *Communication Education*, *50*(4), 374–384. https://doi.org/10.1080/03634520109379262.

Dickinson, G., Ott, B. L., & Aoki, E. (2005). Memory and myth at the Buffalo Bill museum. *Western Journal of Communication*, *69*(2), 85–108. https://doi.org/10.1080/10570310500076684.

Dindia, K., & Canary, D. J. (2006). *Sex differences and similarities in communication*. Mahwah, NJ: Erlbaum.

Domagalski, T. A., & Steelman, L. A. (2007). The impact of gender and organizational status on workplace anger expression. *Management Communication Quarterly*, *20*(3), 297–315. https://doi.org/10.1177/0893318906295681.

Dougherty, D. S. (2001). Sexual harassment as [dys]functional process: A feminist standpoint analysis. *Journal of Applied Communication Research*, *29*(4), 372–402. https://doi.org/10.1080/00909880128116.

Dragojevic, M., Giles, H., & Gasiorek, J. (2016). Communication accommodation theory. In C. R. Berger & M. E. Roloff (Eds.), *The international encyclopedia of interpersonal communication* (pp. 176–196). Dresden, Germany: Wiley-Blackwell.

Duranti, A. (2006). The social ontology of intentions. *Discourse Studies*, *8*(1), 31–40. https://doi.org/10.1177/1461445606059548.

Eagly, A. H., & Karau, S. J. (2002). Role congruity theory of prejudice toward female leaders. *Psychological Review*, *109*(3), 573–598. https://doi.org/10.1037/0033-295X.109.3.573.

Elhami, A. (2020). A socio-pragmatic perspective of Spanish and Persian greeting. *Theory and Practice in Language Studies*, *10*(9), 1009–1014. https://doi.org/http://dx.doi.org/10.17507/tpls.1009.01.

Fitch, K. L. (1998). *Speaking relationally: Culture, communication, and interpersonal connection*. New York: Guilford Press.

Flood-Grady, E., & Koenig Kellas, J. (2019). Sense-making, socialization, and stigma: Exploring narrative told in families about mental illness. *Health Communication*, *34*(6), 607–617. https://doi.org/10.1080/10410236.2018.1431016.

Gallois, C. (2003). Reconciliation through communication in intercultural encounters: Potential or peril. *Journal of Communication*, *53*(1), 5–15. https://doi.org/10.1093/joc/53.1.5.

Gibbs, J. L., Kim, H., & Ki., S. (2019). Investigating the role of control and support mechanisms in members' sense of virtual community. *Communication Research*, *46*(1), 117–145. https://doi.org/10.1177/0093650216644023.

Grossman, P. J., Eckel, C., Komai, M., & Zhan, W. (2019). It pays to be a man: Rewards for leaders in a coordination game. *Journal of Economic Behavior & Organization*, *161*, 197–215. https://doi.org/10.1016/j.jebo.2019.04.002.

Gudykunst, W. B. (1993). Toward a theory of effective interpersonal and intergroup communication: An anxiety/uncertainty management perspective. In R. L. Wiseman & J. Koester (Eds.), *Intercultural communication competence* (pp. 33–71). Newbury Park, CA: Sage.

Gudykunst, W. B. (2005). An anxiety/uncertainty management (AUM) theory of effective communication. In W. B. Gudykunst (Ed.), *Theorizing about intercultural communication* (pp. 281–322). Thousand Oaks, CA: Sage.

Hall, J. A. (2011). Is it something I said? Sense of humor and partner embarrassment. *Journal of Social and Personal Relationships*, *28*(3), 383–405. https://doi.org/10.1177/0265407510384422.

Harkins, D. A., & Ray, S. (2004). An exploratory study of mother-child storytelling in east India and northeast United States. *Narrative Inquiry*, *14*(2), 347–367. https://doi.org/10.1075/ni.14.2.09har.

Hofstede, G. (2001). *Culture's consequences: Comparing values, behaviors, institutions, and organizations across nations* (2nd ed.). Thousand Oaks, CA: Sage.

Hylmö, A. (2006). Telecommuting and the contestability of choice: Employee strategies to legitimize personal decisions to work in a preferred location. *Management Communication Quarterly*, *19*(4), 541–569. https://doi.org/10.1177/0893318905284762.

Jahn, J. L. S., & Black, A. E. (2017). A model of communicative hierarchical foundations of high reliability organizing in wildland firefighting teams. *Management Communication Quarterly*, *31*(3), 356–379. https://doi.org/10.1177/0893318917691358.

Kurchirko, Y. A., Schatz, J. L., Fletcher, K. K., & Tamis-Lemonda, C. S. (2020). Do, say, learn: the functions of mothers' speech to infants. *Journal of Child Language*, *47*(1), 64–84. https://doi.org/10.1017/S0305000919000308.

Lee, C. M., & Gudykunst, W. B. (2001). Attraction in initial interethnic interactions. *International Journal of Intercultural Relations*, *25*(4), 373–387. https://doi.org/10.1016/S0147-1767(01)00011-6.

Li, M. (2018). Maintaining ties and reaffirming unity: Family rituals in the age of migration. *Journal of Family Communication*, *18*(4), 286–301. https://doi.org/10.1080/15267431.2018.1475391.

Lindsey, E. W., Cremeens, P. R., & Caldera, Y. M. (2010). Gender differences in mother-toddler and father-toddler verbal initiations and responses during a caregiving and play context. *Sex Roles*, *63*(5), 399–411. https://doi.org/10.1007/s11199-010-9803-5.

Logan, S., Steel, Z., & Hunt, C. (2014). Investigating the effect of anxiety, uncertainty and ethnocentrism on willingness to interact in an intercultural communication. *Journal of Cross-Cultural Psychology*, *46*(1), 39–52. https://doi.org/10.1177/0022022114555762.

Martin, D. M. (2004). Humor in middle management: Women negotiating the paradoxes of organizational life. *Journal of Applied Communication Research: Organized Irrationality? Coping with Paradox, Contradiction, and Irony in Organizational Communication*, *32*(2), 147–170. https://doi.org/10.1080/0090988042000210034.

McCabe, M. P., & Hardman, L. (2005). Attitudes and perceptions of workers to sexual harassment. *Journal of Social Psychology*, *145*(6), 719–740. https://doi.org/10.3200/SOCP.145.6.719-740.

Mohr, M. (2013). *Holy sh*t: A brief history of swearing*. Oxford: Oxford University Press.

Mongeau, P. A., & Carey, C, M. (1996). Who's wooing whom II: An experimental investigation of date initiation and expectancy violation. *Western Journal of Communication*, *60*(3), 195–213. https://doi.org/10.1080/10570319609374543.

Mongeau, P. A., Hale, J. L., Johnson, K. L, & Hillis, J. D. (1993). Who's wooing whom: An investigation of female initiated dating. In P. J. Kalbfleisch (Ed.), *Interpersonal communication: Evolving interpersonal relationships* (pp. 51–68). Hillsdale, NJ: Lawrence Erlbaum.

Neuliep, J. W., & McCroskey, J. C. (1997). The development of intercultural and interethnic communication apprehension scales. *Communication Research Reports*, *14*(4), 145–156. https://doi.org/10.1080/08824099709388656.

Neuliep, J. W., & Speten-Hansen, K. M. (2013). The influence of enthocentrism on social perceptions of nonnative accents. *Language & Communication*, *33*(3), 167–176. https://doi.org/10.1016/j.langcom.2013.05.001.

Nishida, T. (2016). Anxiety/uncertainty management (AUM) theory. In C. R. Berger & M. E. Roloff (Eds.), *The international encyclopedia of interpersonal communication* (pp. 40–50). Dresden, Germany: Wiley-Blackwell.

Pená, J., & Hancock, J. T. (2006). An analysis of socioemotional and task communication in online multiplayer video games. *Communication Research*, *33*(1), 92–109. https://doi.org/10.1177/0093650205283103.

Peters, K., & Kashima, Y. (2014). Gossiping as moral social action: A functionalist account of gossiper perceptions. In J. P. Forgas, O. Vincze, & J. Laszlo (Eds.), *Social cognition and communication* (pp. 185–201). New York, NY: Psychology Press.

Phillipsen, G. (1997). A theory of speech codes. In G. Phillipsen & T. L. Albrecht (Eds.), *Developing communication theories* (pp. 119–156). Albany: SUNY Press.

Phillipsen, G., Coutu, L. M., & Covarrubias, P. (2005). Speech codes theory: Restatement, revisions, and response to criticisms. In W. B. Gudykunst (Ed.), *Theorizing about intercultural communication* (pp. 55–68). Thousand Oaks, CA: Sage.

Powell, L., Amsbary, J., & Hickson, M. (2014). The Wai in Thai culture: Greeting, status-marking and national identity functions. *Journal of Intercultural Communication*, *34*(1), 46–55. Retrieved from https://immi.se/intercultural/nr34/powell.html.

Razzante, R. J., & Orbe, M. P. (2018). Two sides of the same coin: Conceptualizing dominant group theory in the context of co-cultural theory. *Communication Theory*, *28*(3), 354–375. https://doi.org/10.1093/ct/qtx008.

Reich, S. M., Black, R. W., & Foliaki, T. (2018). Constructing different: Lego® set narratives promote stereotypic gender roles and play. *Sex Roles*, *79*(5), 285–298. https://doi.org/10.1007/s11199-017-0868-2.

Rodgers, S., & Chen, Q. (2005). Internet community group participation: Psychosocial benefits for women with breast cancer. *Journal of Computer-Mediated Communication*, *10*(4). https://doi.org/10.1111/j.1083-6101.2005.tb00268.x.

Rose, S., & Frieze, I. H. (1993). Young singles' contemporary dating scripts. *Sex Roles*, *28*(9–10), 499–509. https://doi.org/10.1007/BF00289677.

Rui, J. R., & Wang, H. (2015). Social network sites and international students' cross-cultural adaptations. *Computers in Human Behavior*, *49*, 400–411. https://doi.org/10.1016/j.chb.2015.03.041.

Rygg, K. (2016). Was Malinowski Norwegian?: Norwegian interpretations of phatic talk. *Journal of Intercultural Communication*, *40*, 1.

Samochowiec, J., Florack, A. (2010). Intercultural contact under uncertainty: The impact of predictability and anxiety on the willingness to interact with a member from an unknown cultural group. *International Journal of Intercultural Relations*, *34*(5), 507–515. https://doi.org/10.1016/j.ijintrel.2010.05.003.

Scott, C., & Myers, K. (2010). Toward an integrative theoretical perspective on organizational membership negotiations socialization, assimilation, and the duality of structure. *Communication Theory*, *20*(1), 79–105. https://doi.org/10.1111/j.1468-2885.2009.01355.x.

Silva, V. T. (2005). In the beginning was the gene: The hegemony of genetic thinking in contemporary culture. *Communication Theory*, *15*(1), 100–123. https://doi.org/10.1093/ct/15.1.100.

Soliz, J. (2016). Convergence/divergence. In C. R. Berger & M. E. Roloff (Eds.), *The international encyclopedia of interpersonal communication* (pp. 430–434). Dresden, Germany: Wiley-Blackwell.

Solomon, D. H. (2006). A relational framing perspective on perceptions of social-sexual communication at work. In R. M. Dailey, & B. A. LePoire (Eds.), *Applied interpersonal communication matters: Family, health, and community relations*. New York: Peter Lang.

Ting-Toomey, S., Yee-Jung, K. K., Shapiro, R. B., Garcia, W., Wright, T. J., & Oetzel, J. G. (2000). Ethnic/cultural identity salience and conflict styles in four US ethnic groups. *International Journal of Intercultural Relations*, *24*(1), 47–81. https://doi.org/10.1016/s0147-1767(99)00023-1.

3 IDENTITY AND INTERPERSONAL COMMUNICATION

Abu-Rayya, H. M. (2006). Ethnic self-identification and psychological well-being among adolescents with European mothers and Arab fathers in Israel. *International Journal of Intercultural Relations*, *30*(5), 545–556. https://doi.org/10.1016/j.ijintrel.2005.10.003.

Ahnallen, J. M., Suyemoto, K. L., & Carter, A. S. (2006). Relationship between physical appearance, sense of belonging and exclusion, and racial/ethnic self-identification among multiracial Japanese European Americans. *Cultural Diversity and Ethnic Minority Psychology*, *12*(4), 673–686. https://doi.org/10.1037/1099-9809.12.4.673.

Alicke, M. D., LoSchiavo, R. M., Zerbst, J., & Zhang, S. (1997). The person who outperforms me is a genius: Maintaining perceived competence in upward social comparison. *Journal of Personality and Social Psychology*, *73*(4), 781–789. https://doi.org/10.1037/0022-3514.73.4.781.

Aloia, L. S., & Strutzenberg, C. (2019). Parent-child communication apprehension: The role of parental alienation and self-esteem. *Communication Reports*, *32*(1), 1–14. https://doi-org/10.1080/08934215.2018.1514641.

Arnett, J. J. (2000). Emerging adulthood. *American Psychologist*, *55*(5), 469–480. ttps://doi.org/10.1037/0003–066X.55.5.469.

Arnett, J. J. (2010). Emerging adulthood (s). In L. A. Jensen (Ed.), *Bridging cultural and developmental approaches to psychology: New syntheses in theory, research, and policy* (pp. 255–275). Oxford: Oxford University Press.

Ashcraft, C. (2006). Ready or not ...?: Teen sexuality and the troubling discourse of readiness. *Anthropology and Education Quarterly*, *37*(4), 328–346. https://doi.org/10.1525/aeq.2006.37.4.328.

Banks, S. P., Louie, E., & Einerson, M. (2000). Constructing personal identities in holiday letters. *Journal of Social and Personal Relationships*, *17*(3), 299–327. https://doi.org/10.1177/0265407500173001.

Beals, K. P., & Peplau, L. A. (2005). Identity support, identity devaluation, and well-being among lesbians. *Psychology of Women Quarterly*, *29*(2), 140–148. https://doi.org/10.1111/j.1471-6402.2005.00176.x.

Beauregard, K. S., & Dunning, D. (1998). Turning up the contrast: Self-enhancement motives prompt egocentric contrast effects in social judgments. *Journal of Personality and Social Psychology*, *74*(3), 606–621. https://doi.org/10.1037/0022-3514.74.3.606.

Bouchard, G., & McNair, J. L. (2016). Dyadic examination of the influence of family relationships on life satisfaction at the empty-nest stage. *Journal of Adult Development*, *23*(3), 174–182. https://doi.org/10.1007/s10804-016-9233-x.

Burke, P. J., & Harrod, M. M. (2005). Too much of a good thing? *Social Psychology Quarterly*, *68*(4), 359–374. https://doi.org/10.1177/019027250506800404.

Carr, C. T., & Foreman, A. C. (2016). Identity shift III: effects of publicness of feedback and relational closeness in computer-mediated communication. *Media Psychology*, *19*, 334–358. DOI:10.1080/15213269.2015.1049276.

Colaner, C. W., & Soliz, J. (2017). A communication-based approach to adoptive identity: Theoretical and empirical support. *Communication Research*, *44*(5), 611–637. https://doi.org/10.1177/0093650215577860.

Constantino, M. J., Wilson, K. R., & Horowitz, L. M. (2006). The direct and stress-buffering effects of self-organization on psychological adjustment. *Journal of Social and Clinical Pscyhology*, *25*(3), 333–360. https://doi.org/10.1521/jscp.2006.25.3.333.

Constantino, M. J., Wilson, K. R., Horowitz, L. M., & Pinel, E. C. (2006). Measures of self-organization and their association with psychological adjustment. *Journal of Social and Clinical Psychology*, *25*, 333–360.

Coyne, S. M., McDaniel, B. T., & Stockdale, L. A. (2017). "Do you dare to compare?" Associations between maternal social comparisons on social networking sites and parenting, mental health, and romantic relationship outcomes. *Computers in Human Behavior*, *70*, 335–340. DOI:10.1016/j.chb.2016.12.081.

Cramer, E. M., Song, H., & Drent, A. M. (2016). Social comparison on Facebook: motivation, affective consequences, self-esteem, and Facebook fatigue. *Computers in Human Behavior*, *64*, 739–746. DOI:10.1016/j.chb.2016.07.049.

Crowley, B. J., Hayslip, B., & Hobdy, J. (2003). Psychological hardiness and adjustment to life events in adulthood. *Journal of Adult Development*, *10*(4), 237–248. https://doi.org/10.1023/A:1026007510134.

Dennerstein, L., Dudley, E., & Guthrie, J. (2002). Empty nest or revolving door? A prospective study of women's quality of life in midlife during the phase of children leaving and re-entering the home. *Psychological Medicine*, *32*(3), 545–550. https://doi.org/10.1017/S0033291701004810.

Gieseler, C. (2018). Gender-reveal parties: performing community identity in pink and blue. *Journal of Gender Studies*, *27*(6), 661–671. https://doi.org/10.1080/09589236.2017.1287066.

Hamwey, M. K., Rolan, E. P., Jensen, A. C., & Whiteman, S. D. (2019). "Absence makes the heart grow fonder": A qualitative examination of sibling relationships during emerging adulthood. *Journal of Social and Personal Relationships*, *36*(8), 2487–2506. https://doi.org/10.1177/0265407518789514.

Harper, G. W., Serrano, P. A., Bruce, D., & Bauermeister, J. A. (2016). The internet's multiple roles in facilitating the sexual orientation identity development of gay and bisexual male adolescents. *American Journal of Men's Health*, *10*(5), 359–376. https://doi.org/10.1177/1557988314566227.

Hecht, M. & Lu, Y. (2014). Communication theory of identity. In T. L. Thompson (Ed.), *Encyclopedia of health communication* (Vol. 1, pp. 226–227). Thousand Oaks, CA: Sage. https://doi.org/10.4135/9781483346427.n85.

Henderson, L. (2011). Sexting and sexual relationships among teens and young adults. *McNair Scholars Research Journal*, *7*(1), 9. Retrieved from https://scholarworks.boisestate.edu/mcnair_journal/vol7/iss1/9.

Holmes, J. (2005). Story-telling at work: A complex discursive resource for integrating personal, professional and social identities. *Discourse Studies*, *7*(6), 671–700. https://doi.org/10.1177/1461445605055422.

Holt, L. F., & Sweitzer, M. D. (2020). More than a black and white issue: Ethnic identity, social dominance orientation, and support for the Black Lives Matter movement. *Self and Identity*, *19*(1), 16–31. https://doi.org/10.1080/15298868.2018.1524788.

Hovick, S. R., & Holt, L. F. (2016). Beyond race and ethnicity: Exploring the effects of ethnic identity and its implications for cancer communication efforts. *Journal of Health Communication*, *21*(2), 199–207. https://doi.org/10.1080/10810730.2015.1058436.

Hsieh, E. (2004). Stories in action and the dialogic management of identities: Storytelling in transplant support group meetings. *Research on Language and Social Interaction*, *37*(1), 39–70. https://doi.org/10.1207/s15327973rlsi3701_2.

Jack, A. (2020). The gender reveal party. *International Journal of Child, Youth and Family Studies*, *11*(2), 82–93. https://doi.org/10.18357/ijcyfs112202019520.

Jensen, L. A., Arnett, J. J., Feldman, S. S., & Cauffman, E. (2004). The right to do wrong: Lying to parents among adolescents and emerging adults. *Journal of Youth and Adolescence*, *33*(2), 101–112. https://doi.org/10.1023/B:JOYO.0000013422.48100.5a.

Johns, M. M., Poteat, V. P., Horn, S. S., & Kosciw, J. (2019). Strengthening our schools to promote resilience and health among LGBTQ youth: Emerging evidence and research priorities from The State of LGBTQ Youth Health and

Wellbeing Symposium. *LGBT Health*, 6(4), 146–155. https://doi.org/10.1089/lgbt.2018.0109.

Jung, E., & Hecht, M. L. (2004a). Elaborating the communication theory of identity: Identity gaps and communication outcomes. *Communication Studies*, *52*(3), 265–283, https://doi.org/10.1080/01463370409370197.

Jung, E., & Hecht, M. L. (2004b). Korean Americans' identity gaps in interethnic interaction and levels of depression. Unpublished manuscript.

Karp, D. A., Holmstrom, L. L., & Gray, P. S. (2004). Of roots and wings: Letting go of the college-bound child. *Symbolic Interaction*, *27*, 357–382.

Kenny, D. A. (2019). *Interpersonal perception, second edition: the foundation of social relationships*. New York: Guilford Press.

King, M. E., & Theiss, J. A. (2016). The communicative and physiological manifestations of relational turbulence during the empty-nest phase of marital relationships. *Communication Quarterly*, *64*(5), 495–517. https://doi.org/10.1080/01463373.2015.1129353.

Knobloch-Westerwick, S., & Hastall, M. R (2006). Social comparisons with news personae: Selective exposure to news portrayals of same-sex and same-age characters. *Communication Research*, *33*(4), 262–284. https://doi.org/10.1177/0093650206289152.

Leary, M. R. (2019). *Self-presentation: Impression management and interpersonal behavior*. London: Routledge.

Lefkowitz, E. S. (2005). "Things have gotten better": Developmental changes among emerging adults after the transition to university. *Journal of Adolescent Research*, *20*(1), 40–63. https://doi.org/10.1177/0743558404271236.

Li, Y., & Samp, J. A. (2019). Predictors and outcomes of initial coming out messages: Testing the theory of coming out message production. *Journal of Applied Communication Research*, *47*(1), 69–89. https://doi.org/10.1080/00909882.2019.1566631.

Lutz, C. J., & Ross, S. R. (2003). Elaboration versus fragmentation: Distinguishing between self complexity and self-concept differentiation. *Journal of Social and Clinical Psychology*, *22*(5), 537–559. https://doi.org/10.1521/jscp.22.5.537.22927.

Maas, M. K., & Lefkowitz, E. S. (2015). Sexual esteem in emerging adulthood: Associations with sexual behavior, contraception use, and romantic relationships. *The Journal of Sex Research*, *52*(7), 795–806. https://doi.org/10.1080/00224499.2014.945112.

Marciano, A. (2014). Living the VirtuReal: negotiating transgender identity in cyberspace. *Journal of Computer-Mediated Communication*, *19*, 824–838. DOI:10.1111/jcc4.12081.

Marsiglia, F. F., Kulis, S., & Hecht, M. L. (2001). Ethnic labels and ethnic identity as predictors of drug use and drug exposure among middle school students in the Southwest. *Journal of Research on Adolescence*, *11*(1), 21–48. https://doi.org/10.1111/1532-7795.00002.

Martey, R. M., & Consalvo, M. (2011). Performing the looking-glass self: Avatar appearance and group identity in Second Life. *Popular Communication*, *9*(3), 165–180. https://doi.org/10.1080/15405702.2011.583830.

McCarthy, M. H., Wood, J. V., & Holmes, J. G. (2017). Dispositional pathways to trust: Self-esteem and agreeableness interact to predict trust and negative emotional disclosure. *Journal of Personality and Social Psychology*, *113*(1), 95–116. https://doi-org/10.1037/pspi0000093.

McConnell, A. R. (2011). The multiple self-aspects framework: Self-concept representation and its implications. *Personality and Social Psychology Review*, *15*(1), 3–27. https://doi.org/10.1177/1088868310371101.

Mehra, B., Merkel, C., & Bishop, A. P. (2004). The internet for empowerment of minority and marginalized users. *New Media and Society*, *6*, 781–802.

Miller-Day, M., & Barnett, J., M. (2004). "I'm not a druggie": Adolescents' ethnicity and (erroneous) beliefs about drug use norms. *Health Communication*, *16*(2), 209–228. https://doi.org/10.1207/S15327027HC1602_5.

Morgan, E. M., Thorne, A., & Zurbriggen, E. L. (2010). A longitudinal study of conversations with parents about sex and dating during college. *Developmental Psychology*, *46*(1), 139–150. https://doi.org/10.1037/a0016931.

Nagy, M. E., & Theiss, J. A. (2013). Applying the relational turbulence model to the empty-nest transition: Sources of relationship change, relational uncertainty, and interference from partners. *Journal of Family Communication*, *13*(4), 280–300. https://doi.org/10.1080/15267431.2013.823430.

Nelson, L. J., & Barry, C. M. (2005). Distinguishing features of emerging adulthood: The role of self-classification as an adult. *Journal of Adolescent Research*, *20*(2), 242–262. https://doi.org/10.1177/0743558404273074.

Palomares, N. A. (2004). Gender schematicity, gender identity salience, and gender-linked language use. *Human Communication Research*, *30*(4), 556–588. https://doi.org/10.1111/j.1468-2958.2004.tb00745.x.

Price-Feeney, M., Green, A. E., & Dorison, S. H. (2020). Suicidality among youth who are questioning, unsure of, or exploring their sexual identity. *Journal of Sex Research*, *58*(5), 581–588. https://doi.org/10.1080/00224499.2020.1832184.

Rosario, M., Schrimshaw, E. W., Hunter, J., & Braun, L. (2006). Sexual identity development among lesbian, gay, and bisexual youths: Consistency and change over time. *Journal of Sex Research*, *43*(1), 46–58. https://doi.org/10.1080/00224490609552298.

Rosenberg, M. (2015). *Society and the adolescent self-image*. Rahway, NJ: Princeton University Press.

Soliz, J., & Harwood, J. (2006). Shared family identity, age salience, and intergroup contact: Investigation of the grandparent-grandchild relationship. *Communication Monographs*, *73*(1), 87–107. https://doi.org/10.1080/03637750500534388.

Subrahmanyam, K., Smahel, D., & Greenfield, P. (2006). Connecting developmental constructions to the Internet: Identity presentation and sexual exploration in online teen chat rooms. *Developmental Psychology*, *42*(3), 395–406. https://doi.org/10.1037/0012-1649.42.3.395.

Swann, W. (2012). Self-verification theory. In P. A. Van LangeA. W. Kruglanski, & E. T. Higgins (Eds.), *Handbook of theories of social psychology* (Vol. 2, pp. 23–42). Thousand Oaks, CA: Sage. www.doi.org/10.4135/9781446249222.n27.

Terán, L., Yan, K., & Aubrey, J. S. (2020). "But first let me take a selfie": US adolescent girls' selfie activities, self-objectification, imaginary audience beliefs, and appearance concerns. *Journal of Children and Media*, *14*(3), 343–360. https://doi.org/10.1080/17482798.2019.1697319.

Tiidenberg, K., & van der Nagel, E. (2020). *Sex and social media*. Emerald Publishing.

Toomey, A., Dorjee, T., & Ting-Toomey, S. (2013). Bicultural identity negotiation, conflicts, and intergroup communication strategies. *Journal of Intercultural Communication Research*, *42*(2), 112–134. https://doi.org/10.1080/17475759.2013.785973.

Tracy, S. J., & Scott, C. (2006). Sexuality, masculinity, and taint management among firefighters and correctional officers: Getting down and dirty with "America's Heroes" and the "Scum of Law Enforcement." *Management Communication Quarterly*, *20*(1), 6–38. https://doi.org/10.1177/0893318906287898.

Virginia Christian Alliance. (2012). *A rainbow of lies*. Retrieved online 11/30/2020 at: https://vachristian.org/at-the-end-of-the-rainbow-refuting-the-homosexual-claims.

4 PERCEPTION AND INTERPERSONAL COMMUNICATION

Albada, K. F., Knapp, M. L., & Theune, K. E. (2002). Interaction appearance theory: Changing perceptions of physical attractiveness through social interaction. *Communication Theory*, *12*(1), 8–40. https://doi.org/10.1093/ct/12.1.8.

April, M., & Schrodt, P. (2019). Person-centered messages, attributions of responsibility, and the willingness to forgive parental infidelity. *Communication Studies*, *70*(1), 79–98. https://doi.org/10.1080/10510974.2018.1469525.

Atkinson, J. L., & Sloan, R. G. (2017). Exploring the impact of age, race, and stereotypes on perceptions of language performance and patronizing speech. *Journal of Language and Social Psychology*, *36*(3), 287–305. https://doi.org/10.1177/0261927X16662967.

Barker, V., Giles, H., & Harwood, J. (2004). Inter- and intragroup perspectives on intergenerational communication. In J. F. Nussbaum, & J. Coupland (Eds.), *Handbook of communication and aging research* (2nd ed., pp. 139–165). Mahwah, NJ: Lawrence Erlbaum.

Baumeister, R. F., Bratslavsky, E., Finkenauer, C., & Vohs, K. D. (2001). Bad is stronger than good. *Review of General Psychology*, *5*(4), 323–370. https://doi.org/10.1037/1089-2680.5.4.323.

Berkos, K. M., Allen, T. H., Kearney, P., & Plax, T. G. (2001). When norms are violated: Imagined interactions as processing and coping mechanisms. *Communication Monographs*, *68*(3), 289–300. https://doi.org/10.1080/03637750128066.

Blair, I. V., Chapleau, K. M., & Judd, C. M. (2005). The use of Afrocentric features as cures for judgment in the presence of diagnostic information. *European Journal of Social Psychology*, *35*(1), 59–68. https://doi.org/10.1002/ejsp.232.

Blair, I. V., Judd, C. M., & Chapleau, K. M. (2004). The influence of Afrocentric facial features in criminal sentencing. *Psychological Science*, *15*(10), 674–679. https://doi.org/10.1111/j.0956-7976.2004.00739.x.

Blanchard-Fields, F., & Horhota, M. (2005). Age differences in the correspondence bias: When a plausible explanation matters. *The Journals of Gerontology. Series B, Psychological Sciences and Social Sciences*, *60*(5), 259–267. https://doi.org/10.1093/geronb/60.5.P259.

Bolkan, S., & Griffin, D. J. (2018). Catch and hold: Instructional interventions and their differential impact on student interest, attention, and autonomous motivation. *Communication Education*, *67*(3), 269–286. https://doi.org/10.1080/03634523.2018.1465193.

Brandone, A. C., & Klimek, B. (2018). The developing theory of mental state control: Changes in beliefs about the controllability of emotional experience from elementary school through adulthood. *Journal of Cognition and Development*, *19*(5), 509–531. https://doi.org/10.1080/15248372.2018.1520711.

Burgers, C., & Beukeboom, C. J. (2016). Stereotype transmission and maintenance through interpersonal communication: The irony bias. *Communication Research*, *43*(3), 414–441. https://doi.org/10.1177/0093650214534975.

Burgoon, J. K. (2016). Expectancy violation theory. In C. R. Berger & M. E. Roloff (Eds.), *International encyclopedia of interpersonal communication* (pp. 596–604). Hoboken, NJ: Wiley Blackwell.

Canary, D. J., & Hause, K. S. (1993). Is there any reason to research sex differences in communication? *Communication Quarterly*, *41*(2), 129–144. https://doi.org/10.1080/01463379309369874.

Carr, C., Vitak, J., & McLaughlin, C. (2013). Strength of social cues in online impression formation: Expanding SIDE research. *Communication Research*, *40*(2), 261–281. https://doi.org/10.1177/0093650211430687.

Chalik, L., Rivera, C., & Rhodes, M. (2014). Children's use of categories and mental states to predict social behavior. *Developmental Psychology*, *50*(10), 2360–2367. https://doi.org/10.1037/a0037729.

Chen, C. Y., Joyce, N., Harwood, J., & Xiang, J. (2017). Stereotype reduction through humor and accommodation during imagined communication with older adults. *Communication Monographs*, *84*(1), 94–109. https://doi.org/10.1080/03637751.2016.1149737.

Cortes, K., Leith, S., & Wilson, A. E. (2018). Relationship satisfaction and the subjective distance of past relational events. *Journal of Social and Personal Relationships*, *35*(8), 1092–1117. https://doi.org/10.1177/0265407517704721.

Davis, M. H. (1980). A multidimensional approach to individual differences in empathy. *JSAS Catalog of Selected Documents in Psychology*, *10*, 85–105.

Edwards, R., Bybee, B. T., Frost, J. K., Harvey, A. J., & Navarro, M. (2017). That's not what I meant: How misunderstanding is related to channel and perspective-taking. *Journal of Language and Social Psychology*, *36*(2), 188–210. https://doi.org/10.1177/0261927X16662968.

Epstein, N. B. (2016). Reattribution. In G. R. Weeks, S. T. Fife, and C. M. Peterson (Eds.), *Techniques for the couple therapist: Essential interventions form the experts* (pp. 87–91). New York, NY: Routledge.

Epstein, N. B., Baucom, D. H., Kirby, J. S., & LaTaillade, J. J. (2019). Cognitive-behavioral therapy. In K. S. Dobson, & D. J. A. Dozois (Ed.), *Handbook of cognitive-behavioral therapies* (4th ed, pp. 433–463). New York, NY: Guilford Press.

Fask, L., A., Reimer, H. M., & Funder, D. C. (2008). The social behavior and reputation of the attributionally complex. *Journal of Research in Personality*, *42*(1), 208–222. https://doi.org/10.1016/j.jrp.2007.05.009.

Finchman, F. D., & Bradbury, T. N. (2004). Marital satisfaction, depression, and attributions: A longitudinal analysis. In R. M. Kowalski & M. R. Leary (Eds.), *The interface of social and clinical psychology: Key readings* (pp. 129–146). New York, NY: Psychology Press.

Fletcher, G. J. O., Danilovics, P., Fernandez, G., Peterson, D., & Reeder, G. D. (1986). Attributional complexity: An individual differences measure. *Journal of Personality and Social Psychology*, *51*(4), 875–884. https://doi.org/10.1037/0022-3514.51.4.875.

Follett, K., & Hess, T. M. (2002). Aging, cognitive complexity, and the fundamental attribution error. *The Journals of Gerontology*, *57*(4), 312–323. https://doi.org/10.1093/geronb/57.4.P312.

Gilbert, P., Irons, C., Olsen, K., Gilbert, J., & McEwan, K. (2006). Interpersonal sensitivities: Their links to mood, anger and gender. *Psychology and Psychotherapy: Theory, Research and Practice*, *79*(1), 37–51. https://doi.org/10.1348/147608305X43856.

Goodboy, A. K., Bolkan, S., & Baker, J. (2018). Instructor misbehaviors impede students' cognitive learning: Testing the causal assumption. *Communication Education*, *67*(3), 308–329. https://doi.org/10.1080/03634523.2018.1465192.

Hamilton, L. M., & Duke, R. A. (2020). Changes in perception accompany the development of music performance skills. *Journal of Research in Music Education*, *68*(2), 175–192. https://doi.org/10.1177/0022429420920567.

Hancock, J. R., & Dunham, P. J. (2001). Impression formation in computer-mediated communication revisited. *Communication Research*, *28*(3), 325–347. https://doi.org/10.1177/009365001028003004.

Hendriks, H., & Yzer, M. (2020). Is involvement a good thing? The undesirable consequences of topical and conversational involvement in the context of alcohol consumption. *Journal of Health Communication*, *25*(1), 66–73. https://doi.org/10.1080/10810730.2019.1701587.

Hong, Y., Benet-Martinez, V., Chiu, C., & Morris, M. W. (2003). Boundaries of cultural influence: Construct activation as a mechanism for cultural differences in social perception. *Journal of Cross-Cultural Psychology*, *34*(4), 453–464. https://doi.org/10.1177/0022022103034004005.

Ishii, K., Reyes, J. A., & Kitayama, S. (2003). Spontaneous attention to word content versus emotional tone: Differences among three cultures. *Psychological Science*, *14*(1), 39–46. https://doi.org/10.1111/1467-9280.01416.

Ito, K., Masuda, T., Man Wai Li, L. (2013). Agency and facial emotion judgment in context. *Personality and Social Psychology Bulletin*, *39*(6), 763–776. https://doi.org/10.1177/0146167213481387.

Joireman, J. (2004). Relationships between attributional complexity and empathy. *Individual Differences Research*, *2*(3), 197–202.

Jones-Eversley, S. D., Rice, J., Adedoyin, A. C., & James-Townes, L. (2020). Premature deaths of young Black males in the United States. *Journal of Black Studies*, *51*(3), 251–272. https://doi.org/10.1177/0021934719895999.

Kashima, Y., Lyons, A., & Clark, A. (2013). The maintenance of cultural stereotypes in the conversational retelling of narratives. *Asian Journal of Social Psychology*, *16*(1), 60–70. https://doi.org/10.1111/ajsp.12004.

Lac, A., & Berger, D. E. (2013). Development and validation of the alcohol myopia scale. *Psychological Assessment*, *25*(3), 738–747. doi.org/10.1037/a0032535.

Lannutti, P. J., & Monahan, J. L. (2002). When the frame paints the picture: Alcohol consumption, relational framing, and sexual communication. *Communication Research*, *29*(4), 390–421. https://doi.org/10.1177/0093650202029004002.

Ledgerwood, A., Easwick, P. W., & Smith, L. K. (2018). Toward an integrative framework for studying human evaluation: Attitudes toward objects and attributes. *Personality and Social Psychology Review*, *22*(4), 378–398. https://doi.org/10.1177/1088868318790718.

Lewandowski, G. W., Aron, A., & Gee, J. (2007). Personality goes a long way: the malleability of opposite-sex physical attractiveness. *Personal Relationships*, *14*(4), 571–585. https://doi.org/10.1111/j.1475-6811.2007.00172.x.

Ma, Y., Xue, W., Zhao, G., Tu, S., & Zheng, Y. (2019). Romantic love and attentional biases toward attractive alternatives and rivals: Long-term relationship maintenance among female Chinese college students. *Evolutionary Psychology*, *17*(4), 1–14. https://doi.org/10.1177/1474704919897601.

Maass, A., Arcuri, L, & Suitner, C. (2014). Shaping intergroup relations through language. In T. M. Holtgraves (Ed.), *The Oxford handbook of language and social psychology* (pp. 157–176). New York, NY: Oxford University Press. https://doi.org/10.1093/oxfordhb/9780199838639.013.036.

MacFadden, A., Elias, L, & Saucier, D. (2003). Males and females scan maps similarly, but give directions differently. *Brain and Cognition*, *53*(2), 297–300. https://doi.org/10.1016/S0278-2626(03)00130-1.

MacGeorge, E. L. (2001). Support providers' interaction goals: The influence of attributions and emotions. *Communication Monographs*, *68*(1), 72–97. https://doi.org/10.1080/03637750128050.

McNulty, J. K., O'Mara, E. M., & Karney, B. R. (2008). Benevolent cognitions as a strategy of relationship maintenance: "Don't sweat the small stuff" … But it is not all small stuff. *Journal of Personality and Social Psychology*, *94*(4), 631–646. https://doi.org/10.1037/0022-3514.94.4.631.

Monahan, J. L., Murphy, S. T., & Miller, L. C. (1999). When women imbibe: Alcohol and the illusory control of HIV risk. *Psychology of Women Quarterly*, *23*(3), 643–651. https://doi.org/10.1111/j.1471-6402.1999.tb00386.x.

Nathanson, A. I., Wilson, B. J., McGee, J., & Sebastian, M. (2002). Counteracting the effects of stereotypes on television via active mediation. *Journal of*

Communication, *52*(4), 922–937. https://doi.org/10.1111/j.1460-2466.2002.tb02581.x.

Nguyen, T. P., Karney, B. R., Kennedy, D. P., & Bradbusy, T. N. (2020). Couples' diminished social and financial capital exacerbate the association between maladaptive attributions and relationship satisfaction. *Cognitive Therapy and Research*, *45*, 529–541. https://doi.org/10.1007/s10608-020-10161-w.

Oliver, M. B., Jackson II, R. L., Moses, N. N., & Dangerfield, C. L. (2004). The face of crime: Viewers' memory of race-related facial features of individuals pictured in the news. *Journal of Communication*, *54*(1), 88–104. https://doi.org/10.1111/j.1460-2466.2004.tb02615.x.

Pansky, A., Oren, Y., Yaniv, H., Landa, O., Gotlieb, A., & Hemed, E. (2019). Positive and negative effects of gender expertise on episodic memory. *Memory & Cognition*, *47*(2), 257–265. https://doi.org/10.3758/s13421-018-0863-z.

Peng, K., & Knowles, E. D. (2003). Culture, education, and the attribution of physical causality. *Personality and Social Psychology Bulletin*, *29*(10), 1272–1284. https://doi.org/10.1177/0146167203254601.

Peterson, R. S., Dvorak, R. D., Stevenson, B. L., Kramer, M. P., Pinto, D. A., Mora, E. T., & Leary, A V. (2020). Protective behavioral strategies and alcohol-related regretted sex among college students. *Experimental and clinical Psychopharmacology*, *28*(1), 6–12. https://doi.org/10.1037/pha0000291.

Pfister, R., Pohl, C., Keisel, A., & Kunde, W. (2012). Your unconscious knows your name. *PlosOne*, *7*(3), e32402. https://doi.org/10.1371/journal.pone.0032402

Purdie, M. P., Norris, J., Davis, K. C., Zawacki, T., Morrison, D. M., George, W. H., & Keikel, P. A. (2011). The effects of acute alcohol intoxication, partner risk level, and general intention to have unprotected sex on women's sexual decision making with a new partner. *Experimental and Clinical Psychopharmacology*, *19*(5), 378–388. https://doi.org/10.1037/a0024792.

Rains, S. A., Tsetsi, E., Akers, C., Pavlich, C. A., & Appelbaum, M. (2019). Factors influencing the quality of social support messages produced online: The role of responsibility for distress and others' support attempts. *Communication Research*, *46*(6), 866–886. https://doi.org/10.1177/0093650218796371

Samp, J. A., & Monahan, J. L. (2011). Communicating about a relational problem while intoxicated: Influences on goal judgements and message features. *Communication Studies*, *62*(3), 328–348. https://doi.org/10.1080/10510974.2010.550667.

Scott-Sheldon, L. A., Carey, K. B., Cunningham, K., Johnson, B. T., & Carey, M. P. (2016). Alcohol use predicts sexual decision-making: A systematic review and meta-analysis of the experimental literature. *AIDS and Behavior*, *20*(S1), 19–39. https://doi.org/10.1007/s10461-015-1108-9.

Senzaki, S., Masuda, T., Takada, A., & Okada, H. (2016). The communication of culturally dominant modes of attention from parents to children: A comparison of Canadian and Japanese parent-child conversations during a joint scene description task. *PLoS ONE*, *11*(1), https://doi.org/10.1371/journal.pone.0147199.

Shapiro, M. A., & Fox, J. R. (2002). The role of typical and atypical events in story memory. *Human Communication Research*, *28*(1), 109–135. https://doi.org/10.1093/hcr/28.1.109.

Steele, C. M., & Josephs, R. A. (1990). Alcohol myopia: Its prized and dangerous effects. *American Psychologist*, *45*(8), 921–933. https://doi.org/10.1037/0003-066X.45.8.921.

Swinton, A. D., Kurtz-Costes, B., Rowley, S. J., & Adeyanju, N. (2011). A longitudinal examination of African American adolescents' attributions about achievement outcomes. *Child Development*, *82*(5), 1486–1500. https://doi.org/10.1111/j.1467-8624.2011.01623.x.

Vanden Abeele, M. M. P., Antheunis, M. L., & Schouten, A. P. (2016). The effect of mobile messaging during a conversation on impression formation and interaction quality. *Computers in Human Behavior*, *62*, 562–569. https://doi.org/10.1016/j.chb.2016.04.005.

Walther, J. B. (2011). Theories of computer-mediated communication and interpersonal relations. In M. L. Knapp & J. A. Daly (Eds.), *The Handbook on Interpersonal Communication* (4th edition, pp. 443–479). Thousand Oaks, CA: Sage.

Walther, J. B., Anderson, J. R., & Park, D. (1994). Interpersonal effects in computer-mediated interaction: A meta-analysis of social and anti-social communication. *Communication Research*, *21*(4), 460–487. https://doi.org/10.1177/009365094021004002.

Weiner, B. (1986). *An attributional theory of motivation and emotion*. New York: Springer-Verlag.

Weiner, B. (1995). *Judgments of responsibility: A foundation for a theory of social conduct*. New York: Guilford Press.

Weiner, B. (2006). *Social motivation, justice, and the moral emotions: An attributional approach*. Mahwah, NJ: Lawrence Erlbaum Associates.

Wigboldus, D. H. J., Semin, G. R., & Spears, R. (2000). How do we communicate stereotypes? Linguistic bases and inferential consequences. *Journal of Personality and Social Psychology*, *78*(1), 5–18. https://doi.org/10.1037/0022-3514.78.1.5.

Wigboldus, D. H. J., Semin, G. R., & Spears, R. (2006). Communicating expectancies about others. *European Journal of Social Psychology*, *36*(6), 815–824. https://doi.org/10.1002/ejsp.323.

Woods, E. (1996). Associations of nonverbal decoding ability with indices of person-centered communicative ability. *Communication Reports*, *9*(1), 13–22. https://doi.org/10.1080/08934219609367631.

5 LANGUAGE AND INTERPERSONAL COMMUNICATION

Allgood, S. M., Seedall, R. B., & Williams, R. B. (2020). Expressive writing and marital satisfaction: A writing sample analysis. *Family Relations*, *69*(2), 380–391. https://doi.org/10.1111/fare.12416.

Babad, E. (1980). Expectancy bias in scoring as a function of ability and ethnic labels. *Psychological Reports*, *46*(2), 625–626. https://doi.org/10.2466/pr0.1980.46.2.625.

Barnes, B., Palmary, I., & Durrheim, K. (2001). The denial of racism: The role of humor, personal experience, and self-censorship. *Journal of Language and Social Psychology*, *20*(3), 321–338. https://doi.org/10.1177/0261927X01020003003.

Bianco, M. (2005). The effects of disability labels on special education and general education teachers' referrals for gifted programs. *Learning Disability Quarterly*, *28*(4), 285–293. https://doi.org/10.2307/4126967.

Bolden, G. B. (2006). Little words that matter: Discourse markers "so" and "oh" and the doing of other-attentiveness in social interaction. *Journal of Communication*, *56*(4), 661–688. https://doi.org/10.1111/j.1460-2466.2006.00314.x.

Boutonnet, B., Dering, B., Viñas-Guasch, N., & Thierry, G. (2013). Seeing objects through the language glass. *Journal of Cognitive Neuroscience*, *25*(10), 1702–1710. https://doi.org/10.1162/jocn_a_00415.

Bowes, A., & Katz, A. (2015). Metaphor creates intimacy and temporarily enhances theory of mind. *Memory & Cognition*, *43*(6), 953–963. https://doi.org/10.3758/s13421-015-0508-4.

Brown, P., & Levinson, S. C. (1987). *Politeness: Some universals in language usage*. Cambridge: Cambridge University Press.

Brownlow, S., Rosamond, J. A., & Parker, J. A. (2003). Gender-linked linguistic behavior in television interviews. *Sex Roles*, *49*(3), 121–132. https://doi.org/10.1023/A:1024404812972.

Carter, S. P., Osborne, L. J., Renshaw, K. D., Allen, E. S., Loew, B. A., Markman, H. J., & Stanley, S. M. (2018). Something to talk about: Topics of conversation between romantic partners during military deployments. *Journal of Family Psychology*, *32*(1), 22–30. https://doi.org/10.1037/fam0000373.

Cate, R. M., & Lloyd, S. A. (1992). *Courtship*. Newbury Park, CA: Sage.

Cralley, E. L., & Ruscher, J. B. (2005). Lady, girl, female, or woman: Sexism and cognitive busyness predict use of gender-biased nouns. *Journal of Language and Social Psychology*, *24*(3), 300–314. https://doi.org/10.1177/0261927X05278391.

Dillard, J. P. (2014). Language, style, and persuasion. In T. M. Holtgraves (Ed.), *The Oxford Handbook of Language and Social Psychology* (pp. 177–187). New York, NY: Oxford University Press.

Dorland, J. M., & Fischer, A. R. (2001). Gay, lesbian, and bisexual individuals' perceptions: An analogue study. *The Counseling Psychologist*, *29*(4), 532–547. https://doi.org/10.1177/0011000001294004.

Douglas, K. M., & Sutton, R. M. (2006). When what you say about others says something about you: Language abstraction and inferences about describers' attitudes and goals. *Journal of Experimental Social Psychology*, *42*(4), 500–508. https://doi.org/10.1016/j.jesp.2005.06.001.

Duck, S., & Usera, D. A. (2014). Language and interpersonal relationships. In T. M. Holtgraves (Ed.), *The Oxford Handbook of Language and Social Psychology* (pp. 188–200). New York, NY: Oxford University Press.

Fehr, B. (2019). Everyday conceptions of love. In R. J. Sternberg, & K. Sternberg (Eds.), *The New Psychology of Love* (2nd ed., pp. 154–182). New York, NY: Cambridge University Press.

Felmlee, D., Rodis, P. I., & Zhang, A. (2020). Sexist slurs: Reinforcing feminine stereotypes online. *Sex Roles*, *83*(1–2), *16–28*. https://doi.org/10.1007/s11199-019-01095-z.

Frey, N. (2005). Retention, social promotion, and academic redshirting: What do we know and need to know? *Remedial and Special Education*, *26*(6), 332–346. https://doi.org/10.1177/07419325050260060401.

Goldsmith, D. J., & Baxter, L A. (1996). Constituting relationships in talk: A taxonomy of speech events in social and personal relationships. *Human Communication Research*, *23*(1), 87–114. https://doi.org/10.1111/j.1468-2958.1996.tb00388.x.

Greiffenhagen, C., & Sharrock, W. (2007). Linguistic relativism: Logic, grammar, and arithmetic in cultural comparison. *Language & Communication*, *27*(1), 81–107. https://doi.org/10.1016/j.langcom.2006.05.001.

Grice, H. P. (1957). Meaning. *The Philosophical Review*, *66*(3), 377–388. https://doi.org/10.2307/2182440.

Grice, H. P. (1975). Logic and conversation. In P. Cole, & J. L. Morgan (Eds.), *Syntax and Semantics 3: Speech acts* (pp. 41–58). New York: Academic Press.

Guerin, B. (2003). Combating prejudice and racism: New interventions from a functional analysis of racist language. *Journal of Community and Applied Social Psychology*, *13*(1), 29–45. https://doi.org/10.1002/casp.699.

Guiller, J., & Durndell, A. (2006). "I totally agree with you": Gender interactions in educational online discussion groups. *Journal of Computer Assisted Learning*, *22*(5), 368–381. https://doi.org/10.1111/j.1365-2729.2006.00184.x.

Hansen, K., Littwitz, C., & Sczesny, S. (2016). The social perception of heroes and murderers: Effects of gender-inclusive language in media reports. *Frontiers in Psychology*, 7, 369. https://doi.org/10.3389/fpsyg.2016.00369.

Harris, T. M., & Moffitt, K. (2019). Centering communication in our understanding of microaggressions, race, and otherness in academe and beyond. *Southern Communication Journal*, *84*(2), 67–71. https://doi.org/10.1080/1041794X.2018.1515978.

Holling, M. A. (2019). "You intimidate me" as a microaggressive controlling image to discipline women of color faculty. *Southern Communication Journal*, *84*(2), 99–112. https://doi.org/10.1080/1041794X.2018.1511748.

Holtgraves, T. (2002). Comprehending speaker meaning. In W. B. Gudykunst (Ed.), *Communication Yearbook 26* (pp. 2–35). Mahwah, NJ: Lawrence Erlbaum.

Horton, W. S. (2007). Metaphor and readers' attributions of intimacy. *Memory & Cognition*, *35*(1), 87–95. https://doi.org/10.3758/BF03195945.

Hosman, L. A., & Siltanen, S. A. (2011). Hedges, tag questions, message processing, and persuasion. *Journal of Language and Social Psychology*, *30*(3), 341–349. https://doi.org/10.1177/0261927X11407169.

Hussey, K. A., & Katz, A. N. (2006). Metaphor production in online conversation: Gender and friendship status. *Discourse Processes*, *42*(1), 75–98. https://doi.org/10.1207/s15326950dp4201_3.

Joshi, P. D., Wakslak, C. J., Appel, G., & Huang, L. (2020). Gender differences in communicative abstraction. *Journal of Personality and Social Psychology*, *118*(3), 417–435. https://doi.org/10.1037/pspa0000177.

Kelly, K. R., & Bailey, A. L. (2012). Becoming independent storytellers: Modeling children's development of narrative macrostructure. *First Language*, *33*(1), 68–88. https://doi.org/10.1177/0142723711433582.

Kesebir, S. (2017). Word order denotes relevance differences: The case of conjoined phrases with lexical gender. *Journal of Personality and Social Psychology*, *113*(3), 262–279. https://doi.org/10.1037/pspi0000094.

Knobloch, L. K., & Solomon, D. H. (2003). Manifestations of relationship conceptualizations in conversation. *Human Communication Research*, *29*(4), 482–515. https://doi.org/10.1093/hcr/29.4.482.

Krieger, J. L., Parrott, R. L., & Nussbaum, J. F. (2011). Metaphor use and health literacy: A pilot study of strategies to explain randomization in cancer clinical trials. *Journal of Health Communication*, *16*(1), 3–16. https://doi.org/10.1080/10810730.2010.529494.

Lakoff, R. (1973). Language and woman's place. *Language in Society*, *1*, 45–80. https://doi.org/10.1017/S0047404500000051.

Leaper, C. (2014). Gender similarities and differences in language. In T. M. Holtgraves (Ed.), *The Oxford handbook of language and social psychology* (pp. 62–81). New York, NY: Oxford University Press. https://doi.org/10.1093/oxfordhb/9780199838639.013.002.

Leaper, C., & Ayres, M. M. (2007). A meta-analytic review of gender variations in adults' language use: Talkativeness, affiliative speech, and assertive speech. *Personality and Social Psychology Review*, *11*(4), 328–363. https://doi.org/10.1177/1088868307302221.

Leaper, C., & Smith, T. E. (2004). A meta-analytic review of gender variations in children's language use: Talkativeness, affiliative speech, and assertive speech. *Developmental Psychology*, *40*(6), 993–1027. https://doi.org/10.1037/0012-1649.40.6.993.

Levine, T. R., Anders, L. N., Banas, J., Baum, K. L., Endo, K., Hu, A. D. S., & Wong, N. C. H. (2000). Norms, expectations, and deception: A norm violation model of veracity judgments. *Communication Monographs*, *67*(2), 123–137. https://doi.org/10.1080/03637750009376500.

Lindqvist, A., Renström, E. A., & Gustafsson Sendén, M. (2019). Reducing a male bias in language? Establishing the efficiency of three different gender-fair language strategies. *Sex Roles*, *81*(1–2), 109–117. https://doi.org/10.1007/s11199-018-0974-9.

Mathies, N., Coleman, T., McKie, R. M., Woodford, M. R., Courtice, E. L., Travers, R., & Renn, K. A. (2019). Hearing "that's so gay" and "no homo" on academic outcomes for LGBQ+ college students. *Journal of LGBT Youth*, *16*(3), 255–277. https://doi.org/10.1080/19361653.2019.1571981.

Miller, C. H., Lane, L. T., Deatrick, L. M., Young, A. M., & Potts, K. A. (2007). Psychological reactance and promotional health messages. *Human Communication Research*, *33*(2), 219–240. https://doi.org/10.1111/j.1468-2958.2007.00297.x.

Morand, D. A. (2000). Language and power: An empirical analysis of linguistic strategies used in superior-subordinate communication. *Journal of Organizational Behavior*, *21*(3), 235–248. https://doi.org/10.1002/(SICI)1099-1379(200005)21:3<235::AID-JOB9>3.0.CO;2-N.

Morand, D. A. (2005). Black holes in social space: The occurrence and effects of name-avoidance in organizations. *Journal of Applied Social Psychology*, *35*(2), 320–334. https://doi.org/10.1111/j.1559-1816.2005.tb02123.x.

Morand, D. A. (2014). Using politeness to model the psychosocial dynamics of power in organizational interaction. *International Journal of Organizational Analysis*, *22*(2), 247–273. https://doi.org/10.1108/IJOA-09-2011-0515.

Morrison, W. F., & Rizza, M. G. (2007). Creating a toolkit for identifying twice-exceptional students. *Journal for the Education of the Gifted*, *31*(1), 57–76. https://doi.org/10.4219/jeg-2007-513.

Mulac, A., & Lundell, T. L. (1986). Linguistic contributors to the gender-linked language effect. *Journal of Language and Social Psychology*, *5*(2), 81–101. https://doi.org/10.1177/0261927X8652001.

Mulac, A., Bradac, J. J., & Gibbons, P. (2001). Empirical support for the gender-as-culture hypothesis: An intercultural analysis of male/female language differences. *Human Communication Research*, *27*(1), 121–152. https://doi.org/10.1111/j.1468-2958.2001.tb00778.x.

Mulac, A., Giles, H., Bradac, J. J., & Palomares, N. A. (2013). The gender-linked language effect: An empirical test of a general process model. *Language Sciences*, *38*, 22–31. https://doi.org/10.1016/j.langsci.2012.12.004.

Parks, J. B., & Roberton, M. A. (2000). Development and validation of an instrument to measure attitudes toward sexist/nonsexist language. *Sex Roles*, *42*(5), 415–438. https://doi.org/10.1023/A:1007002422225.

Patev, A. J., Dunn, C. E., Hood, K. B., & Barber, J. M. (2019). College students' perceptions of gender-inclusive language use predict attitudes toward transgender and gender nonconforming individuals. *Journal of Language and Social Psychology*, *38*(3), 329–352. https://doi.org/10.1177/0261927X18815930.

Pennebaker, J. W., Mehl, M. R., & Niederhoffer, K. G. (2003). Psychological aspects of natural language use: Our words, our selves. *Annual Review of Psychology*, *54*(1), 547–577. ttps://doi.org/10.1146/annurev.psych.54.101601.145041.

Pexman, P. M., & Zvaigzne, M. T. (2004). Does irony go better with friends? *Metaphor and Symbol*, *19*(2), 143–163. https://doi.org/10.1207/s15327868ms1902_3.

Pilling, M., & Davies, I. R. L. (2004). Linguistic relativism and colour cognition. *British Journal of Psychology*, *95*(4), 429–455. https://doi.org/10.1348/0007126042369820.

Prewitt-Freilino, J. L., Caswell, T. A., & Laakso, E. K. (2012). The gender of language: A comparison of gender equality in countries with gendered, natural gender, and genderless language. *Sex Roles*, *66*(3–4), 268–281. https://doi.org/10.1007/s11199-011-0083-5.

Rodriquez, S. R. (2014). "We'll only see parts of each other's lives": The role of mundane talk in maintaining nonresidential parent-child relationships. *Journal of Social and Personal Relationships*, *31*(8), 1134–1152. https://doi.org/10.1177/0265407514522898.

Saalbach, H., & Imai, M. (2012). The relation between linguistic categories and cognition: The case of numeral classifiers. *Language and Cognitive Processes*, *27*(3), 381–428. https://doi.org/10.1080/01690965.2010.546585.

Sahlstein, E. M. (2006). Making plans: Praxis strategies for negotiating uncertainty-certainty in long-distance relationships. *Western Journal of Communication*, *70*(2), 147–165. https://doi.org/10.1080/10570310600710042.

Saygin, A. P., & Cicekli, I. (2002). Pragmatics in human-computer conversations. *Journal of Pragmatics*, *34*(3), 227–258. https://doi.org/10.1016/S0378-2166(02)80001-7.

Schrodt, P., Braithwaite, D. O., Soliz, J., Tye-Williams, S., & Miller, A. (2007). An examination of everyday talk in stepfamily systems. *Western Journal of Communication*, *71*(3), 216–234. https://doi.org/10.1080/10570310701510077.

Scott, C. (2019). Compassionate democrats and tough republicans: How ideology shapes partisan stereotypes. *Political Behavior*, *42*(4), 1269–1293. https://doi.org/10.1007/s11109-019-09542-z.

Seider, B. H., Hirschberger, G., Nelson, K. L., & Levenson, R. W. (2009). We can work it out: Age differences in relational pronouns, physiology, and behavior in marital conflict. *Psychology and Aging*, *24*(3), 604–613. https://doi.org/10.1037/a0016950.

Spengler, E. S., Miller, D. J., & Spengler, P. M. (2016). Microaggressions: Clinical errors with sexual minority clients. *Psychotherapy*, *53*(3), 360–366. https://doi.org/10.1037/pst0000073.

Steuber, K. R., & Solomon, D. H. (2011). Managing information within social networks during infertility. In M. Miller-Day (Ed.), *Family communication, connections, and health transitions* (pp. 297–322). New York: Peter Lang.

Sue, D. W., Alsaidi, S., Awad, M. N., Glaeser, E., Calle, C. Z., & Mandez, N. (2019). Disarming racial microaggressions: Microintervention strategies for targets, white allies, and bystanders. *American Psychologist*, *74*(1), 128–142. https://doi.org/10.1037/amp0000296.

Swim, J. K., Mallett, R., & Stangor, C. (2004). Understanding subtle sexism: Detection and use of sexist language. *Sex Roles*, *51*(3/4), 117–128. https://doi.org/10.1023/b:sers.0000037757.73192.06.

Taliaferro, L. A., McMorris, B. J., Rider, G. N., & Eisenberg, M. E. (2019). Risk and protective factors for self-harm in a population-based sample of transgender youth. *Archives of Suicide Research*, *23*(2), 203–221. https://doi.org/10.1080/13811118.2018.1430639.

Thomas-Tate, S., Daugherty, T. K., & Bartkoski, T. J. (2017). Experimental study of gender effects on language use in college students' email to faculty. *College Student Journal*, *51*(2), 222–226.

Thomson, R. (2006). The effect of topic discussion on gendered language in computer-mediated communication discussion. *Journal of Language and Social Psychology*, *25*(2), 167–178. https://doi.org/10.1177/0261927X06286452.

Thurlow, C. (2001). Naming the "outsider within": Homophobic pejoratives and the verbal abuse of lesbian, gay, and bisexual high-school pupils. *Journal of Adolescence*, *24*, 25–38.

Turpin, R., Boekeloo, B., & Dyer, T. (2019). Sexual identity modifies the association between bullying and suicide among adolescents with same-sex sexual partners. *Journal of LGBT Youth*, *16*(3), 300–316. https://doi.org/10.1080/19361653.2019.1575784.

Van Beusekom, G., Collier, K. L., Box, H. M. W., Sanfort, T. G. M., & Overbeek, G. (2020). Gender nonconformity and peer victimization: Sex and sexual attraction differences by age. *The Journal of Sex Research, 57*(2), 234–246. https://doi.org/10.1080/00224499.2019.1591334.

Vangelisti, A. L., Middleton, A. V., & Ebersole, D. S. (2013). Couples' online cognitions during conflict: Links between what partners think and their relational satisfaction. *Communication Monographs, 80*(2), 125–149. https://doi.org/10.1080/03637751.2013.775698.

Watson, R. J., Wheldon, C. W., & Puhl, R. M. (2020). Evidence of diverse identities in a large national sample of sexual and gender minority adolescents. *Journal of Research on Adolescents, 30*, 431–442. doi/10.1111/jora.12488.

Whorf, B. L. (1956). *Language, thought, and reality: Selected readings*. Cambridge, MA: Technology Press of Massachusetts Institute of Technology.

Willis, M., & Jozkowski, K. N. (2018). Ladies first? Not so fast: Linguistic sexism in peer-reviewed research. *Journal of Sex Research, 55*(2), 137–145. https://doi.org/10.1080/00224499.2017.1346058.

6 NONVERBAL COMMUNICATION

Alexander, M. G., & Wood, W. (2000). Women, men, and positive emotions: A social role interpretation. In A. H. Fischer (Ed.), *Gender and emotion: Social psychological perspectives* (pp. 189–210). Paris: Cambridge University Press.

Andersen, P. A. (1985). Nonverbal immediacy in interpersonal communication. In A. W. Siegman & S. Feldstein (Eds.), *Multichannel integrations of nonverbal behavior* (pp. 1–36). Hillsdale, NJ: Erlbaum.

Andersen, P. A., Guerrero, L. K., & Jones, S. M. (2006). Nonverbal behavior in intimate interactions and intimate relationships. In V. L. Manusov & M. L. Patterson (Eds.), *The Sage handbook of nonverbal communication* (pp. 259–278). Thousand Oaks, CA: Sage.

Andersen, P., Gannon, J., & Kalchik, J. (2013). Proxemic and haptic interaction: the closeness continuum. In *Nonverbal Communication* (pp. 295–330). Berlin: De Gruyter. https://doi.org/10.1515/9783110238150.295.

Bänziger, T., Patel, S., & Scherer, K. (2014). The role of perceived voice and speech characteristics in vocal emotion communication. *Journal of Nonverbal Behavior, 38*(1), 31–52. https://doi-org.proxy.libraries.rutgers.edu/10.1007/s10919-013-0165-x.

Ben-Ari, A., & Lavee, Y. (2007). Dyadic closeness in marriage: From the inside story to a conceptual model. *Journal of Social and Personal Relationships, 24*(5), 627–644. https://doi.org/10.1177/0265407507081451.

Beres, M. A., Herold, E., & Maitland, S. B. (2004). Sexual consent behaviors in samesex relationships. *Archives of Sexual Behavior, 33*(5), 475–486. https://doi.org/10.1023/b:aseb.0000037428.41757.10.

Birdwhistell, R. L. (2010). *Kinesics and Context: Essays on Body Motion Communication*. Philadelphia, PA: University of Pennsylvania Press.

Bodie, G. D., Vickery, A. J., Cannava, K., & Jones, S. M. (2015). The role of "active listening" in informal helping conversations: Impact on perceptions of listener helpfulness, sensitivity, and supportiveness and discloser emotional improvement. *Western Journal of Communication, 79*(2), 151–173. https://doi.org/10.1080/10570314.2014.943429.

Bolmont, M., Cacioppo, J. T., & Cacioppo, S. (2014). Love is in the gaze: An eye-tracking study of love and sexual desire. *Psychological Science, 25*(9), 1748–1756. https://doi.org/10.1177/0956797614539706.

Brescoll, V. L. (2011). Who takes the floor and why: Gender, power, and volubility in organizations. *Administrative Science Quarterly*, *56*(4), 622–641. https://doi.org/10.1177/0001839212439994.

Brody, L. R., & Hall, J. A. (2000). Gender, emotion, and expression. In M. Lewis & J. M. Haviland-Jones (Eds.), *Handbook of emotions* (2nd ed., pp. 338–349). New York: Guilford.

Burgoon, J. K. and Buller, D. B. (2015). Interpersonal deception theory. In C. R. Berger, M. E. Roloff, S. R. Wilson, J. P. Dillard, J. Caughlin and D. Solomon (Eds.), *The international encyclopedia of interpersonal communication* (pp. 1–6). Hoboken, NJ: John Wiley & Sons. https://doi.org/10.1002/9781118540190.wbeic170.

Byers, E. S. (2011). Beyond the birds and the bees and was it good for you?: Thirty years of research on sexual communication. *Canadian Psychology/Psychologie Canadienne*, *52*(1), 20–28. https://doi.org/10.1037/a0022048.

Coates, E. J., & Feldman, R. S. (1996). Gender differences in nonverbal correlates of social status. *Personality and Social Psychology Bulletin*, *22*(10), 1014–1022. https://doi.org/10.1177/01461672962210004.

Cortina, L. M. (2008). Unseen injustice: Incivility as modern discrimination in organizations. *Academy of Management Review*, *33*(1), 55–75. https://doi.org/10.5465/amr.2008.27745097.

Derlega, V. J., Catanzaro, D., & Lewis, R. J. (2001). Perceptions about tactile intimacy in same-sex and opposite-sex pairs based on research participants' sexual orientation. *Psychology of Men & Masculinity*, 2(2), 124–132. https://doi.org/10.1037/1524-9220.2.2.124.

Dunbar, N. E., Jensen, M. L., Conly Tower, D., & Burgoon, J. K. (2014). Synchronization of nonverbal behaviors in detecting mediated and non-mediated deception. *Journal of Nonverbal Behavior*, *38*(3), 355–376. https://doi.org/10.1007/s10919-014-0179-z.

Dunbar, N. E., Giles, H., Bernhold, Q., Adams, A., Giles, M., Zamanzadeh, N., Gangi, K., Coveleski, S., & Fujiwara, K. (2020). Strategic synchrony and rhythmic similarity in lies about ingroup affiliation. *Journal of Nonverbal Behavior*, *44*(1), 153–172. https://doi.org/10.1007/s10919-019-00321-2.

Duncan, S., & Fiske, D. W. (2015). *Face-to-face interaction: Research, methods, and theory*. London: Routledge.

Einarsen, S., Hoel, H., & Notelaersa, G. (2009). Measuring exposure to bullying and harassment at work: Validity, factor structure and psychometric properties of the Negative Acts Questionnaire–Revised. *Work & Stress*, *23*(1), 24–44. https://doi.org/10.1080/02678370902815673.

Floyd, K. (2006). An evolutionary approach to understanding nonverbal communication. In V. Manusov & M. L. Patterson (Eds.), *The Sage handbook of nonverbal communication* (pp. 139–158). Thousand Oaks, CA: Sage.

Floyd, K. (2018). *Affectionate communication in close relationships*. Cambridge: Cambridge University Press.

Floyd, K., Boren, J. P., Hannawa, A. F., Hesse, C., McEwan, B., & Veksler, A. E. (2009). Kissing in marital and cohabitating relationships: Effects on blood lipids, stress, and relationship satisfaction. *Western Journal of Communication*, *73*(2), 113–133. https://doi.org/10.1080/10570310902856071.

Fridlund, A. J., & Russell, J. A. (2006). The functions of facial expressions: What's in a face? In V. Manusov & M. L. Patterson (Eds.), *The Sage handbook of nonverbal communication* (pp. 299–320). Thousand Oaks, CA: Sage.

Hall, J. A., & Gunnery, S. D. (2013). Gender differences in nonverbal communication. In J. A. Hall & M. L. Knapp (Eds.), *Handbooks of communication science. Nonverbal communication* (p. 639–669). Berlin: De Gruyter. https://doi.org/10.1515/9783110238150.639.

Hall, J. A., Coats, E. J., & LeBeau, L. S. (2005). Nonverbal behavior and the vertical dimension of social relations: A meta-analysis. *Psychological Bulletin, 131*(6), 898–924. https://doi.org/10.1037/0033-2909.131.6.898.

Hall, J. A., Murphy, N. A., & Schmid Mast, M. (2006). Recall of nonverbal cues: Exploring a new definition of interpersonal sensitivity. *Journal of Nonverbal Behavior, 30*(4), 141–155. https://doi.org/10.1007/s10919-006-0013-3.

Hartwig, M., &Bond, C. F. (2014). Lie detection from multiple cues: a meta-analysis. *Applied Cognitive Psychology, 28*(5), 661–676. https://doi.org/10.1002/acp.3052.

Henningsen, D. D., Cruz, M. G., & Morr, M. C. (2000). Pattern violations and perceptions of deception. *Communication Reports, 13*(1), 1–9. https://doi.org/10.1080/08934210009367718.

Hertenstein, M. J., & Keltner, D. (2011). Gender and the communication of emotion via touch. *Sex Roles, 64*(1), 70–80. https://doi.org/10.1007/s11199-010-9842-y.

Hess, K. P. (2013). Investigation of nonverbal discrimination against women in simulated initial job interviews. *Journal of Applied Social Psychology, 43*(3), 544–555. https://doi.org/10.1111/j.1559-1816.2013.01034.x.

Hess, U., Adams, R. B., Jr., Grammer, K., & Kleck, R. E. (2009). Face gender and emotion expression: Are angry women more like men? *Journal of Vision, 9*(12), 19. https://doi.org/10.1167/9.12.19.

Humphreys, T. (2007). Perceptions of sexual consent: The impact of relationship history and gender. *Journal of Sex Research, 44*(4), 307–315. https://doi.org/10.1080/00224490701586706.

Humphreys, T. P. (2004). Understanding sexual consent: An empirical investigation of the normative script for young heterosexual adults. In M. C. Cowling & P. R. Reynolds (Eds.), *Making sense of sexual consent* (pp. 209–225). Surrey, UK: Ashgate.

Hurley, C. M., & Frank, M. G. (2011). Executing facial control during deception situations. *Journal of Nonverbal Behavior, 35*(2), 119–131. https://doi.org/10.1007/s10919-010-0102-1.

Jakubiak, B. K., & Feeney, B. C. (2017). Affectionate touch to promote relational, psychological, and physical well-being in adulthood: A theoretical model and review of the research. *Personality and Social Psychology Review, 21*(3), 228–252. https://doi.org/10.1177/1088868316650307.

Jozkowski, K. N. (2013). The influence of consent on college students' perceptions of the quality of sexual intercourse at last event. *International Journal of Sexual Health, 25*(4), 260–272. https://doi.org/10.1080/19317611.2013.799626.

Jozkowski, K. N., & Peterson, Z. D. (2013). College students and sexual consent: Unique insights. *Journal of Sex Research, 50*(6), 517–523. https://doi.org/10.1080/00224499.2012.700739.

Jozkowski, K., Peterson, Z. D., Sanders, S. A., Dennis, B., & Reece, M. (2014). Gender differences in heterosexual college students' conceptualizations and indicators of sexual consent: Implications for contemporary sexual assault prevention education. *The Journal of Sex Research, 51*(8), 904–916. https://doi.org/10.1080/00224499.2013.792326.

Kalish, N. (2004, January). How honest are you? *Reader's Digest*, 114–119.

Klofstad, C. A., & Anderson, R. C. (2018). Voice pitch predicts electability, but does not signal leadership ability. *Evolution and human behavior, 39*(3), 349–354. https://doi.org/10.1016/j.evolhumbehav.2018.02.007.

Knapp, M. L., Hall, J. A., Horgan, T. G. (2014). *Nonverbal Communication in Human Interaction.* Belmont, CA: Wadsworth. 8th ed.

LaFrance, M., Hecht, M. A., & Paluck, E. L. (2003). The contingent smile: a meta-analysis of sex differences in smiling. *Psychological Bulletin*, *129*, 305–334. DOI:10.1037/0033-2909.129.2.305.

LaFrance, B. H., Henningsen, D. D., Oates, A., & Shaw, C. M. (2009). Social–sexual interactions? Meta-analyses of sex differences in perceptions of flirtatiousness, seductiveness, and promiscuousness. *Communication Monographs*, *76*(3), 263–285. https://doi.org/10.1080/03637750903074701.

LaFrance, M., & Vial, A. C. (2016). Gender and nonverbal behavior. In D. Matsumoto, H. C. Hwang, & M. G. Frank (Eds.), *APA handbook of nonverbal communication* (pp. 139–161). American Psychological Association.

Leal, S., & Vrij, A. (2008). Blinking during and after lying. *Journal of Nonverbal Behavior*, *32*(4), 187–194. https://doi.org/10.1007/s10919-008-0051-0.

Leaper, C., & Robnett, R. D. (2011). Women are more likely than men to use tentative language, aren't they? A meta-analysis testing for gender differences and moderators. *Psychology of Women Quarterly*, *35*(1), 129–142. https://doi.org/10.1177/0361684310392728.

Levine, T. R. (2014). Truth-default theory (TDT) a theory of human deception and deception detection. *Journal of Language and Social Psychology*, *33*(4), 378–392. https://doi.org/10.1177/0261927X14535916.

Livingston, R. W., & Pearce, N. A. (2009). The teddy-bear effect: Does having a baby face benefit Black chief executive officers? *Psychological Science*, *20*(10), 1229–1236. https://doi.org/10.1111/j.1467-9280.2009.02431.x.

Loy, J. E., Rohde, H., & Corley, M. (2017). Effects of disfluency in online interpretation of deception. *Cognitive Science*, *41*, 1434–1456. https://doi.org/10.1111/cogs.12378.

Madera, J. M., & Hebel, M. R. (2012). Discrimination against facially stigmatized applicants in interviews: An eye-tracking and face-to-face investigation. *Journal of Applied Psychology*, *97*(2), 317–330. https://doi.org/10.1037/a0025799.

Manusov V., Docan-Morgan T., Harvey J. (2015) Nonverbal firsts: When nonverbal cues are the impetus of relational and personal change in romantic relationships. In A. Kostić, and D. Chadee (Eds.), *The social psychology of nonverbal communication*. London: Palgrave Macmillan. https://doi.org/10.1057/9781137345868_8.

Mast, M. S. (2002). Dominance as expressed and inferred through speaking time: A meta-analysis. *Human Communication Research*, *28*(3), 420–450. https://doi.org/10.1093/hcr/28.3.420.

Matsumoto, D., & Hwang, H. C. (2016). The cultural bases of nonverbal communication. In *APA handbook of nonverbal communication* (pp. 77–101). American Psychological Association.

Montoya, R. M., Kershaw, C., & Prosser, J. L. (2018). A meta-analytic investigation of the relation between interpersonal attraction and enacted behavior. *Psychological bulletin*, *144*(7), 673. https://doi.org/10.1037/bul0000148.

Moore, M. M. (2010). Human nonverbal courtship behavior: A brief historical review. *Journal of Sex Research*, *47*(2–3), 171–180. https://doi.org/10.1080/00224490903402520.

Murphy, M. L., Janicki-Deverts, D., & Cohen, S. (2018). Receiving a hug is associated with the attenuation of negative mood that occurs on days with interpersonal conflict. *PloS one*, *13*(10), e0203522. https://doi.org/10.1371/journal.pone.0203522.

Nadal, K. L. (2011). The Racial and Ethnic Microaggressions Scale (REMS): Construction, reliability, and validity. *Journal of Counseling Psychology*, *58*(4), 470–480. https://doi.org/10.1037/a0025193.

Neuliep, J. W. (1997). A cross-cultural comparison of teacher immediacy in American and Japanese college classrooms. *Communication Research*, *24*(4), 431–451. https://doi.org/10.1177/009365097024004006.

Park, L. E., Sreamer, L., Huang, L., & Galinsky, A.D. (2013). Stand tall, but don't put your feet up: Universal and culturally-specific effects of expansive postures on power. *Journal of Experimental Social Psychology*, *49*(6), 965–971. https://doi.org/10.1016/j.jesp.2013.06.001.

Planalp, S. (1998). Communicating emotion in everyday life: Cues, channels, and processes. In P. A. Andersen & L. K. Guerrero (Eds.), *Handbook of communication and emotion: Research, theory, applications, and contexts* (pp. 29–48). San Diego, CA: Academic Press.

Porter, S., & ten Brinke, L. (2008). Reading between the lies: Identifying concealed and falsified emotions in universal facial expressions. *Psychological science*, *19*(5), 508–514. https://doi.org/10.1111/j.1467-9280.2008.02116.x.

Regan, P. C. (2016). *The mating game: A primer on love, sex, and marriage*. Thousand Oaks, CA: Sage.

Robinson, J. D. (2006). Nonverbal communication and physician–patient interaction. *The Sage handbook of nonverbal communication*, 437–459. Thousand Oaks, CA: Sage. https://doi.org/10.4135/9781412976152.n23.

Rosenberg, E. L., & Ekman, P. (Eds.). (2020). *What the face reveals: Basic and applied studies of spontaneous expression using the facial action coding system (FACS)*. Oxford: Oxford University Press.

Scherer, K. R., Clark-Polner, E., & Mortillaro, M. (2011). In the eye of the beholder? Universality and cultural specificity in the expression and perception of emotion. *International Journal of Psychology*, *46*(6), 401–435. https://doi.org/10.1080/00207594.2011.626049.

Sell, A., Cosmides, L., & Tooby, J. (2014). The human anger face evolved to enhance cues of strength. *Evolution & Human Behavior*, *35*(5), 425–429. https://doi.org/10.1016/j.evolhum behav.2014.05.008.

Serota, K. B., Levine, T. R., & Boster, F. J. (2010). The prevalence of lying in America: Three studies of self-reported lies. *Human Communication Research*, *36*(1), 2–25. https://doi.org/10.1111/j.1468-2958.2009.01366.x.

Soussignan, R., Dollion, N., Schaal, B., Durand, K., Reissland, N., & Baudouin, J. Y. (2018). Mimicking emotions: How 3–12-month-old infants use the facial expressions and eyes of a model. *Cognition and Emotion*, *32*(4), 827–842. https://doi.org/10.1080/02699931.2017.1359015.

Székely, E., Tiemeier, H., Arends, L. R., Jaddoe, V. W. V., Hofman, A., Verhulst, F. C., & Herba, C. M. (2011). Recognition of facial expressions of emotions by 3-year-olds. *Emotion*, *11*(2), 425–435. https://doi.org/10.1037/a0022587.

Tay, P. K. (2015). The adaptive value associated with expressing and perceiving angry-male and happy-female faces. *Frontiers in Psychology*, *6*, 851–851. https://doi.org/10.3389/fpsyg.2015.00851.

Theiss, J. A., & Solomon, D. H. (2007). Communication and the emotional, cognitive, and relational consequences of first sexual encounters between partners. *Communication Quarterly*, *55*(2), 179–206. https://doi.org/10.1080/01463370601036663.

Trifiletti, E., D'Ascenzo, S., Lugli, L., Cocco, V. M., Di Bernardo, G. A., Iani, C., Rubichi, S., Nicoletti, R., & Vezzali, L. (2020). Truth and lies in your eyes: Pupil dilation of White participants in truthful and deceptive responses to White and Black partners. *PLoS ONE*, *15*(10), 1–15. https://doi.org/10.1371/journal.pone.0239512.

Tusing, K. J., & Dillard, J. P. (2000). The sounds of dominance: Vocal precursors of perceived dominance during interpersonal influence. *Human Communication Research*, *26*(1), 148–171. https://doi.org/10.1093/hcr/26.1.148.

Van der Pol, L. D., Groeneveld, M. G., van Berkel, S. R., Endendijk, J. J., Hallers-Haalboom, E. T., Bakermans-Kranenburg, M. J., & Mesman, J. (2015). Fathers' and mothers' emotion talk with their girls and boys from toddlerhood to preschool age. *Emotion, 15*(6), 854–864. https://doi.org/10.1037/emo0000085.

Van Swol, L. M. (2003). The effects of nonverbal mirroring on perceived persuasiveness, agreement with an imitator, and reciprocity in a group discussion. *Communication Research, 30*(4), 461–480. https://doi.org/10.1177/0093650203253318.

Vannier, S. A., & O'Sullivan, L. F. (2011). Communicating interest in sex: Verbal and nonverbal initiation of sexual activity in young adults' romantic dating relationships. *Archives of Sexual Behavior, 40*(5), 961–969. https://doi.org/10.1007/s10508-010-9663-7.

Vrij, A. (2008). *Detecting lies and deceit: Pitfalls and opportunities*. Hoboken, NJ: John Wiley & Sons.

Vrij, A., Akehurst, L., Soukara, S. Bull, R. (2004). Detecting deceit via analyses of verbal and nonverbal behavior in children and adults. *Human Communication Research, 30*(1), 8–41. https://doi.org/10.1093/hcr/30.1.8.

Vrugt, A., & Luyerink, M. (2000). The contribution of bodily posture to gender stereotypic impressions. *Social Behavior and Personality: An International Journal, 28*(1), 91–103. https://doi.org/10.2224/sbp.2000.28.1.91.

Zebrowitz, L. A., Montepare, J. M., & Strom, M. A. 2013. Face and body physiognomy: Nonverbal cues for trait impressions. In J. A. Hall & M. L. Knapp (Eds.), *Nonverbal communication* (pp. 263–294). Boston: DeGruyter. https://doi.org/10.1515/9783110238150.263.

7 EMOTIONS AND COMMUNICATION

Armfield, J. M. (2006). Cognitive vulnerability: a model of the etiology of fear. *Clinical Psychology Review, 26*(6), 746–768. https://doi.org/10.1016/j.cpr.2006.03.007.

Barrett, L. F., Lane, R. D., Sechrest, L., & Schwartz, G. E. (2000). Sex differences in emotional awareness. *Personality and Social Psychology Bulletin, 26*(9), 1027–1035. https://doi.org/10.1177/01461672002611001.

Basinger, E. D., & Knobloch, L. K. (2018). A grounded theory of online coping by parents of military service members. *Journal of Social and Personal Relationships, 35*(5), 702–721. https://doi.org/10.1177/0265407517694769.

Basinger, E. D., Wehrman, E. C., & McAninch, K. G. (2016). Grief communication and privacy rules: Examining the communication of individuals bereaved by the death of a family member. *Journal of Family Communication, 16*(4), 285–302. https://doi.org/10.1080/15267431.2016.1182534.

Bevan, J. L. (2015). Jealousy in Interpersonal Communication. In C.R. Berger, M.E. Roloff, S.R. Wilson, J.P. Dillard, J. Caughlin and D. Solomon (Eds.), *The international encyclopedia of interpersonal communication* (pp. 1–9). Hoboken, NJ: John Wiley & Sons. https://doi.org/10.1002/9781118540190.wbeic214.

Birditt, K. S., & Fingerman, K. L. (2003). Age and gender differences in adults' descriptions of emotional reactions to interpersonal problems. *Journals of Gerontology: Series B: Psychological Sciences & Social Sciences, 58*(4), 237–245. https://doi.org/10.1093/geronb/58.4.P237.

Bodie, G. D., Vickery, A. J., Cannava, K., & Jones, S. M. (2015). The role of "active listening" in informal helping conversations: Impact on perceptions of listener helpfulness, sensitivity, and supportiveness and discloser emotional improvement. *Western Journal of Communication, 79*(2), 151–173. https://doi.org/10.1080/10570314.2014.943429.

Brackett, M. A., Mayer, J. D., & Warner, R. M. (2004). Emotional intelligence and its relation to everyday behaviour. *Personality and Individual Differences*, *36*(6), 1387–1402. https://doi.org/10.1016/s0191-8869(03)00236-8.

Brackett, M. A., Warner, R. M., & Bosco, J. S. (2005). Emotional intelligence and relationship quality among couples. *Personal Relationships*, *12*(2), 197–212. https://doi.org/10.1111/j.1350-4126.2005.00111.x.

Brebner, J. (2003). Gender and emotions. *Personality and Individual Differences*, *34*(3), 387–394. https://doi.org/10.1016/S0191-8869(02)00059-4.

Burleson, B. R., & Planalp, S. (2000). Producing emotion(al) messages. *Communication Theory*, *10*(2), 221–250. https://doi.org/10.1111/j.1468-2885.2000.tb00191.x.

Burleson, B. R., Holmstrom, A. J., & Gilstrap, C. M. (2005). "Guys can't say that to guys": From experiments assessing the normative motivation account for deficiencies in the emotional support provided by men. *Communication Monographs*, *72*(4), 468–501. https://doi.org/10.1080/03637750500322636.

Cappella, J. N. (1993). The facial feedback hypothesis in human interaction: Review and speculation. *Journal of Language and Social Interaction*, *12*(1–2), 13–29. https://doi.org/10.1177/0261927X93121002.

Carmon, A. F., Western, K. J., Miller, A. N., Pearson, J. C., & Fowler, M. R. (2010). Grieving those we've lost: An examination of family communication patterns and grief reactions. *Communication Research Reports*, *27*(3), 253–262. https://doi.org/10.1080/08824096.2010.496329.

Clark, M. S., & Finkel, E. J. (2005). Willingness to express emotion: The impact of relationship type, communal orientation, and their interaction. *Personal Relationships*, *12*(2), 169–180. https://doi.org/10.1111/j.1350-4126.2005.00109.x.

Clore, G. L., & Schnall, S. (2005). The influence of affect on attitude. In D. Albarracín, B. T. Johnson, & M. P. Zanna (Eds.), *The handbook of attitudes* (pp. 437–489). Mahwah, NJ: Lawrence Erlbaum.

Cohen, H., & Samp, J. A. (2018). Grief communication: Exploring disclosure and avoidance across the developmental spectrum. *Western Journal of Communication*, *82*(2), 238–257. https://doi.org/10.1080/10570314.2017.1326622.

Cunningham, M. R., Shamblen, S. R., Barbee, A P., & Ault, L. K. (2005). Social allergies in romantic relationships: Behavioral repetition, emotional sensitization, and dissatisfaction in dating couples. *Personal Relationships*, *12*(2), 273–296. https://doi.org/10.1111/j.1350-4126.2005.00115.x.

Daly, M., & Wilson, M. (1988). *Homicide*. New York: Aldine.

de los Santos, T. M., & Nabi, R. L. (2019). Emotionally charged: Exploring the role of emotion in online news information seeking and processing. *Journal of Broadcasting & Electronic Media*, *63*(1), 39–58. https://doi.org/10.1080/08838151.2019.1566861.

Dillard, J. P., & Peck, E. (2000). Affect and persuasion: Emotional responses to public service announcements. *Communication Research*, 27(4), 461–495. https://doi.org/10.1177/009365000027004003.

Dillard, J. P., & Seo, K. (2013). Affect and persuasion. In J. P. Dillard, & L. Shen (Eds.), *The Sage handbook of persuasion: Developments in theory and practice* (2nd ed, pp. 150–166). Thousand Oaks, CA: Sage.

Feeney, J. A. (2005). Hurt feelings in couple relationships: Exploring the role of attachment and perceptions of personal injury. *Personal Relationships*, *12*, 253–271. DOI:10.1111/j.1350–4126.2005.00114.x.

Fehr, B., & Harasymchuk, C. (2005). The experience of emotion in close relationships: Toward an integration of the emotion-in-relationships and interpersonal script models. *Personal Relationships*, *12*(2), 181–196. https://doi.org/10.1111/j.1350-4126.2005.00110.x.

Flynn, F. J., & Schaumberg, R. L. (2012). When feeling bad leads to feeling good: Guilt-proneness and affective organizational commitment. *Journal of Applied Psychology*, *97*(1), 124–133. https://doi.org/10.1037/a0024166.

Frijda, N. H. (2007). *The laws of emotion*. Mahwah, NJ: Erlbaum.

Goodboy, A. K., & Bolkan, S. (2011). Attachment and the use of negative relational maintenance behaviors in romantic relationships. *Communication Research Reports*, *28*(4), 327–336. https://doi.org/10.1080/08824096.2011.616244.

Guerrero, L. K. (2014). Jealousy and relational satisfaction: Actor effects, partner effects, and the mediating role of destructive communicative responses to jealousy. *Western Journal of Communication*, *78*(5), 586–611. https://doi.org/10.1080/10570314.2014.935468.

Guerrero, L. K., Trost, M. R., & Yoshimura, S. M. (2005). Romantic jealousy: Emotions and communicative responses. *Personal Relationships*, *12*(2), 233–252. https://doi.org/10.1111/j.1350-4126.2005.00113.x

Hall, J. A. (2011). Is it something I said? Sense of humor and partner embarrassment. *Journal of Social and Personal Relationships*, *28*(3), 383–405. https://doi.org/10.1177/0265407510384422.

Harms, P. D., & Credé, M. (2010). Emotional intelligence and transformational and transactional leadership: A meta-analysis. *Journal of Leadership & Organizational Studies*, *17*(1), 5–17. https://doi.org/10.1177/1548051809350894.

Horstman, H. K., & Holman, A. (2018). Communicated sense-making after miscarriage: A dyadic analysis of spousal communicated perspective-taking, well-being, and parenting role salience. *Health Communication*, *33*(10), 1317–1326. https://doi.org/10.1080/10410236.2017.1351852.

Hwang, H. C. and Matsumoto, D. (2020). Cross-cultural emotional expression. In B. J. Carducci, C. S. Nave, J. S. Mio and R. E. Riggio (Eds.), *The Wiley encyclopedia of personality and individual differences* (pp. 257–261). https://doi.org/10.1002/9781118970843.ch308.

Ip, K. I., Miller, A. L., Karasawa, M., Hirabayashi, H., Kazama, M., Wang, L., Olson, S. L., Kessler, D., & Tardif, T. (2020). Emotion expression and regulation in three cultures: Chinese, Japanese, and American preschoolers' reactions to disappointment. *Journal of Experimental Child Psychology*, *201*, 104972. https://doi.org/10.1016/j.jecp.2020.104972.

Jakoby, N. R. (2012). Grief as a social emotion: Theoretical perspectives. *Death Studies*, *36*(8), 679–711. https://doi.org/10.1080/07481187.2011.584013.

Jones, S. M., & Hansen, W. (2015). The impact of mindfulness on supportive communication skills: Three exploratory studies. *Mindfulness*, *6*(5), 1115–1128. https://doi.org/10.1007/s12671-014-0362-7.

Kamm, S., & Vandenberg, B. (2001). Grief communication, grief reactions and marital satisfaction in bereaved parents. *Death Studies*, *25*(7), 569–582. https://doi.org/10.1080/07481180126576.

King, M. E., & La Valley, A. G. (2019). Partner influence, emotion, and relational outcomes: A test of relational turbulence theory in early dating relationships. *Southern Communication Journal*, *84*(5), 287–300. https://doi.org/10.1080/1041794x.2019.1639212.

Knobloch, L. K. (2005). Evaluating a contextual model of responses to relational uncertainty increasing events. *Human Communication Research*, *31*(1), 60–101. https://doi.org/10.1093/hcr/31.1.60.

Kristensen, P., Weisæth, L., & Heir, T. (2012). Bereavement and mental health after sudden and violent losses: A review. *Psychiatry: Interpersonal & Biological Processes*, *75*(1), 76–97. https://doi.org/10.1521/psyc.2012.75.1.76.

Lee, S. Y., & Hawkins, R. P. (2016). Worry as an uncertainty-associated emotion: Exploring the role of worry in health information seeking. *Health*

Communication, *31*(8), 926–933. https://doi.org/10.1080/10410236.2015.1018701.

Lemay Jr, E. P., Overall, N. C., & Clark, M. S. (2012). Experiences and interpersonal consequences of hurt feelings and anger. *Journal of Personality and Social Psychology*, *103*(6), 982. https://doi.org/10.1037/a0030064.

Lepore, S. J., Silver, R. C., Wortman, C. B., & Wayment, H. A. (1996). Social constraints, intrusive thoughts, and depressive symptoms among bereaved mothers. *Journal of Personality and Social Psychology*, *70*(2), 271–282. https://doi.org/10.1037/0022-3514.70.2.271.

Lucas, K., & Buzzanell, P. M. (2012). Memorable messages of hard times: Constructing short-and long-term resiliencies through family communication. *Journal of Family Communication*, *12*(3), 189–208. https://doi.org/10.1080/15267431.2012.687196.

MacGeorge, E. L. (2001). Support providers' interaction goals: The influence of attributions and emotions. *Communication Monographs*, *68*(1), 72–97. https://doi.org/10.1080/03637750128050.

Manusov, V. (2015). Facial feedback hypothesis. In C.R. Berger, M.E. Roloff, S.R. Wilson, J.P. Dillard, J. Caughlin and D. Solomon (Eds.), *The international encyclopedia of interpersonal* communication (pp. 1–5). Hoboken, NJ: John Wiley & Sons. https://doi.org/10.1002/9781118540190.wbeic0107.

Mayer, J. D., Caruso, D. R., & Salovey, P. (2016). The ability model of emotional intelligence: Principles and updates. *Emotion review*, *8*(4), 290–300. https://doi.org/10.1177/1754073916639667.

Mayer, J. D., Salovey, P., & Caruso, D. R. (2004). A further consideration of the issues of emotional intelligence. *Psychological Inquiry*, *15*(3), 249–255. https://doi.org/10.1207/s15327965pli1503_05.

McLaren, R. M., & Sillars, A. (2014). Hurtful episodes in parent-adolescent relationships: How accounts and attributions contribute to the difficulty of talking about hurt. *Communication Monographs*, *81*(3), 359–385. https://doi.org/10.1080/03637751.2014.933244.

McLaren, R. M., & Sillars, A. (2020). Parent and adolescent conversations about hurt: How interaction patterns predict empathic accuracy and perceived understanding. *Communication Monographs*, *87*(3), 312–335. https://doi.org/10.1080/03637751.2020.1722848.

Michinov, E., & Michinov, N. (2020). When emotional intelligence predicts team performance: Further validation of the short version of the Workgroup Emotional Intelligence Profile. *Current Psychology*, 1–14. https://doi.org/10.1007/s12144-020-00659-7.

Moors A. (2020). Appraisal theory of emotion. In V. Zeigler-Hill, & T. K. Shackelford (Eds.) *Encyclopedia of personality and individual differences*. Cham: Springer. https://doi.org/10.1007/978-3-319-24612-3_493.

Netzer, L., Gutentag, T., Kim, M. Y., Solak, N., & Tamir, M. (2018). Evaluations of emotions: Distinguishing between affective, behavioral and cognitive components. *Personality and Individual Differences*, *135*, 13–24. https://doi.org/10.1016/j.paid.2018.06.038.

Park, J., Baek, Y. M., & Cha, M. (2014). Cross-cultural comparison of nonverbal cues in emoticons on twitter: Evidence from big data analysis. *Journal of communication*, *64*(2), 333–354. https://doi.org/10.1111/jcom.12086.

Petrides, K. V., Mikolajczak, M., Mavroveli, S., Sanchez-Ruiz, M. J., Furnham, A., & Pérez-González, J. C. (2016). Developments in trait emotional intelligence research. *Emotion Review*, *8*(4), 335–341. https://doi.org/10.1177/1754073916650493.

Planalp, S., Fitness, J., & Fehr, B. A. (2018). *The roles of emotion in relationships*. In A. L. Vangelisti & D. Perlman (Eds.), *The Cambridge handbook of personal relationships* (p. 256–267). Cambridge University Press. https://doi.org/10.1017/9781316417867.021.

Riordan, M. A. (2017). Emojis as tools for emotion work: communicating affect in text messages. *Journal of Language and Social Psychology*, *36*(5), 549–567. https://doi.org/10.1177/0261927X17704238.

Ruan, Y., Reis, H. T., Clark, M. S., Hirsch, J. L., & Bink, B. D. (2020). Can I tell you how I feel? Perceived partner responsiveness encourages emotional expression. *Emotion*, *20*(3), 329–342. https://doi.org/10.1037/emo0000650.

Ryan, R. M., La Guardia, J. G., Solky-Butzel, J., Chirkov, V., & Kim, Y. (2005). On the interpersonal regulation of emotions: Emotional reliance across gender, relationships, and cultures. *Personal Relationships*, *12*(1), 145–163. https://doi.org/10.1111/j.1350-4126.2005.00106.x.

Safdar, S., Friedlmeier, W., Matsumoto, D., Yoo, S. H., Kwantes, C. T., Kakai, H., & Shigemasu, E. (2009). Variations of emotional display rules within and across cultures: A comparison between Canada, USA, and Japan. *Canadian Journal of Behavioural Science*, *41*(1), 1–10. https://doi.org/10.1037/a0014387.

Scherer, K. R., & Wallbott, H. G. (1994). Evidence for universality and cultural variation of differential emotion response patterning. *Journal of Personality and Social Psychology*, *66*(2), 310–328. https://doi.org/10.1037/0022-3514.66.2.310.

Schneider, T. R., Lyons, J. B., & Khazon, S. (2013). Emotional intelligence and resilience. *Personality and Individual Differences*, *55*(8), 909–914. https://doi.org/10.1016/j.paid.2013.07.460.

Senft, N., Campos, B., Shiota, M. N., & Chentsova-Dutton, Y. E. (2020). Who emphasizes positivity? An exploration of emotion values in people of Latino, Asian, and European heritage living in the United States. *Emotion*. Advance online publication. https://doi.org/10.1037/emo0000737.

Shaver, P. Schwartz, J., Kirson, D., & O'Connor, C. (1987). Emotion knowledge: further exploration of a prototype approach. *Journal of Personality and Social Psychology*, *52*, 1061–1086. DOI:10.1037/0022–3514.52.6.1061.

Sheldon, K. M., Abad, N., & Hinsch, C. (2011). A two-process view of Facebook use and relatedness need-satisfaction: Disconnection drives use, and connection rewards it. *Journal of Personality and Social Psychology*, *100*(4), 766–775. https://doi.org/10.1037/a0022407.

Shiota, M. N., Neufeld, S. L., Yeung, W. H., Moser, S. E., & Perea, E. F. (2011). Feeling good: Autonomic nervous system responding in five positive emotions. *Emotion*, *11*(6), 1368–1378. https://doi.org/10.1037/a0024278.

Solomon, D. H., & Brisini, K. S. C. (2019). Relational uncertainty and interdependence processes in marriage: A test of relational turbulence theory. *Journal of Social and Personal Relationships*, *36*(8), 2416–2436. https://doi.org/10.1177/0265407518788700.

Spitzberg, B. H., & Cupach, W. R. (Eds.). (2013). *The dark side of close relationships*. London: Routledge.

Stanton, S., Selcuk, E., Farrell, A. K., Slatcher, R. B., & Ong, A. D. (2019). Perceived partner responsiveness, daily negative affect reactivity, and all-cause mortality: A 20-year longitudinal study. *Psychosomatic Medicine*, *81*(1), 7–15. https://doi.org/10.1097/PSY.0000000000000618.

Steuber, K. R., & Solomon, D. H. (2011). Factors that predict married partners' disclosures about infertility to social network members. *Journal of Applied Communication Research*, *39*(3), 250–270. https://doi.org/10.1080/00909882.2011.585401.

Stroebe, M., Finkenauer, C., Meij, L., Schut, H., Van den Bout, J., & Stroebe, W. (2013). Partner-oriented self-regulation among bereaved parents: The costs of holding in grief for the partner's sake. *Psychological Science*, *24*(4), 395–402. https:/doi.org/10.1177/0956797612457383.

Szczygieł, D., & Mikolajczak, M. (2017). Why are people high in emotional intelligence happier? They make the most of their positive emotions. *Personality and Individual Differences*, *117*, 177–181. https://doi.org/10.1016/j.paid.2017.05.051.

Thomsen, D. K., Mehlsen, M. Y., Viidik, A., Sommerlund, B., & Zachariae, R. (2005). Age and gender differences in negative affect: Is there a role for emotion regulation? *Personality and Individual Differences*, *38*(8), 1935–1946. https://doi.org/10.1016/j.paid.2004.12.001.

Tian, X., & Solomon, D. H. (2020). A relational turbulence theory perspective on women's grief following miscarriage. *Journal of Social and Personal Relationships*, *37*(6), 1852–1872. https://doi.org/10.1177/0265407520910792.

Torre, J. B., & Lieberman, M. D. (2018). Putting feelings into words: Affect labeling as implicit emotion regulation. *Emotion Review*, *10*(2), 116–124. https://doi.org/10.1177/1754073917742706.

Turner, M. M., Underhill, J. C., & Kaid, L. L. (2013). Mood and reactions to political advertising: A test and extension of the hedonic contingency hypothesis. *The Southern Communication Journal*, *78*(1), 8–24. https://doi.org/10.1080/1041794X.2012.712194.

Turner, M. (2017). Using guilt to motivate individuals to adopt healthy habits. *Oxford research encyclopedia of communication*. https://doi.org/10.1093/acrefore/9780190228613.013.196.

Van Kleef, G. A. (2016). *The interpersonal dynamics of emotion: Toward an integrative theory of emotions as social information*. Cambridge: Cambridge University Press. https://doi.org/10.1017/CBO9781107261396.

Vangelisti, A. L. (2015). Hurtful communication. In C. R. Berger, M. E. Roloff, S. R. Wilson, J. P. Dillard, J. Caughlin and D. Solomon (Eds.), The international encyclopedia of interpersonal communication (pp. 1–9). Hoboken, NJ: John Wiley & Sons. https://doi.org/ 10.1002/9781118540190.wbeic0178.

Vangelisti, A. L., & Young, S. L. (2000). When words hurt: the effects of perceived intentionality on interpersonal relationships. *Journal of Social and Personal Relationships*, *17*, 393–424. DOI:10.1177/0265407500173005.

Vangelisti, A. L., Young, S. L., Carpenter-Theune, K. E., & Alexander, A. L. (2005). Why does it hurt? The perceived causes of hurt feelings. *Communication Research*, *32*(4), 443–477. https://doi.org/10.1177/0093650205277319.

Yan, C., Dillard, J. P., & Shen, F. (2010). The effects of mood, message framing, and behavioral advocacy on persuasion. *Journal of Communication*, *60*(2), 344–363. https://doi.org/10.1111/j.1460-2466.2010.01485.x.

Yih, J., Uusberg, A., Taxer, J. L, & Gross, J. J. (2019) Better together: a unified perspective on appraisal and emotion regulation. *Cognition and Emotion*, *33*(1), 41–47. https://doi.org/10.1080/02699931.2018.1504749.

8 LISTENING AND RESPONDING

Bavelas, J. B., Coates, L., & Johnson, T. (2002). Listener responses as a collaborative process: The role of gaze. *Journal of Communication*, *52*(3), 566–580. https://doi.org/10.1111/j.1460-2466.2002.tb02562.x.

Behrendt, G., & Tuccillo, L. (2004). *He's just not that into you: The no-excuses truth to understanding guys*. New York, NY: Gallery Books.

Bodie, G. D., & Jones, S. M. (2012). The nature of supportive listening II: The role of verbal person centeredness and nonverbal immediacy. *Western Journal of Communication*, *76*(3), 250–269. https://doi.org/10.1080/10570314.2011.651255.

Bodie, G. D., Gearhart, C. C., Denham, J. P., & Vickery, Al J. (2013). The temporal stability and situational contingency of active-empathic listening. *Western Journal of Communication*, *77*(2), 113–138. https://doi.org/10.1080/10570314.2012.656216.

Bodie, G. D., Vickery, An. J., Cannava, K., & Jones, S. M. (2015). The role of "active listening" in informal helping conversations: Impact on perceptions of listener helpfulness, sensitivity, and supportiveness and discloser emotional improvements. *Western Journal of Communication*, *79*(2), 151–173. https://doi.org/10.1080/10570314.2014.943429.

Burleson, B. (2011). A constructivist approach to listening. *International Journal of Listening*, *25*(1–2), 27–46. https://doi.org/10.1080/10904018.2011.536470.

Canpolat, M., Kuzu, S., Yildirim, B., & Canpolat, S. (2015). Active listening strategies of academically successful university students. *Eurasian Journal of Educational Research*, *15*(60), 163–180. https://doi.org/10.14689/ejer.2015.60.10.

Cegala, D. J. (1984). Affective and cognitive manifestations of interaction involvement during unstructured and competitive interactions. *Communication Monographs*, *51*(4), 320–338. https://doi.org/10.1080/03637758409390205.

Clark, C. M., Murfett, U. M., Rogers, P. S., & Ang, S. (2013). Is empathy effective for customer service? Evidence from call center interactions. *Journal of Business and Technical Communication*, *27*(2), 123–153. https://doi.org/10.1177/1050651912468887.

Cohen, E. L., Wilkin, H. A., Tannebaum, M., Plew, M. S., & Haley, L. L. (2013). When patients are impatient: The communication strategies utilized by emergency department employees to manage patients frustrated by wait times. *Health Communication*, *28*(3), 275–285. https://doi.org/10.1080/10410236.2012.680948.

DeMarree, K. G., Clark, C. J., Wheeler, S. C., Briñol, P., & Petty, R. E. (2017). On the pursuit of desired attitudes: Wanting a different attitude affects information processing and behavior. *Journal of Experimental Social Psychology*, *70*, 129–142. https://doi.org/10.1016/j.jesp.2017.01.003.

Edwards, R. (2011). Listening and message interpretation. *International Journal of Listening*, *25*(1–2), 47–65. https://doi.org/10.1080/10904018.2011.536471.

Emanuel, R., Adams, J., Baker, K., Daufin, E. K., Ellington, C., Fitts, E., Himel, J., Holladay, L., & Okeowo, D. (2008). How college students spent their time communicating. *International Journal of Listening*, *22*(1), 13–28. https://doi.org/10.1080/10904010701802139.

Evans, W. G., Tulsky, J. A., Back, A. L., & Arnold, R. M. (2006). Communication at times of transitions: How to help patients cope with loss and redefine hope. *The Cancer Journal*, *12*(5), 417–424. https://doi.org/10.1097/00130404-200609000-00010.

Gearhart, C. C., & Bodie, G. D. (2011). Active-empathic listening as a general social skill: Evidence from bivariate and canonical correlations. *Communication Reports*, *24*(2), 86–98. https://doi.org/10.1080/08934215.2011.610731.

Gearhart, C. C., Denham, J. P., & Bodie, G. D. (2014). Listening as a goal-directed activity. *Western Journal of Communication*, *78*(5), 668–684. https://doi.org/10.1080/10570314.2014.910888.

Geiman, K. L., & Greene, J. O. (2019). Listening and experiences of interpersonal transcendence. *Communication Studies*, *70*(1), 114–128. https://doi.org/10.1080/10510974.2018.1492946.

Glas, N., & Pelachaud, C. (2018). Topic management for an engaging conversational agent. *International Journal of Human-Computer Studies*, *120*, 107–124. https://doi.org/10.1016/j.ijhcs.2018.07.007.

Greene, J. O. (2016). Action assembly theory. In C. R. Berger & M. E. Roloff (Eds.), *International encyclopedia of interpersonal communication* (pp. 8–15). Hoboken, NJ: Wiley Blackwell.

Greene, J. O., & Herbers, L. E. (2011). Conditions of interpersonal transcendence. *International Journal of Listening*, *25*, 66–84.

Greene, J. O., Kirch, M. W., & Grady, C. S. (2000). Cognitive foundations of message encoding: An investigation of message production as coalition formation. *Communication Quarterly*, *48*(3), 256–271. https://doi.org/10.1080/01463370009385596.

Greene, J. O., Morgan, M., McCullough, J., Gill, E., Graves, A. R. (2010). A phrase well turned: Creative facility in narrative production. *Communication Studies*, *61*(1), 118–134.

https://doi.org/10.1080/10510970903400329.

Hale, J. L., Burgoon, J. K., & Householder, B. (2005). The relational communication scale. In V. Manusov (Ed.), *The sourcebook of nonverbal measures: Going beyond words* (pp. 127–139). Mahwah, NJ: Lawrence Erlbaum Associates.

Heritage, J., & Robinson, J. D. (2006). The structure of patients' presenting concerns: Physicians' opening questions. *Health Communication*, *19*(2), 89–102. https://doi.org/10.1207/s15327027hc1902_1.

Hilal, H., Siddiqui, Z., Khan, J., & Hameed, S. (2012). Conversation memory in relation to humorous-nonhumorous version of conversation and listener's mood. *Social Science International*, *28*(2), 275–292.

Huang, K., Yeomans, M., Brooks, A. W., Minson, J., & Gino, F. (2017). It doesn't hurt to ask: Question-asking increases liking. *Journal of Personality and Social Psychology*, *113*(3), 430–452. https://doi.org/10.1037/pspi0000097.

International Listening Association (1996). Retrieved from www.listen.org, March 24, 2011.

Jones, S. M., Bodie, G. D., & Hughes, S. D. (2019). The impact of mindfulness on empathy, active listening, and perceived provisions of emotional support. *Communication Research*, *46*(6), 838–865. https://doi.org/10.1177/0093650215626983.

Knapp, S. J. (2020). *Suicide prevention: An ethically and scientifically informed approach.* Washington, DC: American Psychological Association.

Kwapis, K. (2009). *He's just not that into you.* [Film]. Warner Bros.

Liu, B., & Sundar, S. S. (2018). Should machines express sympathy and empathy? Experiments with a health advice chatbot. *Cyberpsychology, Behavior, and Social Networking*, *21*(10), 625–636. https://doi.org/10.1089/cyber.2018.0110.

Lwi, S. J., Haase, C. M., Shiota, M. N., Newton, S. L., & Levenson, R. W. (2019). Responding to the emotions of others: Age differences in facial expressions and age-specific associations with relational connectedness. *Emotion*, *19*(8), 1437–1449. https://doi.org/10.1037/emo0000534.

McAuliffe, W. H. B., Carter, E. C., Berhane, J., Snihur, A.C., & McCullough, M. E. (2020). Is empathy the default response to suffering? A meta-analytic evaluation of perspective taking's effect of empathic concern. *Personality and Social Psychology Review*, *24*(2), 141–162. https://doi.org/10.1177/1088868319887599.

McKinley, G. L., Brown-Schmidt, S., & Benjamin, A. S. (2017). Memory for conversation and the development of common ground. *Memory & Cognition*, *45*(8), 1281–1294. https://doi.org/10.3758/s13421-017-0730-3.

McLaren, R. M. (2016). Relational framing theory. In C. R. Berger & M. E. Roloff (Eds.), *International encyclopedia of interpersonal communication* (pp. 1451–1459). Wiley Blackwell.

Miller, J. B., & deWinstanley, P. A. (2002). The role of interpersonal competence in memory for conversation. *Personality and Social Psychology Bulletin*, *28*(1), 78–89. https://doi.org/10.1177/0146167202281007

Morgan, M., Greene, J. O., Gill, E. A., & McCullough, J. D. (2009). The creative character of talk: Individual differences in narrative production ability. *Communication Studies*, *60*(2), 180–196. https://doi.org/10.1080/10510970902834908.

Muralidharan, S., & Kim, E. (2020). Can empathy offset low bystander efficacy? Effectiveness of domestic violence prevention narratives in India. *Health Communication*, *35*(10), 1229–1238. https://doi.org/10.1080/10410236.2019.1623645.

Nazione, S., & Pace, K. (2015). An experimental study of medical error explanations: Do apology, empathy, corrective action, and compensation alter intentions and attitudes? *Journal of Health Communication*, *20*(12), 1422–1432. https://doi.org/10.1080/10810730.2015.1018646.

Passalacqua, S. A., & Segrin, C. (2012). The effect of resident physician stress, burnout, and empathy on patient-centered communication during the long-call shift. *Health Communication*, *27*(5), 449–456. https://doi.org/10.1080/10410236.2011.606527.

Priem, J. S., McLaren, R. M., & Solomon, D. H. (2010). Relational messages, perceptions of hurt, and biological stress reactions to a disconfirming interaction. *Communication Research*, *37*(1), 48–72. https://doi.org/10.1177/0093650209351470.

Priem, J. S., Solomon, D. H., & Steuber, K. R. (2009). Accuracy and bias in perceptions of emotionally supportive communication in marriage. *Personal Relationships*, *16*(4), 531–552. https://doi.org/10.1111/j.1475-6811.2009.01238.x.

Reed, V. A., & Trumbo, S. (2020). The relative importance of selected communication skills for positive peer relations: American adolescents' opinions. *Communication Disorders Quarterly*, *41*(3), 135–150. https://doi.org/10.1177/1525740118819684.

Robinson, J. D., & Heritage, J. (2016). How patients understand physicians' solicitations of additional concerns: Implications for up-front agenda setting in primary care. *Health Communication*, *31*(4), 434–444. https://doi.org/10.1080/10410236.2014.960060.

Robinson, J. D., Tate, A., & Heritage, J. (2016). Agenda-setting revisited: When and how do primary-care physicians solicit patients' additional concerns. *Patient Education and Counseling*, *99*(5), 718–723. https://doi.org/10.1016/j.pec.2015.12.009.

Samp, J. A., & Humphreys, L. R. (2007). "I said what?" Partner familiarity, resistance, and accuracy of conversational recall. *Communication Monographs*, *74*(4), 561–581. https://doi.org/10.1080/03637750701716610.

Samp, J. A., & Solomon, D. H. (2005). Toward a theoretical account of goal characteristics in micro-level message features. *Communication Monographs*, *72*(1), 22–45. https://doi.org/10.1080/0363775052000342517.

Sargent, S. L., & Weaver, J. B. (2007). The listening styles profile. In R. A Reynolds, R. Woods, & J. D. Baker (Eds.), *Handbook of research on electronic surveys and measurements* (pp. 334–338). Hershey, PA: Idea Group Reference/IGI Global. https://doi.org/10.4018/978-1-59140-792-8.ch045.

Schneider, B. A., Daneman, M., Murphy, D. R., & Kwong See, S. (2000). Listening to discourse in distracting settings: The effects of aging. *Psychology and Aging*, *15*(1), 110–125. https://doi.org/10.1037/0882-7974.15.1.110.

Sillars, A. (2011). Motivated misunderstanding in family conflict discussions. In J. L. Smith, W. Ickes, J. A. Hall, & S. D. Hodges (Eds.), *Managing interpersonal sensitivity: Knowing when and when not to understand others* (pp. 193–213). Hauppauge, NY: Nova Science Publishers.

Sillars, A. L., Roberts, L. J., Leonard, K. E., & Dun, T. (2000). Cognition during marital conflict: The relationship of thought and talk. *Journal of Social and Personal Relationships, 17*(4–5), 479–502. https://doi.org/10.1177/0265407500174002.

Solomon, D. H., & McLaren, R. M. (2008). Relational framing theory: Drawing inferences about relationships from interpersonal interactions. In L. A. Baxter & D. O. Braithwaite (Eds.), *Engaging theories in interpersonal communication* (pp. 103–115). Thousand Oaks, CA: Sage.

Stafford, L., & Daly, J. A. (1984). Conversational memory: The effects of recall mode and memory expectancies on remembrances of natural conversations. *Human Communication Research, 10*(3), 379–402. https://doi.org/10.1111/j.1468-2958.1984.tb00024.x.

Venaglia, R. B., & Lemay, E. P., (2019). Accurate and biased perceptions of partner's conflict behaviors shape emotional experience. *Journal of Social and Personal Relationships, 36*(10), 3293–3312. https://doi.org/10.1177/0265407518818771.

Villaume, W. A., & Bodie, G. D. (2007). Discovering the listener within us: The impact of traitlike personality variables and communicator styles on preferences for listening style. *International Journal of Listening, 21*(2), 102–123. https://doi.org/10.1080/10904010701302006.

Watson, K. W., Barker, L. L., & Weaver, J. B. (1995). The Listening Styles Profile (LSP-16): Development and validation of an instrument to assess four listening styles. *International Journal of Listening, 9*(1), 1–13. https://doi.org/10.1080/10904018.1995.10499138.

Weaver, J. B., Watson, K. W., & Barker, L. L. (1996). Individual differences in listening styles: Do you hear what I hear? *Personality and Individual Differences, 20*(3), 381–387. https://doi.org/10.1016/0191-8869(95)00194-8.

Wombacher, K., Darnell, W. H., Harrington, N. G., Scott, A. M., & Martin, C. A. (2020). Identifying conversational strategies for psychiatrists in discussing substance use with adolescent patients. *Health Communication, ahead-of-print*, 1–7. https://doi.org/10.1080/10410236.2020.1816309.

Woolley, K., & Risen, J. L. (2018). Closing your eyes to follow your heart; Avoiding information to protect a strong intuitive preference. *Journal of Personality and Social Psychology, 114*(2), 230–245. https://doi.org/10.1037/pspa0000100.

Worthington, D. L. (2005). Exploring the relationship between listening style preference and verbal aggressiveness. *International Journal of Listening, 19*(1), 3–11. https://doi.org/10.1080/10904018.2005.10499069.

Worthington, D. L. (2008). Exploring the relationship between listening styles and need for cognition. *International Journal of Listening*, 22(1), 46–58. https://doi.org/10.1080/10904010701802154.

9 DEVELOPING AND ENDING RELATIONSHIPS

Afifi, W. A., & Faulkner, S. L. (2000). On being "just friends": The frequency and impact of sexual activity in cross-sex friendships. *Journal of Social and Personal Relationships, 17*(2), 205–222. https://doi.org/10.1177/0265407500172003.

Altman, I., & Taylor, D. A. (1973). *Social penetration: The development of interpersonal relationships*. New York: Holt, Rinehart, & Winston.

Alves, H. (2018). Sharing rare attitudes attracts. *Personality and Social Psychology Bulletin, 44*(8), 1270–1283. https://doi.org/10.1177/0146167218766861.

Bahns, A. J., Crandall, C. S., Canevello, A., & Crocker, J. (2013). Deciding to dissolve: Individual- and relationship-level predictors of roommate breakup.

Basic and Applied Social Psychology, *35*(2), 164–175. https://doi.org/10.1080/01973533.2013.764301.

Baruh, L., & Cemalcilar, Z. (2015). Rubbernecking effect of intimate information on Twitter: When getting attention works against interpersonal attraction. *Cyberpsychology, Behavior, and Social Networking*, *18*(9), 506–513. https://doi.org/10.1089/cyber.2015.0099.

Baxter, L. A., & Wilmot, W. W. (1984). "Secret tests": Social strategies for acquiring information about the state of the relationship. *Human Communication Research*, *11*(2), 171–201. https://doi.org/10.1111/j.1468-2958.1984.tb00044.x.

Beckmeyer, J. J., & Jamison, T. B. (2019). Is breaking up hard to do? Exploring emerging adults' perceived abilities to end romantic relationships. *Family Relations*, *69*(5), 1028–1040. https://doi.org/10.1111/fare.12404.

Berger, C. R., & Bradac, J. J. (1982). *Language and social knowledge: Uncertainty in interpersonal relationships*. London: Edward Arnold.

Berger, C. R., & Calabrese, R. J. (1975). Some explorations in initial interaction and beyond: Toward a developmental theory of interpersonal communication. *Human Communication Research*, *1*(2), 99–112. https://doi.org/10.1111/j.1468-2958.1975.tb00258.x.

Berger, L. M., Ferrari, G., Leturcq, M., Panico, L., & Solaz, A. (2021). COVID-19 lockdowns and demographically-relevant Google trends: A cross-national analysis. *PLoS One*, *16*(3), e0248072–e0248072. https://doi.org/10.1371/journal.pone.0248072.

Bevan, J. L., Ang, P, & Fearns, J. B. (2014). Being unfriended on Facebook: An application of expectancy violation theory. *Computers in Human Behavior*, *33*, 171–178. https://doi.org/10.1016/j.chb.2014.01.029.

Blight, M. G., Ruppel, E. K., & Jagiello, K. (2019). "Using Facebook lets me know what he is doing": Relational uncertainty, breakups, and renewals in on-again/off-again relationships. *The Southern Communication Journal*, *84*(5), 328–339. https://doi.org/10.1080/1041794X.2019.1641836.

Boelen, P. A., & Reijntjes, A. (2009). Negative cognitions in emotional problems following romantic relationship breakups. *Stress and Health*, *16*(1), 11–19. https://doi.org/10.1002/smi.1219.

Branje, S. J. T., Frijns, T., Finkenauer, C., Engels, R., & Meeus, W. (2007). You are my best friend: Commitment and stability in adolescents' same-sex friendships. *Personal Relationships*, *14*(4), 587–603. https://doi.org/10.1111/j.1475-6811.2007.00173.x.

Brody, N., LeFebvre, L. E., & Blackburn, K. G. (2016). Social networking site behaviors across the relational lifespan: Measurement and association with relationship escalation and de-escalations. *Social Media + Society*, *2*(4), 1–16. https://doi.org/10.1177/2056305116680004.

Burton-Chellew, M. N., & Dunbar, R. I. M. (2015). Romance and reproduction are socially costly. *Evolutionary Behavioral Sciences*, *9*(4), 229–241. https://doi.org/10.1037/ebs0000046.

Chaulk, K., & Jones, T. (2011). Online obsessive relational intrusion: Further concerns about Facebook. *Journal of Family Violence*, *26*(4), 245–254. https://doi.org/10.1007/s10896-011-9360-x.

Chopik, W. J., Wardecker, B. M., & Edelstien, R. S. (2014). Be mine: Attachment avoidance predicts perceptions of relationship functioning on Valentine's Day. *Personality and Individual Differences*, *63*, 47–52. https://doi.org/10.1016/j.paid.2014.01.035.

Chory-Assad, R. M., & Booth-Butterfield, M. (2001). Secret test use and self-esteem in deteriorating relationships. *Communication Research Reports*, *18*(2), 147–157. https://doi.org/10.1080/08824090109384792.

Connolly, J., & McIsaac, C. (2009). Adolescents' explanations for romantic dissolutions: A developmental perspective. *Journal of Adolescence*, *32*(5), 1209–1223. https://doi.org/10.1016/j.adolescence.2009.01.006.

Cope, M. A., & Mattingly, B. A. (2020). Putting me back together by getting back together: Post-dissolution self-concept confusion predicts rekindling desire among anxiously attached individuals. *Journal of Social and Personal Relationships*, *38*(1), 384–392. https://doi.org/10.1177/0265407520962849.

Coupland, J. (2003). Small talk: Social functions. *Research on Language and Social Interaction*, *36*(1), 1–6. https://doi.org/10.1207/S15327973RLSI3601_1.

Cupach, W. R., Spitzberg, B. H., & Carson, C. L. (2000). Toward a theory of obsessive relational intrusion and stalking. In K. Dindia & S. Duck (Eds.), *Communication and personal relationships* (pp. 131–146). Hoboken, NJ: John Wiley & Sons.

Dai, Y., Shin, S. Y., Kashian, N., Jang, J., & Walther, J. B. (2016). The influence of responses to self-disclosure on liking in computer-mediated communication. *Journal of Language and Social Psychology*, *35*(4), 394–411. https://doi.org/10.1177/0261927X15602515.

Dainton, M. (2019). Equity and relationship maintenance in first marriages and remarriages. *Journal of Divorce & Remarriage*, *60*(8), 583–599. https://doi.org/10.1080/10502556.2019.1586420.

Dainton, M., Goodboy, A. K., Borzea, D., & Goldman, Z. W. (2017). The dyadic effects of relationship uncertainty on negative relational maintenance. *Communication Reports*, *30*(3), 170–181. https://doi.org/10.1080/08934215.2017.1282529.

Derlega, V. J., Anderson, S., Winstead, B. A., & Greene, K. (2011). Positive disclosure among college students: What do they talk about, to whom, and why? *Journal of Positive Psychology*, *6*(2), 119–130. https://doi.org/10.1080/17439760.2010.545430.

Dominguez, J., & Hall, J. A. (2020). Examining context shifts' effects on relationship trajectories in friendships using Turning Point Theory. *Journal of Social and Personal Relationships*, *37*(6), 1892–1909. https://doi.org/10.1177/0265407520909475.

Donaghue, N., & Fallon, B. J. (2003). Gender role self-stereotyping and the relationship between equity and satisfaction in close relationships. *Sex Roles*, *48*(5), 217–230. https://doi.org/10.1023/A:1022869203900.

Finn, C., Johnson, M. D., & Neyer, F. J. (2020). Happily (n)ever after? Codevelopment of romantic partners in continuing and dissolving unions. *Developmental Psychology*, *56*(5), 1022–1028. https://doi.org/10.1037/dev0000897.

Geher, G., Bloodworth, R., Mason, J., Stoaks, C., Downey, H. J., Renstrom, K. L., & Romero, J. F. (2005). Motivational underpinnings of romantic partner perceptions: Psychological and physiological evidence. *Journal of Social and Personal Relationships*, *22*(2), 255–281. https://doi.org/10.1177/0265407505050953.

Gibbs, J. L., Ellison, N. B., & Heino, R. D. (2006). Self-presentations in online personals: The role of anticipated future interaction, self-disclosure, and perceived success in Internet dating. *Communication Research*, *33*(2), 152–177. https://doi.org/10.1177/0093650205285368.

Gomillion, S., Murray, S. L., & Lamarche, V. M. (2015). Losing the wind beneath your wings: The prospective influence of romantic breakup on goal progress. *Social Psychological and Personality Science*, *6*(5), 513–520. https://doi.org/10.1177/1948550614568160.

Greene, K., Derlega, V. L., & Mathews, A. (2006). Self-disclosure in personal relationships. In A. Vangelisti & D. Perlman (Eds.), *Cambridge handbook of personal relationships* (pp. 409–427). Cambridge: Cambridge University Press.

Hall, J. A. (2019). How many hours does it take to make a friend? *Journal of Social and Personal Relationships*, *36*(4), 1278–1296. https://doi.org/10.1177/0265407518761225.

Honeycutt, J. M., & Cantrill, J. G. (2001). *Cognition, communication, and romantic relationships*. Mahwah, NJ: Lawrence Erlbaum Associates.

Hubbard, A. S. E. (2001). Conflict between relationally uncertain romantic partners: The influence of relational responsiveness and empathy. *Communication Monographs*, *68*(4), 400–414. https://doi.org/10.1080/03637750128071.

Hughes, M., Morrison, K., & Asada, K. J. (2005). What's love got to do with it? Exploring the impact of maintenance rules, love attitudes, and network support on friends with benefits. *Western Journal of Communication*, *69*(1), 49–66. https://doi.org/10.1080/10570310500034154.

Ickes, W., Dugosh, J. W., Simpson, J. A., & Wilson, C. L. (2003). Suspicious minds: The motive to acquire relationship threatening information. *Personal Relationships*, *10*(2), 131–148. https://doi.org/10.1111/1475-6811.00042.

Jarvis, S., McClure, M. J., & Bolger, N. (2019). Exploring how exchange orientation affects conflict and intimacy in the daily life of romantic couples. *Journal of Social and Personal Relationships*, *36*(11–12), 3575–3587. https://doi.org/10.1177/0265407519826743.

Johnson, A. J., Wittenberg, E., & Haigh, M. (2004). The process of relationship development and deterioration: Turning points in friendships that have terminated. *Communication Quarterly*, *52*(1), 54–67. https://doi.org/10.1080/01463370409370178.

Johnson, A. J., Wittenberg, E., Villagran, M. M., Mazur, M., & Villagran, P. (2003). Relational progression as a dialectic: Examining turning points in communication among friends. *Communication Monographs*, *70*(3), 230–249. https://doi.org/10.1080/0363775032000167415.

Kansky, J., & Allen, J. P. (2018). Making sense and moving on: The potential for individual and interpersonal growth following emerging adult breakups. *Emerging Adulthood*, *6*(3), 172–190. https://doi.org/10.1177/2167696817711766.

King, M. E., & Theiss, J. A. (2016). The communicative and physiological manifestations of relational turbulence during the empty-nest phase of marital relationships. *Communication Quarterly*, *64*(5), 495–517. https://doi.org/10.1080/01463373.2015.1129353.

Knapp, M. L. (1984). *Interpersonal communication and human relationships*. Boston: Allyn & Bacon.

Knight, K. (2014). Communicative dilemmas in emerging adults' friends with benefits relationships: Challenges to relational talk. *Emerging Adulthood*, *2*(4), 270–279. https://doi.org/10.1177/2167696814549598.

Knobloch, L. K., & McAninch, K. G. (2016). Relational uncertainty. In C. R. Berger & M. E. Roloff (Eds.), *International Encyclopedia of Interpersonal Communication* (pp. 1473–1482). Hoboken, NJ: Wiley Blackwell.

Knobloch, L. K., & Satterlee, K. L. (2009). *Relational uncertainty: Theory and application*. In T. D. Afifi & W. A. Afifi (Eds.), *Uncertainty, information management, and disclosure decisions: Theories and applications* (p. 106–127). London: Routledge/Taylor & Francis Group.

Knobloch, L. K., & Solomon, D. H. (2003). Manifestations of relationship conceptualizations in conversation. *Human Communication Research*, *29*(4), 482–515. https://doi.org/10.1093/hcr/29.4.482.

Knobloch, L. K., Solomon, D. H., & Theiss, J. A. (2006). The role of intimacy in the production and perception of relationship talk within courtship. *Communication Research*, *33*(4), 211–244. https://doi.org/10.1177/0093650206289148.

Koenig Kellas, J., & Manusov, V. (2003). What's in a story? The relationship between narrative completeness and adjustment to relationship dissolution. *Journal of Social and Personal Relationships*, *20*, 285–307.

Laurenceau, J. P., Felcman Barrett, L., & Petromonaco, P. R. (1998). Intimacy as an interpersonal process: The importance of self-disclosure, partner disclosure, and perceived partner responsiveness in interpersonal exchanges. *Journal of Personality and Social Psychology*, *74*(5), 1238–1251. https://doi.org/10.1037/0022-3514.74.5.1238.

LeFebvre, L. E., & Fan, X. (2020). Ghosted?: Navigating strategies for reducing uncertainty and implications surrounding ambiguous loss. *Personal Relationships*, *27*(2), 433–459. https://doi.org/10.1111/pere.12322.

Lewandowski, G. W., Aron, A., Bassis, S., & Kunak, J. (2006). Losing a self-expanding relationship: Implications for the self concept. *Personal Relationships*, *13*(3), 317–331. https://doi.org/10.1111/j.1475-6811.2006.00120.x.

Mikucki-Enyart, S. L., & Caughlin, J. P. (2018). Integrating the relational turbulence model and a multiple goals approach to understand topic avoidance during the transition to extended family. *Communication Research*, *45*(3), 267–296. https://doi.org/10.1177/0093650215595075.

Mongeau, P. A., Ramirez, A., & Vorrell, M. (2003, February). *Friends with benefits: Initial explorations of sexual, non-romantic relationships* [Conference session]. Annual meeting of the Western Communication Association, Salt Lake City, UT, United States.

Mongeau, P., van Raalte, L., Bednarchik, L., & Generous, M. (2019). Investigating and extending variation among friends with benefits relationships: Relationship maintenance and social support. *The Southern Communication Journal*, *84*(5), 275–286. https://doi.org/10.1080/1041794X.2019.1641837.

Morse, K. A., & Neuberg, S. L. (2004). How do holidays influence relationship processes and outcomes?: Examining the instigating and catalytic effect of Valentine's Day. *Personal Relationships*, *11*(4), 509–527. https://doi.org/10.1111/j.1475-6811.2004.00095.x.

Norona, J. C., & Olmstead, S. B. (2017). The aftermath of dating relationship dissolution in emerging adulthood: A review. *Contemporary Perspectives on Family Research*, *11*, 237–261. https://doi.org/10.1108/S1530-353520170000011011.

Norona, J. C., Olmstead, S. B., & Welsh, D. P. (2017). Breaking up in emerging adulthood: A developmental perspective of relationship dissolution. *Emerging Adulthood*, *5*(2), 116–127. https://doi.org/10.1177/2167696816658585.

Ogolsky, B. G., Surra, C. A., 7 Monk, J. K. (2016). Pathways of commitment to wed: The development and dissolution of romantic relationships. *Journal of Marriage and the Family*, *78*(2), 293–310. https://doi.org/10.1111/jomf.12260.

Oswald, D. L., & Clark, E. M. (2003). Best friends forever?: High school best friendships and the transition to college. *Personal Relationships*, *10*(2), 187–196. https://doi.org/10.1111/1475-6811.00045.

Reyns, B. W., Henson, B., & Fisher, B. W. (2012). Stalking in the twilight zone: Extent of cyberstalking victimization and offending among college students. *Deviant Behavior*, *33*(1), 1–25. https://doi.org/10.1080/01639625.2010.538364.

Robinson, M. D., Persich, M. R., Sjoblom-Schmidt, S., & Penzel, I. A. (2020). Love stories: How language us patterns vary by relationship quality. *Discourse Processes*, *57*(1), 81–98. https://doi.org/10.1080/0163853X.2019.1627158.

Roloff, M. E. (2016). Social exchange theories. In C. R. Berger & M. E. Roloff (Eds.), *International encyclopedia of interpersonal communication* (pp. 1615–1633). Hoboken, NJ: Wiley Blackwell.

Roloff, M. E., Soule, K. P., & Carey, C. M. (2001). Reasons for remaining in a relationship and responses to relational transgressions. *Journal of Social and Personal Relationships*, *18*(3), 362–385. https://doi.org/10.1177/0265407501183004.

Rusbult, C. E., Agnew, C. R., & Arriaga, X. B. (2012). The investment model of commitment processes. In P. A. M. Van Lange, A. W. Kruglanski, & T. E. Higgins (Eds.), *Handbook of theories of social psychology* (Vol. 2, pp. 218–231). Thousand Oaks, CA: Sage.

Sbarra, D. A. (2006). Predicting the onset of emotional recovery following nonmarital relationship dissolution: Survival analyses of sadness and anger. *Personality and Social Psychology Bulletin*, *32*(3), 298–312. https://doi.org/10.1177/0146167205280913.

Sharabi, L. L., & Caughlin, J. P. (2017). What predicts first data success? A longitudinal study of modality switching in online dating. *Personal Relationships*, *24*(2), 370–391. https://doi.org/10.1111/pere.12188.

Solomon, D. H. (2016). Relational turbulence model. In C. R. Berger & M. E. Roloff (Eds.), *International encyclopedia of interpersonal communication* (pp. 1460–1468). Hoboken, NJ: Wiley Blackwell.

Solomon, D. H., & Brisini, K. S. (2017). Operationalizing relational turbulence theory: Measurement and construct validation. *Personal Relationships*, *24*(4), 768–789. https://doi.org/10.1111/pere.12212.

Spitzberg, B. H. (2002). The tactical topography of stalking victimization and management. *Trauma, Violence, and Abuse*, *3*(4), 261–288. https://doi.org/10.1177/1524838002237330.

Spitzberg, B. H. (2016). Stalking/obsessive relational intrusion. In C. R. Berger & M. E. Roloff (Eds.), *International encyclopedia of interpersonal communication* (pp. 1688–1696). Hoboken, NJ: Wiley Blackwell.

Spitzberg, B. H., & Veksler, A. E. (2007). The personality of pursuit: Personality attributions of unwanted pursuers and stalkers. *Violence and Victims*, *22*(3), 275–289. https://doi.org/10.1891/088667007780842838.

Sprecher, S. (2001). Equity and social exchange in dating couples: Associations with satisfaction, commitment, and stability. *Journal of Marriage and the Family*, *63*(3), 599–613. https://doi.org/10.1111/j.1741-3737.2001.00599.x.

Sprecher, S. (2018). Inequity leads to distress and a reduction in satisfaction: Evidence from a priming study. *Journal of Family Issues*, *39*(1), 230–244. https://doi.org/10.1177/0192513X16637098.

Sprecher, S., & Hendrick, S. (2004). Self-disclosure in intimate relationships: Associations with individual and relationship characteristics over time. *Journal of Social and Clinical Psychology*, *23*(6), 857–877. https://doi.org/10.1521/jscp.23.6.857.54803.

Sprecher, S., Zimmerman, C., & Fehr, B. (2014). The influence of compassionate love on strategies used to end a relationship. *Journal of Social and Personal Relationships*, *31*(5), 697–705. https://doi.org/10.1177/0265407513517958.

Sprecher, S., Zimmerman, C., Abrahams, E. M. (2010). Choosing compassionate strategies to end a relationship: Effects of compassionate love for partner and the reason for the breakup. *Social Psychology*, *41*(2), 66–75. https://doi.org/10.1027/1864-9335/a000010.

Sunnafrank, M. (1986). Predicted outcome value during initial interactions: A reformulation of uncertainty reduction theory. *Human Communication Research*, *13*(1), 3–13. https://doi.org/10.1111/j.1468-2958.1986.tb00092.x.

Sunnafrank, M. (2016). Predicted outcome value theory. In C. R. Berger & M. E. Roloff (Eds.), *International encyclopedia of interpersonal communication* (pp. 1374–1378). Hoboken, NJ: Wiley Blackwell.

Sunnafrank, M., & Ramirez, A. (2004). At first sight: Persistent relational effects of get-acquainted conversations. *Journal of Social and Personal Relationships*, *21*(3), 361–379. https://doi.org/10.1177/0265407504042837.

Surra, C. A. (1985). Courtship types: Variation in interdependence between partners and social networks. *Journal of Personality and Social Psychology*, *49*(2), 357–375. https://doi.org/10.1037/0022-3514.49.2.357.

Tani, F., Smorti, A., & Peterson, C. (2015). Is friendship quality reflected in memory narratives? *Journal of Social and Personal Relationships*, *32*(3), 281–303. https://doi.org/10.1177/0265407515573601.

Tashiro, T., & Frazier, P. (2003). "I'll never be in a relationship like that again": Personal growth following romantic relationship breakups. *Personal Relationships*, *10*(1), 113–128. https://doi.org/10.1111/1475-6811.00039.

Theiss, J. A., & Estlein, R. (2014). Antecedents and consequences of the perceived threat of sexual communication: A test of the relational turbulence model. *Western Journal of Communication*, *78*(4), 404–425. https://doi.org/10.1080/10570314.2013.845794.

Theiss, J., A., & Nagy, M. E. (2013). A relational turbulence model of partner responsiveness and relationship talk across cultures. *Western Journal of Communication*, *77*(2), 186–209. https://doi.org/10.1080/10570314.2012.720746.

Verswijvel, K., Heirman, W., Hardies, K., & Walrave, M. (2018). Adolescents' reasons to unfriend on Facebook. *Cyberpsychology, Behavior, and Social Networking*, *21*(10), 603–610. https://doi.org/10.1089/cyber.2018.0243.

Weaver, J. R., & Bosson, J. K. (2011). I feel like I know you: Sharing negative attitudes of others promotes feelings of familiarity. *Personality and Social Psychology Bulletin*, *37*(4), 481–491. https://doi.org/10.1177/0146167211398364.

Wilson, S. R., Kunkel, A. D., Robson, S. J., Olufowote, J. O., & Soliz, J. (2009). Identity implications of relationship (re)definition goals: An analysis of face threats and facework as young adults initiate, intensify, and disengage from romantic relationships. *Journal of Language and Social Psychology*, *28*(1), 32–61. https://doi.org/10.1177/0261927X08325746.

10 INTIMACY AND INTERPERSONAL COMMUNICATION

Afifi, T. D., Harrison, K., Zamanzadeh, N., & Acevedo Callejas, M. (2020). Testing the theory of resilience and relational load in dual career families: relationship maintenance as stress management. *Journal of Applied Communication Research*, *48*(1), 5–25. https://doi.org/10.1080/00909882.2019.1706097.

Afifi, W. A., Falato, W. L., & Weiner, J. L. (2001). Identity concerns following a severe relational transgression: The role of discovery method for the relational outcomes of infidelity. *Journal of Social and Personal Relationships*, *18*(2), 291–308. https://doi.org/10.1177/0265407501182007.

Afshordi, N., & Liberman, Z. (2021). Keeping friends in mind: Development of friendship concepts in early childhood. *Social Development*, *30*(2), 331–342. https://doi.org/10.1111/sode.12493.

Alexander, A. (2008). Relationship resources for coping with unfulfilled standards in dating relationships: Commitment, satisfaction, and closeness. *Journal of Social and Personal Relationships*, *25*(5), 725–747. https://doi.org/10.1177/0265407508093783.

Aron, A., Fisher, H., Mashek, D. J., Strong, G., Haifang, L., & Brown, L. L. (2005). Reward, motivation, and emotion systems associated with early-stage intense romantic love. *Journal of Neurophysiology*, *94*(1), 327–337. https://doi.org/10.1152/jn.00838.2004.

Bartholomew, K. (1990). Avoidance of intimacy: An attachment perspective. *Journal of Social and Personal Relationships*, *7*(2), 147–178. https://doi.org/10.1177/0265407590072001.

Baumeister, R. F., Wotman, S. R., & Stillwell, A. M. (1993). Unrequited love: On heartbreak, anger, guilt, scriptlessness, and humiliation. *Journal of Personality and Social Psychology*, *64*(3), 377–394. https://doi.org/10.1037/0022-3514.64.3.377.

Baxter, L. A. (2011). *Voicing relationships: A dialogic perspective*. Thousand Oaks, CA: Sage.

Baxter, L. A., & Norwood, K. M. (2016). Relational dialectics theory. In C. R. Berger & M. E. Roloff (Eds.), *International encyclopedia of interpersonal communication* (pp. 1443–1451). Hoboken, NJ: Wiley Blackwell.

Ben-Ari, A. (2011). Rethinking closeness and distance in intimate relationships: Are they really two opposites? *Journal of Family Issues*, *33*(3), 391–412. https://doi.org/10.1177/0192513X11415357.

Berscheid, E., Snyder, M., & Omoto, A. M. (2004). Measuring closeness: The relationship closeness inventory (RCI). In D. J. Mashek & A. P. Aron (Eds.), *Handbook of closeness and intimacy* (pp. 81–101). Mahwah, NJ: Lawrence Erlbaum.

Bippus, A. M., & Rollin, E. (2003). Attachment style differences in relational maintenance and conflict behaviors: Friends' perceptions. *Communication Reports*, *16*(2), 113–123. https://doi.org/10.1080/08934210309384494.

Bitzan, J. E., & Kruzich, J. M. (1990). Interpersonal relationships of nursing home residents. *Gerontologist*, *30*(3), 385–390. https://doi.org/10.1093/geront/30.3.385.

Branand, B., Mashek, D., & Aron, A. (2019). Pair-bonding as inclusion of other in the self: A literature review. *Frontiers in Psychology*, *10*. https://doi.org/10.3389/fpsyg.2019.02399.

Brinberg, M., & Ram, N. (2021). Do new romantic couples use more similar language over time? Evidence from intensive longitudinal text messages. *Journal of Communication*, *jqab012*, 1–24. https://doi.org/10.1093/joc/jqab012.

Canary, D. J., & Stafford, L. (1992). Relational maintenance strategies and equity in marriage. *Communication Monographs*, *59*(3), 243–267. https://doi.org/10.1080/03637759209376268.

Canary, D. J., & Yum, Y. (2016). Relationship maintenance strategies. In C. R. Berger & M. E. Roloff (Eds.), *International encyclopedia of interpersonal communication* (pp. 1491–1499). Hoboken, NJ: Wiley Blackwell.

Candel, O., & Turliuc, M. N. (2019). Insecure attachment and relationship satisfaction: A meta-analysis of actor and partner associations. *Personality and Individual Differences*, *147*, 190–199. https://doi.org/10.1016/j.paid.2019.04.037.

Cann, A., & Baucom, T. R. (2004). Former partners and new rivals as threats to a relationship: Infidelity type, gender, and commitment as factors related to distress and forgiveness. *Personal Relationships*, *11*(3), 305–318. https://doi.org/10.1111/j.1475-6811.2004.00084.x.

Cantañeda, A. M., Wendel, M. L., & Crockett, E. E. (2015). Overlap in Facebook profiles reflects relationship closeness. *The Journal of Social Psychology*, *155*(4), 395–401. https://doi.org/10.1080/00224545.2015.1008968.

Chango, J. M., Allen, J. P., Szwedo, D., & Schad, M. M. (2015). Early adolescent peer foundations of late adolescent and young adult psychological adjustment. *Journal of Research on Adolescence*, *25*(4), 685–699. https://doi.org/10.1111/jora.12162.

Dainton, M., & Aylor, B. (2002). Routine and strategic maintenance efforts: Behavioral patterns, variations associated with relational length, and the prediction of relational characteristics. *Communication Monographs*, *69*(1), 52–66. https://doi.org/10.1080/03637750216533.

Dainton, M., Zelley, E., & Langan, E. (2003). Maintaining friendships throughout the lifespan. In D. J. Canary & M. Dainton (Eds.), *Maintaining relationships through communication* (pp. 79–102). Mahwah, NJ: Lawrence Erlbaum.

David, B. A., & Weigel, D. J. (2020). Cognitive interdependence and the everyday expression of commitment. *Journal of Social and Personal Relationships*, *37*(3), 1008–1029. https://doi.org/10.1177/0265407519884640.

Deci, E. L., La Guardia, J. G., Moller, A. C., Scheiner, M. J., & Ryan, R. M. (2006). On the benefits of giving as well as receiving autonomy support: Mutuality in close friendships. *Personality and Social Psychology Bulletin*, *32*(3), 313–327. https://doi.org/10.1177/0146167205282148.

Dillow, M. r., Goodboy, A. K., & Bolkan, S. (2014). Attachment and the expression of affection in romantic relationships: The mediating role of romantic love. *Communication Reports*, *27*(2), 102–115. https://doi.org/10.1080/08934215.2014.900096.

Dillow, M. R., Malachowski, C. C., Brann, M., & Weber, K. D. (2011). An experimental examination of the effects of communicative infidelity motives on communication and relational outcomes in romantic relationships. *Western Journal of Communication*, *75*(5), 473–499. https://doi.org/10.1080/10570314.2011.588986.

Dovala, T., Hawrilenko, M., & Cordova, J. V. (2018). Implicit theories of relationships and conflict communication patterns in romantic relationships. *Journal of Relationships Research*, *9*, 1–9. https://doi.org/10.1017/jrr.2018.11.

Drigotas, S. M., Safstrom, C. A., & Gentilita, T. (1999). An investment model prediction of dating infidelity. *Journal of Personal and Social Psychology*, *77*(3), 509–524. https://doi.org/10.1037/0022-3514.77.3.509.

Edwards, T., Pask, E. B., Whitbred, R., & Neuendorf, K. A. (2017). The influence of personal, relational, and contextual factors on forgiveness communication following transgressions. *Personal Relationships*, *25*(1), 4–21. https://doi.org/10.1111/pere.12224.

Farley, S. D., Hughes, S. M., & Lafayette, J. N. (2013). People will know we are in love: Evidence of differences between vocal samples directed toward lovers and friends. *Journal of Nonverbal Behavior*, *37*(3), 123–138. https://doi.org/10.1007/s10919-013-0151-3.

Fehr, B. (2019). Everyday conceptions of love. In R. J. Sternberg & K. Sternberg (Eds.), *The new psychology of love* (2nd ed., pp. 154–182). New York, NY: Cambridge University Press.

Feldman, S. S., & Cauffman, E. (1999). Your cheatin' heart: Attitudes, behaviors, and correlates of sexual betrayal in late adolescents. *Journal of Research on Adolescents*, *9*(3), 227–252. https://doi.org/10.1207/s15327795jra0903_1.

Finchum, T. D. (2005). Keeping the ball in the air: Contact in long-distance friendships. *Journal of Women & Aging*, *17*(3), 91–106. https://doi.org/10.1300/J074v17n03_07.

Floyd, K., Hesse, C., & Generous, M. A. (2015). Affection exchange theory: A bio-evolutionary look at affectionate communication. In D. O. Braithwaite & P. Schrodt (Eds.), *Engaging theories in interpersonal communication: Multiple perspectives* (2nd ed., pp. 303–314). Thousand Oaks, CA: Sage.

Franiuk, R., Cohen, D., & Pomerantz, E. M. (2002). Implicit theories of relationships: Implications for relationship satisfaction and longevity. *Personal Relationships*, *9*(4), 345–367. https://doi.org/10.1111/1475-6811.09401.

Gana, K., Saada, Y., & Untas, A. (2013). Effects of love styles on marital satisfaction in heterosexual couples: A dyadic approach. *Marriage & Family Review*, *49*(8), 754–772. https://doi.org/10.1080/01494929.2013.834025.

Gonzaga, G. C., Turner, R. A., Keltner, D., Campos, B., & Altemus, M. (2006). Romantic love and sexual desire in close relationships. *Emotion*, *6*(2), 163–179. https://doi.org/10.1037/1528-3542.6.2.163.

Goodboy, A. K., Horan, S. M., & Booth-Butterfield, M. (2012). Intentional jealousy-evoking behavior in romantic relationships as a function of received partner affection and love styles. *Communication Quarterly*, *60*(3), 370–385. https://doi.org/10.1080/01463373.2012.688792.

Gray, J. (1992). *Men are from Mars, women are from Venus*. New York: HarperCollins.

Green, M. C., & Sabini, J. (2006). Gender, socioeconomic status, age, and jealousy: Emotional responses to infidelity in a national sample. *Emotion*, *6*(2), 330–334. https://doi.org/10.1037/1528-3542.6.2.330.

Greene, K., Derlega, V. L., & Mathews, A. (2006). Self-disclosure in personal relationships. In A. Vangelisti & D. Perlman (Eds.), *Cambridge handbook of personal relationships* (pp. 409–427). Cambridge: Cambridge University Press.

Guerrero, L. K., & Wiedmaier, B. (2013). Nonverbal intimacy: Affectionate communication, positive involvement behavior, and flirtation. In J. A. Hall & M. L. Knapp (Eds.), *Nonverbal communication* (pp. 577–612). Boston, MA: De Gruyter Mouton. https://doi.org/10.1515/9783110238150.577.

Gunderson, P. R., & Ferrari, J. R. (2008). Forgiveness of sexual cheating in romantic relationships: Effects of discovery method, frequency of offense, and presence of apology. *North American Journal of Psychology*, *10*(1), 1–14.

Gupta, V., & Korte, C. (1994). The effects of a confidant and a peer group on the well-being of single elders. *International Journal of Aging and Human Development*, *39*(4), 293–302. https://doi.org/10.2190/4YYH-9XAU-WQF9-APVT.

Haas, S. M., & Lannutti, P. J. (2019). The impact of minority stress and social support on positive relationship functioning in same-sex relationships. *Health Communication*, *36*(3), 315–323. https://doi.org/10.1080/10410236.2019.1687130.

Hall, J. H., & Fincham, F. D. (2006). Relationship dissolution following infidelity: The roles of attributions and forgiveness. *Journal of Social and Clinical Psychology*, *25*(5), 508–522. https://doi.org/10.1521/jscp.2006.25.5.508.

Hans, J. D. (2008). Do love styles predict lifetime number of sex partners? *American Journal of Sexuality Education*, *3*(2), 149–164. https://doi.org/10.1080/15546120802104328.

Hasim, M. J. M., Mustafa, H., & Hashim, N. H. (2018). From middle childhood to adulthood attachment: Measuring attachment stability in the context of married individuals in Penang, Malaysia. *The Family Journal*, *26*(4), 444–454. https://doi.org/10.1177/1066480718806522.

Hendrick, C., & Hendrick, S. S. (2019). Styles of romantic love. In R. J. Sternberg, & K. Sternberg (Eds.), *The new psychology of love* (2nd ed., pp. 223–239). New York, NY: Cambridge University Press.

Hendrick, S. S., & Hendrick, C. (2002). Linking romantic love with sex: Development of the perceptions of love and sex scale. *Journal of Social and Personal Relationships*, *19*(3), 361–378. https://doi.org/10.1177/0265407502193004.

Hoppe-Nagao, A., & Ting-Toomey, S. (2002). Relational dialectics and management strategies in marital couples. *The Southern Communication Journal*, *67*(2), 142–159. https://doi.org/10.1080/10417940209373226.

Iannone, N. E., McCarty, M. K., & Kelly, J. R. (2017). With a little help from your friend: Transactive memory in best friendships. *Journal of Social and Personal Relationships*, *34*(6), 812–832. https://doi.org/10.1177/0265407516659565.

Jones, J. D., Fraley, R. C., Ehrlich, K. B., Stern, J. A., Lejuez, C. W., Shaver, P. R., & Cassidy, J. (2018). Stability of attachment study in adolescence: An empirical test of alternative developmental processes. *Child Development*, *89*(3), 871–880. https://doi.org/10.1111/cdev.12775.

Kanemasa, Y., Taniguchi, J., Daibo, I., & Ishimori, M. (2004). Love styles and romantic love experiences in Japan. *Social Behavior and Personality: An International Journal*, *32*(3), 265–282. https://doi.org/10.2224/sbp.2004.32.3.265.

Kennedy-Lightsey, C. D., Martin, M. M., LaBelle, S., & Weber, K. (2015). Attachment, identity gaps, and communication and relational outcomes in martial couples' public performances. *Journal of Family Communication*, *15*(3), 232–248. https://doi.org/10.1080/15267431.2015.1043430.

Kenrick, D. T., Trost, M. R., Sundie, J. M. (2004). Sex roles as adaptations: An evolutionary perspective on gender differences and similarities. In A. H. Eagly, A. E. Beall, & R. J. Sternberg (Eds.), *The psychology of gender* (pp. 65–91). New York: Guilford Press.

Keyes, C. L. M. (2002). The exchange of emotional support with age and its relationship with emotional well-being by age. *The Journals of Gerontology: Series B, Psychological Sciences and Social Sciences*, *57*(6), 518–525. https://doi.org/10.1093/geronb/57.6.P518.

Kleine, M. (2021). Accounts and attributions following marital infidelity. *Western Journal of Communication*, *85*(2), 211–229. https://doi.org/10.1080/10570314.2019.1702714.

Knobloch, L. K., & Donovan-Kicken, E. (2006). Perceived involvement of network members in courtships: A test of the relational turbulence model. *Personal Relationships*, *13*(3), 281–302. https://doi.org/10.1111/j.1475-6811.2006.00118.x.

Knobloch, L. K., & Solomon, D. H. (2002). Information seeking beyond initial interaction: Negotiating relational uncertainty within close relationships. *Human Communication Research*, *28*(2), 243–257. https://doi.org/10.1093/hcr/28.2.243.

Komolova, M., & Wainryb, C. (2011). "What I want and what you want": Children's thinking about competing personal preferences. *Social Development*, *20*(2), 334–352. https://doi.org/10.1111/j.1467-9507.2010.00589.x.

Kunkel, A., & Burleson, B. (2003). Relational implications of communication skill evaluations and love styles. *The Southern Communication Journal*, *68*, 1810197.

Kurdek, L. A. (2006). Differences between partners from heterosexual, gay, and lesbian cohabiting couples. *Journal of Marriage and the Family*, *68*(3), 509–528. https://doi.org/10.1080/1041794030937326.

Lewandowski, G. W., & Ackerman, R. A. (2006). Something's missing: Need fulfillment and self-expansion as predictors of susceptibility to infidelity. *Journal of Social Psychology*, *146*(4), 389–403. https://doi.org/10.3200/SOCP.146.4.389-403.

Li, T., Fok, H. K., Fung, H. H. (2011). Is reciprocity always beneficial? Age differences in the association between support balance and life satisfaction. *Aging & Mental Health*, *15*(5), 541–547. https://doi.org/10.1080/13607863.2010.551340.

McAlister, A. R., Pachana, N., & Jackson, C. J. (2005). Predictors of young dating adults' inclination to engage in extradyadic sexual activities: A multiperspective study. *British Journal of Psychology*, *96*(3), 331–350. https://doi.org/10.1348/000712605X47936.

McClanahan, K. K., Gold, J. A., Lenney, E., Ryckman, R. M., Kulberg, G. E. (1990). Infatuation and attraction to a dissimilar other: Why is love blind? *Journal of Social Psychology*, *130*(4), 433–445. https://doi.org/10.1080/00224545.1990.9924604.

Mongeau, P. A., & Schulz, B. E. (1997). What he doesn't know won't hurt him (or me): Verbal responses and attributions following sexual infidelity. *Communication Reports*, *10*(2), 143–152. https://doi.org/10.1080/08934219709367670.

Moskowitz, K., Richmond, K., & Michniewicz, K. (2020). Caught in a bad romance: Endorsement of traditional romantic ideology, internalized heterosexism, and intimate partner violence experiences among sexual minority individuals. *Psychology of Sexual Orientation and Gender Diversity*, *7*(3), 329–336. https://doi.org/10.1037/sgd0000380.

Murray, S. L., Holmes, J. G., & Griffin, D. W. (2004). The benefits of positive illusions: Idealization and the construction of satisfaction in close relationships.

In H. T. Reis and C. E. Rusbult (Eds.), *Close relationships: Key readings* (pp. 317–338). Philadelphia, PA: Taylor & Francis.

Naidoo, R., Coleman, K., & Guyo, C. (2020). Exploring gender discursive struggles about social inclusion in an online gaming community. *Information Technology & People*, *33*(2), 576–601. https://doi.org/10.1108/ITP-04-2019-0163.

Noller, P., Feeney, J. A., & Peterson, C. (2001). *Personal relationships across the lifespan*. Philadelphia, PA: Taylor & Francis.

Nussbaum, J. F. (1991). Communication, language and the institutionalised elderly. *Ageing and Society*, *11*(2), 149–166. https://doi.org/10.1017/S0144686X00003986.

Nussbaum, J. F., Hummert, M. L., Williams, A., & Harwood, J. (1996). Communication and older adults. *Communication Yearbook 19* (pp. 1–47). Thousand Oaks, CA: Sage.

Ogolsky, B. G., & Bowers, J. R. (2013). A meta-analytic review of relationship maintenance and its correlates. *Journal of Social and Personal Relationships*, *30*(3), 343–367. https://doi.org/10.1177/0265407512463338.

Papp, L. J., Liss, M., Erchull, M. J., Godfrey, H., & Waaland-Kreutzer, L. (2017). The dark side of heterosexual romance: Endorsement of romantic beliefs relates to intimate partner violence. *Sex Roles*, *76*(1), 99–109. https://doi.org/10.1007/s11199-016-0668-0.

Patterson, B. R., Bettini, L., & Nussbaum, J. F. (1993). The meaning of friendship across the lifespan: Two studies. *Communication Quarterly*, *41*(2), 145–160. https://doi.org/10.1080/01463379309369875.

Pitts, M. J., Krieger, J., L., & Nussbaum, J. F. (2005). Finding the right place: Social interaction and life transitions among the elderly. In E. B. Ray (Ed.), *Health communication in practice: A case study approach* (pp. 233–242). Mahwah, NJ: Lawrence Erlbaum.

Ramirez, A., & Broneck, K. (2009). "IM me": Instant messaging as relational maintenance and everyday communication. *Journal of Social and Personal Relationships*, *26*(2–3), 291–314. https://doi.org/10.1177/0265407509106719.

Rawlins, W. K. (2004). Friendships in later life. In J. F. Nussbaum & J. Coupland (Eds.), *Handbook of communication and aging research* (2nd ed., pp. 273–299). Mahwah, NJ: Lawrence Erlbaum.

Regan, P. C. (2000). The role of sexual desire and sexual activity in dating relationships. *Social Behavior and Personality*, *28*(1), 51–59. https://doi.org/10.2224/sbp.2000.28.1.51.

Robinson, M. D., Persich, M. R., Sjoblom-Schmidt, S., & Penzel, I. A. (2020). Love stories: How language use patterns vary by relationship quality. *Discourse Processes*, *57*(1), 81–98. https://doi.org/10.1080/0163853X.2019.1627158.

Sahlstein, E., Maguire, K. C., & Timmerman, L. (2009). Contradictions and praxis contextualized by wartime deployment: Wives' perspectives revealed through relational dialectics. *Communication Monographs*, *76*(4), 421–442. https://doi.org/10.1080/03637750903300239.

Samter, W. (2003). Friendship interaction skills across the life span. In J. O. Greene & B. R. Burleson (Eds.), *Handbook of communication and social interaction skills* (pp. 637–684). Mahwah, NJ: Lawrence Erlbaum.

Sanders, R. E. (2007). The composition and sequencing of communicative acts to solve social problems: Functionality and inventiveness in children's interactions. *Communication Monographs*, *74*(4), 464–491. https://doi.org/10.1080/03637750701716628.

Shackelford, T. K., Buss, D. M., & Bennett, K. (2002). Forgiveness or breakup: Sex differences in responses to a partner's infidelity. *Cognition & Emotion*, *16*(2), 299–307. https://doi.org/10.1080/02699930143000202.

Shackelford, T. K., LeBlanc, G. J., & Drass, E. (2000). Emotional reactions to infidelity. *Cognition and Emotion*, *14*(5), 643–659. https://doi.org/10.1080/02699930050117657.

Sprecher, S. (2011). The influence of social networks on romantic relationships: Through the lens of the social network. *Personal Relationships*, *18*(4), 630–644. https://doi.org/10.1111/j.1475-6811.2010.01330.x.

Sprecher, S., & Metts, S. (1999). Romantic beliefs: Their influence on relationships and patterns of change over time. *Journal of Social and Personal Relationships*, *16*(6), 834–851. https://doi.org/10.1177/0265407599166009.

Stafford, L. (2004). Communication competencies and sociocultural priorities of middle childhood. In A. L. Vangelisti (Ed.), *Handbook of family communication* (pp. 311–332). Mahwah, NJ: Lawrence Erlbaum.

Stafford, L. (2011). Measuring relationship maintenance behaviors: Critque and development of the revised relationship maintenance behavior scale. *Journal of Social and Personal Relationships*, *28*(2), 278–303. https://doi.org/10.1177/0265407510378125.

Sternberg, R. J. (2004). A triangular theory of love. In H. T. Reis, & C. E. Rusbult (Eds.), *Close relationships: Key readings* (pp. 213–227). Philadelphia, PA: Taylor & Francis.

Tallis, F. (2005). Crazy for you. *Psychologist*, *18*(2), 72–74.

Thompson, S. A., Gold, J. A., & Ryckman, R. M. (2003). The simulated video interaction technique: A new method for inducing infatuation in the laboratory. *Representative Research in Social Psychology*, *27*, 32–37.

Timmermans, E., De Caluwé, E., & Alexopoulos, C. (2018). Why are you chearing on tinder? Exploring user' motives and (dark) personality traits. *Computers in Human Behavior*, *89*, 129–139. https://doi.org/10.1016/j.chb.2018.07.040.

Väänänen, A., Buunk, A. P., Kivimäki, M., Vahtera, J., & Koskenvuo, M. (2008). Change in reciprocity as a predictor of depressive symptoms: A prospective cohort study of Finnish women and men. *Social Science & Medicine*, *67*(11), 1907–1916. https://doi.org/10.1016/j.socscimed.2008.09.015.

Vannier, S. A., & O'Sullivan, L. F. (2017). Passion, connection, and destiny: How romantic expectations help predict satisfaction and commitment in young adults' dating relationships. *Journal of Social and Personal Relationships*, *34*(2), 235–257. https://doi.org/10.1177/0265407516631156.

Vannier, S. A., & O'Sullivan, L. F. (2018). Great expectations: Examining unmet romantic expectations and dating relationship outcomes using an investment model framework. *Journal of Social and Personal Relationships*, *35*(8), 1045–1066. https://doi.org/10.1177/0265407517703492.

Walters, A. S., & Burger, B. D. (2013). "I love you, and I cheated": Investigating disclosure of infidelity to primary romantic partners. *Sexuality & Culture: An Interdisciplinary Quarterly*, *17*(1), 20–49. https://doi.org/10.1007/s12119-012-9138-1.

Wang, C., Song, S., d'Oleire Uquillas, F., Zilverstand, A., Song, H., Chen, H., Zou, Z. (2020). Altered brain network organization in romantic love as measured with resting-state fMRI and graph theory. *Brain Imaging and Behavior*, *14*(6), 2771–2784. https://doi.org/10.1007/s11682-019-00226-0.

Wang, D., & Gruenewald, T. (2019). The psychological costs of social support imbalance: Variation across relationship context and age. *Journal of Health Psychology*, *24*(12), 1615–1625. https://doi.org/10.1177/1359105317692854.

Weaver, S. E., & Ganong, L. H. (2004). The factor structure of the romantic beliefs scale for African Americans and European Americans. *Journal of Social and Personal Relationships*, *21*(2), 171–185. https://doi.org/10.1177/0265407504041373.

Weiser, D. A., & Weigel, D. J. (2014). Testing a model of communication responses to relationship infidelity. *Communication Quarterly*, *62*(4), 416–435. https://doi.org/10.1080/01463373.2014.922482.

Wieselquist, J. (2007). Commitment and trust in young adult friendships. *Interpersona: An International Journal on Personal Relationships*, *1*(2), 209–220. https://doi.org/10.5964/ijpr.v1i2.14.

Yu, R., Branje, S. J. T., Keijsers, L., & Meeus, W. H. J. (2014). Personality types and development of adolescents' conflict with friends. *European Journal of Personality*, *28*(2), 156–167. https://doi.org/10.1002/per.1913.

11 COMMUNICATION IN FAMILIES

Afifi, T. D., & Olson, L. (2005). The chilling effect in families and the pressure to conceal secrets. *Communication Monographs*, *72*(2), 192–216. https://doi.org/10.1080/0363775050011906.

Afifi, T. D., McManus, T., Hutchinson, S., & Baker, B. (2007). Inappropriate parental divorce disclosures, the factors that prompt them, and their impact on parents' and adolescents' wellbeing. *Communication Monographs*, *74*(1), 78–102. https://doi.org/10.1080/03637750701196870.

Afifi, T. D., Olson, L. N., & Armstrong, C. (2005). The chilling effect and family secrets: Examining the role of self protection, other protection, and communication efficacy. *Human Communication Research*, *31*(4), 564–598. https://doi.org/10.1111/j.1468-2958.2005.tb00883.x.

Aloia, L. S. (2019). The influence of family relationship schemas, parental support, and parental verbal aggression on mental well-being. *Journal of Family Studies*, 1–14. https://doi.org/10.1080/13229400.2019.1702578.

Aloia, L. S. (2020). Parent-child relationship satisfaction: The influence of family communication orientations and relational maintenance behaviors. *The Family Journal*, *28*(1), 83–89. https://doi.org/10.1177/10664807 19896561.

Altgelt, E. E., & Meltzer, A. L. (2019). Associations between premarital factors and first-married, heterosexual newlywed couples' frequency of sex and sexual trajectories. *Journal of Sex Research*, *58*(2), 146–159. https://doi.org/10.1080 /00224499.2019.1695722.

Banchefsky, S., & Park, B. (2016). The "new father": Dynamic stereotypes of fathers. *Psychology of Men & Masculinity*, *17*(1), 103–107. https://doi.org/10.1037/a0038945.

Bethea, L. S., Travis, S. S., & Pecchioni, L. (2000). Family caregivers' use of humor in conveying information about caring for dependent older adults. *Health Communication*, *12*(4), 361–376. https://doi.org/10.1207/S15327027 HC1204_3.

Bozoglan, B. (2015). Spousal intrusion as a predictor of wives' marital satisfaction in their spouses' retirement. *Psychological Reports*, *116*, 921–935. DOI:10.2466/21.PR0.116k28w1.

Brach, E. L., Camara, K. A., Houser, R. F. (2000). Patterns of dinnertime interaction in divorced and nondivorced families. *Journal of Divorce and Remarriage*, *32*(3–4), 125–139. https://doi.org/10.1300/J087v32n03_08.

Brisini, K. S. C., & Solomon, D. H. (2020). Relational transitions and stress: Turbulence over the lifespan of marriage. In L. S. Aloia, A. Denes, & J. P. Crowley (Eds.), *The Oxford handbook of the physiology of interpersonal communication*. Oxford, UK: Oxford University Press. https://doi.org/10.1093/oxfordhb/9780190679446.013.10.

Campbell-Salome, G. (2019). "Yes they have the right to know, but…": Young adult women managing private health information as dependents. *Health Communication*, *34*(9), 1010–1020. https://doi.org/10.1080/10410236.2018.1452092.

Caughlin, J. P., Golish, T. D., Olson, L. N., Sargent, J. E., Cook, J. S., & Petronio, S. (2000). Intrafamily secrets in various family configurations: A communication boundary management perspective. *Communication Studies*, 51, 116–134.

Child Welfare Information Gateway. (2016). *Trends in U.S. adoptions: 2008–2012*. Washington, DC: U.S. Department of Health and Human Services, Children's Bureau.

Cicirelli, V. G. (2006). Caregiving decision making by older mothers and adult children: Process and expected outcomes. *Psychology and Aging*, *21*(2), 209–221. https://doi.org/10.1037/0882-7974.21.2.209.

Crapo, S., & Bradford, K. (2021). Multidimensional family development theory: A reconceptualization of family development. *Journal of Family Theory & Review.* https://doi.org/10.1111/jftr.12414.

Dayan, J., Creveuil, C., Dreyfus, M., Herlicoviez, M., Baleyte, J., & O'Keane, V. (2010). Developmental model of depression applied to prenatal depression: Role of present and past life events, past emotional disorders and pregnancy stress. *PLoS One*, *5*(9), 1–8. https://doi.org/10.1371/journal.pone.0012942.

Dickson, F. C., Christian, A., & Remmo, C. J. (2004). An exploration of the marital and family issues of the later-life adult. In A. Vangelisti (Ed.), *Handbook of family communication* (pp. 153–174). Mahwah, NJ: Lawrence Erlbaum.

Dun, T. (2010). Turning points in parent-grandparent relationships during the start of a new generation. *Journal of Family Communication*, *10*(3), 194–210. https://doi.org/10.1080/15267431.2010.489218.

Ellis, R. R., & Simmons, T. (2014). *Coresident Grandparents and Their Grandchildren: 2012*. U.S. Department of Commerce, Economics and Statistics Administration, U.S. Census Bureau, Washington, DC.

Feeney, J. A., Hohaus, L., Noller, P., & Alexander, R. P. (2001). *Becoming parents: Exploring the bonds between mothers, fathers, and their infants*. Cambridge: Cambridge University Press.

Fitzpatrick, M. A. (1988) *Between husbands and wives: Communication in marriage*. Newbury Park, CA: Sage.

Fitzpatrick, M. A., & Ritchie, L. D. (1994). Communication schemata within the family: Multiple perspectives on family interaction. *Human Communication Research*, *20*(3), 275–301. https://doi.org/10.1111/j.1468-2958.1994.tb00324.x.

Floyd, K, & Mikkelson, A. C. (2005). The affectionate communication index. In V. Manusov (Ed.), *The sourcebook of nonverbal measures* (pp. 47–55). Mahwah, NJ: Lawrence Erlbaum.

Floyd, K. (2006). Human affection exchange: XII. Affectionate communication is associated with diurnal variation in salivary free cortisol. *Western Journal of Communication*, *70*(1), 47–64. https://doi.org/10.1080/10570310500506649.

Floyd, K., Mikkelson, A. C., Hesse, C., & Pauley, P. M. (2007). Affectionate writing reduced total cholesterol: Two randomized, controlled trials. *Human Communication Research*, *33*(2), 119–142. https://doi.org/10.1111/j.1468-2958.2007.00293.x.

Givertz, M., Segrin, C., & Hanzal, A. (2009). The association between satisfaction and commitment differs across marital couple types. *Communication Research*, *36*(4), 561–584. https://doi.org/10.1177/0093650209333035.

Haverfield, M. C., & Theiss, J. A. (2017). Parental communication of responsiveness and control as predictors of adolescents' emotional and behavioral resilience in families with alcoholic versus nonalcoholic parents, *Human Communication Research*, *43*(2), 214–236. https://doi.org/10.1111/hcre.12102.

He, W., Sengupta, M., Velkoff, V. A., & DeBarros, K. A. (2005). 65+ in the United States: 2005. *U.S. Census Bureau* (Series P23–P209). Retrieved from www.census.gov/population/www/socdemo/age.html#elderly.

Hurley, D. (2005). Divorce rate: It's not as high as you think. *New York Times*, April 19.

Huston, T. L., & Holmes, E. K. (2004). Becoming parents. In A. L. Vangelisti (Ed.), *Handbook of family communication* (pp. 105–133). Mahwah, NJ: Lawrence Erlbaum.

Jackl, J. A. (2018). "Do you understand why I don't share that?": Exploring tellability within untellable romantic relationship origin tales. *Western Journal of Communication*, *82*(3), 315–335. https://doi.org/10.1080/10570314.2017.1347274.

Kaźmeirczak, M., & Karasiewicz, K. (2019). Making space for a new role: Gender differences in identity changes in couples transitioning to parenthood. *Journal of Gender Studies*, *28*(3), 271–287. https://doi.org/10.1080/09589236.2018.1441015.

Koerner, A. F. (2016). Family typologies. In C. R. Berger & M. E. Roloff (Eds.), *International encyclopedia of interpersonal communication* (pp. 671–675). Hoboken, NJ: Wiley Blackwell.

Korporaal, M., Broese van Groenou, M. I., & van Tilburg, T. G. (2013). Health problems and marital satisfaction among older couples. *Journal of Aging and Health*, *25*, 1279–1298. https://doi.org/10.1177/0898264313501387.

Kreider, R. M. (2010). Increase in opposite-sex cohabiting couples from 2009 to 2010 in the Annual Social and Economic Supplement (ASEC) to the Current Population Survey (CPS). *Housing and Household Economic Statistics Division Working Paper*, available at: www.census.gov/population/www/socdemo/Inc-Opp-sex-2009-to-2010.pdf.

Lavner, J. A., Karney, B. R., & Bradbury, T. N. (2014). Relationship problems over the early years of marriage: Stability or change? *Journal of Family Psychology*, *28*(6), 979–985. https://doi.org/10.1037/a0037752.

Ledbetter, A. M., & Vik, T. A. (2012). Parental invasive behaviors and emerging adults' privacy defenses: Instrument development and validation. *Journal of Family Communication*, *12*(3), 227–247. https://doi.org/10.1080/15267431.2012.686943.

Lévesque, S., Bisson, V., Charton, L., & Fernet, M. (2020). Parenting and relational well-being during the transition to parenthood: Challenges for first-time parents. *Journal of Child and Family Studies*, *29*(7), 1938–1956. https://doi.org/10.1007/s10826-020-01727-z.

Liberman, Z. (2020). Keep the cat in the bag: Children understand that telling a friend's secret can harm the friendship. *Developmental Psychology*, *56*(7), 1290–1304. https://doi.org/10.1037/dev0000960.

Lorber, M. F., Eckardt Erlanger, A. C., Heyman, R. E., & O'Leary, K. D. (2015). The honeymoon effect: Does it exist and can it be predicted? *Prevention Science*, *16*(4), 550–559. https://doi.org/10.1007/s11121-014-0480-4.

Mather, M. (2010). U.S. children in single mother families. *Population Reference Bureau*, available at: www.prb.org/pdf10/single-motherfamilies.pdf.

Mather, M., & Lavery, D. (2010). In U.S., proportion married at lowest recorded levels. *Population Reference Bureau*, available at: www.prb.org/Articles/2010/usmarriagedecline.aspx.

Mayol-Garcia, Y., Gurrentz, B., & Kreider, R. M. (2021). Number, timing, and duration of marriages and divorces: 2016. *Current Population Reports*, 70–167. U.S. Census Bureau. Washington, DC.

Miller-Ott, A. E. (2020). "Just a heads up, my father has Alzheimer's": Changes in communication and identity of adult children of parents with Alzheimer's Disease. *Health Communication*, *35*(1), 119–126, https://doi.org/10.1080/10410236.2018.1547676.

Morman, M. T., & Floyd, K., (2006). Good fathering: Father and son perceptions of what it means to be a good father. *Fathering*, *4*(2), 113–136. https://doi.org/10.3149/fth.0402.113.

Mustafa, H., Hasim, M. J. M., Aripin, N., & Hamid, H. A. (2013). Couple types, ethnicity and marital satisfaction in Malaysia. *Applied Research in Quality of Life*, *8*(3), 299–317. https://doi.org/10.1007/s11482-012-9200-z.

Petronio, S. (2002). *Boundaries of privacy: Dialectics of disclosure*. Albany, NY: SUNY Press.

Petronio, S. (2010). Communication privacy management theory: What do we know about family privacy regulation? *Journal of Family Theory & Review*, *2*, 175–196.

Petronio, S., & Child, J. T. (2020). Conceptualization and operationalization: Utility of communication privacy management theory. *Current Opinion in Psychology*, *31*, 76–82. https://doi.org/10.1016/j.copsyc.2019.08.009.

Pylyser, C., Buysse, A., & Loeys, T. (2018). Stepfamilies doing family: A meta-ethnography. *Family Process*, *57*(2), 496–509. https://doi.org/10.1111/famp.12293.

Rafferty, K. A., Hutton, K., & Heller, S. (2019). "I will communication with you, but let me be in control": Understanding how parents manage private information about their chronically ill children. *Health Communication*, *34*(1), 100–109. https://doi.org/10.1080/10410236.2017.1384432.

Rauch-Anderegg, V., Kuhn, R., Milek, A. W., Halford, W. K., & Bodenmann, G. (2020). Relationship behaviors across the transition to parenthood. *Journal of Family Issues*, *41*(1), 483–506. https://doi.org/10.1177/0192513X19878864.

Rauscher, E. A., Schrodt, P., Campbell-Salome, G., & Freytag, J. (2020). The intergenerational transmission of family communication patterns: (In)consistencies in conversation and conformity orientations across two generations of family. *Journal of Family Communication*, *20*(2), 97–113. https://doi.org/10.1080/15267431.2019.1683563.

Ritchie, L. D., & Fitzpatrick, M. A. (1990). Family communication patterns: Measuring interpersonal perceptions of interpersonal relationships. *Communication Research*, *17*(4), 523–544. https://doi.org/10.1177/009365090017004007.

Romo, L. K. (2016). Family secrets. In C. R. Berger & M. E. Roloff (Eds.), *International encyclopedia of interpersonal communication* (pp. 655–663). Hoboken, NJ: Wiley Blackwell.

Rossetto, K. R, Manning, J., & Green, E. W. (2017). Perceptions of paternal support after transitioning to college: Interpretations based on the generative fathering framework. *Western Journal of Communication*, *81*(4), 405–425. https://doi.org/10.1080/10570314.2017.1283047.

Sabey, A. K., & Rauer, A. J. (2018). Changes in older couples' compassionate love over a year: The roles of gender, health, and attachment avoidance. *Journal of Social and Personal Relationships*, *35*(8), 1139–1158. https://doi.org/10.1177/0265407517705491.

Samek, D. R., & Rueter, M. A. (2011). Associations between family communication patterns, sibling closeness, and adoptive status. *Journal of Marriage and Family*, *73*(5), 1015–1031. https://doi.org/10.1111/j.1741-3737.2011.00865.x.

Sillars, A., Holman, A. J., Richards, A., Jacobs, K. A., Koerner, A., & Reynolds-Dyk, A. (2014). Conversation and conformity orientations as predictors of observed conflict tactics in parent-adolescent discussions. *Journal of Family Communication*, *14*(1), 16–31. https://doi.org/10.1080/15267431.2013.857327.

Travis, S. S., Bethea, L. S., & Winn, P. (2000). Medication administration hassles reported by family caregivers of dependent elderly persons. *The Journals of Gerontology*, *55*(7), M412–M417. https://doi.org/10.1093/gerona/55.7.M412.

Van Egeren, L. A., & Barratt, M. S. (2004). The developmental origins of communication: Interactional systems in infancy. In A. L. Vangelisti (Ed.), *Handbook of family communication* (pp. 287–310). Mahwah, NJ: Lawrence Erlbaum.

Vangelisti, A. L., Caughlin, J. P., & Timmerman, L. (2001). Criteria for revealing family secrets. *Communication Monographs*, *68*(1), 1–27. https://doi.org/10.1080/03637750128052.

Wong, J. D., Marshall, A. D., & Feinberg, M. E. (2021). Intimate partner aggression during the early parenting years: The role of dissatisfaction with division of labor and childcare. *Couple and Family Psychology: Research and Practice*, *10*(1), 1–10. https://doi.org/10.1037/cfp0000156.

12 INTERPERSONAL INFLUENCE

Afifi, W. A., & Lee, J. W. (2000). Balancing instrumental and identity goals in relationships: The role of request directness and request persistence in the selection of sexual resistance strategies. *Communications Monographs*, *67*(3), 284–305. https://doi.org/10.1080/03637750009376511.

Anderson, R. E., & Huang, W. (2006). Empowering salespeople: Personal, managerial, and organizational perspectives. *Psychology & Marketing*, *23*(2), 139–159. https://doi.org/10.1002/mar.20104.

Boster, F. J., Shaw, A. S., Hughes, M., Kotowski, M. R., Strom, R. E., & Deatrick, L. M. (2009). Dump-and-chase: The effectiveness of persistence as a sequential request compliance-gaining strategy. *Communication Studies*, *60*(3), 219–234, https://doi.org/10.1080/10510970902955976.

Brown, P., & Levinson, S. (1987). *Politeness: Some universals in language use*. New York: Cambridge University Press.

Brown, R. F., & Bylund, C. L. (2008). Communication skills training: describing a new conceptual model. *Academic Medicine*, *83*(1), 37–44. https://doi.org/10.1097/ACM.0b013e31815c631e.

Burgoon, M., Alvaro, E., Grandpre, J., & Voulodakis, M. (2002). Revisiting the theory of psychological reactance. In J. P. Dillard & M. Pfau (Eds.), *The persuasion handbook* (pp. 213–232). Thousand Oaks, CA: Sage.

Caughlin, J. P. (2010). Invited Review Article: A multiple goals theory of personal relationships: Conceptual integration and program overview. *Journal of Social and Personal Relationships*, *27*(6), 824–848. https://doi.org/10.1177/0265407510373262.

Dillard, J. P. (2008). Goals-plans-action theory of message production: Making influence messages. In L. Baxter & D. Braithewaite (Eds.), *Engaging theories of interpersonal communication: Multiple perspectives*. Thousand Oaks, CA: Sage.

Dillard, J. P. (2015c). Goals-plans-action theory of message production: Making influence messages. In D. O. Braithwaite & P. Schrodt (Eds.), *Engaging theories in interpersonal communication: Multiple perspectives* (2nd ed., pp. 63–74). Thousand Oaks, CA: Sage. https://doi.org/10.4135/9781483329529.n5.

Dillard, J. P. (2015a). Goals–Plan–Action Theory. In C. R. Berger, M. E. Roloff, S. R. Wilson, J. P. Dillard, J. Caughlin and D. Solomon (eds.), *The international encyclopedia of interpersonal communication* (pp. 1–5). Hoboken, NJ: John Wiley & Sons. https://doi.org/10.1002/9781118540190.wbeic148.

Dillard, J. P. (2015b). Influence goals and plans. In C. R. Berger, M. E. Roloff, S. R. Wilson, J. P. Dillard, J. Caughlin and D. Solomon (eds.), *The international encyclopedia of interpersonal communication* (pp. 1–9). Hoboken, NJ: John Wiley & Sons. https://doi.org/10.1002/9781118540190.wbeic114.

Dillard, J. P., & Wilson, S. R. (2014). Interpersonal influence. In P. J. Schultz & P. Cobley (Series Eds.) & C. R. Berger (Vol. Ed.), *Handbooks of communication science: Vol. 6. Interpersonal communication* (pp. 155–176). Berlin: De Gruyter Mouton.

Dunbar, N. E. (2015). Power and dominance in nonverbal communication. In C. R. Berger, M. E. Roloff, S. R. Wilson, J. P. Dillard, J. Caughlin and D. Solomon (eds.), *The international encyclopedia of interpersonal communication* (pp. 1–5). Hoboken, NJ: John Wiley & Sons, Inc. https://doi.org/10.1002/9781118540190.wbeic146.

Epitropaki, O., & Martin, R. (2013). Transformational–transactional leadership and upward influence: The role of relative leader–member exchanges (RLMX) and perceived organizational support (POS). *The Leadership Quarterly*, *24*(2), 299–315. https://doi.org/10.1016/j.leaqua.2012.11.007.

Goldsmith, D. J., Bute, J. J., & Lindholm, K.A. (2012). Patient and partner strategies for talking about lifestyle change following a cardiac event. *Journal of Applied Communication Research*, *40*(1), 65–86, https://doi.org/10.1080/00909882.2011.636373.

Goldsmith, D. J., Lindholm, K. A., & Bute, J. J. (2006). Dilemmas of talking about lifestyle changes among couples coping with a cardiac event. *Social science & medicine*, *63*(8), 2079–2090.

Guadagno, R. E., & Cialdini, R. B. (2007). Persuade him by email, but see her in person: Online persuasion revisited. *Computers in Human Behavior*, *23*(2), 999–1015. https://doi.org/10.1016/j.chb.2005.08.006.

Guntzviller, L. M., & MacGeorge, E. L. (2013). Modeling interactional influence in advice exchanges: Advice giver goals and recipient evaluations. *Communication Monographs*, *80*(1), 83–100, https://doi.org/10.1080/03637751.2012.739707.

Hendrickson, B., & Goei, R. (2009). Reciprocity and dating: Explaining the effects of favor and status on compliance with a date request. *Communication Research*, *36*(4), 585–608. https://doi.org/10.1177/0093650209333036.

Johnson, D. I. (2007). Politeness theory and conversational refusals: Associations between various types of face threat and perceived competence. *Western Journal of Communication*, *71*(3), 196–215, https://doi.org/10.1080/10570310701518427.

Johnson, D. I. (2015). Obstacle Hypothesis. In C. R. Berger, M. E. Roloff, S. R. Wilson, J. P. Dillard, J. Caughlin and D. Solomon (eds.), *The international encyclopedia of interpersonal communication* (pp. 1–8). Hoboken, NJ: John Wiley & Sons. https://doi.org/10.1002/9781118540190.wbeic196

Johnson, D. I., Roloff, M. E., & Riffee, M. A. (2004). Responses to refusals of requests: Face threat and persistence, persuasion and forgiving statements. *Communication Quarterly*, *52*(4), 347–356, https://doi.org/10.1080/01463370409370205.

Kellermann, K. (2004). A goal-directed approach to gaining compliance: Relating differences among goals to differences in behaviors. *Communication Research*, *31*(4), 397–445. https://doi.org/10.1177/0093650204266093.

Kunkel, A. D., Wilson, S. R., Olufowote, J., & Robson, S. (2003). Identity implications of influence goals: Initiating, intensifying, and ending romantic relationships. *Western Journal of Communication*, *67*(4), 382–412. https://doi.org/10.1080/10570310309374780.

Lansford, J. E., Staples, A. D., Bates, J. E., Pettit, G. S., & Dodge, K. A. (2013). Trajectories of mothers' discipline strategies and interparental conflict:

Interrelated change during middle childhood. *Journal of Family Communication*, *13*(3), 178–195. https://doi.org/10.1080/15267431.2013.796947.

Lee, H. E., & Park, H. S. (2011). Why Koreans are more likely to favor "apology," while Americans are more likely to favor "thank you". *Human Communication Research*, *37*(1), 125–146, https://doi.org/10.1111/j.1468-2958.2010.01396.x.

Lee, H. E., Park, H. S., Imai, T., & Dolan, D. (2012). Cultural differences between Japan and the United States in uses of "apology" and "thank you" in favor asking messages. *Journal of Language and Social Psychology*, *31*(3), 263–289. https://doi.org/10.1177/0261927X12446595.

McCormick, M., & McElroy, T. (2009). Healthy choices in context: How contextual cues can influence the persuasiveness of framed health messages. *Judgment and Decision Making*, *4*(3), 248–255.

Miller, C. H., Lane, L. T., Deatrick, L. M., Young, A. M., & Potts, K. A. (2007). Psychological reactance and promotional health messages: The effects of controlling language, lexical concreteness, and the restoration of freedom. *Human Communication Research*, *33*(2), 219–240. https://doi.org/10.1111/j.1468-2958.2007.00297.x.

Oh, H. J., & LaRose, R. (2016) Impression management concerns and support-seeking on social network sites. *Computers in Human Behavior*, *57*, 38–47. https://doi.org/10.1016/j.chb.2015.12.005.

Postmes, T., Spears, R., Lee, A. T., & Novak, R. J. (2005). Individuality and social influence in groups: Inductive and deductive routes to group identity. *Journal of Personality and Social Psychology*, *89*(5), 747–763. https://doi.org/10.1037/0022-3514.89.5.747.

Sanders, R. E., & Fitch, K. L. (2001). The actual practice of compliance seeking. *Communication Theory*, *11*(3), 263–289. https://doi.org/10.1111/j.1468-2885.2001.tb00243.x.

Scott, A. M., & Caughlin, J. P. (2012). Managing multiple goals in family discourse About end-of-life health decisions. *Research on Aging*, *34*(6), 670–691. https://doi.org/10.1177/0164027512446942.

Smith, R. A., Fink, E. L., Romano, A., & Mikanatha, N, M. (2020). Precise persuasion: Investigating incentive appeals for the promotion of antibiotic stewardship with message-induced transitions. *Journal of Health Communication*, *25*(5), 430–443. https://doi.org/10.1080/10810730.2020.1778821.

Stratmoen, E., Rivera, E. D., & Saucier, D. A. (2020). "Sorry, I already have a boyfriend": Masculine honor beliefs and perceptions of women's use of deceptive rejection behaviors to avert unwanted romantic advances. *Journal of Social and Personal Relationships*, *37*(2), 467–490. https://doi.org/10.1177/0265407519865615.

Terkourafi, M. (2015). Conventionalism: A new agenda for im/politeness research. *Journal of Pragmatics*, *86*, 11–18. https://doi.org/10.1016/j.pragma.2015.06.004.

Thompson, C. M., Romo, L. K., & Dailey, R. M. (2013) The effectiveness of weight management influence messages in romantic relationships. *Communication Research Reports*, *30*(1), 34–45, https://doi.org/10.1080/08824096.2012.746222.

Tong, S. T., & Walther, J. B. (2010). Just say "no thanks": Romantic rejection in computer-mediated communication. *Journal of Social and Personal Relationships*, *28*(4), 488–506. https://doi.org/10.1177/0265407510384895.

Waldron, V. R. (1999). Communication practices of leaders, members, and protégés: The case of upward influence tactics. In M. E. Roloff (Ed.), *Communication Yearbook 22* (pp. 251–299). Thousand Oaks, CA: Sage.

Waldron, V. R., & Sanderson, J. (2011). The role of subjective threat in upward influence situations. *Communication Quarterly*, *59*(2), 239–254, https://doi.org/10.1080/01463373.2011.563444.

Wilson, S. R., Hall, E. D., Gettings, P. E., & Pastor, R. G. (2019). A multiple goals analysis of families attempting to encourage U.S. service members to seek behavioral health care: Linking the GPA model and confirmation theory. *Communication Research*, *46*(4), 525–554. https://doi.org/10.1177/0093650215617507.

Yu, K. (2011). Culture-specific concepts of politeness: Indirectness and politeness in English, Hebrew and Korean requests. *Intercultural Pragmatics*, *8*(3), 385–409. https://doi.org/10.1515/iprg.2011.018.

13 INTERPERSONAL CONFLICT

Afifi, T. D., & McManus, T., Steber, K., & Coho, A. (2009). Verbal avoidance and dissatisfaction in intimate conflict situations. *Human Communication Research*, *35*(3), 357–383. https://doi.org/10.1111/j.1468-2958.2009.01355.x.

Afifi, T. D., & Olsen, L. (2005). The chilling effect and the pressure to conceal secrets in families. *Communication Monographs*, *72*(2), 192–216. https://doi.org/10.1080/03637750500111906.

Afifi, T. D., Olson, L. N., & Armstrong, C. (2005). The chilling effect and family secrets: Examining the role of self protections, other protection, and communication efficacy. *Human Communication Research*, *31*(4), 564–598. https://doi.org/10.1111/j.1468-2958.2005.tb00883.x.

Allen, T. H., & Berkos, K. M. (2005). Ruminating about symbolic conflict through imagined interactions. *Imagination, Cognition and Personality*, *25*(4), 307–320. https://doi.org/10.2190/F760-0671-2402-K65N.

Barki, H., & Hartwick, J. (2004). Conceptualizing the construct of interpersonal conflict. *International Journal of Conflict Management*, *15*(3), 216–244. https://doi.org/10.1108/eb022913.

Barsky, A. E., & Wood, L. (2005). Conflict avoidance in a university setting. *Higher Education Research & Development*, *24*(3), 249–264. https://doi.org/10.1080/07294360500153984.

Caughlin, J. P., & Reznik, R. M. (2016). Demand-withdrawal sequences in conflict. In C. R. Berger & M. E. Roloff (Eds.), *International encyclopedia of interpersonal communication* (pp. 473–478). Hoboken, NJ: Wiley Blackwell.

Corcoran, K. O., & Mallinckrodt, B. (2000). Adult attachment, self-efficacy, perspective-taking, and conflict resolution. *Journal of Counseling & Development*, *78*(4), 473–483. https://doi.org/10.1002/j.1556-6676.2000.tb01931.x.

Cupach, W. R., Canary, D. J., & Spitzberg, B. H. (2010). *Competence in interpersonal conflict* (2nd ed.). Long Grove, IL: Waveland Press.

de Wied, M., Branje, S. J. T., & Meeus, W. H. J. (2006). Empathy and conflict resolution in friendship relations among adolescents. *Aggressive Behavior*, *33*(1), 48–55. https://doi.org/10.1002/ab.20166.

DiPaola, B. M., Roloff, M. E., & Peters, K. M. (2010). College students' expectations of conflict intensity: A self-fulfilling prophecy. *Communication Quarterly*, *58*(1), 59–76. https://doi.org/10.1080/01463370903532245.

Ebesu Hubbard, A. S. (2001). Conflict between relational uncertain romantic partners: The influence of relational responsiveness and empathy. *Communication Monographs*, *68*(4), 400–411. https://doi.org/10.1080/03637750128071.

Edelenbos, J., & Klijn, E. (2007). Trust in complex decision-making networks: A theoretical and empirical exploration. *Administration & Society*, *39*(1), 25–50. https://doi.org/10.1177/0095399706294460.

Farnish, K. A., & Neff, L. A. (2020). Shake it off: The role of optimistic expectations for conflict recovery. *Personal Relationships*, *27*(4), 820–845. https://doi.org/10.1111/pere.12342.

Garcia, A. B., Munduate, L., Elgoibar, P., Wendt, H., & Euwema, M. (2017). Competent or competitive? How employee representatives gain influence in organizational decision-making. *Negotiation and Conflict Management Research*, *10*(2), 107–125. https://doi.org/10.1111/ncmr.12093.

Gottman, J. M., Gottman, J. S., Cole, C., & Preciado, M. (2020). Gay, lesbian, and heterosexual couples about to begin couples therapy: An online relationship assessment of 40,681 couples. *Journal of Marital and Family Therapy*, *46*(2), 218–239. https://doi.org/10.1111/jmft.12395.

Grych, J. H., Wachsmuth-Schlaefer, T., & Klockow, L. L. (2002). Interparental aggression and young children's representations of family relationships. *Journal of Family Psychology*, *16*(3), 259–272. https://doi.org/10.1037/0893-3200.16.3.259.

Guerrero, L. K., & Gross, M. A. (2014). Argumentativeness, avoidance, verbal aggressiveness, and verbal benevolence as predictors of partner perceptions of an individual's conflict style. *Negotiation and Conflict Management Research*, *7*(2), 99–120. https://doi.org/10.1111/ncmr.12029.

Guerrero, L. K., Trost, M. R, & Yoshimura, S. M. (2005). Romantic jealousy: Emotions and communicative responses. *Personal Relationships*, *12*(2), 233–252. https://doi.org/10.1111/j.1350-4126.2005.00113.x.

Halpert, J. A., Stuhlmacher, A. F., Crenshaw, J. L., Litcher, C. D., & Bortel, R. (2010). Paths to negotiation success. *Negotiation and Conflict Management Research*, *3*(2), 91–116. https://doi.org/10.1111/j.1750-4716.2010.00051.x.

Holt, J. L., & DeVore, C. J. (2005). Culture, gender, organizational role, and styles of conflict resolution: A meta-analysis. *International Journal of Intercultural Relations*, *29*(2), 165–196. https://doi.org/10.1016/j.ijintrel.2005.06.002.

Johnson, K. L., & Roloff, M. E. (2000). Correlates of the perceived resolvability and relational consequences of serial arguing in dating relationships: Argumentative features and the use of coping strategies. *Journal of Social and Personal Relationships*, *17*(4–5), 676–686. https://doi.org/10.1177/0265407500174011.

Keck, K. L., & Samp, J. A. (2007). The dynamic nature of goals and message production as revealed in a sequential analysis of conflict interactions. *Human Communication Research*, 33, 27–47.

Kim, W., Nicotera, A. M., & McNulty, J. (2015). Nurses' perceptions of conflict as constructive or destructive. *Journal of Advanced Nursing*, *71*(9), 2073–2083. https://doi.org/10.1111/jan.12672.

Kirmayer, M. H., Khullar, t. H., & Dirks, M. A. (2021). Initial development of a situation-based measure of emerging adults' social competence in their same-gender friendships. *Journal of Research on Adolescence*, *31*(2), 451–468. https://doi.org/10.1111/jora.12616.

Knobloch, L. K. (2005). Evaluating a contextual model of responses to relational uncertainty increasing events: The role of intimacy, appraisals, and emotions. *Human Communication Research*, *31*(1), 60–101. https://doi.org/10.1093/hcr/31.1.60.

Laforest, M. (2002). Scenes of family life: Complaining in everyday conversation. *Journal of Pragmatics*, 34, 1595–1620.

Lopes, G. S., Shackelford, T. K., Buss, D. M., & Abed, M. G. (2020). Individual differences and disagreement in romantic relationships. *Personality and Individual Differences*, *155*, 109735. https://doi.org/10.1016/j.paid.2019.109735.

Makoul, G., & Roloff, M. E. (1998). The role of efficacy and outcome expectations in the decision to withhold relational complaints. *Communication Research*, *25*(1), 5–29. https://doi.org/10.1177/009365098025001001.

Malie, J., Heyman, R. E., & Slep, A. M. A. (2020). Emotional flooding in response to negative affect in couple conflicts: Individual differences and correlates.

Journal of Family Psychology, *34*(2), 145–154. https://doi.org/10.1037/fam0000584.

Malik, J., Heyman, R. E., Smith Slep, A. M. (2020). Emotional flooding in response to negative affect in couple conflicts: Individual differences and correlates. *Journal of Family Psychology*, 34, 145–154. DOI:10.1037/fam0000584.

Marshall, A. D., Jones, D. E., & Feinberg, M. E. (2011). Enduring vulnerabilities, relationship attributions, and couple conflict: An integrative model of the occurrence and frequency of intimate partner violence. *Journal of Family Psychology*, *25*(5), 709–718. https://doi.org/10.1037/a0025279.

McLaren, R. M., & Sillars, A. (2014). Hurtful episodes in parent-adolescent relationships: How accounts and attributions contribute to the difficulty of talking about hurt. *Communication Monographs*, *81*(3), 359–385. https://doi.org/10.1080/03637751.2014.933244.

Morman, M. T., & Whitely, M. (2012). An exploratory analysis of critical incidents of closeness in the mother/son relationship. *Journal of Family Communication*, *12*(1), 22–39. https://doi.org/10.1080/15267431.2011.629969.

O'Leary, K. D., Smith Slep, A. M., & O'Leary, S. G. (2007). Multivariate models of men's and women's partner aggression. *Journal of Consulting and Clinical Psychology*, *75*, 752–764.

Parmer, L. (2018). Relationships between philosophical values and conflict management styles. *International Journal of Conflict Management*, *29*(2), 236–252. https://doi.org/10.1108/IJCMA-11-2016-0091.

Rahim, M. A. (1983). A measure of styles of handling interpersonal conflict. *Academy of Management Journal*, *26*(2), 368–376. https://doi.org/10.2307/255985.

Roloff, M. E., & Ifert, D. E. (2000). Conflict management through avoidance: Withholding complaints, suppressing arguments, and declaring topics taboo. In S. Petronio (Ed.), *Balancing the secrets of private disclosures* (pp. 151–163). Mahwah, NJ: Lawrence Erlbaum.

Samp, J. A. (2013). Goal variability and message content during relational discussions: A sequential analysis. *Communication Studies*, *64*(1), 86–105. https://doi.org/10.1080/10510974.2012.732186.

Samp, J. A., & Palevitz, C. E. (2014). Managing relational transgressions as revealed on Facebook: The influence of dependence power on verbal versus nonverbal responses. *Journal of Nonverbal Behavior*, *38*(4), 477–493. https://doi.org/10.1007/s10919-014-0197-x.

Sanford, K. (2012). The communication of emotion during conflict in married couples. *Journal of Family Psychology*, *26*(3), 297–307. https://doi.org/10.1037/a0028139.

Schütz, A. (1999). It was your fault! Self-serving biases in autobiographical accounts of conflicts in married couples. *Journal of Social and Personal Relationships*, *16*(2), 193–208. https://doi.org/10.1177/0265407599162004.

Siegert, J. R., & Stamp, G. H. (1994). "Our first big fight" as a milestone in the development of close relationship. *Communication Monographs*, *61*(4), 345–360. https://doi.org/10.1080/03637759409376342.

Smith Slep, A. M., & O'Leary, S. G. (2007). Multivariate models of mothers' and fathers' aggression toward their children. *Journal of Consulting and Clinical Psychology*, 75, 739–751.

Solomon, D. H., & Roloff, M. E. (2019). Power and interpersonal communication. In C. R. Agnew & J. J. Harman (Eds.), *Power and interpersonal communication* (pp. 241–260). New York, NY: Cambridge University Press. https://doi.org/10.1017/9781108131490.012.

Waldron, V. R., & Kelley, D. L. (2005). Forgiving communication as a response to relational transgressions. *Journal of Social and Personal Relationships*, *22*(6), 723–742. https://doi.org/10.1177/0265407505056445.

Worcel, S. D., Shields, S. A., & Paterson, C. A. (1999). "She looked at me crazy": Escalation of conflict through telegraphed emotion. *Adolescence*, *34*(136), 689–697.

Worley, T., & Samp, J. (2018). Initial goals, goal trajectories, and serial argument resolvability: A growth curve analysis. *Personal Relationships*, *25*(2), 249–267. https://doi.org/10.1111/pere.12239.

Worley, T. R. (2017). Complaint expression in close relationships: A depending power perspective. In J. A. Samp (Ed.). *Communicating interpersonal conflict in close relationships: Contexts, challenges, and opportunities* (pp. 93–108). New York: Taylor & Francis.

Yip, J. A., Schweitzer, M. E., & Nurmohamed, S. (2018). Trash-talking: Competitive incivility motives rivalry, performance, and unethical behavior. *Organizational Behavior and Human Decision Processes*, *144*, 125–144. https://doi.org/10.1016/j.obhdp.2017.06.002.

Zornoza, A., Ripoll, P., & Peiro, J. M. (2002). Conflict management in groups that work in two different communication contexts: Face-to-face and computer-mediated communication. *Small Group Research*, *33*(5), 481–508. https://doi.org/10.1177/104649602237167.

14 COMMUNICATING COMFORT AND SUPPORT

Arora, N. K., Rutten, L. J. F., Gustafson, D. H., Moser, R., & Hawkins, R. P. (2007). Perceived helpfulness and impact of social support provided by family, friends, and health care providers to women newly diagnosed with breast cancer. *Psycho-Oncology*, *16*(5), 474–486. https://doi.org/10.1002/pon.1084.

Barbee, A. P., Fallat, M. E., Forest, R., McClure, M. E., Henry, K., & Cunningham, M. R. (2016). EMS perspectives on coping with child death in an out-of-hospital setting. *Journal of Loss and Trauma*, *21*(6), 455–470. https://doi.org/10.1080/15325024.2015.1117929.

Bodie, G. D. (2012). Task stressfulness moderate the effects of verbal person centeredness on cardiovascular reactivity: A dual-process account of the reactivity hypothesis. *Health Communication*, *27*(6), 569–580. https://doi.org/10.1080/10410236.2011.618433.

Bodie, G. D. (2013). The role of thinking in the comforting process: An empirical test of a dual-process framework. *Communication Research*, *40*(4), 533–558. https://doi.org/10.1177/0093650211427030.

Bodie, G. D., Jones, S. M., Brinberg, M., Joyer, A. M., Solomon, D. H., & Ram, N. (2020). Discovering the fabric of supportive conversations: A typology of speaking turns and their contingencies. *Journal of Language and Social Psychology*, *40*(2), 214–237. https://doi.org/10.1177/0261927X20953604.

Buehler, E. M., Crowley, J. L., Peterson, A. M., & High, A. C. (2019). Broadcasting for help: A typology of support-seeking strategies on Facebook. *New Media & Society*, *21*(11–12), 2566–2588. https://doi.org/10.1177/1461444819853821.

Burleson, B. R., & Mortenson, S. (2003). Explaining cultural differences in evaluations of emotional support behaviors: Exploring the mediating influences of value systems and interaction goals. *Communication Research*, *30*(2), 113–146. https://doi.org/10.1177/0093650202250873.

Chen, W., & Choi, A. S. K. (2011). Internet and social support among Chinese immigrants in Singapore. *New Media and Society*, *13*(7), 1067–1084. https://doi.org/10.1177/1461444810396311.

Crowley, J. L., & High, A. C., & Thomas, L. J. (2019). Desired, expected, and received support: How support gaps impact affect improvement and perceived stigma in the context of unintended pregnancy. *Health Communication*, *34*(12), 1441–1453. https://doi.org/10.1080/10410236.2018.1495162.

Derlega, V. J., Winstead, B. A., Oldfield, E. C., & Barbee, A. P. (2003). Close relationships and social support in coping with HIV: A test of sensitive interaction systems theory. *AIDS and Behavior*, *7*(2), 119–129. https://doi.org/10.1023/a:1023990107075.

Elwell, L., Grogan, S., & Coulson, N. (2011). Adolescents living with cancer: The role of computer mediated support groups. *Journal of Health Psychology*, *16*(2), 236–248. https://doi.org/10.1177/1359105310371398.

Feng, B., & MacGeorge, E. L. (2006). Predicting receptiveness to advice: Characteristics of the problem, the advice-giver, and the recipient. *Southern Journal of Communication*, *71*(1), 67–85. https://doi.org/10.1080/10417940500503548.

High, A. C. (2011). The production and reception of verbal person-centered social support in face-to-face and computer-mediated dyadic conversations. *Unpublished doctoral dissertation*, The Pennsylvania State University, University Park.

High, A. C., & Dillard, J. P. (2012). A review and meta-analysis of person-centered messages and social support outcomes. *Communication Studies*, *63*(1), 99–118. https://doi.org/10.1080/10510974.2011.598208.

High, A. C., & Scharp, K. M. (2015). Examining family communication patterns and seeking social support: Direct and indirect effects through ability and motivation. *Human Communication Research*, *41*(4), 459–479. https://doi.org/10.1111/hcre.12061.

High, A. C., & Solomon, D. H. (2011). Locating computer-mediated social support within online communication environments. In K. Wright & L. M. Webb (Eds.), *Computer-mediated communication in personal relationships* (pp. 119–155). New York: Peter Lang Publishing.

Holmstrom, A. J. (2016). Emotional appraisal/reappraisal in social support. In C. R. Berger & M. E. Roloff (Eds.), *International encyclopedia of interpersonal communication* (pp. 549–558). Hoboken, NJ: Wiley Blackwell.

Holmstrom, A. J., Bodie, G. D., Burleson, B. R., McCullough, J. D., Rack, J. J., Hanasono, L. K., & Rosier, J. G. (2015). Testing a dual-process theory of supportive communication outcomes: How multiple factors influence outcomes in support situations. *Communication Research*, 42(4), 526–546. https://doi.org/10.1177/0093650213476293.

Jabloo, V. G., Alibhai, S. M. H., Fitch, M., Tourangeau, A. E., Ayala, A. P., & Puts, M. T. E. (2017). Antecedents and outcomes of uncertainty in older adults with cancer: A scoping review of the literature. *Oncology Nursing Forum*, 44(4), E152–E167. https://doi.org/10.1188/17.ONF.E152-E167.

Jefferson, G. (2015). *Talking about troubles in conversation*. P. Drew, J. Heritage, G. Lerner, & A. Pomerantz (Eds.). Oxford: Oxford University Press.

Jones, S. M., & Koerner, A. F. (2016). Support types. In C. R. Berger & M. E. Roloff (Eds.), *International encyclopedia of interpersonal communication* (pp. 1711–1719). Hoboken, NJ: Wiley Blackwell.

Jones, S. M., & Wirtz, J. G. (2006). How does the comforting process work? An empirical test of an appraisal-based model of comforting. *Human Communication Research*, 32(3), 217–243. https://doi.org/10.1111/j.1468-2958.2006.00274.x.

Kaul, M., & Lakey, B. (2003). Where is the support in perceived support? The role of generic relationship satisfaction and enacted support in perceived support's relation to low distress. *Journal of Social and Clinical Psychology*, 22(1), 59–78. https://doi.org/10.1521/jscp.22.1.59.22761.

McCullough, J. D. (2019). "When you care enough to send the very best": Examining he person-centered quality of message features provided in sympathy cards. *Communication Reports*, 32(3), 148–160. https://doi.org/10.1080/08934215.2019.1636106.

McLaren, R. M., & High, A. C. (2019). The effect of under-and over-benefited support gaps on hurt feelings, esteem, and relationships. *Communication Research*, 46(6), 785–810. https://doi.org/10.1177/0093650215605155.

Mesquita, B. (2001). Emotions in collectivist and individualist cultures. *Journal of Personality and Social Psychology*, 80(1), 68–74. https://doi.org/10.1037/0022-3514.80.1.68.

Mortenson, S. (2006). Cultural differences and similarities in seeking social support as a response to academic failure: A comparison of American and Chinese college students. *Communication Education*, 55(2), 127–147. https://doi.org/10.1080/03634520600565811.

Mortenson, S., Liu, M., Burleson, B. R., & Liu, Y. (2006). A fluency of feeling: Exploring cultural and individual differences (and similarities) related to skilled emotional support. *Journal of Cross-Cultural Psychology*, 37(4), 366–385. https://doi.org/10.1177/0022022106288475.

Powers, S. R., Buck, R., Kiehl, K., & Schaich-Borg, J. (2007, November). *An fMRI study of neural responses to spontaneous emotional expressions: Evidence for a communicative theory of empathy* [Conference session]. Annual meeting of the National Communication Association, Chicago, IL, United States.

Priem, J. S., & Solomon, D. H. (2018). What is supportive about supportive conversation? Qualities of interaction that predict emotional and physiological outcomes. *Communication Research*, 45(3), 443–473. https://doi.org/10.1177/0093650215595074.

Priem, J. S., Solomon, D. H., & Steuber, K. R. (2009). Accuracy and bias in perceptions of emotionally supportive communication in marriage. *Personal Relationships*, 16(4), 531–552. https://doi.org/10.1111/j.1475-6811.2009.01238.x.

Rack, J. J., Burleson, B. R., Brodie, G. D., Holmstrom, A. J., & Servaty-Seib, H. (2008). Bereaved adults' evaluations of grief management messages: Effects of message person-centeredness, recipient individual differences, and contextual factors. *Death Studies*, 32(5), 399–427. https://doi.org/10.1080/07481180802006711.

Rains, S. A., & Young, V. (2009). A meta-analysis of research on formal computer-mediated support groups: Examining group characteristics and health outcomes. *Human Communication Research*, 35(3), 309–336. https://doi.org/10.1111/j.1468-2958.2009.01353.x.

Rains, S. A., Brunner, S. R., Akers, C., Pavlich, C. A., & Tsetsi, E. (2016). The implications of computer-mediate communication (CMC) for social support message processing and outcomes: When and why are effects of support messages strengthened during CMC? *Human Communication Research*, 42(4), 553–576. https://doi.org/10.1111/hcre.12087.

Servaty-Seib, H., & Burleson, B. R. (2007). Bereaved adolescents' evaluations of the helpfulness of support-intended statements: Associations with person-centeredness and demographic, personality, and contextual factors. *Journal of Social and Personal Relationships*, 24(2), 207–223. https://doi.org/10.1177/0265407507075411.

Solomon, D. H., Priem, J. S., & Steuber, K. R. (2008, November). *Perceptions of supportive communication in marital interactions: Accuracy, projection, and sentiment override* [Conference session]. Annual meeting of the National Communication Association, San Diego, CA, United States.

Tian, X. (2021). The role of person-centered supportive communication and personal disclosures in coping with the dean of a parent. *Unpublished doctoral dissertation.* Penn State University.

Uchino, B. N. (2006). Social support and health: A review of physiological processes potentially underlying links to disease outcomes. *Journal of Behavioral Medicine*, *29*(4), 377–387. https://doi.org/10.1007/s10865-006-9056-5.

Wang, N. (2019). Emerging adults' received and desired support from parents: Evidence for optimal received-desired support matching and optimal support surpluses. *Journal of Social and Personal Relationships*, *36*(11–12), 3448–3470. https://doi.org/10.1177/0265407518822784.

Weber, K. M., & Solomon, D. H. (2008). Locating relationship and communication issues among stressors associated with breast cancer. *Health Communication*, *23*(6), 548–559. https://doi.org/10.1080/10410230802465233.

Williams, S. L., Mickelson, K. D. (2008) A paradox of support seeking and rejection among the stigmatized. *Personal Relationships*, *15*(4), 493–509. https://doi.org/10.1111/j.1475-6811.2008.00212.x.

Youngvorst, L. J., & High, A. C. (2018) "Anyone free to chat?" using technological features to elicit quality support online. *Communication Monographs*, *85*(2), 203–223. https://doi.org/10.1080/03637751.2018.1426871.

Index

Entries in *italics* denote figures; entries in **bold** denote tables.

9780815386971